C0-AOF-074

MANDATES UNDER THE LEAGUE OF NATIONS

MANDATES UNDER THE LEAGUE OF NATIONS

By QUINCY WRIGHT
The University of Chicago

GREENWOOD PRESS, PUBLISHERS
NEW YORK

First Greenwood Reprinting, 1968

Library of Congress Catalogue Card Number: 68-57649

PRINTED IN THE UNITED STATES OF AMERICA

TO P. G. W.

BY SHOWING THAT ENTHUSIASM CAN BE COMBINED
WITH PRECISION, POETRY WITH MATHEMATICS,
HE HAS ENCOURAGED RESEARCH

PREFACE

The new institution of mandates established by the peace treaties and the League of Nations Covenant has attracted interest from a number of different points of view. Its establishment was an interesting incident of recent diplomatic history. Its conception was a notable triumph of statesmanship in solving perhaps the most difficult dilemma of the Peace Conference.

In addition to this, the operation of the system throws light on the problem of international administration. Sovereign states have not been accustomed to submit to systematic supervision, and this effort of the League of Nations to develop a procedure by which the greatest powers may be effectively supervised in the very delicate field of colonial administration is significant.

Furthermore, the mandates system marks perhaps the most important innovation wrought by the peace treaties and the Covenant in the system of international law. Territory unless undiscovered or unoccupied *res nullius* has, heretofore, been regarded as nominally under the exclusive sovereignty of some state. Yet here are vast territories, aggregating one-third the area and one-sixth the population of the United States, not under the sovereignty of any state but in a status new to international law. Does this innovation mark a step away from the conception of exclusive territorial sovereignty which has characterized international law at least since the time of Grotius?

Finally, the mandates system has given wide publicity to discussions, of the actual and ideal policy of European civilization toward the cultures of Asia, Africa, and the Pacific, by competent administrators and responsible government representatives. The problem of peaceful and mutually beneficial contact between these divergent cultures is one of the great problems brought on by modern means of communication and economic enterprise. The contribution which the mandates system may make to its solution will be watched with interest.

The four parts of this book are designed to approach the subject successively from the standpoint of these four types of interest. Part I attempts to trace the origin of the mandates system and to survey its development. Part II describes the structure of the system and the activity of its constituent entities. Part III seeks to define the system with legal precision and to fit it into existing conceptions of international law. Part IV attempts to evaluate the objects aimed at by the system, to appraise its success in achieving them in the regions now under mandate, and to suggest the possibilities of further development. It is hoped that the effort to present the subject adequately from each point of view has not resulted in undue repetition.

The writer wishes to thank the editors and publishers of the *American Journal of International Law*, the *Southwestern Political and Social Science Review*, and the *Michigan Law Review* for the privilege of using material from articles published in those periodicals and the Carnegie Endowment for International Peace for the privilege of using maps published in *The Trustees of Peace, 1919–1923*, New York, 1924. He also wishes to acknowledge his indebtedness to the John Simon Guggenheim Memorial Foundation which made it possible for him to visit Geneva and the near eastern mandated territories during the summer and autumn of 1925. The direct contacts made at that time have proved invaluable supplements to documentary study.

Numerous friends in Europe, in the Near East, and in America have generously contributed of their time in supplying information and documents, in criticizing his published articles on the subject, and in discussing the problem with him. They have made this work possible, and while he cannot mention them individually, he appreciates their assistance and encouragement. The staff of the University of Chicago Press has given cheerful assistance on matters of form and detail. To his wife, who has borne with the book from its initial stages to the final revision of the proof, he owes thanks for numerous and valuable suggestions both in substance and in style and for unfailing encouragement.

QUINCY WRIGHT

LIST OF ABBREVIATIONS

Acad. D.I.—*Académie de droit international, Recueil des Cours*
A.J.I.L.—*American Journal of International Law*
A.P.S.R.—*American Political Science Review*
Am. Hist. Rev.—*American Historical Review*
Am. Law School Rev.—*American Law School Review*
Annals—*Annals of the American Academy of Social and Political Science*
Br. and For. St. Pap.—*British and Foreign State Papers*
B.Y.B.I.L.—*British Year Book of International Law*
B.I.I.I.—*Bulletin de l'institut intermédiaire international*
Cornell L. Q.—*Cornell Law Quarterly*
F.P.A., Inf. Ser.—*Foreign Policy Association, Information Service*
For. Aff.—*Foreign Affairs, An American Quarterly Review*
G.B., Parl. Deb., H. of C.—*Great Britain, Parliamentary Debates, House of Commons*
G.B., Parl. Pap.—*Great Britain, Parliamentary Papers*
Grotius Soc.—*Transactions of the Grotius Society*
I.L.A., Rep.—*International Law Association, Reports*
J.O.—*Journal officiel de la Republique Française*
J.B.I.I.A.—*Journal of the British Institute of International Affairs*
J.C.L.—*Journal of Comparative Legislation and International Law*
J.P.E.—*Journal of the Parliaments of the Empire*
J.R.S.A.—*Journal of the Royal Society of Arts*
L.Q.R.—*Law Quarterly Review*
L. of N., Assembly, Rec.—*League of Nations, Assembly, Records*
L. of N., Council, Min.—*League of Nations, Council, Minutes*
L. of N., Monthly Summary—*League of Nations, Monthly Summary*
L. of N. News—*League of Nations News*
L. of N., Sec. Gen., Rep.—*League of Nations, Secretary General, Report to the Assembly*
L. of N., T.S.—*League of Nations, Treaty Series*
L. of N. Y.B.—*League of Nations Year Book*
M.D.G.V.—*Mitteilungen der Deutschen Gesellschaft für Völkerrecht*
Mich. L.R.—*Michigan Law Review*
Minn. L.R.—*Minnesota Law Review*
O.J.—*League of Nations, Official Journal*
P.C.I.J.—*Permanent Court of International Justice, Publications.*
P.M.C., Min. (or *Rep.*)—*League of Nations, Permanent Mandates Commission, Minutes* (or *Report*)

Proc. A.P.S.A.—Proceedings American Political Science Association
Proc. A.S.I.L.—Proceedings American Society of International Law
P.S.Q.—Political Science Quarterly
R.D.I.—Revue de Droit international et de Législation comparée
R.G.D.I.P.—Revue générale de Droit international public
S. de N., R.M.D.—Société des Nations, Revue Mensuelle Documentaire
U.S., For. Rel.—United States, Foreign Relations
W.A.—Weltwirtschaftliches Archiv
Yale L.J.—Yale Law Journal
Z.O.R.—Zeitschrift für öffentliches Recht
Z.V.—Zeitschrift für Völkerrecht

TABLE OF CONTENTS

PART I. ORIGIN AND DEVELOPMENT OF THE MANDATES SYSTEM

PART II. ORGANIZATION OF THE MANDATES SYSTEM

PART I

ORIGIN AND DEVELOPMENT OF THE MANDATES SYSTEM

CHAPTER I

ORIGIN OF THE IDEA

The mandates system is the form of control established by the League of Nations Covenant for the non-European territories yielded by Germany and Turkey as a result of the World War. It contemplates administration of each of these areas by a mandatory selected by the Principal Allied (and Associated)[1] Powers, guided by certain principles and restrictions formulated in the Covenant and the mandate and subject to supervision by the League of Nations. This system, like most other political innovations, was not a product of disinterested juristic thought nor of detached scientific investigation but was a compromise invented by the Versailles statesmen to meet an immediate political dilemma. The factors in this political dilemma will be considered in the next chapter.

Few inventions, however, whether political or mechanical, are wholly new. The elements of this particular invention had been evolving for years in the thoughts and writings of administrators, statesmen, jurists, and idealists, and even their co-ordination in the form adopted at Versailles had been to some extent anticipated. Let us consider the progress of thought on this subject of governing dependencies.

1. Government of Dependencies

A dependency may result from any one of three processes which may be denominated "expansion," "colonization," and "imperialism." Expansion occurs where a people with a naturally increasing population gradually extends its frontiers over adjacent, vacant or almost vacant, territory. The expansion of the United States over

[1] This term appears in the mandates assigning former German territory but not in those assigning former Turkish territory, thus conforming to the treaties of peace which in the case of Germany with which the United States was at war ceded the territory to the Principal Allied and Associated Powers but in the case of Turkey with which the United States was not at war referred only to the Principal Allied Powers. Whether the United States, the only "principal associated power," was legally entitled to a voice in the selection of any mandatories is debatable. See *infra*, chap. xiii, sec. 4*a*.

its present continental area and of Russia over much of Siberia is of this character. Apart from possible diplomatic complications due to the prior claims of other states over the territory, the problem of government is comparatively simple. The "dependency" because of the continuity of its territory and the identity of its inhabitants with those of the motherland is really not a dependency at all but merely a part of the motherland, and the latter's institutions can usually be gradually enlarged sufficiently to provide for the new territories as they are occupied.

Colonization is much the same but with the difference that the colony is not territorially continuous with the motherland. It is separated by such natural barriers as a range of mountains, a desert, or a sea. Seeley in his *Expansion of England* attempted to identify this colonization with the type of expansion just considered,[2] but in fact geographical separation has made the problem of political incorporation more difficult, as witness the separation of the United States from Great Britain, of Latin America from Spain and Portugal, and the steady differentiation of the British dominions from the mother-country.[3] Nevertheless, whether the new colony is con-

[2] "Greater Britain is a real enlargement of the English state; it carries across the seas not merely the English race, but the authority of the English government. . . . . It does not consist of a congeries of nations held together by force, but in the main of one nation, as much as if it were no Empire but an ordinary state. This fact is fundamental when we look to the future and enquire whether it is calculated for duration. . . . The question is often asked, What is the good of colonies? but no such question could possibly be raised if colonies were such a simple extension of the mother state" (*op. cit.* [London, 1883], pp. 43, 51, 57).

[3] Seeley recognized this fact but thought it could be overcome by the cohesive influence of common nationality and religion (*ibid.*, pp. 50, 154, 159). However, in 1926 the British Imperial Conference recognized that "geographic and other conditions made attainment of equal status [of Great Britain and the dominions] by way of federation impossible. Consequently it could only be sought by way of autonomy" (see British Imperial Conference, *Summary of Proceedings* [1926], Cmd. 2768). In the light of certain investigations which seem to show that through direct influence as well as selection even physical characteristics are eventually as much a product of environment as of blood (Boas, "Changes in Bodily Form of Descendants of Immigrants," *Report of the United States Immigration Commission*, Vol. XXXVIII [Washington, 1911]; Huntington, *The Character of Races* [1925]) and of the universal biological and sociological observation that geographic separation has led to differentiation it is impossible to assume that distant colonies will permanently retain the parent-nationality even if there is no infusion of foreign blood.

ceived as naturally independent, as was the case among the ancient Greek cities, or as naturally attached to the mother-country, as has been true in modern colonization, the problem of political institutions is not difficult. The colonists carry adequate laws and institutions with them. People will not colonize to any extent in a region so different in climate or geography that wholly new institutions are necessary.

Imperialism occurs when a state attempts to control territory which may be adjacent or separated but which is inhabited by a people of different characteristics and institutions. Expansion may be likened to the growth of an organism and colonization to reproduction, but imperialism more nearly resembles the acquisition of property. The people in a state's expanded area are but peripheral cells of the leviathan, colonies are its children, but the inhabitants of its empire tend to become its slaves. Imperialism is not always easy to distinguish from expansion and colonization. If the original inhabitants of a new area climatically suitable for colonization are of inefficient civilization and not too numerous they are likely to be exterminated, driven out, or confined to reservations by colonists or to lose their identity through intermarriage with the latter, and the territory ceases to be an imperial domain in the usual sense and becomes a part of the mother-country or a colony. Or, if the original inhabitants are not widely different from the people of the imperial state, the two may coalesce sufficiently for permanent political union as have the English, Scotch, and Welsh in Great Britain; the British and Dutch in South Africa; the French and British in Canada; and the Germans, French, and Italians in Switzerland. Such a result is clearly more likely to occur when the territories are adjacent and the divergent effect of environmental differences is not present; but is not always easy even then, as witness German pre-war efforts to assimilate Lorraine and Posen, and French and Italian post-war efforts to assimilate, respectively, Alsace and the southern Tyrol.[3a]

The major difficulty, however, in administering dependencies

[3a] The Negro race in America even though diluted by an ever increasing amount of white blood has tended to segregate and form a distinct nationality (Reuter, *The Mulatto in the United States*, Boston, 1918). The assimilation of Indian and Spanish civilizations in Latin America has been by no means complete (Gamio, in Vasconcelos and Gamio, *Aspects of Mexican Civilization*, Chicago, 1926).

arises in the case of geographically separated areas, well populated by people of a culture different from that in the imperial state. The mandated areas lie for the most part in this relation to the mandatory.[4] How has Europe treated such areas in the past?

When the European states with the new energy of the Renaissance began to extend their control into America, Asia, and Africa, they knew no principles of law, policy, or morality to restrain them. At an age when Machiavelli was suggesting that European princes shape their conduct toward each other by a scientific estimate of immediate consequences regardless of traditional conceptions and blind to a distant future, it is not surprising that the adventurers who blazed the path of empire should have taken the shortest cut to their goal, whether that goal was pecuniary profit, political aggrandizement, or merit in heaven.[5] The shortest cut usually seemed to be conquest and annexation followed by sufficiently strong administration to destroy or to convert and assimilate the natives, and to direct production and commerce to the immediate profit of the conquering state.[6] When imperialism was a novelty the possible remote advantages of a more deliberate approach could hardly be foreseen. European monarchs willing to accept the advantages of colonies were prepared to acquiesce in the means by which they were acquired and maintained. This was the practice, and international law, imperial policy, and moral standards accommodated themselves to it.

[4] European colonization is possible in some of the Pacific islands, parts of Southwest Africa, the highlands of East Africa, and parts of the Arab countries, especially the Lebanon. It is actually being attempted by the Zionists in Palestine.

[5] As an evidence of impelling motives it is interesting to note that British and Dutch colonies were frequently acquired by private initiative and their administration carried on for considerable periods by chartered commercial companies whereas royal and church patronage played a larger part in the Spanish, Portuguese, and French acquisitions which were usually administered directly by the home government.

[6] Seeley, *op. cit.*, p. 44. Modern imperialism is an outgrowth of medieval imperialism manifested in the Crusades and the commercial expansion of Italian city states into the Levant; which in turn grew from Roman imperialism over the Mediterranean, but it was so distinct in direction, method, and participants that the experience of past imperialisms was of little influence at its beginning, though in recent times men like Seeley, Bryce, and Cromer have compared ancient and modern imperialism (see also Moon, *Imperialism and World Politics* [New York, 1926], pp. 9–14).

International law, which was just beginning to form with the age of discovery, was in practice a law between the Christian states of Europe.[7] Even among them war and conquest might create new conditions which could become rights through forced treaties or general acquiescence.[8] Peoples outside of European Christian civilization hardly came within its sphere at all.[9] They could be massacred and their villages pillaged without regard to the law of war.[9a] Conquest of their territory was considered meritorious.[10] After annexation, though the imperial master might insist that foreign states accord them the benefits of international law, they had no protection against him except his humanity and sense of expediency.

The latter were uncertain guaranties. The sense of humanity

[7] Walker, *A History of the Law of Nations* (Cambridge, 1899), pp. 138, 331; Oppenheim, *International Law* (3d ed.; London, 1920), pp. 31–36, 61. There were theoretical writers who took a different view (see *infra*, n. 9).

[8] This is still the case. Duress against a state does not invalidate a treaty (Venezuela preferential-claims case before Hague Court of Arbitration, 1904, in Scott, *Hague Court Reports*, p. 55; Phillipson, *Termination of War and Treatise of Peace*, p. 162) and conquest of territory if acquiesced in gives good title. Some writers hold that subjugation and annexation give title irrespective of the attitude of third states (Oppenheim, *op. cit.*, pp. 399–400; Lindley, *Acquisition and Government of Backward Territory in International Law* [1925], p. 160; Cobbett, *Leading Cases on International Law*, II [1913], 245; Phillipson, *op. cit.*, p. 9) while others hold that protracted acquiescence (prescription) or cession are necessary to give title to conquered territory (Hall, *International Law* [8th ed.], pp. 142–44, 681; John Fischer Williams, *B.Y.B.I.L.* [1926], pp. 38–42). For members of the League this is changed by article 10 of the Covenant (Wright, *A.P.S.R.*, XIII, 559).

[9] Though treating international law primarily as a law between European Christian states, theoretical writers usually denied a right to fight and plunder infidels and Indians indiscriminately but apparently on the basis of *jus naturale* rather than *jus gentium* for practice was to the contrary. See Victoria, *De Indis, relectio prior* (1557), sec. 1, par. 24; Ayala, *De jure et officiis bellicis et disciplina militari* (1582), Lib. I, c. 3, pars. 28, 29, also c. 5, par. 19; Gentilis, *De jure belli* (1588), Lib. I, c. 9, 12, 19; Grotius, *De jure belli ac pacis*, Lib. II, c. 20, secs. 40, 41, 48, and c. 22, secs. 9, 10, 12; Vattel, *Le Droit des gens*, Lib. I, c. 18, par. 209, and Lib. II, c. 3, par. 34; Walker, *op. cit.*, p. 331; Lindley, *op. cit.*, pp. 10–24, 328.

[9a] F. W. Hirst, *Arbiter in Council*, p. 230; Colby, "How To Fight Savage Tribes," *A.J.I.L.*, XXI, 279.

[10] *Johnson* v. *Mackintosh*, 8 Wheat. 543 (1823); Oppenheim, *op. cit.*, I, 36, 180; Westlake, *International Law*, II, 59, 87; Lindley, *op. cit.*, p. 24. Most writers have recognized natives as enjoying some title which may only be extinguished by complete conquest, though some have considered their territory as *res nullius* subject to the acquisition of civilized states by occupation (Lindley, *op. cit.*, pp. 11–23).

was narrowly limited by race and religion. People of different blood and different faith were hardly to be considered human beings at all, and the highest moral requirements were satisfied by tendering them the blessings of Christianity and civilization. The Supreme Court of the United States said through Chief Justice Marshall:

> On the discovery of this immense continent the nations of Europe were eager to appropriate to themselves so much of it as they could respectively acquire. Its vast extent offered an ample field to the ambition and enterprise of all; and the character and religion of its inhabitants afforded an apology for considering them as a people over whom the superior genius of Europe might claim an ascendency. The potentates of the old world found no difficulty in convincing themselves that they made ample compensation to the inhabitants of the new, by bestowing on them civilization and Christianity, in exchange for unlimited independence.[11]

As for policy, colonies were considered tributary to the parent-state supplying its raw materials and taking its manufactures. The welfare of the latter was the object of policy, and little consideration was given to the needs or desires of the colony that ran counter to this welfare as interpreted by mercantilist statesmen. If this was true of colonies largely populated by migrants from the mother-country, much more was it true of dependencies whose population continued of alien race and culture.[12]

In brief, the principles governing the relations of European and non-European peoples at the beginning of the modern period was that described by Seeley: "Everywhere the country fell into the hands of the immigrating race and was disposed of as so much plunder," thus furnishing "one of the most terrible pages to the annals of the world."[13]

2. Trusteeship of Backward Peoples

In the succeeding four centuries changes took place. First of these was the development of a sense of responsibility toward the world for the just government of subject territories and their native inhabitants; in fact, if we judge by the current terminology we may

[11] *Johnson* v. *Mackintosh,* 8 Wheat. 543 (1823).

[12] Moon, *op. cit.*, pp. 9–14. Sir Cecil Hurst, *Great Britain and the Dominions,* "Harris Foundation Lectures" (1928), p. 14.

[13] Seeley, *op. cit.*, p. 44; Lindley, *op. cit.*, p. 328.

suppose that dependencies have ceased entirely to be a right of the imperial state but have become a responsibility, a trust of civilization, the white man's burden. The change, however, has not been only in terminology. Humanitarian, economic, and political influences have tended to make it a reality.

Humanitarian consideration for subject races was from the first demanded by moralists and theologians. Queen Isabella in her letter of February 10, 1495, urged generous treatment of the Indians. The Missionary Bartolome de las Casas and the half-blood Inca, Garcilaso de la Vega, popularized the cause of the Indian in Spain while the learned theologian Francis de Victoria assured his students at Salamanca that the law of nations protected the Indians even though they were infidels.[14] It was not, however, until the latter eighteenth century that humanitarianism became organized and effective. Through the efforts of the Quakers John Woolman (1720–73) and Anthony Benezet (1713–84) in America; the Christian philanthropists Thomas Clarkson (1760–1846), William Wilberforce (1759–1833), and Thomas Fowell Buxton (1786–1845) in England; and the revolutionary humanitarians Condorcet (1743–94), L'Abbe Gregoire (1750–1831), and Mirabeau (1749–91) in France: societies were formed in these countries to abolish the slave trade and protect the aborigines. Their agitation brought legislation against the slave trade early in the nineteenth century, and their scrutiny was a continuous stimulus to colonial offices. Although barbarities against natives were still frequent enough, public sentiment was sometimes successfully mobilized for reform, as in the Congo in the early twentieth century.[15]

Presently humanitarianism was strengthened by a new appreciation of economic expediency. In the exploitation of thinly populated temperate regions extermination of the natives was little loss to the imperial power and perhaps a gain. Immigrants could fill the gap,

[14] See *supra*, n. 9.

[15] Snow, *The Question of Aborigines in the Law and Practice of Nations* (Washington, 1919), chaps. i, ii. This work, originally prepared for the American delegation at the Paris Peace Conference, was reprinted (New York, 1921). Lindley (*op. cit.*, p. 330) credits Burke with the first formulation of the duties of a colonial power in terms of trusteeship in debating Fox's India bill in 1783 (Hansard, *Parliamentary History*, Vol. XXIII, cols. 1316–17).

supplying better labor than the natives and also relieving population pressure in the home territory. But with thickly settled acquisitions like India or tropical acquisitions like Central Africa it began to be seen that the native was an important economic asset. Without his labor the territory could not produce. Thus the ablest administrators like Sir Frederick Lugard in Nigeria began to study the native and cater not only to his material but to his psychological welfare with highly gratifying economic results. Everywhere the devastating and uneconomic effects of trade spirits and firearms among the natives came to be recognized and their importation controlled. In some parts of Africa, especially the west coast, the more fundamental problems of an equitable land system and a liberal and humane labor policy were studied and in a measure solved.[16]

With the scramble for African colonies which began in the 1880's political expediency prompted the application of mutually beneficial principles to certain dependencies. None of the highly industrialized states was satisfied with the markets and raw materials supplied by its own colonies alone, and a tendency toward economic equalization, neutralization, or internationalization was observable. The open door, although practiced in a minority of colonies, had a prominent place in the foreign policy of certain states and was recognized in a few treaties. Colonial neutralization and demilitarization were also discussed and in fact given a certain approval in the Congo, but the attempt could not stand the strain of the World War. A few areas like Samoa and the New Hebrides were placed under international administration but without marked success.[17]

The principle that dependencies are a trust of civilization had influenced theory more than practice when the World War broke out. Economic and military exploitation of natives and various devices for monopolizing colonial trade were still the rule, but the

[16] Beer, *African Questions at the Peace Conference* (New York, 1923), pp. 27, 180. This is a compilation of documents prepared for the American delegation at the Paris Peace Conference See also Lugard, *The Dual Mandate in Central Africa* (2d ed., 1923), chaps. xix, xx.

[17] Beer, *op. cit.*, pp. 189–286.

principle was generally accepted in terms and was beginning to have effects in practice.[18]

3. Tutelage of Backward Communities

Not only was the conception of dependency administration shifting from that of a right to a responsibility, but the conception of the dependency itself was shifting from that of a piece of property to a personality. The dependency came to be looked upon not merely as real estate but as a community with a corporate personality—adolescent perhaps, unprepared for immediate independence but capable of organic development. Thus the trust undertaken by the imperial power was not only for the administration of property but for the development of a ward. It resembled guardianship or tutelage.[19]

The rise of nationalism largely accounts for this change. In Greek times where the state was the city, a colony naturally became independent upon its establishment. Modern colonies built up under

[18] Snow, *op. cit.*, p. 69. Queen Victoria's proclamation of November 1, 1858, assuming the government of India said: "We hold ourselves bound to the natives of our Indian territories by the same obligations of duty which bind us to all our other subjects, which Seeley notes, "imposes upon us vast and almost intolerable responsibilities" (*op. cit.*, p. 183). W. F. Willoughby says the first principle of American colonial policy has been administration "primarily with a view to its [the colony's] own benefit or advancement and in no way as constituting a field for exploitation in the interest of the mother country" (*Territories and Dependencies of the U.S.* [1905], p. 11; see also Potter, "The Nature of American Territorial Expansion," *A.J.I.L.*, XV, 196). The American theory is set forth in the Northwest Ordinance, July 3, 1787, art. III, and in President McKinley's message of December 3, 1900, containing his instructions to the second Philippine commission, April 7, 1900. Professor Miono Yamamota, of the Imperial University of Kyoto, Japan, writes: "The past history of colonial policies has been that of the policy of assimilation, its aim being to further the interest of the mother countries. . . . . The ideal of liberty, equality, and fraternity should be the controlling principle of the future colonial policies of nations, and the relations between mother countries and their colonies or dependencies should be so regulated as to bring about the general welfare of mankind, co-operation and friendship being its keynote. . . . . Should our country fail to adopt this fundamental colonial policy at present, we shall some day face disastrous consequences" (*Kyoto University Economic Review*, I [July, 1926], 90). See also *infra*, nn. 23, 24.

[19] Snow, *op. cit.*, p. 109; Lindley, *op. cit.*, p. 330. The relation of the Indians to the United States was considered analogous to that of a ward to his guardian by Chief Justice Marshall in *Cherokee Nation* v. *Georgia*, 5 Pet. 17 (1831).

the patronage of national states just as naturally remained attached.[19a] But when they were distant and subject to a new geographic and climatic environment from the parent-state the colony began to develop an individuality of its own, to resent treatment as a subordinate, and generally to break away as in the case of the United States and the Latin-American countries. Turgot had anticipated this a quarter of a century before the Declaration of Independence, saying, "Colonies are like fruits, which cling to the tree only till they ripen." The subsequent verification of his statement impressed governments, and after the Napoleonic wars empires confidently awaited dissolution.[20]

In fact, the western empires converted to the cause of nationality in Europe somewhat assisted the process in the case of Turkey by successively recognizing her subject nationalities in the Balkans as quasi- or wholly independent states. Although European states did not during the nineteenth century think of applying the principle of nationality to subject peoples of non-European civilization, still there was serious doubt of the expediency of holding such dependencies. So ardent an imperialist as Seeley could say in 1883, "When the state advances beyond the limits of nationality, its power becomes precarious and artificial. This is the condition of most empires; it is the condition for example of our own in India."[21] The notion that the eventual independence of dependencies was inevitable and expedient tended to the notion that it was a right. Not only was Turkey compelled to give her subject communities independence. Great Britain began to recognize the right of her dominions to full self-government not only in domestic affairs but finally in foreign affairs.[22] The United States in 1898 asserted that Cuba is

[19a] Under modern international law *res nullius* occupied by individuals or corporations of a state come within that state's sovereignty (Lindley, *op. cit.*, pp. 84–113).

[20] Seeley, *op. cit.*, pp. 37–42.

[21] *Ibid.*, p. 46.

[22] *Report of the Imperial Conference* (1926), Cmd. 2768. "From the point of view of the dominions the important point to note is the evolution from a position of dependence to one of freedom from control. These great communities have all the time been climbing a ladder. Now they have reached the top; but the climbing process is common to all the communities which form part of the Empire. Each of them, whether the population is predominantly white or predominantly colored, is gradually, as it develops in strength and capacity, passing upward from the stage in which the community is wholly subject to control exercised from London to that in which the measure

and of right ought to be free and independent of Spain and in 1902, after a temporary occupation as "trustee" for the Cubans, withdrew her own forces from the island.[23] The same power declared in 1899, but not with such speedy effectiveness, that the Philippines were entitled to eventual independence,[24] and a year later insisted on the

---

of control diminishes, and so on to that in which the control has ceased entirely. The dominions of today were but crown colonies in the past. The crown colonies of today will be dominions in days to come. There is nothing static about the British Empire" (Sir Cecil Hurst, *Great Britain and the Dominions* [1928], p. 12).

[23] The Supreme Court held in *Neeley* v. *Henkel*, 180 U.S. 109 (1901): "As between the United States and Cuba that is territory held in trust for the inhabitants of Cuba to whom it rightfully belongs and to whose exclusive control it will be surrendered when a stable government shall have been established by their voluntary action. . . . Indeed, the Treaty of Paris contemplated only a temporary occupancy and control of Cuba by the United States. While it was taken for granted by the treaty that, upon evacuation by Spain, the island would be occupied by the United States, the treaty provided that 'so long as such occupation shall last,' the United States should 'assume and discharge the obligations that may, under international law, result from the fact of its occupation for the protection of life and property.' " Wilson (*International Law* [2d ed., 1927], p. 32) classifies Cuba during this period with the mandates as "Entities in Trust." See also "Report of Secretary of War Root, 1902," printed in Root, *Military and Colonial Policy of the United States*, p. 221. The theory of British occupation of Egypt was much the same. Though it lasted for forty years it was always considered temporary (Moon, *op. cit.*, pp. 229 ff.).

[24] A majority of the Senate on February 14, 1899, soon after the ratification of the treaty of peace with Spain resolved: "That by the ratification of the treaty of peace with Spain it is not intended to incorporate the inhabitants of the Philippine Islands into citizenship of the United States, nor is it intended to permanently annex said islands as an integral part of the territory of the United States; but it is the intention of the United States to establish on said islands a government suitable to the wants and conditions of the inhabitants of said islands to prepare them for local self government, and in due time to make such disposition of said islands as will best promote the interests of the United States and the inhabitants of said islands" (*Congressional Record*, XXXII, 1847). In *Fourteen Diamond Rings* v. *U.S.*, 183, U.S. 176 (1901), the Supreme Court held this resolution to be of no legal effect, but that the islands "came under the complete and absolute sovereignty and dominion of the United States, and so became territory of the United States over which civil government could be established." President McKinley in his message of December 3, 1900, described American possession of the Philippines as "an unsought trust which should be unselfishly discharged and devolved upon this Government a moral as well as material responsibility toward these millions whom we have freed from an oppressive yoke." The Filipinos he described as "the wards of the nation. Our obligation as guardian was not lightly assumed; it must not be otherwise than honestly fulfilled, aiming first of all to benefit those who have come under our fostering care" (Richardson, *Messages and Papers of the Presidents*, X, 222). President Roosevelt on December 6, 1904, "earnestly hoped that in the end they

territorial integrity and administrative entity of China.[25] The Powers, including the United States, did the same for Morocco at Algeciras.[26]

The movement of nationalism, which began in Western Europe and spread first across the Atlantic and then to Eastern Europe and the Balkans, reached a climax during the World War in the broad announcements of self-determination not only for peoples of European civilization but for peoples of Asia and Africa.[27] The announcements were both declaratory and effective. They described movements which could be faintly observed and in doing so stimulated them into renewed activity. Nationalism, accompanied by an insistent demand for self-determination, is now a fact to be seriously reckoned with in many parts of Asia and Africa.[28]

Long before the war, however, nationalism or its antecedent, government by consent of the governed, had begun to change the terminology and administration of dependencies. The term "protectorate" which had been used for small states of Europe too weak to defend themselves was, in deference to the recognition by international jurists of native titles, applied to African acquisitions, and to conform to the theory of protectorates and to an American suggestion at the Berlin conference of 1885 the authority of the protector

---

will be able to stand, if not entirely alone, yet in some such relation to the United States as Cuba now stands" and he distinguished American work from that of other "civilized powers" with possessions in the Orient by its "endeavor to develop the natives themselves so that they shall take an ever-increasing share in their own government" (*ibid.*, p. 836). President Taft in December, 1912, had said, "We are seeking to arouse a national spirit and not, as under the older colonial theory, to suppress such a spirit," and President Wilson had in 1915 referred to the United States as "trustee of the Filipino people" (Baker, *Woodrow Wilson and World Settlement*, I [1922], 263–65). The Jones Act passed by Congress in 1916 declared, "It is as it always has been, the purpose of the people of the United States to withdraw their sovereignty from the Philippines and to recognize their independence as soon as a stable government can be established therein" (see Moon, *op. cit.*, pp. 392–99, and Snow, *op. cit.*, p. 200).

[25] Circular note to the Powers, July 3, 1900 (Moore, *Digest of International Law*, V, 481–82).

[26] Preamble to Algeciras convention, 1906 (Malloy, *Treaties, Conventions, etc.*, II, 2159). See *infra*, nn. 44, 45.

[27] See chap. ii *infra*.

[28] Chirol, *The Occident and the Orient* (1924), pp. 86 (Egypt), 101 (Sudan), 185 (Turkey), 197 (Afghanistan), 199 (Central Asia). Nationalist movements have since taken military form in Morocco (1925), Syria (1925), and China (1926).

was based on treaties with the native chiefs.[29] Earlier the United States and Great Britain had given similar recognition to the personality of native Indian communities in America and in India. The United States introduced a new term in referring to her "quasi-parental" relation to Liberia.[30] In some instances, colonial officers experimented with institutions of limited self-government in colonies of non-European or quasi-European civilization.[31] Native rulers were preserved with many of the externals of independence under the French protectorates in Tunis and Morocco and under the British control in Egypt. Although some protectorates like Madagascar, Brunei, and Korea rapidly glided toward annexation, thus justifying the impression that the term was a mere subterfuge, others like Abyssinia, Afghanistan, and Egypt have emerged into a status of recognized independence.

Thus the theory existed, though it was not universally accepted, and seldom applied, that every considerable people of distinct culture is potentially an independent state and that imperial powers can properly exercise only tutelage over them pending their maturity.[32]

4. International Mandate of Backward Territories.

A third change was the growing conviction that imperial responsibilities of trusteeship and tutelage toward dependencies is not

[29] The American representative, Mr. Kasson, said during the conference: "Modern international law follows closely a line which leads to the recognition of the rights of native tribes to dispose freely of themselves and of their hereditary territory. In conformity with this principle, my government would gladly adhere to a more extended rule to be based on a principle which should aim at the voluntary consent of the natives whose country is taken possession of in all cases where they have not provoked the aggression" (Snow, *op. cit.*, p. 152). For the method of negotiating such treaties see Moon, *op. cit.*, p. 101. The subject is treated in detail by Lindley, *op. cit.*, chaps. v, xxiii.

[30] Secretary of State Frelinghuysen to the French minister Roustan, August 22, 1884 (Moore, *Digest*, V, 773).

[31] The United States did so in Porto Rico and the Philippines and Great Britain in Fiji, Jamaica, other West Indian Islands, and in India, especially under the Montague-Chelmsford Act of 1919.

[32] W. F. Willoughby says the second principle of American colonial policy has been the "conferring on territory the largest measure of self government that the condition and character of its inhabitants render feasible," and the third principle has been eventually to admit such territory to statehood within the union or if that is not practical or desired by the people "to grant them that measure of autonomy or independence which they are fitted to enjoy, and which conditions render safe" (*op. cit.*, pp. 11–12). See also *supra*, nn. 18, 23, 24.

merely a moral responsibility but is a responsibility under international law which can properly be sanctioned by legal guaranties. Aborigines and their territory have tended to come under the protection of international law as evidenced not only by the gradual growth of custom but also by the conventional recognition of principles and the establishment of international procedures for enforcing them.

International law was originally confined in practice, though not in theory, to the Christian states of Europe.[33] The recognition of the United States and then of the Latin-American states as full members of the family of nations carried it out of Europe while the admission of Turkey to the "advantages of the public law and concert of Europe" in 1856 carried it out of the world of Christian nations, though the full equality of Turkey was not recognized until termination of the capitulations by the treaty of Lausanne in 1923. Japan was recognized as fully within the protection of international law by the treaties which became effective in 1899, and at the Hague conference of that year China, Korea, Siam, and Persia were present though all of them were still subject to extraterritoriality. Liberia was present at the second Hague conference, and Abyssinia was admitted to the League of Nations in 1923. Thus international law is no longer limited by geographical position or type of civilization, although judged by practice complete equality cannot be asserted of all its subjects.[34]

Some writers have attempted to classify on the basis of practice the international status of different communities according to their degree of civilization. Thus Lorimer distinguishes civilized, barbarous, and savage communities to each of which certain but different rights and duties are assigned. "The right of undeveloped races," he says, "like the right of undeveloped individuals, is a right not to recognition as what they are not, but to guardianship—that is, to guidance—in becoming that of which they are capable, in realising their special ideals."[35] To the same effect writes Alpheus H. Snow

[33] See *supra*, nn. 7, 9.

[34] See Dickinson, *The Equality of States in International Law* (Cambridge, 1920).

[35] *Institutes of the Law of Nations* (Edinburgh, 1883), I, 157.

after a careful examination of the principles actually applied in administering dependencies:

> It would seem, therefore, that the general nature of the jural relationship which a civilized state exercises over all its colonies and all its dependent communities, whether these communities be in colonies, or within its domestic territory or located externally to both, is best described by the word trusteeship, using this word in its literal sense as implying a fiduciary relationship essentially personal, though extending to property as well as person; that the fiduciary power is plenary, in the sense that it is adequate to the needs of the situation of the particular personality to which it is applied, though limited to those needs; that as a power over political personalities it is an incident of the sovereignty of each civilized State, and is governed by the law of nations, though not by the body of rules which apply between civilized States to which the name international law is properly applied, and that the closest analogies to this relationship which occur in the private law are those of patron and apprentice and guardian and ward.[36]

More specifically he found that the law of nations assured aborigines the right of occupying land subject to restrictions imposed by the guardian, the right to protection from the slave trade though not from all forms of domestic slavery or corporal punishment, the right to education and to sanitary conditions, and the right to have their treaties and agreements with civilized states respected. After a detailed study of practice Lindley also concludes that natives are within the protection of international law, not only prior to the extension of the influence of a civilized state, but under the terms of protectorate treaties and even after their incorporation in the state, though in the latter case the international duty is owed not to the natives but to other members of the family of nations.[36a]

Treaties have to an ever increasing extent established further

[36] *Op. cit.*, p. 70. The rather unusual distinction made here between "the law of nations" and "international law" is explained by the writer in *A.J.I.L.*, VI, 890, and VII, 315.

[36a] Lindley, *op. cit.*, pp. 45, 322, 324. He recognizes that territories nominally under colonial protectorate are sometimes within the protector's domain under international law (pp. 203–6). The Institute of International Law recognizes the duty of colonizing powers to avoid useless severities, to respect native individual and collective property, to educate and improve their moral and material conditions, to respect liberty of conscience, to prepare for the abolition of slavery, and to prohibit slave and liquor trade (Resolution, 1888).

rights of certain dependent native communities. Most important is the Berlin act of 1885 which sought to protect the natives of the conventional basin of the Congo "in their moral and material well being." The parties to the treaty agreed "to co-operate in the suppression of slavery and the slave trade, to further education and civilization of the natives; to protect missionaries, scientists and explorers." It also assured the open door in this region and equal rights in the navigation of the Congo and Niger rivers. Other general conventions have attempted to regulate the trade in slaves, liquor, and firearms among native races and to extend farther the open door.[37]

These conventional regulations have not been applied to all dependent areas and have been very indifferently observed in the regions to which they apply. Thus international supervision has been suggested and in some cases provided. The congress of Vienna had in 1815 deputed Great Britain to protect the Ionian Islands though no very definite supervision was provided.[38] In 1860 the Powers authorized France to land troops in the Lebanon to protect the Christians,[39] and the congress of Berlin in 1878 reserved some supervision over Turkey's administration of certain subject nationalities.[40] Proposals for neutralization of the conventional basin

[37] See Beer, *op. cit.*, Part III, and Snow, *op. cit.*, chaps. xi–xiii; Lindley, *op. cit.*, chaps. xxxvi–xlii.

[38] The treaty of Paris of November 5, 1815, declared them "an independent state . . . . under the immediate and exclusive protection of the King of Great Britain and Ireland." The Protector, however, continually extended his authority until the manifest desire of the people to unite with Greece led to a conference at London which resolved on August 1, 1863, that the islands should be united to Greece "under the sanction of a European Act" which was forthcoming in the treaty of November 14, 1863 (Holland, *European Concert in the Eastern Question* [1885], pp. 23, 45).

[39] Protocol 1 of the Paris conference, August 3, 1860. This limited the intervention to six months but was extended on March 19, 1861, to June 5, 1861, at which time the French forces withdrew (*ibid.*, p. 206).

[40] Art. 6 required the collaboration of the European powers in controlling the provisional régime of Bulgaria; arts. 17–19 and 23 provided a European commission to assist in setting up a new régime in Eastern Roumelia and Crete; art. 61 required Turkey "periodically to make known the steps taken to [guarantee the security of Armenians] to the powers who will superintend their application." Holland points out that little was done to carry out this article in spite of Mr. Bryce's repeated allusions to the subject in the House of Commons (*op. cit.*, pp. 283, 392, 306). The treaty of Paris

of the Congo and the establishment of a permanent international commission with general powers of supervision were so qualified before adoption at the Berlin congress of 1885 as to be meaningless. The congress did however consider itself in the position of a *tuteur officieux* or guardian of the natives who were entitled to the protection of international law.[41] This congress recognized the International Association of the Congo under Leopold of Belgium as competent to administer the Congo free state according to the terms of the Berlin act, but unfortunately without supervision.[42] In 1887 Ger-

---

of 1856, art. 9, had noted the Sultan's "generous intention toward the Christian populations of his empire" and his resolution to communicate firmans on the subject to the Powers, but while recognizing the high value of these communications the Powers "clearly understood" that it gave them no right "to interfere either collectively or separately" in Turkey. Nevertheless this article was referred to in the second protocol of the Paris conference of 1860 authorizing intervention in the Lebanon (*ibid.*, pp. 208, 246). "The assumption of a collective authority on the part of the powers to supervise the solution of the eastern question," says Holland, "has been exercised tentatively since 1826, systematically since 1856" (*ibid.*, p. 2). It was applied not only over certain regions such as Egypt, Syria, the Danubian principalities, and Armenia while they remained within Turkey but to new states like Greece, Serbia, Montenegro, Bulgaria, Roumania, and Albania recognized as "independent" by the concert. In the first type of case the supervision was usually to protect Christians and in the latter to fix boundaries and assure financial obligations. Similar supervision has been provided by the minority treaties since the World War over the succession states, but here as in the mandates the League of Nations provides a permanent machinery for exercising this supervision (see De Visscher, *The Stabilization of Europe* [1924], chap. ii). International supervision of China's finances, customs, and treatment of foreigners has been established by custom and treaty, especially the Boxer protocol of 1900 and the Washington conference treaties and resolutions of 1922.

[41] Beer, *op. cit.*, p. 259; Snow, *op. cit.*, p. 155; Lindley, *op. cit.*, p. 327.

[42] Lugard notes the analogy of the Congo arrangement with the mandates system (*The Dual Mandate in British Tropical Africa* [2d ed., 1923], p. 53). Since Stanley, an American citizen, had first explored the Congo, the United States took a major interest in the political destiny of this region and according to Snow desired: "First, that all nations should unite in founding 'a great state in the heart of western Africa whose organization and administration [should] afford a guarantee that it is to be held for all time, as it were, in trust for the benefit of all peoples'; second, that the obligations of this international trusteeship should be 'the civilization of the native races' and the assurance of 'equal privileges for all' as respects 'commercial enterprises'; third, that the proposed trustee State, in order to fulfill its international trusteeship, should be 'neutralized against aggression' " (*op. cit.*, p. 131). Apparently convinced that the International Association of the Congo could carry out these purposes, the United States was first to recognize it on April 22, 1884 (Malloy, *Treaties*, I, 327) and took a

many proposed that the Powers appoint a "mandatory" for Samoa, and in 1898 Italy suggested that Prince George of Greece be made "mandatory" of the Powers to administer Crete.[43] During the Russo-Japanese War, Dr. Ariga published a book entitled *Mandate System in Manchuria* urging Japan to assume the administration of that country on the basis of a treaty with China whereby the latter's sovereignty would be formally preserved and certain limitations would be imposed upon the Japanese administration, though international supervision seems not to have been contemplated.[43a] President Roosevelt and Secretary Root, doubtless with the proposals of the Berlin congress in mind, suggested that France and Spain be made "the mandatory of all the powers for the purpose of at once maintaining order and preserving equal commercial opportunities for all of them" in Morocco.[44] The Algeciras convention somewhat followed this suggestion but neglected to provide an effective system of supervision.[45]

In certain cases a single power had assumed supervision of

---

prominent part in the Berlin conference but failed to ratify its general act. Leopoldian administration of the Congo not only failed to live up to the requirements of the trust but presently became an international scandal (see Beer, *op. cit.*, p. 78; Moon, *op. cit.*, pp. 79–90; Buell, *The Native Problem in Africa*, New York, 1928).

[43] *British and Foreign State Papers*, LXXIX, 904; XCII, 1224–34; *J.C.L.* (3d ser., 1921), III, 327. See Batsell, "The United States and the System of Mandates," *Revue de Droit International* (Geneva), July–September, 1926, and comments thereon (Potter, *A.P.S.R.*, XX, 844).

[43a] This book is published in the Japanese language and the writer has become acquainted with it only through an article by Toji Manabe, entitled "Dr. Ariga and the Mandate System," which appeared in *Gaiko Jiho* (Tokio, 1927), XLVI, 107–21, and was translated for the writer by Sterling T. Takeuchi.

[44] Bishop, *Theodore Roosevelt, and His Times*, I, 494; Potter, *A.P.S.R.*, XVI, 580; XX, 846. The United States referred to itself as "the mandatory of civilization" to build the Panama Canal and to its "moral mandate" under the Central American treaty of 1907 to maintain order in Nicaragua (*U.S. For. Rel.* [1903], pp. 275–76; *ibid.* [1912], pp. 1042–43).

[45] Moon, *op. cit.*, pp. 202–18; Beer, *op. cit.*, pp. 105–6. Snow says: "The action of the Algeciras conference in formulating and declaring 'the triple principle' will no doubt prove to be of great importance in the development of the law of nations, as giving a concrete and practical interpretation of the rights and duties implied in mutual and reciprocal trusteeship" (p. 218). "The 'triple principle,' " he says, "of 'the sovereignty and independence' of each State once recognized as a State, 'the integrity of its domains,' and 'economic liberty' for all states in their dealings with the state, without any inequality, would seem to be a universal principle of the social law of nations" (p. 217).

another's administration of native races. Thus in 1860 Great Britain by treaty reserved the right to supervise Nicaragua's administration of the Mosquito Indians.[46] The same power reserved the right to enforce explicit conditions protecting natives and prohibiting differential customs duties in granting Queensland the right to administer British New Guinea in 1887[47] and in granting South Africa the right to administer Basutoland and Bechuanaland in 1909.[48] So also in their treaties establishing protectorates over native chiefs, European powers in addition to assuming responsibility for the foreign affairs of the native state have sometimes assumed supervision of the international administration of the native chief in respect to certain matters specified in the treaty such as abolition of the slave trade, administration of justice, and internal development.[48a]

Various writers such as J. A. Hobson,[49] Walter Lippman,[50]

[46] By this treaty Great Britain renounced her protectorate but specified certain rights for the natives. The legal opinion on which Emperor Francis Joseph based his award in the British-Nicaraguan arbitration of July 2, 1881, said that in insisting on Nicaraguan observance of the treaty Great Britain was not "intermeddling with the internal affairs" of Nicaragua and was not claiming "a continued exercise of the relinquished protectorate" but was merely claiming "a right of its own" to insist upon the fulfilment of the treaty clauses assuring "certain political and pecuniary advantages for the Mosquitoes" (Moore, *Digest of International Arbitrations,* V, 4965).

[47] Temperley, *History of the Peace Conference,* II, 236; *New Statesmen,* March 26, 1921.

[48] The South African Act, 1909, Part IX, sec. 151; D. Campbell Lee, *The Mandate for Mesopotamia and the Principle of Trusteeship in English Law,* p. 8. J. Stoyanovsky (*La Théorie générale des mandats internationaux* [Paris, 1925], p. 12) suggests that General Smuts found the prototype of the mandate system in these arrangements within the British Empire, and Sir Frederick Lugard says, "The British and Dutch Royal charters to companies—and indeed the orders issued to colonial governors—were written instruments conferring authority to govern as delegates" (*J.R.S.A.,* LXXII [June 27, 1924], 537). The relation of the South African company in the administration of Southern Rhodesia was described as a mandate by the Judicial Committee of the Privy Council (*In re Southern Rhodesia,* L.R. [1919], A.L. 244–45). See also Luther H. Evans, "Some Legal and Historical Antecedents of the Mandatory System," *Proceedings of the Fifth Annual Conference* (Southwestern Political Science Association, March, 1928), and denial of the force of the analogy (Potter, *A.P.S.R.,* XX, 843).

[48a] See "Treaty of Great Britain and Warsangali, 1886," *Br. and For. St. Pap.,* LXXVII, 1263; Lindley, *op. cit.,* p. 184.

[49] *Toward International Government* (New York, 1915), pp. 138–41, and *Towards a Lasting Settlement* (New York, 1916), pp. 106–7, discussed by Potter, *A.P.S.R.,* XVI, 574.

[50] *The Stakes of Diplomacy* (1915), chap. x.

Alpheus H. Snow,[51] and some of the British Round Table group,[52] in searching means to assure such principles as native protection and the open door in colonial areas without incurring the demonstrated inefficiencies of direct international administration, suggested conventional regulation similar to that of Algeciras with the addition of a permanent machinery for supervision. On January 1, 1918, G. L. Beer in a report to the "House inquiry" preliminary to the Paris Peace Conference dealt at length with the problem of the German colonies and elaborated the mandates system as eventually adopted using that term. He wrote:

> Under modern political conditions apparently the only way to determine the problem of politically backward peoples, who require not only outside political control but also foreign capital to reorganize their stagnant economic systems, is to entrust the task of government to that state whose interests are most directly involved. . . . . If, however, such backward regions are entrusted by international mandate to one state, there should be embodied in the deed of trust most rigid safeguards both to protect the native population from exploitation and also to ensure that the interests of other foreign states are not injured either positively or negatively.[53]

These ideas were developed before an informal conference participated in by several British and American experts on international affairs at London in November, 1918. The British protagonist of the plan wished to learn the views of the Americans as to the acceptability in America of certain mandates to be administered by the United States. Both the proposal and the views of two Americans were subsequently published in the *Round Table*. The words tutelage, trustee, wardship, and mandatory were all used; prohibition of forced labor, liquor traffic, militarization of natives, and education for self government were to be dealt with in the covenants; and the League was empowered to exercise continuous supervision and to dismiss a mandatory and appoint its successor in case the terms of the mandate were violated.[53a]

[51] *Op. cit.*, chap. xv.

[52] See *infra* n. 53a and Philip Kerr in Grant *et al.*, *International Relations* (London, 1916), chap. v.

[53] *Op. cit.*, pp. 424–25.

[53a] "Windows of Freedom" and succeeding articles, *Round Table*, December, 1918, March, 1919, pp. 26–28, 33, 97, 249, 259. The editor of the *Round Table*, Mr. Lionel

This plan was more precisely set forth by General Jan Smuts, of South Africa, in his proposal for a League of Nations published on December 16, 1918,[54] which was in large measure taken over by President Wilson in his second draft covenant of January 10, 1919.[55] These documents are undoubtedly the immediate source of article 22 of the League of Nations Covenant.[56]

The ideas of trusteeship, tutelage, and international mandate had all been discussed with reference to the administration of backward territory and had all been given actual trial before the Peace Conference. But General Smuts had a great advantage over previous speculators on the subject in the imminent presence of the League of Nations. An instrument for continuous international supervision of the mandatory which was lacking at Berlin in 1878 and 1885 and at Algeciras in 1906 seemed now certain. "What sharply distinguishes the Mandatory system from all such international arrangements of the past," writes Temperley, "is the unqualified right of intervention possessed by the League of Nations. The mandatories act on its behalf. They have not sovereign powers, but are responsible to the League for the execution of the terms of the mandate."[57]

Curtis, has informed the writer that he absorbed many of the ideas expressed in this article from conversations with Philip Kerr and others during 1918 and that General Smuts had read it before preparing his own memorandum.

[54] *The League of Nations, a Practical Suggestion* (London, 1918), reprinted in *New York Nation*, February 8, 1919; Baker, *Woodrow Wilson and World Settlement*, III (1922), 94; D. H. Miller, *The Drafting of the Covenant* (New York, 1928), II, 23. General Smuts is said to have collaborated with the Round Table group in preparing his plan (D. H. Miller, in House and Seymour, *What Really Happened at Paris* [New York, 1921], p. 402; Potter, *op. cit.*, p. 572).

[55] For text see Baker, *op. cit.*, III, 108; Miller, *op. cit.*, II, 87.

[56] See chap. ii, *infra.*

[57] *Op. cit.*, II, 236.

CHAPTER II

ESTABLISHMENT OF THE INSTITUTION

"The mandatory system," said M. Rappard, first director of the mandates section of the League Secretariat, "formed a kind of compromise between the proposition advanced by the advocates of annexation and the proposition put forward by those who wished to entrust the colonial territories to international administration."[1] Annexation and internationalization were doubtless the solutions most strongly advocated at the Peace Conference, but others such as independence or even restoration to the former owners were also suggested. Each of these solutions, however, was impossible.

1. COMPROMISES IN THE MANDATES SYSTEM

Annexation, though demanded by several of the Allies, was barred by specific pledges. The principle of no annexations and self-determination of peoples, proclaimed by the Russian Revolution,[2] had been emphasized by President Wilson,[3] and the Allies were com-

[1] *P.M.C.*, *Min.*, I, 4; Lugard, *The Dual Mandates in British Tropical Africa* (London, 1923), p. 53.

[2] See *Memorandum* (April 10, 1917), by Prince Lvoff, president of Russian Council; *Peace Terms of Russian Council of Workmen's and Soldiers Delegates* (October 20, 1917); *Proposal for Armistice* (November 22, 1917), by Trotsky, Bolshevik commissar for foreign affairs; Dickinson, *Documents and Statements Relating to Peace Proposals and War Aims* (1919), pp. 43, 79, 80–81. See also Baker, *Woodrow Wilson and World Settlement* (New York, 1922), I, 51; Temperley, *A History of the Peace Conference at Paris*, I, 235. In his address to the Senate on January 22, 1917, President Wilson had said, "No peace can last or ought to last, which does not recognize and accept the principle that governments derive all their just powers from the consent of the governed and that no right anywhere exists to hand peoples about from sovereignty to sovereignty as if they were property" (Scott, *Official Statements of War Aims and Peace Proposals* [Washington, 1921], p. 56; Temperley, *op. cit.*, pp. 431–48).

[3] In his address of February 11, 1918, President Wilson said: "Peoples and provinces are not to be bartered about from sovereignty to sovereignty as if they were mere chattels and pawns in a game, even the great game, now forever discredited of the balance of power; but every territorial settlement involved in this war must be made in the interest and for the benefit of the populations concerned, and not as a part of any mere adjustment or compromise of claims amongst rival states." See also addresses on April

mitted to it by the pre-Armistice agreement which formally accepted with specified modifications President Wilson's fourteen points and other speeches as the basis for peace.[4] The President's twelfth point of January 8, 1918, had declared "the Nationalities which are now under Turkish rule should be assured an undoubted security of life and an absolutely unmolested opportunity of autonomous development," and the fifth point referring to colonies declared that "the interest of the populations concerned must have equal weight with the equitable claims of the government whose title is to be determined." Lloyd George had gone even further in declaring "the general principle of national self determination is as applicable in their cases [the German colonies] as in those of occupied European territories."[5] President Wilson at the Conference was prepared to insist on fulfilments of these pledges.[6]

6, 1918, July 4, 1918, September 27, 1918; extracts collected, Temperley, *op. cit.*, I, 398–99. For texts of these addresses see Dickinson and Scott, *op. cit.;* Temperley, *op. cit.*, I, 431–48. See also President Wilson's conference with experts on the high seas while going to Paris, December 10, 1918, in which "self-determination" was spoken of as the first of the two central ideas on the President's program (Baker, *op. cit.*, I, 11). Dr. Isaiah Bowman's notes of this conference are printed in Miller, *The Drafting of the Covenant*, I, 41.

[4] Note, November 5, 1918 (Scott, *op. cit.*, p. 456; Temperley, *op. cit.*, I, 378–83; II, 246). The specified exceptions related to "freedom of the seas" and reparations and did not affect the territorial provisions. This agreement, made before the German armistice, legally superseded all conflicting agreements, secret or otherwise, with respect to Germany (see correspondence between Germany and Principal Allied and Associated Powers, May 29 and June 16, 1919, *Senate Doc. 149* [66th Cong., 1st sess.], pp. 83, 101; Temperley, *op. cit.*, I, 133–35, 417–20). The Turkish and Austrian armistices, however, had been made earlier, and these states were not parties to the agreement of November 5, as was Germany. Thus legally the conference was not bound to apply these principles to them. Both Turkey and Austria, however, had expressly referred to the Wilsonian principles in asking for peace, and the Allies, having propagandized them among the subject peoples of the two empires for war purposes, could not wholly repudiate them (Austrian note, October 7, 1918; Turkish note, October 14, 1918 [Scott, *op. cit.*, pp. 418–19]).

[5] Address, January 5, 1918 (Temperley, *op. cit.*, II, 226–27, also in Dickinson and Scott, *op. cit.*). This was expressly denied by Smuts, who, however, recognized the principle of self-determination (*op. cit.*, par. 2).

[6] "The point of view of the United States of America was indifferent to the claims of both Great Britain and France over peoples unless those people wanted them. One of the fundamental principles to which the United States of America adhered was the consent of the governed" (President Wilson in Conference of the Four, March 20, 1919 [Baker, *op. cit.*, III, 12; see also *ibid.*, I, 260]).

Internationalization of Palestine had been proposed in the Sykes-Picot agreement of 1916, and a similar treatment of ex-German colonies had been especially advocated in Socialist and labor circles,[7] but this solution was also barred not only by several practical demonstrations of the inefficiency of direct international administration of territory[8] but even more by the desire of certain allied belligerents to annex or at least to administer enemy colonies—a desire supported by actual occupation, by the public opinion of some of the Allies, and by various secret treaties. When the Peace Conference met Japan was in occupation of the North Pacific islands and had secret treaties made in February and March, 1917, with Great Britain, France, Russia, and Italy agreeing to support her claim to acquire them.

[7] A declaration of the Executive Committee of the British Labour party, December, 1917, after repudiating all imperialistic control over Central Africa, suggested the transfer of all the present colonies there "to the supra national authority of the League of Nations. . . . . Their administration will be organized under the authority of the Legislative council into an independent African state with its government based on the following principles: (1) Taking account in each locality of the wishes of the people when they can be determined, (2) protection of the natives against exploitation and oppression and preservation of their tribal interests, (3) all the revenues will be employed for the well-being and development of the African state itself, (4) permanent neutralization of the African state and its abstention from all participation in international rivalries or future wars." A similar declaration was made by the National Council of French socialist parties on February 18, 1918 (Schneider, *Das völkerrechtliche Mandat* [Stuttgart, 1926], p. 21; Furukaki, *Les Mandats internationaux de la société de nations* [Lyons, 1923], p. 25; Antonelli, *L'Afrique et la paix de Versailles* [Paris, 1923], p. 215; Stoyanovsky, *La Théorie générale des mandats internationaux* [Paris, 1925], p. 7; Woolf, *Empire and Commerce in Africa*, p. 355; Moon, *Imperialism and World Politics*, p. 476; Temperley, *op. cit.*, I, 217–18; VI, 502). See also statement of Lord Balfour, May, 1917 (Hendrick, *Life and Letters of Walter Hines Page*, II, 246).

[8] As in Samoa and the New Hebrides (see Beer, *African Questions at the Peace Conference* [1923], pp. 421–23; Temperley, *op. cit.*, II, 232; Hudson, in House and Seymour, *What Really Happened at Paris* [1921], p. 225; Hicks, *The New World Order* [1920], pp. 185–92; Smuts, *The League of Nations, a Practical Suggestion*, sec. 4; Stoyanovsky, *op. cit.*, pp. 7–8; Lugard, *J.R.S.A.*, LXXII, 536). "The experience of the world in regard to international administration had shown the unsatisfactory nature of such a form of government owing to the difficulty of fixing responsibility upon any one of the participating powers" (Temperley, *op. cit.*, VI, 502, and to the same effect Ormsby Gore, *The League of Nations Starts*, p. 111). A more favorable view of the possibility of direct international administration is given by Sayre (*Experiments in International Administration* [1919], chap. vi, and *The League of Nations Starts*, chap. vi), but see Sayre's later criticism of the international commission "which the experience of the past has shown to be too often the mere sport of international politics and from its very nature unsuited to the task" of colonial administration (Duggan, *The League of Nations*, p. 151).

Australian forces were in occupation of German New Guinea and Nauru and New Zealand forces were occupying German Samoa, while the secret treaty with Japan had recognized Britain's claim to the German islands south of the Equator. South African troops under General Botha had occupied German Southwest Africa and South African public opinion vigorously demanded annexation. British forces under General Smuts had occupied East Africa with the exception of a small region on the Congo border held by Belgians. The French and British had occupied Cameroons and Togoland and M. Simon, colonial minister of that power, argued for "annexation pure and simple." British forces under Maude and Allenby were holding Mesopotamia, Palestine, and Syria but the British had invited French forces under Gouraud to occupy the Lebanese and Syrian littoral and Cilicia in 1919 in pursuance of various secret treaties distributing Turkish territory made in 1915 and 1916. These states having sacrificed blood and treasure for the territories were not inclined to accept internationalization.[9]

Independence was barred by the same considerations. The German colonies were clearly in no condition to organize fully independent states and in any case the occupying powers would not withdraw. Nevertheless statements by allied leaders on self-determination[10] and specific pledges of independence made to some of the Arab chiefs could not be wholly ignored.[11] Feisal, the second son of King Hussein of the Hedjaz, was at the Conference to recall these pledges.

[9] Baker, *op. cit.*, Vol. I, chap. iii ("Principal Secret Treaties"); chap. iv ("The Turkish Empire as Booty"); chap. xv ("War Spoils at Paris"), esp. pp. 267–68; also Temperley, *op. cit.*, VI, 350–52; Condliffe, *Problems of the Pacific* (Chicago, 1928), pp. 192 ff.

[10] See *supra*, nn. 3–6.

[11] Exchange of notes between Sir Henry MacMahon representing Great Britain and King Hussein of the Hedjaz, October, 1915, and Anglo-French Declaration, November 9, 1918 (see Temperley, *op. cit.*, VI, 140, 174; George Kampffmeyer, "Urkunden und Berichte zur Gegenwartsgeschichte des arabischen Orients," *Mitteilungen des Seminars für orientalische Sprächen an der Friederich-Wilhelm Universität zu Berlin*, XXVI-XXVII (1924), II, 83–136. "Arab Petition to League of Nations, April 12, 1925," *P.M.C., Min.*, VII, 172; Wright, "The Palestine Problem," *P.S.Q.*, XLI, 392; Loder, *The Truth about Mesopotamia, Palestine and Syria* [London, 1923], chap. i; "Minutes of the Secret Conference, March 20, 1919," Baker, *op. cit.*, III, 4, 10). On this occasion Lloyd George recognized this agreement and admitted it gave the interior of Syria to the Arabs. France was not a party to the agreement and refused to be bound by it, and insisted on the whole of Syria as a mandate. The Arabs who were occupying the inte-

Finally, restoration of the colonies to Germany and Turkey was barred by the course of allied war propaganda as well as by the insistence of the present occupants. The Allies had persistently alleged during the war that Germany had proved herself hopelessly incompetent and brutal as a colonial power and that the natives wished to be rid of her. Though these allegations hardly bear historical scrutiny if comparison is made with the colonial administration of some of the Allied Powers,[12] they were so thoroughly believed among the allied peoples that the Peace Conference was bound by them[13] and Germany's plea for restoration or at least a mandate of her colonies was in vain.[14] Allegations in regard to Turkish misrule in the Arab countries and Armenia were more sustainable, and there was no doubt of the desire of most of the inhabitants to be rid of Turkey.[15]

---

rior felt betrayed. General Allenby said at the March 20 conference, "If the French were given a mandate in Syria there would be serious trouble and probably war." Colonel Lawrence while with the Arabs in 1917 wondered at the peoples' "attitude of accepting the result naturally and trustingly" and had to persuade himself "that the British government would really keep the spirit of its promises" (T. E. Lawrence, *Revolt in the Desert*, 1927, p. 189).

[12] See Schnee (*German Colonization Past and Future* [London, 1926]), a former governor of German East Africa who vigorously denies the allied charges. See also *infra*, chap. iii, sec. 3.

[13] Beer, *op. cit.*, pp. 38, 58; Temperley, *op. cit.*, II, 227; Hudson, *op. cit.*, p. 224; Smuts, *op. cit.*, sec. 2. At the meeting of the Council of Ten on January 24, 1919, Lloyd George attempted to show that the German colonial policy had been a bad one and opposed the return of any of her colonies. President Wilson "thought all were agreed to oppose the restoration of the German colonies." Orlando for Italy and Makino for Japan agreed and the principle was adopted by formal resolution on January 30, 1919 (see Baker, *op. cit.*, I, 255, and text of resolution in King-Crane report on Near East, 1919, *Editor and Publisher*, LV [December 2, 1922], 12; Miller, *Foreign Affairs*, January, 1928, p. 284).

[14] See German observations on the conditions of peace, May 29, 1919, sec. 10, requesting an impartial hearing of the colonial question as required by President Wilson's fifth point and allied reply of June 16, 1919, expressing the conviction that "the native inhabitants of the German colonies are strongly opposed to being again brought under Germany's sway" ("Conditions of Peace with Germany," *U.S. Sen. Doc. 149* [66th Cong., 1st sess.], pp. 81, 89, 102, 118). For minute of agreement in the Council of Ten on January 24, 1919, not to restore the German colonies, see Miller, *The Drafting of the Covenant*, I, 105.

[15] Bryce report on treatment of the Armenians in the Ottoman Empire, 1915–16, and King-Crane report on the Near East (*op. cit.*, pp. 12–13) which quotes the resolution of the Peace Conference of January 30, 1919, "Because of the historical misgovern-

Thus annexation, internationalization, independence, and restoration were all impossible though each was desired in certain quarters. This was a dilemma and a dilemma which, as Lord Milner pointed out, had to be solved compatibly with "the idealistic spirit in which immediately after the war a great many people had approached the problem of world settlement."[16] This idealistic spirit was insisting on the principles of trusteeship, tutelage, and international supervision referred to in the last chapter. Writers, organizations, and even government experts were demanding that the natives be protected against exploitation, especially against military conscription, and that they be given every opportunity for self-development. The abolition of colonial monopolies and the maintenance of the open door for the trade and investment of all countries was insisted upon as was the creation of adequate international guaranties to assure these conditions.[17] These idealistic demands had been indorsed in President Wilson's speeches with more or less definiteness and were reiterated by him at the Peace Conference.[18]

A solution compatible with both the negative and positive requirements of allied commitments was not easy to devise but this

---

ment by the Turks of subject peoples and the terrible massacres of Armenians and others in recent years, the allied and associated powers are agreed that Armenia, Syria, Mesopotamia, Palestine, and Arabia must be completely severed from the Turkish empire."

[16] *J.R.S.A.*, LXXII (June 27, 1924), 548; see also Ormsby-Gore, in *The League of Nations Starts* (1920), p. 105–6.

[17] See British writers Hobson and Kerr, and American experts Beer, Snow, and Lippmann, *supra*, chap. i, nn. 49–53. The conference of allied associations for a League of Nations held at Paris, January 25–30, 1919, resolved that the League Council should be invested with "the moral tutelage of uncivilized races" and should assure the conclusion and execution of international conventions "necessary for the protection and the progress of these races." A similar resolution was adopted on February 6, 1919, by the International Socialist Conference at Berne, and the League Constitution proposed by the German delegation at the Peace Conference provided for an international bureau to supervise the protection of natives and the open door in all colonies (arts. 57–61) (see "Conditions of Peace with Germany," *U.S. Sen. Doc. 149* [66th Cong., 1st sess.]; Stoyanovsky, *op. cit.*, pp. 9, 14).

[18] See *supra*, n. 3, and *infra*, n. 36. President Wilson's third point of January 8, 1918, had called for "the removal as far as possible of all economic barriers and the establishment of an equality of trade conditions among all the nations consenting to the peace and associating themselves for its maintenance." See also addresses of February 11, 1918, and April 6, 1918; extracts collected in Temperley, *op. cit.*, I, 416.

solution was found in General Smut's proposal published on the very eve of the Conference. This proposal consisted of twenty-one articles organizing a League of Nations, the first nine of which dealt with mandates. Each article was preceded by an extensive "argument or comment . . . . written in a moving and appealing style, tending indeed to disarm criticism of the text of the articles." The setting up of a League of Nations was envisaged as "the primary and basic task" of the Peace Conference, and the League was to "be considered as the reversionary in the most general sense" of the "peoples and territories formerly belonging to Russia, Austria-Hungary and Turkey" and "as clothed with the right of ultimate disposal in accordance with certain fundamental principles. Reversion to the League of Nations should be substituted for any policy of national annexation." General Smuts, however, did not wish to push his proposal too far. As "the German colonies in the Pacific and Africa are inhabited by barbarians, who not only cannot possibly govern themselves but to whom it would be impracticable to apply any idea of political self-determination in the European sense," they were excluded. Thus, though the "interests of the populations" should be considered as required by Wilson's fifth point, General Smuts would not have interfered with the interest of Great Britain and her dominions in annexing these colonies.[19]

General Smut's plan doubtless grew from suggestions from many sources[20] as well as from his own understanding of the dilemma in

[19] Smuts, *The League of Nations, a Practical Suggestion* (London, 1918), reprinted in *New York Nation* (February 8, 1919); Baker, *op. cit.*, III, 94; Miller, *The Drafting of the Covenant*, II, 23; see comments of Miller and Scott in this document, *ibid.*, I, 34). For accounts of the making of art. 22 of the Covenant see Miller, *Foreign Affairs*, January, 1928; *The Drafting of the Covenant*, I, 100–117; Baker, *op. cit.*, Vol. I, chaps. xiii–xv; Temperley, *op. cit.*, II, 21–31, 231–36; VI, 351, 500–525; House and Seymour, *What Really Happened at Paris* (1921), pp. 223–26, 398–424; Lansing, *The Peace Negotiations* (1921), chap. xiii; Potter, "Origin of the System of Mandates under the League of Nations," *P.S.R.*, XVI, 563–83; XX, 842–46. Stoyanovsky, *La Théorie générale des mandats internationaux* (Paris, 1925), chap. i; Schneider, *op. cit.* (Stuttgart, 1926), pp. 12–32; Lugard, "The Mandate System and the British Mandates," *J.R.S.A.*, LXII (June 27, 1924), 535–40; Evans, *Proceedings of the Fifth Annual Convention of Southwestern Political Science Association*, March, 1924; Batsell, *Revue de Droit International* (Geneva), July–September, 1924.

[20] Potter (*op. cit.*, XVI, 583) thinks Smuts got his idea from the Roosevelt-Root mandate plan for Morocco transmitted by Hobson and the British Round Table group

which the allied statesmen found themselves. It was forwarded to President Wilson and incorporated with some modifications in his second draft covenant circulated on January 10, 1919.[21] Earlier British plans such as the Phillimore draft convention prepared by a committee under the Foreign Office on March 20, 1918, and Lord Robert Cecil's plan circulated to the war cabinet on December 17, 1918, made no mention of mandates though the first draft of the latter suggested "an African commission." The official British draft of January 20, 1919, utilized all three of these plans and "recognized the duty encumbent upon the more advanced members of the family of nations to render help and guidance under the sanction of the League in the development of the administration of states and territories which have not yet attained to stable government." To define the "responsibility of mandatory states" it suggested an annexed convention. This document divided the areas into "vested territories" and "assisted states" and suggested a commission established by the League council to examine reports of mandatories and to recommend thereon to the council.[22] In the amalgamation of this plan with Wilson's second draft worked out by Lord Eustace Percy, the British plan was followed in respect to mandates, and in the

---

and reinforced by the Wilson principles for the peace settlement. Schneider (*op. cit.*, p. 31) follows Potter but doubts the influence of the Roosevelt-Root plan which he says "remained without permanent practical significance and fell again into oblivion." Stoyanovsky suggests that General Smuts found the prototype of the mandate system in arrangements within the British Empire (*op. cit.*, p. 12), and Lugard thinks the method of chartered companies and international supervision of the Congo may have been suggestive (*op. cit.*, p. 537). These precedents were suggested in the *Round Table* article of December, 1918. *Supra*, chap. i, nn. 53a, 54.

[21] For text see Miller, *op. cit.*, II, 87; Baker, *op. cit.*, III, 108. President Wilson's third draft is similar (Miller, *op. cit.*, II, 103; Baker, *op. cit.*, III, 126; see also "Hearings, Committee on Foreign Relations U.S. Senate, 1919," *Sen. Doc. 106* [66th Cong., 1st sess.], pp. 259, 1169, 1175, 1218, 1225). In a discussion with the American experts while on the high seas in December, 1918, before seeing the Smuts plan, President Wilson thought "the German colonies should be declared the common property of the League of Nations and administered by small nations. The resources of each colony should be available to all members of the League" (Baker, *op. cit.*, I, 10; Miller, *op. cit.*, I, 43).

[22] Miller, *op. cit.*, I, 106; Schneider (*op. cit.*, p. 27, referring to Furukaki, *op. cit.*, p. 25.) refers to a memorandum to the British Colonial Office which recognized three classes of mandates. He must have meant this document though it only refers to two types of territory.

Miller-Cecil revision of this document produced on January 27, 1919, the question of mandates was reserved. Wilson's fourth draft of February 2, 1919, was made after the resolution of the Commission of Ten on mandates, and incorporated most of the latter, though it added two paragraphs authorizing the League to issue mandates and to hear petitions and stating that the "object" of all such tutelary oversight and administration by the League "shall be to build up in as short a time as possible out of the people or territory under its guardianship a political unit which can take charge of its own affairs, determine its own connections, and choose its own policies." The League was empowered to release such people from tutelage at any time and the people were entitled to petition for this purpose.[23]

This document, however, was not used as the basis of the deliberations of the League of Nations Commission as President Wilson had at first intended but instead the Hurst-Miller draft which he had seen before preparing his and which had been worked out by the legal advisers of the British and American delegations on the basis of the Miller-Cecil draft during the night of February 1 and 2. The Hurst-Miller draft contained a brief article on mandates evidently with the thought of supplementing it by an annexed convention.[24] French and Italian draft covenants were submitted to the League of Nations Commission but they contained nothing on mandates.[25] The text actually adopted was introduced in the League of Nations Commission on February 8 by General Smuts as a substitute for the brief Hurst-Miller article. Like Wilson's fourth draft it incorporated almost verbatim the resolution adopted by the Commission of Ten on January 30. The latter had been introduced by Lloyd George and was actually drafted in the main by General Smuts. Thus both the original proposal and the final form of article 22 is largely the work of General Smuts. There are, however, notable differences with respect to the territories covered, to the rôle of the League, and to the principles applied which developed out of the proposal mentioned between December 16, 1918, and January 30, 1919.[26]

[23] For texts of the documents here referred see Miller, *op. cit.*, II, 62, 106, 129, 140, 151–53, and comments, I, 38, 60, 73.

[24] Miller, *op. cit.*, I, 68; II, 236.

[25] *Ibid.*, II, 238–46.

[26] Temperley says, "The actual wording is due to the main to General Smuts and M. Philip Kerr" (*op. cit.*, VI, 501; see Miller, *op. cit.*, I, 105, 109; Potter, *A.P.S.R.*, XVI, 570–71; Moon, *op. cit.*, pp. 480–83).

Whereas General Smuts originally thought of applying the mandatory system to the broken empires of Austria-Hungary, Russia, and Turkey from which he expressly "distinguished in principle" the German Colonial empire, the Wilson draft, benefiting by a memorandum prepared by Messrs. D. H. Miller and J. B. Scott, omitted Russia and added the former German colonies. Baker writes:

The President when he used General Smuts' suggestion had pressed it further than General Smuts ever intended. He universalized it. General Smuts never thought of applying the principle to the former German colonies but only to the old empires that were to be liquidated. But the President perceived the direct annexation of these vast colonial territories in Africa, Asia, and the Pacific, with their millions of population and their great strategic political and economic values, to be quite as dangerous in practice and as likely to be the cause of future wars as the annexation of parts of Turkey, Russia, or Austria. He clearly foresaw the difficulties which could later arise over the control of the Pacific and of China—if the new principle was not adopted at the start.[27]

The final text of article 22 follows a suggestion by David Hunter Miller and the desire of Italy in omitting Austria-Hungary as well as Russia,[28] and one by General Bliss in avoiding the names of the former sovereigns so that "color would not be given to the idea that the League of Nations has for one of its principal objects the control of situations growing out of the present war."[29] Thus it applies the system "to those colonies and territories which as a consequence of the late war have ceased to be under the sovereignty of the states which formerly governed them and which are inhabited by peoples not yet able to stand by themselves under the strenuous conditions of the modern world." The system originally proposed by General Smuts for solving the nationality problem of Eastern Europe and the Near East was in fact utilized for solving the colonial problem in parts of Asia, Africa, and the Pacific.

Furthermore, the rôle of the League had been considerably re-

[27] Baker, *op. cit.*, I, 266; Miller, *op. cit.*, I, 34–39, 101–2; Batsell, *op. cit.*, II, 265; Rappard, "The League of Nations as an Historical Fact," *International Conciliation*, No. 231 (June, 1927), p. 291; Temperley, *op. cit.*, VI, 351. The *Round Table* proposal applied the system to all German colonies except Southwest Africa (IX, 28).

[28] Miller, *op. cit.*, I, 65, 102; II, 87; "Senate Hearings," *op. cit.*, p. 1202, and Hurst-Miller draft, *supra*, n. 24. Signor Orlando had objected that "if the Trentino and Trieste were to be handed over to a Mandatory by the League of Nations, it would seriously compromise Italy's dignity" and the President had promised to make a change.

[29] Miller, *op. cit.*, II, 96; Baker, *op. cit.*, III, 114.

duced in the final draft. By the original Smuts and Wilson proposals the League was "reversionary of the empires" and had the right of allocating the mandates and of substituting a new mandatory in case of breach of mandate. Under the Covenant and treaties the first of these powers is vested in the principal Allies while the last is not expressly referred to. These changes arose from the insistence of the British dominions that their *de facto* possession be imediately legitimatized and from Lloyd George's argument that the financial responsibility of his government toward Parliament required an immediate determination of the status of occupying troops in German East Africa and the Arab countries.[30]

The original mandates proposals also clearly contemplated approval of the mandatory by the natives of the territory but the Covenant requires this only for A mandates. The failure to specify the open door for A and C mandated territories and to prohibit the military use of natives by the mandatory in A mandated territories are also modifications of the original Wilson-Smuts idea, though the A mandates in fact went further than the Covenant and with certain exceptions required the open door. These changes can easily be explained by the desire of the prospective mandatories to get *de jure* possession without delay and to be as little limited as possible in their future government of the areas. The C class mandates was in fact created in order to permit the British dominions to close the door to immigration and trade in their areas, prerogatives which they claimed under the secret treaties.[31] Though the text adopted forbids the "military training of the natives [in B and C territories] for other than police purposes and defense of territory," the Council of Ten accepted an interpretation which appears to justify the exceptional provision in the French mandates for Cameroons and Togoland permitting the use of such troops for "defense of the territory outside that subject to the mandate."[32]

2. Peace Conference Negotiations

In spite of the reductions of the League's power, as originally contemplated by Smuts and Wilson, the mandatory system was applied

[30] Miller, *op. cit.*, II, 222.

[31] Moon, *op. cit.*, pp. 482, 502; Miller, *op. cit.*, I, 106, and *Foreign Affairs* (January, 1928), p. 280; Temperley, *op. cit.*, VI, 351, 515.

[32] See *infra*, n. 40.

by the treaties and subsequent documents to nearly all[33] non-European enemy territories. President Wilson's successful struggle to achieve this result is one of the most dramatic incidents of the Peace Conference.[34] Forgetting their commitments during the war some of the Allies made a vigorous drive for outright annexation of certain territories. In this the British dominions with Hughes of Australia and Massey of New Zealand as their leading protagonists took a prominent part. To achieve this end, in opposition to President Wilson's plan, which put the League of Nations first and the colonies last on the Peace Conference agenda,[35] Lloyd George raised the colonial question on January 23, 1919, in the Council of Ten before the Covenant was drafted. Urged to favor annexation of much of this territory by the dominions and by France and Japan who had been assured territories by secret treaties, it required all the strategy of President Wilson to prevent the mandatory idea, already accepted in principle, from being "negated in detail."[36] On January 27, before the Council of Ten, President Wilson expounded his conception of the mandatory system:

> The basis of this idea was the feeling which had sprung up all over the world against further annexation. Yet, if the Colonies were not to be returned to Germany (as all were agreed), some other basis must be found to develop them and to take care of the inhabitants of these backward territories. It was with this object that the idea of administration through mandatories acting on behalf of the League of Nations arose. . . . . Some institution must be found to carry out the ideas all had in mind, namely, the development of the country for the benefit of those already in it, and for the advantage of those who would live there later. . . . .
>
> The purpose was to serve the people in undeveloped parts, to safeguard them against abuses such as had occurred under German administration and such as might be found under other administrations. Further, where people

[33] For a few exceptions see *infra*, nn. 51, 59.

[34] See Baker, *op. cit.*, chaps. iv, xv.

[35] *Ibid.*, I, 198; Temperley, *op. cit.*, I, 252. At the opening session of the Conference, January 18, 1919, Clemenceau, as president of the Conference, announced that the next session would begin with discussion of the League of Nations. At the second plenary session, January 25, a resolution was passed declaring that a League of Nations should be created as an integral part of the peace treaty and a committee was appointed to work out a plan (see Miller, *op. cit.*, I, 76; II, 155 ff.; *International Conciliation*, No. 139 [June, 1919], pp. 805 ff.).

[36] President Wilson's remarks in Council of Ten, January 28, 1919 (Baker, *op. cit.*, I, 268, and *supra*, n. 18).

and territories were undeveloped, to assure their development so that, when the time came, their interests, as they saw them, might qualify them to express a wish as to their ultimate relations—perhaps lead them to desire their union with the mandatory power. . . . .

In the first place, the League of Nations would lay down certain general principles in the mandate, namely, that districts be administered primarily with a view to the betterment of the conditions of the inhabitants. Secondly, that there should be no discrimination against members of the League of Nations so as to restrict economic access to the resources of the districts. . . . . All countries would pay the same duties, all would have the same right of access. . . . .

If the process of annexation went on, the League of Nations would be discredited from the beginning. Many false rumours had been set about regarding the Peace Conference. Those who were hostile to it said that its purpose was merely to divide up the spoils. If they justified that statement in any degree, that would discredit the Conference.

His audience was by no means enthusiastic for the proposal. There was no serious conflict of interest as to the distribution of the territory. This, it was understood, would follow the secret treaties in any case with possible exception of the special interest of the United States (not a party to those treaties) in the cable situation of Yap and the strategic importance of the other North Pacific islands for Philippine's defense, but on the form of tenure there was diversity. France wanted to annex part of Togo and the Cameroons in pursuance of her black-army policy, the three British dominions wanted to annex the South Pacific islands and Southwest Africa, and Japan seems to have preferred annexation of the North Pacific islands. The government of Great Britain was in a mixed position. It wanted to keep peace in the commonwealth family but aside from that, according to David Hunter Miller,

it cared very little about annexation as distinguished from mandates either in Africa or in the Pacific, indeed, while committed to the Japanese claim for islands north of the equator, the British probably preferred the mandate system to annexation in either locality.[37]

He continues:

Turkey was another matter; Egypt, the Suez Canal, the Persian Gulf, the Balfour declaration regarding Palestine, the rather vague commitments to the

[37] Miller, *op. cit.*, I, 104. See also "Minutes of Council of Ten, January 30, 1919," *ibid.*, II, 194–228, and Miller's notes made at the time (I, 112–13) on which the following is based.

Arabs and the various agreements with the French and the Italians about Syria or Cilicia or Anatolia, were all factors.

Furthermore there was a good deal of difference in public opinion in Great Britain on this general question. During the election campaign in December [1918] it had been bluntly asserted, for example, that Mesopotamia was a very rich country and if the British took it over, it would help pay the cost of the war. . . . . On the other hand, there was a feeling which was pretty strong even in 1919 against the extension of British colonial rule in any form whatever, anywhere. "The British Empire is big enough," is the way this sentiment was reflected among some of the most responsible British representatives at Paris.

On January 29, Lloyd George met with the dominion representatives who indicated their desire to annex the German territories they were occupying but finally accepted a compromise prepared by General Smuts. This extended the mandates principle to all the conquered German colonies and Turkish territories but created the C class to include the colonies occupied by the dominions which would be allotted to them as mandatories to be governed as "integral parts of their territory" without any obligation to maintain the open door. Colonel House had been shown this proposal and regarded it as a "fair compromise."[38]

On the next day the dominion representatives appeared before the Council of Ten and Lloyd George presented the document stating that it did not represent the views of the dominions but had been accepted by them as a compromise. Hughes of Australia agreed and President Wilson expressed doubt whether a final decision could be made on the mandates until the League of Nations was completed. Lloyd George thought this would take too long and asked at least for a provisional acceptance of the resolution. To this President Wilson agreed. Orlando of Italy then said he was not clear whether provisional acceptance of the resolution meant that the status until final action of the League would be that of military occupation or a temporary mandate, but in either case Italy must "obtain her share." Clemenceau assumed that the resolution was accepted and suggested they proceed to the next question. Makino of Japan "expressed satisfaction" with the provisional agreement on the question of mandatories.

Hughes of Australia then arose and said President Wilson's re-

[38] Miller, *op. cit.*, I, 109.

marks "had disturbed" the compromise which he had accepted. He would not accept a provisional mandate the nature of which was unknown. "Was not the *de facto* League of Nations already in existence in that room? . . . . No League of Nations could be superior to the members of the conference. . . . . The world looked to them for decisions." Sir Robert Borden of Canada professed high regard for the League of Nations but thought it should not be burdened in infancy with too much and hoped the mandates matter might be determined as speedily as possible.

The meeting then recessed to the afternoon when Massey of New Zealand referred to the clause in the resolution dealing with C mandates and said it was only on the basis of that article that the dominions had accepted the mandate principle. "It was a matter of life and death to many of them." He personally preferred direct annexation because that would enable them "to proceed very much more quickly with the development of the territories" and to "educate the native races not only in secular matters but also in the principles of Christianity which he believed was necessary for the welfare of all nations."[39] Consequently he regretted that he had not heard definitely whether President Wilson accepted that article. "President Wilson then asked if he was to understand that New Zealand and Australia had presented an ultimatum to the conference." Massey said, "No," but Hughes said he felt he ought not to concede more than the resolution. Botha of South Africa made a conciliatory speech and said in spite of his interest in Southwest Africa he had been willing to accept this resolution because he believed the "League of Nations would consist mostly of the same people who were present there that day, who understood the position and who would not make it impossible for any mandatory to govern the country." Massey then said he never used threats, but without further instructions he could not concede any more than the resolution.

France now voiced her desire through Pichon and Clemenceau to recruit native troops in her mandated territories in case of general

[39] This recalls President McKinley's remark to a group of Methodist clergymen in 1898 that he prayed for light on the Philippine question and arose converted to annexation in order to "uplift, civilize and christianize" the Filipinos (Garner, *American Foreign Policies* [1928], p. 77).

war. It was agreed that this was implied from the resolution as amended on suggestion of Sir Robert Borden of Canada. Though ostensibly introduced merely to clarify the text by rearrangement of clauses, this amendment inserted the words "and the defense of territory" in the phrase prohibiting military training of natives "for other than police purposes and the defense of territory." Lloyd George said:

He really thought that those words would cover the case of France. There was nothing in the document which would prevent their doing exactly the same thing as they had done before. What it did prevent was the kind of thing the Germans were likely to do, namely, organize great black armies in Africa, which they could use for the purpose of clearing everybody else out of that country. That was their proclaimed policy and if that was encouraged amongst the other nations even though they might not have wars in Europe, they would have the sort of thing that happened in the 17th and 18th century in India when France and Great Britain were at war in India, whilst being fairly good friends in Europe. Then they were always raising great native armies against each other. That must now be stopped. There was nothing in this document which prevented France doing what she did before. The defense of the territory was provided for.

M. Clemenceau said that if he could raise troops, that was all he wanted.

Mr. Lloyd George replied that he had exactly the same power as previously. It only prevented any country drilling the natives and raising great armies.

M. Clemenceau said that he did not want to do that. All that he wished was that the matter should be made quite plain, and he did not want anybody to come and tell him afterward that he had broken away from the agreement. If this clause meant that he had a right of raising troops in case of general war, he was satisfied.

Mr. Lloyd George said that so long as M. Clemenceau did not train big "nigger" armies, for the purpose of aggression, that was all the clause was intended to guard against.

M. Clemenceau said that he did not want to do that. He therefore understood that Mr. Lloyd George's interpretation was adopted.

President Wilson said that Mr. Lloyd George's interpretation was consistent with the phraseology.

M. Clemenceau said that he was quite satisfied.[40]

[40] Miller, *op. cit.*, II, 218. Mr. Miller, who was present at the January 30 meeting, made a pencil note during the discussion as follows: "Clemenceau and Pichon speak against the clause preventing voluntary recruiting in colonies—they want this right in mandatories as well as present colonies. This right is admitted by L.G. and W.W." (*ibid.*, I, 116). Though the omission of the word "the" from the phrase "defense of territory" in the English text of the Covenant suggests that territory outside of the

Orlando's suggestion interpreted by Clemenceau to mean that as "France, England and her dominions had their share, Italy wanted to have her own share" was reiterated and supported by Clemenceau and Lloyd George in a demand for immediate allocation of the near eastern mandates. The latter "put the British position again":

The German colonies did not matter very much, although the maintenance of troops in German East Africa was a very considerable burden. He could not say exactly how many troops they had in that theatre, but he knew it was a very considerable number. Coming to the Turkish empire, he had handed some figures to the President of the United States and to M. Clemenceau, and he had also told M. Orlando that they had 1,084,000 men there. It was true that only between 250,000 and 300,000 were British troops, but they had to maintain the lot, and it was an enormous expense. The difficulty was to keep all these various tribes in some sort of peace with each other. If they kept them there until they had made peace with Turkey, and until the League of Nations had been constituted and had started business, and until it was able to dispose of this question, the expense would be something enormous and they really could not face it, especially as they had not the slightest intention of being Mandatories of a considerable number of territories they now occupied, such as Syria and parts of Armenia. He thought the same thing applied to Kurdistan and the Caucasus, although they had rich oil-wells. He did not think that they had the slightest intention of being mandatories even for the oil-wells of Baku, but somebody had to be there to protect the Armenians and to keep the tribes and sects in Lebanon from cutting each other's throats and attacking the French or Turks, or whoever else might be there. Therefore, he was afraid that they must insist (he was not using that word in a military sense but from the point of view of those who had to pay taxes in the United Kingdom, and to propose it to parliament). He was afraid, however, that Parliament would want to know why they should keep 1,084,000 men there? Did they really mean to occupy the country? Why should they do so when they had no intention of having a permanent garrison there? This question specially affected them, and unless the Conference was prepared to relieve them of that responsibility, he would really have to press very hard for a definite appointment of the mandatories,

---

mandated area is included, a contrary impression might be gained from the official French text which reads *defense du territoire*, though perhaps the argument is weakened by the fact that the phrase *defense de territoire* would not be very good French. See Diena ("Les Mandats internationaux," *Acad. D.I.*, V, 249) who thinks no conclusion one way or the other can be drawn from the phraseology. The failure of M. Clemenceau's later attempt to insert more specific words in the text of art. 22 somewhat weakens the argument drawn from the dialogue here quoted (see *infra*, n. 45).

which he should have thought was the most satisfactory way of dealing with it. They could clear out, and leave the mandatory to undertake the job."[41]

The problem was, however, settled after Wilson had pointed out that administration of mandates would be in many cases a burden not a privilege and that formal assumption of these burdens, certainly in the case of the United States, could not be undertaken without further consideration and instruction of public opinion. Adequate military control was all that was necessary now and he suggested that the military advisers of the powers report on the "most equitable and economical distribution among the powers of the burden of supplying military forces for the purpose of maintaining order in the Turkish Empire and Trans-Caucasia" pending final decision of the Peace Conference. This was accepted as was Lloyd George's resolution as amended.[42]

President Wilson had thus prevented annexation, got the principle of mandates accepted for all the territories, and postponed final allocation of mandates until the League of Nations was in operation though he had been obliged to recognize the prior claim of the occupying powers to receive mandates, the special claim of the dominions in respect to the open door and of France in respect to recruiting natives.

The resolution of the Council of Ten with elimination of the first two paragraphs which recited the misgovernment of Germany and Turkey in their colonies and the addition of two paragraphs dealing with the powers of the League Council and the Permanent Mandates Commission was proposed by General Smuts in the commission on the League of Nations as a substitute for the mandates article in the Hurst-Miller draft and accepted on February 8 with a few modifications.[43] General Smuts had modified the text by omitting the word "yet" in the qualification of the peoples of the areas subject to mandate as "not yet able to stand by themselves" thus applying this

[41] See *supra*, n. 30.

[42] Miller, *op. cit.*, II, 227; Baker, *op. cit.*, I, 261, 272; Temperley, *op. cit.*, II, 233–39. The text of the resolution is printed in Miller, *op. cit.*, I, 109, and in part in the King-Crane report, p. 12 (see *supra*, n. 13).

[43] Miller, *op. cit.*, II, 274. The "Minutes of the League of Nations Commission" are printed in full (see II, 272–76, 283, 306, 323, 333, 355, 384, and I, 501–4).

qualification only to the former Turkish territory, but the original text was subsequently re-established by the drafting committee. Smuts had also inserted the word "if" in the paragraph authorizing the administration of C mandates "under the law of the mandatory state as *if* integral portions thereof." This was eliminated on the suggestion of the Japanese delegate. Specific mention of the former sovereigns of the territory was eliminated on the suggestion of President Wilson to accord with the desires expressed by Signor Orlando of Italy. After publication of the draft Covenant on February 14 the words "and who are willing to accept it" were inserted as a further qualification of mandatories on motion of the British representative. These changes had both been strongly urged by General Bliss in a memorandum to President Wilson, and the latter was demanded by elements of the American public which did not want the country saddled with a mandate against its will.[44]

President Wilson, thinking of certain former Russian territories, proposed on February 8 an additional paragraph permitting the application of the mandate system "in respect of other peoples and territories which are not otherwise disposed of in the treaty of peace of which the covenant forms a part, or are not definitely constituted in autonomous states" but did not press it after the representatives of Portugal and Belgium had "pointed out the consequences which might follow in the future from too broad a wording." M. Vesnitch of Serbia proposed an amendment to facilitate the complete emancipation of the mandated peoples and their admission to the League but did not insist after Lord Robert Cecil had besought him not to "for reasons of expediency."

During the course of discussion of the article in the League of Nations Commission M. Hymans of Belgium suggested that the open door be applied to C as well as B mandates but did not insist when informed by Smuts that the matter "had been the object of long discussions in the council of ten," and the same question was later raised by Viscount Chinda of Japan. In the initial discussion of the article in the Commission M. Bourgeois of France suggested a

[44] Miller, *op. cit.*, II, 96, 226. Smuts himself later referred to the elimination of the "if" as evidence of the practical sovereignty of the mandatory over the C territories (*P.M.C.*, *Min.*, IX, 33).

more general draft eliminating details including that on reference to military recruiting of natives but did not press it after vigorous opposition from President Wilson and Lord Robert Cecil. On May 5, after the final text of the Covenant had been agreed upon, Clemenceau of France on his own authority ordered insertion of words permitting recruiting of natives for "defense of the territory of the mother country." President Wilson was informed of this by Sir Maurice Hankey, the British expert on the drafting staff, and took prompt measures to eliminate the phrase from the document which was already in press. The persistent French effort to assure herself the right to recruit natives beyond equivocation continued during the drafting of the mandate texts.[45]

3. Assignment and Drafting of Mandates

In conformity with the understanding reached by the Council of Ten on January 30 the Supreme Council, consisting of the principal Powers at the Peace Conference, began allotting the mandates before the treaty was signed; Germany was required to renounce her colonies in favor of the Principal Allied and Associated Powers by the peace treaty (art. 119), and the League Council was given power by the Covenant (art. 22) to define the "authority, control or administration to be exercised by the mandatory" only in so far as "not previously agreed upon by the members of the League" which for this purpose was held to mean the Principal Allied and Associated Powers.[46]

These Powers, acting through the Supreme Council, allotted mandates for the German possessions on May 7, 1919, adhering in the main to existing occupations and secret treaties and before the treaty of Versailles was in effect or even signed.[47] The Pacific islands

[45] Miller, *op. cit.*, I, 502. (See *supra*, n. 40, and *infra*, n. 50).

[46] *O.J.*, I, 338–39. "The original intention of the authors of the Covenant had been that the terms of the mandates should be embodied in the peace treaties, but this was subsequently abandoned and the treaties signed without the inclusion of the terms" (*L. of N., Information Section, Mandates* [Geneva, 1924], p. 14). See also Philip Baker in Munch, *Les Origines et l'œuvre de la Société des nations* (Copenhagen, 1924), II, 57; Temperley, *op. cit.*, VI, 506; see also *infra*, chap. iv.

[47] Transcript of minutes of meeting, *L. of N., Assembly, Rec.*, sess. I (Sixth Committee), p. 375. See also Temperley, *op. cit.*, II, 241; VI, 503; Hudson, in House and Seymour, *op. cit.*, p. 226; Levermore, in *L. of N., Y.B.*, I, 9, 64–68.

were distributed among Great Britain, Australia, New Zealand, and Japan. President Wilson had made a reservation on the island of Yap, which he thought should be kept as an international cable center, at an earlier meeting in the presence of the Japanese delegate, and did not withdraw it on this occasion though it seems not to have been recorded in the minute assigning the islands north of the Equator to Japanese mandate.[48] German Southwest Africa was assigned to the Union of South Africa, German East Africa to Great Britain, and Great Britain and France were requested to make a joint recommendation with regard to Togoland and Cameroons. France contended that full sovereignty of these territories and not merely mandatory powers were to be divided but this interpretation was later relinquished except in regard to the German acquisition of 1911.[49] France, however, has continued to insist on her right to recruit natives for general defensive purposes in these territories in spite of the apparent conflict with provisions in article 22 of the Covenant.[50] Belgium objected to the decision with regard to German East Africa and on May 30, 1919, reached an agreement with Great Britain approved by the Supreme Council on August 21, 1919, for division of the mandate, Belgium obtaining the territories of Ruanda and Urundi adjacent to the Congo. Portugal likewise claimed a mandate but was given none though she was accorded full sovereignty of the Kionga triangle, a small territory adjacent to Mozambique which she claimed under the treaty of 1886 with Germany though by the treaty of 1894 she had recognized German sovereignty.[51] This and the part of Cameroons acquired by Germany from French Equatorial Africa by the treaty of 1911 seem to be the only German colonial territory to which the mandatory principle was not applied. The political difficulty which arose made it impossible to draft texts of

[48] See *infra*, nn. 80, 84.

[49] Moon, *op. cit.*, pp. 214, 498.

[50] See art. 3 of French mandates for Cameroons and Togo, *Suppl.*, *A.J.I.L*, XVII, 146, 191 and *infra*, Appendix II; Baker, *op. cit.*, Vol. I, chap. xxiv; Temperley, *op. cit.*, II, 242; *P.M.C.*, *Min.*, I, 24; III, 6, 311, 219; Lugard, *J.R.S.A.*, LXXII, 543. See *supra*, nn. 40, 45, and *infra*, chap. iv, n. 32.

[51] Moon, *op. cit.*, p. 131; *L. of N.*, *Council*, *Min.*, sess. XII, p. 10; Martin, *The Treaties of Peace*, *1919–1923* (Washington, 1924).

the mandates in time for inclusion in the treaty of Versailles as had been originally intended.[52]

Turkish territory was allotted to mandatories by the Principal Allied Powers at San Remo on April 25, 1920,[53] after the United States had withdrawn from official participation in the Supreme Council.[54] President Wilson had attempted to get an allied commission to ascertain the wishes of the inhabitants of the Arab countries as was required by the Covenant, but though they accepted in principle, France and Great Britain failed to co-operate.[55] He then sent an American commission under Henry Churchill King and Charles R. Crane which received 1,863 petitions and had numerous interviews with native delegations in Palestine and Syria during June and July, 1919. The report of this commission was elaborate and informing. It showed a strong sentiment favorable to complete independence for a United Syria (including Palestine), but if supervision was necessary, the United States was preferred, then Great Britain. France had few friends outside of the Lebanese Christians who, indeed, had sent a delegation to Paris requesting a French mandate. Strong opposition to the Zionist proposal was also indicated. The report made specific recommendations not only on Syria and Palestine but on Mesopotamia, Armenia, and Anatolia.[56] It, however, was

[52] See *supra*, n. 46.

[53] Temperley notes that the assignment became final on May 5, 1920 (*op. cit.*, VI, 505).

[54] The United States withdrew from official participation in the Council on December 9, 1919, but continued an unofficial observer until January 11, 1921 (Levermore, *op. cit.*, II, 7).

[55] The minutes of the Council of Four meeting on March 20, 1919, at which this proposal was made are printed in full in Baker, *op. cit.*, III, 1–19. See also *ibid.*, I, 77.

[56] It recommended that all parts of the Turkish Empire in Asia and Europe be placed under mandate for a limited term; that united Syria (including Lebanon and Palestine but excluding Cilicia) be made a kingdom under Feisal with United States as mandatory or, if it refused, Great Britain, and if absolutely necessary to preserve peace France might be given a mandate of the Lebanon (not enlarged) alone; that united Mesopotamia (including Mosul) be placed under a constitutional monarchy to be selected by plebiscite under British mandate; that an Armenian state including both Russian and Turkish territory, a Constantinopolitan state, and a Turkish state each with a separate administration be all placed under United States mandate (see *Editor and Publisher*, Vol. LV [December 2, 1922], and Baker, *op. cit.*, Vol. II, chap. xxiv).

kept secret until 1922 and had no apparent influence on the San Remo decision, which in the main followed secret treaties among the Allies. France was assigned Syria and the Lebanon; Great Britain, Palestine and Mesopotamia; and the United States was asked to accept Armenia. The United States Senate rejected President Wilson's recommendation in compliance with this request on June 1, 1920,[57] and no other power was found to accept the responsibility.[58] Of the remaining territories relinquished by Turkey,[59] Egypt, which was declared a protectorate by Great Britain early in the war, has been recognized as an independent state as has the part of Arabia containing the holy cities of Mecca and Medina known as the Hedjaz. The rest of Arabia is divided among independent semi-nomadic states, such as Nejd, Yemen, Asir, and Koweit, the first of which under the Wahabi chief Ibn Saud drove out the Hashemite family and annexed the Hedjaz in 1925.[60] Under the treaty of Sèvres Greece claimed a sphere about Smyrna, Italy in Adalia, and France in Cilicia.[61] These, however, were not assigned as mandates and all have reverted to the full sovereignty of Turkey as a result of Mustapha Kemal's conquests and diplomacy, ratified by the treaty of Lausanne in 1923.[62] There was during this development a plan to assign Albania as a mandate to Italy, but this was not done and Albania con-

---

In the case of Mesopotamia alone was this recommendation carried out, and it is worth noticing that it has progressed the most satisfactorily of the Eastern mandates since.

[57] The vote was 52 to 23 (Cong. Rec. LIX, 8073). The President's address of May 24, 1920, the Senate Resolution of June 1, 1920, and General Harbord's report on Armenia are printed in *International Conciliation*, No. 151 (June, 1920), pp. 271 ff. For the latter see also *Sen. Doc. 266* (66th Cong., 2d sess.).

[58] The League itself was offered a mandate of Armenia but declined on April 11, 1920 (*O.J.*, I, No. 8 [November–December, 1920], 89). Armenia was in part reconquered by the Turkish nationalists and recognized as part of Turkey by the treaty of Lausanne and in part organized as a soviet republic in the Union of Soviet Republics.

[59] See Chirol, *The Occident and the Orient*, chaps. iii, v; treaty of Sèvres, arts. 98–122; *Supp., A.J.I.L.*, XV, 198 ff.

[60] Moon, *op. cit.*, pp. 269–72.

[61] The Greek sphere is defined in arts. 65–83 of the treaty of Sèvres but the French and Italian spheres were defined in a separate agreement dependent on that treaty (Secretary of State Colby, note of February 21, 1921; *L. of N., Council, Min.*, sess. XII, p. 70; see also Levermore, *L. of N., Y.B.*, II, 24; III, 195). The Balfour proposal of May 17, 1919, proposing spheres of influence in Turkey is printed in Baker, *op. cit.*, III, 303; see also *ibid.*, Vol. II, chap. xxxiii.

[62] For French and Italian agreements with Turkey in the spring of 1921 see *Current History*, XIV (May, 1921), 203–5; French agreement of October, 1921 (Franklin-Bouil-

tinued as an independent state though in close treaty relations with Italy.[63]

The work of drafting mandates was intrusted by the Supreme Council to a commission representing the Principal Allied and Associated Powers under Lord Milner on June 28, 1919.[64] Three types of mandates were prepared designated as "A," "B," and "C" corresponding to the three classes of territory described in article 22 of the Covenant. The first included former Turkish territory, the second Central African territory, and the third Southwest Africa and the Pacific islands. Japan objected to the C draft because it omitted guaranties for the open door, thus permitting the British dominions to discriminate with regard to immigration and commerce.[65] France objected to the B draft because recruiting of natives for service outside the mandated territory was forbidden.[66] The applicability of the A draft could not be determined until peace was made with Turkey, and this draft was finally abandoned because of divergent views.[67]

---

lon), *ibid.*, XV (January, 1922), 661; *Supp., A.J.I.L.*, XVII, 48; treaty of Lausanne, arts. 2–22, *ibid.*, XVIII, 6–11.

[63] See Ormsby Gore, in *The League of Nations Starts*, (1920), p. 104.

[64] House, in House and Seymour, *op. cit.*, pp. 440–43; Temperley, *op. cit.*, II, 237; Philip Baker, in P. Munch, *op. cit.* (Copenhagen, 1924), II, 57; Kluyver, *Documents on the League of Nations* (Leiden, 1920), pp. 290–92.

[65] See Philip Baker, *op. cit.*, p. 56; Rappard, *P.M.C., Min.*, I, 47; Viscount Ishii explained the Japanese position at the eleventh session of the League Council on November 14, 1920 (p. 15), as follows: "Japanese interests in the Pacific islands south of the Equator, which were very important—were before the war and under German administration in a more favorable position than they would be at present in spite of the sacrifices made by Japan in the Pacific during the war in order to safeguard the allies' common interests. Japan would wish to see Japanese interests in these islands placed in at least as secure a position as before the war." Balfour of Great Britain said he appreciated this sentiment but thought par. 6 of art. 22 should be applied. Ishii asked whether Great Britain had a reply from her representations to Australia. The Council decided to sent a telegram urging the Powers to reach agreement (see also Temperley, *op. cit.*, VI, 515). The United States was entitled to insist under the Samoan agreement between Germany, Great Britain, and the United States in 1899 that the open door should be maintained in the New Zealand mandated territory of Samoa, but it has been suggested that the United States was itself violating this agreement by limiting trade from the United States to American Samoa to American vessels. No treaty has been negotiated, and it appears that each party is content to let the other continue its violation of the 1899 treaty (see *infra*, chap. xiii, sec. 4*d*).

[66] Hudson, in House and Seymour, *op. cit.*, p. 227; Temperley, *op. cit.*, p. 239; see *supra*, n. 50.

[67] See note of Lord Curzon, July 28, 1920, *International Conciliation*, No. 160 (September, 1921), p. 315.

The treaty of Versailles went into effect and the League of Nations was inaugurated on January 10, 1920, with the United States not a member. The question of mandates was raised by a memorandum from the Secretary General in January, and at its eighth session, August 5, 1920, the Council addressed a letter to the Principal Allied Powers, Great Britain, France, Italy, and Japan, calling attention to the duties given the Principal Allied and Associated Powers by articles 22 and 119 of the Versailles Treaty and suggesting that they communicate as soon as possible the mandatories assigned and the terms of the mandates. "It is much to be desired," ran the letter, "that the application of the mandatory system provided by article 22 of the Covenant should not be further delayed.[68]

A reply was received from the French Prime Minister on October 16 explaining that Great Britain and France had not yet agreed upon the delimitation of their mandated territories in Syria, Mesopotamia, and Palestine nor upon the French reservation with regard to the draft mandates for Cameroon and Togoland, while Great Britain and Japan were still debating the Japanese reservation on the C mandate draft.[69] Draft mandates following closely the drafts of the Milner commission were however submitted to the Council early in December. France was given certain exceptional privileges in regard to use of troops from her African mandated territories and Japan accepted the C drafts with a reservation. The C drafts were formally approved by the Council on December 17, 1920, with, however, no mention of the United States reservation on Yap and no provision for the open door. These mandates, together with the A and B drafts, were published in January.[70]

4. Claims of the United States

In the meantime the United States had begun a discussion with Great Britain in regard to the open door in former Turkish territory[71]

[68] *L. of N., Assembly, Rec.* (Sixth Committee), I, 386. See also reports by Secretary-General and M. Hymans of Belgium, July 30 and August 5, 1920 (*ibid.*, pp. 375–83).

[69] *Ibid.*, p. 387.

[70] *L. of N., Sec. Gen. Report to Second Assembly* (August 18, 1921), p. 45, and Japanese reservation, p. 46. The C mandates are printed in *International Conciliation*, No. 166, pp. 288 ff., and all the mandates except Iraq, and the Japanese reservation, are printed in *Supp., A.J.I.L.*, XVII, 138–44, and *infra*, Appendix II.

[71] This correspondence was published in *British White Paper* (1921), Cmd. 675, and is reprinted in *International Conciliation*, No. 166 (September, 1921), pp. 304 ff.

with the assertion that "the unfortunate impression had been created in the minds of the American Public" that the British authorities in the occupied regions of Palestine and Mesopotamia "had given advantage to British oil interests which were not accorded to American companies and further that Great Britain had been preparing quietly for exclusive control of the oil resources in this region." Ambassador Davis added on May 12, 1920:

> The Government of the United States desires to point out that during the peace negotiations at Paris leading up to the treaty of Versailles, it consistently took the position that the future peace of the world required that, as a general principle, any alien territory which should be acquired pursuant to the Treaties of Peace with the Central Powers, must be held and governed in such a way as to assure equal treatment in law, and in fact to the commerce of all nations. It was on account of, and subject to, this understanding that the United States felt itself able and willing to agree that the acquisition of certain enemy territory by the victorious Powers would be consistent with the best interests of the world. The representatives of the Principal Allied Powers, in the discussion of the mandate principles, expressed in no indefinite manner their recognition of the justice and farsightedness of such a principle, and agreed to its application to the mandates over Turkish territory.

Concrete propositions embodying the open-door doctrine which "the United States would be pleased to see applied in the occupied or mandated regions" were then laid down as a basis of discussion. On July 28 Ambassador Davis recalled the note of May 12 and regretted the San Remo oil agreement between Great Britain and France,[72] published in the meantime, which had not served "to diminish the concern felt by the government and people of the United States." Lord Curzon replied on August 9, 1920, denying the facts alleged as evidence that the door was closed, asserting that the only British interests recognized were those vested before the war, comparing the

---

It is discussed by W. R. Batsell in an article entitled "The United States and the System of Mandates," *Revue de Droit International* (Geneva), II, 264–87, and Temperley, *op. cit.*, VI, 506–19.

[72] Text printed (*ibid.*). This agreement related to oil in Rumania, Russia, North Africa, and other French colonies, and British crown colonies as well as Mesopotamia. Great Britain agreed to allow France 25 per cent of the oil or if a private company developed it to allow France a 25 per cent share in the company. This concession was in consideration of French relinquishment on December, 1918, of her secret-treaty claim to Mosul though the latter is not mentioned in the agreement (Moon, *op. cit.*, pp. 263–67; Baker, *op. cit.*, III, 4–8; see agreement, December 23, 1920, *infra*, n. 78).

80 per cent of world's oil output in American control with 4½ per cent in British control, alluding to the exclusion of foreign interests from American-controlled oil fields in the United States, Haiti, and Costa Rica, and explaining the San Remo oil agreement as wholly within the conditional interpretation of the most favored nation clause adhered to by the United States, but expressing full sympathy with the propositions laid down for securing the open door with due consideration for interests vested before the war. Lord Curzon asserted also that the draft mandates included provisions securing the open door for members of the League and that as soon as agreed to by the Allied Powers interested they would be transmitted to the League Council, which in his opinion was the proper place for discussing their terms.

On November 20, 1920, Secretary of State Colby wrote an extended answer which reasserted the American doctrine of the open door generally accepted at the Peace Conference with respect to mandatories and assumed that though not a member of the League the "United States can not be excluded from the benefits of the principle of equality of treatment." He denied that the subject of mandatories could be discussed only in the League Council, saying:[73]

> Such powers as the Allied and Associated nations may enjoy or wield in the determination of the governmental status of the mandated areas accrued to them as a direct result of the war against the Central Powers. The United States as a participant in that conflict and as a contributor to its successful issue cannot consider any of the Associated Powers, the smallest not less than itself, debarred from the discussions of any of its consequences, or from participation in the rights and privileges secured under the mandates provided for in the Treaties of Peace.

He consequently requested that "draft mandate forms be communicated to this government for its consideration before their submission to the Council of the League" and emphasized the need of frank discussion of the oil question because it is an "outstanding illustration of the kind of economic question with reference to which the mandate principle was especially designed." The note then reasserted the objections to the San Remo oil agreement and contraverted Lord Curzon's criticism of American oil policy in the United States and the Caribbean. A copy of the note was sent to France

[73] *L. of N., Council, Min.*, sess. XII (February and March, 1921), p. 72.

and Italy with a request for an interpretation of the Sèvres agreement of August 10, 1920, creating spheres of interest in Turkey.[74]

The Colby letter was made public to the League Assembly on November 26, and at about the same time notice was taken of a recent German protest to the Assembly against the assumption that the Principal Allied Powers rather than the League had the right to determine mandates.[75] The assembly led by Dr. Nansen of Norway discussed the subject at length on the basis of a report from the Council. It appeared that Japan also objected to the draft A mandates because of the lack of adequate assurance of the open door.[76] The Assembly reluctantly recognized that under the Covenant control of mandates is given to the Council but in its resolution on the subject regretted the refusal of the Council to publish draft mandates before they came into force, deplored the delay in putting the system into effect, and expressed the strong feeling that a mandatory "should not be allowed to make use of its position in order to increase its military strength" and "must not be allowed to use its power under the mandate in order to exploit for itself or its friends the natural resources of a mandated territory."[77]

On December 23 Great Britain and France made an agreement readjusting the boundaries of the mandated areas of Palestine, Mesopotamia, and Syria,[78] so as to allow Great Britain to construct a railway and pipe line entirely in her mandated area connecting the Hedjaz Railway with the Mosul oil region and to permit France also to tap this oil region within her mandated territory.

On February 28, 1921, Lord Curzon replied to Secretary Colby's note of November 20 emphasizing the need of respecting vested interests in Mesopotamia and asserting that the Turkish Petroleum Company's rights were of that character. "His Majesty's Government are, nevertheless," he explained, "glad to find themselves in

[74] Secretary of State Colby, note, February 21, 1921 (*infra*, n. 80; see also *supra*, n. 61).

[75] *L. of N., Assembly, Rec.*, sess. I (Plenary Meetings), pp. 204, 210; *ibid.* (Sixth Committee), p. 301.

[76] Levermore, *op. cit.*, I, 40 (*infra*, chap. iv).

[77] These recommendations applied especially to A mandates (*L. of N., Assembly, Rec.*, sess. I (Plenary Meetings), pp. 725, 735.

[78] *British White Papers* (1921), Cmd. 1195, reprinted in *International Conciliation*, No. 166, p. 297, and discussed in Levermore, *op. cit.*, I, 62; II, 416.

general agreement with the contention of the United States Government, that the world's oil resources should be thrown open for development without reference to nationality." But he found American policy in Philippines, Haiti, and Costa Rica out of harmony with this principle.[79]

Before reception of this note Secretary Colby had addressed a note to the League Council on February 21, recalling the note to Great Britain of November 20 and insisting that "approval of the United States is essential to the validity of any determination which may be reached" on the form of mandates. Specifically the note objected to the omission of the Yap reservation in the Japanese mandate for the North Pacific islands. The note runs:

> The United States, which is distinctly included in the very definite and constantly used descriptive phrase 'the Principal Allied and Associated Powers,' had not agreed to the terms or provisions of the mandate which is embodied in this text, nor has it agreed that a mandate should be conferred upon Japan covering all the former German islands situated in the Pacific Ocean and lying north of the equator. The United States has never given its consent to the inclusion of the Island of Yap in any proposed mandate to Japan.[80]

President Wilson's reservation in the Supreme Council and its reassertion in subsequent notes is then referred to. The note was received while the Council at its twelfth session was preparing to confirm the A and B mandates. This action was postponed, and the Council replied that "the rights which the United States acquired as one of the leading actors both in the war and in the negotiations for peace were not likely to be challenged in any quarter" but the situation was complicated by the failure of the United States to ratify the treaty and its consequent absence from the Council. It therefore had postponed consideration of the mandates until its June meeting which the United States was invited to attend. With regard to C mandates, however, which had already been confirmed, the League had no power except to supervise their administration. It had consequently forwarded the note to Great Britain, France, Italy, and Japan.[81] Japan replied on February 26, asserting that the allocation

[79] *International Conciliation*, No. 166, p. 330.

[80] *L. of N., Council, Min.*, sess. XII, p. 70.

[81] *Ibid.*, pp. 10, 28, 75; *L. of N., Report of Sec. Gen. to Second Assembly*, p. 46. See also statement by Bonar Law in British House of Commons, March 8, 1921, asserting

of the mandate on May 7, 1919, and its confirmation by the League Council on December 17, 1920, were final.[82]

On April 2, 1921, soon after the beginning of the Harding administration at Washington, Secretary of State Hughes addressed identical notes[83] to Great Britain, France, Italy, and Japan reiterating Secretary Colby's contention with regard to Yap, and asserting America's right to a voice in the disposition of the German colonies because of her "participation in the victory" through which alone "the right to dispose of the overseas possessions of Germany was acquired." He pointed out further that article 119 of the treaty of Versailles "confirms the position of the government of the United States," and added that as the United States had never consented to the Japanese mandate of Yap the confirmation of this mandate by the League Council of which the United States was not a member could "not be regarded as having efficacy with respect to the United States." The note adds to the evidence cited by Secretary Colby by quotation from a memorandum by President Wilson on March 3, 1921, explaining his reservations on Yap in the Supreme Council in April and May, 1919, and by reference to the reiteration of this reservation by the American government when the question of Yap was raised in the conference on electrical communications in October and November, 1920.[84]

A French reply to this note on April 19 affirmed President Wilson's "categorical reservation concerning the island of Yap" prior to May 7, 1919, in the presence of the Japanese representative.[85]

In the meantime League confirmation of the A and B mandates was pending but the United States gave no reply to the invitation to attend the June meeting of the Council and at that meeting the sub-

---

that because of the part of the United States in the war "it is quite reasonable that it should consider these mandates" (*Parl. Deb., H. of C.*, CXXXIX, 238; "Société des Nations," *R.M.D.*, III [1921], 526).

[82] *New York Times*, April 19, 1921; Levermore, *op. cit.*, II, 59.

[83] *New York Times*, April 7, 1921, summarized in Levermore, *op. cit.*, II, 59.

[84] On the conference see Levermore, *op. cit.*, I, 37. The political and technical importance of Yap as a cable center is emphasized in memoranda by Walter S. Rogers, technical expert at the Paris conference to President Wilson on February 12 and May 2, 1919, printed in Baker, *op. cit.*, III, 437, 444; see also *ibid.*, II, 480.

[85] Levermore, *op. cit.*, II, 59.

ject was again postponed.[86] In August, Secretary Hughes addressed an identical note to the Principal Allied Powers insisting on the right of the United States to an equal voice in deciding the mandates over Turkish territory because of its contribution to the victory over Germany.[87] The note then suggested with regard to the terms of the draft mandates that the capitulations be retained until the mandatory governments were organized, that religious guaranties be extended to future as well as existing charitable organizations, that the open-door guaranty be extended to all states mentioned in the annex to the Covenant and not merely to members of the League, and that American approval be recognized as necessary for the allotment and modification of mandates.[88]

In the September meeting of the Council it was disclosed that the Powers had reached no agreement with the United States,[89] and in the Assembly meeting on September 7 Lord Robert Cecil regretted the fact that no progress had been made in the confirmation of mandates since the last assembly, adding: "The whole cause of that delay is not in the council. It is perfectly clear that the delay has been entirely due to the attitude of the Government of the United States of America."[90] He saw no objection to the American demands except that they were not made earlier. He continued:

I mention all this not in the least for the purpose of criticizing the United States Government, which is entitled, of course, to pursue its own policy, but merely for the purpose of calling the attention of the Assembly to the way in which this delay affects the reputation and the actual work of the League. Everyone must admit that it is desirable that the inhabitants of those territories should receive the protection which was designed for them and which was embodied in principle in Article 22, and the League cannot afford to have it said, largely in the very country whose government has rightly or wrongly caused the delay, that this whole talk about mandates is a mere deception, merely camouflage for naked annexation. I venture to urge upon the Council, now that they have received or will shortly receive, if they have not already done so, the criti-

[86] *L. of N., Sec. Gen. Report to Second Assembly*, p. 46. On June 25, 1921, the Council decided that the mandatory Powers might transmit texts of the mandates to the United States without the Council's consent.

[87] The United States was never at war with Turkey.

[88] Levermore, *op. cit.*, II, 137.

[89] *L. of N., Council, Min.*, sess. XIV (August–September, 1921), p. 16.

[90] *L. of N., Assembly, Rec.*, sess. II (Plenary Meetings), pp. 64–65. Batsell thinks the actions of the United States "violated international comity" (*op. cit.*, II, 275).

cism and suggestions of the United States Government, to proceed immediately to define the remaining mandates.

The Assembly passed a resolution to the effect on September 23 and the Council approved the draft mandates "in principle" and hoped their spirit would be observed but refused to confirm the mandates until agreement had been reached with the United States. The United States continued unwilling to discuss the question in the Council and carried on separate negotiations with each of the mandatory powers with the object of securing American rights in the territories by separate treaties. Such treaties were signed with Japan dealing especially with Yap on February 11, 1922, as a result of negotiations during the Washington conference on limitation of armament.[91] Treaties with France dealing with Cameroons, Togoland, and Syria; with Belgium on Ruanda-Urundi; and with Great Britain on Palestine, Tanganyika, Cameroons, and Togo were negotiated in the next three years.[92] Negotiations in regard to Iraq were delayed by America's hesitation to conform to the British desire that King Feisal's government be a party but on January 9, 1930, a tripartite treaty was signed. Negotiations with the British dominions, Australia, New Zealand, and South Africa seem not to have been begun. The United States had not exchanged diplomatic representatives with these dominions, and because of the non-application of the open door by those mandates is not discriminated against with respect to League members in the absence of treaty.[93] In a campaign speech on October 23, 1924, Secretary Hughes said:

> The delay has not been caused by us nor has it affected the administration of the mandated territories which has gone on. We have had treaties ratified with Belgium and France with respect to the territories under what are called "B" mandates in Africa, and with France as to the "A" mandate for Syria. The situation in Mesopotamia has been such that for local reasons and because of the setting up of a native Arab government in Iraq or Mesopotamia, the definition

[91] The four-power Pacific pact signed at the Washington conference before this date extended protection to the mandated islands but was not "deemed to be an assent on the part of the United States of America to the mandates," and did not preclude agreements by the United States with mandatories on the subject.

[92] Belgium did not complete her negotiations with the United States in reference to the Kisaka area transferred to her after the mandate was in effect until 1925 (*P.M.C., Min.*, IV, 65).

[93] See *supra*, n. 38.

of the form of control to be exercised was delayed by the mandatory power itself. With regard to the other mandates, our position is clear and we are ready to sign the remaining treaties whenever the Governments concerned will agree to give this Government the equal treatment that it feels it has a right to ask.[94]

To provide a government for the B and C territories during the period of negotiation which it foresaw, the League Council on October 2, 1921, recommended a provisional régime in accordance with article 22 of the Covenant.[95] In fact, the Mandates Commission which had been organized by the Council in December, 1920, met on October 4, 1921, and examined reports from several of the actual or prospective mandatories, submitting recommendations which were considered by the Council on October 10.[96]

It appears that the American negotiations were the main elements in delaying final confirmation of the class B mandates. By July 20, 1922, however, after a final modification of the missionary article in British mandates to conform to American wishes, the prospective B mandatories had succeeded in getting American consent to the drafts and the mandates were confirmed by the League Council.[97] With regard to A mandates, however, delay arose in part from other causes as suggested by Secretary Hughes.

5. "A" Mandate Negotiations

The terms of the Palestine mandate were objected to by the papacy on May 23, 1922, as giving too great privileges to the Jews who had been promised a "national home" in that region, by the

[94] *New York Times*, October 24, 1924. This was in reply to an article by Raymond Fosdick in the *ibid.*, October 19, 1924, which concluded a review of American policy on the mandates with the remark, "Instead of settling the question around a common table with all the nations present Mr. Hughes elected to flout the League and spend three or four years and an infinite amount of diplomatic energy in conducting a series of separate treaties only a few of which are yet completed." Batsell suggests that treaties have not been concluded with the British dominions because of American reluctance to recognize their treaty-making status (*op. cit.*, II, 286).

[95] *L. of N., Council, Min.*, sess. XIV, pp. 119, 168; *Sec. Gen. Report to the Third Assembly*, p. 51.

[96] *L. of N., Council, Min.*, sess. XIV, pp. 124, 178; *Sec. Gen. Report to the Second Assembly*, p. 44; *Sec. Gen. Report to the Third Assembly*, p. 49.

[97] *O.J.*, III, 793, 810, 862; *Sec. Gen. Supp. Report to the Third Assembly* (August 28, 1922), p. 12. The French had submitted their drafts to the United States on June 29, 1927 (Levermore, *op. cit.*, III, 163).

Balfour declaration of November 2, 1917, by various Moslem organizations for the same reason, by several Jewish organizations as limiting the privileges of the Jews too much, and by the British House of Lords as contrary to the wishes of the majority of the inhabitants of Palestine. The British announced agreement with the United States on the terms of this mandate in May, 1922.[98]

The United States approved the French draft of the Syrian mandate in July, 1922, but Italy objected to its confirmation, as also that of Palestine, until title was cleared through ratification of a peace treaty with Turkey.[99] Apparently she also objected because the failure of the treaty of Sèvres had deprived her of the spheres of interest which she had been accorded in compensation for her approval of the French and British spheres by the agreement of August 10, 1920, dependent on that treaty.[100] Italy apparently wished a renewal of the assurances with regard to economic, educational, and missionary privileges in Syria and Palestine which she had renounced in the sphere of interest agreement. Great Britain had already given assurances to Italy with regard to Palestine, and during the Council meeting in July, 1922, Italy and France began negotiations with the result that the Syrian and Palestine mandates were confirmed with assurances that Catholic and Moslem interests in Palestine would be protected, on July 24, to go into effect when Franco-Italian agreement was announced.[101] This announcement was made on September 29, 1923,[102] the peace treaty with Turkey having been signed at Lausanne on July 24, 1923.

The tentative confirmation of the Palestine and Syrian mandates on July 22, 1922, was due in large measure to the diplomacy of Lord Balfour.[103] On May 17, 1922, he suggested that the Council take

[98] *L. of N., Sec. Gen. Report to the Third Assembly*, pp. 51–52.

[99] *O.J.*, III (August, 1922), 799; Stoyanovsky, *op. cit.*, p. 27.

[100] See *supra*, n. 61. In a note of August 9, 1920, Lord Curzon, British foreign minister, had answered Ambassador Davis' information that "the assignment to Great Britain of the mandate for Mesopotamia was made subject to a friendly agreement with the Italian government regarding economic rights" by a "categorical denial" (*International Conciliation*, No. 166, p. 312).

[101] *L. of N., Sec. Gen. Report to the Third Assembly, Supp.* (August, 29, 1922), p. 13.

[102] *L. of N., Sec. Gen. Report to the Fifth Assembly* (June 10, 1924), p. 45.

[103] *O.J.*, III, 798, 817, 823, 846.

definite action on the Palestine mandate in six weeks. The United States, he pointed out, had agreed, and the want of a definitive treaty with Turkey was merely a technical difficulty. Public opinion did not understand the situation. Japan supported him as did France and Italy though they urged more time which resulted in an informal agreement to consider the question on July 15. The next session of the Council was held in London, and on July 18 the Council considered a letter from H. Wilson Harris, an Englishman and president of the Association of Journalists, accredited to the League of Nations asking that the mandates question be considered in public session, and adding: "The fact that certain of the mandates have recently been the subject of discussion and resolution in both houses of the British parliament and I believe also in both houses of the American Congress makes the avoidance of open discussion by the League Council particularly regrettable." Imperiali of Italy and Viviani of France thought conciliation was not promoted by public discussion. Balfour admitted that private discussion was necessary to conciliate differences, but insisted that if such discussions were unsuccessful the public should know the reasons. It was decided to hold a public session on the B mandates but the session on A mandates the next day was private. At this session Viviani wished to postpone discussion of Palestine until the Syrian mandate was confirmed, and Italy was not ready to confirm that mandate until pending negotiations with France were concluded. Balfour pointed out that "it would be tantamount to a breach of an understanding arrived at between the members of the Council if the Palestine mandate were not immediately discussed." Furthermore, he thought "the Marquis Imperiali would agree upon reflection that when the question came to be discussed in a public session—as it would inevitably have to be discussed—his defense of the Italian government's attitude might seem somewhat inadequate." There had been no new factor during the two years in which confirmation had been held up by the United States. The Italian attitude came as a surprise to him. He feared "the immense powers—he would not say of obstruction but of delay accorded to the members of the Council—had been in this instance used in a manner which would bring, if not discredit upon the working of the League, at least a feeling of something approaching despair to those who had to work the machinery." He asked the Marquis Imperiali to reconsider, but the latter said he couldn't act in a matter of "high policy" without new instructions. Viscount Ishii of Japan then called attention to the possibility of confirming the mandate with a reservation as his country had done in the case of the C mandates. The representatives of Belgium, China, and Brazil joined Balfour in urging Imperiali to get instructions at once, saying that the peace of Asia and the reputation of the League were at stake.

On July 22 the Italian representative expressed his willingness to confirm the Palestine and Syrian mandates under reservation of certain assurances from France. Difficulties then arose over the clause of the Palestine mandate with regard to holy places but finally agreement was reached through the simple expedient of omitting all mention of the organization of the commission in control of this matter. Public announcement of the confirmation of the Syrian and Palestine mandates was made on July 24 by Viviani who said the amount of secrecy indulged in was not dangerous because "sooner or later the Council had to give an account of its proceedings." Balfour followed with a plea for reconciliation between the Arabs and Jews in Palestine. Thus through an adroit threat of publicity, the support of disinterested members of the Council and an appeal to the prestige of the League, Lord Balfour had induced Italy to withdraw from her obstructive position. League diplomacy had been successful.

During these discussions Balfour stated that the mandate for Mesopotamia was not reported by Great Britain because negotiations with the United States were still pending.[104] Other factors, however, seem to have been in part responsible. The Arabs objected to the British mandate in Mesopotamia and revolted in 1920 with the result that on August 23, 1921, Great Britain recognized the kingdom of Iraq with Feisal, the third son of King Hussein of the Hedjaz, at its head. A treaty was signed with that country on October 10, 1922, defining British powers. This was to be in effect for twenty years or until Iraq was admitted to the League of Nations, but a protocol of April 30, 1922, shortened the term to four years

[104] *Ibid.*, pp. 547, 800, 823.

from the ratification of peace with Turkey.[105] These transactions placed the status of Iraq in some doubt, especially as the British in that country, knowing the unpopularity of the term "mandate" among the inhabitants, encouraged the notion that the recognition of Feisal's government terminated mandatory relations. Great Britain was thus in the rather ambiguous position of having a mandate for Iraq vis-à-vis the League, and not having one vis-à-vis Iraq: an ambiguity evident in Lord Parmour's extraordinary speech before the Council on September 19, 1924, in which he said:

> Iraq has advanced too far along the path laid down in Article 22 of the Covenant for the particular form of control contemplated in that article to be any longer appropriate. . . . . The treaty and connected documents place the British government in a position vis-à-vis Iraq to discharge their obligations toward the League. . . . . It will be found that the various documents taken together cover all the points embodied in the original draft mandate.[106]

Nevertheless, on September 27, 1924, the Council approved a document which appears to be a mandate in substance if not wholly in form. It accepts the treaty and supplementary British pledges as defining the mandatory's obligations.[107] Though some doubts were expressed in the seventh session of the Mandates Commission, the final opinion of that body, as well as the documents, make it clear that Great Britain has a mandate in Iraq.[108] In fact, the form of the documents seems to comply more accurately with the terms of article 22, paragraph 4, of the Covenant than is the case with any other class A mandate.

The negotiations with the United States in regard to the open door begun in 1920 in protest against the San Remo oil agreement were still pending when the Iraq mandate was confirmed, but agreement was reached in November, 1925, whereby American oil in-

[105] *Great Britain*, "Treaty Series," No. 17 (1925), Cmd. 2370, and declaration, *O.J.*, III (December, 1922), 1506, 1509. The Council took note of this treaty on November 17, 1922, and on this occasion the British representative said the treaty was not a substitute for the mandate which would remain the operative instrument as between Great Britain and the League (*L. of N.*, *Council*, *Min.*, sess. XV, p. 11).

[106] *O.J.*, V, 1314–15.

[107] "Iraq, Papers Relating to the Application to Iraq of the Principles of Article 22 of the Covenant of the League of Nations, 1925," *Great Britain*, Cmd. 2317; *infra*, Appendix II.

[108] *P.M.C.*, *Min.*, VII, 10–14, 123.

terests were permitted to acquire 25 per cent of the shares of the Turkish Petroleum Company, which had obtained from Iraq an exclusive concession for oil development in the Bagdad and Mosul villayets on March 14, 1925. In April, 1926, an American group, including Rockefeller, Sinclair, and Doheny interests, took advantage of this agreement and the Turkish Petroleum Company began operations.[109]

The northern boundary of Iraq remained unsettled by the treaty of Lausanne (1923), but under the terms of that treaty the question was submitted to the League of Nations Council which awarded most of Mosul to Iraq on December 16, 1925. The award, however, was contingent upon British continuance of the mandate for twenty-five years unless Iraq earlier became a member of the League. A new treaty complying with this requirement was concluded between Great Britain and Iraq in January, 1926, and on March 11, 1926, the Council finally ratified the Mosul award. By an agreement of June 5, 1926, between Great Britain, Iraq, and Turkey, the latter recognized this boundary with slight rectifications in return for 10 per cent of Iraq oil royalties and neutralization of the frontier.[110] On December 14, 1927, Great Britain signed a new treaty with Iraq. This, however, was not ratified and on November 4, 1929, the British government announced that it would recommend Iraq for admission to the League in 1932 according to article 3 (1) of the treaty of January 13, 1926 (*P.M.C., Min.*, XVI, 183).

The mandatory principle as set forth in the Smuts and Wilson proposals of 1919 had not remained wholly intact. It had been ac-

[109] The remainder of the shares were held 25 per cent by the Anglo-Persian Oil Co. (controlled by the British government), 25 per cent by the Royal Dutch Shell (two-fifths British), and 25 per cent by the Compagnie Française des Pétroles (representing sixty-seven French companies). The 5 per cent beneficiary interest of Mr. C. S. Gulbenkian who had served as mediator between the Turkish government and the promoters when the company was formed held up American participation for some time, but in April, 1926, was given up for a royalty on production (see Earle, "The Turkish Petroleum Co., a Study in Oleaginous Diplomacy," *P.S.Q.*, XXXIX, No. 2, June, 1924; Moon, *op. cit.*, pp. 266–67; Turkish Petroleum Co., Ltd., *Convention with Government of Iraq Made March, 1925* [London and Bagdad, 1925]; "American Oil Interests in Mesopotamia," *Foreign Policy Association Information Service*, II, No. 6, May 22, 1926.

[110] *Great Britain*, "Treaty Series" (1926), Cmd. 2679; Wright, "The Mosul Dispute," *A.J.I.L.*, XX (July, 1926), 453–64; *infra*, Appendix II.

cepted by the Peace Conference not so much from conviction of its merits as from conviction of its expediency to solve an immediate political dilemma. Thus not unnaturally opportunities were seized by the mandatories to whittle it down to the semblance of annexation. The Covenant itself departed from some of the principles in some of the territories and somewhat reduced the rôle of the League.[111] Further whittlings took place in putting the system into effect. The opinion of the inhabitants was ignored in selecting the mandatories though the Covenant required that it be a "principle consideration" in the case of A mandated territories.[112] The French mandates for Togoland and Cameroons permit the use of native troops outside the territory in case of a general war though the Covenant forbids "military training of the natives for other than police purposes and the defense of territory."[113] The British mandate for Palestine requires the development of a national home for the Jews there, which in view of the widespread Arab opposition is hardly compatible with the covenant's insistence that the well-being and development of the inhabitants is the main object of the mandates and that A mandated communities should be provisionally recognized as independent nations.[114]

Furthermore, some of the phraseology of the Covenant, the text of some of the mandates, and the declarations of some statesmen seemed to assimilate mandates to annexations.[115] Apparently on this

[111] See *supra*, nn. 26–32. [112] See *supra*, nn. 55–56. [113] See *supra*, n. 50.

[114] This was noted in the first report of the Permanent Mandates Commission on Palestine, *O.J.*, VI, 211, and in many petitions from the Arabs; but see the statement of Lord Finlay prepared for the Zionist organization (*ibid.*, II, 443, and Stoyanovsky, *The Mandate for Palestine*, pp. 42–47.

[115] Art. 22 of the Covenant says class C mandated territories may be "administered under the laws of the mandatory as integral portions of its territory" and most of the B as well as the C mandates contain this phrase. General Smuts, though the father of the mandate system, wrote on July 4, 1922, " 'C' mandates are in effect not far removed from annexation" (*P.M.C.*, *Min.*, II [1922], 91), and Lord Balfour referred to mandates as "self imposed limitations by the conquerors on the sovereignty which they obtained over conquered territory" (Levermore, *op. cit.*, III, 138). The official paraphrase, substitutes the word "exercised" for "obtained" (*O.J.*, III, 547). Secretary of State Lansing wrote, "If the advocates of the system intended to avoid through its operation the appearance of taking enemy territory as the spoils of war, it was a subterfuge which deceived no one" (*The Peace Negotiations* [New York, 1921], p. 155). In a discussion of the mandatory system led by Sir Frederick Lugard at a meeting of the Royal Society of Arts on June 27, 1924, Lord Milner thought the mandatory system "was likely as time

assumption Great Britain and France considered themselves bound to "compensate" Italy as required by the pact of London of 1915 in case those powers augmented their African possessions.[116] The former ceded Jubaland in Kenya colony and the Jarabub Oasis in Egypt while France rectified the boundary of Tunis.[117] "Mandated territories," writes Sir Frederick Lugard, "are not 'possessions' and it would seem, therefore, equitable that the territory thus added to Italy in compensation for the acquisition of Mandates by England and France, should be held under mandate by Italy, but the promise was made in 1915 before the Mandates system was devised, and it is too late to alter its conditions now." Further he points out it revived the "immoral idea that territories in Africa could be exchanged as mere chattels or make-weights in a political bargain," that "pledges of protection and treaties with the natives could be set aside and transferred to another without their knowledge or consent" thus "giving color to the assertions of cynics who sneered at the allies' professions of trusteeship." The same implication that mandates are but veiled annexations was made by Lloyd George when he alleged that "France would be 'compensated' for the oil wells of Iraq by her Mandate for Syria."[118] But though mutilated in details, sullied by the spirit of barter, delayed in confirmation, and minified by the mandatories, the system was finally put in operation. It remained to be seen what the League of Nations would do with it.

---

went on to be contracted and to prove in many cases a mere transitory stage." Lord Askwith thought the system "had arisen from some of those unfortunate phrases like 'no annexations,' 'self-determination' and so on. . . . . The time might come when with the progress of the world the people in these mandatory countries, one country after another, would ask for a change themselves. . . . . He confessed he would not care to be a citizen in a mandatory country, and not be able to say that he belonged to a great nation." Sir Robert W. Hamilton wished discussion on "the inevitable tendency for a mandated territory to be absorbed into the government of the mandatory." Sir Frederick Lugard, however, thought the Mandates Commission "should in course of time become a valuable body" and that the discussions before it "have served and will continue to serve a useful purpose" (*J.R.S.A.*, LXXII, 546, 549–50).

[116] Baker, *op. cit.*, I, 54.

[117] Moon, *op. cit.*, pp. 137, 222; Martin, *The Treaties of Peace, 1919–1923* (New York, 1924), pp. xvi–xix. At first the Powers tried to avoid compensating Italy on the ground that mandates were not possessions (Gibbons, *Annals* [July, 1921], p. 84; Stoyanovsky, *La Théorie générale des Mandats Internationaux*, p. 17).

[118] Lugard, *J.R.S.A.*, LXXII, 540.

CHAPTER III

RECEPTION OF THE SYSTEM

The mandates system according to the terms of article 22 of the League of Nations Covenant and the statements of its advocates aims to establish a better system for the administration of backward areas than has existed under the régime of colonies, protectorates, or spheres of influence—better in the sense that it would more effectively secure the liberty, material welfare, and opportunity for development of the native inhabitants, and that it would more effectively secure the opportunity of all states of the world to equal participation in the trade and resources of these areas. While the system applies as yet only to the territories yielded by Germany and Turkey, with which alone the conference was directly concerned, advocates have looked upon it as a revolution in the relations of civilized and backward peoples which, if successful in these limited areas, may furnish an example for the government of other areas of similar character.[1]

The distinctive feature of the system is undoubtedly the League's supervision.[2] The principles of trusteeship and tutelage have often been avowed before and sometimes practiced but only as self-limitations. Systematic international supervision was not possible prior to the creation of the League of Nations. Whether in fact the supervision of the League of Nations has curbed the tendency toward

[1] M. Yanaghita of the Mandates Commission, *P.M.C., Min.*, III, 282; Roden Buxton, remarks in Sixth Committee of Fifth Assembly, *ibid.*, V, 8; M. Rappard, *ibid.*, p. 10; VI, 122–23; Hon. W. Ormsby Gore, *The League of Nations Starts* (1920), p. 118; Captain Benn, M.P., House of Commons, December 14, 1926, *Parliamentary Debates* (5th ser.), Vol. CC, col. 2881; M. Moutet of France and Sir Beddoe Rees of Great Britain, Interparliamentary Union, 22d Conference, 1924, *Compte rendu*, pp. 464, 467; H. N. Brailsford and Salvador de Madariaga, Foreign Policy Association, New York, luncheon discussion, February 4, 1928, *Pamphlet 50*, pp. 13, 16; P. J. N. Baker, *The League of Nations at Work*, p. 96; F. W. Eggleston, opening address of the Australian Delegation, and data paper, "International Relations in the Pacific," *Institute of Pacific Relations Conference* (Kyoto, 1929); Hocking, *Yale Review*, XIX (1930), 268.

[2] See *supra*, chap. i; *infra*, chaps. x, xiv.

abuse of natives and selfish exploitation of economic and military resources heretofore common will not be considered here. It is proposed rather to consider the progress of public opinion upon which the effectiveness of this supervision in large measure depends.

Is there a substantial public opinion back of the system? Have the mandatories accepted the system in good faith? The answer to these questions depends in part on the League itself. It is today the most important instrumentality through which a world-opinion may be organized, educated, and maintained. It is the agency by which the mandatories may be led to take a view of their interests more in accord with the principles of the Covenant than has heretofore been the case,[2a] and it may be added, upon the League's success in this effort depends in no small degree its own prestige and influence.[3] Let

[2a] "If there is an alternative to imperialism, there is far greater strength in anti-imperialistic public opinion. If there is nothing in the world but 'each for himself,' if there is no other way of dealing with the economic, the financial, the political, the military problems than the unguarded and the uncounciled will of each particular nation, then we cannot expect to find at home the necessary leverage for anti-imperialistic opinion to curb imperialistic opinion. But if there is a League of Nations, if it is fully developed, if it contains within itself all the political and judicial organizations capable of dealing with every possible problem in international life, then public opinion at home will be able to take up the point and will be able to conquer, because it will be on the side of reason and the future against the side of animal impulses and the past" (Salvador de Madariaga, *op. cit.*, p. 14).

[3] "With all my colleagues, I hope and trust that, thanks to your experience, your impartiality and your zeal, the welfare of the inhabitants of the mandated areas may be furthered, the administration of the Mandatory Powers facilitated and encouraged, the interests of all the Members of the League protected and advanced, in short all the ideals of Article 22 of the Covenant may be realized. You will thus most powerfully have enhanced the prestige of the League itself by strengthening its hold upon the confidence and the affection of the peoples of the world" (Wellington Koo, representative of China and acting president of the Council opening the first session, *P.M.C.*, *Min.*, I, 3). "The League of Nations, which is the outcome of a general movement of public opinion, will live and develop for the benefit of mankind according to its success in gaining and retaining popular confidence. Nothing so develops and strengthens that confidence as to make manifest the sincerity with which the tutelary provisions of the Covenant are applied. Among all these provisions, there are none perhaps upon which the sarcasm of skeptics and cynics has been expended with more bitter joy than those of article 22. If, as they were wont to assert before your commission took up its work, this text has no other purpose than to cloak in high sounding and pseudo-humanitarian phrases the intention of rapacious conquerors to exploit for their own ends; if the institution of mandates were nothing more than a hypocritical cover for ill-disguised annexation, the League of Nations as a whole would suffer a considerable and well-merited set-back to

us attempt to sketch the course of opinion toward the system (1) in the world at large, (2) in the League organs, (3) in the mandated communities, and (4) in the mandatory governments.

1. World-Opinion on the Mandates System

Has world-opinion supported the system? Public opinion with occasional setbacks in certain countries has apparently given steadily greater support to the League of Nations since its inauguration in 1920. The membership of the League increased each year up to the sixth assembly in 1925, and though Costa Rica announced its withdrawal in that year and Brazil and Spain did likewise at the seventh assembly this was more than offset by the entry of Germany. Before the two-year period had expired Spain withdrew her resignation and Costa Rica has intimated an intention of re-entering. Though the United States has not become a member it has participated to an ever increasing extent in the League's non-political work and even in some of its political work such as disarmament. The same is true of the Soviet Union.

The League's budget, which may be taken as roughly indicating the importance attached to it by the nations, has been comparatively stable but has shown a slight tendency to increase. Beginning at a little over $3,000,000 in 1920 it rose to $4,028,671 in 1922 and $4,954,987 in 1923, which was not again attained for several years doubtless because of a decline in the Swiss price-level. In 1925 the budget was $4,424,542; in 1926, $4,729,738; in 1927, $4,902,522;

---

its prestige and moral authority. If, on the contrary, it were to become more and more evident that the administration of peoples 'not yet able to stand by themselves' really constituted a 'sacred trust of civilization' and a tutelage exercised by the mandatories on behalf of the League, with full consciousness of their responsibilities, both towards the League, and towards the peoples under their care, the League itself and, consequently, the peace of the world would reap the benefit. Now the only tangible link provided for by the Covenant between the League of Nations and the mandatory powers is represented by the annual reports of the powers, the preliminary examination of which has been entrusted to this commission by the council. Thanks to the high distinction of its members, thanks also to the diligent care and admirable devotion which the Commission has displayed from the outset in carrying out its appointed task, this link, which neglect on its part might have weakened to breaking-point, has, on the contrary, been strengthened and tightened every year" (remarks of M. Rappard on retiring from direction of mandates section of Secretariat, *ibid.*, V, 10).

and in 1928, $5,066,733.[4] Another evidence of confidence in the League may be found in the fact that the seven government loans issued under its auspices have appreciated over 11 per cent on the average, while non-league loans of similarly situated countries issued during the same period with the same average yield at issue price have appreciated less than 8 per cent.[4a] As measured by the amount of newspaper space devoted to it, interest in the League has been variable, but apparently has tended to increase. Newspaper publicity, however, is a poor measure of the importance of an institution. Those most solidly established and most successful do not generally make news. Their activities have become habits and lack the novelty sought by correspondents.

The importance attached to the League can perhaps better be judged by the increasing regularity with which prime ministers and foreign ministers of the great as well as the small countries have attended its sessions. The prime ministers of Great Britain and France set an example by attending the fifth assembly. Sixteen foreign ministers were present the next year, seventeen in 1926, and the 1927 assembly was attended by one chief of state, two prime ministers, and twenty-one foreign ministers including those from Great Britain, France, and Germany.[5] The confidence in the League of enlightened statesmen even in non-League countries was admirably illustrated by former Secretary Hughes's remarks as president

[4] The Budget Committee pointed out to the Assembly in 1928 that the increase in budget had not kept pace with the new work intrusted to the League. "Between 1922 and 1926 the budget had increased by 5% and the staff by 27%; during the same period the number of documents translated into French increased by 89% and that of documents translated into English by 71%. During the same period the documents passing through the registry increased by 48% and the number of days during which committees and subcommittees held meetings by 175%. Statistics for the first months of 1927 indicated that there had been no falling off in this progressive movement since the end of 1926" (*L. of N.*, *Monthly Summary*, VII [October, 1927], 305).

[4a] Max Winkler, *The Investor and League Loans* (Foreign Policy Association, Information Service, Special Supplement, June, 1928), pp. 25–26. The figures given differ because I have not considered the German loan a League loan and have based appreciation on issue price rather than par value. Winkler's table, correcting an error in calculation, shows 12.3 per cent appreciation for League loans and 7 per cent for non-League loans.

[5] *L. of N.*, *News* (New York, October, 1925), p. 4; *ibid.* (November, 1926), p. 9; *ibid.* (November, 1927), p. 14.

of the American Society of International Law on April 20, 1927. He said:

> In the final analysis the Locarno agreements give ground for assurance because the parties have ready at hand the permanent Court of International Justice for disputes as to legal rights, and, for the composing of other differences, the organization of the Council of the League, with membership of a character affording a practical guaranty that the interests of each of the parties to the agreements will have appropriate attention in formulating proposals and reaching decisions. And thus, in the extra-legal sphere, diplomacy with new institutions at its command will control the issue. Success will depend upon the wisdom and far-sightedness of this diplomacy, but it is difficult to see how peace in Europe could be better assured than by such opportunities of adjustment, though involving, inevitably as it would seem, the balancing of interests.[6]

Confidence in the League may be presumed to beget confidence in its activities. It is not easy to determine whether in fact the mandates system has won as much approval as the League in general. The system has not thus far been applied to any territories other than these referred to in article 22 of the Covenant[7] though it has been applied to all of them[8] and government representatives before the Mandates Commission have seriously discussed its extension.[9]

As an indication of opinion on the subject the views of different classes of people may be sampled.

Jurists, historians, and philanthropists, even those of German nationality, quite generally support the system. "The best defense of the system," writes the French jurist Stoyanovsky, "consists in expounding the juridical principles."[10] "The mandate system may be toothless but it is not bootless," says Moon, an American historian,

[6] *Proc., A.S.I.L.*, 1927, p. 14.

[7] With the exception of Walvis Bay, an enclave in Southwest Africa, which though part of South Africa before the war is now administered as part of the mandated territory (*Statutes of Union of South Africa* [1920], p. 62).

[8] Except the Kionga triangle ceded by Portugal to Germany in 1894 and the part of French Equatorial Africa ceded to Germany in 1911, which were returned to Portugal and France, respectively (see *supra*, chap. ii, n. 51).

[9] *P.M.C., Min.*, VI, 121–24, *supra*, n. 1.

[10] Stoyanovsky, *La Théorie générale des mandats internationaux*, p. 237. M. Van Rees of the Mandates Commission characterizes it as "one of the happiest innovations born of the war and universally recognized as one of the noblest results of the treaty of Versailles" (*Les Mandats internationaux*, I [1927], 2).

after a survey of modern imperialism.[11] "On the whole," writes John H. Harris, of the British Anti-Slavery and Aborigines Protective Society, "The League of Nations may be justly proud of the success of the mandatory system."[12] "In spite of the origin of the system," said Professor Mendelssohn-Bartholdy of Hamburg in the 1925 meeting of the German association of international law, "I believe it will free itself gradually of its imperfections and will prove one of the greatest creations of international law in modern times."[13]

Among specialists the experiment has aroused extraordinary interest. The head of the mandates section of the League Secretariat has drawn attention to the "countless requests for information both bibliographic and other on mandates questions. Many scholars and students," he added, "come to the league of nations library to study the documents and I need not say that the secretariat endeavours to grant them every facility in their work."[13a] Scores of treaties and articles have appeared on the juridical character of the system, its historical development, and its humanitarian achievements and possibilities, in all languages and mostly in an optimistic tone. Though German writers of which there have been many are likely to be reserved in their praise or even cynical, they displayed even before Germany entered the League an increasing tendency to accept the system, to insist that Germany, as a party to the Versailles Treaty, demand full adherence to its principles, and to urge that the League supervision be strengthened. Their criticism has been of the one-sided application of the system to German and Turkish territory alone rather than of the system itself.[14]

[11] Moon, *Imperialism and World Politics*, p. 509.

[12] Harris, "The Mandates System after Five Years' Working," reprinted from *Contemporary Review*, 1925. See also Sir Sydney Olivier, "Mandates under the League of Nations," in Marvin, *Western Races and the World* (1922), p. 252.

[13] *Germania*, June 25, 1925. See also Moritz Bileski, "The Work of the Mandates Commission of the League of Nations," *Die Gesellschaft*, November, 1924; *Zeitschrift für Politik*, XIII, 408; *Zeitschrift für Völkerrecht*, XII, 65; XIII, 77.

[13a] *P.M.C., Min.*, X, 12; see also *ibid.*, IV, 10.

[14] See Resolution of German Association for International Law, June 6, 1925, *Kölnische Volkszeitung*, June 7, 1925, and statements by Gunzert, Fleischman, and Mendelssohn-Bartholdy on the occasion.

Statesmen and politicians, as one might expect, exhibit a wider divergence of opinion. Their views usually reflect personal or national disappointments, ambitions, or policies. The most pessimistic statements have come from Americans, Germans, and Russians. Secretary Lansing of the American delegation at Paris in 1919, whose advice against the system was rejected by President Wilson, has offered such a sweeping criticism of the system as to require extensive quotation:

The mandatory system, a product of the creative mind of General Smuts, was a novelty in international relations which appealed strongly to those who preferred to adopt unusual and untried methods rather than to accept those which had been tested by experience and found practical of operation. The self-satisfaction of inventing something new or of evolving a new theory is inherent with not a few men. . . . . Many reformers suffer from this form of vanity.

In the case of the system of mandates its adoption by the conference and the conferring on the League of Nations the power to issue mandates seemed at least to the more conservative thinkers at Paris a very doubtful venture. It appeared to possess no peculiar advantages over the old method of transferring and exercising sovereign control either in providing added protection to the inhabitants of territory subject to a mandate or greater certainty of international equality in the matter of commerce and trade, the two principal arguments urged in favor of the proposed system.

If the advocates of the system intended to avoid through its operation the appearance of taking enemy territory as the spoils of war, it was a subterfuge which deceived no one. It seemed obvious from the very first that the Powers, which under the old practice would have obtained sovereignty over certain conquered territories, would not be denied mandates over those territories. The League of Nations might reserve in the mandate a right of supervision of administration and even of revocation of authority, but that right would be nominal and of little, if any, real value provided the mandatory was one of the Great Powers as it undoubtedly would be. . . . .

It may appear surprising that the Great Powers so readily gave their support to the new method of obtaining an apparently limited control over the conquered territories, and did not seek to obtain complete sovereignty over them. It is not necessary to look far for a sufficient and very practical reason. If the colonial possessions of Germany had, under the old practice, been divided among the victorious powers and been ceded to them indirectly in full sovereignty, Germany might justly have asked that the value of such territorial cessions be applied on any war indemnities to which the Powers were entitled. On the other hand, the League of Nations in the distribution of mandates would presumably do so in the interests of the inhabitants of the colonies and the mandates could be accepted by the Powers as a duty and not to obtain new possessions. Thus under the mandatory system Germany lost her territorial assets, which might have greatly reduced her financial debt to the Allies, while the latter obtained the German colonial possessions without the loss of any of their claims for indemnity. In actual operation the apparent altruism of the mandatory system worked in favor of the selfish and material interests of the Powers which accepted the mandates. And the same may be said of the dismemberment of Turkey. . . . .

In the tentative distribution of mandates among the Powers, which took place on the strong presumption that the mandatory system would be adopted, the principal European Powers appeared to be willing and even eager to become mandatories over territories possessing natural resources which could be profitably developed and showed an unwillingness to accept mandates for territories which, barren of mineral or agricultural wealth, would be continuing liabilities rather than assets. This is not stated by way of criticism, but only in explanation of what took place. . . . .

On the other hand, there was a sustained propaganda—for it amounted to that—in favor of the United States assuming mandates over Armenia and the municipal district of Constantinople, both of which, if limited by the boundaries which it was then purposed to draw, would be a constant financial burden to the Power accepting the mandate, and, in the case of Armenia, would require that Power to furnish a military force estimated at not less than 50,000 men to prevent the aggression of warlike neighbors and to preserve domestic order and peace. . . . .

Reading the situation thus and convinced of the objections against the mandatory system from the point of view of international law, of policy and of American interests, I opposed the inclusion of the system in the plan for a League of Nations.[15]

Dr. Heinrich Schnee, former governor of German East Africa, indorses Secretary Lansing's view of the system though he believes that the "subterfuge" which may not have deceived the members of the conference did deceive the outside world and thus involved a threefold deception: upon the German nation, upon the native populations, and upon the general public.[16] As to practice under the system, he asserts that pre-war economic conditions were not reattained in any of the former German colonies until 1926, and then

[15] Lansing, *The Peace Negotiations*, pp. 155–60. David Hunter Miller, legal adviser to the American delegation, expressed a similarly cynical opinion of the mandates system as set forth in President Wilson's second draft covenant on January 14, 1919 (*The Drafting of the Covenant*, I, 47), but his considered judgment is that "the world took a very long step forward when Article 22 of the covenant came into force" (*ibid.*, p. 105).

[16] Schnee, *German Colonization Past and Future*, pp. 59–61.

only in the best governed, while "the humanitarian conditions—especially those relating to sanitation and education—are still far behind our standard." Emphasizing the French military policy in her African mandated territories, he says:

Henceforth, until the conscience of the world awakens in righteous indignation, France will be able to employ the natives of the German colonies, so long as they remain under her rule, as of her other colonies, in warfare of any kind, aggressive or defensive, in any part of the globe, including the European continent. . . . . The drafting of late German native subjects into the French army has already begun. . . . . Such proceedings turn the whole Mandate project into a horrible mockery. They are in crassest contradiction to all that the League of Nations claims to stand for, above all to that "sacred trust of civilization," to the fulfillment of which the mandatory powers solemnly pledged themselves.[17]

This point of view seems to be fully adopted by the leaders of the Soviet Union. In an interview with foreign workmen's delegates published in Pravda for November 13, 1927, Stalin replied to the question "Why does the Soviet Union not take part in the League of Nations" in part as follows:

The soviet union is not a member of the League of Nations and does not participate in the League of Nations, first of all because it does not wish to assume responsibility for the imperialistic policy of the League of Nations, for the "mandates" which are issued by the League of Nations for the object of the exploitation and oppression of the colonial countries. The Soviet Union does not participate in the League of Nations since it stands wholly and completely against imperialism, against the oppression of colonies and dependent countries.

Even among the allied statesmen there have been pessimistic utterances. Lord Milner, former British colonial secretary, perhaps expressed the natural predisposition of an ardent imperialist against any limitation upon Britain's colonial activity when in 1924 he referred to the discouraging influence of the long delay in putting the system into effect and of the return of imperial rivalries. He says:

Had it not been for this, the mandatory system might have acquired a prestige which would have enabled it to be gradually extended to other portions of the world in which it seems that the native population were incapable, without external aid, of evolving a decent form of government. But fate had willed it otherwise. As things had actually turned out, it seemed to him that the mandatory system, so far from obtaining greater extension, was likely as time went on

[17] *Ibid.*, p. 99.

to be contracted and to prove in many cases a mere transitory state. Nevertheless [he added more hopefully], it remains even in its curtailed and more or less mutilated form—he meant as compared with the original big conception—a very important factor in the international situation.[18]

The pessimism which has been expressed by the colonial officers may reflect the imperialism and dislike to any limitations upon discretion natural to the profession.[19] It is thus especially significant that Sir Frederick Lugard described as "a man who for more than a generation has had great faith in the British Empire, a great belief in British commerce, and a great trust in British administration," and who at first approached the mandate system with skepticism, after experience on the Mandates Commission became its supporter. The discussions before this Commission he thought

have served and will continue to serve a useful purpose. Each mandatory has been anxious to show that it has not been backward in carrying out its pledges. It is no mean achievement that the conquerors have (as Lord Balfour said) agreed to a self-imposed limitation of the sovereignty which they obtained over conquered territories, and consented to the supervision of the League. The high standards embodied in the Covenant must obviously in the future be regarded as principles of general application. . . . . The mandates system stands as an

[18] *J.R.S.A.*, CLXXII (June 27, 1924), 548–49.

[19] See statements by Mr. Amery, British colonial secretary, criticized by Labour members in Parliament, December 14, 1926, in Hansard, *Parliamentary Debates* (5th ser.), Vol. CC, col. 2883, and statement by W. Ormsby-Gore, under-secretary for colonies in 1924, *J.R.S.A.*, LXXII, 550. "The main obstacle, as he saw it, was the lack of a sense of security in the title of the mandate. Practically all the troubles and difficulties had arisen from that fact. . . . . People were suspicious of it. They had it in the back of their minds that such territories might possibly go back to Germany." Contrast this with the same man's attitude before the mandates system had been put in operation and before he was in the colonial office. "There are few, if any, European countries that have not made mistakes in the past in their government of the native races of Africa, and there still exist in the Dark Continent many abuses which require the searchlight of public opinion throughout the civilized world. The example of successful administration in any one of the Mandatory Areas on the basis of 'trusteeship for the Native Races' will go far to encourage the raising of the standard of administration in other parts of Africa to a higher level. The League of Nations will, therefore, have an opportunity of taking in hand the great task of educating and uplifting the backward races of the world and in securing them against national or individual exploitation by others; while as regards the more highly developed races, such as the Arabs of Mesopotamia, it will be the means of their gradual evolution to restored independent national existence after four hundred years of oppression by an alien conqueror" (*The League of Nations Starts*, pp. 118–19).

international acknowledgment that civilization must be made to mean something higher to backward races than the aims and methods of the development syndicate, or the assiduous cultivation of new wants to afford markets for European commerce.[20]

A similar optimism has been expressed by statesmen of such varied background as President Wilson, Lord Balfour, and Fritjoff Nansen.[21] The official attitude of the mandatory governments will be considered presently.

What has been the attitude among the peoples of different nations? Materials are not available for an adequate survey. Detailed studies should be made of parliamentary debates, the press, journals of opinion, educational books—such as atlases, gazetteers, encyclopedias, and school textbooks—the publications and proceedings of relevant associations, both national and international. The writer is able to give merely a few indications.

National parliaments of the mandatories have paid attention to the system especially on the occurrence of incidents like the Bondelzwart affair, the Mesopotamian troubles, the Arab-Druse insurrection, and the Mosul dispute. Usually such debates have hinged on questions of responsibility for the trouble and expense with evident desire of the opposition to make political capital. Debates in the House of Commons in 1921 disclosed a strong opinion favorable to withdrawal from Mesopotamia,[22] and French Chamber debates on the Druse affair in 1925 brought out considerable sentiment in favor of immediate withdrawal of France from Syria.[23] The questionnaire issue at Geneva in 1926 precipitated a debate in the British House of Commons on the mandatory principles. The Labour members insisted that mandates were trusts and that the conservative government was tending to assimilate them to colonies contrary

[20] *J.R.S.A.*, LXXII, 547. See also Lord Askwith's comment (*ibid.*, p. 550).

[21] Baker, *Woodrow Wilson and World Settlement*, I, 268. See *supra*, chap. ii, n. 36; Balfour, *L. of N.*, *O.J.*, III, 546–48; *infra*, n. 60 and chap. iv, n. 12; Nansen, in *L. of N.*, *Assembly*, *infra*, n. 66.

[22] Gibbons, *An Introduction to World Politics* (1922), p. 507. During this period there were also repeated efforts by the House of Commons to get the government to submit the various mandates to it. Some of these debates are reported in *Société des Nations, Revue mensuelle documentaire*, 1921.

[23] *L'Asie Française*, January, 1926, pp. 9–30.

to the Covenant. The government denied the charge and reiterated its loyalty to the system.[24] On the East African loan question debated at about the same time the Labour party induced the government to introduce an amendment insuring protection for native labor on any works undertaken as a result of the loan, and on the question of confining purchases made with the loan money to the Empire they were more considerate of the open-door provision in the Tanganyika mandate than the conservatives. In fact, some of the latter proposed an amendment requiring that purchases be made within the Empire, though the government induced its withdrawal by declaring that it would effect the policy by executive order.[25] Judging from the attitudes of the conservative and labor parties when in power as well as from parliamentary debates, it appears that the latter has offered a more whole-hearted recognition of the special status of mandated territories and the League's supervisory functions though it has sometimes displayed reluctance to accept mandatory responsibilities.[26]

Thus within the mandatory states opinion has varied with parties and political exigencies. The average man has not taken a very profound interest in the matter. Judging from his usual sources of information—the press and educational material—he probably does not very clearly distinguish mandated areas from colonies. In Great Britain and France parliamentary and popular interest has probably been the greatest. The British dominions were originally anxious to annex the areas, and apparently much of their public thinks they did. Parliamentary interest was stirred in South Africa by the Bondelzwart affair of 1923 and in New Zealand by the Samoan deportations of 1927.[27] In Japan there have been a number

[24] *G. B., Parl. Deb.* (5th ser., 1926), Vol. CC, cols. 2876–98.

[25] *Ibid.*, cols. 2370–89, 2438, especially Colonial Secretary Amery's remarks, col. 2373, and Mr. Harris' remarks, col. 2377.

[26] "We want to see the Mandate system, first of all rendered more effective and then extended to all the non-self governing possessions of the Great empires. That actually was a proposal of the British Labour Party, which suggested that the whole of our tropical possessions in Africa should be brought directly under the League of Nations in that form" (H. N. Brailsford, *op. cit.*, p. 16).

[27] *Great Britain and the Dominions*, "Harris Foundation Lectures" (1927), on Australia by Sir W. Harrison Moore, p. 333; on New Zealand by J. B. Condliffe, p. 376; on

of articles on the subject, some of them recalling suggestions that Manchuria be placed under the mandate of Japan.[28] To a question at the twelfth session of the Mandates Commission the accredited representative of Japan said:

When the budget of the islands was submitted to parliament a discussion on the mandate in general took place. These discussions were never heated, not even as regarded the speeches of the opposition. . . . In view of the great distance separating the islands from Japan and the very small resources they possessed, the Japanese population did not very clearly realize the importance of the mandate. Its interest, therefore, in these islands was not comparable to that shown regarding Formosa and Korea.[29]

Among the non-mandatory League powers, Italy has taken an especial interest in the Mandates. Italians have been led to think that Italy failed to get her share from the victory and to demand compensation. Both France and England have given Italy such compensation in Africa, and Italy has not offered to place the territory given her under mandate.[30] But, on the other hand, as the only Principal Allied Power without a mandate, she has sought to make the system real by strengthening the League's control. The Marquis Theodoli, chairman of the Commission, an Italian though not an official representative of Italy, has been a vigorous defender of the League's competence on mandates questions, of the interests of the natives, and of the open door.[31] In this he has been perhaps most heartily seconded by the other members of the Commission from non-mandatory states. Thus during the extensive debates on economic equality in the twelfth session the members from non-

---

South Africa by Angus S. Fletcher, p. 453; and *supra*, chap. ii. The important debates are conveniently summarized in *J.P.E.*

[28] Togi Manabe, "Dr. Ariga and the Mandates System," *Gaiko Jiho* (Tokio, 1927), XLVI, 107, and *supra*, chap. i, n. 43*a*.

[29] *P.M.C.*, *Min.*, XII, 47.

[30] *O.J.*, III, 798 ff.; Sir F. Lugard, *J.R.S.A.*, LXXII, 540; W. E. Rappard, *J.B.I.I.A.*, 1925, p. 223; *supra*, chap. ii, nn. 99, 100, 116–18.

[31] In accepting the chair at the first meeting of the Commission the Marquis Theodoli "thanked his colleagues for the honor which they had bestowed upon him, an honor which reflected on his country, the only non-mandatory power among those permanently represented on the council" (*P.M.C.*, *Min.*, I, 4). See also his position on the Bondelzwart affair (*ibid.*, III, 205); on the long questionnaire (X, 14); and on economic equality (XII, 168).

mandatory states were the most vigorous defenders of that régime and M. Orts, a Belgian, felt it necessary "to warn his colleagues against the idea that, as regards the principle of economic equality, the different countries could be classified as being its supporters ready to safeguard it and its adversaries wishing to circumvent it according as they had or had not a mandate."[32] The non-mandatory League members in the Council and Assembly have perhaps manifested most confidence in the system and their attitude has dominated the Assembly.[33]

Opinion among non-members of the League has been more skeptical. In the United States, though there has been considerable sympathetic interest among scholars, probably the average man follows Secretary Lansing in considering mandates slightly veiled annexations.[34] Journals of opinion are inclined to assume an ironic attitude in articles with such titles as "France and Her Black Empire," "Thumbs down for Syria."[35] The government, though insisting on certain rights as a participant in the war, has since 1921 refused to deal with the League on the matter though invited to do so, but has negotiated with the mandatories individually.[36] Officials of the Soviet Union and Turkey have expressed hostility to the system.[37] In Germany, where a similar attitude might be expected opinion has been more mixed. A recent survey[38] of German peri-

[32] *P.M.C., Min.*, XII, 69.

[33] During the twenty-second conference of the Interparliamentary Union, Sir Beddoe Rees of Great Britain said, "The success or failure of this mandatory system will depend very largely upon the non-mandatory powers; there are something like 27 of them represented in this conference. It is for you to criticize the powers who are carrying out mandates under the control of the League of Nations, and therefore I think it is for this Conference to be the watchdog of the mandatory system" (*Compte rendu*, p. 465). See also *infra*, n. 65.

[34] See *supra*, n. 15.

[35] *New Republic*, January 23, 1924; *ibid.*, January 19, 1927.

[36] Wright, "The United States and the Mandates," *Mich.L.R.*, *ibid.*, May, 1925, and *supra*, chap. ii.

[37] Statement of Stalin *supra* and statement of Tewfic Rouschdy Bey, Turkish foreign minister in relation to the Mosul controversy, in *L. of N., Council, Min.* (35th sess.; September 3, 1925), *infra*, chap. xv.

[38] Mary E. Townsend, "The Contemporary Colonial Movement in Germany," *P.S.Q.*, XLIII (March, 1928), 64–76. Articles on the subject by Millot have appeared in *L'Afrique française*, 1927–28.

odicals and papers emphasized the strong colonial movement in Germany represented by such men as Schnee, former governor of East Africa, and supported by "literature and propaganda in the shape of colonial histories, treaties, novels depicting life in Africa and in the South Seas, pamphlets replete with statistics, magazines and newspaper articles . . . . telling the Germans more about their former colonies than they ever knew when those lands were German soil." "On the other hand," notes this survey, "both signs of apathy and expressions of positive antagonism to a colonial policy are not lacking today among the German populace as a whole."

> There is as yet no official pronouncement of support from either the government or parties, ... nor is there a definitive promulgation of any plan or program for the recovery of the oversea possessions. From the literature and from the speakers of the movement, one gathers that the present objectives range all the way from the return of the lost territories in toto to Germany, to the more modest restitution of, perhaps, only one colony (preferably East Africa) to be administered as a mandate by Germany, and to the very general granting to Germany of colonial opportunity or economic concession in any part of the world, or else a share in a future internationalization of colonial territories. Whatever the objectives of a colonial policy mentioned in Germany today, however, it is distinctly noticeable that they stress no longer imperialistic or aggressive aims but the economic uses and the cultural responsibilities of oversea possessions. . . . . Many financial and economic experts insist that colonial or mandated territories would at present prove too costly for Germany.[39]

The German government insisted that the Covenant be observed and that as a party to the treaty of Versailles it had the right to protest to the League on the subject, even before it became a member of the League.[40] On Germany's entering the League the Council appointed a German on the Permanent Mandates Commission, without however arousing great enthusiasm among German colonial advocates. The Kolonialgesellschaft, with twenty-five thousand members, announced it as a "step forward for Germany, certainly, but as no reason for great joy and as still less reason for expectant hopes that Germany would regain her colonies or acquire mandates."[41]

[39] Townsend, *op. cit.*, pp. 65, 74.

[40] *L. of N., Assembly, Rec.*, sess. I (Plenary Meetings), 213; *O.J.*, VIII, 316–17; *supra*, chap. xiii.

[41] *Der Kolonialdeutsche* (organ of the Kolonialgesellschaft) September 15, 1927, cited Townsend, *op. cit.*, p. 73.

Probably the general attitude in Germany combines resentment at the forced yielding of her colonies just as they were becoming profitable and at the stigma of colonial maladministration cast on her by the Allies, with a feeling that mandates are better than annexation by the Allies and consequently the system should be supported. This has generally been the attitude of jurists and apparently it is also of officials. The Auswärtige Institut of Hamburg sent out a questionnaire to 280 officials in 1927 asking (*a*) shall Germany strive for colonies, (*b*) shall she strive for them in the form of mandates, (*c*) shall she limit her colonial activity to demanding equal rights with other nations in all colonial territories as well as mandates? Only fifty replies were received, and they were almost evenly divided between the affirmative and the negative in regard to waging of any colonial activity. The affirmative, for the most part, indorsed the mandate form of colonies as the best that can be done under the circumstances.[42]

The press appears to have manifested a growing interest. At its tenth session on November 4, 1926, the Chairman called the Mandates Commission's attention to the review of press comments recently distributed which showed "the great interest which public opinion in several countries is taking on the question of mandates. This," he added, "is very satisfactory for perhaps in no other field of League work is the support of well informed public opinion more vital than in the matter of mandates."[43] It should not be inferred, however, that newspaper comment has always been favorable. Like parliaments, the press has given most attention to dramatic incidents which often reflect on the success of the system. Undoubtedly the publicity of the League's proceedings assures more publicity to hostilities and violent controversy in mandated areas than in colonies—a situation which while assisting in the elimination of abuses may give the public a distorted impression of the relative amount of unrest in mandated and other backward areas.

The situation with respect to educational and reference books indicates anything but adequate public understanding of the man-

[42] *Europäische Gespräche*, December, 1927, cited Townsend, *op. cit.*, p. 75.

[43] *P.M.C.*, *Min.*, X, 10. The Marquis Theodoli of the Mandates Commission emphasized the importance of world public opinion (*ibid.*, VI, 140), as did Mr. Huntington Gilchrist of the mandates section in an article in *Advocate of Peace*, 1926, p. 170.

dates system. An article in *La Paix par le droit* in February, 1927, by M. Proudhommeaux draws attention to the scant respect paid to the mandates system by school textbooks. He reports:

> We have discovered with nothing short of stupefaction that seven years after the signature of the treaty of Versailles and the establishment of the League of Nations, most of the geographical textbooks intended for primary and secondary schools systematically ignore the colonial mandates and regard them as nothing more than a form of annexation. . . . . Thanks to our text books on geography, one whole generation of French people will be persuaded, from what they have learnt at school that Togoland, the Cameroons and Syria have been purely and simply incorporated in the colonial domain of France. . . . . It is useless to insist on the possible consequences of this disastrous error.[44]

This statement was considered by the Mandates Commission at its twelfth session, and though the members generally realized the importance of the matter the feeling was unanimous that it should be considered by the Committee on Intellectual Co-operation rather than the Commission. During the discussion M. Rappard informed the Commission that certain of the French geography texts had been prepared by M. Maurette, of the International Labor Office, and on the latter's attention being drawn to the matter he had explained "that the text books in question had been issued several years before the war and had been rapidly and imperfectly re-edited at the close of hostilities. New editions, however, would certainly show that the statements regarding mandated territories had been corrected." Mr. Grimshaw said he had noted many deformations of the mandates idea in British school manuals and had drawn the matter to the attention of the League of Nations union with the suggestion that they point out the errors to the editors as there existed no official school manuals in Great Britain.[45]

A similar criticism of official and unofficial European atlases has been made by Lieutenant Colonel Lawrence Martin, an American geographer, who notes that in the United States alone do atlases ordinarily distinguish mandated territories from colonies.[46] He writes in an Introduction to the texts of the peace treaties:

[44] *Le Paix par le droit*, XXXVII, 60–65, quoted in *P.M.C., Min.*, XII, 13.

[45] *Ibid.*, pp. 15, 99.

[46] *The Treaties of Peace, 1919–1923* (New York: Carnegie Endowment for International Peace, 1924), pp. xxii–xxiii. The two following notes are by Martin.

It is important to record that, whether by accident or by design, the latest editions of the principal foreign atlases uniformly treat mandates as if they were colonies, dependencies or protectorates of the several mandatory powers. . . . .

The political maps of the continent of Africa as a whole, and the detailed maps of parts of this continent, in atlases published by British, French and Italian map-houses since the World War are illustrative of this treatment of mandates as colonies. It is interesting to note, also, that the leading German atlas treats the mandates over the former German colonies in Africa as if they were possession of Great Britain, France or Belgium.[47]

Likewise in all these atlases the mandates over the former German and Turkish possessions in the Pacific Ocean and in the Arabian Peninsula of Asia are shown uniformly as if they were British, Japanese or French possessions rather than mandates. Philip's "New Commercial Map of the World on Mercator's Projection" equatorial scale 1:20,000,000, published in London, marks the mandates separately under the caption: "Boundaries of Territories administered by or under Mandates of the League of Nations"; but Bartholomew's "Chart of the World on Mercator's Projection," equatorial scale 1:23,000,000 published in Edinburgh, shows no mandates whatever in Africa, the Pacific Ocean, or Arabia, including all fourteen mandates in the colors which cover the adjacent British, French, Belgium, and Japanese possessions.

Quite in contrast, the official American maps, published since the world war, which cover the mandates, and the best American post war atlas, all agree in showing the mandates in Africa, in the Pacific Ocean, and in Asia as separate administrative entities rather than as possessions of Great Britain, France, Belgium or Japan.[48]

The *Statesman's Year Book*, a well-known British manual, treats the B and C mandated areas with the colonies of the mandatory but gives an independent position to the A mandated areas. The most

[47] "See Bartholomew's 'Times Survey Atlas of the World,' 1922, Plate 68; Schrader and St. Martin's 'Atlas Universel de Géographie,' 1923, Carte 53; Baratta-Visintin's 'Grande Atlante Geografico,' 1922, Carta 67; Andree's 'Allgemeine Handatlas,' 1922, Seite 172–3; see also map facing p. 1 in the Belgian 'Annuaire Officiel pour 1923' issued by the Ministère des Colonies."

[48] "See U.S. Army's map entitled 'Europe and Asia Minor, with inserts of Africa and Oceanica,' January 15, 1921; *Ibid.*, 'The Pacific,' 1921, scale 1:23, 546, 157; *Ibid.*, 'The Atlantic,' 1923, scale 1:23, 443, 200; Department of State's 'Map of the Pacific, showing Sovereignties, Mandates, and Claims,' 1921; U.S. Tariff Commission's 'Colonial Tariff Policies,' Government Printing Office, Washington, 2nd edition, 1922, maps facing pp. 4, 26, 310; *Ibid.*, 'Territories held under mandates of the League of Nations,' pp. 10–12, and present status of former German colonies and of other mandated territories,' pp. 265–278; U.S. Navy's 'Outline Chart of the World,' Hydrographic Office, No. 5188, June 2, 1923; *Ibid.*, No. 1262*a*, October 1, 1923; Goode's 'School Atlas, Physical, Political and Economic,' 1923, pages 84, 87, and 94."

recent edition of the *Encyclopaedia Britannica* contains an excellent article under the head "Mandates" by Sir Frederick Lugard.

A considerable number of associations, both national and international, have taken an interest in the mandates system. While some of them refrain from passing resolutions, others commit themselves to definite opinions. In the former class one may gather the tone of the association's opinion somewhat from its publications. Thus in the articles and discussions published by such national and imperial associations as the British Round Table, the Royal Colonial Institute, Le Comité de l'Afrique Française, and Le Comité de l'Asie Française one finds a tendency to minimize the distinction between mandates and colonies though statements are usually formally correct,[49] while in the publications of associations devoted to international law and relations like the Grotius Society, the Royal Institute of International affairs, the Society of Comparative Legislation and International Law, the distinctive features of the mandates are likely to be emphasized.[50] American organizations of the latter type, such as the American Society of International Law, the Council on Foreign Relations, the Foreign Policy Association, have stressed the significance and novelty of the mandates system in their publications.[50a]

Among unofficial associations of an opinion-forming character, those devoted to protection of indigenies, peace, and international co-operation have taken an interest in the mandates system, generally favorable. The British Anti-Slavery and Aborigines Protective Society is perhaps the most important of the first type. In February and April, 1921, it passed resolutions urging that the system be put into full effect as soon as possible.[51] Since then it has taken a steady interest in the system, its officers have written favor-

[49] See *The Round Table, Proceedings of the Royal Colonial Institute, United Empire, L'Afrique française*, and *L'Asie française*.

[50] *Grotius Soc., B.Y.B.I.L., J.B.I.I.A., J.C.L.*

[50a] *A.J.I.L.* and *Proc. A.S.I.L.*, Foreign Affairs (U.S.), Foreign Policy Association, Information Service. The leading international associations of this type, l'Institut de Droit International and the International Law Association, have dealt very little with the mandates in their publications.

[51] See the *Anti-Slavery Reporter and Aborigines' Friend*, April–July, 1921; *S. des N., R.M.D.*, III, 304, 483.

ably of it, and on several occasions it has sent memoranda to the League suggesting measures in the interest of the natives. Its policy is to strengthen the League's control.[52]

The attitude of peace societies is illustrated by the resolution submitted to the twenty-fifth Universal Peace Congress in August, 1926, which asserted that the mandates system "represented an appreciable progress in the field of colonial policy."[53] This resolution indorsed the system because it laid down that colonial policy may not be carried on solely in the selfish interest of a single state, provided a control which aimed to prevent the exploitation of indigenous races, and created the possibility of putting an end to colonial dependence when the indigenous race is developed sufficiently to govern itself. It recommended the extension of the system to all colonies.

Among the important unofficial societies devoted to the promotion of international co-operation is the Interparliamentary Union. It has given serious study to the mandates system since its twentieth session in 1922. In the following session a resolution was passed "registering the conference's satisfaction at the institution of colonial mandates, whereby a new phase of colonial policy is inaugurated in accordance with the principles of the League of Nations Covenant." The resolution "most heartily approved the creation of the Permanent Mandates Commission whose duty is to control the proper administration of mandates" and expressed the earnest hope that the mandatory powers may fulfil their " 'sacred mission of civilization' and that the institution of colonial mandates

[52] "Some of our main work had been concentrated upon the question of the mandates. It had been truly said that the mandatory system opens a new door and establishes a new principle but if it is a new chapter, it takes a very long time to open, and while progress has been made and certain steps have been taken, yet a good deal more requires to be done and it was our duty as a society to continue to press the question of the mandates until we got a satisfactory adjustment" (Charles Robert, president of the Society in meeting, April 27, 1921, *supra*, n. 51). See also John H. Harris, organizing secretary of the Society, *op. cit.*, and Charles Roden Buxton, vice-chairman of the General Committee of the Society, *The Exploitation of the Colored Man* (1925), both printed under the auspices of the Society. The Society has presented memoranda to the Mandates Commission on native lands, the Bondelzwart rebellion, and the Samoan deportations (*P.M.C., Min.*, II, 88–90; III, 287–88; XII, 196).

[53] *25me Congress Universel de la Paix*, August, 1926.

may prove a powerful factor in the establishment of world solidarity and in the maintenance of peace." While "approving the general principle of mandates" the conference referred the question of possible improvements to its Permanent Commission on Racial and Colonial Questions whose report to the twenty-second conference in 1924 was adopted. This resolution considered that the "system could only be crowned with full success through loyal and disinterested co-operation between the League of Nations and the mandatory powers in accordance with article 22 of the covenant," and recommended that the Assembly be empowered to modify and revoke mandates and that the Permanent Mandates Commission be authorized to inspect mandated areas on the spot and to establish direct relations with the Assembly and with the mandatory powers. It also recommended that C mandates be assimilated to B mandates, that all mandated areas have full fiscal autonomy, that the right of petition be unrestricted, that the land of a mandated territory be not mortgaged for security, and natural resources be given in security only with the assent of the assembly, that native recruitment be restricted to police forces for the defense of the mandated territory, that the open-door principle be extended to all mandated territories and to the benefit of all states, and that reports of the mandatories be more detailed. It further requested its Committee on Racial and Colonial Questions to consider the "question of extending the principle of colonial mandates to other regions . . . . in the interest of the peace of the world and of the well-being of coloured races."[54]

Of the various unofficial associations supporting the League of Nations the British League of Nations Union has taken an especially active interest in the mandates question. On January 20, 1922, it resolved that "the mandatory system should be forthwith brought into full operation in Africa and provisionally in Asia." During the Syrian insurrection of 1925 it passed a resolution, later considered by the Permanent Mandates Commission, suggesting that a mandatory should immediately notify the League if "it finds it necessary at any time to suspend its ordinary laws."[55] The Union's publica-

[54] Interparliamentary Union, *Compte rendu* (20th sess., 1922), p. 55; *ibid.* (22d sess., 1924), pp. 68, 667. See also *S. des N., R.M.D.*, VI (1924), 47, 664.

[55] *S. des N., R.M.D.*, IV (1922), 298; *P.M.C., Min.*, XII, 152.

tions indicate confidence in the system. Miss Freda White, whose book is sponsored by this organization, writes:

> The mandatory system will have reached the period of steady, gradual growth. Its principles are defined already; the fine work of the mandates commission has ensured its actuality in international affairs; its application in the territories, on the whole, is well begun. But it will be long enough before it comes to perfection, and in the meantime the surest guarantee of its sound development would be general interest and knowledge.[56]

The Federation of League of Nations Associations which includes this and similar organizations in other countries has also passed resolutions on the mandates question. In June, 1921, it insisted that "articles 22 of the covenant be applied in the letter and the spirit by the mandatory states" and that the system be put in full effect as soon as possible. It urged the Permanent Mandates Commission to give especial attention to the question of developing self-government in mandated territories.[57]

Perhaps the best evidence of the public opinion of the world is to be found in the resolutions and debates of the League of Nations Assembly itself. As will be noted in the next section, these have from year to year expressed increasing confidence in the mandates system.[58]

The data considered perhaps justifies the following conclusions. (1) Learned opinion is generally favorable to the mandates system. (2) Humanitarian, peace, and internationally minded groups support the system. (3) National, colonial, and imperial-minded groups are frequently skeptical. (4) The average man knows little about the subject and hardly distinguishes "mandates" from "colonies." (5) Moderate political parties tend to support the system while extreme reactionaries and extreme radicals are hostile or skeptical. (6) Public opinion within League of Nations members has been more favorable than outside. (7) Within the League, opinion in non-mandatory powers has been more favorable than in mandatory powers. (8) The most vigorous criticism has come from groups within the expropriated powers, from imperialists within the mandatories, and from

[56] Freda White, *Mandates*, pp. 176–77.

[57] *S. des N.*, *R.M.D.*, III (1921), 586.

[58] See *infra*, nn. 64–66.

radical agitators, though even these groups have not been unanimously against the system. In general it appears that the majority of people are favorable or indifferent. Opposition comes from special-interest groups. The system has commended itself to reasonably informed people without an ax to grind.

2. Attitude of the League of Nations

Have the League agencies themselves taken the system seriously? Their attitude has been disclosed by their actions, and they have labored to make the system a success. There seems to have been from the first a recognition within the League that the mandates would be its first acid test.[59] The skeptics looked at them as veiled annexations and not a little in the Peace Conference confirmed this view. With the passage of time the veil would naturally wear out rather than become a fabric discernible to the disillusioned eye of the world and to the equally scrutinizing if differently placed eyes of the mandatories and the natives. Thus the League has bent its efforts to make the system a reality. "The machinery of the mandates commission," said Lord Balfour in the Council, "the machinery of the Council of the League of Nations, and the machinery of the assembly of the League are all contrived to make it quite impossible that any transaction of general interest should take place except in the full glare of the noonday sun of public opinion."[60]

But beyond publicity there has been continuous discovery of facts and supervision. The mandates section of the secretariat has received and collected material about the mandates including not only reports from the mandatories but also petitions and comments from other sources. The Mandates Commission, the majority of whose members are natives of non-mandatory states, have independently examined the reports of mandatories, cross-examined their representatives, prepared reports meticulously pointing out abuses and sometimes formulating general principles. The Assembly has discussed and given wide publicity to the more important

[59] Memorandum of Secretary General, July 30, 1920, *Assembly Doc. 161* (December, 1920), p. 11 (responsibilities of the League arising out of art. 22); see also Rappard, *P.M.C., Min.*, I, 6; V, 10.

[60] *L. of N., Council,* sess. XVIII, *O.J.*, III, 547; Levermore, *L. of N., Y.B.*, III (1923), 129.

of these abuses. The Council has not failed to give practical effect to most of the recommendations of the Mandates Commission, and before confirming the mandates has scrutinized them with lawyer-like care and made efforts to bring them into conformity with article 22 of the Covenant, although it must be confessed that it has not been embarrassingly insistent upon changes which would upset difficult political compromises.[61]

These activities cannot be considered in detail here.[62] Suffice it to say that they disclose differences in the attitude of the various League organs. These organs are not all eventually responsible to a supreme authority. They are mutually independent. The League's organization exemplifies the American theory of separation of powers rather than the European practice of unified responsibility. The Assembly, the Council, the Mandates Commission, the Secretariat, and the Court all enjoy certain independent powers under the Covenant, the mandates, and other constitutional documents.[63]

The Council, which has the major control, contains three mandatory powers among its permanent members. A fourth mandatory power, Belgium, up to 1927 occupied one of the elective seats, and though the three mandatory dominions have not been members of the Council and theoretically are not represented in League activities by the British Empire representative, they are under the Covenant entitled to temporary membership while their interests are being discussed and their interests have in fact been actively supported at least by the conservative government of Great Britain. The British member of the Council has even suggested that he might represent them in the absence of their own delegates. Thus

[61] The Council contented itself with mild comment on the privilege of recruiting natives in case of general war in the French African mandates, and did not object to the incorporation of the Balfour declaration in the Palestine mandate nor to the selection of A mandatories without making the wishes of the natives "a principal consideration" though all of these seem contrary to art. 22. The Permanent Mandates Commission has mentioned these matters but considers itself incompetent to go back of the mandates approved by the Council to art. 22 (see *infra*, chap. iv).

[62] *Infra*, Part II.

[63] See *infra*, chap. v. See report on relation of the Council to the Assembly, *L. of N., Assembly, Rec.* (First Committee), I, 12, 93, 95 and (Plenary Meetings), pp. 318–20. See also remarks by M. Rappard, director of the mandates section on the difficult position of the Secretariat when other organs of the League disagree, *P.M.C., Min.*, III, 11.

the Council has represented the mandatories' point of view to a considerable extent. Italy, the only principal Ally without a mandate, has furnished a useful check though she is also a colonial power. Germany can perhaps be expected to do likewise. Sweden, whose representative has often been *rapporteur* on mandatory affairs, has shown a persistent desire to support the Commission and a certain *esprit de corps* of the Council springing from the frequency of its meetings, and the continuity of its personnel, as well as from the fact that the majority since 1922 has been non-mandatory has prevented it from being merely a rubber stamp for the mandatories. It has occasionally modified the Commission's recommendations in accord with the mandatories' desires and has always in important cases been ready to delay action until these desires were known, but it has usually supported the commission. In cases where two or more mandatories have disagreed this would be the natural solution.[63a]

The Mandates Commission has displayed the characteristics of a technical body. Even the citizens of mandatory states in its membership have wished to maintain its independence and impartiality. Suggestions that it is but a tool of the Council have been promptly denied by reference to its express establishment by the Covenant. It has little interest except in an impartial application of the system, and although its members have sometimes differed as to the scope

[63a] Urging a strengthening of the powers of the Commission as against those of the Council, H. N. Brailsford, of the British Independent Labour party, pointed out that "the council is dominated by the great imperial powers. . . . . When you compose your governing council of the empires themselves, inevitably the interests of empire, the assumptions of empire, the ethics of empire will govern its decisions." With this Senor de Madariaga, formerly of the League Secretariat, said he had agreed on first reading art. 22 of the Covenant. It seemed to him "by far the worst fig leaf of the whole show." "I am now," he added, "bound to confess that I was wrong. The mandates commission has achieved so much that we want it to achieve more, and the criticisms that are directed to the mandatory régime of the League are today, in my opinion, only a proof of the confidence in its workability which has grown up among many of us. We are finding it incomplete, but that is because we are finding it alive. At first, so far as I was concerned, I thought it would not be worth criticizing. I have seen it at work, I believe it is a very courageous commission. It considers itself, as it has every right to do, as a free and independent commission having its charter from the Covenant, appointed of necessity by the Council but not by the members of the Council, composed of men who must be free from their governments and, therefore not officials, and free to advise the council on whatever they want the Council to be advised and not on what the Council wants advice" (*op. cit.*, pp. 7, 12).

of its powers, as to the interpretation of the mandate principles, and as to the best means of making them effective in the various territories, there seems little doubt that they have honestly tried to make these principles their guide. The Commission is the real center of the system. Upon it alone can the natives rely. The Council is not likely to do more for them than the Commission recommends. Though the Assembly may voice their interest it cannot directly affect the policy of the mandatories except through the Commission and the Council. Secretariat officials may acquire knowledge but they can make it effective only through passing it on to Commission members.

Though the Assembly and the Secretariat exercise only an indirect influence their importance should not be underestimated. The alertness of certain members of the Assembly, especially those of race or civilization allied to the peoples under mandates, can be relied on to disclose serious abuses and force the Council to institute an investigation through the Commission.[64] Most of the members of the League have no colonies and can afford to rejoice over limitations upon imperialism. Even in imperial states most of the citizens take little interest in colonies. Equality of man and self-determination of peoples, conflicting though they may be, appeal equally to the sentiment of the day, and both seem to be given some recognition by the mandatory system. Thus the Assembly can be relied upon to support all proposals to strengthen the League's supervision.[65] It has never failed to express its full confidence in the Commission, and when the Council has shown an inclination to wink at abuses by the mandatory or block proposals of the Commission it has sometimes passed resolutions strengthening the latter's hand.

Thus the first Assembly sought to protect the members of the Commission from dismissal without Assembly consent and to prevent the mandatories from securing military or commercial advan-

[64] See activity of Haitian delegate on native rights and especially on the Bondelzwart affair, *L. of N.*, *Assembly*, *Rec.*, sess. I (Plenary Meetings), p. 715; sess. II (Plenary Meetings), p. 355; Levermore, *op. cit.*, III (1923), 276, 278, and remarks of Srinavasa Sastri of India in the Second Assembly, September 12, 1921, on the denial of the open door in C mandates, commented on by M. Rappard, *J.B.I.I.A.*, IV, 218.

[65] As has been noted, the Interparliamentary Union favors increasing the assemblies' functions in the mandates system (see *supra*, n. 54; see also *supra*, n. 33).

tage from the mandate. The second Assembly urged confirmation of mandates at the earliest possible moment and respect for the principles of the Covenant in the territories even prior to confirmation. The third Assembly urged investigation of the Bondelzwart affair and definition of a system of petition. The fourth Assembly again referred to the Bondelzwart incident and urged a special effort to ameliorate the condition of the natives. The fifth Assembly drew attention to the right of petition and urged wider publicity for mandatory reports, rapid definition of principles in regard to loans and liquor traffic, and the presence of responsible officials of the territory before the Commission. The sixth Assembly urged that the benefit of special international conventions be extended to mandated territory. The seventh Assembly confined itself to a general expression of confidence in the Commission, although animated debates in the Sixth Committee and in the Assembly indicated wide sympathy for the position of the Commission in the pending difference with the Council over the new questionnaire and the hearing of petitions. Mr. Nansen of Norway said:

> I desire to say that by the resolution which is now before it the Assembly is expressing its confidence in the Mandates Commission both in respect to the work which has been done in the past year and that which confronts it in the year to come and that it is expressing its approval of the action taken by the Commission during all its sessions both ordinary and special held during the past year.

The eighth and ninth assemblies urged more rigorous enforcement of the liquor-traffic provisions in B and C mandates and the latter urged, in addition, active consideration of the question of economic equality in mandated areas and the completion of statistical tables for judging the results of mandatory administration. The tenth assembly regretted the recent disturbances in Palestine and trusted the mandatory would take measures to prevent the recurrence of such incidents.[66]

Members of the Assembly have frequently expressed approval of the mandates system in debate. Dr. Nansen of Norway, who has

[66] The Assembly resolutions are reported in the *Records* of the assemblies now published as supplements of *O.J.*, and in the annual Assembly number (October) of *L. of N., Monthly Summary*.

usually been *rapporteur* to the Assembly on mandates questions, has never failed to draw particular attention to the importance of the system. On September 25, 1926, he said:

> The assembly is also, as I understand it, expressing its unabated confidence in the rightness of the mandates system, by means of which, we all believe, the mandatory Powers may be able to build up new principles of co-operation between the advanced and backward peoples of the world for the mutual benefit of both. No one who follows these matters can doubt that these relations constitute one of the gravest of the problems which the twentieth century has to face, and that toward its solution the Mandates Commission may have a great contribution to make.

The Secretariat section on mandates, which is always in touch with the situation, knows the documents and history and keeps abreast of periodical and technical discussions of the question, is in a position to influence the Commission by supplying information though it attempts to observe the utmost impartiality in this work.[67] Its international character and natural interest in maintaining the prestige of the League give ample assurance that its influence will be in the direction of supporting the system.

The Permanent Court of International Justice has no immediate control of mandatory policy but the fact that it is the final authority on disputes over the interpretation of the mandates is a valuable safeguard against destructive interpretations by the mandatories. The three cases involving mandates which have come before it, all relating to the Mavromatis Palestine concession, indicate its willingness to give its compulsory jurisdiction in this regard a sufficiently broad interpretation and to be unaffected by the relative power of litigants before it.

We may conclude that the League organs vary in their attitude toward the mandates system but have generally shown an inclination to support it against assaults by the mandatories. Have their efforts been appreciated by the natives?

3. Attitude of the Mandated Peoples

In most of the mandated regions education, communications, and social organization are so undeveloped that there is nothing

[67] Rappard, *P.M.C.*, *Min.*, II, 5.

which can be called public opinion.[68] The opinion of very few of the natives extends beyond private, family, local, or tribal matters. The native culture is so remote from that of the Western world that the people or even the chiefs do not readily understand the League of Nations or the mandate system. Even the words are unknown to most. It certainly cannot be said that the new régime has been received with enthusiasm in any of the territories. Native disturbances have occurred in most of them since the war, and in Syria and Southwest Africa insurrections of considerable seriousness have taken place since confirmation of the mandates.[69]

To the Arab nationalists of Palestine, Syria, and Iraq the system was at first associated with the breach of allied pledges for a united Arab state, with repressive French and British military measures and with the hated Zionist program.[70] Today they understand the League of Nations very little but believe it has ignored their petitions, has palliated such atrocities as the bombardment of Damascus, has by the word "mandate" bracketed them with African tribes of inferior civilization, and instead of preparing them for independence has led to their economic and political retrogression.[71]

The term "mandate" was so unpopular in Iraq that upon recognition of Feisal's government the British found it convenient to abandon it in the country and to assert that Iraq had become independent, its relation with Great Britain being governed only by the

[68] In his original memorandum of December 17, 1918, General Smuts wrote: "The German colonies in the Pacific and Africa are inhabited by barbarians who not only can not possibly govern themselves, but to whom it would be impracticable to apply any idea of political self-determination in the European sense"; thus he suggested that the mandates system be applied only to "territories formerly belonging to Russia, Austria and Turkey" (*The Nation* [New York, February 8, 1919], p. 227). Even in the Arab countries political opinion is organized among only a small part of the population.

[69] On the Bondelzwart affair in Southwest Africa see *P.M.C.*, *Min.*, III, and on the Druse insurrection in Syria, *ibid.*, VIII. A minor revolt was reported in Ruanda in 1922 (*ibid.*, III, 96, 313) and in Western Samoa in 1927 (*ibid.*, XII, 105–10, 123, 126–27, 203). See also *infra*, chap. vii.

[70] See *infra*, chap. ii. See also Wright, "The Palestine Problem," *P.S.Q.*, XLI, 388 ff.; "The Bombardment of Damascus," *A.J.I.L.*, XX, 263; "Syrian Grievances," *Current History*, XXIII (February, 1926), 687–93.

[71] See typical petitions from Palestine, *P.M.C.*, *Min.*, VII, 160; IX, 203, and from Syria, *ibid.*, VIII, 174; X, 189; XI, 195.

Anglo-Iraq Treaty.[72] In this the British government gave heed to the opinion of its agents on the spot. Miss Gertrude Bell wrote in 1920:

> The king and the Naquib have proclaimed to the listening universe that they will never, so help them God, accept the mandate. His Majesty's Government have replied that they can conclude no treaty except by reason of the right to do so given to them by the League of Nations, i.e., the mandate. I think I've said before, but anyway, I'll say right here, that I'm convinced that no country in the world can work a mandate. . . . The Arabs won't submit to any diminution of their sovereign rights such as being placed in tutelage under the League of Nations. They are ready to exercise those rights in such manner as to bind themselves by treaty to accept advice in return for help.[73]

In Syria and Palestine, the Arab nationalists who constitute the bulk of the population regard the system as but another name for older forms of imperial control. The Syro-Palestinian congress wrote to the sixth Assembly of the League:

> The mandate system imposed on our countries cannot achieve the praiseworthy ends aimed at by the League of Nations. In practice and owing chiefly to the way in which it is applied, the mandate has only led to their political and economic retrogression. In its essence it is a system of colonization pure and simple, instead of being a means of helping these countries towards the attainment of the dearest of their aspirations—complete independence.[74]

The Jews of Palestine in general support the system though they feel that the League is not sufficiently energetic in requiring the mandatory to fulfil its obligations in reference to the Balfour declaration. The Christian communities, though containing many ardent Arab nationalists, are in the Lebanon less hostile to the mandatory and the system than the Moslems and Druses.

In Central Africa and the Pacific islands there is no evidence that the natives as yet distinguish the system from older forms of imperial control. The right of petition has been very little utilized, practically only by ex-German settlers who have gained no satisfaction by it and view the mandates system as a crude bit of hypocrisy designed to reconcile their expulsion and expropriation with Wilson-

[72] See *supra*, chap. ii. Wright, "The Government of Iraq." *A.P.S.R.*, XX, 765.

[73] Gertrude Bell, *Letters*, II, 643–44.

[74] *P.M.C.*, *Min.*, VIII, 174.

ian phrases. In Southwest Africa alone have the ex-Germans been allowed to remain, and here they have been practically forced to accept South African citizenship.[75]

Some effort was made in 1918 to get the opinion of the natives of former German territories under British occupation upon their future governments, but the results were unconclusive.[76] The Allies found in this report justification for depriving Germany of all her colonies,[77] and the report seems to indicate that the chiefs interviewed in Cameroons, Togo, Southwest Africa, Samoa, and Nauru expressed a preference for British rule. In East Africa and New Guinea the report is far from convincing, and German writers interpret it as an indorsement of their government.[78] In June, 1921, after the mandate had been in effect for six months, the Samoan native council was so dissatisfied with New Zealand that it petitioned the King of England to put them under the colonial office.[79] From such evidence, private communications of natives to former German missionaries and colonists and the reception accorded to such persons who have returned, Dr. Heinrich Schnee, former German governor of East Africa, concludes:

> The small community of the Samoan people is the only group of inhabitants of the German colonies which is sufficiently organized politically to be in a position to express its wishes in a united manner calculated to make a strong public

[75] See *supra*, chap. vii. See also *O.J.*, IV (1923), 568–72, 603, 659, and Wright, "Status of Inhabitants of Mandated Territory," *A.J.I.L.*, XVIII, 314.

[76] Correspondence relating to the wishes of the natives of the German colonies as to their future government, *G.B.*, *Parl. Pap.* (Colonial Office, 1918), Cd. 9210, and report on the natives of Southwest Africa and their treatment by Germany (*ibid.*, Cd. 9146).

[77] "The Allied and Associated powers are satisfied that the native inhabitants of the German Colonies are strongly opposed to being again brought under Germany's sway" (allied note to Germany, June 16, 1919, *U.S. Sen. Doc. 149* [66th Cong., 1st sess.], p. 102; see also p. 118). In his original proposal of the mandates system, General Smuts said the natives of the German colonies "might be consulted as to whether they want their German masters back, but the result would be so much a foregone conclusion that the consultation would be quite superfluous" (*The Nation* [New York, February 8, 1919], p. 227).

[78] Schnee, *German Colonization, Past and Future*, chap. viii. With respect to East Africa this contention is hardly supported by the observation made on the spot by Buell in 1925–26 (*The Native Problem in Africa*, I [New York, 1928], 448 ff.).

[79] *P.M.C.*, *Min.*, XII, 123.

impression. Such united protests are unthinkable in the other colonies, where the natives are on a lower plane of civilization and divided into numerous petty tribes. Nevertheless, sufficient evidence comes from all the former colonies that the natives are weary of Mandate administration and long for the return of the Germans.[80]

The evidence presented hardly supports this sweeping assertion. Probably the natives distinguish little between their former and present administrators and none at all between the constitutional system formerly and now prevailing.

4. Attitude of the Mandatory Governments

Have the mandatory governments supported the system? Lord Milner noticed in 1924 that the "spirit of cordial and unselfish co-operation" attained by the Allies during the war had during the protracted period of putting the system into effect been "not always apparent" but "very often submerged by a return of the old rivalries and ambitions."[81] Since the system has been in effect, have the mandatories been willing to assume the burdens it imposes without material reward? It is notable that Armenia, which lacked material resources, went begging for a mandatory.[82] Lord Balfour has repeatedly pointed out that the mandatory system cannot succeed if so worked as to impose an actual loss on the mandatory.[83] British public opinion in the face of overwhelming budgets has given much attention to the subject of profits and necessary expenses of the mandate in Mesopotamia.[84] The French parliament has commented acrimoniously on expenses in Syria.[85] The Honorable Ormsby-Gore of the British Colonial Office says: "it is difficult to get a penny out of the treasury for the colonies; it is still more difficult to do so for the protectorates, and it is quite impossible to do so for mandated territories.[86]

[80] Schnee, *op. cit.*, p. 170.

[81] *J.R.S.A.*, LXXII (June 27, 1924), 548.

[82] See *supra*, chap. ii. The United States Congress refused to accept the Mandate on June 1, 1920, and the League did the same (*O.J.*, I, No. 8 [1920], 89).

[83] *L. of N., Assembly, Rec.*, sess. I (Plenary Meetings), p. 721.

[84] Lee, *The Mandate for Mesopotamia and the Principle of Trusteeship in English Law* (League of Nations Union, 1921).

[85] See *supra*, n. 23.

[86] *J.R.S.A.*, LXII, 550.

Doubtless a mandatory is entitled to recoup the necessary expenses of administration from the mandated territories.[87] The Permanent Mandates Commission has made it clear, however, that the mandatory is entitled to no more. If the revenues of the mandated territory show a surplus at any time, such surplus may be utilized only for the good of the territory.[88] Countries have heretofore been willing to meet large colonial deficits because of the advantages colonies afforded their citizens for profitable trade and capital investment in time of peace, and because of the national advantages of strategic position, military resources, and necessary raw material in time of war. Yet under the principle of the open door, unquestionably applicable to B mandates, in most respects to A mandates and, according to the Japanese contention, which has, however, not been generally accepted, to C mandates,[89] the former of these advantages would seem doubtful and under the demilitarization provisions mandates would seem a military liability rather than an asset.[90] If these provisions are enforced may not mandatories show an inclination to resign? It is interesting to notice that in the United States, different from Great Britain, the legislation of most states allows the trustee, to which a mandatory has been compared, to receive remuneration for his services.[91]

However, the open door does not apply in C mandated territories, and even where it does it is chimerical to suppose that it will or can be so rigorously enforced that nationals of the mandatory will not enjoy a certain advantage through greater familiarity with the administration. Certainly it has not in practice. The open door aims to prohibit only unfair competition and thus does not exclude advantages coming to citizens of a mandatory from closer acquaintance with local conditions. No mandatory has resigned though there

[87] Palestine Mandate, art. 28; Syria Mandate, arts. 15, 19 (*P.M.C., Min.*, XI, 173, 192; *infra*, chap. xiii).

[88] *P.M.C., Min.*, I, 14; Lee, *op. cit.;* see *infra*, chap. xiii, sec. 2*f*, *g*.

[89] *P.M.C., Min.*, I, 36; III, 83; see also *supra*, chap. ii, and *infra*, chap. xiii.

[90] *Ibid.*, I, 24; *Recommendation No. 4, L. of N., Assembly, Rec.*, sess. I (Plenary Meetings), p. 725.

[91] The common-law agency differs from the Roman-law mandate in presuming remuneration for the agent (Holland, *Jurisprudence* [11th ed.], p. 298, and *infra*, chap. xii).

have been occasional press rumors that such action was contemplated.[92] But have they loyally submitted to the restrictions of the system? Have not the "imperial ambitions" referred to by Lord Milner made them restive?

The mandatory dominions of the British Empire never concealed their desire for outright annexation. Statements assimilating C mandates to annexation have not been uncommon among their representatives.[93] This restiveness was especially noticeable in their comments upon the more searching questionnaire prepared by the Commission in 1926.[94] The British conservative government with its imperial traditions has naturally supported this attitude of the dominions. This, coupled with the historic conservative policy of expanding the Empire, doubtless accounts for the apparent efforts made by Great Britain since 1926 to reduce the rôle of the League with respect to mandates. Belgium has been accused of covert annexation in her legislation organizing Ruanda-Urundi.[95] France was openly hostile to the system at the Peace Conference[96] though she took her severe grilling over Syria with grace and her representative especially noted that mandated territories are not under the sovereignty of the mandatory, so there could be no occasion for sensitiveness.[97] The Japanese attitude has always been extremely correct.

Probably none of the mandatory governments has been enthusiastic for the system. They prefer mandates to nothing but doubtless would prefer colonies to mandates. Preparing reports and answering questions is a nuisance for overworked colonial officials. Prestige may be injured by the disclosure of inhumanities to a public

92 The American press reported that France was considering resigning the Syrian mandate in the fall of 1926 and in December, 1927, and that Great Britain was contemplating resigning her near eastern mandates in the spring of 1927 (see *New Palestine* [New York, May 20, 1927], XII, 468).

93 See *supra*, chap. ii. See, e.g., statement by General Smuts of South Africa (*P.M.C.*, *Min.*, II, 92).

94 See *infra*, chap. vi; *O.J.*, VII, 1235, 1646, 1647.

95 See *infra*, chap. xiii; German notes, 1925; discussed (*P.M.C.*, *Min.*, VII, 53–61).

96 See *supra*, chap. ii; D. H. Miller, *The Drafting of the Covenant* (New York, 1928), I, 103.

97 *L. of N., Council, Min.*, sess. XXXIX (1926); *O.J.*, VII, 524.

which knows little of normal colonial conditions. Budgetary or commercial prosperity may be thwarted. It may even be that sound administration will be interfered with by advice from League agencies ignorant of local conditions.[98]

But in spite of these considerations no mandatory has failed to fulfil its duties of reporting annually to the League, of answering questions and of transmitting petitions.[99] The mandatories have regularly sent experts to Commission meetings. Often these have been administrators of the territories and they have always cheerfully responded to rigorous cross-questioning. The mandatory governments have generally given heed to Commission suggestions when formally approved by the Council. Whether in all cases the spirit of mandatory administration has been observed in full cannot be considered in this place. Suffice it to say that formally the mandatories have shown good faith to the system. "Even those like Great Britain," said M. Rappard, in the eleventh session of the Commission, "which had most severely criticised the commission, had shown particular attention and care in drawing up the documents submitted to it. Hence it would be erroneous to imagine that the mandatory Powers were hampering the Commission's activities. On the contrary, they were co-operating with the Commission on increasingly closer terms."[100]

The world is interested and expectant, the League organs are optimistic and faithful to the Covenant, the natives are skeptical or wholly ignorant, the mandatories though indifferent if not antagonistic recognize their obligations. It is now time to leave the world of opinion for that of action. What opinion is justified by the facts? What has the League actually done in respect to mandates?

[98] In their report to the British government on the third Assembly, the British delegates said, "The question of mandates is of course one which interests, more than any other members of the League, the British self-governing dominions but speaking generally it may be said that the Dominion delegates seemed to have no serious charge to make against the good faith of the Permanent Mandates Commission. Their main criticisms would probably be:—(*a*) That the Permanent Mandates Commission is a body which has little knowledge of local conditions and local difficulties, (*b*) That a mandatory power should not be publicly arraigned before the world in the report of the Permanent Mandates Commission" *G.B., Parl. Pap.* [Misc. No. 52, 1923], Cmd. 1807, p. 32. See also speech of Sir Francis Bell of New Zealand in third Assembly.

[99] See *supra*, chap. vi, for a few minor lapses.

[100] *P.M.C., Min.*, XI, 20; Van Rees, *op. cit.*, I, 49.

PART II

ORGANIZATION OF THE MANDATES SYSTEM

CHAPTER IV

THE CONFIRMATION OF MANDATES

1. ANALOGOUS LEAGUE ACTIVITIES

The League's activity in relation to mandates bears some resemblance to other of its activities and has been to some extent affected by them. The peace treaties and subsequent treaties have burdened the League with a number of problems of territorial administration and these may be classified in three types: (1) the mandates provided for in the Covenant itself, (2) the minorities provided for in a number of treaties and declarations relating to Central and Eastern European countries made soon after the war, and (3) special territorial settlements such as the Saar Valley, Dantzig, the Aaland Islands, Upper Silesia, and Memel. In all, the League has to see that certain rights of the inhabitants guaranteed by treaty, agreement, or declaration are respected and in most it receives petitions from the inhabitants. In the Saar Valley it is directly responsible for the government and appoints the governing commission, but the régime is expected to be temporary. In Dantzig it appoints a high commissioner who serves as arbiter between Poland and the Dantzig government, the latter being responsible to a locally elected assembly. In Upper Silesia it confirms the appointment of the president of the mixed commission to supervise transitional measures and the chairman of an arbitral tribunal. In other special settlements its duties are confined to guaranteeing the provisions of treaties assuring such things as civil rights to the inhabitants, demilitarization, and commercial opportunities.[1]

Under the minority treaties and agreements the League merely supervises the execution of certain guaranties for minorities within the territories of certain states of Central and Eastern Europe.[2] Al-

[1] *Saar Basin and Free City of Dantzig* (L. of N., Information Section); Maurice Fanshawe, *Reconstruction* (London, 1925), pp. 229–44, 259, 261, 282; F. M. Russell, *The International Government of the Saar.*

[2] *The League of Nations and Minorities* (L. of N., Information Service); Fanshawe, *op. cit.*, pp. 244–50; Rappard, *International Relations as Viewed from Geneva* (1925),

though these treaties contain no time limitations it appears that the régime is thought of as transitional. The minorities are not considered to have a corporate entity but, according to Austen Chamberlain, the object is to secure them "that measure of protection and justice which would gradually prepare them to be merged in the national community to which they belonged."[3]

The mandates differ from the minority agreements in that they require unanimous rather than majority vote of the Council for modifications, and in that each mandated community occupies definite territory not within the mandatory's sovereignty and, in the case of A mandates at least, has a recognized corporate existence. The provision, however, in the C mandates and in some of the B mandates that the territory may be administered as an integral part of the mandatory's territory creates a close resemblance between these communities and the minorities. The opinion has also been expressed that the mandates like the minority agreements are transitional measures and that eventually the territories will come under the full sovereignty of the mandatories.[4] Others, however, insist and certainly the documents indicate, that the mandatory régime was intended to be permanent unless terminated by the recognition of the full independence of the mandated community—a situation distinctly previsioned in the Covenant's description of them as "not yet able to stand by themselves" and its "provisional recognition" of the A mandated communities as "independent nations." The future recognition of complete independence is concretely specified in the Iraq mandate. "The covenant," said M. Adatci of Japan while the Council was discussing the national status of inhabitants, "meant

---

pp. 40–58; Rosting, "Protection of Minorities by the League of Nations," *A.J.I.L.*, XVII (October, 1923), 641; De Visscher, *The Stabilization of Europe* (Chicago, 1924), chap. ii; "The Problem of Minorities," *International Conciliation Pamphlet 222*, September, 1926.

[3] L. of N., Council, December 9, 1925, sess. XXXVII, *O.J.*, VII, 144. Count Apponyi of Hungary has sought to gain for the minorities a corporate status but has not been successful. See statement of M. Mello Franco of Brazil, *rapporteur*, *ibid.*, pp. 138–44, and De Visscher, *op. cit.*

[4] Lord Milner, *J.R.S.A.*, LXXII (June 27, 1924), 549. Some of the mandates required consent of only a majority of the Council for modification in the drafts originally proposed by the mandatories (see *infra*, chap. v, n. 17).

that at some future data, more or less distant, these peoples would become independent and enjoy full political freedom. The League must keep this distant end in view."[5]

Thus while the minority régime is designed to ease the process of assimilation, the mandatory régime is to ease the process of self-determination. From this point of view the mandated communities have some resemblance to Dantzig which though under League supervision is recognized as at least nominally independent, while the Saar Valley, Upper Silesia, and Memel are more analogous to the minorities.

Partly no doubt, in view of these differences, the League's procedure in regard to mandates differs radically from that in regard to minorities through the requirement of annual reports and the establishment of an independent commission to examine them. A minority matter cannot get before the League except on the initiative of a member of the Council and can only be considered by the Council itself or a committee of its members. Considering the political character of the Council it is not surprising that only the most serious abuses are considered at all. Each mandate, on the other hand, must be considered at least once a year and by a body whose members have no political responsibilities to consider. Thus it is not surprising that the League's activity in relation to mandates has been infinitely more effective. Sir Austen Chamberlain in the Council will naturally hesitate to jeopardize the friendly relations of his country with Roumania or Czechoslovakia by pressing the grievances of some Jew or Hungarian in one of these countries but Sir Frederick Lugard in the Mandates Commission is not worried by such considerations when he is presented with complaints from natives in the Cameroons or Syria.[6]

Furthermore, the fact that the mandated communities are geographically separated and are not under the sovereignty of the mandatory government renders the latter less sensitive to criticism

[5] L. of N., Council, April 20, 1923, sess. XXIV, *O.J.*, IV, 570. See also Sir F. Lugard, *P.M.C.*, *Min.*, VII, 195. General Smuts tried to eliminate the "yet" from the foregoing phrase in the Peace Conference (see *supra*, chap. ii).

[6] See remarks by Count Apponyi of Hungary, *L. of N.*, *Assembly*, *Rec.*, Vol. V (September 9, 1924), and M. Rappard, *op. cit.*, pp. 57–58.

than is the case with governments within whose territory dwell minorities. Rapid assimilation of the minorities seems to these governments a natural policy or even a vital necessity. The mandatories are not affected by this sentiment except in the few cases where their own citizens would like to colonize the mandated territory. The mandatories, it is true, are for the most part great powers permanently represented on the Council while the minority states are not—a fact which may account for the more vigorous opposition in the former case to League investigation of conditions on the spot.[7] The obstacles, however, which the power of the mandatories might be supposed to offer to effective League supervision of mandates have not, in fact, proved as important as those hampering the supervision of minorities.

In view of these differences the powers and procedure of League organs with respect to mandates cannot be implied by analogy to the other situations in which they supervise territorial administrations. They can only be learned from a study of the documents and precedents relating to the mandates themselves; in fact, the situation with reference to different classes of mandated communities or even different communities (especially in the A class) has been thought sufficiently divergent to warrant variations in the terms of each mandate and consequently in the League's powers. The League of Nations, like the British Empire, inclines to regard each territorial situation as *sui generis* and to be wary of generalizing its procedure.

This was emphasized in the Council discussion in March, 1926, on the procedure for answering petitioners. Objection was raised by M. Boncour, the French representative, to the Commission's proposal to forward its entire report on the Syrian situation in answer to certain Syrian petitions. Chamberlain of Great Britain supported this objection and was surprised to discover that the procedure for answering mandate petitions differed from that in the case of minorities. Scialoja of Italy demurred to the reproof implied by this observation and noted that the minorities were under the sovereignty of the administering state which was not true of the people under mandate. "There was accordingly an essential difference between the two cases, which might very well justify a difference of method in re-

[7] See *infra*, chap. vi.

gard to the communication of resolutions."[8] The Commission's suggestion was not followed, but at the next Council meeting the procedure for answering petitions in various cases was discussed and the existing procedure evolved by the Secretariat wa approved, thus apparently recognizing that the procedure of minority and mandate petitions should differ.[9]

In spite of these differences certain similarities exist between the League's supervisory function in these various territorial situations, and it is possible that with experience the procedure may be somewhat assimilated.[10] In view, however, of the greater success of the mandates system up to date it is likely that it will serve as the precedent rather than the others. The suggestion has in fact been made that a minority commission similar to the Mandates Commission be established.[11] Thus in this volume we will have little occasion to refer to the less advanced methods employed by the League in its other activities analogous to mandatory supervision.

2. League Functions in the Mandates System

The League's functions in respect to mandates have consisted of (1) confirming the original mandates and subsequent modifications, (2) organizing agencies for supervising the mandatories, (3) discovering and verifying facts in regard to the mandated communities, (4) assuring the continuous application of the mandate provisions, and to this end (5) ascertaining and formulating standards, principles, and rules for governing the mandated areas.

The first of these functions is clearly implied by the Covenant stipulation that the mandatories act "in behalf of the League" and that "the degree of authority, control or administration to be exercised by the mandatory shall, if not previously agreed upon by the

[8] *O.J.*, VII (1926), 526.

[9] *Ibid.*, p. 878.

[10] When the Council was considering the procedure for mandate petitions it asked the Secretary-General to prepare a memorandum on the procedure adopted for petitions from the minorities and the Saar Valley (L. of N., Council, September 2, 1922, sess. XX, *O.J.*, III, 1176, 1245. The Mandates Commission suggested modification of the British proposal in regard to mandate petitions in view of the procedure in those other two cases and this was accepted in the Council.

[11] H. Wilson Harris, *What the League of Nations Is* (1925), reprinted in *International Conciliation Pamphlet 222* (September, 1926), p. 347.

members of the league, be explicitly defined in each case by the council." It has proved a political function. The prospective mandatory government often had wishes with regard to the frontiers of the territory and the policies to be pursued there, which conflicted with the real or purported wishes of other countries or with the principles of the Covenant. Compromises were necessary, and in order to get the system into operation the League organs had to exhibit a high order of diplomacy.

The third function is implied by the requirement that the mandatory "render to the council an annual report in reference to the territory committed to its charge" and that the Commission "receive and examine" these reports. Fact-finding has been the major activity of the Commission, and it has been mainly of a technical character though occasionally diplomatic *finesse* has been necessary.

The fourth function is the *raison d'être* of the League's activity in respect to mandates and follows from the very conception of "mandatories in behalf of the League" and from the requirement that the Commission "advise the council in all matters relating to the observance of the mandates." It is a semi-judicial function though the Commission and Council have preferred a spirit of co-operation and advice to one of criticism and reproof.

It might seem that the second and fifth functions do not belong to the League at all. The Covenant itself establishes the Council and the Permanent Commission with certain powers, and that document together with the mandates drafted by the Principal Allied and Associated Powers lays down the principles to be applied. Why, then, is further organization of machinery and formulation of principles necessary? A negative answer appears to have been in Lord Balfour's mind, when, in the eighteenth session of the Council in order to correct "errors as to powers of the League," he said:

> Mandates are not our creation. The mandates are neither made by the League, nor can they in substance be altered by the League. Our duties are of two kinds. It is our business in the first place to see that the specific and detailed terms of the mandates are in accordance with the decisions come to by the Allied and Associated Powers in Article 22 of the treaty of Versailles; and, in the second place, to see that in carrying out those mandates, the mandatory powers shall be under the supervision—not the control, but the supervision of the League of Nations, which possess an admirable organization through which it

can obtain the fullest information as to the method in which each mandatory power fulfills the duties which are entrusted to it.

Remember that a mandate is a self-imposed limitation by the conquerors on the sovereignty which they obtained over conquered territories. It is imposed by the Allied and Associated Powers themselves in the interests of what they conceive the general welfare of mankind; and they have asked the League of Nations to assist them in seeing that this policy should be carried into effect. But the League of Nations is not the author of the policy, but its instrument. It is not they who invented the system of the mandates; it is not they who have laid down the general lines on which the three classes are framed. Their duty, let me repeat, is to see in the first place that the terms of the mandate conform to the principles of the Covenant, and in the second place that these terms shall, in fact, regulate the policy of the mandatory powers in the mandated territories.[12]

Lord Balfour said this while defending the Balfour declaration in the Palestine mandate. In view of the difficulty of reconciling this declaration, requiring a national home for the Jews in Palestine, with the Covenant, which provides that A mandated territories be "provisionally recognized as independent," he wished to convince the Council that the reconciliation was not their business. The Zionist policy, he insisted, had been definitively adopted by a power beyond them. "The general lines of policy stand and must stand."

Although he may have been right in contending that principles once in the mandates are legally beyond the power of the League to change on its own responsibility, nevertheless experience has shown that the principles so established are not exhaustive and require interpretation. The Commission has spent much of its time in studying so-called "general questions" in which it includes general principles of land tenure, education, labor regulation, etc., applicable to mandated territories, and on several occasions when it found provisions of the mandates which it thought conflicted with the Covenant or with sound principles it has so reported and sometimes succeeded in bringing about modifications. Although the mandatory powers and their representatives on the Council have occasionally expressed the fear that the League was giving too broad an interpretation to its powers,[13] practice has borne out M. Bourgeois' con-

[12] Levermore, *L.N.*, *Y.B.*, III, 138, based on stenographic reports of the meeting furnished the press. The official paraphrase in *O.J.*, III, 546–48, is somewhat modified.

[13] See discussion of the questionnaire proposed by the Permanent Mandates Commission (*supra*, chap. v, sec. 4).

tention on August 4, 1920, that the League's control was not limited to "verifying whether mandatory powers strictly observed the term of their mandates" but had a moral significance. "A mandate had not for its object to increase the power of certain states but to guarantee the well being and development of the interested populations."[14] This theory was in fact formally approved by the Council on August 5, 1920, when it adopted M. Hymans' report containing the following sentences:

What will be the responsibility of the Mandatory Power before the League of Nations, or in other words, in what direction will the League's right of control be exercised? Is the Council to content itself with ascertaining that the Mandatory Power has remained within the limits of the powers which were conferred upon it, or is it to ascertain also whether the Mandatory Power has made good use of these powers, and whether its administration has conformed to the interests of the native population?

It appears to me that the wider interpretation should be adopted. Paragraphs 1 and 2 of Article 22 have indicated the spirit which should inspire those who are entrusted with administering peoples not yet capable of governing themselves, and have determined that this tutelage should be exercised by the States in question, as Mandatories and in the name of the League. The Annual Report stipulated for in Art. 7 should certainly include a statement as to the whole moral and material situation of the peoples under the Mandate. It is clear, therefore, that the Council also should examine the question of the whole administration. In this matter the Council will obviously have to display extreme prudence so that the exercise of its right of control should not provoke any justifiable complaints, and thus increase the difficulties of the task undertaken by the Mandatory Power.[15]

Experience has also shown that the broad description of the machinery for supervision to be found in the Covenant needed supplementing. The constitution of the Permanent Mandates Commission had to be provided and its powers more clearly defined. To acquire needed information a secretariat section, a procedure for petitions, a questionnaire for the guidance of mandatories and other things were needed. To sanction decisions, means of publicity through the assembly, publications, etc., had to be provided. Thus in fact the League has done much work in each of the five fields. This activity

[14] *L. of N., Council, Min.*, sess. VIII, p. 39.

[15] Responsibilities of the League arising out of art. 22, *L. of N., 1st Assembly, Doc. 161*, p. 17 (reprinted in *L. of N., Assembly, Rec.* [Sixth Committee], sess. I, pp. 371–97).

will be considered in detail in the next chapters, attention here being devoted to the confirmation of mandates.

3. Original Confirmation of Mandates

The long delay in confirming the mandates has been discussed in chapter ii. For this delay the League was not responsible. In fact, it made every effort to accelerate action. On January 30, 1920, twenty days after the League came into official existence, the Secretary-General laid before the Council a memorandum outlining its responsibilities under article 22 of the Covenant, suggesting a procedure for meeting them, and concluding: "The late German overseas possessions are being governed by the prospective mandatory powers as if the powers conferred on the League under the Covenant were not existent. If the mandatory system is to be established before the meeting of the assembly, the measures indicated above must be taken as soon as possible." The memorandum suggested that if the Principal Allied and Associated Powers did not soon submit draft mandates for confirmation, the Council "could on its own initiative draw up the mandates itself and inform the principal allied and associated powers as to the terms upon which the mandatory powers selected shall have to govern." With regard to the territories "of the late Turkish Empire" the Secretary-General thought it clear that nothing could be done by the League until the Turkish treaty was "finally signed," but suggested that the Council ask the Principal Powers what they were doing toward nominating the mandatory powers and drawing up the mandates.[16]

The Council considered the question at San Sebastian in August, 1920. It recognized that "draft mandates adopted by the Allied and Associated Powers would not be definitive until they had been considered and approved by the League," and at the same time it recognized its own incompetence to supervise mandatory administration until they had been confirmed. The latter decision was taken in reply to a letter from King Hussein of the Hedjaz who protested against the arrest and court-martial under French authority of the Lebonese administrative council. "The League," wrote the King, "is morally responsible for the injustice and I am confident that it will

[16] *Ibid.*, pp. 8–11.

take this just request into consideration." Balfour of England in the Council thought this was "the first time a small nation had addressed an appeal to the League. Public opinion would expect the League to answer it with courtesy," but nothing must be done to increase French difficulties in Syria. Bourgeois of France characterized the letter as a "political manœuvre" and the Council replied on the suggestion of Imperiali of Italy: "It is beyond their province to intervene where, in international law, war still continues, and where the new system to be established at the peace is not yet in operation. They can not take any action on a matter which thus seems to them wholly outside their jurisdiction."[17] Nevertheless, as has been noticed, in October, 1921, stimulated by discussions in the first Assembly, the Council did recommend a provisional régime for the mandates still unconfirmed and examined the report of the Commission on several provisional reports submitted to it by prospective mandatories. The Council and Commission, however, both recognized that submission to this procedure was entirely discretionary with the mandatory prior to confirmation.[18]

At the San Sebastian meeting the Council also adopted an elaborate and important report by M. Hymans of Belgium.[19] This report examined the legal foundations of the mandates system in article 22 of the Covenant which specified that the mandatories should exercise their functions "on behalf of the League" and in article 119 of the treaty of Versailles by which "Germany renounces in favor of the Principal Allied and Associated Powers all her rights and titles over her overseas possessions." From these provisions it concluded that "the legal title held by the mandatory Power must be a double one: one conferred by the Principal Powers and the other conferred by the League of Nations." Thus three steps were necessary to put the system into effect:

(1) The Principal Allied and Associated Powers confer a mandate on one of their number or on a third power; (2) the principal powers officially notify the council of the League of Nations that a certain power has been appointed

[17] *L. of N., Council, Min.*, sess. VIII, pp. 53, 55, 239, 241.

[18] See *infra*, nn. 24, 42.

[19] Text in responsibilities arising out of art. 22, *supra*, pp. 12–18; *L. of N., Council, Min.*, sess. VIII, pp. 177–89, and *O.J.*, I, 334–41.

mandatory for such a certain defined territory; (3) the council of the League of Nations takes official cognisance of the appointment of the mandatory power and informs the latter that it [the council] considers it as invested with the mandate, and at the same time notifies it of the terms of the mandate, after ascertaining whether they are in accordance with the provisions of the covenant.

The report then inquires, "By whom shall the terms of the mandates be determined?" In the case of B and C mandates this is in large measure done by paragraphs 5 and 6 of article 22 of the Covenant. These provisions may need "amplifying and defining," but it would seem desirable that in the mandates for the same category and in the provisions in favor of the indigenous inhabitants in the two categories "these prescriptions should be identical." In the case of A mandates, however, the Covenant is less specific. The notion of "provisional independence" provided for by paragraph 4 is "capable of an infinite series of differences in interpretation" and might vary "according to the degree of civilization of the people concerned and even according to the principles and system of government of the respective mandatory powers."

Paragraph 8 of the Covenant authorizes the Council "explicitly to define in each case the degree of authority control or administration to be exercised by the mandatory, if not previously agreed upon by the members of the League." This last expression if taken literally would mean the Assembly since it alone brings all the members of the League together, but this was probably not the intention of those who drew up the article because (1) if they had meant the Assembly they would not have used such an "obscure paraphrase," (2) soon after drawing up the article the Principal Allied and Associated Powers indicated their intention by summoning a meeting of colonial experts in London to draw up draft mandates, and (3) because of its numbers the Assembly is not adapted to "the difficult task of working out the details of the three kinds of mandates." It seemed more likely that by "members of the League" the authors of the article meant "the signatories of the treaty of Versailles who are members of the League," for when they drew up the article in January, 1919, they expected that the mandates would be included in the treaty itself or form annexes to it and that only the Allied and Associated Powers would be considered original members of the League. Thus it was anticipated that these members of the League would have agreed to the mandates by their signature of the treaty.[20]

As the procedure intended by the authors of article 22 had not been followed and as it would now be impracticable to get the ratification of all the signatories of the treaty who were members of the League, it was "theoretically incontestable" that the Council had the right to draw up the mandates as suggested by the Secretary-General. But in view of the practical impossibility of drawing up the terms until the mandate was assigned, the territory defined, and the opinion of experts at hand it seemed "inopportune to exercise this right." It would be "more reasonable to take advantage of the work which has already been accomplished by the experts of the principal powers." But before going into effect the mandates must certainly be "submitted for the approval of the council, and if the latter appears reluctant to take the matter up, it might incur the censure of the Assembly."

In conformity with this report the Council passed a resolution

> requesting the principal powers to be so good as to: (*a*) name the powers to whom they have decided to allocate the mandates provided for in article 22; (*b*) to inform it as to the frontiers of the territories to come under these mandates; (*c*) to communicate to it the terms and the conditions of the mandates that they propose should be adopted by the council from following the prescriptions of article 22.

Thus practically the drawing up of mandates as well as their assignment and territorial definition was left to the Principal Powers; in fact, M. Bourgeois, at the Council meeting August 4, 1920, thought that by the expression "members of the League" in article 22 the Principal Powers whose delegates had in fact drawn the article at the conference meant themselves.[21]

The French Prime Minister replied to this resolution on October 16, 1920, indicating the difficulties which the Principal Powers had met in reaching agreement on the terms of mandates. At the same time he officially communicated their decision in regard to the assignment of mandatories. M. Hymans of the Council on October 27

[20] This interpretation is further borne out by the use of the term "High Contracting parties" rather than "Members of the League" in the draft of the Covenant, published February 14, 1919 (Miller, *The Drafting of the Covenant*, II, 334).

[21] *L. of N., Council, Min.*, sess. VIII, p. 39.

and November 30 again urged the Principal Powers to hurry with the drafts, and early in December these were received for all the mandates.[22]

At the first Assembly meeting in November and December, 1920, the question of mandates was discussed with some heat. Certain members thought the Principal Powers should have reported the state of their negotiations with the United States to the Council and that the Council should be more frank with the Assembly. Dr. Nansen of Norway on the subcommittee on mandates of the Assembly's Sixth Committee twice asked the Council for the texts of the draft mandates and finally these were transmitted with the understanding that they be kept confidential with the subcommittee and with the implication that the subject was within the exclusive jurisdiction of the Council. To this Nansen replied that the Assembly could "discuss any matter within the competence of the League."[23] Perhaps under this stimulus the Council on December 17, 1920, confirmed the C mandates and forthwith published their texts.

On the next day the Assembly resolved that "future draft mandates should be published before they are decided on by the council." The theory had been expressed by Lord Robert Cecil and others that the Assembly as the only organ representing all "members of the League" could draw up the mandates, but eventually a compromise was reached according to which Lord Robert ceased to press his point in the Sixth Committee upon hearing from Mr. Fisher of Great Britain, Mr. Reynold of France, and Mr. Poullet of Belgium that their governments would submit reports to the Commission even though the mandates were not confirmed. "In virtue," said the director of the mandates section, "of a tacit agreement, the commission would be enabled to consider the administration of the mandatory powers, but . . . . there would be no legal obligation for the latter to accept the observations of the council, nor to submit their reports officially before the end of the first year of their administration."[24]

[22] Responsibilities arising out of art. 22, *supra*, pp. 20, 31, 32. See also letter from Japan of November 4, 1920, asserting that she had been "definitely allotted" the North Pacific islands (*ibid.*, p. 23; Rappard, *P.M.C., Min.*, I, 6; Levermore, *op. cit.* [1921], p. 59).

[23] *L. of N., Council, Min.*, sess. XI, pp. 28, 95, 96, and *L. of N., Assembly, Rec.* (Sixth Committee), sess. I, p. 351. See also *infra*, chap. v, nn. 22–23.

[24] *P.M.C., Min.*, I, 6; see *supra*, chap. ii, n. 96.

The Assembly then passed resolutions relating to the composition of the Mandates Commission, suggesting that the mandatories be asked to submit reports on their administration of the territories even though not confirmed, and proposing certain principles for the A mandates. The texts of the draft A and B mandates were submitted to the Secretariat for comparison with the terms of the Covenant in December and soon after were published, thus conforming to the Assembly's resolution.[25]

In chapter ii attention has been given to the course of negotiations, especially between the mandatories and the United States which under continuous Council urging led to the confirmation of B mandates on July 20, 1922; of Syria and Palestine tentatively on July 22, 1922, and finally on September 29, 1923; and of Iraq on September 27, 1924. In confirming the mandates the Council in the main adopted the draft supplied by the prospective mandatory and already approved by the Principal Allied and Associated Powers, but on each occasion the draft was scrutinized by a subcommittee of the Council with the assistance of the Secretariat and in some cases minor modifications were suggested.

4. Responsibility for the Terms of the Mandates

The drafts were not formally submitted to the Permanent Mandates Commission for its advice. A suggestion in the Council meeting of October 23, 1920, that this be done, was answered by Viscount Ishii and Lord Balfour who said "the jurists of the secretariat will be able to complete the examination of these terms and conditions in five minutes."[26] Nevertheless some of the draft mandates were still unconfirmed when the Commission held its first meeting in October, 1921, and it actually made some suggestions on the texts.[27]

The texts of C mandates gave the Council little trouble but Viscount Ishii's report on A and B mandates in July, 1922, indicated more than five minutes' scrutiny. He said:

> In submitting my proposals my principal aim is to bring the mandates in all points into conformity with the covenant. While thus protecting the in-

[25] See *supra*, chap. ii, n. 77.

[26] *L. of N., Council, Min.*, sess. X, p. 25.

[27] *Ibid.*, sess. XIV, pp. 124, 180.

tegrity of the natives and of all the members of the league we shall place an institution with such important duties of guaranteeship over colonial mandates above the criticism to which our work has continually been subjected through the skeptical cynicism of opponents.[28]

The Viscount's reports[29] pointed out lack of uniformity in form, as some of the drafts failed to recite the League's confirmation in the preamble; in procedure, as some required only a majority of the Council for change; and also in substance. Some regulated but did not prohibit liquor traffic, some of the B mandates did not sufficiently safeguard the open door especially in allowing customs unions with adjacent territory, and some did not sufficiently limit forced labor. Thus the English text confining forced labor to "essential public works and services" was not reproduced by the French text *travaux public et services essentiels*. Most of these suggestions were adopted in revised drafts proposed by a committee consisting of a representative of the mandatory, the Council *rapporteur*, and the director of the mandates section. The open door was strengthened in the B mandates. More protection was given to missionaries in accordance with the wish of the United States and the mandates were made more difficult to change and more uniform.[30] The C mandates, after the preamble, are precisely identical; the B mandates are identical with these and with one another in many articles; and the A mandates in a few. Certain divergencies, however, were overlooked. Thus in the Mavromatis case some of the judges of the Permanent Court of International Justice noted that the article defining its jurisdiction was the same in all the mandates except that for Tanganyika, but in this case apparently no difference was intended.[31]

There were, however, cases in which differences in text resulted not from faulty drafting but from political compromises and these in some cases seemed to involve departures from the Covenant. This was true of the French African mandates which allowed natives re-

[28] *Ibid.*, sess. XIX (July 18, 1922), *O.J.*, III, 850.

[29] Submitted at eleventh session of the Council, December, 1920; twelfth session, February, 1921; seventeenth session, February, 1922; and nineteenth session, July, 1922 (*O.J.*, III, 791, 821, 847–62).

[30] *Ibid.*, p. 793.

[31] *P.C.I.J.* (Ser. A), No. 2, dissenting opinions of Judges Moore, Bustamente, and Oda, pp. 60, 82; *P.M.C.*, *Min.*, VI, 56, 159. See *infra*, chap. v, sec. 5 and Appendix II.

cruited in mandated territory to be used for defense of outside territory in case of a general war. The French sought to justify this divergence by noting that the Supreme Council's resolution of May 7, 1919, did not expressly confer a mandate on France and Great Britain for Togo and Cameroons but asked them to make a joint recommendation on these territories. The Covenant, however, required all the former German territories to be put under mandate from which "apparent contradiction" the two powers in the joint recommendation "deduced" that they retained a certain amount of latitude in the application of the "mandate system" in these areas. Viscount Ishii, the *rapporteur*, was certain that the League was bound by the Covenant alone and "compelled to supervise the application of the provisions of this article [22] to all the territories forming part of the former German colonies overseas." Nevertheless, when noting the exceptional provision in the two French mandates he only said, "although it appears difficult to reconcile this paragraph with the spirit of the covenant we hope that the future will show that this is not the case."[32]

The Council's power to insist on changes in the draft texts agreed on by the Principal Powers was not unchallenged. In the twelfth session of the Council on February 22, 1921, when Viscount Ishii gave his first report on B-mandates texts, Bourgeois of France said he thought the criticism of the texts was unprecedented.[33] The objection, however, was not pressed, and it seems clear that the Council could refuse confirmation if changes it thought required by the Covenant were not agreed to.[34] Where, however, draft texts were known to have been the result of difficult compromises the Council was caught in the dilemma of indefinitely holding up final application of the system or compromising. Thus, as already noted, it permitted several provisions in the mandates, especially in the A mandates where conflicting political interests were most active, which hardly conform to the Covenant. That overscrupulousness on this point would have indefinitely delayed confirmation can be seen by

[32] *O.J.*, III, 855, 858.

[33] *L. of N.*, *Council*, *Min.*, sess. XII, p. 10.

[34] Though after confirmation the League is incompetent to modify the text on its own responsibility. See *infra*, chap. xiii, sec. 1d.

recalling the great difficulties mentioned in chapter ii in getting agreement among the Principal Powers and especially with the United States.

The League has in fact refused to accept responsibility for divergencies between the mandates and the Covenant or for departures from the latter in putting the system into effect. "Mandates," said Lord Balfour in the Council, "are not our creation. . . . . They are imposed by the allied and associated powers themselves."[35] In conformity with this conception the Italian representative declared in the Council in 1920 that he could not consider the draft mandates formally before the Council until all the Principal Allied and Associated Powers had agreed on them, and the Council in 1921 refused to consider suggestions of the Commission in regard to the terms of draft mandates but forwarded them to the allied governments.[36] It has done the same with subsequent suggestions of the Commission for the modification of mandates, though its discussions have undoubtedly had the effect of putting pressure upon the mandatories to act in some cases. Its confirmation is of course recognized as necessary before such changes agreed on by the interested mandatories can go into effect.

In view of this attitude it is interesting to notice that Great Britain and Belgium, after agreeing to modify the common frontier of their East African mandated areas, "requested the council of the League of Nations to amend the British and Belgium mandates" accordingly.[37] It seems clear that amendment of a mandate requires the consent of the mandatory and the Council, but it is not clear which has the initiative. In practice the real impetus has sometimes come from one and sometimes from the other.

At the first session of the Permanent Mandates Commission the

[35] See *supra*, n. 12.

[36] *L. of N., Council, Min.*, sess. XI, p. 28; sess. XIV, pp. 124–25. The Council has been especially anxious to make it clear that it is not responsible for the boundaries of mandated territories. Before confirming the texts, it has insisted that the boundary definitions should be stated in the preambles as facts and not as its decisions. When it has assisted in settling such definitions, as in the Mosul controversy, it has acted as an arbiter or mediator on the basis of art. 11 or 15 of the Covenant or a special treaty and not by virtue of its authority under art. 22 of the Covenant (see *O.J.*, III, 850).

[37] Letter of August 3, 1923 (L. of N., Council, XXVII, *O.J.*, IV, 409.

question was raised by M. Van Rees of the Netherlands whether that body "had authority to lay before the council proposals with a view to the eventual modification of the terms of the mandates." The Covenant authorized it to advise only on "the observance" of mandates. He was in favor of abiding by the letter of the Covenant but noted that a different interpretation might be drawn from the Commission's constitution approved by the Council. Paragraph (*h*) authorized the Commission "to utilize such a meeting of the representatives of the mandatory powers to lay before them any other matter connected with mandates which, in their opinion, should be submitted to the council, to the mandatory powers and to the other states members of the League." M. Orts of Belgium thought the terms of the mandates was a question solely for the governments, and the Commission agreed that it could not give formal advice on the terms of mandates to the Council. Nevertheless, this was not deemed to preclude suggestions on that subject. This rather obscure distinction was explained by M. Rappard:

> Some had proposed that draft mandates should be submitted to the Permanent Commission. The Council did not appear to view such a scheme with favour, as the Commission had only to consider the observance of mandates, and not the way in which they were drawn up. But it was evident that if, during the process of examining the reports, certain clauses in the Mandates should appear liable to interpretations differing from, or contrary to, article 22, the Council could not take exception to questions or opinions with regard to this matter presented by the Commission in a purely advisory capacity, for the Council would doubtless desire that the Commission should be its watchful counsellor.[38]

On this theory, in its report to the Council the Commission actually drew attention to provisions in the draft B mandates which might not precisely conform to Covenant requirements on economic equality, forced labor, and slavery.[39] Subsequently it has noticed the unfortunate consequences to the natives of certain frontiers defined in mandates, the possible inconsistence with the Covenant of the military recruiting provision in the French African mandates, the Balfour declaration in the Palestine mandate, and the lack of uniformity

[38] *P.M.C., Min.*, I, 11.

[39] *L. of N., Council, Min.*, sess. XIV, pp. 180–81.

in certain provisions in different mandates evidently intended to be identical.[40]

In acting upon petitions, however, the stricter view has been maintained. The Commission has refused to consider numerous petitions from the Arabs of Palestine protesting the inclusion of the Balfour declaration in the mandate and from Arabs of Syria and the Lebanon protesting the granting of the mandate to France contrary to the express wishes of the inhabitants.[41]

Prior to confirmation, all the mandatories who were actually governing the territories had assured the Council of their intention to observe the spirit of article 22 of the Covenant, and in some cases they published reports which were examined by the Mandates Commission and the Council. Submission of such reports had been recommended by the League Assembly in December, 1920, and by the Council on June 21, 1921. On this occasion the Belgian, French, and British governments in a reservation declared that prior to confirmation of mandates "the league does not possess the right to ask for a report," but they indicated an intention to publish reports which would be at the disposal of the League.[42]

5. Modification of Mandates

In addition to confirming the original mandates, the Council has several times been called on to confirm subsequent amendments. Each mandate stipulates that "the consent of the council of the League of Nations is required for any modification of the terms of this mandate."[43] The most important occasion for the application of this rule was the discovery that the boundary between the Belgian

[40] *P.M.C., Report*, sess. I (*L. of N., Council, Min.*, sess. XIV, pp. 180–81); *Min.*, II, 75; III, 196, 199, 309, 311, 316; V, 188; VI, 56.

[41] *P.M.C., Min.*, V, 196; VIII, 47, 200. Whatever may be true of members of the League, it seems clear that the inhabitants of the area have rights only under the mandate not under the treaty (see *infra*, chap. xiii, nn. 70*a*, 118).

[42] *L. of N. Council, Min.*, XIII, 26, and *supra*, nn. 17, 24.

[43] As the Council looks upon the territorial limits of mandates as facts for which it is not responsible (see *supra*, n. 36), it might be argued that its consent is not necessary for the modification of frontiers but the practice is to the contrary. The A mandates do not state the boundaries (see *infra*, n. 46).

and British mandates in East Africa divided an area formerly under the United rule of Musinga, King of Ruanda. The natives had protested this arrangement, and local missionaries drew the attention of the Mandates Commission to the serious racial, economic, and political consequences that might follow. It appeared that by the Orts-Milner agreement of December 31, 1921, defining the boundary between the prospective mandatory territories, Belgium had acquiesced in the British desire to have control of the territory west of the Kagera River (Kissaka district), which appeared to be the most suitable route for the proposed Cape to Cairo railroad. After the Commission and the Council had drawn the attention of the two governments to the unfortunate consequences of this arrangement a negotiation was entered into with the result that on August 3, 1923, they asked the Council to amend the mandate in conformity with their agreement which placed this territory in the Belgian area. Great Britain had apparently discovered that the railway could be constructed elsewhere. The Council at once confirmed this modification.[44]

Similar problems have arisen in connection with the boundaries between the British and French mandated areas in West Africa. The French representative displayed some irritation at the Commission's mention of this matter, asserting that it was beyond its competence, but the Council thought the Commission could draw attention to any matter affecting the welfare of natives of the area. Negotiations were begun on the Cameroons boundary and on the French suggestion in the thirtieth Council meeting the boundary of Togoland was included.[45] The modification of the boundary between Palestine, Iraq, and Syria by the Franco-British Treaty of December 23, 1920, occurred before the mandates were confirmed as did the retrocession of Cilicia to Turkey by the Franklin-Bouillon Treaty of 1921.[46]

[44] *G.B., Parl. Pap.* (1923), Cmd. 1974; L. of N., Council, Min., sess. XXVI, *O.J.*, IV, 1273. The consent of the United States was also deemed necessary for this change (*P.M.C., Min.*, IV, 65).

[45] *P.M.C., Min.*, III, 199–200; IV, 133; L. of N., Council, Min., sess. XX, XXVII, XXX, *O.J.*, III, 1269; IV, 335; V, 1399.

[46] See *supra*, chap. ii, nn. 62, 78. Although the boundary of the territories is not described in the A mandates as is done in B and C mandates, the mandatory is responsible

The British declaration of September 16, 1922, modifying the Palestine mandate so as to exclude the Jewish national home from trans-Jordan was formally confirmed. The agreement between Great Britain and Turkey of June 7, 1926, finally establishing the Mosul boundary and that of 1926 between South Africa and Portugal establishing the boundary between Southwest Africa and Portuguese Angola were confirmed by the Council though in the latter case exception was taken to the allegation in the preamble that South Africa "possesses sovereignty" in the mandated area.[47] At its fourth session the Commission urged the Powers to hasten agreement on this boundary which had never been defined but recognized that "any rectification of boundaries which would remove a portion of a mandated territory and attach it to a colony is impossible."[48] The same conclusion was reached in reference to the suggestion made by Sir Frederick Lugard in the sixth session that the boundary of Tanganyika and the British colony of Kenya be rectified in order to unify the Masai tribe. The matter was under discussion between the governors of these two areas. The Commission expressed its readiness to consider any proposal for achieving this "provided that it does not involve any limitation of the control exercised by the League of Nations under the mandate."[49] As political boundaries in Africa and elsewhere have been drawn with little regard for the geographical division of native tribes, demands for boundary rectifications in the interest of the natives have continually arisen and the Commission has always taken a sympathetic interest.[50]

There is room for difference of opinion as to what constitutes a modification of a mandate. The terms of almost any treaty or agree-

---

for preserving the territorial integrity of the former once their boundaries are fixed by express provision of the mandates (Palestine, art. 5; Syria, art. 4 [Stoyanovsky, *Mandate for Palestine*, p. 202]).

[47] L. of N., Council, September 16, 1922, Min., sess. XX, *O.J.*, III, 1189, 1390; June 7, 1926, *O.J.*, VII, 859; March 7, 1927, XLIV, *O.J.*, VIII, 347; September 8, 1927, XLVI, *O.J.*, VIII, 1120.

[48] *P.M.C.*, *Report*, sess. IV; *O.J.*, V, 1405.

[49] *P.M.C.*, *Min.*, VI, 121–22, 176.

[50] In 1925 Mr. Ormsby-Gore, British accredited representative, suggested a rectification of the Tanganyika-Kenya boundary to unite the Baganda tribe (*ibid.*, p. 124).

ment applicable to the territory may modify or conflict with the existing terms of the mandate and, as a treaty (unlike legislation) cannot be unilaterally altered by the mandatory in case such inconsistency is discovered, it would appear that every treaty or agreement relating to mandated territory should be scrutinized by the Council before ratification. In September, 1924, Australia asked the Council to confirm a loan of 167,000 to New Guinea thinking it "desirable" that the "sanction" be obtained "before doing anything which will result in the administration [of the mandated territory] being under any formal obligation to the commonwealth." Viscount Ishii of Japan thought "for the council to sanction the raising of a loan would be to concern itself with questions" of administration beyond its competence. Consequently the Council did not sanction the loan but merely noted the Australian communication.[51] Subsequently, on advice of the Commission and most of the mandatories, the Council took the position that the mandatory is primarily responsible for the observance of the mandate and has power, not as sovereign but in the capacity of mandatory, to make treaties or agreements with respect to mandated territory or to pledge its resources for loans without prior Council consent.[52] This, however, does not apply to boundary or other agreements directly affecting the terms of mandates. The Council intimated that it should be given the opportunity to confirm the agreement pending in March, 1926, between France and Turkey defining the boundary of Syria. The exclusive control of the mandatory over the foreign relations of the territory, said M. Sjoberg of Sweden, the *rapporteur*, "do not include power to cede or lease on its sole authority, any part, however small of the territory." M. Boncour asserted that the treaty in question was merely for the delimitation on the spot of the Angora agreement of 1921 and did not involve any cession of territory.[53] This contention was indorsed by the Mandates Commission at its eighth session.[54]

The transfer or termination of a mandate as well as the modifi-

[51] L. of N., Council, XXX, *O.J.*, III, 1596–97.

[52] *P.M.C.*, *Min.*, VI, 172; L. of N., Council, September, 1925, *O.J.*, VI, 1510.

[53] L. of N., Council, March, 1926, XXXIX, *O.J.*, VII, 522.

[54] *P.M.C.*, *Min.*, VIII, 204; X, 192.

cation of its boundaries is a modification which undoubtedly requires Council confirmation. The Commission recognized this in considering the transfer of administration of Nauru to Australia for five years without notifying the League. This mandate, like the British B mandates, had been given to "His Britannic Majesty" without naming any government to act in his behalf, as had been done in the other C mandates. The Australian representative explained that there had been no transfer but merely temporary delegation of authority to an agent. The British delegation at Paris in plenary session had agreed to vest the government of Nauru in the United Kingdom, Australia, and New Zealand, and these three governments had agreed on July 2, 1919, to nominate the Australian government as agent for the three to administer the island for the first five years. "But on all matters relating to major policy, reference was to be made to all the governments concerned whose concurrence was essential."[55] This agreement was ratified by act of the British Parliament on August 4, 1920.[56] This explanation was apparently accepted, but it raises the interesting question whether the A and B mandates similarly assigned to "His Britannic Majesty" and now administered by the government of Great Britain might be delegated temporarily or permanently to the government of one of the dominions without first obtaining the Council's consent. This would seem to be implied from the statement of Mr. Ormsby Gore, then on the Commission. "There was no government of 'The British Empire.' In this case it was presumably for the British Empire to choose one of its constituent governments to administer the mandate."[57]

A similar question arose in connection with the transfer by the government of South Africa of the administration of the Caprivi Zipfel to the high commissioner of South Africa, who is appointed by the British government and is not responsible to South Africa. The latter, however, explained that in respect to the administration of this area he was responsible to South Africa and to the League Council.[58]

None of the mandates has so far been terminated, but clearly such action would require Council confirmation, as is expressly

[55] *Ibid.*, II, 46; *Report*, II, 4.

[56] 10–11 Geo. V, c. 27.

[57] *P.M.C.*, *Min.*, II, 46.

[58] *Ibid.*, VII, 16.

stated in the Iraq mandate, which alone expressly contemplates termination after a period of years.

Council confirmation is undoubtedly necessary for the extension of a mandate either for a longer time or to new territory, or for the creation of new mandates. The Anglo-Iraq Treaty accepted by the Council as defining the mandate originally provided for termination in four years but as a result of the Council recommendation in the Mosul dispute it was extended for twenty-five years by agreement of the parties. This extension was subsequently accepted by the Council.[59]

The mandates system has not thus far been extended to any new areas; the possibility of such action was foreseen by some members of the Commission when discussing the rectification of the Tanganyika-Kenya boundary suggested by Sir Frederick Lugard at the sixth session in order to unite the area occupied by the Masai tribe. "The commission," said M. Rappard on this occasion, "had not yet had before it a question which was of such importance for the future of the mandates system." The commission, he thought, should favor boundary changes in the interest of the native inhabitants as it had done in the Ruanda case. Such a change might be affected in this case (1) by annexing part of Kenya to Tanganyika, (2) by extending the Kenya administration at the expense of Tanganyika but with the understanding that it would be responsible to the League for the whole Masai area, or (3) by the creation of a new mandate for the Masai area alone which would necessitate complicated international arrangements. He continued:

> Whatever the solution which might eventually be adopted, the Commission could he thought congratulate itself on the possibility of seeing the principle of the mandates system extended to new territories. In his view, the mandates system was not fully justified by the circumstances which had called it into being. Those circumstances alone would not be sufficient to perpetuate the mandates system. It was a question of one of two possibilities. Either the system could be pronounced to be excellent for those under administration in which case there was no reason why the extension of the system to peoples who did not yet enjoy its benefits should not be a source of congratulation; or, on the other hand, there were faults and weak points in the system, in which case there was no reason why it should be continued. As the members of the com-

[59] L. of N., Council, March 11, 1926, sess. XXXIX, *O.J.*, VII, 552.

mission were undoubtedly convinced of the excellence of the mandates system it seemed that they should not fear the arrival of a time when the execution of the principle which the commission was called upon to supervise would be more widely applied.

M. Freire d' Andrade of Portugal did not understand to what territory M. Rappard was alluding as all people were now subject to some administration. M. Rappard replied that he had no thought of depriving any state of "the right to administer territory of which it was sovereign" but merely wished to point out that "the originality of the mandate system consisted in placing the administration of backward peoples by national governments under a supervision exercised on behalf of the League according to certain principles defined in an international instrument. It was obvious that, in putting forward this suggestion, he was looking far into the future." The Chairman thought perhaps it was inopportune if not discourteous to discuss this question in the presence of an accredited representative. M. Orts felt obliged to make some reservations to M. Rappard's enthusiasm for extension of the mandate principle to fresh territories. "It had been in effect only five years and experience of several decades was necessary to test it. It would as yet be premature to say that the system was superior, in every respect, to that of colonies administered in full sovereignty." Sir Frederick indicated a preference for either of the first two alternatives suggested by M. Rappard as against the third, and Mr. Ormsby-Gore, the accredited representative from Great Britain, called attention to the expediency of transferring to Kenya a portion of Tanganyika formerly under the king of Baganda "but of course a separate report could not be submitted in regard to these thousand persons." M. Rappard then summarized his opinion. A mandatory had suggested the question of frontier rectification, and he thought the Commission could properly express an opinion. To do so it should be influenced by two considerations: (1) the welfare of the natives which was beyond discussion and (2) its attitude toward extending the system.

Should it say that it would never admit the possibility of an extension of the principle the application of which it had to supervise, or should it say, on the contrary, that the question was one for the future, the development of which it considered favorably? Certain of his colleagues had understood that he was of the opinion that the mandates system had already given full proof of its value.

He had never dreamed of proposing at this moment the drawing up of any recommendation whatever, but simply to emphasize the importance of the question raised by Mr. Ormsby-Gore and to outline the principles which might guide the commission in its future examination of the question.

The chairman thought the Commission should confine itself to expressing a favorable attitude toward measures in the interest of the natives on condition that the League's supervision over areas now under mandate was not reduced.[60]

Voluntary utilization of the principles of colonial administration developed under the mandates system by the administration of similar areas not under mandate is of course another method by which the influence of the system might extend without any of the difficulties inherent in a legal subjection of new territory to the system.

[60] *P.M.C.*, *Min.*, VI, 123–24. Extension of the mandates system to other territories was foreseen in the British official commentary on the Covenant (see Pollock, *The League of Nations*, London, 1920, p. 217; Stoyanovsky, *La Théorie générale des mandates internationaux*, p. 50).

CHAPTER V

THE AGENCIES OF LEAGUE SUPERVISION

The Covenant declares that the tutelage of the communities in question shall be exercised by "mandatories in behalf of the League" who shall each "render the council an annual report in reference to the territory committed to its charge." The Council shall "if not previously agreed upon by the members of the League, explicitly define in each case, the degree of authority, control, or administration to be exercised by the mandatory," and shall be advised "in all matters relating to the observance of mandates" by a "permanent commission" which "shall be constituted to receive and examine the annual reports." It is recognized that these provisions give the League powers of supervision but not of direct administration. The distinction, however, is easier to state than to define—in fact, the meaning of supervision can only be discovered by studying the methods which the League organs have actually observed.

The League's activity in relation to mandates is carried on through (1) the Council, (2) the Assembly, (3) the Secretariat, (4) the Permanent Mandates Commission, and (5) the Permanent Court of International Justice. The advice of other agencies of the League has occasionally been utilized. The International Labor Office is regularly represented on the Mandates Commission and many of its investigations apply to labor in the mandated areas.[1] The health organization assisted the Commission in drawing up the parts of its questionnaire on public health.[2] The Temporary Commission on Slavery set up by the Council in 1924 following suggestions of the third and fourth Assemblies was closely integrated with the Mandates Commission through incorporating some of its members. The same is true of the Committee on Native Labor set up in 1927 by the International Labor Office following a suggestion of the seventh Assembly.[3] The League's agencies dealing with disarmament, traffic in

[1] *P.M.C., Min.*, I, 8, 36 (see *infra*, n. 34).

[2] *Ibid.*, II, 64; III, 9–10; VI, 10.

[3] *Ibid.*, XI, 11.

arms, promotion of economic equality, traffic in women and children, and opium also sometimes exchange data with the Permanent Mandates Commission. A Council resolution of October 1, 1924, suggested that the Commission collaborate with the Committee on Intellectual Co-operation in archaeological matters.[4] The Commission has sometimes resented the invasion of its field by other bodies fearing that its autonomy might be interfered with. "It might perhaps be well for the commission to make a stand against the tendency shown by other committees of the League to intervene in its work," said M. d'Andrade on the latter occasion, but in general a spirit of co-operation has prevailed.[5]

1. The Council

The Council, which is the authoritative organ of the League in supervising the administration of mandates, utilizes the same methods which it employs in other fields of its work. It discusses and accepts or rejects, usually in public session, resolutions prepared by a *rapporteur* who is now likely to be the same for a particular topic from session to session and the representative of a state not directly interested in the subject. During the period of confirmation, M. Hymans of Belgium, Viscount Ishii of Japan, M. Quinones de Leon of Spain, and Marquis Imperiali and M. Salandra of Italy served successively as *rapporteur*. From 1923 to 1927 M. Branting, Unden, and Sjoberg of Sweden served in this capacity, and since Sweden's retirement from the Council the Netherlands' representative has so acted. The Council's resolutions are tactfully worded as suggestions or invitations to the mandatories and usually simply indorse the Commission's reports. The Council's attitude toward the Commission whose chairman or vice-chairman has usually been present during consideration of mandates, was stated by M. Branting in 1923:

> The council which is called upon to take a decision concerning the recommendations of the permanent mandates commission, will doubtless attach great weight to the authoritative opinions of the committee of experts on colonial questions which it has itself constituted for this purpose and whose duty it is, under the terms of the covenant "to advise the council on all matters relating

[4] *Ibid.*, V, 126; VI, 55.

[5] *Ibid.;* see also comment by M. Orts on co-operation with health organization (II, 64).

to the observance of the mandates." I believe that it would be wise to carry out its recommendations whenever political considerations—with which necessarily our advisory committee is not concerned—do not render such a course impossible.[6]

The resolutions are accompanied and explained by a more or less extended report by the *rapporteur* in an informal manner. The usual form of resolution is indicated by the following example:

The Council of the League of Nations,

Having examined the report of the second session of the Permanent Mandates Commission, and the documents annexed thereto:

I. Desires to thank the Permanent Mandates Commission for the great zeal and admirable impartiality which it has displayed;

II. Instructs the President of the Council to transmit to the mandatory Powers, on its behalf, the recommendations expressed in the Report and in the annexed documents, with the request that they will be good enough to carry out these recommendations;

III. Instructs the President of the Council to transmit for the information of the Belgian and British Governments the observations of the commission with reference to the situation on the frontier of Ruanda, under Belgian mandate, and British Tanganyika.[7]

Article 4 of the Covenant allows members of the League not on the Council to sit as members of that body during the consideration of matters especially affecting their interests, and by resolution of August 31, 1923, the Council decided to allow each mandatory not on the Council to have a representative present when its mandate is under discussion.[8] Thus the British dominions, which alone of the mandatories have not been continuously members of the Council, have frequently sat when their mandated territories were under consideration.[9] It seems clear that the British dominions are not repre-

[6] L. of N., Council, December 11, 1923, Min., sess. XXVIII, *O.J.*, IV, 385. A typical proposal was that of M. Sjoberg, *rapporteur*, on the report of the Commission on Syria, March 11, 1926, that "in accordance with usual practice the report of the commission be forwarded to the mandatory power with a request that it take the requisite action" (*ibid.*, Min., sess. XXXIX, *O.J.*, VII, 522).

[7] *Ibid.*, September 4, 1923, Min., sess. XX, *O.J.*, III, 1263. See also *infra*, chap. vii, secs. 2, 3.

[8] *Ibid.*, Min., sess. XXVI, *O.J.*, IV, 1328.

[9] Belgium ceased to be a member of the Council in 1927 but her representative has continued to be present during the discussion of her mandate (see *ibid.*, sess. XLIX, min. 2117).

sented on the Council by the British Empire representative. At the first meeting of the Mandates Commission M. Rappard, then chief of the mandates section of the Secretariat, pointed out that all the British mandates had been intrusted to "His Britannic Majesty" but certain of them "were to be exercised on his behalf by one of the dominions." Whom should the Council deal with in respect to the latter? Mr. Ormsby-Gore of Great Britain, then a member of the Commission, replied: "The government of the dominions should be directly approached. For instance, if a question should arise with regard to Southwest Africa, the view would have to be adopted that the British crown was represented solely by his Britannic Majesty's government at the Cape. The British Parliament would refuse to consider such a question since it would be within the jurisdiction of the South African Parliament."[10] This interpretation seems to be required by the independent membership of the dominions in the League including not only independent representation in the Assembly but also eligibility to election in the Council.[11] It is also amply supported by the conclusions of the imperial conferences of 1923 and 1926 which insisted that "the part of the empire in respect of which obligations are to be undertaken" should be clearly indicated, and that in League conferences if the dominion members attend they "are represented separately by separate delegations." The 1926 conference commented on the "obscurity and misunderstanding" which resulted from the use of the term "British Empire" in the annex to the Covenant without specific mention of the government intended and recommended that in the future "Great Britain and Northern Ireland and all parts of the British Empire which are not separate members of the League" should be mentioned on a parity with the dominion members of the League and India.[12]

[10] *P.M.C., Min.*, I, 5.

[11] Miller, *The Drafting of the Covenant*, I, 689; Allin, "International Status of the British Dominions, with Respect to the League of Nations," *Minn. L.R.*, IV, 217; Sir Cecil Hurst, *Great Britain and the Dominions* (Chicago, 1928), p. 97; Baker, *The Present Juridical Status of the British Dominions in International Law* (London, 1929), pp. 107, 349. Canada became a member of the Council in 1928.

[12] "Report of Inter Imperial Relations Committee, Imperial Conference, 1926," *G.B., Parl. Pap.* (1926), Cmd. 2768, reprinted in *International Conciliation 228*, pp. 119, 121, 124, 125. See comments by Sir Cecil Hurst, *op. cit.*, pp. 92–93.

Perhaps because of this obscurity of the British Empire representative's position in the Council, that person has occasionally assumed the right to speak in behalf of dominion mandatories who were not present. On October 21, 1920, Lord Balfour said he wished to consult the dominions before deciding on the organization of the Mandates Commission. On December 12, 1923, Lord Robert Cecil asked to be permitted to represent Australia on questions in which she was interested as mandatory. On this occasion M. Hanotaux of France said he thought it should be understood that "Lord Robert Cecil acting as representative of the Australian Government would not have a right to vote," and this was agreed to. Later in the same meeting Lord Robert read a telegram from the Australian Prime Minister asking that decision on a legal question interesting to Australia be delayed. On September 3, 1926, Sir Austen Chamberlain said he might have to ask that certain questions interesting to Australia be postponed until the representative of that country arrived.[13]

From these instances it appears that the British Empire representative in reality represents only those parts of the Empire not independent members of the League but it appears also that the dominions receive a certain advantage from their imperial connection.[14]

The chairman or vice-chairman of the Mandates Commission has taken part in the discussion of the Commission's report at Council meetings and the secretary-general as well as the chief and other members of the mandates section are present when mandate matters are being considered though of course they do not vote.

[13] *L. of N., Council, Min.*, sess. X, p. 23; sess. XXVII, *O.J.*, IV, 333, 337; sess. XLI, *ibid.*, VII, 1230.

[14] Sir Cecil Hurst has pointed out that under the constitutional practice of the Empire in matters "which are of importance to the empire as a whole . . . . the British Member of the council is something more than a mere representative of Great Britain. While nominated by His Majesty's Government in Great Britain and primarily responsible to them, he is bound in view of the constitutional position of the British Empire and the established practice of foreign affairs, to consult fully with the dominions before agreeing to any action which may affect their interest. On the other hand, in matters which specially affect a dominion, the dominion, like all other members of the League, gets the benefit of the rule in article 4 of the Covenant that any member of the League not represented in the council shall be invited to send a representative to sit as a member at any meeting of the council during the consideration of matters specially affecting its interest." The dominion interest in their mandates is cited as an example (*op. cit.*, pp. 95–96). But see Baker, *op. cit.*, pp. 89, 365, 366.

The Council acts by unanimous vote as required by article 5 of the Covenant in mandate questions, though there is a tendency to give wider application to the rule of article 15, which excludes the vote of interested parties from the required unanimity in recommending on political disputes. The Permanent Court of International Justice in the Mosul advisory opinion applied this rule to the procedure of the Council in exercising the jurisdiction given it by article 2 of the Treaty of Lausanne on the principle that a party should not be judge in his own case.[15] Thus it is possible that a resolution dealing with a particular mandatory might be effective over the adverse vote of that mandatory. On the other hand, it may be thought that the Council in dealing with mandates acts in an administrative rather than a quasi-judicial character in which case absolute unanimity might be required. It is probable that the character of the particular question before the Council would determine the matter but up to date there has always been absolute unanimity.[16]

The provision originally in the draft mandates requiring consent of only a majority of the Council for modification of the mandates has been modified to read "the consent of the Council," and in the discussion this was assumed to mean unanimity.[17] Nevertheless, during the debate of July, 1922, M. Viviani of France suggested that the tentative confirmation of the Palestine and Syrian mandates was a question of procedure requiring a mere majority.[18] The suggestion was not acted on and mandate questions seem to have been considered substantive rather than procedural.

[15] *P.C.I.J.* (Ser. B), No. 12. For discussion of the dilemma presented by the principle that a party should not be judge in his own case in relation to the principle that a state cannot be sued without its consent see Wright, *Control of American Foreign Relations* (1922), pp. 209–15.

[16] For discussion of the unanimity rule and its qualifications see *O.J.*, VI (October, 1925), 1381–83; *ibid.*, VII (February, 1926), 127–28; Wright, "The Mosul Dispute," *A.J.I.L.*, XX, 461; "The United States and the Permanent Court of International Justice," *ibid.*, XXI, 14; Sir John Fischer Williams, "The League of Nations and Unanimity," *ibid.*, XIX, 484; Norman L. Hill, "Unanimous Consent in International Organization," *ibid.*, XXII, 327; McNair, *B.Y.B.I.L.* (1926), pp. 1–13.

[17] See report by Viscount Ishii and statement by M. Rappard, L. of N., Council, Min., sess. XIX, July, 1922; *O.J.*, III, 821. Changes in provisions of minority treaties require consent of only a majority of the Council.

[18] *Ibid.*, *O.J.*, III, 819.

2. THE ASSEMBLY

The Assembly has devoted attention to mandates at every regular session. Frequently there is considerable debate on the subject in discussing the secretary-general's report. The sixth committee on political questions has always framed a resolution on the subject, frequently acting on the advice of a subcommittee, and this resolution has then been reported, usually by Dr. Nansen of Norway, to the plenary session and adopted. As has been noticed, the suggestion made by Lord Robert Cecil and also by Germany in 1920 that the Assembly had power to define the terms of the mandates was not accepted by the Council.[19] The latter has in fact displayed considerable jealousy of its prerogative in regard to mandates. Thus at its tenth meeting a proposal by Hymans of Belgium that the non-mandatory members of the Commission be appointed by the Assembly was opposed by Balfour, who thought the Covenant left this task to the Council alone and his opinion was accepted by the Council. Later in this session, when deciding to give the Assembly information on the mandates, the Council worded its communication "so as not to appear to confer upon the Assembly powers which belonged to the Council."[20] Again at its twenty-sixth meeting the members of the Council were reluctant to submit mandates documents to the Assembly before they had been examined by the Council though eventually this was done, thus giving the Assembly an opportunity to discuss the report on the Bondelzwart affair before it had been considered by the Council.[21]

The Assembly has not entirely acquiesced in this attitude and, as had been noticed, when the Council refused to submit the draft mandates to the first Assembly and intimated that mandate questions vested wholly in the Council, Dr. Nansen of Norway replied by quoting a resolution approved by the Council on the relative power of the two bodies: "Neither body has jurisdiction to render a decision on a matter which has been expressly committed to the other organ of the

[19] See *supra*, chap. ii, n. 75; chap. iv, n. 24.

[20] *L. of N., Council, Min.*, sess. X, October 24, 1920, 23, 25, 101. See also remarks by Mr. Balfour in the first Assembly (*L. of N., Assembly, Rec.*, sess. I [Plenary Meetings], p. 719).

[21] *Ibid.*, August 31, 1923, Min., sess. XXVI, *O.J.*, IV, 1376.

League. But either body may discuss and examine any matter which is within the competence of the League."[22] The resolution quoted was adopted by the first Assembly after extensive debate, and the final sentence was added in plenary session on motion of Lord Robert Cecil in order to "make it absolutely clear that every matter, whether it is left to the decision of the council or otherwise, within the general competence of the League, may be investigated and discussed and adopted in this assembly." M. Viviani of France, the *rapporteur*, thought Lord Robert's proposal so far as it related to "discussion" was implied by the report but feared "anarchy and discord" would result if the Assembly tried to "investigate" matters decided by the Council. Mr. Balfour then proposed substitution of the word "examine" for "investigate," stating that this was acceptable to the Council committee that had considered the matter, and the resolution was adopted by the Assembly.[23]

Every Assembly has actually passed resolutions on mandates and these have sometimes been addressed to the mandatory powers, sometimes to the Council, but most frequently to the Mandates Commission. The mandatory powers, whose representatives of course are entitled to participate in debate and vote on Assembly resolutions, have acquiesced in them. The Council has given prompt effect to such resolutions when addressed to it. The Commission has taken cognizance of Assembly resolutions which apply to it but has not attempted to solve the dilemma which would be presented in case they conflicted with a Council resolution. Thus far there has been no conflict and so long as there is not and the Assembly resolution clearly relates to the observance of mandates the commission would have no difficulty in considering it.

The Covenant authorizes the Commission to advise only the "council on all matters relating to the observance of mandates."

[22] *L. of N., Assembly, Rec.* (Sixth committee), sess. I, 351.

[23] *Ibid.*, sess. I, 286, 288, 296. Lord Robert referred to the mandates question as one of those on which Assembly discussion was particularly desirable. See also his remarks (*ibid.*, p. 722). For Balfour's report on relation of Council to Assembly accepted by the Council in August, 1920, see *L. of N., Council, Min.*, sess. VIII, pp. 11, 25, 119. This as well as the report of the Secretary-General on the subject, the proposal of Mr. Rowell of Canada, the Viviani-Rowell report, and the resolution finally accepted by the Assembly are printed in *L. of N., Assembly, Rec.* (First Committee), sess. I, pp. 12, 93, 95; *ibid.* (Plenary Meetings), pp. 318–20.

During the fifth session of the Commission M. d'Andrade referred to "recommendations addressed to the commission" as "the sole prerogative of the council and of the assembly."[24] In the third session the chairman called attention to the Assembly resolution on the Bondelzwart affair and discussion proceeded on the theory that this limited the Commission's investigations of that subject but M. Rappard pointed out:

> The assembly has voted a resolution in very precise terms addressed to the mandates commission. This resolution, however, did not relieve the Commission of its chief responsibility, which was a responsibility towards the council. The council had asked the Commission for its opinion on everything which concerned the administration of the territories under mandate. The commission had, therefore, to deal even with points which did not fall within the scope of the assembly resolution.[25]

Thus it appears that the Commission feels obliged to consider "all matters relating to the observance of mandates" raised by resolutions of the Assembly as well as of the Council, but can direct its advice only to the Council.

The usual form of Assembly resolution is indicated by the following example:

> The Assembly:
>
> Having taken cognizance of the report to the council relating to the mandated territories and of the discussion on the subject which has taken place in the Council;
>
> And having heard the Vice-chairman of the Permanent Mandates Commission:
>
> Thanks the Permanent Mandates Commission for the devotion and zeal with which is has carried out its delicate task;
>
> Has confidence in the members of this Commission as well as in the Members of the Council to assure the application of the principles of article 22 of the Covenant in a cordial spirit of co-operation with the mandatory Powers.[26]

3. The Secretariat

The Secretariat organized a mandates section even before the Covenant went into effect with G. L. Beer, the colonial expert of the

[24] *P.M.C., Min.*, V, 150.

[25] *Ibid.*, III, 63.

[26] Resolutions of the Seventh Assembly (*L. of N., Monthly Summary*, VI, 238). For substance of Assembly resolutions see *supra*, chap. iii, sec. 2.

American peace delegation, provisionally at its head.[27] Upon the failure of the United States to ratify the Covenant the position was given to a Swiss, Professor W. L. Rappard, whose energy was of the very greatest importance in giving the mandates system reality. In 1925 Professor Rappard retired as director of the section to become rector of the University of Geneva and a special member of the Commission. His place was taken by Signor Catastini, an Italian who was given the title of chief of the mandates section. During the formative years there were two other members of the section, Mr. Hunington Gilchrist, an American who retired in 1928, and Mr. Friis, a Dane.

Apart from serving the Commission in a secretarial capacity at its meetings the chief of the section usually begins the discussion by a review of the work since the last meeting and takes an active part in the discussion. He is supposed to be, and has been, a mine of information. At the fifth session of the Commission it was decided that the Secretariat should regularly prepare for each future session an indexed file including the replies of the mandatories and their representatives to Commission observations and the minutes of Council and Assembly meetings and of Assembly committee meetings on the subject.[28]

During the interim of Commission meetings the section gathers miscellaneous material about mandates and mandated areas from government documents, the press, periodicals, reports of travelers, etc. The most important of this material is mimeographed and distributed to the Commission members, thus supplying them with an almost embarrassing mass of data. During the sixth session of the Commission Sir Frederick Lugard suggested a classification of this material in order of importance, putting laws and decrees applicable to the territory first, official statements and debates in national assemblies second, authoritative lectures and articles third, and newspaper comments and articles last. The Commission did not, however, indicate complete agreement with this classification.[29] The Sec-

[27] Ormsby-Gore, *The League of Nations Starts, an Outline by Its Organizers* (London, 1920), p. 119, and Beer, *African Questions at the Paris Peace Conference*, Editor's Introduction, p. xliii.

[28] *P.M.C.*, *Min.*, V, 128.

[29] *Ibid.*, VI, 149, and debate, p. 140. See also *infra*, chap. vi, sec. 5.

retariat also has important functions in connection with petitions, correspondence, and publications.

4. The Permanent Mandates Commission

The Permanent Mandates Commission is in fact the center of mandatory supervision. The Council seldom acts except on the basis of its advice and usually accepts this when given. One of the first tasks of the Council was to organize this Commission, which though mentioned by the Covenant was not organized by it. The high standard which the Commission must meet was generally recognized. Thus wrote Hon. Ormsby-Gore, member of the British Parliament, later to become a member of the Commission and then undersecretary of the colonies, before the Commission was organized:

The commission must be so constituted that it can constantly bear in mind three points of view: international interests, since in modern civilization what affects one region of the world has repercussions in every other portion; national interests, since the rights and dignity of the Mandatory Power or the Mandatory Dominion are intimately concerned; native interest, since the promotion of the welfare of the Mandated Territories is the primary object. Further, each of these must be considered from at least two aspects: the general and the special. Each area has its peculiar problems; for example, the native legal systems prevailing in tropical Africa are entirely unlike those which obtain in the ex-Ottoman territories. For all such questions experts are necessary, but it must be borne in mind that the expert is liable to grave errors as a result of his very specialization. He is apt to lose his sense of perspective and to force facts to agree with theories, rather than to shape theories according to facts; he inclines to become either unduly enthusiastic—even sentimental—or morbidly hostile and hypercritical. It is necessary, then, that the contributions of the experts—who are absolutely indispensable, and whose investigations, conclusions, and advice should in all cases be sought and carefully considered—be controlled and correlated from a general point of view; and that experts and general advisers bear patiently the buffetings that each must give the other to attain the common weal.

But the Mandates Commission must be more than a group of experts and general advisers studying problems at the seat of the League of Nations. This Commission is not, in a sense, dealing with problems at all; at least, it is not investigating them as abstract questions. It is concerned with human beings, and—whatever else it may forget—this it must always remember. Its members must possess all knowledge—native law, native religion, native psychology, native customs, methods of combating disease and vice, understanding of climatic, geographical and economic conditions, principles of colonial administration throughout the world from the beginning; all this, and more, must be familiar to them—but their knowledge is nothing unless it serves for the promotion of the welfare of those over whom for a time they exercise tutelage. They must, then, possess the greater gifts of understanding and of tact—tact not only to understand and to sympathize with their wards, but to reconcile differences that conceivably may arise, not merely between peoples within a given mandated territory, but between that territory and the mandatory, or even between neighboring territories or between neighboring mandatories. . . . .

If, however, the Mandates Commission stands for certain things, there are other things for which it does *not* stand. As we have seen, it is not a complicated machine, nor is it an obtrusive and meddlesome organization. Neither is it a court of appeal for complaints of minor importance. . . . .

It is equally requisite that the Mandates Commission shall not degenerate into a bureaucracy. Both its competence and its limitations must be clearly and publicly defined with the utmost possible exactness, with all provision, of course, for such modifications as future circumstances may direct. But, at the same time, it must avoid the danger of becoming a closed circle. It must cooperate in fullest measure with its fellow commissions; and if it draws help from them, it must be ready to assist them in return. It will do well to consider all problems concerning backward countries, whether they are under foreign tutelage as colonies or protectorates; or whether they are independent but in need of advice, assistance, or administration; and general international conventions for the promotion of the welfare of backward peoples, such as the convention for control of traffic in arms and ammunition, or conventions which may prove necessary in future for the advancement of the less progressive nations, will best come within its domain. All peoples, whether in Mandated Territories or not, may perhaps come to seek from it needed advice and counsel; and the reports which it publishes should not be merely perfunctory records, but must be fertile in suggestion for the future as well as data regarding past and present conditions.

The task of the mandate commission is not an easy one, but it can and must be done. Much naturally depends on the personnel of the commission itself and on those members of the secretariat of the League who are associated with it.[30]

In view of these high requirements it is not surprising that considerable differences of opinion were disclosed in the Council as to the organization of the Commission. Hymans of Belgium thought that the mandatories if represented on the Commission ought not to vote in cases where they were interested in order to convince the public that mandates are not "a convenient fiction of a temporary char-

[30] *Op. cit.*, pp. 116–19. Huntington Gilchrist, a member of the mandates section of the Secretariat, considered "the character of the Permanent Mandates Commission of first importance" (*Advocate of Peace*, 1926, p. 170).

acter" but that the League is a "reality." Mitsui of Japan and Balfour of England demurred and Tittoni of Italy suggested that the non-mandatories should have a majority.[31] Hymans proposed two months later that the Assembly appoint the non-mandatory members but this was quickly vetoed. Tittoni then made the extraordinary proposal that the mandatories should pay the expenses of the Commission but should not vote on it, and Ishii of Japan suggested that there was no need of setting up the Commission at all until the mandates were confirmed. Hymans, however, pointed out the deplorable consequences if the public is given the impression that the "League was unwilling to accept the duty of supervision entrusted to it by the covenant." Thus a plan was drawn up for a commission of fifteen, seven to be elected by the mandatories and eight by the Council, on nomination of non-mandatory powers.[32]

At the next session Mr. H. A. L. Fisher of Great Britain proposed a commission of only five, all non-mandatories, to save expense, but the Secretary-General pointed out that the mandatories would have to send representatives in that case which would be as expensive. Furthermore, such a reduction in size would increase the personal responsibility of the members and make it difficult for them to criticize a great power. Finally, "it did not seem advisable that the commission should have no function but criticism. . . . . The intention had been that the commission should be able to co-operate positively in all matters concerning the progress and well-being of the populations placed under mandates." Bourgeois of France added that mandatories were needed in the Commission to insure "uniformity in the jurisprudence which would be created by the decisions of the commission." Its "moral authority" would be endangered if it were out of touch with the mandatories. He suggested a commission of seven, three appointed by the mandatories.[33]

On November 26, 1920, Hymans reported a suggestion prepared by the secretary-general for a commission of nine, a majority non-

[31] *L. of N., Council, Min.*, sess. VIII, 41, 43. See Van Rees, *Les Mandats internationaux* (Paris, 1927), I, 57 ff.

[32] *L. of N., Council, Min.*, sess. X, pp. 23, 191; "Responsibilities of the League Arising out of Art. 22," pp. 24, 29.

[33] *L. of N., Council, Min.*, sess. XI, pp. 5–6.

mandatory, all to be appointed by the Council on expert qualifications. Thus only four of the seven mandatories would have a member. In practice the three British dominion mandatories, Australia, New Zealand, and South Africa, have had no national on the Commission, while Great Britain, France, Japan, and Belgium have each had one. Inasmuch as the Commission members from mandatory Powers were not to be representatives of those Powers, it was proposed that these Powers be entitled to send a representative before the Commission when their mandates were being considered. These accredited representatives would take part in the discussions and, at Balfour's suggestion, it was added that they be permitted to append comments to the Commission's report before it was submitted to the Council. At the same time the Director of the Labor Office referring to articles XXII and XXIII (*a*) of the Covenant as well as articles 421 and 427 of the treaty of Versailles asked that a member of the Labor Office be appointed on the Commission. The Council agreed that the Labor Office might appoint an expert "to be present in an advisory capacity at all meetings where labor questions were discussed." The resolution was adopted on December 1 and forms the Commission's constitution.[34] The first Assembly suggested that members of the Commission should not be dismissed without consent of a majority of the Assembly and that one member should be a woman. A later proposal by a representative of Haiti that one member be a negro was not approved.[35]

During the next year the Commission was established. All of the appointees from the mandatory states were men of experience in colonial administration. The non-mandatory members were chosen from colonial states (Italy, Netherlands, Portugal, and Spain) with the exception of a woman member from Sweden.[36] Some of the Powers had in fact suggested to the Council the propriety of appointing one of their citizens.[37] Mr. Cameron Forbes of the United States had

[34] *Ibid.*, pp. 13–15, 19, 88, 92; "Responsibilities of the League Arising out of Art. 22," p. 34. See *infra*, Appendix III.

[35] *L. of N., Assembly, Rec.* (Plenary Meetings), I, 734.

[36] See list of members in Appendix III.

[37] See letters from Netherlands government, January 12 and March 29, 1920 and from Portuguese government, September 11, 1920, *O.J.*, I (October, 1920), 441.

originally been nominated for the place later filled by the Spanish member but declined.[38] Mr. Grimshaw, an Englishman, was named as delegate from the International Labor Office. In 1925 M. Rappard, upon his retirement as director of the mandates section, was made a special member of the Commission, thus increasing its members to ten. Upon Germany's admission to the League the question of increasing the membership so as to include a German member was at once considered, and at its eleventh session the Commission saw no technical objections to such a course but recognized that the matter was within the exclusive competence of the Council. In September, 1927, the latter appointed a German member.[39]

The members of the Commission are appointed on the basis of personal qualifications, thus attendance through substitutes would seem impossible. At the eighth session M. Beau, the member of French nationality, was unable to attend on account of health and suggested to the President of the Council that M. Roume be authorized to represent him. In view of the importance of having a French member on the Commission at this meeting on Syria, M. Scialoja, the president of the Council, agreed to the proposal.[40] Discussion of the question of substitutes, put on the agenda of the tenth session, was adjourned *sine die* without reported debate.[41] The representative of the Labor Office is not strictly a member of the Commission and during the ninth session the Commission agreed to the appointment of a substitute for Mr. Grimshaw.[42]

The Commission and Council have each emphasized the expert as distinguished from the representative qualifications of the members. Expert knowledge of the members is assured not only by their experience but by the continuous supply of reading matter supplied them by the Secretariat. The members also keep themselves *en rapport* with colonial questions by maintaining personal contacts with

[38] *L. of N., Council, Min.*, sess. XIII, pp. 25, 73; *O.J.*, II, 254.

[39] The Commission discussed the question at length and could not reach unanimous agreement. It had before it a communication from the Union Coloniale Française vigorously protesting such an appointment.

[40] *P.M.C., Min.*, VIII, 8, 171.

[41] *Ibid.*, X, 17; Van Rees (*op. cit.*) mentions the matter (p. 77) but expresses no opinion.

[42] *P.M.C., Min.*, IX, 20.

official and private organizations dealing with these subjects. In opening the eleventh session the Chairman said:

I think further that it is highly important to maintain personal relations with the various semi-official and unofficial institutions dealing with colonial problems in general. Last year, Sir Frederick Lugard and M. Orts attended the big international missionary congress at LeZoute in Belgium. M. VanRees and the Head of the Mandates Section of the Secretariat have just attended the plenary meetings of the International Colonial Institute at the Hague where the question of mandates was included in the agenda and several interesting reports on the subject were submitted. At the opening meeting in particular, M. VanRees gave a very lucid account of the mandates system.

While it is perfectly true that here in the commission we have only to deal with the mandated territories, it is quite natural that we should endeavour individually to follow the development, under its various aspects, of colonial policy in general.

We shall undoubtedly be very much interested to hear the results of the recent study tour of our colleague, Mme. Wicksell, who has just visited the United States, at the invitation of the Phelps-Stokes Foundation, in order to study the methods and results of the education of members of the black race.

We may also note with very special satisfaction that no less than four members of the commission, namely, Sir F. Lugard, M. Freire d'Andrade, M. Merlin and M. VanRees, have been invited by the international labor organization to assist in the work of the committee of experts on native labor of which Mr. Grimshaw is Secretary General. We see in this not only a tribute to the personal competence of our colleagues but a recognition of the fact that the work done by the Mandates Commission in this sphere has not passed unnoticed.[43]

The technical and impartial attitude of the members is given an additional guaranty in the provision that they may not hold any official position under their governments.[44] Doubtless the fact that most of them have held such positions in the past gives each a certain prejudice in favor of his government's policy. The Commission selects its chairman and vice-chairman annually, and the Marquis Theodoli of Italy and M. Van Rees of the Netherlands have been continuously re-elected for these positions.

The question of salaries for the Commission has been a thorny one. The Council's resolution of December 1, 1920, provided that the League should give them traveling expenses plus 100 gold francs

[43] *Ibid.*, XI, 6, 7.

[44] See Van Rees, *op. cit.*, p. 60; Stoyanovsky, *op. cit.*, p. 134. The Assembly resolution urging that its consent by majority vote be required for dismissal is also important (see *supra*, n. 35).

per diem during meetings. In pursuance of general economies urged by the Assembly this was reduced to 70 francs *per diem* by the Council resolution of January 10, 1922. It is not customary for League commissions to receive more than expenses, but in view of the increasing burden on the members of this Commission, in view of the fact that the Commission was especially mentioned in the Covenant, and particularly in view of the provision in its constitution that the members could not occupy positions in the service of their states, the Council in 1926 after a long discussion recommended an exception which was approved by the Supervisory Commission and the seventh Assembly. Thus the members of the Commission were given 2,000 gold francs a year provided that they sit over thirty days.[45]

The Commission was authorized by the Council resolution of December 1, 1920, to make its own rules of procedure, which it did at its first session. These rules were approved by the Council in January, 1922. In August, 1923, the Commission proposed several amendments to these rules, changing the time of its annual meeting from August to June, changing the time for receiving reports from the last of June to May 20, increasing the number of copies of the report to be submitted by the mandatories from twenty to one hundred, and making the plenary public meeting required by its constitution and rules optional. The Council approved these changes on December 12, 1923, though Lord Robert Cecil expressed the hope that the Commission would "exercise as little as possible its right to restrict the publicity given to its meetings."[46] At its twelfth session the Commission proposed further minor modifications to bring them into conformity with the usual practice of two annual meetings, with the increase of its constitutional membership to ten and with the changed dates for reception of reports. These were accepted by the Council.[46a]

The revised rules provide for at least one annual session in the second half of June and extraordinary sessions on request of a mem-

[45] L. of N., Council, June 7, 1926, Min., sess. XL, *O.J.*, VII, 856.

[46] L. of N., Council, Min., sess. XXVII, *O.J.*, IV, 338. The rules were printed by the League on February 20, 1924, as *Doc. C.P.M.*, 8(1). Van Rees prints the French text (pp. 68–71). See also Appendix III.

[46a] *P.M.C.*, *Min.*, XII, 97–98, 158, 199–200; L. of N., Council, March 5, 1928, sess. XXIX, min. 2117.

ber approved by the majority of the Commission and the president of the Council. Six members constitute a quorum and decisions may be taken by a majority of those present, the chairman having a casting vote. The minority have the right to transmit their views to the Council. The chairman and vice-chairman are selected for a year at the first ordinary session by secret ballot. Reports of each mandatory are to be in the hands of each commissioner by May 20 of each year in certain cases and by September 1 in others, and at the same time one hundred copies are to be sent to the Secretariat. The agenda is prepared by the Secretariat with approval of the chairman, and new items may be added by two-thirds vote. A separate examination of each report takes place in the presence of the accredited representative of the mandatory, and the Commission's observations are communicated to the accredited representative who may add his remarks. The Commission may hold public meetings by majority vote. French and English are both official languages. Subject to approval of the Council, the rules may be modified by a vote of five members of the Commission.

At first the Commission held only one session a year but since 1923 it has held two, one in June, so that its reports may be considered by the Council in time to submit to the September Assembly, and a second in October. In February, 1926, a third session was held to consider the situation in Syria. The custom of regularly holding a second session was due to the large amount of business and the difficulty of the members getting away for long meetings and also because the reports of all the mandatories, on account of their distance, could not be available for the June meeting.[47]

The Commission has always sat at Geneva, as required by its constitution, except at the special session on Syria which was held at Rome. Some objection was made to this change on the ground of expense and possible political influence but the majority of the Commission preferred it, ostensibly because of climatic conditions in the winter.[48] It was voted that the fifth session be held in London in

[47] This practice was noted by the Council on September 3, 1925 (Min., sess. XXXV, *O.J.*, VI, 1312).

[48] *P.M.C.*, *Min.*, VII, 130–32. The Council noted that this was not to be regarded as a precedent, December 9, 1925 (L. of N., Council, Min., sess. XXXVII, *O.J.*, VII, 269).

1924 although similar objection was made, but in fact the session was at Geneva, "both," said the Chairman, "to give evidence of our good will and to set a good example, without in any way prejudicing our freedom in regard to this point in the future."[49]

The Commission's rules provide for public meetings at the desire of a majority of the Commission, and the opening meeting has been public in every session except the first and the eighth which was an extraordinary session called to deal with the Syrian situation. At these opening meetings the work of the League on mandates since the last meeting is reviewed by the chairman and the chief of the mandates section, the agenda of the session is adopted, and if it is the first ordinary session of the year the chairman and vice-chairman are elected. At the second and third sessions public meetings were arranged for the discussion of general questions but these meetings proved rather uninteresting because of the extreme reserve of everyone, though one was the occasion of what was later described as a "disagreeable incident." During the seventh session it was suggested that the Belgian representative make a public statement in refutation of the German charge that the law organizing Ruanda-Urundi was in derogation of the mandate, but the Commission decided against such action. Nevertheless, during the ninth session, at his request M. de Jouvenal, French high commissioner for Syria, was permitted to be heard in public though it was felt necessary to have the police in the committee-room and an "unfortunate incident occurred."[49a]

At its first meeting the Commission decided that meetings should generally be private, and after the experience mentioned and extensive discussion in the third, fifth, seventh, and twelfth sessions this policy was reaffirmed in spite of expressions in both the Council and Assembly favorable to public meetings.[49b]

This decision was supported by arguments of law, efficiency, and prudence. The Commission was advisory to the Council, and if the meetings were public it would in fact be presenting its opinions to the

[49] *P.M.C., Min.*, IV, 158; V., 6.

[49a] See remarks of M. Orts (*ibid.*, XII, 60) and report of actual and suggested public meetings (II, 56; III, 191; VII, 52–54; IX, 54, 109–24).

[49b] Especially by Lord Robert Cecil in the Council and Dr. Nansen in the Assembly (see *supra*, n. 46, and *P.M.C., Min.*, XII, 60).

public in general before they reached that body, thus embarrassing the latter's action.[49c] Furthermore, neither the accredited representatives nor the members of the Commission would talk with the openness necessary for real understanding in public. Close and cordial relations of the Commission with the accredited representatives have been considered a *sine qua non* of successful operation of the mandates system, and such relations would only be possible if the Commission preserved the character of "a laboratory rather than a parliament." Finally, if the public were excluded from meetings at which the representatives of the mandatory were present and at which important conclusions were reached, there would not be much left to interest them. The Commission would find itself in the dilemma of making its public meetings either "dull or indiscreet," and this had actually been borne out by experience.

The Commission realized the general value of publicity for the League's work but thought the character of its own work presented peculiar difficulties and the full minutes published within three months of the session would ordinarily be sufficient. All the commissioners, however, were insistent that their existing discretion to have public meetings should be preserved.[49d] Even in the private meetings the Commission has allowed accredited representatives of mandatories to be present on request on occasions other than those when their mandates were being examined. On such occasions, however, they may not enter into discussion. M. Rappard once remarked that such requests should be "noted with great satisfaction" by the Commission, "for it showed a desire to understand and cooperate with the commission upon which the commission should congratulate itself."[49e]

The Commission divides its work into (1) general questions comprising questions of procedure, law, and general principles of mandatory administration in which it acts upon the basis of reports by a member or subcommittee; (2) reports of the mandatories which are examined by the members before the Commission meets and which furnish the basis for interrogations to the mandatory's accredited

[49c] *Ibid.*, III, 48; VII, 53; XII, 60.

[49d] *Ibid.*, XII, 60–62; see also I, 7; III, 48; V, 141; VII, 52–54.

[49e] *Ibid.*, IX, 31.

representative during the meeting; and (3) petitions which are similarly handled.

The Commission's results are submitted to the Council in a report of ten to twenty pages, but this is accompanied by the full minutes of the session which, with appendixes, forms a volume of two or three hundred pages. The report is tactfully worded. Criticism is likely to be in the form of requests for further information on the question—a practice the advantage of which is indicated by a discussion in the Council of the Commission's second report. Resolutions to request the mandatories "to be good enough to carry out the recommendations" of the Commission had been proposed. "Lord Balfour said he did not wish to be associated with any criticism when he had no opportunity to consider the evidence concerning the criticism." Marquis Imperiali of Italy pointed out that the recommendations were merely requests for "supplementary information" and Balfour acquiesced in the resolution.[50] Occasionally the Commission finds a direct violation of the mandate, in which case it says so.[51]

In September, 1926, the Council suggested that a careful distinction be made between general observations by the Commission and the parts of the report directed to particular mandatories or petitions. The inclusion of a general statement of its functions in the report on Syria had brought some criticism from Sir Austen Chamberlain, especially when it was suggested that the whole report be forwarded in answer to certain petitioners.[52]

The powers of the Commission have not been fully defined by either the Covenant or the Council resolution of December 1, 1920, and differences of opinion have arisen in regard to four questions: (1) Is the Commission an independent body or merely an instrument of the Council? (2) Is the Commission limited to advice on the observance of the mandates or can it recommend improvements in the texts? (3) Is the Commission limited to the investigation of written documents and the interrogation of representatives of the mandates, or can it hear petitions orally and conduct investigations in the mandated areas? (4) Is the Commission limited to consideration of the

[50] *L. of N., Council, Min.,* sess. XV, p. 178.

[51] See *infra,* chap. vii.

[52] L. of N. Council, June 2, 1926, Min., sess. XL, *O.J.,* VII, 879.

activities of the mandatory on matters mentioned in the mandates or can it advise on the entire administration of the areas?

On the first question the Commission made its position clear in the first report to the Council, and this has never been seriously challenged.

The Covenant provides that "the Permanent Commission shall be constituted to receive and examine the annual report" which the mandatory powers are pledged to send to the Council concerning the territories under their charge, and "to advise the Council on all matters relating to the observance of the mandates." Such investigations and such advice can only be of value if inspired by absolute independence and impartiality of judgment concerning the data furnished to us. We know that the Council intended us to act in that spirit, since it insisted that the Commission should be composed of experts answerable only to the League of Nations as a body, and, further, insisted that the majority of these members should be nationals of non-mandatory states.

Allow me, Mr. President and Gentlemen, to assure you that this is the manner in which we as a commission unanimously interpret the mission entrusted to us, a mission of which we hope to prove ourselves worthy.[53]

In the tenth session of the Commission in November, 1926, M. Rappard, while discussing the questionnaire issue, said:

The Permanent Mandates Commission had duties, and the only rights which it possessed were the result of such duties. It was simply and solely the servant of the Council and its competent adviser for all mandates questions, and this position gave rise to certain misunderstandings regarding the interpretation of the decisions which it had taken.

To this, exception was promptly taken by Freire d'Andrade of Portugal and the chairman, Marquis Theodoli of Italy, who said:

M. Rappard had used a word which, so far as he was concerned, he could not accept. M. Rappard had maintained that the Commission was the servant of the Council. The Permanent Mandates Commission differed from the other advisory Commissions of the League, as it was an organization of a peculiar kind, expressly mentioned in the covenant, and which, once constituted, could not be dissolved either by the mandatory powers or by the council. It was therefore a very special form of instrument, entirely independent, and whose duty it was to give advice to the Council. The Council was free to follow or reject the advice which it received.

M. Rappard then regretted the misunderstanding which had occurred. He fully agreed with the chairman regarding the complete independence of the

[53] *Ibid.*, sess. XIV, p. 178.

Permanent Mandates Commission in respect to the Council—an independence which had been expressly desired by the Council itself. He had merely wished to emphasize the fact that it was the sole duty of the Commission to give advice and, in this way, to be of service to the Council.[54]

On the second question the Commission and Council have been clear that the former's duties are limited to advice on "the observance of mandates" but as already noted the Commission has felt itself free to tender suggestions for the modification of the mandates, which the Council has often transmitted to the mandatory powers.[55]

On the third question there has been much discussion, which will be considered in a later chapter. After discussing the oral hearing of petitioners at its fourth, seventh, eighth, and ninth sessions the Commission finally made a tentative suggestion to the Council favoring the practice, but the latter after consulting the mandatories disapproved. The feasibility of an investigation on the spot was considered in the third and again in the seventh sessions, but the Commission doubted whether it had the power without express council authorization. It appears that either of these sources of information might be opened to the Commission by the Council, but the latter has been unfavorable mainly on the ground that the mandatory's prestige in the territory might be compromised.[56]

The fourth question has proved the most difficult to answer. In his original report, accepted by the Council in August, 1920, M. Hymans emphasized the importance of the Commission examining the entire administration of the mandated territories, and this conception was frequently indorsed in the early meetings of the Council. Thus on November 14, 1920, M. Hymans said that the Commission should have wide latitude in the form of its report. It might be a general report on the administration of a power or a report on a question involved in the application of article 22 or an extraordinary report in case of abuses or complaints. The constitution of the Commission adopted at this time by the Council seems to contemplate the same wide scope, and thus the Commission had considered itself

[54] *P.M.C., Min.*, X, 14.

[55] See *supra*, chap. iv, n. 38.

[56] Report of Sir Frederick Lugard, *P.M.C., Min.*, IX, 190; see *infra*, chap. vi, secs. 3, 4.

competent to consider all phases of administration in the mandated territories.[57]

The first opposition to this theory occurred in a Council meeting of December 12, 1923. The report of the Mandates Commission which was under consideration made a series of positive recommendations, and M. Hanotaux of France said, "The mandates commission had a tendency to go beyond the powers with which it was entrusted. Its duty was to advise the council on questions relating to the execution of the mandates. The mandates commission could not on its own initiative make proposals in regard to the general administration of the mandated territory as a whole." The Marquis Theodoli, chairman of the Commission, read the text of the Covenant and said, "The commission has assumed that when it discovered there were certain difficulties in the administration of a mandated country it was its duty to offer the council suggestions which might have the effect of lessening or removing such difficulties." Hanotaux agreed but pointed out that "the commission could only make observations on action taken and not take the initiative in anticipation of such action." The Commission, in fact, should give its opinion in regard to the execution of the mandates and should keep strictly within these limits. Lord Cecil agreed to this, "but thought that the task of the commission would be very difficult if it were not able to make suggestions for the better execution of the mandates. He would not like to contemplate anything which might tend to restrict the liberty of the mandates commission and diminish the value of its work." Theodoli then said that he would be glad to have definite instructions from the Council as to the Commission's powers. Count Bonin-Longare of Italy noticed that the Commission's proposals were all addressed to the Council and were merely recommendations, consequently the initiative of the governments was entirely reserved. M. Hanotaux "thought the mandatory governments should be first informed and that the council should subsequently study the problems in question." To this Lord Robert Cecil promptly demurred insisting that the "commission could not communicate directly with the governments. Such a procedure would be strongly resented. The commission should report to the council and it was

[57] *L. of N., Council, Min.*, sess. XI, pp. 13, 90. See also *supra*, chap. iv, n. 15.

for the council to decide whether its recommendations should be forwarded to the governments or not." Hanotaux agreed "so far as the execution of the mandates was concerned," and Branting of Sweden reiterated that the Council had discretion to forward the Commission's recommendations or not.[58]

Later in the meeting Hanotaux repeatedly accused the Commission of going beyond its functions in suggesting a change in the boundary of French and British mandated territories in West Africa and in recommending principles with regard to loans for mandated territories and the extension of special conventions to them. He thought the Commission's function should be limited "to an examination of the execution of mandates," but the Italian representative pointed out that "great care must be taken not to limit it unduly," and Lord Robert Cecil repeated that "the mandates commission was responsible for the good administration of the territory under mandate and might perfectly well examine facts which were likely to react on the welfare of the natives and draw the attention of the interested powers to these facts." Hanotaux then made a definite request for a study of the Commission's powers.[59]

The question of competence arose again in the summer of 1926 when Chamberlain of Great Britain took exception to the Commission's definition of its functions in the report on Syria and in September, 1926,[60] when a suggestion of the Commission on the subject of oral hearings of petitioners and a recommendation for a more extensive questionnaire for the use of mandatories raised a storm. Chamberlain was again the main objector. This "immense" questionnaire, he said, was

> infinitely more detailed, infinitely more inquisitorial than that which had hitherto been in force with the sanction of the council—it raised the question of the true relative position of the mandatory governments in a mandated territory and the mandates commission which examined their reports, and the council which took action as guardian under terms of the covenant. . . . . It seemed to him that there was a tendency on the part of the commission to extend its authority where the government would no longer be vested in the mandatory

[58] *Ibid.*, sess. XXVII, *O.J.*, IV, 333–36, Balfour's Opinion (see *supra*, chap. iv, n. 12) was similar to that of M. Hanotaux.

[59] *Ibid.*, p. 336.

[60] *Ibid.*, June 2, 1926, sess. XL, *O.J.*, VII, 879.

power but in the mandates commission. He was sure that was not the intention of the covenant. It was clear from that document that these territories were to be put under the tutelage of advanced powers and that they would exercise their authority under the supervision of the League, for which the League would have a commission to assist it. But it was not according to his reading of that document, intended that the governing authority of those territories should be any other than the government which had received the mandate.

Briand of France, Ishii of Japan, and Vandervelde of Belgium agreed. Sir Francis Bell of New Zealand said, "New Zealand which had always received the commendation of the mandates commission and of the council was becoming impatient at the minute investigation by the commission of administrative detail." Mr. Smit of South Africa added:

The impression had grown in the mandated territory that the more it developed constitutionally the greater the assumption by the permanent mandates commission of power to direct the government in the territory. In cases where the mandated territory had its own legislative body, such a body would not like such questions as the hearing of the petitioners orally and the questionnaire to be settled without its having been consulted and without having been asked for observations. . . . . He would urge the council not to overlook the fact that in this very exhaustive questionnaire matters were touched upon which did not really concern the permanent mandates commission and which really constituted an investigation of the policy of the mandatory in its own territory. C mandates were administered as integral parts of the territory and some questions—54 for example (Is local labor supply adequate for industrial development or must enterprises be restricted for a time with a care for health of native races?)—inquired into the future policy of, for instance, the Union Government. To have such questions put before the Union Government in that way would create a great deal of sentiment.

M. Van Rees, the vice-chairman of the Commission, defended that body with ample reference to the documents defining its powers. "The reproach which he had heard addressed to the mandates commission after five years of hard and conscientious work had moved him very deeply." Chamberlain and Briand then expressed their appreciation of the Commission's services, and the Council decided to submit the Commission's suggestions to the mandatory powers before taking action. Scialoja of Italy said he had to make reservations to some of the remarks made by his colleagues.[61]

[61] *Ibid.*, September 3, 1926, *O.J.*, VII, 1233, 1235, 1240.

The mandatory powers later replied, Great Britain and her Dominions objecting to the questionnaire as "inquisitorial, unnecessary, and extending to details of administration not within the purview of the League," and supporting the position taken by their representatives in the Council. Both the present proposals, said the British note, are based "on a misconception of the duties and responsibilities of the commission and the council." A rather unconvincing effort was then made to discover a departure in present practice from the proposal of the original Hymans report adopted by the Council in 1920. As has been noticed, that document declared that "the annual reports should certainly include a statement as to the whole moral and material situation of the people under the mandate." The British note commented:

> In the light of this purpose and the terms of the covenant should be read Hyman's further statement "The council should examine the question of the whole administration"—it was not called upon to check and examine the detailed administration nor has it the means to discharge such a Herculean task. Its duty was to see that the administration was conducted generally in accordance with the ideas enunciated in article 22. If it should have reason to suppose that these ideals were not being realized it would naturally pursue its inquiries in such detail as might be found necessary to ascertain the facts, and would make such recommendations as it thought proper for remedying any particular abuse that might be revealed. But there was no need of submitting in annual reports all the details of legislative and administrative activity.[62]

Belgium, France, and Japan objected to the proposal for hearing petitions orally but were less opposed to the questionnaire. The latter was resubmitted to the Commission but the question of competence was not decided.[63] It appears, however, that the mandatories are becoming increasingly restive under the Commission's detailed supervision.

The Commission itself has not been oblivious to these criticisms, in fact it anticipated them, but it has been reluctant to press the issue or formulate its position. At its first session, M. Van Rees raised the question whether in discussing the reports of prospective mandatories the Commission was limited to points mentioned in the draft mandates and called attention to the liberal view of the Com-

[62] *O.J.*, VII, 1646, 1649.

[63] *Ibid.*, and *P.M.C.*, *Min.*, XI, 200.

mission's competence taken by the Council in accepting the Hymans report of 1920. The chairman, Marquis Theodoli of Italy, thought the Hymans report should be followed, and M. Orts of Belgium agreed, adding that the mandatory powers seemed to have accepted this interpretation in explaining their whole administration in the reports.[64] The issue, however, was not raised in the report submitted to the Council.

At the fourth session of the Commission the question of competence was put on the agenda after M. Van Rees had drawn attention to M. Hanotaux's disagreement in the Council from the Commission's opinion on the subject. The matter, however, was not considered until the fifth session when the chairman expressed the opinion that "according to the terms of the constitution of the mandates commission and certain other decisions taken by the council itself the competence of the commission was not and was not intended to be limited as M. Hanotaux had suggested." Several members, however, objected to further consideration of the subject, especially in public, and it was stricken off the agenda after M. Rappard had pointed out that since no one really called in question the competence of the Commission and since raising the question might result in limiting its sphere of usefulness, "discussion at this stage would either be useless or dangerous."[65]

At the eleventh session in July, 1927, M. Van Rees, referring to the mandatories' replies to the Council's request for their views on the proposed new questionnaire, again asked that the question be put on the agenda, but other members considered it preferable to allow the Commission's opinion in the matter to be disclosed by its comments on particular problems. This was accepted though M. Orts of Belgium insisted that the Commission could not "function properly when the scope of its competence was constantly under discussion." He referred to the Council's acceptance of the Hymans report of 1920 which had until recently been unchallenged, and thought it important that the Commission "affirm its determination to exercise its supervision in conformity with the decisions of the council." The report of the Commission pointed out that the questionnaire was prepared only to assist the mandatories, and they were therefore

[64] *P.M.C., Min.*, I, 12.

[65] *Ibid.*, IV, 14; V, 142.

free to use it or not. The Council was equally free to make such recommendations as it saw fit with regard to its use.[66]

5. The Permanent Court of International Justice

The Permanent Court of International Justice is recognized by the mandates themselves as the final interpreter of their terms. By these instruments:

> The mandatory agrees that if any dispute whatever should arise between the mandatory and another member of the League of Nations relating to the interpretation or the application of the provisions of the mandate, such dispute, if it can not be settled by negotiation, shall be submitted to the Permanent Court of International Justice provided for by article 14 of the Covenant of the League of Nations.

The original drafts of the mandates presented by the Principal Powers all contained this provision in identical terms which were not modified upon final confirmation. The British mandate for Tanganyika, however, both in its original drafts and final form contains the additional paragraph:

> States members of the League of Nations may likewise bring any claims in behalf of their nationals for infraction of their rights under the mandate before the said court for decision.[67]

The meaning of these terms was discussed by the Court in the Mavromatis Palestine concessions case. Greece brought action against Great Britain on the basis of this article (26) in the Palestine mandate, alleging that the latter had infringed article 11 of the mandate by granting the various Rutenberg concessions. Mavromatis, a Greek national, had a concession given by the Turkish government which was encroached upon by the Rutenberg grant. Greece claimed that this must be respected under article 11, which gave the mandatory "full power to provide for public ownership or control" of natural resources or public works "subject to any international obligations accepted by the mandatory."

[66] *Ibid.*, XI, 14–15, 166–69, 177–78, 200.

[67] Judge Oda said this paragraph was in all the original draft B mandates (*P.C.I.J.* [Ser. A], No. 2, pp. 86–87, and *P.M.C.*, *Min.*, VI, 161), but this is not shown by Ishii's report to the Council on the drafts (*O.J.*, III, 860 ff.), nor by the texts printed in Levermore, *L. of N.*, *Y.B.*, I, 59 ff. See especially Secretariat's comment on art. 12 of Belgium mandate (*ibid.*, p. 67).

It was admitted that article 26 of the mandate came within article 36 of the Court statute, which extended the latter's jurisdiction to "matters specially provided for in treaties and conventions in force," and that Greece had complied with article 40 of the statute and article 35, paragraph 2, of the rules prescribing the formalities for invoking the Court's jurisdiction. But Great Britain objected to the jurisdiction on other grounds. The Court sustained its jurisdiction, however, holding that there was a dispute between the states since Greece had the "right to ensure, in the person of its subjects, respect for the rules of international law," and that it was a dispute which "can not be settled by negotiation" because, although only one exchange had taken place between the two governments, this was based on earlier correspondence between Great Britain and Mavromatis which made it apparent that a deadlock had been reached. Finally, the court held that since Great Britain had agreed by Protocol XII of the Lausanne Treaty to maintain concessionary contracts concluded before October 29, 1914, and since the Jerusalem, but not the Jaffa, concession of Mavromatis came within that description, it appeared that "international obligations accepted by the mandatory" and consequently the application of article 11 of the mandate were involved. The Court subsequently heard the case in regard to the Jerusalem concession on its merits and sustained the contention of Greece with regard to the validity of the concession but not with regard to compensation.

Five judges dissented from the Court's preliminary decision on the jurisdiction, and among them Judges Moore, De Bustamente, and Oda directed attention to the absence in the Palestine mandate of the additional paragraph found in the Tanganyika mandate. Moore drew no conclusions from this, but De Bustamente and Oda thought it indicated that the Court had no compulsory jurisdiction over cases under the Palestine mandate in which a member of the League claimed in behalf of its nationals.[68]

The Director of the mandates section called the attention of the Mandates Commission to this case at its fifth session and said he had "every reason to believe that this difference is entirely due to accident in the drafting of the Tanganyika mandate," consequently he suggested that the Commission point it out to the Council "with a

[68] *P.C.I.J.* (Ser. A), No. 2, pp. 61, 82, 86.

view to its removal, provided other and more important factors do not intervene." The Commission discussed the matter at its sixth session but made no suggestion to the Council. M. Van Rees thought the difference in text carried legal consequences and if any change were recommended it should be the addition of the clause now in the Tanganyika document to the other mandates. Sir Frederick Lugard said he had been informed by the British government that they considered it "incorrect to assert that the clause was accidental," but had no objection to its excision from the Tanganyika mandate. Mme Bugge-Wicksell considered the courts opinion "regarding the interpretation to be given on the non-introduction of this clause" in the Palestine mandate conclusive, and thus there was no reason for changing the texts. This view seems to have prevailed.[69]

In 1927 the Court was again presented with an issue arising out of the Mavromatis concession. In accordance with the 1925 decision Great Britain had readapted the concession by granting a new concession in 1926 which canceled the original Mavromatis concession. Mavromatis, however, alleged that delays by the Palestinian authorities in the execution of the new concession had amounted to their cancellation causing him serious losses for which he asked damages. Negotiations by the Greek government having failed, the latter invoked the Court's jurisdiction. Great Britain entered a plea to the jurisdiction and this time was sustained by the Court.

The Court distinguished this case from the earlier one on the ground that in this case no action by the mandatory government was involved which could be considered an exercise of its "full power to provide for public ownership or control" of natural resources or public works in the country. The grant of the new Mavromatis concession was not such an act, for under it the government retained merely the normal supervision of concessions, not any special powers of control such as it had under the Rutenberg concessions. Through this definition of "public control" the Court somewhat narrowed possible implications of the earlier decision. Furthermore, the Court considered it doubtful whether delays of the Palestinian authorities in executing the new Mavromatis concession could be considered such an act, even if proved, but it held that the Greek government did not make even a prima facie case on the facts.

[69] *P.M.C., Min.*, V, 9; VI, 56, 159–61.

Thus as the alleged violations of "international obligations accepted by the mandatory" did not in any case result from the exercise by the mandatory of the "full powers" referred to in article 11 of the mandate, the Court was able to conclude that no question of the application of the mandate was involved irrespective of the accuracy of these allegations. Hence it had no jurisdiction from article 26 of that instrument.[70]

From these cases it would appear that a mandatory can be brought before the Court by unilateral arraignment of another member of the League on questions involving not only the interpretation but the application of a mandate provision, and that any member may adopt the claim of its national as its own, consequently, whenever such a national is adversely affected by acts of the mandatory's administration contrary to requirements of the mandate, the Court's interpretation may be sought. Whether every member of the League can be considered to have a legal interest in the observance of the mandate, entitling it to raise a dispute and eventually to invoke the Court's jurisdiction even where no citizen and no material interest of its own is involved, has not been decided. It might be argued that the interest of every member of the League in maintaining the complete integrity of the Covenant and the mandate is sufficient.[71] Undoubtedly the Council could ask the Court for an advisory opinion on the interpretation of any clause in the mandates but the Court might, according to its jurisprudence,[72] refuse to respond to the request. The Court evidently regards a mandate as a document limiting the competence of the mandatory and susceptible of judicial interpretation in all its parts—a conclusion which has also been reached by courts of some of the mandatory governments.[73]

[70] *P.C.I.J.* (Ser. A), No. 11.

[71] The preliminary counter case filed by the British government in the Mavromatis case said, "It would have been open to any member of the League to question provisions in those [Mr. Rutenberg's] concessions which infringed the international obligations which His Britannic Majesty as mandatory for Palestine had accepted" (*ibid.* [Ser. C], No. 5-I, p. 445; Stoyanovsky, *The Mandate for Palestine*, p. 145; see *infra*, chap. xiii, sec. 4*a*). It is doubtful whether a League Member whose national is not involved can bring a "dispute" before the Council in regard to the observance of minority treaties, but the situation in respect to mandates is not identical. See *infra*, chap. xiv, n. 74a.

[72] In The Eastern Carelia Advisory Opinion, *ibid.* (Ser. B), No. 5.

[73] See *infra*, chap. xii.

CHAPTER VI

THE DISCOVERY OF FACTS

The procedure of the various League organs in regard to mandates has been evolved to acquire information, to establish standards, and to assure observance of the mandates. The first of these is fundamental and occupies most of the Commission's effort. The fear has been expressed that the League's supervision would be detrimental because of the unfamiliarity of its organs with local conditions in the territories.[1] In practice the Commission had made every effort to ascertain the facts and has shown great reluctance to make any recommendation when it did not feel itself in complete possession of them. It is worth noting that some of these critics have been the very governments most anxious to limit the Commission's understanding of local conditions by restricting the scope or method of its investigations.[2]

At present the League acquires information (1) from the written reports of the mandatories, (2) from oral hearing of their representatives, (3) from written petitions, (4) from reports of special committees and commissions, and (5) from miscellaneous materials gathered by the Secretariat. Oral hearing of petitioners and commissions of inquiry in the areas are additional methods which have been discussed but not utilized as yet.

[1] The existence of this fear in South Africa was implied by General Botha's statement in the Council of Ten at the Peace Conference that he had confidence the League of Nations would consist of people "who understood the position and who would not make it impossible for any mandatory to govern the country" (Miller, *The Drafting of the Covenant*, II, 213; see also report of Great Britain on the third Assembly, *G.B.*, *Parl. Pap.*, Misc. 2 [1923], Cmd. 1807, p. 32; *supra*, chap. iii, n. 98).

[2] The British dominions which have been most worried about the possible ignorance of the Commission were most hostile to the Commission's efforts to enlarge its information by the oral hearing of petitioners and the more detailed list of questions. See especially statement of Smit of South Africa and Briand's recognition of the Commission's need of information (L. of N., Council, September 3, 1926, Min. sess. XLI, *O.J.*, VII, 1234–36).

1. Reports of the Mandatories

The Covenant requires the mandatory to "render to the council an annual report in reference to the territory committed to its charge." The B and C mandates add that this report shall be "to the satisfaction of the council" and shall "contain full information concerning the measures taken to apply the provisions of this mandate." The A mandates add to this "copies of all laws and regulations promulgated or issued during the year shall be communicated with the report." The Commission has sought to guide the form and content of the reports, the date of presentation, and the number presented.

Before confirmation of the mandates, tentative reports were submitted by most of the prospective mandatories with the understanding, however, that in respect to them the prospective mandatories were not subject to League supervision.[3] These reports were usually addressed by the local administrations to the governments. The Commission has insisted with indorsement of the Council that the reports since confirmation of the mandates be addressed to the Council of the League by the mandatory government, which thereby assumes responsibility for it.[4] The Commission felt considerable embarrassment in considering the reports by local administrators and commissions submitted by South Africa on the Bondelzwart affair during its third session because of doubt whether the South African government assumed responsibility for them.[5] In spite of the Commission's and Council's insistence the form of address was not satisfactory in all cases by 1927.[6]

The Commission has also tried to bring about a certain uniformity in the order of treatment in reports by requesting that the order of the questionnaire be followed. The order of the brief questionnaire on B and C mandates approved by the Commission during its first session and by the Council in its fourteenth session[7] was not

[3] See *supra*, chap. iv, nn. 24, 42; *L. of N.*, *Council*, *Min.*, sess. XIV, p. 179.

[4] *P.M.C.*, *Min.*, III, 102; VI, 172; VII, 98; L. of N., Council, September 15, 1925, Min., sess. XXXV, *O.J.*, p. 1510.

[5] *P.M.C.*, *Min.*, III, 290.

[6] Statement of Chief of mandates section (*ibid.*, IX, 11; XI, 13).

[7] *L. of N.*, *Council*, *Min.*, sess. XIV, pp. 124, 125, 179, 181; *P.M.C.*, *Min.*, II, 81.

suitable for the body of the report and the mandatories usually appended a final chapter giving brief answers. A more elaborate list of questions was published by the Commission at its ninth session in 1926 following an order similar to that actually followed by the reports, especially those from Belgium. After some discussion the Commission declared in the preamble that it "considered it desirable that the reports should be drawn up in accordance with the general plan of the questionnaire" though it did not ask that the question be necessarily reproduced in the report.[8] This list of questions has not been indorsed by the Council but some of the mandatories have agreed to follow its order in preparing annual reports.[9]

There has in fact been considerable diversity in the form of reports. The British reports tend to a narrative statement of the activities in various fields during the year and are printed in octavo size varying from 50 to 100 pages for the African areas and from 150 to 200 for Palestine and Iraq. Miss Gertrude Bell wrote the earlier reports on Iraq, which are readable and dramatic documents in marked contrast to the schematically arranged descriptive folio prepared by the French government on Syria. The French and Belgium reports have in general been schematically arranged and have included elaborate statistics and legislative texts. The French reports on Togo and Cameroons have been folios from 200 to 250 pages, and the Belgian are of similar type though less voluminous. Of the C mandatories Australia has produced a handsomely illustrated folio of 300 pages on New Guinea. Her reports on Nauru have been brief folios. New Zealand sends a 50-page folio on Western Samoa sometimes with maps and illustrations of native life. South Africa's reports have been wrongly addressed and were quite brief until 1925. These reports have been of a descriptive and narrative character. Japan at first sent laconic reports with many statistical tables and occasional pictures and maps. Later they have become more voluminous.

The Commission has urged that the reports be made more available to the public, and on an Assembly recommendation the 1925

[8] *P.M.C., Min.*, IX, 128, 231.

[9] *L. of N., Council, Min.*, sess. XLII, XLIII, XLIV, *O.J.*, VII, 1239; VIII, 1119; *P.M.C., Min.*, XI, 10; XIV, 17, 205; *supra*, chap. v, nn. 61–66.

reports were reprinted at the League's expense in uniform typography. This was discontinued on account of the expense, but with the understanding that the mandatory governments would supply sufficient copies for distribution through League agencies.[10]

The reports differ in content as much as in form, and the Commission has repeatedly had to request that essential material be included. Special questionnaires for Syria and Palestine were drawn up at the second session and one for Iraq was prepared by the *rapporteur* of the Commission, M. Orts, at the tenth session but its consideration was postponed.[11] The questionnaires on B and C mandates prepared at the first session of the Commission and approved by the Council were soon found to be inadequate as guides to the content of reports,[12] but the more detailed list of questions suggested by the Commission in 1926 met with Council opposition. As has been noted,[13] Great Britain and her dominions thought the Commission was prying into matters of administration beyond its competence, and imposing an expensive and unnecessary burden of question answering upon the administrations. Great Britain declared that the questionnaire called for a detailed report on certain matters on which, in her unrivaled colonial experience, she had found it unwise to interfere with local administrations. Belgium, however, saw no objection to the questionnaire and said, "The mandates commission can not give the council effective assistance in its work of supervision unless the council accords it wide powers of discretion as to the questions which it may think fit to ask the mandatory states." France made little objection though it saw some advantage in the greater latitude given the mandatories by the old questionnaire. Japan thought the new list of questions somewhat too detailed and that it might impose an undue burden on overworked officials.[14] The Commission had made it clear in its discussions that the questions were intended merely as suggestions to produce uniformity of order and the inclusion of important material without any implication that all

[10] *P.M.C., Min.*, IX, 9.

[11] *Ibid.*, II, 74; X, 17; *Report*, II, 7.

[12] Amendments were suggested at the second session (*P.M.C., Min.*, II, 64).

[13] See *supra*, chap. v, sec. 4.

[14] *O.J.*, VII, 1646 ff.

must be answered in every report. In its eleventh session, after considering the objections of certain mandatories, it said that of course the mandatories had full discretion to use it or not and the Council was free to make such recommendations as it saw fit.[15]

The Commission has frequently urged the inclusion of maps and legislative texts in the reports, and the latter are required by the terms of the A mandates. Great Britain and her dominions have had an especial difficulty in complying with the latter requirement, apparently because the laws are voluminous, often apply to more than the mandated area, and are not normally published until after the reports are submitted. At its sixth session the Commission, having found that the practice suggested at the fifth session of submitting the official gazettes containing the legislation for mandated territories to the Secretariat was impracticable, suggested that the laws be printed as an appendix to the reports, or submitted in bound volumes to each member of the Commission and three to the Secretariat. At the ninth session the director of the mandates section announced that France, Belgium, Australia, South Africa, and Great Britain, after special negotiations, had accepted this proposal.[16]

Great Britain and her dominions have been least responsive to Council and Commission suggestions in regard to the form and content of reports. From reading these documents as well as from their expressed attitude one gets the impression that British administrators are less systematic, though perhaps for that reason more adaptable, in their methods of administrative reporting than the French, Belgians, or Japanese. They chafe under rigorous requirements of form and act on the theory that the man on the job be allowed to develop his own method. Efforts to achieve uniformity of method have little place in British practice.

The reports were originally prepared for different periods in the different areas and though several of the mandatories have changed to the calendar year, the Australian report on New Guinea still runs from July 1 to June 30 and the New Zealand report on Western Samoa from April 1 to March 31. Partly because of this variation, partly because of the remote position of some of the territories, and in the case of Iraq because of the desire of the native government to

[15] *P.M.C., Min.*, XI, 200. [16] *Ibid.*, VI, 173; IX, 11.

examine the report before submission, there has been difficulty in getting all the reports to the Commission by the required time, May 20. The fall meeting of the Commission was arranged partly to allow more time for certain reports, and the Commission has been willing to meet the convenience of the mandatories. Rulings of the Commission and Council up to 1927 allowed the New Guinea report until the following May 20, that is, nearly a year from its closing date, and postponed reports on Samoa, Japanese islands, British Cameroons and Togo, Ruanda-Urundi, and Iraq until September 1.[17]

The Commission is naturally insistent that when a date for reception of reports has been agreed upon it be observed. Obviously the efficiency of the Commission's work depends on the members having time to read the reports before the meeting begins. In fact, the mandatories have been quite delinquent in this respect. At the eleventh session only three of the eight reports due on May 20 had been received by that date, and one was not received until June 7. The Commission has also had to complain occasionally that even when the reports are received they are not sent in sufficient numbers. The rules of procedure require that a copy be sent to each member of the Commission and 100 to the Secretariat.[18]

In addition to the annual reports the Commission has sometimes asked for special reports upon emergency situations, such as the Bondelzwart insurrection in Southwest Africa in 1923 and the insurrection in Syria in 1925–26. On the first of these occasions the Commission complained of the failure of the mandatory government to express its attitude toward the reports prepared by its commissions and administrator but on the latter occasion it seemed to find sufficient guaranty of the accuracy of facts and reliability of positive conclusions in the character of the officers who wrote the reports. In both cases, apparently, the reports were submitted as evidence by impartial witnesses rather than as conclusions of the mandatory.[19]

The report itself usually stimulates the Commission to ask for

[17] *Ibid.*, VI, 6, 172; VII, 6, 211; L. of N., Council, December 9, 1925, Min., sess. XXXVII, *O.J.*, VII, 269.

[18] *P.M.C.*, *Min.*, VII, 8, 211; IX, 9; X, 13; XII, 13; L. of N., Council, September, 1925, Min., sess. XXXV, p. 1510.

[19] *P.M.C.*, *Min.*, III, 290–91; X, 131–33, 185.

more information on certain points, and such requests are usually answered by special communications to the Council published in the *Official Journal*, and this practice was requested by the Council in September, 1925. Answers to specific requests, if submerged in the next annual report or given orally by accredited representatives, were found to involve serious inconvenience.[20]

As has been noted, the mandatories are frequently asked by the Council, usually on suggestion of the Commission, to express opinions on general questions of mandatory procedure, law, or policy. Because of delay in answering by some of the mandatories the Council has often had to repeat such requests.[21] The Commission has sought to complete statistical tables of the mandated areas in order that progress in various directions may be tested and at the ninth session asked the Council to authorize the Secretariat to request the mandatories to submit supplementary data not included in the reports. By the twelfth session this data had been received from all the mandated areas except Syria.[22]

2. Hearing of the Mandatories

Written material from the mandatories is the main source of information, but the oral hearing of the mandatories' accredited representatives is of great importance. The constitution of the Commission says the mandatory powers "should send" their annual reports to the Commission through duly authorized representatives prepared to offer any supplementary explanations or information and the Commission "shall examine" each report in the presence of the duly authorized representative. The Commission's rules of procedure say that it "shall undertake" a separate examination and discussion of each annual report in the presence of the accredited representative. Accredited representatives have always been present except on the consideration of the first report from South Africa during the second session and again when the report on the Caprivi Zipfel

[20] L. of N., Council, September, 1925, Min., sess. XXXV, *O.J.*, VI, 1511; *P.M.C.*, *Min.*, VI, 10; XVI, 290.

[21] *P.M.C.*, *Min.*,VI, 10; IX, 9–11, summarizing status of such questions still pending.

[22] *Ibid.*, VII, 141; IX, 216; XI, 12; XII, 13. See suggestions of M. Yanaghita on the value of such data (III, 285).

was considered during the seventh session. On this first occasion the Commission expressed its regret, and on the latter expressed some doubt whether it could proceed with the examination of this report in such circumstances but decided it could.[23] At the tenth session Sir Frederick Lugard suggested that examination of reports from certain of the smaller areas like Nauru might be dispensed with on some years but withdrew it after several members had expressed the opinion that to do so would be constitutionally impossible as well as politically unwise. The opinion seemed to prevail that the Commission's duty to examine the reports would not be affected by the failure of a mandatory to send a representative.[24] It may, of course, postpone consideration of a report for sufficient reason. Thus at its seventh session it complied with the British request that consideration of the first report on Iraq be postponed until the Mosul question, which involved a quarter of the territory, was settled. It also postponed the Syrian report in view of the insurrection which had arisen since its publication and its decision to have a special session for the consideration of the latter.[25] The Commission has interpreted its rule to mean that a mandatory can have only one accredited representative before the Commission at a time, and that his statements engage the responsibility of his government but the mandatory may send experts in addition.[26]

The Commission has often expressed the hope that mandatories would send the administrator on the spot or a leading subordinate as their representatives as often as possible. This has frequently been done. In its ninth report the Commission had the satisfaction of noting that five of the eight reports considered at that session had been in the presence of such representatives.[27] Among such officials who have attended Commission sessions have been the high commissioners of Iraq, Palestine, Syria, Ruanda-Urundi, and French Togoland and the administrator of Southwest Africa. The preliminary statements of these officials in the minutes of the Commission meetings give important insight into the policy actually followed by the colonial powers. After this the representatives are subjected to

[23] *Ibid.*, II, 16; *Report*, II, 3; *Min.*, VII, 16, 134, 216.

[24] *Ibid.*, X, 17–18.

[25] *Ibid.*, VII, 9–16, 212, 214.

[26] *Ibid.*, III, 101–2.

[27] *Ibid.*, IX, 216.

cross-questioning by the members of the Commission who are themselves, for the most part, experienced colonial administrators. The Commission, it may be noted, urged the revised questionnaire in part to relieve the representatives. If the reports are meager, they will be questioned at length, and it is interesting to note that the accredited representatives seem not always to share their governments' views of the proper scope of the Commission's questions. During the tenth session, after Mr. Ormsby-Gore had been catechized at length and in detail upon the policy of his government in the West African mandated territories, the Chairman hoped he would not take away the impression that the questions asked "were outside the scope of the terms of reference of the committee." Mr. Ormsby-Gore replied that

> he certainly had not received the impression that the commission had exceeded the limits of the interest which it was bound to take in the administration of mandated territory. Personally, he preferred, in his statements to the commission to be able to base his replies on concrete questions of detail. Such a method of examination was greatly to be preferred to any mere excursion into generalities.[28]

The oral questioning serves not only to supplement the Commission's information but also gives the mandatory governments an opportunity to sell their policy to the Commission. Mr. Hofmeyer during the fourth session put the South African policy in relation to the Bondelzwarts in a much more favorable light than the Commission had derived from written documents. Sir Herbert Samuel's exposition of the Zionist policy in Palestine during the next session seems to have had considerable influence on the Commission. M. Robert de Caix had perhaps too great success in winning the Commission's approval of French policy in Syria in 1924. After the insurrection of the next year, at the eighth session, M. Rappard wondered whether the Commission "had fulfilled its responsibilities" in "congratulating itself on the French administration in Syria" at the

[28] *Ibid.*, X, 105. At the fourth session Mr. Hofmeyer, administrator of Southwest Africa, asked the Commission for instructions as to the reports. "The government has always told me to make it very short, saying that the members of the Mandates Commission are very busy people and can not read all the details I wanted to put in my report and so my report has been cut down. I want, however, to give the fullest possible information to this commission and I should like to know in what direction the report could be improved, or what additional information the commission might desire" (IV, 50–51).

very period to which M. de Caix now said that the origin of the recent extremely serious events "went back." It required all of M. de Caix's dexterity to reply that while he agreed that "deep social and political factors had long existed among the Jebel Druse which might at any moment give rise to a rebellion," he had contended after careful reflection that "it was impossible to attribute to the mandatory power, among the causes which had provoked the rebellion of the Druses, a responsibility reaching far back."[29] Perhaps warned by this experience the Commission was on its guard against the engaging manner of M. de Jouvenal at its ninth session. He made an excellent impression in the public meeting on Syria but hardly sustained it under the rigorous cross-questioning to which he was subjected in private. Nevertheless, through these personal contacts the relations of the mandatory and the League can become ones of genuine co-operation, but only if there is complete frankness on both sides. Apparently there generally has been.

With the thought that division of labor and specialization within the Commission would promote efficiency, the Commission decided at its second meeting on suggestion of M. Van Rees and M. Beau to divide the subjects on the questionnaire among the members.[30] This specialization was intended to apply both to the examination of the reports and the interrogation of the accredited representatives. The *rapporteur* for each subject might also receive written memoranda from other members and prepare memoranda on the subject for distribution. Assignment of topics was made at this time, and a series of valuable memoranda by the members resulted at the third session. After 1923, owing to the advent of new members in the Commission, these efforts at specialization somewhat broke down but its renovation was suggested by the chairman, the Marquis Theodoli, at the tenth session. This proposal contemplated *rapporteurs* for all subjects of the questionnaire except general administration, with the understanding that assignments would be reallotted every three years. The questioning in a particular field would normally be confined to the *rapporteur*, and the *dossiers* sent out by the Secretariat would also be somewhat specialized. This proposal was accepted

[29] *Ibid.*, V, 186; VIII, 51, 53.

[30] *Ibid.*, II, 62, and appointment of *rapporteurs* (III, 211).

with exception of the last item and with the understanding that members other than the *rapporteur* were free to ask questions. M. Rappard insisted on this for constitutional as well as practical reasons. The examinations, he thought, must be by the Commission as a whole.[31]

3. Petitions

A third source of information is petitions. At the first session of the Commission the Director of the mandates section inquired in regard to the treatment of complaints which reached the Secretariat, but the Commission thought the matter had better be deferred. An opportunity for petitions from the mandated areas was urged by the second Assembly. In 1922 the British government presented a memorandum on petitions to the Council suggesting that the Permanent Mandates Commission might want to discuss it, but the latter feared political issues might be involved and it would have to await an express instruction from the Council. This the Council gave in September, 1922, and to avoid delay the Chairman of the Commission consulted his colleagues by correspondence and submitted the British proposal slightly modified to the Council. After considerable debate which indicated that the subject was a delicate one, the Council accepted this procedure with minor modifications in January, 1923.[32] Under it, petitions from inhabitants of a mandated area are received only if submitted through the mandatory which is requested to append comments before sending it to the Commission.[32a] Petitions from other sources are sent to the chairman of the Mandates Commission who decides which are of sufficient importance to demand the attention of the Commission. The mandatories concerned are requested to make such comments as they consider desirable within six months.

[31] *Ibid.*, X, 18, 123, 173–74.

[32] *Ibid.*, I, 28; II, 15, 36; *Report*, II, 8; L. of N., Council, Min., XX, *O.J.*, III, 1176, 1245; XXIII, *O.J.*, IV, 200, 211; *P.M.C.*, *Min.*, XII, 176–77.

[32a] The Secretariat, in fact, receives copies of petitions from the petitioners and has reported to the Commission a few cases in which the mandatory has failed to forward the petition. The Commission drew the attention of the mandatory in question to those cases and explanations were given (*P.M.C.*, *Min.*, XII, 62–63). The Commission also discussed apparent efforts by the administrator to discourage the natives of Western Samoa from petitioning the League during the disturbances of 1927 (*ibid.*, XIII, 123, 133). See also XVI, 144, 201.

The commissioners and the Secretariat receive a great deal of material not only from inhabitants of the mandated areas but from travelers, investigators, writers, lawyers, humanitarian, religious and other associations with varying degrees and types of interest in the mandated areas, the mandates system, native welfare, missions, business, political propaganda, etc. How much of this material is to be regarded as petitions and so subject to the procedure laid down in that regard? Much of it is obviously intended merely for the information of the Commission and no specific action is necessary, but the line is not always easy to draw. The question was discussed in the fifth and seventh sessions of the Commission in relation to various communications from organizations interested in Palestine and Syria. Though some of these documents were mainly of an informational character, they were all treated as "petitions." The memoranda from the Zionist organization were in fact treated as petitions coming from the area and so to be submitted through the mandatory power even though the seat of that organization was in London.[33] Thus the term "petition" was given a broad definition as including "memoranda, memorials or other communications," and this definition was accepted by the Council.[34]

The question was more fully discussed during the twelfth session of the Commission in connection with a resolution of the British League of Nations Union placed on the agenda of the meeting at request of Sir Frederick Lugard, a member of the Commission. This resolution, obviously suggested by the recent insurrection in Syria, recommended that the Mandates Commission suggest to the Council the propriety of requiring that any mandatory "immediately notify the League" if it "finds it necessary to suspend its ordinary laws." After noting the delicacy of the problem involved by the substance of the resolution, M. Palacios, the *rapporteur*, expressed the opinion that the document was a petition not from the inhabitants of a mandated area and consequently it should be submitted to the mandatories for their comments. M. Van Rees thought the document was not a petition because not addressed to the League. M. Merlin agreed, adding that it did not have the definite object of righting a wrong in

[33] *Ibid.*, VII, 112–13.

[34] *Ibid.*, V, 115–16; VII, 130, 211; XII, 176; XVI, 19.

the territory. M. Rappard thought all documents in the supposed interest of the inhabitants might be considered petitions. Mme Wicksell thought it was not a petition since it did not refer to "some grievance concerning a particular mandated territory." M. Freire d' Andrade considered it a petition and Dr. Kastl did not. M. Orts was non-committal, and the Chairman announced that a majority of the Commission thought it was not a petition. In that case he looked upon it as a general question, brought before the Commission by one of its members, but as Sir Frederick Lugard was not present, the Commission decided to postpone discussion.[35]

Even though the distinction is recognized between petitions, which involve definite grievances in the application of the mandates system, and suggestions or information of a more general character, the Commission has treated petitions as primarily a source of information. It has sought to avoid giving itself the character of a court of appeal for complainants.[36] Thus petitions dealing with ordinary civil rights for which the local courts give a remedy are not considered. It is, however, recognized that this principle cannot be adhered to too rigidly. The courts of the mandatory may violate the mandate themselves in giving a decision either through misinterpretation of the law or because the law is in conflict with the mandate, and in such cases petition to the League would seem appropriate. This principle was expressed in a resolution drawn up by M. Rappard in the sixth session of the Commission after considerable discussion, and the resolution was approved by the Commission though it was not sent to the Council. There seemed to be a feeling that the Commission could make its own rules in regard to the non-consideration of petitions because of their substance though definition of the procedure necessary to make them receivable was a matter for the Council.[37]

The Commission has also adopted the policy of refusing to consider petitions that oppose the mandate itself or its principles, on the theory that the Commission's functions are confined to advice on the observance of mandates. The Arab protest against the Balfour dec-

[35] *Ibid.*, XII, 153–54.

[36] *Ibid.*, VIII, 201; see also Ormsby-Gore in *The League of Nations Starts*, p. 118.

[37] *P.M.C., Min.*, VI, 96–97, 168–69.

laration in the Palestine mandate was held to come especially under this objection.[38] Anonymous petitions and those merely repeating the allegations and information of earlier petitions are also refused. This practice was formally codified by the Commission at its seventh session, especially for the guidance of the chairman in disposing of petitions from outside the mandated area, and it was understood that he also had discretion to refuse a petition on grounds of violent or indecent language, though this was not mentioned in the resolution. It was specified, however, that if the petition was found unreceivable it must be returned to the petitioner with the reasons for its non-acceptance but it should not be sent, in such case, to the mandatory. The same rules, it was understood, should apply to petitions from the inhabitants of the area though the fact that they came through the mandatory would doubtless create a presumption that they were proper for consideration.[39] A codification of the rules in regard to petitions drawn up by the Secretariat was adopted after a few modifications by the Commission at its twelfth session.[40]

Petitions on being received through the proper channels are referred by the chairman of the Commission to a member who acts as *rapporteur*. There is usually discussion of the petition in the presence of the accredited representative of the mandatory concerned after which the *rapporteur* draws up a report which is considered by the Commission in private. Often difficulty is met because of inadequate data. At the seventh session the Commission recommended that the mandatory always give its opinion on all points raised by the petitioners, but this is after all *ex parte* evidence.[41] The petitions from the various Jewish and Arab groups of Palestine have been especially puzzling. In this case the Commission considered a visit to the spot, but the Council advised it to give an opinion on the data it had.[42]

The question of oral hearing of petitioners has been discussed at several meetings of the Commission, and was definitely raised by the request of the Anti-Slavery and Aborigines Protective Society of

[38] *Ibid.*, VII, 219, 220.

[39] *Ibid.*, p. 133.

[40] *Ibid.*, XII, 57–58, 176–78.

[41] *Ibid.*, VII, 211; VIII, 201.

[42] *Ibid.*, VII, 219; L. of N., Council, December 9, 1925, Min. sess. XXXVII, *O.J.*, VII, 270.

London to be heard in behalf of the Bondelzwarts during the third session. MM. d'Andrade and Orts favored a hearing but the Commission finally decided to invite only written information.[43] During the seventh session a petition from the Arabs of Palestine alleged unfairness in the one-sided procedure on its earlier petition and asked for a study on the spot in the presence of both parties. This was not done, but some members of the Commission thought an oral hearing might be desirable. To this there was some dissent though all agreed that the members of the Commission might hear petitioners individually provided no official use was made of the information received. The Secretary-General was consequently asked to reply to petitioners "that the Mandates Commission did not think it its duty to receive petitioners; but it was understood that the chairman would always be happy to hear what they had to say."[44] The question was again raised by the presence of a "Syrian delegation" at Rome during the eighth session with a request to be heard officially. The Commission was unanimously of the opinion that it would be inexpedient to give them an official hearing because of the precedent in the Bondelzwart case and because their information had actually been communicated by written petitions and informal interviews with the members of the Commission. The Commission was divided as to its legal competence and decided to consider this at its next meeting.[45]

At the ninth session the Jewish national council of Palestine asked to be heard and an extensive debate followed in the Commission.[46] Sir Frederick Lugard thought "it was entirely within the competence of the commission to hear anyone it might desire to hear" and presented a memorandum reiterating the view he had expressed at the eighth session "that not only could I see no objection in principle to this course but I found it difficult to reconcile an attitude of complete impartiality with a denial of audience to a petitioner, while hearing the representative of the mandatory, unless there were special reasons for the denial, as, for instance, in the Syrian case, when the allegations had already been exhaustively examined." He sug-

[43] *P.M.C., Min.*, III, 162–67; see also VII, 34–35; VIII, 157.

[44] *Ibid.*, VII, 35, 128, 164, 180.

[45] *Ibid.*, VIII, 156–60, 168; see especially remarks of M. Rappard, p. 158.

[46] *Ibid.*, IX, 47–50, 52–56, 130.

gested a procedure for hearing deserving petitioners in order to secure for the Commission valuable information and to give "satisfaction" to "those who have genuine cause for submitting a petition," while frustrating the maneuvers of "agitators who seek notoriety and self advertisement." A subcommittee was to consider whether the petition "contained only allegations of a general nature or any specific accusations" and to recommend whether an audience be given. He wrote:

If audience is granted to any petitioner or memorialist it is in order that he may oppose his own version of the circumstances to that of the accredited representative, and perhaps inform the latter of matters within his knowledge which invite further investigation. He should, therefore, be heard in the presence of the representative and allowed to question him. How far a verbatim record of such a discussion should appear in the Minutes it will be for the commission to decide in each case; probably a brief summary will suffice.

On the other hand, if the Permanent Mandates Commission decides that a memorial contains only general allegations, which can be adequately dealt with without the personal presence and oral evidence of the petitioners before the commission, there would be no objection to the chairman or any member giving a private interview to them, provided that it is clearly understood that the member is acting in his private capacity and that no communication is made to the press.

Sir Frederick noted that the right of petition through the mandatory did "not in fact exceed the right which exists in every British colony to petition the Secretary of State through the governor." Though reaching a favorable conclusion, he alluded to the great burden which careful consideration of petitions would throw on the Commission and to the

fear lest this right of petition should create in the minds of the people the idea that the mandatory power is subordinate to the League, which can overrule its decisions and set aside the reply which it may have already given to the petitioners. Such an idea would be fatal to the authority of the mandatory. Agitators seeking notoriety would endeavour to use this right of petition in order to embarrass the mandatory.

These considerations, however, applied to the consideration of petitions at all and not merely to oral hearings. "So long," he thought, "as the right of petition or memorial exists, it should not be concealed but made widely known, and at the same time the conditions should be equally made known."[47]

[47] *Ibid.*, pp. 190–91.

M. Merlin disagreed as on earlier occasions had the other French commissioners, M. Beau and M. Roume. He divided petitions into those coming (1) from individuals in the territory with a specific complaint which ought never to get to the Commission until local remedies were exhausted; (2) from philanthropic and other associations which complained of the mandatory's policy (these should go to the mandatory first, who presumably would satisfy the complainants and would only rarely reach the Commission); (3) from political organizations objecting to the mandatory's acts and policy. These were likely to be most numerous and in considering them the commission could "not be too prudent." He considered the existing procedure adequate. Oral hearings would enable such petitioners

to confront the mandatory power and would give them in the minds of their fellow-countrymen a position of which they would not fail to make the greatest use in combatting the local authority. The consequences would be many, and grave and perhaps without end, and would deliver a fierce attack on the authority of the mandatory power, which was already weak enough in itself owing to the institution of the mandate.

Furthermore, if hearings were given

a long line of pilgrims would march to Geneva on the pretext of obtaining justice and would fill the secretariat to overflowing with their intrigues during each session of the commission. The commission would end by collapsing beneath the weight of too heavy a load which it would itself have been responsible for shouldering.[48]

M. Van Rees considered the hearing of petitions an "executive" function given the Commission by special resolution of the Council and distinct from its ordinary "advisory" functions which flowed from the Covenant. The procedure could not therefore be modified without express Council consent.[49] With this the Commission eventually agreed, but it was more difficult to reach agreement on the expediency of asking the Council to modify the existing procedure. Finally, M. Rappard prepared a memorandum suggesting that the existing procedure be first followed in every case, but in order to guard the League of Nations against the charge of apparent partiality, which might in certain cases be brought on account of this somewhat one-sided procedure, and to dispel genuine misunderstanding which might not be removed by this procedure," the Coun-

[48] *Ibid.*, p. 49. [49] *Ibid.*, p. 50.

cil might be requested to consider permitting an oral hearing to petitioners, who remained dissatisfied and "returned to the attack." He thought the Commission should have discretion to refuse such a hearing and should never grant it unless it was "genuinely likely to clear up a situation which would otherwise remain obscure."[50]

After further discussion the Commission agreed that the hearing of petitioners in exceptional cases might be desirable and consequently drafted the following suggestion to the Council in its report:

> Experience having shown that sometimes the commission has been unable to form a definite opinion as to whether certain petitions are well founded or not, the commission is of opinion that in these cases it might appear indispensable to allow the petitioners to be heard by it. The commission, however, would not desire to formulate a definite recommendation on this subject before being informed of the views of the council.[51]

This suggestion called forth vigorous opposition from the representatives of mandatory powers on the Council though the *rapporteur* M. Unden of Sweden saw merit in the suggestion. The matter was submitted to the mandatory governments who unanimously denounced it. They thought their prestige would be injured by being put on a parity with petitioners as litigants. The British said they had a wide experience on petitions from the colonies and found that written evidence was sufficient—if more was necessary the Commission could ask the mandatory for it. Thus at its meeting in March, 1927, the Council decided that there was no occasion to modify the existing procedure.[52]

The question of publicity to petitions and the form of answer to petitioners has also caused considerable discussion in the Commission. At its fourth session it decided not to publish the text of petitions but departed from this rule at the next session and now exercises discretion according to the character and length of the petition. Marquis Theodoli said at the seventh session:

> With regard to petitioners, the commission should remember that in reality they did not obtain much satisfaction. In any dispute it ought to be the rule

[50] *Ibid.*, pp. 53, 192.

[51] *Ibid.*, pp. 56, 130, 216.

[52] L. of N., Council, September 3, 1926, Min., sess. XLI, *O.J.*, VII, 1232–37, 1240; letters from the mandatories (*ibid.*, pp. 1646–50; Council, March, 1927, sess. XLIV, *O.J.*, VIII, 438; *P.M.C., Min.*, XI, 10–11.

that both parties should be given the same facilities for representing their views. When the dispute concerned grave questions which interested communities or involved religious matters, the least the commission could do would be to publish the protests, in order to show how conscientiously the commission was performing its task.[53]

The Commission reports on petitions only to the Council, consequently its observations are not transmitted to the petitioners until approved by that body. The Council, however, provided by resolution of September 15, 1925, that its decision on petitions should be communicated "to the petitioners and to the mandatory powers."[54] The secretary-general has in compliance with this ordinarily communicated the Commission's observations when approved by the Council to the petitioner individually and sent a copy of the letter to the mandatory. In some cases, however, as the Rehoboth community petition considered in the sixth session, the Commission recommended transmission to the petitioners through the mandatory.[55] In a report adopted at its seventh session and approved by the Council the Commission reserved discretion to recommend either procedure.[56] Some objection was raised in the Council to the Commission's recommendation that the entire report on its eighth session, which dealt exclusively with Syria, be forwarded as an answer to certain Syrian petitioners. A detailed description of existing practice, drawn up by the Secretariat, was however accepted.[57] At first the Commission did not publish reports on petitions in its minutes but since a discussion in the sixth session this has generally been done though the Commission reserves discretion.[58]

Petitions have been most numerous from Syria and Palestine where they proceed from organized groups. The Arab executive and the Jewish executive in Palestine have each sent at least one petition a year, and several petitions have been received from the Agudath Israel, a Jewish sect which dissents from the Zionist majority. The

[53] *P.M.C., Min.*, IV, 146; VI, 57; VII, 137–38; IX, 191.

[54] *O.J.*, VI, 1366, 1512.

[55] *P.M.C., Min.*, VI, 83.

[56] *Ibid.*, VII, 134.

[57] *Ibid.*, L. of N., Council, March, 1926, Min., sess. XXXIX, *O.J.*, VII, 524–26; June, 1926, sess. XL, *O.J.*, VII, 878, 879, 988–89.

[58] *P.M.C., Min.*, VI, 141; XII, 177.

Syrian committee in Cairo has sent numerous petitions voicing the claims of the Arab nationalists of Syria and the Lebanon. The Commission has commented on the fact that the Syrian petitions came from outside Syria, apparently taking that as evidence that dissatisfaction was not so great within the territory.[59]

Another interpretation points out that Arab nationalists in Syria might be in an embarrassing if not dangerous position if they criticized the administration, especially in the midst of insurrection. At the eighth session the French representative admitted among reasons for the lack of petitions from the territory "fear owing to the customs of the country and the apprehension inspired by the authorities among populations long subjected to the oppression of the old régime."[60] From Southwest Africa the Rehoboth community has petitioned, but petitions from Central Africa and the Pacific islands have generally come from individuals, often Germans who think they have been illegally deprived of their property. In most cases, the Commission has found little merit in the complaints of petitioners.

4. Special Commissions

The League and the International Labor Office have set up a number of permanent as well as temporary commissions and committees to deal with subjects which require data on the mandated areas. Among these is the health organization, which has instituted investigations into the health conditions of annual pilgrimages to Mecca and Palestine and into the incidence of sleeping sickness and tuberculosis in Equatorial Africa. This organization regularly distributes epidemological information from all parts of the world. The opium commission publishes regular information on opium and narcotic seizures. The various armament commissions publish data on armaments and arms trade. The temporary slavery commission set up by the Council in 1925 made extensive investigations into the existence of slavery and analogous conditions. The native labor committee set up by the governing body of the International Labor Office in 1927 has collected data in regard to forced labor. As these commissions do not confine their data to mandated areas, although including them, their reports give a valuable basis for comparison of

[59] *Ibid.*, X, 189.

[60] *Ibid.*, VIII, 201; IX, 191.

conditions in these and other similar areas. The Mandates Commission has utilized the data from such commissions and occasionally some of its members have served on them. The activity of such specialized commissions, manned by experts and designed to establish solid bases for policy through the exhaustive collection of data, should be of great value to the Mandates Commission, especially in its work of developing standards of mandatory administration.[61]

Another type of League commission is that which, instead of investigating a problem of significance over a broad area, investigates a particular incident or area. Members of the Secretariat have visited certain of the minority areas of Europe on invitation of those countries, epidemic commissions and refugee commissions have visited parts of Eastern Europe, special commissions including League appointees have been set up to supervise the exchange of certain populations in Eastern Europe, permanent League officials reside at Dantzig and the Saar, and special commissions of inquiry have been sent to investigate on the spot the situation in the Aaland Islands, Vilna, Albania, Memel, Mosul, the Graeco-Bulgarian frontier, and other disputes before the Council. Such commissions have to do with the application of proper standards rather than with their formulation and may furnish useful precedents for the League's supervisory work in connection with mandates.

Several proposals for a regular scheme for inspecting mandated areas on the spot have been made. Toynbee and others have suggested resident League commissioners in each area. The Mosul boundary commission recommended such a commission in the Mosul area, and at the first Assembly M. Doret of Haiti proposed that the parliament of each mandatory should organize a regular inspection.[62]

It was originally planned that members of the mandates section should visit the areas regularly and report on them. This was not

[61] See *supra*, chap. v, nn. 1–5.

[62] A. J. Toynbee, *The League in the East*, pp. 19–20; Georges Cioriceanu, *Les Mandats internationaux* (Paris, 1921), p. 92; Leonard Woolf, *I.L.A.*, *Rep.* (29th sess., 1920); E. M. Earl, *The Nation* (New York), January 13, 1926, p. 29; W. E. Hocking, *Yale Review*, XIX (1930), 266; L. of N., *Question of the Frontier between Turkey and Iraq*, Report, July 16, 1925, p. 89; *L. of N. Assembly, Rec.* (December, 1920), sess. I, Plenary Meetings, pp. 738–41; Stoyanovsky, *op. cit.*, pp. 152–57.

provided for, but M. Rappard while director of the mandates section made a visit to Palestine. Such expeditions would seem to involve no political complications and would give a valuable background for detailed information.[63]

The Commission has occasionally discussed the question of sending a commission of inquiry or visiting a mandated area itself. At the third session it decided, apparently with little debate, that it had no power to send a commission and that in the case of the Bondelzwart insurrection which was under consideration it would be inexpedient to do so apart from the constitutional objection.[64] During the seventh session a petition from the Arabs of Palestine criticized the one-sided character of the Commission's procedure on an earlier petition and suggested that the Commission visit the country to examine the complaints on the spot in the presence of all parties concerned. The *rapporteur* of the Commission, M. Palacios, thought this proposal should be taken into consideration as "it would not only enable the commission to hear personally the Arabs and the other elements of the population but would also give the committee some idea of the atmosphere and the numerous imponderable factors which are of the first importance in solving the problem." Proper circumstances, he thought, should be awaited for such a visit and the time would be a matter for the Commission itself and the Council to decide.[65] M. Van Rees thought that theoretically to bestow upon the Commission power to make such visits would be a step forward, but pointed out the danger to the mandatory's prestige and the difficulty of getting adequate results from such an inquiry. Furthermore, the Commission was merely an advisory body consequently he reserved his opinion. Sir Frederick Lugard considered the suggestion quite impracticable:

> No mandatory power could accept such a procedure. Its prestige would inevitably suffer, for the commission or sub-committee would be in the position of a court of enquiry in which the mandatory power was the defendant. If there were any specific point, such as a disputed frontier, or punitive action, an en-

[63] Beer, *African Questions at the Paris Peace Conference*, Editor's Introduction, xliii; Ormsby-Gore, in *The League of Nations Starts*, p. 102.

[64] *P.M.C.*, *Min.*, III, 291.

[65] *Ibid.*, VII, 181. For debate see *ibid.*, pp. 124–29. See also Sir Frederick Lugard's Introduction to Freda White, *Mandates* (1926), p. 8.

quiry might conceivably be desirable, but in that case it would be for the council to nominate the commission of enquiry, which might or might not consist of members of the Permanent Mandates Commission, and the duty of the Permanent Mandates Commission would be limited to informing the council that in its opinion an enquiry on the spot was necessary. Further, material difficulties would make it almost impossible for an adequate number of the members of the Commission to visit Palestine or any other mandated territory.

The Marquis Theodoli thought that clearly the Commission could advise the Council to send a commission, and the commission which investigated the Mosul boundary was a precedent. Furthermore, it might ask that the commission be composed in whole or in part of its own members. M. Freire d' Andrade agreed, citing the Council's decision to send a commission to investigate the Graeco-Bulgarian dispute—these were not mandated territories but the principle would apply *a fortiori* to "mandates of the League."

M. Rappard agreed with M. Van Rees that the Commission was wholly an advisory body and thought if the information before the Commission was inadequate the best procedure would be to state that fact and let the Council decide whether measures should be taken to get more. The Marquis Theodoli agreed, pointing out that when the nationality question arose the Council had appointed three members of the Commission and the director of the mandates section as a committee to visit the capitals and get the views of the mandatories.

M. Palacios then pointed out that he had suggested a "visit" to the territory not an "enquiry." The object was co-operation not criticism. Sir Frederick Lugard thought if additional information was wanted the specific points should be mentioned, but M. Palacios insisted that what was needed was understanding of the whole situation, which required a visit.

M. Rappard from his own visit realized the value of personal visits to the territory and hoped members of the Commission might occasionally travel to the mandated areas as individuals, but he feared a proposal for the whole Commission to visit the territory would excite political feeling in Palestine. Sir Frederick Lugard continued to insist that an official visit was impracticable. The analogy of the Mosul commission was not accurate as that was in connection with a dispute before the Council. Members of the Commission might of course visit mandated territory on invitation of the mandatory. The chairman, Marquis Theodoli, was afraid such visits would not have the guaranty of impartiality which would be assured by a commission sent by the Council. Sir Frederick Lugard then expressed the view that it would be better to hear the petitioners personally than to send a commission.

M. Van Rees thought a compromise might be effected by noting the inadequacy of the Commission's information and its inability to appreciate what was going on in Palestine because of the dual nature of the mandate in such a way as to suggest to the Council that it would be appropriate to permit a visit to the territory. This was adopted. "The commission," said the report to the Council, "doubts whether it can make any adequate recommendation on so complex and delicate a subject on the sole basis of written documents, even by examining these documents in conjunction with the accredited representative of the mandatory power against whom the petitioners feel they have cause for complaint." The Council's reply simply recognized that the Commission acted "under certain limitations" and that consequently it could only be expected to give a "statement of the best judgment it could form from the information placed at its disposal." At the ninth session the Commission reported on the Palestine petition in accordance with these instructions.[66] In view of the intense interest which the Catholic church is known to take in the Palestine situation, and its tendency to sympathize with the Arabs as against the Zionists, it is interesting to note that the members of the Commission, in spite of the Chairman's effort to confine consideration to the general question, tended to divide on religious lines.

At the eighth session the question of an inquiry on the spot was again considered in connection with the Syrian insurrection. In its report the Commission pointed out that if it were merely charged with the duty of "supervising the administration of mandated territories it would be natural that in all difficult cases it should propose to visit this territory itself, or should recommend the holding of inquiries on the spot," but in fact it was also obliged to co-operate with

[66] *P.M.C.*, *Min.*, VII, 219; IX, 222; L. of N., Council, December 9, 1925, Min., sess. XXXVII, *O.J.*, VII, 269–70.

the mandatory, consequently it must avoid action which "might create embarrassment and render the task of the government more difficult of execution. Thus in spite of the doubtful situation in Syria it refrained from recommending the council to set up a commission of enquiry independent of the mandatory power," although it did not "feel able to abstain from expressing certain criticisms."[67] Unfortunately, the debate which led to these important conclusions is not printed in the *Minutes*.[68]

During the ninth session the question was brought up in connection with the problem of oral hearing of petitions. Some members thought the latter procedure was less objectionable than investigations on the spot.[69] At the sixteenth session the Commission declined to endorse a British proposal to appoint with consent of the Council an *ad hoc* commission to decide on claims in regard to the Wailing Wall in Jerusalem. It thought such an *ad hoc* commission could not be given the powers contemplated for the Commission on Holy places by article 14 of the Palestine mandate. The Council, however, gave its consent on the understanding that the Commission would deal only with this one urgent matter.[69a]

Apparently the Commission agrees that it has no power to visit or send a committee to mandated territory unless expressly authorized by the Council, and is divided on the general expediency of such procedure. The Council has on occasion sent special investigating commissions, especially in connection with disputes before it, but has shown no inclination to authorize a commission to examine general conditions in mandated areas. Commissions of inquiry if frequent and if vested with authority to require the giving of evidence on the general administration of the mandatory might undermine the latter's authority and tend to change the League's action from that of supervision to direct administration. A commission, however, sent to investigate a particular incident or fairly authenticated allegations of malfeasance would seem to come under other League precedents.[70]

[67] *P.M.C.*, *Min.*, VIII, 200.

[68] *Ibid.*, pp. 167–69.

[69] *Ibid.*, VII, 128; IX, 56, 190.

[69a] *P.M.C.*, XVI, 202; L. of N. Council, January 14, 1930, sess. LVIII, item 2571.

[70] Wright, "The Bombardment of Damascus," *A.J.I.L.*, XX (April, 1926), 279.

Unofficial visits by members of the Secretariat or of the Commission, merely to gain a general appreciation of conditions in the areas, would not seem to involve political complications and have actually been made. The British, French, and Japanese members of the Commission expressed confidence that their governments would welcome visits by Members of the Commission in their colonies or mandated territories.[70a]

5. Miscellaneous Information

As has been noted, the Secretariat indefatigably collects information about the mandated areas and the mandates system from all sources, culls it, and sends what seems important to the members of the Commission. This material is quite voluminous. Between the ninth and tenth sessions three *dossiers* were circulated, and between the tenth and eleventh sessions, six. This material is of great importance to supplement the accounts given by the mandatory and by petitions and to assist the members of the Commission in formulating standards.[71]

During the sixth session Sir Frederick Lugard submitted a suggestion for the improvement of this service:

> With regard to the work of the Secretariat, I submit that we do not derive the full benefit of the extremely able and efficient staff. A bundle of papers is periodically circulated, some in French and some in English and some on flimsy paper, which often arrives crumpled or mutilated. Probably few members find time to read all in both languages, and they are difficult to file for reference. I suggest that every document which is considered to be of sufficient importance to be circulated should be either translated in full or a *précis*, more or less full according to the importance of the subject, should be made.
>
> *a*) The laws which are enacted by the Mandatory are the most important of all, and each member desires to have a complete file of these laws, either in the form of decrees and ordinances or of *arrêtés* and regulations having the force of law. These will be received separately either as an annex to the report or in a separate volume for each year.
>
> *b*) Next in order of importance are official statements and the views expressed by responsible Ministers in debates in National Assemblies. Of these, a *précis* can be made, only the more important passages being quoted verbatim.
>
> *c*) Next in importance are public lectures and articles in responsible journals by eminent authorities. A brief *précis* in French of such an article if written in English—*and vice versa*—should be circulated *with the original.*
>
> *d*) Finally, newspaper comments and articles, of which a brief *précis* in the alternative language would suffice.

[70a] *P.M.C., Min.*, XIV, 16–17.

[71] *Ibid.*, II, 6; X, 12; XI, 12.

In discussing this the Marquis Theodoli thought it was of great importance to follow the public opinion of the world and that press extracts should not be merely summarized. M. Catastini, the director of the section, said only selected press extracts would be given but these would be given in full.[72]

It is to be regretted that there was not more debate on this subject. The character of the work of the Commission doubtless depends in no small measure on the character of reading done by its members in the interims between meetings. Close attention to public opinion as manifested by parliamentary and press comment would give one bias. Exclusive attention to the laws and administrative measures of the mandatory and of analogous colonial administrations would give another. Intensive reading of scientific articles on the population, geography, economic resources, anthropology, education, labor, and land policy, etc., of the mandated and similar areas would give a different point of view. And still another would flow from a perusal of juristic analyses of the mandates system and its relation to the League's other activities, to other systems for the regulation of colonial administration, and to international law. Doubtless the opinions of the different members of the Commission vary considerably and their practices even more on both the quantity and quality of written material proper to consume.[73]

In spite of these several sources of information the Commission has often lamented the insufficiency of the data at its disposal. The most serious incidents with which it has had to deal have been the Bondelzwart rebellion in Southwest Africa in 1923 and the Druse and Arab revolt in Syria in 1925. In both cases certain members of the Commission doubted whether the information at hand was sufficient to warrant any judgment at all on the causes of the disturbances and the measures taken by the mandatory to suppress them. Though the Commission eventually refused to accept this position and expressed an opinion it prefaced its report in each case by a severe arraignment of the mandatory for furnishing so little data.[74]

[72] *Ibid.*, VI, 140, 149.

[73] M. Van Rees believes that this auxiliary documentation cannot compare in value with the information furnished officially by the mandatory and so should be used with the "greatest circumspection" (*Les Mandats internationaux*, I, 118–19).

[74] *P.M.C., Min.*, III, 290–91; VIII, 201.

This same difficulty has been met in answering petitions. As has been noted, the first report on one Palestine Arab petition expressed the opinion that the data at hand did not permit of an answer. To remedy this the Commission has discussed the additional procedures of oral hearing of petitioners and visitation of the areas but has not pressed the matter against Council opposition.

As time has gone on the Commission seems to have come more and more to the opinion that the activity of the mandatory could not be judged properly, even with the most complete data on specific acts and incidents. Its activity can only be properly appreciated in the light of the entire situation—not merely from its conformity to the texts of the mandate. A practical interpretation of the texts is itself in question, and this requires a full understanding of the conditions of the territory.

If the law of mandatory administration were developed by precise interpretations, and if the Commission had the power to hear not only the mandatory but also complaints, it might function as a court, but neither of these conditions exists and it does not appear to have been the intention of the system that the Commission should act as a court. If, however, its functions are to be those of an adviser, it must understand the entire situation which the mandatory has to meet in order to appreciate the practicability of realizing certain principles of the mandates with greater or less speed.

This evolution of the Commission's attitude is indicated by a comparison of the first and second questionnaires on the B and C mandates. The first document prepared during the first session was drafted, as the Director of the section explained, on the mandate texts. It had thirteen sections of which the first seven dealt with the special guaranties of the Covenant and the mandates—slavery, labor, arms traffic, trade and manufacture of alcohol and drugs, liberty of conscience, military clauses, and economic equality. The next five sections dealt with general provisions implied by the letter or spirit of these documents—education; public health; land tenure; moral, social, and material welfare; public finance. Only the last section, demographic statistics, covered general information not immediately suggested by the texts. In the discussion of this questionnaire the Commission, and especially the Director of the section, seemed to be preoccupied with the need of conforming the questions, especially when they dealt with such controversial matters as military recruiting and immigration to the texts in order to avoid offending the mandatory powers.[75]

The revised questionnaire completed in the ninth session differs materially in order and emphasis and considerably in content and method. Instead of beginning with the particular and moving to the general guaranties of the Covenant it begins with questions on the legal conceptions and governmental policy of the mandatory. Even questions that deal with the specific guaranties of the Covenant are often subsumed under broader titles, e.g., instead of a title on "Military Clauses" there are two heads, "Police" and "Defense of the Territory." The questions on slavery are subsumed in the title "Social, Moral and Material Condition of the Natives," and those on economic equality under "International Relations." Not only are some of these special heads given less emphasis, but the number of questions under them are in some cases reduced. This is true of the questions on economic equality and armaments. On the other hand, matters of general information about the territory, not touched on in the first questionnaire, such as status of the territory and its native inhabitants, general administration, trade statistics, judicial organization, are given full heads in the revision, and other subjects, such as public finance and taxation, labor, education, public health, land tenure, and population, are greatly expanded.

Furthermore, questions designed to bring out the mandatories— general policy in such matters as native status, centralization of administration, native participation in government, taxation, preservation of native authorities, labor, land, health, and education—are inserted under appropriate heads. One of these, which was discussed at length in the Commission, deals with the relation of economic development and native welfare in the following form:

54. Does the local supply of labor, in quantity, physical powers of resistance and aptitude for industrial and agricultural work conducted on modern lines appear to indicate that it is adequate as far as can be foreseen, for the economic development of the territory?

Or does the Government consider it possible that sooner or later a proper

[75] *Ibid.*, I, 32, 47.

care for the preservation and development of the native races may make it necessary to restrict for a time the establishment of new enterprises or the extension of existing enterprises and to spread over a longer term of years the execution of such large public works as are not of immediate and urgent necessity?

This question called forth a special criticism from the representative of the South African government in the Council on the ground that it "enquired into the future policy" of the mandatory.[76]

The revised questionnaire is considerably longer than the original document comprising 22 heads as against 13, and 118 numbered questions as against 51. As in each case some of the numbers contain actually more than one question, the second document really has some 275 questions as against 61 in the first.

The revised questionnaire is clearly intended to elicit the facts necessary to give an accurate indication of the entire political, administrative, economic, and social situation in the territory, not merely the specific steps taken by the mandatory in respect to the provisions of the mandate. As M. Orts, *rapporteur* of this questionnaire, said, it "constituted a kind of inventory of the position of the territory and its legislation" and was intended to "elicit indications in regard to the general lines of policy."[77] The increase in length gave some concern to members of the Commission, but the *rapporteur* pointed out that great compression had been employed. Each member had submitted questions on the field of his special interest, and the result was, as M. Merlin pointed out, like that achieved in framing the scholastic program in France, "Each professor was quite naturally led to increase the volume of the subjects which he taught and the final result was a swollen program which overburdened the minds of the pupils." This tendency he thought must be warned against but as the questionnaire showed efforts at compression he accepted it, merely suggesting that in the future "something less rigid" might be introduced. M. Merlin also pointed, out as indeed did M. Yanaghita, in regard to the first questionnaire[78] that some of the questions dealt with relatively unchanging conditions, so that an answer in each report would involve useless repetition. To obviate

[76] *Ibid.*, IX, 234; L. of N., Council, Min., sess. XLI, *O.J.*, VII, 1235.

[77] *P.M.C.*, *Min.*, IX, 51.

[78] *Ibid.*, III, 281.

this difficulty the preamble made clear that answers to all questions were not expected in each report. Reference might merely be made to earlier reports.[79]

The title of the new questionnaires caused some discussion for fear that the mandatories might be offended, and eventually it was not called a questionnaire but "a list of questions which the Permanent Mandates Commission desires should be dealt with in the annual reports of the mandatory powers."[80] As has been noted, the Council has refused to recommend this list of questions to the mandatories and several of the latter have expressed their disapproval of its character,[81] but nevertheless it probably indicates the Commission's present conception of the data necessary for its work, and if this is not furnished in the reports, it will be sought from the accredited representatives during the oral hearing.[82] At the eleventh session of the Commission attention was drawn to the fact that many of the mandatories actually had supplied the fuller information indicated by these questions in their reports.[83] Genuine cooperation seems to require that the Commission should be informed of the entire situation in the areas.

[79] *Ibid.*, IX, 51.

[80] *Ibid.*, pp. 51, 128, 231.

[81] See *supra*, nn. 9, 13.

[82] *P.M.C., Min.*, X, 14.

[83] *Ibid.*, XI, 200; see also 166–68, 177.

CHAPTER VII

THE SUPERVISION OF MANDATORY ADMINISTRATION

The ultimate object of the League's action in regard to mandated territories is to improve conditions in those areas. To do this the League organs must know the facts and have in mind some standards by which they may be criticized, using criticism in the broad sense of suggesting improvements as well as pointing out mistakes. Complete knowledge of the circumstances leading up to an incident or of the conditions in the territory cannot yield any constructive suggestions unless they are compared with some principle or standard of conduct or culture. Such standards are not necessarily formulated. They may exist only in the subconscious mind and doubtless usually do in the case of men whose judgments are based on practical experience rather than book learning.

Standards of colonial administration have been formulated to a very limited extent and the principles embodied in the Covenant and mandates are both meager and vague, consequently judgments of the League organs have been to some extent based upon the rather imperfectly defined standards in the minds of the members of the Council and especially of the Commission. The value of these judgments thus depends in no small degree upon the ability and experience of these men. As standards become more formulated the personal equation will become less dominant. The League's supervision will become a supervision of law rather than of men, but for the time being its value depends to a large extent upon the wisdom of the Commission's members.

1. Methods of Supervision

Supervision is difficult to distinguish from control[1]—the difference in fact is only one of degree, depending on the manner in which

[1] The English word "control," implying power to effect results, to govern, differs greatly in meaning from the French word *contrôle*, which implies only power to acquire

influence is exerted. In making this distinction, Lord Balfour seemed to assume that it rested on the fact that the League had no responsibility for the administration in the territories.[2] But the mandatories, it must be remembered, act "in behalf of the League," and the world has held the League in a measure responsible for conditions in the areas. The A mandates, in fact, specifically impose some responsibility upon the League for financial obligations of the territory in case the mandate terminates and the League organs have been inclined to accept responsibility and to exercise sufficient authority to meet it.[3]

Nor has M. Hanotaux's assertion that the League's functions are limited to criticism of "action taken" by the mandatory been accepted in practice.[4] The Commission has in fact emphasized its function of advice and co-operation beyond that of censure and supervision.[5]

Equally inapplicable in practice has been the distinction made by Sir Austen Chamberlain and the British memorandum of 1926 between a consideration of results and of details of administration.[6] Such a distinction has often been recognized as applicable to the relation of a business directorate or a parliament to the actual administration. "The business of parliament," writes E. H. Davenport, "remains to control policy, its business with administration to judge and approve after the event."[7] But while a business directo-

information, to verify, although the two are used as equivalent in the official texts of art. 22, par. 8 of the Covenant. The French word is thus nearly equivalent to supervision with which the English word may be contrasted—a fact which is likely to lead to confusion in discussions carried on in the two languages. Balfour, for instance, said in the Council in May, 1922, that the League "supervised" but did not "control" the mandatories, although in a report adopted by the Council in August, 1920, M. Hymans had defined the League's *droit de contrôle* of the mandatories, a phrase translated in the English text as "right of control" (L. of N., Council, Min., sess. XVIII, *O.J.*, III, 547; Responsibilities of the League under Article 22, p. 17, *O.J.*, I, 339; Mavromatis Palestine concession case, *P.C.I.J.* [Ser. A], No. 2, pp. 18–20, 69).

[2] See *supra*, n. 1.

[3] See *infra*, chap. xiv, sec. 2.

[4] See *infra*, chap. v, n. 58.

[5] See *P.M.C.*, *Min.*, VIII, 200.

[6] See *supra*, chap. v, n. 62.

[7] *Parliament and the Tax Payer* (1918), p. 24, quoted in White, *Public Administration* (1926), p. 25.

rate or the Parliament of England may judge of the activity of the administration by results and bring about improvement through the simple expedient of substituting a more capable executive, this course is not open to the League in relation to mandatories. In the complex conditions of colonial administration the responsibility for results from year to year cannot be allocated with precision. The great difficulty of placing responsibility for specific incidents was disclosed by the investigations of the Bondelzwart and Druse insurrections in Southwest Africa and Syria. Much more difficult would be the attribution of responsibility for the general conditions of the area. Nor has the League power to transfer mandates on the basis of inefficiency. If it has that power at all it is only after definite proof of persistent violation of the mandate. If the power exists at all it resembles a judgment rather than an act of administrative discretion. Thus the League has been obliged to meet its responsibility by suggestions of reform in detail and this, as the British memorandum admitted, requires examination of the administration in detail.

The distinction between the League's function of supervision and the mandatory's function of administration can only be defined by a scrutiny of the means of influence available to the former.

In a broad way the methods of government action may be defined as "legalistic" and "administrative."[8] The first lays down general rules and enforces them ordinarily through the legislature and the courts. The second declares general policies and carries them out ordinarily through the executive and the administration. Clearly, the League's relation to the mandatories cannot be defined as exclusively in either of these categories. The League gives validity to general rules by confirming and interpreting the mandates and judges the acts of the mandatories according to their conformity with these rules, possibly in extreme cases sanctioning its judgment by transferring a mandate, but at the same time it gives general advice on policy and criticizes the activity of the mandatory according to its results. The first type of activity is mainly performed through the Council and the Permanent Court of International Justice; the second through the Council and the Permanent Mandates Commission,

[8] See Roscoe Pound, "Inherent and Acquired Difficulties in the Administration of Punitive Justice," *Proc., A.P.S.A.*, IV (1907), 222–39.

but the line of division is not strict. The Council and Commission each perform functions of both a judicial and administrative character.

This, in fact, is true of all government agencies. All over the world we find legislatures and courts performing functions of an administrative character while at the same time executives and administrative officers make decisions of a legislative or judicial character. To define the functions of the League in terms of ordinary governmental action a more detailed analysis is necessary.

Legislatures act (1) by enacting statutes which may lay dowr broad policies, standards, and principles, or, on the other hand, may minutely prescribe details of administrative organization, compe tence, and procedure; (2) by criticizing administrative action throug' investigating committees, parliamentary debate, and, in parliamentary governments, by question or interpellation; (3) by control of personnel through dismissal of the cabinet because of want of confidence or through detailed control by confirmation of appointments or impeachment; and (4) by the control of appropriations either by broad heads or by minute specification. The League does not appropriate for mandatory administration, and can neither appoint nor dismiss the administrative personnel. Nor can it dismiss the mandatory merely from lack of confidence. Though it possibly might take such action on legal grounds, the practical influence of this control is even slighter than is that of impeachment in most modern governments. On the other hand, the Council and especially the Assembly do debate acts of the mandatory and the Commission examines reports and questions accredited representatives of the mandatory. The Council also confirms the original mandates and passes interpretive resolutions which approach the character of legislation. Whether they would be regarded as legally binding interpretations of the mandates by the Permanent Court of International Justice has not been determined.[9] Undoubtedly the principle, recognized by administrative experts, that legislative rules should not unduly limit the discretion of the administration[10] should be and has been ob-

[9] Such resolutions have usually been examined and approved by the mandatories before acceptance by the Council. See *infra*, chap. xiii, n. 3.

[10] White, *op. cit.*, pp. 25–26.

served by the Council. The League's influence on the mandatory thus has some characteristics suggestive of legislative control of administration but is much less far reaching.

Courts act (1) by nullifying illegal acts of the administration through power of review or injunction, (2) by requiring performance of legal duties through mandamus or other process, (3) by holding the administration financially responsible for illegal acts, (4) by holding officials criminally or financially responsible for illegal acts, (5) by performing administrative functions themselves. In all but the last of these methods courts have no initiative. They can act only incidentally to the settlement of controversies initiated by individuals, by government agents, or by the state itself. The League clearly has no functions of the fourth or fifth class in relation to mandates. It does not act directly on officials in the mandated areas, though the Commission may reach conclusions on the responsibility of such officials as it did in the Syrian investigation of 1926. Nor can the League or any of its organs perform administrative functions in the areas. It would seem that the Permanent Court of International Justice might employ any of the first three methods in litigations before it arising out of the interpretation or application of a mandate. Examples may be cited from its jurisprudence of each of these types of action.[11] The organs of the League itself have been anxious to avoid an appearance of judicial control of the mandatories. The Council and Commission have both insisted that the procedure on petitions is not to be considered a case between the petitioner and the mandatory but a means of acquiring information. This attitude is emphasized by the Council's refusal to allow the oral hearing of petitioners by the Commission. Nevertheless, the appearance of a litigation cannot be wholly avoided, and for this reason the Commission has feared that its impartiality might be jeopardized if it refused to give the petitioners the same privileges of presenting evidence as the mandatory.[12] The Commission's reports on petitions do

[11] Thus in the Polish German case over the Chorzow factory and other German interests in Upper Silesia the Court gave a declaratory judgment holding certain Polish laws contrary to German treaty rights, and indicated a willingness to define the attitude toward these properties which Poland ought to take and to assess damages against Poland for injuries resulting from contrary action (*P.C.I.J.* [Ser. A], Nos. 7, 9). Damages actually were assessed against Germany in the Wimbledon case (*ibid.*, No. 1).

[12] See *supra*, chap. vi, sec. 3.

not have the authoritative character of judgments, though if indorsed by the Council they approach that character.[13]

A recent study of public administration enumerates nine methods by which central administrative authorities influence or control local administrations: (1) advice and information, (2) requirement of reports, (3) inspection without specific power of control, (4) inspection with conditional grant of money, (5) audit of accounts, (6) requirement of prior permission, (7) authoritative review, (8) issuance of orders with power to compel performance, (9) partial or total assumption of activity.[14] Of these methods the League has on occasion utilized all but the fourth, eighth, and ninth in relation to mandates, and there appears to be nothing in its constitution to prevent use of the fourth method. The Covenant imposes no limitation upon the purposes for which the Assembly may appropriate money, and conditional grants in aid might be made for use by mandatories in their areas. The League's ordinary activity in relation to mandates clearly has a closer resemblance to administrative than to either legislative or judicial methods.

These nine methods indicate a progression from advice (1) and supervision (2, 3, 4) to control (5, 6, 7) and direct administration (8, 9). Advice is the method on which the League has most relied. Processes that savor of criticism or compulsion have been so far as possible avoided. A spirit of co-operation has been sought and to a considerable extent achieved. The wisdom of this attitude is in fact indorsed by experience in ordinary public administration when international susceptibilities are not involved. White writes:

> More and more clearly it is becoming evident that administration must proceed on the basis of consent. . . . . The achievement of administrative discretion has opened the door wide to the opportunity for conference with interested groups in order to enable the official to proceed where possible with a prior understanding and agreement. For assent is fundamentally a matter of conference, discussion, adjustment, all leading toward the establishment of confidence through understanding. . . . . The importance of conference in matters of administration has been greatly stressed in the last two decades.[15]

Advice is more likely to be useful if anticipatory than if merely remedial. "Advisory boards," continues White, "must be discouraged

[13] Sir Frederick Lugard of the Commission assumed that "council decisions had the same force as the mandate itself" (*P.M.C., Min.*, VII, 58).

[14] White, *op. cit.*, pp. 85–87.

[15] *Ibid.*, p. 187.

from attempting to govern; on the other hand, they must be encouraged to take an initiative in developing plans." They may, thinks Laski, "use the rule making power to build up over and above certain minima established by law, higher standards which the social opinion of a given group will approve."[16]

2. The Form of the League's Comments

To this conception the Mandates Commission has in large measure conformed. "We shall endeavor," reads the first report of the Commission, "to exercise our authority less as a judge from whom critical pronouncements are expected, than as collaborators who are resolved to devote their experience and their energies to a joint endeavor."[17] The Commission, however, has discovered that its desire to co-operate and its duty to supervise may present a dilemma. This was true of the Syrian investigation during the eighth session, and the following conclusions were reported and approved by the Council:

The task of the commission is one of supervision and of co-operation. It is its duty, when carefully examining the reports of the mandatory Powers, to determine how far the principles of the Covenant and of the mandates have been truly applied in the administration of the different territories. But at the same time it is its duty to do the utmost that lies in its power to assist the mandatory Governments in carrying out the important and difficult tasks which they are accomplishing on behalf of the League of Nations, and on which they render reports to the Council.

Supervision and co-operation are functions which, though neither incompatible nor in conflict with one another, may yet be accompanied with genuine difficulties when they have to be carried out simultaneously. If the task of the Mandates Commission were merely to supervise the administration of the mandated territories, it would be natural that, in all difficult cases, it should propose to visit these territories itself, or should recommend the holding of inquiries on the spot. If, on the other hand, the rôle of the Mandates Commission were merely to facilitate the task of the mandatory Power, it should offer it lavish encouragement and abstain from passing any critical judgments which, if conveyed to the population under mandate, might create embarrassment and render the task of the Government more difficult of execution.

The procedure followed by the Commission and the character of the observations which it has the honor to submit to the council have been dictated by

[16] *Ibid.*, p. 189, citing H. J. Laski, *Grammar of Politics* (1925), pp. 376–87.

[17] *L. of N., Council, Min.*, sess. XIV, p. 178; see also *P.M.C., Min.*, III, 183.

its desire to carry out, so far as the circumstances enable it do to so, this double mission of supervision and co-operation. As it is anxious not to make the task of France in Syria and the Lebanon impossible of performance, it does not in the present instance recommend the Council to set up a commission of enquiry independent of the mandatory Power. Nevertheless, recognizing its duty of supervision, it has not felt able to abstain from expressing certain criticisms.[18]

In supervising the mandates the Commission has felt obliged to limit its criticism by law. It does not censure the mandatory unless the latter's orders or their application are in definite conflict with the mandate or other authoritative text, but if such a conflict is reported by the Commission and the report is adopted by the Council the mandatory is bound to recognize it. It becomes an authoritative interpretation of the latter's obligations unless, indeed, overruled by a subsequent determination of the Permanent Court of International Justice.[19]

In co-operating with the mandatories, however, though the League's powers are more limited, the scope of its suggestions is infinitely wider. It has not considered itself limited by authoritative documents but has formulated standards of good administration from the widest sources, and suggested whatever practical steps it deems expedient to give them effect. Such suggestions, however, even when indorsed by the Council, never have more than the character of advice. The mandatory is free to differ from them, though if based on an adequate understanding of the situation he will do well to consider them.

In practice the Commission has displayed caution in making comments not based on legal texts. While it has received reports from its members and discussed many general questions of policy, it has but rarely attempted to formulate general principles and almost never made recommendations with respect to particular incidents on matters that do not involve a suspected breach of mandate.

The Commission has been particularly cautious in criticizing acts of the mandatory which are ostensibly for the maintenance of order.[20]

[18] *P.M.C., Min.*, VIII, 200, and discussion, *ibid.*, pp. 47–52. See also opinion of Secretary-General, *L. of N., Council, Min.*, sess. XI, pp. 5–6, and *supra*, chap. v, n. 33.

[19] See *supra*, nn. 9, 13, and Van Rees, *P.M.C., Min.*, VIII, 48.

[20] See interpretation of religious-liberty provisions as subordinate to maintenance of order (*ibid.*, III, 311) and cautious attitude toward suggestion that mandatories be required immediately to report a state of siege to the League (*ibid.*, XII, 152–54).

It has been ready to criticize well-authenticated acts or policy of the administrator which contributed to unrest or insurrection, as it did in the Bondelzwart and Syrian cases, but acts committed in the suppression of such incidents are usually considered within the discretion of the official on the spot. The opinion expressed by Major Herbst in defending the conduct of the South African administrator during the Bondelzwart incident has apparently been indorsed:

> In ordinary circumstances, the opinion of an administrator, where a matter of discretion is involved, is almost always regarded as final. He is the only person who is capable of judging a situation as it is presented at the particular moment. He is entirely responsible for his actions, and it is only afterwards, when his action is criticized by another body, that he is required to give an account of the happenings of the particular moment, and to justify his action. I may say that in the whole of my experience—and I have thirty years' experience of administration in South Africa—I do not think that there are many—certainly not more than two or three—cases where a commission of any body of men has laterally condemned an official on the question of exercise of discretion, and then only on the clearest and most undoubted evidence that he has been guilty of bad judgment in the exercise of his discretion.[21]

In this case the Commission thought the administrator acted wisely after hostilities with the Bondelzwarts were inevitable "in taking prompt and effective steps to uphold government authority and to prevent the spread of disaffection," though because of the absence of native evidence no opinion could be expressed "whether these operations were conducted with needless severity."[22]

Again, after considering many petitions and three French investigations on measures employed in suppressing the Syrian insurrection of 1925–26, the Commission "concluded that there is no reason to affirm" that it was carried out "in an abnormal manner or was accompanied by reprehensible excesses."[23] Before examining the French report of investigations the Commission noted that the mandatory's duty to preserve order might oblige it to adopt measures which are "particularly painful when they are taken by a guardian against his ward" and that "such measures are only defensible in so far as they

[21] *Ibid.*, III, 184.

[22] *Ibid.*, p. 294. For Council comment see *infra*, n. 54.

[23] *Ibid.*, IX, 186.

are necessary for the restoration of peace and do not create unnecessary suffering or arouse justifiable resentment." Later, in answering a petition the Commission "concluded that the mandatory authorities should have recourse to such extreme measures as air bombardment, burning, destruction of villages, and collective fines only in case of absolute necessity and then only under the direct supervision of French officers." It noted with pleasure the accredited representative's statement that so far as he was aware the French military authorities were guided by these views.[24]

A similar view was taken by the Commission in answering a petition alleging cruelty by the mandatory in transporting certain members of the Adjigo tribe in French Togoland. It noted that "the government is responsible for public order and except for serious reasons, which do not arise in this case, we are not called upon to discuss the propriety of such measures as it thinks fit to take to ensure the maintenance of order."[25]

In view of the wide publicity and popular criticism which has and will continue to be accorded severe repressive measures such as the aerial bombardment of Bondelzwart villages and the bombardment and burning of Syrian cities and villages, it would seem worth while to develop standards defining the limits of coercive measures which are justifiable even in situations of necessity. In cases where actual insurrection exists, it would seem that the law of war furnished just such a body of standards, but the Commission does not seem to have attempted to judge the activity of the French military in Syria on this basis.[26]

Even where the Commission does intend criticism it is likely to preserve the form of co-operation. It requests information or explanations but seldom gives formal judgments or definite recommendations.[27] Only where evidence of abuse is unquestionable are the latter forms employed, and on these as on all occasions the accredited representative and his government are given full opportunity not only to be heard by the Commission but to append com-

[24] *Ibid.*, VIII, 206; X, 190. [25] *Ibid.*, IX, 230.

[26] Wright, "The Bombardment of Damascus," *A.J.I.L.*, XX (April, 1926), 263–80.

[27] See *supra*, chap. v, n. 50.

ments to the report before it reaches the Council. The latter privilege has frequently been utilized.

The comments of the Commission directed to particular mandatories have nearly always been formally approved and communicated to the mandatories by the Council, though in some cases the conclusions of the Commission have been somewhat softened as was the case in the Bondelzwart report.[28] These comments are brief and definite, usually referring to a particular paragraph of the mandatory's report, to a statement of the accredited representative, to a provision of legislation, or to the allegation of a petitioner. In view of their brevity the report always states that reference to the minutes of Commission meetings, which accompany the report, is necessary fully to understand them. Whether arising from consideration of reports, hearings, petitions, or other material these comments fall into four classes: (*a*) commendations, (*b*) requests, (*c*) criticisms, and (*d*) recommendations.

a) Approval or commendation of the mandatory's policy is sometimes expressed both generally or in regard to particular acts. The statement of the High Commissioner, says the first report on Iraq in 1926, "could not but make a favorable impression on the commission."[29] Words of general commendation are often introduced before or after a specific criticism. "If the present events," reads the eighth report, "appear to be attributable in a certain measure to the representatives of the mandatory power in Syria, it would be unjust not to refer, in noting this point, to the sacrifices made by France on behalf of the country."[30] Occasionally experiments attempted by one mandatory are favorably commented on in order to draw the attention of other mandatories. Thus the Australian action in attaching an anthropologist to the staff in New Guinea and of sub-

[28] In his report which dealt with this incident M. Branting, the *rapporteur*, said he believed "it would be wise to carry out [the commissions] recommendations whenever political considerations, with which necessarily our advisory committee is not concerned do not render such a course impossible" (L. of N., Council, December 11, 1923, Min., sess. XXVII, *O.J.*, IV, 380; *supra*, chap. v, n. 6). In this case, however, the Commission, because of insufficiency of the evidence, was unable to make a unanimous report, consequently the Council could hardly recommend on details (see *supra*, n. 54; see also Freda White, *Mandates*, p. 31).

[29] *P.M.C.*, *Min.*, X, 183.

[30] *Ibid.*, VIII, 208.

stituting "job contracts" in the Manus district for indentured labor is commended.[31] Sometimes the practice of one mandatory is specifically suggested to another. The comment on the Nauru report of 1924 invites the mandatory's attention to the substitution in Western Samoa of civil for criminal action in breach-of-labor-contract cases.[32]

b) The effort at compression, however, usually reduces words of praise to the minimum demanded by courtesy or the advertising of promising experiments. Much more frequent are requests for further information on or explanation of legislation, statistics, incidents, or the mandatory's opinion or policy. Three-fourths of the comments are in this form, and they often imply a criticism, either of the report for failing to include essential material or of the administration for suspected lapses from the requirements of the mandate. The Commission has tried to get the mandatories to indicate the general objectives of their policy but more commonly information is asked on specific points. "The commission," says the report of the tenth session on Samoa, "would appreciate further information with regard to Clause 47 of the Native Regulations [Samoa] Order of 1925, and concerning the compulsory labor imposed by the District Councils in connection with sanitation and the upkeep of communications."[33] In the ninth report we read in reference to Tanganyika: "The commission would appreciate an explanation concerning the difference in the rates applicable to letters and certain other postal matter destined for 'British possessions' and 'foreign countries.'"[34]

c) Less frequently the Commission formally criticizes the decisions, policy, or acts of the mandatory as inconsistent with the letter or spirit of the mandate. Such a criticism, of course, implies a recommendation to reform. Failure to address the report properly or to submit it at the required time has been the most common subject of such criticism. The impropriety of terms used in legislation, decrees, or treaties has sometimes been noted. "The commission," reads the tenth report in reference to the South African Portuguese boundary treaty, "doubts whether such an expression as 'possesses sovereignty'

[31] *Ibid.*, V, 193; VI, 197. The Australian effort to provide anthropological experts is explained further (*ibid.*, IX, 22 ff.).

[32] *Ibid.*, V, 193.

[33] *Ibid.*, X, 188.

[34] *Ibid.*, IX, 219.

used in the preamble to the above mentioned agreement, even when limited by such a phrase as that used in the above quoted passage can be held to define correctly, having regard to the terms of the covenant, the relation existing between the mandatory power and the territory placed under its mandate."[35] The Commission criticized the administrators for negligence or bad judgment in allowing conditions which led to the Bondelzwart and Syrian rebellion. In each case it discussed in considerable detail the governors' and administrators' conduct involved. In the Bondelzwart case it brought out the inadequacy of the mandatory's remedial measures after the incident by quoting a page of the colloquy between members of the Commission and the mandatory's accredited representative. During the Council's discussion of this report the Chairman of the Commission replied to the complaint of "unjustifiable censure" by the South African representative that because of the method, if there was censure, it was administered by the accredited representative himself.[36] As has been noticed, the Commission often sugar-coats criticism by associating it with general commendation or proferring it in the form of requests. Its extreme reluctance to criticize measures for the preservation of order has also been alluded to.[37]

d) Rarely a definite recommendation for change of law, policy, or administrative method is made. Such a recommendation if directed to a particular mandatory of course implies criticism and may arouse susceptibilities. Thus the matter is often converted into a general question, and when the recommendation finally emerges it applies to all mandatories in form, and those whom the cap fits are trusted to act accordingly. Sometimes this trust is in vain. After the Council with consent of all the mandatories had approved a resolution defining the mandatories' tenure of former German public property in the areas, the Commission reiterated what it had said in two earlier sessions "as to the desirability of bringing the text of the Southwest African River and Harbors act, 1922, into conformity with the interpretation given by the mandatory power."[38] At the

[35] *Ibid.*, X, 182.

[36] *Ibid.*, VIII, 205–8; III, 294; L. of N., Council, December 11, 1923, Min., sess. XXVII, *O.J.*, IV, 340.

[37] See *supra*, nn. 21–26, 27, 30.

[38] *P.M.C.*, *Min.*, IX, 320.

fifth session the Commission recommended a definite method for reporting the finances of British Togoland and Cameroons so as to disentangle them from the finances of the adjoining colonies with which they were administered.

In putting forward this suggestion the commission is fully aware that its fulfilment would increase the labor of bookkeeping for the administration concerned and that the statistics obtained would necessarily be of an approximate character. At the same time, it is compelled to recommend the adoption of this method, for otherwise it would be driven to the conclusion that the policy adopted by the mandatory power would render inadequate the supervision entrusted to the commission.[39]

3. The Substance of the League's Comments

Do the Commission's comments indicate persistent differences in attitude toward the system by the various mandatory powers? Apparently not. Great Britain and her dominions have nine of the fourteen mandates, but the character and amount of comment upon their reports have varied greatly; as much in fact as that upon the reports of the three French, the Belgium, and the Japanese mandates. The French and Belgium reports have perhaps conformed most to the Commission's liking in form, promptness, and completeness, especially in respect to legislative texts. South Africa has probably received the most criticism for her administration in Southwest Africa while Great Britain for Iraq and New Zealand for Samoa prior to 1927 perhaps received the least criticism and the most praise. These differences, however, may reflect the varying conditions of the areas more than the varying abilities of the mandatories. Let us now consider the general character of the comments on the A, B, and C territories.

Consideration of the first report on Iraq after confirmation of the mandate was postponed in the fall of 1925 on account of the pendency of the Mosul dispute before the Council and was not taken up until the tenth session in the fall of 1926. The high commissioner, Sir Henry Dobbs, then appeared as accredited representative and gained commendation for his policy of "Iraq governed for Iraqi and by Iraqi helped by small numbers of British advisers and inspectors."[40] The Commission found nothing to criticize though it ex-

[39] *Ibid.*, V, 190. [40] *Ibid.*, X, 50, 183.

pressed an especial interest in the provisions for assuring minority rights to the Kurds which had been recommended by the Mosul commission, the method of settling tribal disputes, the determination of Iraq's share of the Ottoman debt, the delimitation of her remaining frontiers, and the progress of land-tax reform and education.

At the twelfth session Iraq was again considered by the Commission, and information was requested on the protection of minorities suggested by the League's commission on the Mosul dispute and on economic equality with respect to the customs drawback law of 1926 and various oil concessions. The extension of the Anglo-Persian oil concession to 1996 was approved at the fourteenth session, but on this occasion, examination of a petition from the Bahais indicated a "serious denial of justice" arising from "religious fanaticism" and "a weakening of the mandatory's control." The mandatory was called upon to "redress" the wrong "without delay" and the incident predisposed the Commission against further reduction of the mandatory's control as proposed by the draft Anglo-Iraq treaty of December 14, 1927. At the sixteenth session Great Britain announced the abandonment of the treaty and its intention to recommend the admission of Iraq to the League in 1932.[40a]

Palestine has been considered among the most difficult of the mandates because of the somewhat conflicting principles of self-determination and Zionism to which the mandatory is bound, but Great Britain's effort to compromise has on the whole been commended. Proper restriction of Jewish immigration and a steady effort to develop local autonomy and representative institutions have been urged by the Commission. The commission has also been interested in the progress of the land survey which may open vacant land to Jewish settlement, in the health and educational programs, and in the development of labor legislation. As in all the mandates it continuously urges fuller reporting of government finance. Petitions which have come from the Arab executive, the Zionist executive, the Agudath Israel, the Waad Leumi, and the National party of Tulkarem have kept the Commission alive to the complicated religious and sectarian situation in Palestine, and have caused it to urge great caution upon the mandatory in grouping and recognizing religious

[40a] *Ibid.*, XIV, 247, 264, 270, 276; XVI, 183, 203.

communities. To allow all the religious communities the autonomy demanded by religious liberty and yet to keep them from quarreling and disturbing the peace "will require," says the Commission, "much wisdom, much patience and much willingness to acknowledge mistakes, qualities that are rarer still in a state than in individuals."[41] The gravity of the situation was demonstrated by disputes in regard to the Jewish use of the "Wailing Wall" which resulted in widespread violence in the summer of 1929, the Council's consent to a special commission to settle the matter, and the decision of the Mandates Commission to hold an extraordinary session on the question in March, 1930. The special status of Trans-jordan has frequently been discussed, especially in connection with the Agreement of February 20, 1928, recognizing the independence of the Arab government.[41a]

The reports on Syria at first caused the Commission to "note with satisfaction the success with which the mandatory power has tried to conduct its administration in conformity with the terms of the mandate."[42] It did urge amnesty for political exiles, hoped for rapid promulgation of the law of antiquities, and noted an apparent violation of the open door in customs discrimination against goods from countries adjacent to Germany. It also expressed great interest in labor laws, education, public health, and public finance. Discriminations against Syrian traders and goods in the territory of some League members has induced the suggestion in the Commission that League members accord privileges to the mandated territories and peoples reciprocal to those which their trade and citizens enjoy in those areas.[42a] The insurrection of 1925–26, however, was not in any way anticipated by its comments nor indeed by the mandatory's reports. The blame for this it imputed in part to the vacillating policy of the mandatory in repeatedly changing the constitutional structure and the high commissioner; in part to the incoherence and inexperience of minor officials; in part to grievances arising out of faulty organization of the judicial system, the depreciation of currency, and the

[41] *Ibid.*, IX, 235. The Commission, however, held in response to an Arab petition, that neither the mandate nor the Covenant specifically requires a "democratic and parliamentary government" in Palestine (*ibid.*, XIV, 246).

[41a] *Ibid.*, XIII, 225; XV, 291; XVI, 201.

[42] *Ibid.*, V, 187.

[42a] *Ibid.*, XIV, 236–40.

detailed intervention of mandatory officials in the native administration, but immediately and particularly to the incompetence of General Sarrail and Captain Carbillet in the Jebel Druse. The Commission refrained from criticizing the bombardment of Damascus and other incidents in suppressing the insurrection. The policy declared by the French representative after the insurrection was commended by the Commission, and the natives of Syria were urged to co-operate with France in its execution.[43]

For the six B mandates, two British and two French in West Africa and a British and Belgian in East Africa, the Commission's comments have a family resemblance. The problem of assuring that all the territory's assets go to its benefit has been difficult in view of the customs and administrative union of most of these territories with adjacent colonies. The Commission has insisted that a fair proportion of the combined customs revenue be credited to the mandated territory and a separate account of receipts and expenditures for the area be exhibited even though some of the items are merely estimates from the combined budget. In French Togoland and Cameroons a surplus has accrued giving the Commission some concern, especially when this credit depreciated with the franc to the loss of the mandated area. The customs union of these Central African areas with adjacent colonies has also raised the question of the open door. The Commission has concluded that the required equality of commercial opportunity is not affected if the colony in question offers no preference to the mother-country. The colonies within the free-trade zone of the Congo are precluded by general conventions from offering such preferences, but Nigeria, Dahomey, and the Gold Coast to which British Cameroons, French Togoland, and British Togoland are respectively attached are not in this zone, consequently the Commission has gained assurances that no preferences are given in these colonies. Attention of the mandatories has been called to specific preferences permitted by the laws of Tanganyika, French Cameroons, and Togoland, and these have been rectified.[44] The legislation of Ruanda-Urundi establishing an administrative union with the Congo and that of French Togoland and Cameroons relating to "domain lands" contained terms suggesting that the mandatory

[43] *Ibid.*, VIII, 202 ff.

[44] *Ibid.*, III, 314.

claimed sovereignty over the areas, and the Commission has requested rectification.[45] Reports on British Togoland and Cameroons in dealing with the administrative union suggested a similar interpretation which induced the Commission to comment that administered "as an integral portion of its territory" does not mean "have become integral portions of the neighboring colonies."

> While the commission desires to bring this matter to the notice of the council, it does not exaggerate its importance. As, however, the passage referred to might lead to annexationist aims being attributed quite erroneously to the mandatory powers, it appears to the commission that their own interest, no less than that of the League of Nations, requires that in the future any formula should be avoided which might give rise to doubts on the subject in the minds of ill-informed or ill-intentioned readers.[46]

The military clauses, especially in the French mandates, the proper regulation of missionary activity especially in Tanganyika; the rectification of boundaries so as to preserve the unity of native tribes; the regulation of liquor imports and prevention of smuggling between the areas especially in West Africa; the preservation of native rights and interests in the land; the maintenance of a sufficient force of doctors and nurses in the areas; the protection of native labor against efforts at too rapid development of the economic possibilities of the country and the definition of "forced labor"; the effort to train native teachers and to develop practical and agricultural education rather than "thinking in French" or other European language; the utilization of native advisory or representative institutions but with maintenance of sufficient control by the mandatory to prevent abuses like slavery and cannibalism have all been subjects of comment in relation to most of the B areas. In connection with the last point the Commission asked in its fifth report whether the "very wide margin of freedom allowed to the native chiefs in the north [of British Cameroons] might not possibly result in the toleration of abuses and the perpetuation of practices which it is incumbent upon the mandatory Power, in virtue of its mission of civilization, to suppress or modify," consequently it wished "detailed information re-

[45] *Ibid.*, VII, 21; III, 22, 37, 222–23; Rep., sess. IV, *O.J.*, V, 1407–8.

[46] *P.M.C.*, *Min.*, V, 190. Concern was expressed over the federation, proposed by the Hilton Young report, of Tanganyika with the British East African Colonies. *Ibid.*, XV, 292; XVI, 202.

garding the numbers and duties of the European staff intrusted with the supervision of native administration."[47] A similar question has been raised with regard to Ruanda-Urundi and a proposal to transfer natives from overpopulated regions in that territory to the Congo has been frowned upon by the Commission.[47a]

Among the C mandatories South Africa has contended with the difficult problem of reconciling the interests of a considerable white population, half of it disgruntled ex-German farmers, with those of the natives in the vast dry region of Southwest Africa. The frequent assertion of practical sovereignty of the area in the mandatory's laws and treaties, and in the declarations of statesmen has given the commission grave concern[48] as has the anomalous situation of the Caprivi Zipfel, the finger which projects west to the Zambesi and until 1929 was administered separately from the rest of the area under the governor-general of South Africa. As this official is appointed by Great Britain, is not responsible to the South African Parliament, and is administrator of the Bechuanaland protectorate the arrangement suggested a cession of the area by the mandatory to the latter. However, South Africa assumed responsibility and submitted special reports on the area to the Commission.[49] The Mandatory's policy toward the German inhabitants permitted to remain has been discussed. As an exception South Africa was permitted to naturalize *en bloc* those that did not opt out but the law of 1927 seemed to withdraw the option in some cases. Inconsistencies in official statements at different times as to the treatment of ex-enemy landed-estates have also been noted.[49a]

[47] *Ibid.*, V, 191. [47a] *Ibid.*, XIV, 271.

[48] *Ibid.*, Rep., sess. IV (*O.J.*, V, 1412); Min., VI, 178; IX, 220; XI, 104, 204.

[49] *Ibid.*, VI, 177; VII, 17; XI, 96, 205, and opinion of law adviser of South African government communicated to the League, November 20, 1925, holding that as the union of South Africa had under the mandate full legislative power in the mandated territory it could properly delegate the government of part of that territory to the high commissioner who was also the governor-general of South Africa, and that that official could properly delegate the administration of the area to the resident commissioner of Bechuanaland protectorate though on the doctrine *delegatus non potest delegari* he could not have delegated legislative power (*O.J.*, VII, 375).

[49a] See *infra*, chap. xiii, secs. 2*c*, 3*b*, and *P.M.C.*, *Min.*, XIV, 260, 277; XVI, 141, 203.

The policy of segregating blacks on reserves where it is not certain that the "civilizing influence" of the mandatory will penetrate; the policy of compelling missionaries to be propagandists of loyalty to Union policies and of the native duty to labor; and the apparent assumption by the white population that "natives exist chiefly for the purpose of labor for the whites" have all caused the Commission grave concern.[50] In its third report made after the Bondelzwart incident we read:

> The commission deplores the unfortunate relations which the report discloses between the white population and a large proportion of the natives of the mandated territory. It trusts that the administration will resist the influence of these deplorable relations which are largely the heritage of past events in Southwest Africa and which are so much opposed to the essential principles of Article 22 of the Covenant. It hopes that future reports will be able to disclose better relations between the two races.[51]

The Bondelzwart insurrection of 1922 called forth resolutions from the Assembly, stimulated by the remarks of M. Bellegarde of Haiti, which hoped that the Commission would consider the question and that the mandatory would remedy conditions, while expressing "profound satisfaction" with the South African representative's statement that a full and impartial inquiry into all the facts would be made.[52] The results of this investigation were regarded as inadequate by the Mandates Commission because the South African government did not assume responsibility for any of the conflicting reports which it submitted. Nevertheless, after cross-questioning the accredited representative, a majority of the Commission (five out of eight present) agreed that the trouble was due fundamentally to native grievances arising in part from legislative and administrative action in behalf of the white settlers and immediately to mistakes of the administrator after the situation had become serious. Though not criticizing the severe measures of repression, the majority of the Commission indicated the inadequacy of remedial measures by quoting the replies to questions of the accredited representative. M. d'Andrade, though admitting that the natives had cause for grievance, was less critical of the administration; M. Van Rees thought

[50] *P.M.C.*, *Min.*, III, 292; XI, 95, 97–100.

[51] *Ibid.*, III, 325; Rep., sess. IV, *O.J.*, V, 1412.

[52] *Ibid.*

the evidence was not sufficient to reach any conclusion; and the chairman, Marquis Theodoli, insisted that while the mandatory's first duty should be to the natives, in this case it had "pursued a policy of force rather than of persuasion and further that the policy has always been conceived and applied in the interests of the colonists rather than in the interests of the natives."[53]

In the Council M. Branting thought in view of the division in the Commission the Council "could not express any final opinion on the essence of the dispute" though apparently the ultimate causes lay in the unstable conditions among the native population "subjected for years to a harsh régime" and the lack of comprehension between the two elements of the population. He passed lightly over the "administrative measures which may have contributed to the outbreak of discontent" and followed the Commission in reserving judgment on the measures of repression, though he thought the mandatory should note the Commission's remark on the inexpediency of allowing the administrator himself to lead the troops engaged in this work, thus depriving the natives of appeal to him as an impartial authority, in case of excesses. M. Branting proposed a mild resolution which, however, was criticized by Sir Edgar Walton, representative of South Africa, because it failed to mention the "great efforts to improve the situation of the Bondelzwarts" made by his government and "might appear to contain an unjustifiable censure" of his government "which was anxious to collaborate with the League of Nations in every possible manner." By the resolution, as amended on motion of Lord Robert Cecil, to note the "efforts" of the mandatory, the Council expressed the hope that in its annual reports the mandatory government might be able to record a satisfactory result of its efforts on behalf of the Bondelzwart people and a steady and continuous advancement in civilization and in moral and material well being.[54]

The Rehoboth community of half-breeds in the center of South-

[53] *P.M.C., Min.*, III, 293, 296.

[54] L. of N., Council, Min., sess. XXVII, *O.J.*, IV, 341, 393. In agreeing to the resolution M. Quinones de Leon of Spain "wished to testify to the great zeal and efficiency of the commission, which enjoyed the entire confidence of the council. Nothing should be done to impair or limit its valuable work."

west Africa, like the Druses of Syria, had been granted a high degree of autonomy by the administration soon after the war. They petitioned the League in 1924 when they thought these privileges were being encroached upon, but before the Commission considered the petition they prepared for armed resistance and in the spring of 1925 the administrator sent out a large military force. Profiting by the Bondelzwart experience, active hostilities were delayed and the Rehoboth's finding themselves outnumbered surrendered without bloodshed. The Commission answered the petition by approving the mandatory's policy of negotiating a new agreement after the Rehoboth leaders had regularized their position by an election. Concern was expressed for the Rehoboth prisoners taken, and at the ninth session the Commission noted the accredited representative's promise to furnish the report of an inquiry into their situation. The delay of this report under preparation by Justice de Villiers was noted during the tenth and eleventh sessions, and when it was finally received at the twelfth session action was impossible because the mandatory's attitude toward it and toward a new petition received from the Rehoboths in November, 1926, was not made clear. The Commission indicated considerable irritation at these long delays by the mandatory but was satisfied with the mandatory's detailed statement of policy toward the Rehoboths considered at the fourteenth session.[55]

The usual African mandate problems of land tenure, forced labor, suppression of slavery and liquor traffic, development of education, and public-health service have arisen in Southwest Africa in aggravated form. The Commission has inquired into the reason for the very high mortality of native labor in the diamond mines and for the unrest and desertion among the Xoxas tribe. It has intimated that an insufficient proportion of the revenue received from the natives is spent for their welfare. The Commission has also had difficulty in assuring itself, in view of the union of the customs, railway, and harbor system of the territory with those of South Africa, that a proper proportion of the receipts from these public works and customs were credited to the territory.[56] In its sixth report the Commission com-

[55] *P.M.C., Min.*, VI, 181; IX, 220; X, 86; XI, 217–18; XII, 195; XIV, 243, 277.

[56] See especially P.M.C., Rep., II, 11; Min., II, 325; Rep., sess. IV (*O.J.*, V, 1412); Min., VI, 178; IX, 220; XI, 100 f. and 205.

mented on the proposal to transform the advisory council into a legislative council elected in part by the British subjects (most of the white population since the Germans have been naturalized) in the area. This action, it insisted, could not derogate from the undivided responsibility of the mandatory toward the League.[57] It is quite probable that the resident whites when in authority will be even less considerate of the natives than the Union government. Because of this white minority, and the temperate climate of Southwest Africa which makes possible its increase, the League's problem in protecting the natives in this area is likely to become even more difficult as time goes on.

The four groups of Pacific islands under mandate, which are also in most cases suitable for white or Asiatic population, have given rise to similar but less serious comments. Protection of Chinese contract labor, development of education and public health, especially the control of venereal disease, the control of arms and liquor trade, and the presentation of accurate accounts have frequently been mentioned, but on the whole conditions seem to be fairly good in these respects. New Zealand prohibits the importation of alcoholic beverages to both natives and whites in Samoa, though the mandate requires it only for the former.[58] The utilization of native advisory councils has been carried to the greatest extent in Samoa, and has been commended for consideration of the other mandatories.[59] In New Guinea the Commission has been interested in protecting native labor from the ill-effects of transportation to new climatic conditions, from too long indentures (which are likely to break up the tribal organization), and in a scientific study of native customs.[60] In Nauru the exploitation of phosphates by a syndicate of the three mandatory governments Great Britain, Australia, and New Zealand raised a question of the propriety of the mandatory's exploiting the territory's only resource for its own profit. The mandatory pointed out that the exploitation of this product in Nauru had always been a monopoly first of a German then of a British corporation, and that

[57] *Ibid.*, VI, 177.

[58] *Ibid.*, III, 260.

[59] *Ibid.*, VII, 19–21, 77; X, 26–27.

[60] *Ibid.*, V, 130, 192; VI, 180; IX, 221. Unsatisfactory conditions were commented on in 1929 (XV, 293).

the phosphate commissioners were merely business executives subject to control in labor-recruiting and other matters by the administrator.[61] The open door is not required in the C mandated areas except in so far as it is a necessary means for promoting the interests of the natives. A comment on the Australian exclusion of foreign vessels from the trade with New Guinea, however, brought prompt modification of the law.[62] Inquiries from the Commission as to whether in view of the sparse population and difficulties of white settlement the bars against Asiatic immigration might not be let down in New Guinea brought out a statement that the "white Australia policy" applied to the mandated area and there was no intention of modifying it.[63] The Commission seems to consider the appropriation made by Australia in developing the territory inadequate though it welcomed the annual grant of £10,000 noticed in the sixth session.[64] The large expropriated enemy estates in New Guinea and Samoa raised an issue as to title, control of labor conditions, and the incidence of profit or loss from their exploitation. The Commission has concluded that the mandatory may acquire title to them but is obliged to submit to the same regulation as private enterprises in operating them.[65]

Up to the twelfth session, when serious disturbances in Samoa were discussed, there was less comment about Samoa and the Japanese islands than about any other mandates. In the former the special interest has been the progress of the native institutions, the effort to change from communal to private land tenure, the policy of substituting free for contract Chinese labor and reducing the amount,[66] but members of the Commission have occasionally found it necessary to comment on the inaccurate view of the League's position in the mandates system given with sanction of the mandatory authorities to the natives. After examining a Royal Commission report and a number of petitions and after quizzing the administrator of Western Samoa, the Mandates Commission exonerated the mandatory from all charges made against it in connection with the native

[61] *Ibid.*, Rep., II, 5.

[62] *Ibid.*, VI, 87, 180; VII, 8.

[63] *Ibid.*, VI, 86.

[64] *Ibid.*, pp. 86, 180.

[65] *Ibid.*, III, 321, 324; Rep., sess. IV (*O.J.*, V, 1412) and *infra*, chap. xiii, sec. 2*c*.

[66] *Ibid.*, X, 188; XIII, 23, 133.

disturbances of 1926–27. While holding that Nelson and other half-blood local leaders by "propagandizing an impressionable people" for selfish objects were primarily responsible, it suggested "insufficient psychological insight" by the administrator and provision by the mandatory of inadequate means to enable him to enforce the law as contributory conditions.[66a]

In the Japanese reports the Commission has had difficulty in getting sufficiently detailed financial accounts, and has taken especial interest in the number and condition of Japanese immigrants, in the condition of labor in the newly developed sugar-cane industry, and in the status of the South Seas Bureau. The latter appears to be a branch of the mandatory government. In its report for 1924 Japan stated that revenue and expenditure of this bureau for public works was treated as revenue and expenditure of the Japanese government, not as mandatory. The Commission promptly commented that this was contrary to the opinion of Japan and other mandatories of a mandatory's power.[67]

From a perusal of the Commission's comments it appears that its efforts are mainly directed at four objects.

a) In the first place, it has been anxious to maintain the League's authority. It has insisted that reports be sent promptly and in proper form, that its questions be answered definitely, and that the mandatories keep steadily aware that they are not sovereigns of the areas but only mandatories. Any law or treaty employing terms which seem to imply sovereignty is promptly pounced upon by the Commission. The mandatory is not to be allowed to develop prescriptive title through acquiescence by the League in claims of sovereignty.

b) In the second place, and as a direct corollary to the lack of sovereignty and acceptance of trusteeship, the Commission has been insistent that the mandatory make no direct profit from the territory. The budget of the territory must be kept separate and all revenues from taxes, customs, public works, or services used for its betterment. Domain lands are held by the mandatory only in that capacity, profits from them belong to the territory, and if the mandate terminates, the present mandatory retains no claim to such lands. Lands or other property owned and exploited by the mandatory as a

[66a] *Ibid.*, XIII, 229–30; XVI, 207.

[67] *Ibid.*, V, 195.

business venture must enjoy no special privileges, can impose no burden on the territory in case of loss, and their accounts must be kept in a separate budget. In A and B mandated territories economic privileges must not be given to the mandatory's nationals and the door must be kept open to the trade of all members of the League. Even in C territories economic discriminations are scrutinized to see that they are not against the interests of the inhabitants of the area. The areas must be demilitarized and the natives may not be recruited for the mandatory's military service even voluntarily and outside the area. Thus every effort is made to eliminate all financial, economic, or military profit so far as required by the mandates.

c) The Commission has regarded the natives as its special charge and has in fact displayed more solicitude for them than for the European settlers which form an important element of the population only in Southwest Africa and Palestine. In the latter mandate Jewish immigrants are given special privileges which the Commission has recognized while noting its conflict with the basic principle of article 22 of the Covenant. It has censored unsympathetic treatment of natives leading to insurrection and has scrutinized the methods of suppression employed but with due consideration for the claims of order. It has taken great interest in the land, labor, health, and educational policies of the mandatory and has leaned toward indirect administration with preservation of native organizations and customs where not abhorrent to civilization and provided the mandatory does not neglect its "civilizing mission." The specific provisions of B and C mandates with regard to arms, liquor and slave trade, slavery and forced labor, religious freedom, respect for native rights to land, and military recruiting it has defined and interpreted in a spirit favorable to native interests.

d) Finally, the Commission has been mindful of the mandatory's duty to develop the economic potentialities of the territory, though most of the members believe this must be subordinated to respect for native welfare. It has approved measures necessary to preserve order even though harsh and regulative of religious liberty, and has sought to avoid action which would injure the mandatory's prestige in the area. It has sought to give assurance to financial interests by declaring that obligations on or investments in the territory will remain valid in case the mandate terminates or is transferred.

4. The Effectiveness of the League's Comments

What assurance has the League that its recommendations will not be ignored? Is there a sanction to the system?

The mandates system, like all international law, rests on intelligent co-operation and good faith rather than on coercion. It may be that the League has an eventual sanction by its power to transfer a mandate. This will be discussed later.[68] But whether it does or not, the power could hardly be exercised in times of peace without the mandatory's consent.

Publicity is a valuable sanction. World public opinion, whether manifested through learned writing, through newspaper comment, or through assembly debates, is kept informed through the regular publication of the reports and minutes of the Commission, through the distribution by the League of mandatory reports, through the publication of important petitions and the replies given on them, through the publication of Council and Assembly proceedings, and through the admission of the press and public to Assembly sessions and some sessions of the Council and of the Commission. The development and statement in more succinct form of approved principles and standards and the publication of a journal devoted to mandatory matters have been discussed in the Commission as additional means of publicity.[69] The question of publicity in Commission meetings has been discussed, but the opinion has prevailed that the examination of the accredited representative must be in private to preserve freedom of discussion.[70]

Nations do not like to endure the contempt or disgust of the world, and the certainty that any malfeasance in the mandated areas will be widely known is a deterrent which will become steadily more important as world-opinion becomes more organized through the League.[71]

[68] See *infra*, chap. xiv, sec. 3*b*.

[69] *P.M.C., Min.*, V, 8, 118, 150–52, 175.

[70] See *supra*, chap. v, sec. 4.

[71] "A colonial office debate in the British House of Commons seldom gets into a foreign newspaper, but when the mandates commission speaks, it speaks with a united voice upon a single issue, and from a forum which may extend not only to England but around the world. This 'functional' type of control promises to be much more effective in enforcing the obligations of trusteeship than parliamentary control" (Buell, *The Native Problem in Africa*, I, 540). See also Hocking, *Yale Review*, XIX, 258.

Apart from publicity, however, good faith is not wholly wanting in nations. Statesmen do not like to break the recognized principles of international law or solemnly pledged agreements of their nation, especially those made with other civilized nations. It is not good form. The mandatories have solemnly agreed to the obligations of the Covenant and the mandates. Furthermore, the Council takes pains to get their consent to important interpretations before passing a resolution on them. The mandatories are permitted to participate in Council discussions of their mandates, and most of them, being members of that body, can vote. Thus the mandatories are seldom asked to do more than carry out their own specific agreements. Furthermore, the application of these agreements to specific circumstances is made clear. Obligations are defined in written documents, subject to the interpretation of the Permanent Court of International Justice. Recommendations are not binding until formally approved by the Council. Thus the mandatory knows precisely what is expected of him and to make assurance doubly sure has been asked to reply specifically in writing to comments bearing on his mandate so that misunderstandings may be promptly corrected.[72]

But even more than good faith is intelligence a sanction. The system hopes to rest on reason rather than conscience. The Commission is designed to be a body whose advice will be intrinsically valuable. The mandatories are given every opportunity to keep in close touch with it and to give as well as to receive advice. If the spirit of co-operation can really obtain, the mandatory may be expected to follow the Commission's advice, not because it is compelled to, or feels it ought to, but because it thinks it is sound administration to do so. If the mandatories really learn something which they consider valuable from the Commission discussions they may be expected to use it.

Accredited representatives have often expressed appreciation of the Commission meetings; but to increase the probability that their results will be put to work, the mandatories have been requested to send administrators from the area to Commission meetings and to distribute all relevant reports, answers to petitions, minutes, and

[72] See L. of N. Council, December, 1925, *Min.*, sess. XXXVII, *O.J.*, VI, p. 383.

other documents to all the responsible officials of the area.[73] Thus it is hoped that good advice will not be barren through neglect. Those who can put it in effect will read it.

These sanctions, publicity, good faith, and intelligence are those which must be mainly relied on in all international co-operation, though as time goes on they are aided by the powerful influence of custom. In the mandates system there is room for improving their efficiency especially by increasing the sources of information available to the Commission and by the scientific development of standards of administration applicable to mandated areas, so that the Commission's advice will be even wiser than it has been. To date the League's recommendations seem to have been fairly well observed, and with the habituation of the mandatories and their officials to its procedure and objectives they are not likely to become less so.

[73] *P.M.C, Min.*, V, 186; VI, 173; L. of N. Council, August, 1924, *Min.*, sess. XXX, *O.J.*, V, 1402; September, 1925, sess. XXXV, *O.J.*, VI, 1512.

CHAPTER VIII

THE ESTABLISHMENT OF STANDARDS

Article 22 of the Covenant declares that the mandates system exists to secure "the principle that the well-being and development" of the peoples in the area "not yet able to stand by themselves" form "a sacred trust of civilization," and article 23 requires the members of the League administering mandates to "endeavor to secure and maintain fair and humane conditions of labor for men, women and children" and to "undertake to secure just treatment of native inhabitants" in these areas as well as others under their control. Furthermore, the mandatories as well as other members of the League agree by this article to "entrust the League with general supervision over the execution of agreements" with regard to the traffic in women and children, in opium and narcotic drugs, and in arms and ammunition; "to secure and maintain freedom of communications and transit and equitable treatment for the commerce" of League members; and to "take steps in matters of international concern for the prevention and control of disease."

These broad principles are developed in more detail with respect to certain mandated territories by other provisions in article 22, by the mandates, and by various general conventions such as the Berlin Central African general act of 1885, the Brussels slave-trade general act of 1890, the St. Germain conventions of 1919 revising these and regulating liquor traffic in Africa, the Geneva slavery convention of 1926, and others dealing with labor, white slavery, opium, arms trade, etc. To what extent has the League developed this inchoate material into standards capable of guiding policy and action in the mandated areas?

1. Methods of Establishing Standards

For establishing such standards three distinct procedures have evolved: (*a*) the growth of a jurisprudence from decisions on particular questions, (*b*) the agreement on principles for its own use by the Commission, and (*c*) the passage of formal resolutions by the Council or Assembly.[1] The first is a quasi-judicial, the second a technical, and the third a quasi-legislative process.

a) PRECEDENTS

In the fifth Assembly, Mr. Roden Buxton of the British delegation urged that the Mandates Commission organize its work so as to command greater public attention and to this end suggested that "broad principles be laid down." "We should keep in view," he said, "the idea that the improved principles of administration which are gradually being worked out in the mandated territories should be looked upon as a model for other territories in the future." In discussing this suggestion, however, several members of the Commission expressed the fear that such an effort to codify mandatory principles might prove impracticable in view of the varied conditions in the different territories, and preferred to allow standards and principles gradually to emerge from precedents.[2] The same point was made during discussions in the ninth session.[3] It is thus mainly from a comparison of the pronouncements of the Commission, Council, and Assembly on particular incidents that guiding principles can be discovered.

b) CONCLUSIONS OF THE COMMISSION

The Commission, however, has found it necessary to establish certain standards for its own use in full realization that these are in no sense binding but subject to modification by experience. The attainment of a collective judgment on each incident of mandatory administration by a body of ten men with varied training and expe-

[1] The effect of Assembly resolutions on mandate problems is a matter of doubt. They do not have the lawmaking effect of Council resolutions, and they are usually very general in character, but in fact they are usually observed (see *supra*, chap. v, sec. 2).

[2] *P.M.C., Min.*, V, 8, 151.

[3] "This commission was working on a live question which was changing. It had, therefore, not to take decisions of a general kind, but decisions to meet each particular case. It was not for the commission to establish a general doctrine nor to choose a certain number of principles to be applied indifferently to all cases. In a word, it was not an academy but a commission of control. . . . . It should be careful not to establish a doctrine before dealing with the facts" (M. Merlin, *P.M.C., Min.*, IX, 134, who, however, agreed with M. Van Rees that an exact interpretation of certain provisions of the mandates was essential; the chairman, the Marquis Theodoli, and M. Orts agreed with M. Merlin).

rience would require a great deal of time unless these ten men had agreed in advance, at least tentatively, upon certain standards. This was emphasized by M. Van Rees in a memorandum presented at the seventh session.

The study of such questions by the Mandates Commission, with the object of gradually and methodically establishing for its own use what, in my opinion, would constitute its jurisprudence, seems to me to be not only of great value but really indispensable for its work in general and particularly for its discussions with the accredited representatives of the mandatory powers.

We must not lose sight of the fact that some of the provisions whose application the Commission has to supervise are not, as I have already said, couched in a clear and concise form, and that there is no official commentary to inform us as to their origin. Under these circumstances, it is for the Commission to study them and to interpret them for its own use whenever it meets with an obscure clause, so as to obtain a set of guiding principles which may enable it to appraise the administration of the mandatory powers.

It is possible that these interpretations, when finally adopted, may not be accepted by the Powers in question or by the Council; that is certainly possible, but do not forget that, even in cases in which the Commission might find itself obliged to revise or reject certain of its pronouncements, the work will not have been useless since, as the proverb says, "truth springs from conflicting opinions."[4]

M. Van Rees had earlier expressed concern at the difficulty which would arise in case the Commission disagreed on a question of principle in the presence of an accredited representative.[5] Such disagreements have frequently taken place as, for example, on the question of the propriety of labor levies commutable for taxes which arose in the discussion on French Togoland during the sixth session.[6] It may be questioned whether these disagreements have been wholly a disadvantage. They perhaps tend to preserve a spirit of co-operation with the mandatory as it helps the latter's accredited representative to feel himself a member of a body of experts exploring a problem and trying to find a solution rather than as an advocate defending his government before a united commission.[7] However this may be,

[4] *Ibid.*, VII, 152. [5] *Ibid.*, VI, 138. [6] *Ibid.*, p. 20.

[7] The latter atmosphere has prevailed in the few public meetings, on which occasions the Commission naturally attempts to display unanimity. M. Van Rees suggested that "the three representatives present at the public meeting of August 7, 1922, had the appearance if not of persons who were accused at least of defendants. Such a position appeared unacceptable" (*ibid.*, III, 49). See also remarks of M. Rappard

when such differences arise within the Commission they require a solution and the subject is usually put on the agenda of the next session as a general question. Occasionally the Commission has considered general questions from a theoretical point of view before a practical difference has arisen but has not favored this practice.[8]

Though the stimulus may come from different sources, at almost every session the Commission has discussed certain general topics, usually on the basis of reports prepared by one or more of its members. At the fifth session, under the inspiration of Mr. Roden Buxton's suggestion, consideration was begun of a regular procedure for this work. M. Freire d'Andrade suggested that the Secretariat section regularly extract the principles evolving from the Commission's work. Sir Frederick Lugard thought if the Commission were competent to lay down general principles, one particular subject should be selected in advance for each session and each member should prepare a report on that subject for discussion. If agreement were reached this could be submitted to the Council. The Chairman suggested that a subcommittee of the Commission give preliminary consideration to these reports.[9]

At the sixth session, Sir Frederick Lugard again raised the issue, suggesting that a *rapporteur* be appointed to whom other members should submit their views in advance. The Secretariat should prepare a *dossier* including discussions in the Commission, Council, Assembly, and its committees regarding the selected question. The *rapporteur*'s report would be debated and the final conclusions recorded in the Commission's minutes, or if the matter required action forwarded to the Council. This suggestion was accepted by the Commission though it was pointed out that it merely codified existing practice.[10]

During the ninth session a significant debate took place on the type of question to which this procedure should apply. The Chairman pointed out that

---

on this occasion and of M. Palacios at the twelfth session who recalled that a "well qualified newspaper had written of 'the proconsul at the inquisitor's bar' " (*ibid.*, XII, 62).

[8] See *supra*, n. 3.

[9] *P.M.C.*, *Min.*, V, 149–52.

[10] *Ibid.*, VI, 137–40, 149.

the commission was not a legal body having the duty of giving opinions for the use of the council on questions of interpretation before these questions had even arisen in practice. The Permanent mandates commission was a committee of control, whose duty it was to supervise the application of the provisions of the mandates. If one of those provisions was obscure it was not for the commission to explain it unless a definite point with regard to a special case arose in connection with it. . . . . It was important for the prestige of the commission that it should not engage in endless discussion concerning questions of theory.

M. Van Rees emphasized again the danger to the "prestige" of the Commission if continual disagreement on principle were manifested by the members in the presence of representatives of the mandatory powers. M. Orts agreed with this but thought reports on general matters should be confined to the definition of concrete terms such as "liquor traffic," "trade spirits," "forced labor," etc., and that discussion of such broad phrases as "the well-being and development" of peoples under mandate "form a sacred trust of civilization" be discontinued. He said:

The improvement in the material conditions of existence of the peoples they administered and their moral and intellectual development were the objects which the conscience of the modern world assigned to all colonising Powers. The covenant merely recalled this duty to those powers invested with a mandate to administer a territory in the name of the League of Nations. He did not think that this was a matter for interpretation.

The above proposal comprised a very definite obligation, and it would be a mistake to try to determine rigidly the means which each mandatory power should use in order to fulfil it. The development of primitive peoples could be carried on by different means, and these means would be such as were proper to the native genius, traditions, and the political and philosophical conceptions of each mandatory State. Such means might be all equally good. The mandatory states would fail in their task if a system and method foreign to their mentality were imposed upon them.

The duty of the commission was confined to discovering whether the mandatory powers conformed to the definite obligations imposed upon them by the covenant and by the mandates, and in addition, whether within the limits of these acts, they were honestly performing their task in order to justify the confidence reposed in them.

M. Merlin agreed, emphasizing that "the members of the commission were not lawyers but persons who had lived in colonies and who placed the benefit of their experience at the disposal of the League of

Nations." M. Van Rees then agreed to the distinction made by M. Orts.[11]

c) RESOLUTIONS OF THE LEAGUE

Decisions of a legislative character, binding both the League and the mandatories, have occasionally been made. The Covenant itself establishes certain principles, and in confirming the mandates the Council established others. For the establishment of further principles of general application the League has evolved a process assuring thorough consideration by the League organs and the mandatories.

Recognition that a general question requires authoritative definition may occur in the Assembly, the Council, or the Commission, but in any case the effort to formulate such a definition is first made by the Commission, sometimes on the basis of an Assembly or Council resolution. At the thirty-ninth session of the Council, some objection was made to the inclusion by the Commission of general comments in its report on the Syrian situation, and at the following session the Council agreed that such matters should not be included in answers to petitions. Sir Austen Chamberlain hoped that "when the Permanent Mandates Commission desired to lay before the council any statement concerning the general principles which it followed in carrying out its work and which were applicable, therefore, to the general discharge of that work and not to a particular mandated territory it would consider it convenient and more conducive to a clear discussion of such matters to include those statements in a separate report." Thus the Commission's procedure in regard to general questions has become distinct from that in regard to particular mandates.[12]

An authoritative formulation of doctrine is a long process. It usually involves (1) preparation by the Secretariat of a memorandum resuming all pertinent decisions and discussion by the Commission, Council, or assembly on the subject; (2) informal discussion of the subject by the Commission; (3) preparation of a report with draft recommendation by a *rapporteur* or subcommittee of the Commission; (4) discussion and action upon this resolution by the Commission. This preliminary formulation is then considered by the Council

[11] *Ibid.*, IX, 133–34, and *supra*, n. 3.

[12] L. of N., Council, Min., sess. XXXIX, XL, *O.J.*, VII, 526, 879.

which may approve it but if of importance generally (5) submits it to all the mandatory governments for their consideration. (6) The replies of the mandatories unless they all agree with the recommendation are then submitted to the Commission which (7) reconsiders the matter and makes a new recommendation for (8) final action by the Council. This process is employed quite rarely and may consume several years, but as colonial policy has been little standardized and conditions vary greatly this extreme caution and deliberation is doubtless of advantage.[13]

The evolution of general standards will be perhaps the most important development of the mandates system, but to be of value they must be practical. Principles savoring of doctrinairism would not only be useless, but might do great damage to the mandated areas and even more to the Commission and the League.

d) PROCEDURE, LAW, AND POLICY

The general subjects considered by the League organs fall into three categories, which may be denominated (1) procedure, (2) law, and (3) policy. The organization and competence of League organs, the procedure of reports, petitions, and discussions, the form of reso-

[13] This process was, for instance, employed with respect to the definition of terms concerning the liquor traffic, the ambiguity of which had been referred to by the Council on confirming the B mandates on July 18, 1922. The Commission considered the matter at its third and fourth sessions and made a preliminary recommendation to the Council on the latter occasion in July, 1924 (*P.M.C., Min.*, III, 256–61; IV, 156, 180), on the basis of which the Council submitted the problem to the mandatories on August 29, 1924 (*O.J.*, V, 1398). The Commission discussed the question at length at its seventh session (*P.M.C., Min.*, VII, 87–91, 152–54), and on June 5, 1926, the Council, having received replies from the mandatories asked the Commission to consider them (*O.J.*, VII, 944; *P.M.C., Min.*, IX, 32). This the Commission did at its tenth session, and made a recommendation based on a report of Sir Frederick Lugard (X, 138, 175) which was "noted" by the Council on March 7, 1927, and forwarded to the mandatories nearly five years after the problem was first raised (XI, 10) and it was not settled yet. The eighth Assembly, however, indorsed the Commission's recommendation in September, 1927 (*P.M.C., Min.*, XII, 12). The Commission again discussed the matter in its twelfth session, summarized progress to date in its thirteenth session, and made further recommendations in its fourteenth session (*ibid.*, pp. 129–30, 184–93; XIII, 208, 224; XIV, 269).

The chief of the mandates section ordinarily summarizes the stage which pending general questions have reached at the opening meeting of the Commission. Among other problems thus treated have been status of ex-enemy property, land tenure, and state domain, loans, military recruiting, equalization of liquor duties, education, and extension of international conventions to mandated territories (*ibid.*, sess. IX, pp. 9–11).

lutions and publications are of major importance for the operation of the system and have consumed much time, but such matters have little bearing on the general problem of colonial administration. The League decisions on them are considered in other chapters of this part.

The Covenant and the mandates define the relations of the League, the mandatories, the mandated communities, and the members of the League in a general way; declare certain principles and together with applicable conventions lay down a few specific rules which the mandatory must follow in his administration. These legal requirements, as M. Van Rees pointed out, "are not couched in a clear and concise form."[14] Consequently, the Commission has had to interpret them. This definition and deduction of legal principles from the terms of the constitutional documents has been the most common type of general question considered by the Commission. A legalistic spirit has prevailed. The Commission has not usually inquired what ought to be done in territory with these potentialities and among natives of this stage of culture but rather "what does the covenant and the mandate declare must or must not be done." Inasmuch as the mandates differ, conclusions are often limited to one type of mandate or even to one mandate though certain principles of the Covenant apply to all types.

Conclusions reached from this manner of reasoning are of value for territories not under mandate only in so far as the principles of the Covenant are generally accepted or proved to be sound through practical application under varied conditions. These legal principles will be considered in the third part of this book.

In fact, the prescriptions of the Covenant and of the mandates vary greatly in definiteness. Some regulations like those on slave, arms and liquor traffic, military bases, recruiting, and the open door are quite definite; but, on the other hand, certain principles like "the well-being and development" of the inhabitants and "provisional recognition of independence" are so vague as to admit of a broad variety of policies. Thus in discussing such principles the League organs in fact and of necessity depart from the legalistic spirit. As has been noticed, the Commission has felt obliged to study the entire

[14] *Ibid.*, VII, 152.

administration of the mandatory and in order to form an opinion upon it has extended general inquiries beyond the legal limitations upon the mandatory's powers into the proper manner of their exercise.[15] What, in view of the general principles of the Covenant, ought the mandatory to do for the welfare and development of the natives? What policy should be pursued in regard to labor, land tenure, economic development, public health, etc.? It is true the general principles of the Covenant and mandate may furnish guides, but clearly the main source for such formulations is not the documents but the data, not deduction but induction. The different direction of study suggested by this scientific approach, in contrast to a legalistic approach, is well indicated by two suggestions for proposed studies by the Commission. At the seventh session M. Van Rees suggested the following legal studies.

1. Are the clauses of the mandates in harmony with the distinctive conception of the B and C mandates which appear in article 22 of the covenant?

2. Is it allowable to give the territory a political organization which would make it practically independent of the mandatory state?

3. Do the clauses of the covenant and of the mandates oblige the mandatory powers to devote themselves to the development of the territory and of its population exclusively in the interest of the natives?

4. Is there any contradiction between the clauses concerning the liquor traffic which appear in the covenant and those which appear in the mandates?

5. Is the tax known as the labour levy [*prestation en nature*] allowable in a mandated territory?

6. What is the import of the special military clauses which have been inserted in the mandates for French Togoland and French Cameroons?

7. Is it contrary to the principle of economic equality to authorize the recruiting of natives in order to supply additional labor in a colony belonging to the mandatory powers while forbidding such recruiting in a case in which another country would benefit thereby?

8. What are the obligations which result from the principle that the mandatory powers, having been made trustees by the League of Nations, shall derive no profit from this trusteeship?

9. Is it allowable for the mandatory power to establish in a mandated territory a system of taxation designed to yield a large annual budgetary surplus?

10. Do the full legislative powers conferred on the mandatory allow it to appropriate by legal measures assets in the territory under mandate?

11. Is the mandatory authorized to establish on its own account in a territory under mandate *public* undertakings of its own?

[15] See *supra*, chap. vi, sec. 5.

12. Is it open to the mandatory to take security of any kind in a mandated territory in respect of a guaranteed loan or of an advance?[16]

With these contrast the suggestions of M. Yanaghita made at the third session:

1. Enumeration of population according to tribal divisions, or to the stage of development attained by the various tribes.

2. General tendencies of emigration, immigration, and movements of population in the interior.

3. Progress of the development of the land, shown in reference to localities or native groups.

4. Principles adopted for the maintenance of common law.

5. Program of general native education.

6. Regulations for the official language, and for interpreting.

7. Steps taken in connection with ethnographical and linguistic studies.[17]

The Commission has naturally been reluctant to deduce policy from the broad terms of the mandate but formulations based on studies of the latter type and upon practical experience, of which the Mandates Commission has an abundance, should be of the greatest value not only to the mandatories but to the administrators of other territories where similar conditions prevail. This was, in fact, recognized by the Council in accepting the report of M. Unden on the Commission's sixth report:

I have examined the minutes of the recent session with some care and I have found them of the greatest possible assistance and interest. Moreover, I believe that they illustrate in a particularly striking way the far reaching value of these annual meetings of experts on colonial questions from different parts of the world. The preliminary discussion, which will be found in one of the early meetings, on the question of the development of colonial territories in relation to the supply of labor, is an example of the contribution which the commission makes to some of the fundamental problems which those powers directly responsible for conditions in Africa and the Pacific have to face.[18]

The same point was emphasized by Mr. Roden Buxton in the fifth Assembly and by Mr. Yanaghita of the Commission who noticed that "the successful results which could be obtained within a short time in some territories where circumstances are favorable would be of great use, not only as regards other mandates but also for the

[16] *P.M.C., Min.*, VII, 151.

[17] *Ibid.*, III, 286.

[18] L. of N., Council, Min., XXXV, *O.J.*, VI, 1509.

Colonies of the whole world."[19] Nothing less than a science of colonial administration based on a deductive and experimental method was here contemplated. The discovery by such a method and verification by practical application of useful principles and standards is probably the most important contribution which the mandates system could make. In such work the Commission should utilize the results and co-operate in the investigations of private scholars and unofficial organizations as well as those of government and League agencies. The specialized work of the latter in tropical diseases, slavery, native labor, etc., should be of the greatest value, and in fact the Mandates Commission has been in close contact with the League committees working in these fields.[20] With the merits of the various policies which have actually been applied in the mandated areas we shall again be interested in the fourth part of this volume. Here the efforts of the League organs to formulate policies will be considered.

Obviously it is not always easy to distinguish principles of procedure, law, and policy. The Commission is reluctant to go beyond the four corners of the mandates, and, as the dispute on the questionnaire matter indicated, the Council and the mandatories are not anxious that it shall.[21] Thus if the Commission wishes to express an opinion on wise colonial policy it is likely to treat it as a question of law by hinging it to a clause of the mandate or Covenant.

Furthermore, the close relation of procedure and substantive law must be borne in mind. Organization of an adequate system of petitions and mandatory reporting may be a more practical guaranty of substantive justice to the natives than a formal declaration of principles. Rules of law gain their meaning, in no small measure, from the character of the authority that interprets and applies them. Thus the classification of the general questions which the League has considered formally or developed practically is not always easy. It may be noticed that questions of organization and procedure are most likely to be the subject of formal resolutions. Thus the organization and procedure of the Mandates Commission and the procedure with regard to petitions, reports, hearings, etc., have been established by this method.

[19] See *supra*, nn. 2, 17.

[20] See *supra*, chap. v.

[21] See *supra*, chap. vi, sec. 5.

In some cases interpretations of substantive law have been made the subject of formal resolution—for example, certain questions in regard to liquor traffic, military recruitment, loans, nationality of inhabitants—but more often such interpretations develop by informal discussion and practice, and this is generally the case with standards of policy. They are not so much made as emerge from discussion and experience, though on the more technical problems of health and education the Commission has made succinct recommendations.

2. Ultimate Objectives

The Commission has occasionally discussed the policy which the mandatory ought to pursue in conformity with the general principles of the Covenant and the mandates, and members of the Commission have written a number of valuable memoranda on particular aspects of mandatory policy, but few formulations sufficiently concise for recommendation and Council resolution have so far emerged.

During the sixth session MM. Orts and Rappard raised the question of whether more effort ought not to be made to obtain from the accredited representatives "statements covering the general policy pursued in the mandated territories." M. Beau "sympathized with this desire" but thought an attempt in this direction would "undoubtedly be premature at the moment."

> The majority of the governments were not yet in a position to make a general plan of their policy as regards the territories under mandate. They were not yet beyond the experimental stage. This had transpired in the course of certain conversations which he had had with the administrators of some of the mandated territories, who had recognized in perfect good faith, that many of the measures adopted were nothing more than trial schemes. If this were true of small territories such as those under French mandate, it was obvious that it would be still more true of administrations which were responsible for larger territories. Moreover, the various mandatory powers had different methods of administration. The British method differed in many respects from the French. Was it wise to emphasize now the contrast between the two systems, and could the commission express an opinion in favor of either the one or the other? The mandatory powers must be allowed a certain time in which to adapt to the particular requirements of each mandate the administrative system which they preferred.

M. Orts then pointed out that his suggestion was designed to give the mandatories an opportunity to justify their policies.

One could readily understand that the mandatory powers considered it reasonable to undertake their task with[out] preconceived ideas and to carry out a study of local conditions before establishing a definite policy. A statement in this sense made before the commission could not fail to have an excellent effect.[22]

Efforts have in fact been made to get such statements with some success. The Commission, however, has discovered that its members are not wholly agreed upon the ultimate goal contemplated by the Covenant. Does it envisage self-contained national cultures developed and maintained by the effort of the people who now live there and their descendants on the roots of their existing cultures? Or, on the other hand, does it envisage communities, efficiently governed and utilizing their natural and human resources to the full, composed of the people, native or immigrant, who have shown the greatest capacity to develop the territory? Self-determination or civilization —the two ideals perhaps ought not to be in conflict and often they are not, but so long as civilization is interpreted by each nation in its own image they are likely to be.

The first ideal seems clearly envisaged for the A mandates by article 22 of the Covenant, and Iraq has in fact been recognized as provisionally independent under a native administration as have, though to a less degree, the Republic of the Lebanon and the Emirate of Transjordan. At the eighth session of the Commission the accredited representative of France declared:

The idea which has governed, if not the whole exercise of the mandate, at any rate all the efforts made to organize it, is the following: The mandate is a provisional system designed to enable populations which, politically speaking, are still minors to educate themselves so as to arrive one day at full self-government. This presupposes that the mandatory power will gradually create native organizations in the mandated territory such as may, when complete, be able to ensure entirely the government of the country and such as may, if they carry out their duties in a proper manner, render the intervention of the mandatory unnecessary. It appears from this that there should not be any intervention on the part of the organs of the mandatory power in the internal affairs of the native governments.

This declaration gave the Commission "great satisfaction" as it was in "strict harmony with the letter and spirit of article 22 of the cove-

[22] *P.M.C., Min.*, VI, 13–14.

nant and also of the mandate for Syria and the Lebanon," and in its opinion "appeared the real solution of the difficult problem which has arisen in those countries."[23]

In Palestine, as the Commission noted,[24] the mandate departs from this principle by including the Balfour declaration, a pronouncement which as interpreted by many of the Zionists, at least, savors of the second ideal given above. Civilization, they say, has stagnated in Palestine under the hands of the Arabs. Give a more able and energetic people an opportunity to develop the country's potentialities not only for themselves but also for the present inhabitants and for the world in general.[25]

For the B and C mandates the Commission has been more divided. Sir Frederick Lugard has expressed the hope of eventual though perhaps distant self-determination.

> The administration, while assisting private enterprise in every reasonable way, must not allow itself to be dominated by the utilitarian spirit, for its special function is to frame its policy for the future and not exclusively to immediate economic success. The time when the bulk of the population of Tropical Africa will be "able to stand alone in the strenuous conditions of the modern world" may not yet be visible on the horizon, but the mandates impose upon the powers which have accepted them the obligation to conduct the people towards that goal.[26]

[23] *Ibid.*, VII, 202. Hocking, *Yale Review*, XIX (1930), 250.

[24] *Ibid.*, V, 188. Keith, *J.C.L.*, IV, Part I, 78.

[25] Q. Wright, "The Palestine Problem," *P.S.Q.*, XLI (September, 1926), 405. Stoyanovsky suggests that the Balfour declaration conforms to the "principles of nationality and self-determination upon which the Covenant of the League of Nations largely rests" by assuring self-determination for the Jews in the only practicable manner (*The Mandate for Palestine*, p. 43). The present writer has suggested that it constitutes a "frank recognition" that "self-determination" is inapplicable in Palestine because of the world-importance of "outside religious interests" (*op. cit.*, p. 411), a situation apparently admitted by Lord Balfour with reference to the provision of the mandate on holy places. This, he thought, "was of interest mainly to people outside Palestine," though recognizing that "the system of mandates had been concerned in the interests of the populations living in the mandated territory, he suggested that "in so far as this mandate was concerned [this principle] might be regarded as of secondary importance" (*O.J.*, III, 820).

[26] *P.M.C.*, *Min.*, VII, 196. Precisely this ideal is said to govern the British Empire with respect to its parts (see *supra*, chap. i, n. 22), and the Commission has indorsed "the British Colonial view in accordance with which a colony ought to be self-supporting and have recourse as seldom as possible to the home country for financial

To M. Freire d'Andrade this seemed hopeless. "The ideal," he wrote, "is the slow, unforced assimilation of weak or inferior communities by strong or more highly developed communities."

> I do not think it is an effective system to try to bring about the development of native races by preserving their customs, provided these are not cruel or inhuman, and their organization, under supervision and guidance, and thus creating two classes—one the supervised and the other the supervisors—who will send out punitive expeditions if their orders are not obeyed. History teaches us that by these methods black communities have never learnt to govern themselves, and I very much doubt whether this result could be attained among African natives or Indians except after centuries of development, as was the case with the European peoples. . . . . In North America racial differences are a thorn in the flesh of the great American nation. In South America there is no race problem. Why? Because in North America the natives or negroes are regarded as inferior; in South America they are looked upon as individually equal. Thus I think that in Africa natives and Europeans must go side by side on a footing of individual equality.[27]

Thus the difference seems to depend on whether emphasis is given to the equality of communities or to the equality of men. One interpretation of the Covenant emphasizes the former. It holds that communities are equal in the sense that each has the right to exist and to develop its potentialities. It regards the culture groups of Asia,

---

support" as applicable to all mandated territories, apparently with the thought that financial independence was a prerequisite of political independence (*P.M.C.*, *Min.*, I, 23; Stoyanovsky, *op. cit.*, p. 219).

[27] *P.M.C.*, *Min.*, VII, 207, 208. This idea is further developed in a memorandum sent by the Portuguese government stating its attitude toward the slavery convention on August 27, 1926. This document emphasized the cruelty to the native of "race prejudice," the right of all men to equality of legal status, the duty of all to labor, the backwardness of natives, and the necessity that backward territories be developed, consequently "colonial labor legislation should be framed with a view to ensuring not merely the well being of the native but also his physical and moral development and at the same time furthering the economic progress of the country which is an essential condition of general prosperity" (*O.J.*, VII, 1539–45). With this contrast Sir Frederick Lugard's opinion of "the true conception of the inter-relation of color: complete uniformity in ideals, absolute equality in the paths of knowledge and culture, equal opportunity for those who strive, equal admiration for those who achieve; in matters social and racial a separate path, each pursuing his own inherited traditions, preserving his own race-purity and race pride; equality in things spiritual, agreed divergence in the physical and material" (*Edin. R.*, April, 1921, quoted by President Harding as "the true way out," speech at Birmingham, Ala., October 26, 1921, and in Lugard, *The Dual Mandate* [1923], p. 86).

Africa, and the Pacific, not as bad but as adolescent. It desires not their extermination or their supplanting, but their cultivation and development. The League, according to this interpretation, is engaged in a mission not of separating the sheep from the goats with a view to survival or suppression, but of universal education of nations whether infant, adolescent, or mature.

This conception apparently conforms more to Anglo-Saxon than to Latin conceptions. To the latter cultures are ephemeral. Men are the units to consider and should be given equal opportunities. Some of the blacks of Africa can be educated to take their place in a civilization like that of Europe. Some will intermarry with the white man and their descendants will do so more easily. Those who can or will do neither are dying out and will continue to do so. All men should be treated alike by the law. The aborigine should be entitled to the civil rights and the opportunities for advancement according to capacity the same as the civilized man, but also he should be required to recognize the same obligations. "The law of labor is a law of nature," wrote M. Freire d'Andrade, "which no one should be allowed to evade. And if this is true of organized and highly developed societies, the same must be admitted for the peoples on the road to civilization and for countries which are on the threshold of development."[28] By this process those capable of civilization will survive and the countries will be developed.

To adherents of this point of view the Covenant calls not for the preservation and development of exotic communities, most of which are useful only as museum specimens for the ethnologist, but for the "well-being and development of peoples—that is to say, all the inhabitants of territories to be placed under mandate, irrespective of their race or their stage of development." To which interpretation Sir Frederick Lugard replies, "The reference to '*such* peoples' in the first paragraph of article 22 of the covenant refers explicitly to the 'peoples' just mentioned—e.g. those 'not able to stand alone'—and not to *all* inhabitants of the mandated territory—but I concur that the mandatory is responsible for all the inhabitants."[29]

Whether "peoples" in the Covenant refers to communities or inhabitants, clearly neither ideal can be consistently applied to all the

[28] *P.M.C., Min.*, VII, 201. [29] *Ibid.*, pp. 198, 206.

mandated areas in practice. "The character of the Mandate," says the Covenant, "must differ according to the stage of development of the people, the geographical situation of the territory, its economic development and other similar circumstances." Some of these areas have a homogeneous culture which can be developed; others have a medley of races and of divergent village cultures presenting few roots for development. Others are very sparsely populated, and migrants of a different culture from the present inhabitants may become the majority. After noting this "chaotic situation," M. Yanaghita of the Commission in an able memorandum presented at the third session wrote:

> These facts must convince us that the term "peoples" referred to in all simplicity in article 22 of the covenant, acquires an exceedingly complicated meaning, and we should be mistaken in believing that a simple administrative measure of a general nature can successfully be applied to numerous groups possessing such dissimilar interests. . . . . It may be conjectured that the mixture of races, already great, will be still further augmented by migrations. Moreover tribes whose intellectual level is similar, and which therefore call for equal treatment at present, may later display many points of dissimilarity due to different conditions and to outside influences. From the point of view of the task of civilizing these races, in view of which the inferior races have been placed under the tutelage of more advanced peoples, the conflicting interests of groups of different intellectual capacity cannot be left to find their natural development, as is the case among civilized nations. In my view there is only one principle which can serve as a guide in the establishment of complete equity in these areas—the principle laid down in Article 22 of the covenant, which divides mandates into categories A, B and C, granting protection to the natives in proportion to the level reached by their civilization. In other words, the least developed or weakest peoples call for the greatest amount of protection.[30]

Opinions differ as to whether it is their own, the mandatory's, or someone else's view of the welfare of the peoples of these areas which should especially attract the League's solicitude. Apparently the Covenant intends that for the "communities" under A mandate it is the first, for the "territories" under C mandate the second, and for the "peoples" under B mandate variation according to their "stage of development."

The Commission seems to be agreed that whoever may be the judge of welfare, the "peoples" of the area must be the main bene-

[30] *Ibid.*, III, 280.

ficiaries of the system, not the mandatory or outside peoples.[30a] Mandatory government is established for the good of the governed, not for the good of the mandatory or even for the good of the world, though the latter is considered not only on the hypothesis that it is for the good of the world that the interests of backward peoples be protected, but also in the requirement that the mandatory give consideration to certain interests of other members of the League of Nations, especially in commercial, religious, and military matters. The prevention, in the interests of world-peace, of inequitable discriminations and of bases of military attack is thus an object of the system, but that it is secondary is indicated by three considerations. First, the "well-being and development of the 'peoples' under mandate" is stated as the *raison d'être* of the system in the Covenant and applies to all mandates while no direct third-state interest as such is universally recognized. The open door, for instance, does not apply generally to C mandates. Second, the interests of the "peoples" protected by the Covenant and the mandates are more comprehensive and are specified in more detail than are any direct third-state interests. Finally, the specified protection of third-state interests in certain mandates, as, for instance, the open door for trade and missions, and demilitarization, are expressly limited by the mandatory's duty to maintain order and to administer the territory efficiently in the interests of the inhabitants. Thus the open-door provisions do not limit the mandatory's discretion to provide for public works and to form customs unions with neighboring territories, nor do the religious freedom and demilitarization provisions prevent local recruiting for police and defensive purposes and the regulation of missionary activity in the interests of order. While these exceptions may in some cases have been recognized because of the mandatory's view of his own interest, their theoretical justification lies in the interests of the inhabitants.

Thus the proper policy of mandatory administration includes consideration first of native policy and then of policy toward third states. It must be emphasized that the line of distinction is not sharp.[31] Religious freedom and demilitarization have been regarded

[30a] For special situation in Palestine see *supra*, nn. 24, 25.

[31] Van Rees, *Les Mandats internationaux*, I, 1–2.

as "in the interests of the indigenous populations," as that term is used in paragraph 6 of article 22 of the Covenant, though the third-state interest in toleration for their missionaries and demilitarization have frequently been manifested. Third states, especially if blessed by humanitarian and aborigines' protective associations, are likely to show an interest in native protection and progress while, on the other hand, the native's interest in the open door has on several occasions been emphasized by the Mandates Commission.

In fact, League discussions have usually proceeded from the standpoint of native interests. From these it appears that the mandates system contemplates a policy (1) assuring the native against certain abuses and forms of exploitation of which he has been a victim in the past, (2) facilitating his political development on the roots of his own wishes and institutions, (3) affording him the opportunity for economic and social progress. Here, again, sharp distinctions are impossible. These three prescriptions of native policy are interdependent. Protection of the native from abuse and exploitation should facilitate his political, economic, and social progress, and advance in any of these directions should assist in the others. There may, however, be conflicts. Premature self-government might lead to the increase of such practices as slavery, intoxication, religious oppression and intertribal warfare, and to economic and social retrogression; while artificially stimulated economic and social progress might lead to such dependence on foreign administration, destruction of self-reliance, tribal loyalty, and interest in life, and deterioration of indigenous institutions that self-government would become impossible and depopulation would be probable. Unless these policies are driven in harness they may prove incompatible.

Possibly the ultimate objectives of mandatory policy can be better discovered by analysis of provisions and discussions on specific problems than from the general terms of the documents and the Commission's discussion of them. The attitude of the League, especially as manifested in the Mandates Commission, will be considered with respect to certain outstanding problems, classified as above indicated. The first group of problems, however, is determined by law rather than policy. The trade in intoxicants, arms, and slaves is regulated or prohibited by the terms of all B and C mandates. Specific provisions in regard to slavery and forced labor, religious freedom, and military and financial exploitation of natives are inserted in most of the mandates. In regard to these matters the proper mandatory policy is to observe the law, as properly interpreted. While some variations in the method of enforcement may be legitimate, and while in some cases the League has recommended protection of natives beyond the strict requirements of law, as, for instance, the non-recruitment of natives who have voluntarily gone into the mandatory's own territory, discussion of these problems is reserved for Part III of this book. Attention will here be given to native policy in respect to political and administrative matters, and in respect to economic and social matters, after which policy discussed with express reference to third-state interests will be considered.

3. Native Policy: Political and Administrative

The native would have little opportunity for political development if he were swamped by alien immigration, if he were subordinated to the white inhabitants of the area, if his customs and institutions were ruthlessly destroyed, and if he were allowed no participation in the government of the country. That the mandate policy recommended by the League seeks to protect him from such catastrophes will, it is believed, be evident from the following discussions.

a) Immigration

Immigration policy has necessarily been discussed in connection with efforts to answer the question, Who are to be considered the inhabitants of the mandated areas? "The word 'Inhabitants' in article 22," wrote Sir Frederick Lugard, "means those persons who are permanently domiciled in the country and does not include persons who are there only temporarily."[32] Permanently domiciled since when? M. Yanaghita had earlier replied:

> Peoples who were, even by chance, in the mandated areas when the covenant was signed are legally entitled to be guaranteed protection under the new system. In other words, the privileges of the mandated peoples cannot be

[32] *P.M.C., Min.*, VII, 206. But see *infra*, chap. xiii, n. 84*a*.

shared by those who have come into the areas in question after June, 1919. If therefore it happens that the interests of the two classes of inhabitants—those previously living in the mandated areas and those arriving there later—prove irreconcilable, the mandatory administration will naturally give first consideration to those of the original inhabitants.

Thus, he pointed out, the immigration and emigration policy adopted by the mandatory is of fundamental importance and as probably the principle of individual authorization for migrants in or out cannot be maintained, a permanent principle should be adopted.[33]

This question has not been generally discussed by the Commission, but in its fifth session when Palestine was for the first time considered, the bearing of the Zionist policy upon the immigration policy proper to mandates was discussed. The Commission noted the conflict between the exceptional provision of the mandate requiring the mandatory to "encourage—as well as to regulate—Jewish immigration into Palestine" and the "fundamental principle of article 22" by which the "paramount duty of the mandatory power is to ensure the development of the mandated territory by administering them in conformity with the interests of their inhabitants." The policy adopted to reconcile these incompatible provisions had given "rise to acute controversy."

It does not afford entire satisfaction to the Zionists who feel that the establishment in Palestine of a Jewish National Home is the first duty of the mandatory Power and manifest a certain impatience at the restrictions which are placed in the way of immigration and in respect of the granting of land to immigrants. This policy is, on the other hand, rejected by the Arab majority in the country, which refuses to accept the idea of a Jewish National Home and regards the action of the administration as a menace to its traditional patrimony.

Inasmuch as the Commission does not feel competent to criticize the terms of mandates, it could only note that "the consequences of this conflict of interests are mitigated by the wisdom and impartiality displayed by the High Commissioner" and the "discontent in Palestine" cannot be attributed to him. Thus its only specific observation on this point was a request for further information because of its "concern with the fact that immigration had not perhaps always been in proportion to the capacity of the economic absorption of the country."[34]

[33] *Ibid.*, III, 280.

[34] *Ibid.*, V, 188–89.

But if the present inhabitants are to be preferred to immigrants, are they to be preferred to their own descendants? "The only criterion for any work of improvement should be whether it was likely to have the effect of damaging materially or morally the present population," said Mr. Grimshaw referring to the common argument of concessionaires that oppressive measures to force economic development were justified because of the benefit to future generations. M. Orts replied that the Commission "had not the right to indulge in considerations which were exclusively philanthropic." Its supervisory work would have "unfortunate results if it did not always take account of the practical aspects of the colonial problem as well as the moral aspect." M. Freire d'Andrade "did not entirely agree with Mr. Grimshaw. If the construction of railway lines were undertaken it might happen that certain natives were sacrificed to the work, just as the Europeans were sacrificed. It should not be concluded that the construction of railways should be stopped." The question raised the fundamental conflict between native interests and economic development, which will be considered presently.[35]

b) RELATION TO WHITE SETTLERS

In some mandated areas, especially Southwest Africa, the inhabitants at the time the system went into effect included both natives and white settlers. The Commission seems to agree that both types of inhabitants are entitled to protection, but is there a difference in the degree? The Covenant refers to "people not yet able to stand by themselves," "communities formerly belonging to the Turkish empire," "peoples of central Africa," and "indigenous populations" of Southwest Africa and the Pacific islands. M. Yanaghita seemed to think that this gave the "least developed or weakest peoples" the greatest protection, and M. Rappard insisted that "it was the first duty of the commission to look after the welfare of the natives."[36] During the discussion of the Bondelzwart rebellion in Southwest Africa the question aroused acute discussion. The Marquis Theodoli, chairman of the Commission, expressed the conviction that the mandate system marked an innovation in colonial policy in that it required the interest of the natives to take preced-

[35] *Ibid.*, VI, 49–50.

[36] *Ibid.*, II, 280; VI, 48.

ence of that of the whites." To this M. Orts took exception, pointing out that the Covenant or mandates made no such distinction but referred to all peoples of the territory.

What were the actual words of the Covenant: "the well-being and development of such peoples form a sacred trust of civilization." Nothing more. As to the mandate for southwest Africa, it confined itself to defining as follows the duty of the mandatory Power as regards the natives: "The mandatory shall promote to the utmost the material and moral well-being and the assured progress of the inhabitants of the territory subject to the present mandate." The Commission should beware of stating opinions not justified by existing texts, otherwise the mandatory Power could say with justice: "Where did you find that? Did you find it in the Covenant, the only document which, together with mandates, you are justified in indicating? Or have you found any provision whatever which would allow you to state that in the territories in question the whole preoccupation of the administration should be in the first instance for the blacks, and that care for the prosperity of the European community should only be a secondary consideration?"

MM. Beau and Van Rees agreed with this but the Marquis Theodoli "maintained his point of view."

It was inconceivable that the illustrious authors of the covenant had produced a work which was anything but an entire departure from precedent. The spirit of the mandates required as a fundamental principle the material and moral progress of the natives; the white population ought only to be considered in so far as it assisted in achieving this progress.

Inasmuch as his colleagues would not agree to this principle or to the deductions he drew from it in reference to the handling of the Bondelzwart affair by the South African government, he refused to associate himself with the report on that subject and withdrew from further meetings of that session of the Commission.[37] The decision on this question is clearly fundamental for determining both the policy of immigration and the proper native policy in mandated areas where there are whites, or where whites have been permitted to migrate.

The Commission's position on the matter of migration has been noted. In regard to the relations of domiciled whites and natives the policy of assimilation has been opposed to the policy of segregation through native reserves. M. d'Andrade wrote:

[37] *Ibid.*, III, 204–7. M. Orts, interpretation of the term "peoples" in article 22 of the Covenant is doubtful (see *supra*, nn. 29 and 36).

There is no question of forming separate organizations of natives and whites; a complete amalgamation of the two races would be the best means of furthering the development and well-being of such peoples. . . . . So far from creating a number of small organizations living side by side in mutual rivalry and detestation, it is desirable to endeavour to secure the co-operation of all and the amalgamation of the various interests in order to make the peoples capable of self government.

To which replied Sir Frederick Lugard:

Why should communities living side by side "detest" each other? The rivalry may be entirely wholesome and lead to progress. Natural causes will no doubt lead in many cases to the absorption of less virile tribes by others but I see no reason why it should be an object of policy to hasten the process.[38]

c) NATIVE CUSTOMS

Agreement has not been reached on this question, nor has it on the closely related question: What respect should the mandatory give to native customs and institutions? The Commission considers the development of a sound administration of justice as a first task of the mandatory, but the members seem to recognize that native custom and conceptions of justice cannot be ignored. M. Yanaghita emphasized the need of a careful integration of the mandatory's standards of justice with those of native custom.

Although the mandatory governments with the support of public opinion in Europe have decided in principle that certain native customs which conflict with humanitarian ideals should be abolished, they do not seem to have sufficient firmness to suppress everything which is repugnant to civilized nations. Thus, polygamy, with an average of two wives, is tolerated as a vice capable of gradual correction, whereas ritual cannibalism is condemned in every case. Savages who have not had the opportunity of coming into contact with the Christian missions will find it just as incomprehensible to be regarded as criminals for practicing the one custom as the other. Nevertheless, the natives are given notice of new kinds of punishable offences which they find extremely surprising.

At the same time, it will be impossible for the new courts of Justice to take any decision whereby the violation of the customary rules, which are so dear to the native social body, would go unpunished. That part at least of the native law which does not hinder the march of progress should be allowed to remain in

[38] *Ibid.*, VII, 201, 204, 206. The policy of confining the natives to reserves has been farthest developed in Southwest Africa, where the Commission has watched it with some concern (*ibid.*, IV, 62; IX, 36). It has also been discussed in connection with Tanganyika (*ibid.*, IV, 91).

force. For a long time two taboo systems of totally different origins will continue to exist side by side. A very curious compromise is being reached between European common-sense and native conservatism, and its inevitable result will be an increase of criminal cases.

In the case of less serious offences it would sometimes be necessary to compare the two legal methods which are now employed by the various mandatory governments: (1) That of native courts in which seats are given to a certain number of natives; (2) that of jurisdiction by tribal chiefs. By the first method it might be possible, by patiently listening to the native jury, to avoid the double punishment of a single crime. By the second, if careful supervision were maintained it would be possible to conform more closely to the native customs. It is not necessarily correct to suppose that the second method is more liberal than the first: the question depends on the effect of each method on the welfare of the common people.

The only satisfactory result which can at present be expected from the new judicial system is the deliverance of the natives from the troubles which are common to all uncivilized peoples, and which arise from the capricious jurisdiction of tyrannical chiefs. It would, however, be a long time before the essential part of the work which this system was intended to accomplish was realized. It will not, in any case, be realized until the natives are capable of distinguishing good from evil, and of comprehending the attitude of the administrators. For the time being we must be content with the secondary results of the judicial reform—results which are more of an instructive nature.

Another obstacle to judicial reform is the fact that certain emoluments are attached to the old system of tribal jurisdiction. This obstacle cannot be removed as long as the governments continue to observe the principle of maintaining the powers of chiefs. It must, however, be admitted that the chief is often the best judge on matters which affect the customs of his tribe, and we have already observed that for the present a certain number of ancient customs, on which native life is founded, must be preserved in the interests of peace in the territory.

M. Yanaghita calls especial attention to the difficulty, in connection with judicial and other administration, of interpretation. Officials often fail to understand native grievances or conceptions. Interpreters become a privileged class with interests of their own. Thus it is desirable that administrators familiarize themselves with at least some phrases of the local idiom.[39]

d) NATIVE PARTICIPATION IN GOVERNMENT

If much of the native custom should be preserved, at least for the time, should the traditional native authorities be retained to

[39] *Ibid.*, III, 282–83, 285.

apply it? In other words, should the mandatory's administration be direct or indirect? Clearly a substitution would in any case take time, but some members of the Commission have intimated that it should take place as rapidly as possible. M. Van Rees said:

> There was a truth to which all colonial administrations of all countries which had any occasion to judge of European and native methods were obliged to subscribe, namely, that the least perfect European administration was one hundred times better than a purely native administration. It was clear that, in general, European civilization was based on principles diametrically opposed to those of the natives, and it resulted from this that a European administration had not and could not have the welfare of the natives as conceived by the natives themselves, for its sole object.[40]

M. d'Andrade said:

> While keeping the native organization as far as may be, it is also possible by degrees for the action of the native chief to be superseded by that of the administration of the mandatory, which governs the community with the help of advisory or executive councils which include the principal natives chosen either by the administration or by the natives themselves. This creates an effective co-operation which will further the work of the community and promote the development of the native races.

Sir Frederick Lugard, however, wrote in reference to this statement:

> A second point on which I do not share M. d'Andrade's view is that it is desirable to supersede by degrees the action of the native chiefs by the administration of the mandatory. This appears to me contrary to the conception that the mandatory should endeavour to render the people able to stand alone.[41]

A compromise policy was favored by M. Yanaghita in an able résumé of the problem. As has been noticed, he recognized that "the chief is often the best judge in matters which affect the customs of his tribe" and that many of these customs should be preserved, but, on the other hand:

> It is an undoubted fact that the long established organization of despotism under chiefs has frequently hampered the working of mandatory administration. We are sometimes inclined to think that the welfare of the common body of natives cannot be guaranteed unless the old system is definitely abolished. Regarded from this point of view, the present system of "native officials," which has been adopted by almost all the mandatory governments, is open to criticism as being a palliative. But, in point of fact, the wisdom and skill displayed by the governments is worthy of admiration. We find that under this

[40] *Ibid.*, III, 50.

[41] *Ibid.*, VII, 201, 206.

system many chiefs, both great and small, are given charge of matters of minor importance connected with village administration. They are permitted to carry out these duties in a most imposing manner, taking advantage of the great traditional respect which they still receive from those under them. Scarcely aware of the fact that their little sovereignty has been transferred to a higher group, they will assist in the work of the mandatory government and will be content with the empty title and the modest stipend. This method may thus be regarded as a suitable means of carrying out the transition to the new era, while disguising the bitterness of the fall from power. As, however, it is only an adaptation to present conditions, and not a definite system, it would be wrong to exaggerate its value, or to suppose that it represents an adequate means of safeguarding the general interest of the people.[42]

The recognition given to native authorities in fact varies considerably in the mandated territories. Iraq and Transjordan have been recognized as native kingdoms and Arab authorities are in control though obliged to consider the advice of advisers provided by the mandatory and in certain specified cases to follow it. In Syria and Palestine the administrative and legislative authority has been far more concentrated in the hands of the mandatories' officials, and native authorities have correspondingly suffered, to the great discontent of the Arabs. In 1926 and 1927, however, native representative governments were set up in the Lebanon and Syria. As has been noted, the mandatories have expressed allegiance to the principle of eventual native independence declared by the Covenant for these areas.[43] Ruanda, among the B mandates, enjoys the most independence of mandatory control, King Musinga's authority having been little impaired. At the second session of the Commission Mr. Ormsby-Gore pointed out that here "the administration of the territory was analogous to that of a territory under an A mandate since the Belgian government would appear to be only in an advisory capacity to a well organized government." M. Van Rees thought in such a case there should be a convention defining the relative powers of the mandatory and the native kingdoms, "otherwise the mandatory might act in breach of rights actually in existence." M. Orts noticed that "these little negro states had never been recognized as such; their territories were absorbed in the general administrative organization."[44] Apparently the Belgian policy has

[42] *Ibid.*, III, 283. [43] See *supra*, n. 23. [44] *P.M.C., Min.*, II, 70.

been gradually to extend the sphere of direct administration in this region, though according to the report of 1925 it has avoided "too brusque an intervention" which would "diminish the authority of the chiefs and be contrary to the desires of the permanent mandates commission which was in favor of preserving a system of indirect administration." Commenting on this passage in the ninth session, M. d'Andrade doubted whether the Commission had unitedly expressed such a preference though admitting that certain members had done so.[45]

The Commission has on occasion noticed that a policy of allowing the native governments to proceed in reservations without any mandatory supervision whatever would hardly be compatible with the civilizing duty of the mandatory,[46] but, on the other hand, it has undoubtedly shown a preference for indirect administration, especially in A mandated territories where it is required by the Covenant.[47] Such institutions, however, cannot be allowed to derogate from the sole responsibility of the mandatory toward the League.[48]

If native governmental institutions are to be in part supplanted, should the substitute institutions set up by the mandatory give the natives opportunity to voice their opinion and participate in the government? The conception of self-determination prevalent at the Peace Conference has been associated with the conception of self-government and representative institutions.[49] The term "tutelage"

[45] *Ibid.*, VII, 63; IX, 102. During the seventh session, the Belgian representative said his government had no "wish to change the policy of indirect administration.... which experience had so far shown to have given such happy results" (*ibid.*, VII, 215). As to the native sultanates in French Cameroons, see *ibid.*, III, 16.

[46] M. Yanaghita referred to the value of "cultural contacts" (*ibid.*, III, 281; see also M. Van Rees, *ibid.*, p. 15, and report on British Cameroons, *ibid.*, V, 191).

[47] *Ibid.*, VIII, 207. The Commission's interest in maintaining tribal integrity and the authority of chiefs is well shown by its effort to rectify boundaries which cut tribes in two (see *supra*, chap. iv, sec. 5).

[48] In regard to Iraq see *ibid.*, VII, 10–12, 123, and in regard to Southwest Africa, *ibid.*, VI, 177.

[49] Strictly self-determination would seem to mean the right of every national unit occupying a definite territory to choose its form of government independently of any external control. As such a choice might result in an autocracy as well as a representative or democratic form of government, self-determination appears to resemble the principle of "nationality" as used by Mazzini rather than the principle of popular government, though there is a relation between the two since under a long established autoc-

of the Covenant may imply a duty to develop such institutions.[50] The mandates of Iraq and Syria provide for the framing of organic laws with the consent of the natives, and the latter requires the encouragement of local autonomy. While the mandate for Palestine gives the mandatory "full powers of legislation and administration save as may be limited by the terms of the mandate," it requires "the development of self-governing institutions" and the "encouragement of local autonomy." The B and C mandates give the mandatory full power of administration and legislation and permit him to administer the area as an integral part of his territory subject to the provisions of the mandates. Thus, except for the A territories the mandates seem not to require native representation or participation in government.

In Syria the delay in framing the organic law and the inadequacy of native representation in the provisional governments has been a cause of serious protest by the Arabs and Druses and of comment by the Commission. "It is clear," says the Commission's eighth report, "that these passages [of the mandate], so far from forbidding the mandatory power to set up a system of the widest local self-government in the mandated territories, actually require it to do so," and to the accredited representative's declaration that France was planning gradually to create "native organizations" which in time would "render the intervention of the mandatory unnecessary" the Commission said this was not only in harmony with the letter and spirit of the mandate but "offered the real solution of the difficult problem in those countries."[51] In Palestine, while noticing the conflict of the Zionist policy and the provisions of article 22 in the case of immigration, the Commission has said:

> The divergencies which bring Zionism and the Arab majority into conflict on the subject of immigration may also be observed in connection with other manifestations of the collective life of Palestine. They produced particularly

racy it would be difficult to discover whether the people still constitute a national unity and whether it still has the form of government it wants. Even with the most advanced techniques of plebiscites, elections, constitutionalism, and scientific definitions of historic, geographic, ethnic, linguistic, cultural, economic, and psychological nationality it is sufficiently difficult to determine these problems.

[50] See *infra*, chap. xi, sec. 3*b*.

[51] *P.M.C.*, *Min.*, VIII, 202–4, see also X, 122, 144, 186.

unfortunate results when an attempt was made to create an advisory or legislative council. The Arabs, appealing to Article 2 of the mandate, which guarantees the development of self governing institutions, declined to co-operate unless they were assured of representation which should be in proportion to their numerical strength and which should at the same time give them an absolute majority on such a body, whereas the administration could not agree to the admission of a majority resolved to oppose the establishment in Palestine of a National Home for the Jewish People and the application of the mandatory system in the country.[52]

In some of the B and C territories native advisory councils of chiefs have been established, and in Western Samoa a quite elaborate system of native councils exists. Of such institutions M. Yanaghita expressed some doubt in a memorandum presented at the third session of the Commission.

The system of the popular assembly, which is of a purely advisory character, and in which certain native notables are invited to take part, may be accepted as the first symptom of the adoption of a liberal and equitable principle. At present, however, we cannot expect great results from the work of this organization. Owing to the nature of their public life, which gives evidence of inveterate habits of indiscipline, the chiefs seem utterly incapable of representing native interests. As they do not show themselves equal to their task in connection with the affairs of their own tribe, it is obvious that they are not fit to deal with those of other tribes living under different conditions; and this would be true even if their opinions were gratefully received by their colleagues and by the government.

We have very scanty information as to the direction taken by the movement for autonomy which was initiated some time ago in the islands of Western Samoa by a number of natives who imagined that they represented their countrymen. It is not, on the whole, an unfavorable sign that certain political terms belonging to the new era have penetrated to this remote island. Although these terms are used indifferently on all occasions, they nevertheless show the direction in which the natives wish to move. We must consider, however, what result is to be expected from the excessive measure of political liberty which has been granted to them, in view of present conditions, under which the whole inexperienced mass of the people is guided and agitated by a few enlightened natives. The result will be an outbreak of oppression and fraud, victimising the innocent, and the poverty of the people will be as great as ever. Until an educational effort improves their personal character and awakens their sense of collective responsibility, the working of the administration will continue to be

[52] *Ibid.*, VI, 188. Later, in response to an Arab petition the Commission found it "obvious that a form of democratic and parliamentary government is not provided for either by the Covenant or by the mandate" for Palestine (*ibid.*, XIV, 247, 276).

hampered by fruitless and unfounded discontent. And although they cannot profit by all the painful experiments through which the peoples of civilized countries have had to pass in order to attain their political ideals, yet they should have a certain preparatory training. How, and in what order, must we proceed to form in every individual native the character which the new organization requires? The study of this problem will be one of the most serious considerations of the future.[53]

In its reports, however, the Commission has undoubtedly favored native participation in the government through advisory councils of notables or where practicable through legislative councils and the appointment of natives to responsible positions in the courts and administration. It has been much interested in the native advisory institutions of Western Samoa, and its discussion of the 1927 disturbances in that area gave no indication that these institutions were responsible though the agitators complained that they did not properly represent the native.[54] The development of representative institutions confined to the white minority in Southwest Africa and Tanganyika has raised more doubt in the Commission.[55]

4. Native Policy: Economic and Social

From the material side the natives' main assets are labor and land. Capital, technology, and industrial organization are undeveloped. Thus his material progress depends in large measure upon land and labor policies which induce him to produce a surplus without destroying his independence and interest in life and which assure the utilization of this surplus to his benefit. Material progress may be accelerated by the importation of goods, capital, and technical skill, and the League has sought to create such confidence in the mandate status, and such an application of commercial treaties and the open door, that the benefit of such importations would not be denied the inhabitants of mandated territory.[56] These problems, as also the problem of eliminating such abuses as forced labor and the expropriation of native lands, are regulated by mandatory law and will be considered in Part III of this book. The positive program

[53] *Ibid.*, III, 283.

[54] *Ibid.*, XII, 109–12, XIII, 126.

[55] *Ibid.*, VI, 177.

[56] See *infra*, Part III. On the importance of capital to undeveloped areas see H. K. Norton, *Foreign Investments*, "Harris Foundation Lectures," Chicago, 1928.

which the mandatory system contemplates is gradually emerging from the Commission's discussion of labor and land policy.

Material progress facilitates and also depends on social progress, though here again one may be overstimulated to the detriment of the other. Thus too extensive a devotion of the territory's financial resources to education and public health would discourage the accumulation of capital and the construction of roads, ports, and other public works, thus preventing economic progress, while exclusive attention to the latter would be equally against the interest of the native. The Mandates Commission has looked upon native education and health as of outstanding importance and has reached general conclusions as to the most useful policy in this regard in the B and C territories. The importance of the legal provisions for preventing drunkenness, slavery, tribal warfare, etc., in the social progress of the native have been fully appreciated by the Commission.

a) LABOR

The economic development of backward areas involves the more intensive utilization of the natives' two economic assets, labor and land. Colonial officials and entrepreneurs have often proceeded on the theory that this end can be achieved by depriving the native of his land, thus compelling him to work. This is especially true in areas capable of white settlement. Elsewhere forced labor has been resorted to. Sometimes wants may be stimulated and labor induced by acquainting the native with imported products which can be bought for money. In any case, if the territory is to develop, the native must be induced to work more than he has in the past or else be crowded out by immigrant laborers. Thus the Mandates Commission has faced the question: What if any derogation from native freedom should be permitted for the sake of economic development?[57]

[57] See, for instance, discussion between Sir Frederick Lugard and the British accredited representative Mr. Ormsby-Gore (who had been Sir Frederick's predecessor on the Mandates Commission) on the question "whether the demands made on the present generation of natives [in Tanganyika] for labor by reason of the rapidity of the material development of the country were not pressing too heavily upon the people." Mr. Ormsby-Gore emphasized the need of railways to relieve the labor wastage in head porterage, thus meeting the "fundamental problem in Africa arising from the small population in such huge areas." Sir Frederick agreed that "economic development was most

This issue was discussed at length in connection with the preparation of the new questionnaire during the sixth session of the Commission. M. Orts wished to introduce a question calling the attention of the mandatory powers "to the necessity of maintaining a just proportion between the rate at which the economic equipment and development of the mandated territories should be proceeded with and the amount of work which might reasonably be required from the native population." When noting the intensive way in which the mandatories were developing their territories he felt considerable apprehension.

The development of the mandated territories constituted for the mandatory powers a duty, alongside their other duty of securing the welfare of the natives. These two duties must be reconciled, and the two tasks must progress side by side. For this purpose it was necessary to find a just criterion. Certain public works had a general and immediate interest, so they justified the most cruel sacrifices. There were, on the other hand, enterprises, public as well as private, the extension or realization of which might without disadvantage be postponed until the native was able to support without injury the burden they involved, and to draw from them a profit, at least indirect.

Sir Frederick Lugard agreed that some control should be exercised on the rate of economic development, but did not admit "that the majority of Africans were physically incapable of work or that they disliked it"; on the contrary, he thought, speaking generally, "the African native was industrious and hardworking," though he admitted exceptions in certain tribes and individuals.

M. Freire d'Andrade pointed out that the native capacity for work varied greatly but disagreed with Sir Frederick:

In a general way, the native preferred not to cultivate the land or to engage in continuous labor. It was the duty of the men to watch over the construction of the villages, to hunt, make war, to drink, to take snuff and indulge in interminable discussions during their councils, in which the negroes showed themselves as orators of a very loquacious habit.

M. Rappard thought the only basis to judge upon was mortality and morbidity statistics, which should be more complete. Probably native populations were decreasing, but whether from liquor, dis-

---

necessary but it must take a secondary place, since it was dependent on the labor supply and the increase of native population" (*P.M.C.*, *Min.*, VI, 124–25).

eases, or "to an intensive effort to develop the country" was not clear.

M. Van Rees, speaking from thirty-five years' experience in the Dutch East Indies, was inclined to agree with M. d'Andrade's conception of the native.

Mr. Grimshaw heartily indorsed M. Orts's suggestion and repudiated the argument often made by prospective concessionaires that the present native population should be sacrificed for future generations.

To which M. d'Andrade replied:

The natives of South Africa who had at their disposal roads and railways, in the construction of which they had collaborated, were much more civilized and were in a much more comfortable position materially than those which inhabited the countries of Central Africa, where civilization had scarcely begun to penetrate.

It was all a question of degree. If there were races unable to work, then without any doubt the very impact of civilization would show them that they were not equipped for the struggle of life and they would end by disappearing. As regards the other races, it was essential to require from them the work which they were able to give in order to assist the mandatory power in the mission with which it was entrusted under the covenant. This mission would not be accomplished if the mandatory power contented itself, for philanthropic reasons, with leaving the natives to drink and to indulge in endless debates and inactivity, under the pretext that they were happier in this mode of life and that it must be respected.

The African races tended to diminish and to disappear. According to statistics it seemed that their disappearance was predestined. Personally, he was persuaded that this was due to alcohol and to syphilis, which prevailed everywhere where Europeans were found. It was from this cause, and not owing to work which was beyond their physical capacity, that the native races were suffering from contact with civilization and disappearing.

M. Rappard thought

if the commission asked an administrator whether the effect of the administration of his government was to cause a decrease in the population, he would probably be obliged to reply in the negative under pain of dismissal. The only criterion lay in the mortality and morbidity tables. If these tables showed abnormal figures it would be for the mandatory power to explain them. It was the duty of the commission to protect the native, and if the native races were dying out, it was clear that their moral and material welfare was being sacrificed.[58]

[58] *Ibid.*, VI, 47–50.

As a result of this discussion, Sir Frederick Lugard and M. d' Andrade prepared extensive memoranda on the question. The former distinguished public works such as arterial railways, harbors, telegraphs, and public buildings which were essential and justified any sacrifice from private enterprises. Wage labor he admitted caused high mortality and the break-up of social restraints through withdrawing many of the men from the tribes for considerable periods.

In order to diminish these disastrous results, it is desirable: (*a*) that the recruiting of laborers should be strictly regulated, especially as to the number that may be withdrawn from a village or tribe without detriment to the native welfare; that they should be medically examined before engagement; that the conditions of transport to the scene of labor should not impose a severe strain; that their food, housing, medical care and hours and conditions of service should be of the best; (*b*) that when once the absolutely essential works (referred to above) are completed, further progress in development should be strictly limited to the capacity of the people to bear the burden without involving either a decrease in population or the premature breakdown of tribal and social organization.

Thus both government and private enterprise should be content to progress slowly, and every effort should be made to introduce labor-saving devices such as caterpillar vehicles which do not require roads or railways. "The best criterion as to whether the demand for labor is excessive or not is that all wage labor should be absolutely free (except for vitally essential services) and that no compulsion should be used either under the guise of a fiscal tax or by indirect pressure. If adequately remunerated, and if the conditions are made sufficiently attractive, there is little fear that the laborers who voluntarily present themselves for work will, by so doing, contribute to the causes which result in a decrease in the population." By prohibiting slavery and forced labor except for essential public services the mandates go far toward requiring this standard.[59]

Apparently M. d'Andrade doubts its practicability. He asks:

Is it always possible to obtain free labor, and is education the only means of obtaining it? In that case the government should begin by setting the example, from which I conclude that compulsory labor should not be al-

[59] *Ibid.*, VII, 195. French experience seems to indicate the practicability of such a policy (*ibid.*, IV, 18).

lowed for public works any more than for private works. That is the point at which we must try to arrive.

Sooner or later foreign enterprise and foreign capital will come into the country. They will need labor. No matter what legislation there may be, if voluntary labor is not forthcoming, abuses of every kind will occur. That, I think, is inevitable, and we are all sufficiently experienced to recognize the fact.

Indeed, Sir F. Lugard himself, with all his authority, admits that natives should work, though he says that this should be brought about by education, using that term in its broadest sense.

I entirely agree. But the education of the colored man must take scores of years, or even centuries. In the meantime, his moral development and civilization can only progress hand-in-hand with the economic development of the country and will occasion expenditure which it is only fair that the native himself should defray, at least in part. The money for that purpose must be earned by labor.

All these facts were in my mind when I said that the native must not be allowed to live in idleness at the expense of his womenfolk or of his more deserving fellows who work. . . .

I also stated that idleness should be a punishable offence and that vagrancy is punishable in civilized countries. Sir F. Lugard says that this is not the case in England. I would like to point out that my remarks should be interpreted in a very broad sense. In civilized countries, those who do not work cannot gain their livelihood; at the same time, they must live. Consequently, they will either beg or steal. In either case they are punished. I am not speaking of those who, by thrift or inheritance, are in possession of assured incomes; though even in their case there is a tendency to withdraw the privilege, either by depriving them of the income or by taxing it.

And consider the number of people in civilized countries who are anxious to work but cannot find employment! How many men and women, too, are forced by the inexorable law of labor to accept employment which is very heavy, unhealthy, and often killing!

I consider, therefore, that the native should work—wherever he likes, for himself or for a master of his own choosing—but that he should not be permitted to idle.[60]

b) LAND

Thus, the Commission is divided on the fundamentals of native labor policy. This is less true of land policy. M. Yanaghita pointed out the problem in the conflict between the native's need for "reserve lands" and his need for "culture contacts." He wrote:

Sooner or later their development guaranteed as it is by the covenant will be accomplished and one of its principal consequences will be a more pronounced

[60] *Ibid.*, VII, 207; see also *ibid.*, I, 37.

need to possess a sufficient quantity of land. It is impossible to foresee accurately in what manner this need will arise; the only safe plan which could be adopted in present circumstances would appear to be to "reserve" areas of land as large as possible in order to provide for future needs, whatever they may be.

On the other hand, the natives need what may be termed "culture contact" for their development if the new civilization must be able to exercise its influence. There is only one condition which can conceivably allow good guides, advisers and employers from civilized countries to settle among the natives—considerable liberality must be shown when concessions of land are made. . . .

In order that the plantations may provide desirable conditions for the natives, and at the same time prove profitable for the capitalists, it will in some cases be necessary to encroach upon the future interests of the natives, or at least upon those interests connected with vacant and unowned land. . . .

The question at issue regards the practical benefits of the land system rather than its legal theory, which the natives will in any case fail to understand. It is as important to make sure that the principle is well applied as to determine the justice of the principle itself. What is desirable is that the mandatory administrators should prove their capability and good will in dealing with the future welfare of the inhabitants, and in taking the necessary steps to provide for their land "reserve."[61]

The Commission seems to be agreed that "land reserves" must be preserved for the natives, not only to care for future increase in population, but to permit his habitual practices of grazing flocks and hunting forest products over a wide area. This is expressly provided in B mandates which require the mandatory to "take into consideration native laws and customs" and to "respect the right and safeguard the interests of the native population" in regard to land. The transfer or creation of real rights in a non-native requires the previous consent of the authorities.

A memorandum from the Aborigines Protective Society received in the second session of the Commission urged the necessity of a broad interpretation of native rights to land and a correspondingly narrow definition of vacant lands so as to limit the acquisition of titles either by the government or concessionaires. This memorandum said:

The term [vacant] may be quite legitimately applied to lands without occupants and without superficial values, but it would raise precisely the danger which we have indicated if the term vacant lands were applied to those large

[61] *Ibid.*, sess. III, p. 281.

areas of tropical lands upon which are found today forest products normally gathered by the natives and forming the basis of their physical, social and economic existence.

In an extended memorandum approaching the question from the legal point of view, M. Van Rees gave a more limited interpretation:

> The imperative recommendation contained in this article is simply that the land settlement should be so carried out as to respect such genuine native rights as had been practically demonstrated in virtue of their customs and uses and to guarantee their interests, both immediate and more remote.

He pointed out that the granting of titles to vacant lands was not incompatible with respect for natives rights to use them and that consequently "state property" declarations would be proper if made "in a manner which satisfies the sense of justice of the native, for whom not theoretical possession but practical advantages are of importance."[62] With this, as we have noticed, M. Yanaghita agreed, though insisting on the need of ample reserves. He recognized the divergent conditions and native customs in different areas and the possibility of success in different policies, such as transporting populations from dense to thinly populated areas. In general, land legislation closely integrated with the existing native customs was recommended.[63]

It seems to be recognized that in regions suitable for agriculture tribal or communal interests in land will gradually give way to private ownership, but the Commission has frequently indicated the hope that in this evolution cultivation by native proprietors be fostered rather than development by native labor on European-owned plantations.

c) EDUCATION

Consideration has been given to educational and public-health policy and the Commission has had little difficulty in reaching agreement. Mme Bugge-Wicksell prepared a memorandum at the third session outlining the educational policy actually followed by the mandatories, and M. Yanaghita drew attention to the dangers of education conducted wholly by missionaries or foreigners which was likely to alienate the educated class from the tribe. The training

[62] *Ibid.*, pp. 238–39. [63] *Ibid.*, pp. 281–82.

of native teachers should be attempted, he thought, and education should be practical and related to daily pursuits. Furthermore, nationalistic propaganda for the mandatory government should be avoided.

The general tendency is certainly to abandon the old methods, which were too nationalistic, and too much directed toward the assimilation of the two races—methods such as the insistent teaching of patriotic songs and the names of emperors to the native children. We shall be interested to observe how the mentality of the natives will be altered by the well organized teaching of history and geography; for they will not realize their individual existence and its meaning until they understand the position they occupy in the vast expanses of Africa or the Pacific, and in the age long history of mankind.

The language of instruction, he thought, should be a native *lingua franca* such as Swahili in East Africa, rather than the mandatory's language, because being like the native dialect it would be easier to learn and would not have a tendency toward creating a special privileged class.[64] The Commission has generally expressed agreement with this point.

At the fourth session the Commission agreed upon a policy suggested by Mme Wicksell in the following terms:

The permanent mandates commission notes with satisfaction a growing tendency in several mandated territories in Africa to give prominence to the daily work and needs of the native boys and girls in the course of their instruction. The commission is of opinion that, by making character training and discipline, the teaching of agriculture, animal husbandry, arts and crafts, and elementary hygiene, the keynote of educational policy, the gradual civilization of the native populations as well as the economic development of the countries will be furthered in the best possible manner. The commission therefore asks the council to call the attention of all the mandatory powers to this system of education as being in its opinion particularly suitable to the conditions of life of backward peoples.

The Council indorsed this resolution, which was accompanied by a note in which Mme Wicksell attributed the development of this new educational policy to American experiments with negro education and its introduction into Africa to Sir Frederick Lugard's book *The Dual Mandate in Africa* and the report of the Commission sent

[64] *Ibid.*, pp. 239–56, 284. The mandates for Syria (art. 8) and Palestine (art. 15) expressly provide for education in the native languages and, subject to general educational requirements, by the native communities.

to West Africa in 1920–21 by the Phelps-Stokes fund entitled *Education in Africa*. She wrote:

> According to these authors, education in tropical countries has the double end, on the one side of teaching the indigenous population itself to develop the economic resources of these rich countries to its own profit and the benefit of the world in general, and, on the other hand, of raising the status of the population to gradually higher civilization by making them, even their rank and file out in the remote little villages, more healthy and wealthy and wise than they are at present.[65]

d) HEALTH

Public health in the mandated areas has attracted the Commission's interest, and at the third session Count de Ballobar wrote a memorandum urging co-operation with the health organization of the League and both he and M. Beau have emphasized the importance of adequate expenditure in this field by the mandatories.[66] At the third session resolutions were approved calling attention to the spread of venereal diseases among the natives and to the prejudicial effect on health through employing workers in a region appreciably different climatically from that in which they were recruited. The hope was expressed that this would engage the sympathetic attention of the mandatories.[67] These resolutions were approved by the Council.

The shortage of medical practicioners in some of the areas has often been alluded to and at the fourteenth session general resolutions, justified both by native health and by economic equality considerations, urging the mandatories to welcome trained physicians of non-mandatory nationality and to encourage missionary medical work were proposed in the Commission by Dr. Kastl of Germany, M. Rappard, and Lord Lugard. The determined opposition of M. Merlin of France, who seemed to fear political complications, delayed action until the fifteenth session.[67a]

The Commission is not agreed on the ideal of culture in the

[65] *Ibid.*, IV, 184.

[66] *Ibid.*, III, 197, 297–305. Both points have been frequently emphasized in subsequent discussions and reports on particular areas. See, for instance, *ibid.*, XIV, 14, 270, 275.

[67] *Ibid.*, III, 310–11.

[67a] *Ibid.*, XIV, 227–29, 265–67; XV, 289.

mandated areas ultimately envisaged by the Covenant, nor on precisely who the "inhabitants" to benefit by the mandatory administration are or will be. With regard to the political, material, and social progress of the native, clearly the first presents the greatest divergence of interest between the European and the native, while with respect to the last there is little conflict. States are usually prepared to look upon problems of health and education as technical rather than political though the political importance of the latter is commanding increasing attention.[68] Thus it is not surprising that the Commission has found it easiest to agree on the proper policy with respect to them. Perhaps, after all, sound foundations in education and sanitation should be the first step in native progress; without this start economic progress can hardly proceed without exploitation, and self-government in the present stage of world-integration implies a certain minimum of both education and economic surplus.

5. Policy with Respect to Third States

What policy should the mandatory observe with reference to the interests of outside states? The legal requirements with respect to the gratuitousness of the mandatory's services, non-military use of the territory and its inhabitants, and the open door for trade, missions, and archaeologists will be considered in Part III. Apart from insistence on the observance of these requirements, League organs have seldom discussed this aspect of policy, and even these problems have frequently been considered from the standpoint of native rather than third-state interests. Discrimination against third states is a problem of international politics, and League organs hesitate to criticize the mandatories unless buttressed by clear provisions of law to which the latter have agreed though their courage in this respect has increased with time.[69]

It has not been considered that the conception of the mandates

[68] See remarks of M. Yanaghita, *supra*, n. 64, and studies on civic education under the direction of C. E. Merriam, Chicago, 1929.

[69] The Commission in its third session (1923) did not include economic equality among the eleven subjects for general resolution and hesitated to criticize certain departures from the open door in the Japanese mandated area. Although the open door is not required in C mandates, the Japanese reservation on this question had favored it (*P.M.C.*, *Min.*, III, 83–84, 309–12). Contrast this with conditions five years later (see *infra*, n. 76).

system implies any duties by the mandatory toward League members or other states beyond those specified in the mandates or flowing from general international law and applicable treaties. As has been noted, the system has been considered to imply certain general duties toward natives, but the terminology of article 22 gives considerable support to the conclusion that duties owed to third states must rest on specific provisions. The right of League members to insist on the League's supervision and the Court's interpretation of mandates rests on that foundation. The mandates conception as first set forth by General Smuts and President Wilson did carry a general requirement of the open door, and the United States subsequently insisted that it was only after this requirement had become an "understanding" of the Peace Conference that it "felt itself able and willing to agree that the assignment of certain enemy territory by the victorious powers would be consistent with the best interests of the world." A similar implication was drawn "from the fundamental spirit of the League of Nations" by Japan in the reservation attached to her acceptance of the C-mandate texts, but the League has considered itself bound by the texts as adopted.[70]

It is clear, however, that by confining trade or loans to its own markets the mandatory might compel the natives to pay higher prices for their requirements and gain a profit for himself or his people. This possibility was emphasized by Japan in objecting to the non-inclusion of the open-door requirement in C mandates, and the question has several times been raised in the Commission. Thus it was decided to include questions in regard to economic equality and freedom of immigration in the C questionnaire, and as, from the standpoint of native interests, there is no reason for confining the open door to members of the League, the B and C questionnaires on the subject included no such limitation.[71] The United States has by treaty succeeeded in securing the open-door privilege in A and B mandated areas. The Council, on suggestion of the Commission, has urged the mandatories to extend bilateral commercial conventions for the benefit of mandated territories as well as general conventions.[72]

[70] See *supra*, chap. ii, nn. 31, 36, 71; chap. iv, sec. 4.

[71] *P.M.C., Min.*, I, 32, 47.

[72] See *infra*, chap. xiii, sec. 3*h*, and *P.M.C., Min.*, III, 309; XIV, 236.

In its report on its second session the Commission "desired to know" whether the establishment of the phosphates monopoly by the mandatory governments in Nauru, although not formally forbidden under the C mandates, "is fully in keeping with the disinterested spirit which should characterize the mission of a mandatory state."[73] On other occasions economic discriminations in C mandated areas have been referred to[74] and, in connection with the proposed requirement of the Tanganyika loan of 1927 that purchases from its proceeds be made in the British Empire, M. Orts of the Commission pointed out: "A sovereign state negotiating a loan in another country accepted the conditions of the loan in a convention freely debated. A mandated territory, however, being a ward of a mandatory state, was not in a position to discuss conditions."[75]

Thus it is clear that the external economic policy of a mandated territory, as well as its internal policy, in addition to conforming to the specific requirements of the mandate must take into consideration the interests of the natives and the gratuitous character of the mandatory's mission. Third states may benefit incidentally from this.

It may be that gradually the full equality for all states and their nationals in the exploitation, trade, cultural development, and scientific study of mandated areas will become an established mandate policy. The original conception of the system, the gratuitous character of the mandatory's mission, and the native's interest in an unrestricted opportunity to secure goods, capital, skill, and ideas from every part of the world suggests that it ought to be, while the practical success of the United States in gaining recognition for certain interests in most of the areas by special treaty, and the practical opportunity of League members to press their interests through the League's Assembly and council, suggests that it may be.[76] At present, however, the mandatory's policy with respect to

[73] *P.M.C., Rep.*, sess. II, p. 5. See *infra*, chap. xiii, secs. 2 f.

[74] See *supra*, n. 69.

[75] *P.M.C., Min.*, XI, 79.

[76] The Ninth Assembly hoped that the Commission would "actively pursue" its work on "the application of the principle of economic equality" and that "the mandatory powers would supply all the information requested" (*L. of N., Monthly Summary*, October, 1928, VIII, 294). The Commission discussed the subject extensively at its ses-

third states seems to be limited only by the interests of the inhabitants of the territory, by the principle prohibiting direct profit to the mandatory and by the specific provisions of the mandates which vary and which permit the mandatory special privileges in certain cases, especially in C-mandated territories.

---

sion which followed even in connection with topics not directly covered by any text (*P.M.C., Min.*, XIV, 139, 157, 236, 266).

PART III

THE LAW OF THE MANDATES SYSTEM

CHAPTER IX

THE SYSTEM OF INTERNATIONAL LAW

It is easy to exaggerate the importance of precise description of institutions in terms of existing law. They can often function without it—in fact, they can sometimes function better without it because their natural development is less restricted. The ingenuity of statesmen usually outstrips the classificatory skill of jurists.[1] Statesmen sometimes even display an aversion to jurists, perhaps from an instinct that the latter by confining them to traditional forms will blind them to useful innovations. Statesmen ask the assistance of lawyers to draw up what they have decided upon not to tell them what they can or cannot do, and, like Lord Salisbury in establishing the condominium of the Soudan, they sometimes look with "joy" upon "hybrid" arrangements "eminently calculated to shock the susceptibilities" of jurists.[2]

The United States government was able to function for years with the divided sovereignty devised by Madison and Hamilton in spite of the insistence of legal purists that divided sovereignty was impossible. The British commonwealth of nations seems able to do business in spite of the doubt as to whether sovereignty has or has not passed to the self-governing dominions. So also the mandatory system has worked successfully for nearly a decade though there has never been an official assertion as to the location of sovereignty and though the opinions of unofficial jurists on the subject have been almost as numerous and as diverse as the jurists who have devoted themselves to the study.

On the other hand, accurate legal description is not without value. By previsioning situations and their solution conflicts may be avoided, and the ascription of institutions to legal categories which have been tested by many situations in the past permits of

[1] Lawrence, *The Principles of International Law* (7th ed., 1923), p. 79; Butler, *B.Y.B.I.L.* (1920–21), pp. 35 ff.

[2] Cited from Lord Cromer by David Hunter Miller, *For. Aff.*, January, 1928, p. 277.

this prevision. Although the United States functioned in the absence of a clear understanding of the location of sovereignty in its government the doubt on this point may have contributed toward rendering civil war inevitable. Furthermore, economic progress is the product of confidence, and confidence rests on the possibility of forecasting the future of social relations. Law, by discouraging innovations the results of which cannot be foreseen, has proved the best agency for making the future like the past and so comprehensible. By reducing the probability of fortuitous change in human relations it has widened the opportunity for intelligent modification of human conditions.

The lawyers might well have strangled the mandates system at birth, but now that that danger is happily passed, their services can only be of benefit in solidifying the system in public confidence and in disclosing its meaning, its possibilities, and its limitations. Because of the loose drafting of article 22 of the Covenant this service is particularly needed.[3] No matter how carefully a document is drawn some powers will always be undefined, but with this product of haste, politics, and compromise it is particularly important to develop some general conceptions by which the terms can be construed and interpreted.

Though the mandates system has not been wholly integrated with the system of international law it has not been without law. In fact, the law in regard to it has been rapidly developing, especially by authoritative utterances of League bodies and voluminous juristic discussions. Possibly if the major legal implications of the system had been even clearer, conflicts such as that in Syria might have been avoided and economic progress in all the areas might have been more rapid than it has.

Before attempting to analyze the law of mandates in terms of existing international law we must recall certain characteristics of the latter. It has developed on the assumption of territorial sovereignty, and we will first examine the necessity of that assumption in the conditions of the modern world. Next the theory of international law as it has developed on this assumption will be considered. After this, the method of ascertaining international law from the sources will be explained.

[3] See *supra*, chap. xiv.

1. The Idea of Territorial Sovereignty

The international lawyer thinks of the world as composed of sixty-odd states members of the family of nations each of which occupies a territory within which it is sovereign in the sense of having the legal capacity to organize and exercise authority as it sees fit and of being alone responsible to other states for whatever happens in that territory. The rights and duties of all persons and officials within the territory are governed by the states internal law alone and the state is responsible under international law alone.[4]

He thus recognizes a sharp distinction between internal or municipal law which governs individuals and organs of government and which each state can change at will and international law which governs states and cannot be changed except by the express or tacit consent of all those bound.

This simple picture is of course modified by the habits of travel, trade, diplomacy, and war which bring citizens and officials of one state into the territory of another with the result that international rights, privileges, and immunities for the benefit of such persons have grown up by treaty and practice, subtracting somewhat from the completeness with which states can exercise their sovereignty in their territory. In such cases, however, the observance and en-enforcement of these rights belong primarily to the territorial sovereign and are sanctioned only by that state's international responsibility, which, because of the presence of such persons within its borders, is somewhat increased. Sometimes this responsibility has been even further increased by the undertaking of states to perform acts, enact laws, or pursue policies in their territories such as disarming, dredging rivers, extraditing criminals, establishing labor standards, or respecting minority rights; but still the doing of these things is left to the state within whose territory they are to be done acting through its own agencies. It alone is sovereign in its territory, and all territory is under the sovereignty of some state. This in broad outlines is the international lawyer's conception. He may admit that there are exceptions like extraterritorial jurisdiction, protectorates, leases, servitudes, condominiums, but he is likely to

[4] Wright, *The Enforcement of International Law through Municipal Law in the United States*, "University of Illinois, Studies in the Social Sciences," V (March, 1916), 11, 21; Willoughby, *Fundamental Concepts of Public Law* (New York, 1924), chap. xvi.

look upon them as anomalies, as blemishes in the picture, to be removed as society approaches the ideal.

This ideal is based not merely on conservatism and taste. It is useful to have everywhere some authority with plenary power to act in the presence of novel conditions unprovided for by any legal document or precedent. Sovereignty is the medium whereby law is kept *en rapport* with changing conditions. Since the inadequacy of communications, the insufficiency of recorded data, and the meager understanding of human behavior in the varied conditions of climate, race and culture have made a single sovereignty of the world impracticable, division has been necessary. Theoretically this division might be defined in terms of persons or activities as well as areas, but in settled societies geography has proved the most natural basis for human grouping. Practically it is difficult to maintain order without exclusive control of an area. Jurisdictional lines between persons and activities in the same area are less precise than geographical boundaries. Authorities far removed from a locality are not likely to understand its changing conditions.

Thus territorial division has proved the most convenient method for organizing government and avoiding conflict between sovereigns. It is justified not merely by custom but by practical considerations and will doubtless continue as the dominant form of political organization for a long time.[5]

Convenient as territorial sovereignty may be, it is neither necessary nor is it a condition actually existing in every part of the world. The international lawyer's conception of the world is merely a description, not a demonstration, and a description which is less accurate today than it was a century ago. Whether it is an idol whose worship is blocking the onward movement of progress or an ideal for the more perfect realization of which sacrifices should be made is the basis of the most profound political controversy of the twentieth century. On this men differ as did President Wilson and his Secretary of State.[6]

[5] For references on the convenience of territorial sovereignty see Wright, *op. cit.*, p. 21. Lowie finds that the territorial tie, though sometimes dwarfed by the kinship ties among primitive peoples, is never eliminated (*The Origin of the State*, p. 73).

[6] Secretary Lansing wrote a memorandum upon the difficulty of reconciling the mandates system with the doctrine of sovereignty which Wilson called mere "legal technicalities" (Lansing, *The Peace Negotiations*, pp. 151–53).

But whether an idol or an ideal the lawyer's assumption of territorial sovereignty is not an idea in the Platonic sense. Its validity is not absolute but relative to particular conditions. There seems to be nothing in human nature, political organization, social grouping, or logic which renders the assumption permanently and universally inevitable.

It is often assumed that political organization is impossible unless ultimate legal power over a territory is vested in an individual or group with a single will and adequate physical power to enforce it.[7] This hypothesis rests on the psychological assumption that men and groups can be induced to act together only by coercion or threats of coercion, a hypothesis which is not supported by the findings of social psychologists,[8] by the practice of modern advertisers, propagandists, and educators,[9] by the theory of liberals who would emphasize persuasion and consent rather than coercion,[10] or by the theory of conservatives who noting that custom was the only social control in primitive communities would continue it as the most important.[11] Human action may in fact be directed by many methods other than coercion. The possibilities of these methods are just on the threshold of exploration but it may be that some will be found as effective as coercion and less geographically limited in application. In fact, if the force theory were true, international relations would today be wholly anarchic and the triumph of law would be

[7] This is the basis of Hobbes's theory of law and sovereignty and is usually associated with the views of John Austin though, as Dunning points out, somewhat unjustly (*A History of Political Theories, from Rousseau to Spencer* [New York, 1920], p. 228). It is emphasized by the statement of Hans Delbrueck that "the decisive question in determining the inner character of a state always is 'whom does the army obey?' " (*Regierung und Volkswille*, pp. 133–39, cited in Beer, *The English Speaking Peoples*, p. 127.)

[8] See, for instance, Graham Wallas, *The Great Society* (New York, 1917), chap. vi on "Fear"; E. A. Ross, *Social Control;* and Charles E. Gehlke's review of recent writers on "Social Psychology and Political Theory," in Merriam and Barnes, *A History of Political Theories, Recent Times*, chap. x.

[9] The importance of propaganda as compared with force, even in the prosecution of war, is emphasized by Lasswell (*The Technique of War Time Propaganda*, New York, 1927).

[10] See John Stuart Mill, *On Liberty*, chap. i, discussed in Dunning, *op. cit.*, p. 238.

[11] Maine, *Early History of Institutions*, pp. 52, 252, 286; *Popular Government* (London, 1886), pp. 137 ff. Maine, however, considered force a useful adjunct of habit (*ibid.*, pp. 63–64; see also Graham Wallas, *op. cit.*, chap. v, "Habit").

impossible without a single world-state. "Unlimited power over its subjects," wrote Burgess, "is the very essence" of the state, and "from the standpoint of the idea, the territorial basis of the state is the world." He admits that the "concept" of the state does not attain this universality, an admission which suggests that territorial sovereignty is not a necessary idea.[12]

But though unified coercive power may not be a psychological necessity for political order, it has been suggested that some ultimate jurisdiction for settling all disputes which may arise in a territory is a practical necessity of political organization.[13] Otherwise it is said the dispute will remain unsettled and the political order will be in danger. This argument, it is submitted, rests on too limited an imagination. Without denying the convenience of courts or other bodies with ultimate obligatory jurisdiction over every possible dispute in a given territory, the possibilities of political organization which relies on ultimate settlement by negotiation or suspension until the dispute becomes obsolete, rather than on the exercise of compulsory jurisdiction, should not be overlooked. This argument also denies the possibility of political order in the family of nations as now organized.[14] Even within the state, disputes between powerful organizations such as those of labor and capital, are usually settled by negotiation, conciliation, or voluntary arbitration. What does the checks-and-balance system in the American Constitution mean but that disputes on competence between co-ordinate departments of the government can only be settled by agreement and voluntary co-operation?[15] Political science may even be capable of

[12] J. W. Burgess, *Political Science and Constitutional Law* (Boston, 1890), I, 50, 56.

[13] John Dickinson, "A Working Theory of Sovereignty," *P.S.Q.*, XLII, 5; W. W. Willoughby, *Fundamental Concepts of Public Law* (New York, 1924), p. 72; F. W. Coker, in Merriam and Barnes, *op. cit.*, p. 83.

[14] The Permanent Court of International Justice has held that "it is well established in international law that no state can, without its consent, be compelled to submit its disputes with other states either to mediation or to arbitration or to any other kind of pacific settlement" (Eastern Carelia case, *P.C.I.J.* [Ser. B], No. 5, p. 27). Consent has of course been given by many states for the compulsory arbitration of many disputes in recent years.

[15] See Wright, *The Control of American Foreign Relations* (New York, 1922), p. 126 and chap. xviii on "Understandings Concerning the Relation of the Independent Departments."

discovering procedures and organs for settling disputes quite different from the courts, the executive, the legislature, and elections as customarily found today, without falling back on the *ultima ratio* of battle or the perils of indefinite watchful waiting. In fact, the experiments made by the League of Nations in methods of deliberation, inquiry, conciliation, mediation, collective resolution, advisory opinion, etc., illustrate the possibilities in this direction. All human institutions are fallible. The decision of the Supreme Court of the United States in the Dred Scott case failed to settle the controversy which led to the Civil War.[16] British labor unions after failing to gain their point in the courts were successful in Parliament.[17] Negotiation was successful where arbitration failed to settle the Maine-boundary dispute.[18] Courts are useful but neither all sufficient nor indispensable. Political order may exist, not only between territorial groups but also between functional, racial, religious, or other groups in the same territory, when negotiation is more important than jurisdiction in settling disputes.[19]

Apart from practical problems of control and organization it has been suggested that territorial propinquity is the most "natural" basis for human grouping.[20] People tend to resemble, to understand, and to associate most with those near at hand. Agriculture which is the basis of modern societies attaches people to the land, and this attachment develops into patriotism, love of the homeland. In nomadic tribes, however, kinship has been the natural basis of grouping, and the sentiment of nationality with its creation of isolated minorities in Europe has often run counter to patriotism, while

[16] *Dred Scott* v. *Sanford,* 19 How. 393 (1857). See T. W. Balch, *A World Court in the Light of the United States Supreme Court,* Philadelphia, 1918.

[17] See the discussion of the Taff Vale case (1901) and the Osborne judgment (1909) in Ogg, *Social Progress in Contemporary Europe* (1912), pp. 299–300.

[18] Fish, *American Diplomacy* (New York, 1923), pp. 228–35; Hill, *Leading American Treaties* (New York, 1922), pp. 175–82.

[19] Political pluralists would emphasize the importance of negotiation (see G. H. Sabine, *A.P.S.R.,* XVII [February, 1923], 39). For a review of pluralistic theories see F. W. Coker, in Merriam and Barnes, *op. cit.,* pp. 80–119.

[20] See Dunning's discussion of writers who have looked upon "The Nation as a Geographic Unit" (*op. cit.,* pp. 316–20) and Franklin Thomas, in "Contributions of Anthropogeography to Modern Political Theory," Merriam and Barnes, *op. cit.,* chap. xii, especially discussion of Ratzel, pp. 471–78.

imperialism has extended political control of persons and processes without regard to geography. The natural grouping of city people is less with their neighbors than with widely dispersed social and business associates and perhaps in the highly organized societies of the future, with great mobility, universal communication, and extensive division of labor, functional groupings will be most "natural" over large areas if not over the whole world. Such groupings are in fact gaining in importance not only nationally but internationally.[21]

Perhaps the most potent argument for the necessary division of the world into territorial sovereignties is that it has always been so. Custom often creates a conviction of necessary truth; in fact, Hume thought it was the only basis of necessary truth.[22] It may be the basis of both physical law and human law but if so it but shows that neither are governed by any logical necessity.[23] The latter has to do only with the relation of concepts, not with their reality or the possibility of their realization. The truth of mathematical and logical conclusions is as universal and eternal as acceptance of the axioms and definitions on which they are based. The truth of the conclusions of physical and social science, on the other hand, is probably limited, in strict accuracy to the time and place in which the observations were made on which a particular "truth" is based. It is merely the customary inertia of things and people which gives a probability of repetition in other times and places— a probability which varies with the nature of the data. Atoms can be relied on to act according to custom more than men, and men more than states.

Custom must not be confused with necessity, and in the present case, as has been pointed out, territorial sovereignty does not even have the authority of universal custom. The personality of laws

[21] C. E. Merriam, in Merriam and Barnes, *op. cit.*, pp. 27–29. Associational grouping based on sex, age, occupation, or other characteristics of the individual has been important in most primitive societies though not so important as kinship and neighborhood groupings (Lowie, *The Origin of the State*, chap. v).

[22] *Treatise of Human Nature*, Book I, Part III, par. 14, entitled "Of the Idea of Necessary Connection" (*Works* [Boston, 1854], I, 199).

[23] Karl Pearson, *Grammar of Science*, chap. iii; W. G. Sumner, *Folkways*, pp. 29–30.

was the rule of Europe on the fall of the Roman Empire.[24] Medieval Europe acted on the theory that temporal and spiritual sovereignty could exist in the same territory.[25] Today theories of functional distribution of sovereignty among economic groups have been developed in Western Europe.[26] In Palestine an independent political organization of the three religious groups is being considered.[27] In South Africa a similar independent organization of racial groups has been proposed.[28] Federations, confederations, and other types of union have distributed functions between central and local governments in the same territory, and in some of them, like the British Empire today, the line of distribution is not interpretable by any superauthority but by negotiation and general consent as the case arises.[29] The dominance of territorial sovereignty is not a necessity. It is not even a universal custom. It is merely a common practice and under present conditions a convenience.[30]

Thus we are unable to find any psychological, political, sociological, or logical necessity for attributing sovereignty of the mandates to a single state. Science and philosophy impose no prohibitions upon the jurist in defining the status of these areas.

The task before us, however, is to integrate the mandates system with existing international law. What limitations does that law impose?

[24] E. Jenks, *Law and Politics in the Midale Ages* (New York, 1913), pp. 13 ff. R. T. Crane, *The State in Constitutional and International Law*, "Johns Hopkins University Studies in Historical and Political Science" (25th ser., 1907), p. 47.

[25] Dunning, *A History of Political Theories, Present and Medieval*, chap. vi.

[26] Coker, in Merriam and Barnes, *op. cit.*, pp. 89–98.

[27] Lieut.-Col. Symes, accredited representative from Palestine (*P.M.C.*, *Min.*, IX, 153–158). See also Wright, "The Palestine Problem," *P.S.Q.*, XLI (September, 1926, 411–412).

[28] Eric H. Louw, in *Great Britain and the Dominions* (Chicago), pp. 444 ff.; Buell, *The Race Problem in South Africa* (F.P.A., Information Service; August 21, 1928), IV, 273–76.

[29] Sir Cecil J. B. Hurst, in *Great Britain and the Dominions*, pp. 24 ff.

[30] "That the possession of a fixed territory is a distinct requirement [of the state] must be looked upon as the result of more general, but not strictly necessary circumstances" (W. E. Hall, *International Law* [8th ed., 1924], p. 18). See also Vinogradoff, *Outlines of Historical Jurisprudence* (Oxford, 1920), I, 122–23; Lowie, *op. cit.*, chap. iii; Crane, *op. cit.*, p. 60.

2. Sovereignty under International Law

In considering the attitude of international law toward sovereignty (*a*) the historic changes in the character of sovereignty will be examined first, after which (*b*) the term will be defined; (*c*) the concept will be analyzed; (*d*) the criteria for determining the sovereignty of territory, persons, and governments will be suggested; and finally, (*e*) the special difficulties of divided and collective sovereignty will be considered.

a) changes in the character of sovereignty

Historically, modern international law though formed of materials handed down from earlier times began with the break-up of the medieval system and the fact of states asserting the right to do whatever they wanted, whenever they pleased, wherever they could. Might was right for Machiavelli and the princes of his time. As Hall remarks, "International relations was fast resolving itself into a struggle for existence in it barest form."[31] International law has developed through the recognition by states of limitations upon these originally unlimited powers or upon their exercise. The true character of international law can thus be best understood through a study of these limitations and the duties and responsibilities which they imply though writers have often followed the contrary practice of emphasizing the so-called fundamental rights and powers of states.[32]

Territorial limitations were first recognized. Thus while protected in the right to its own domain, each state found itself bound to respect the domain of others. Personal jurisdiction, however, which had prevailed among the barbarians who invaded the Roman Empire, could not be entirely eliminated. Thus in order to claim the allegiance of and to extend protection to citizens abroad states had to recognize limitations upon their power over foreigners within the domain. At the same time the development of international

[31] *Ibid.*, p. 18; Lawrence, *op. cit.*, pp. 21, 24.

[32] Wright, *The Enforcement of International Law through Municipal Law in the United States* (1916), chap. i. "All that can be required of a state is that it should not overstep the limits which international law places upon its jurisdiction. Within these limits its title to exercise jurisdiction rests in its sovereignty" (The Lotus, *P.C.I.J.* [Pub. Ser. A], No. 10).

contacts necessitated officials abroad to whom special immunities were accorded and the common use of the sea required limitations upon the exercise of power at a defined distance beyond the shore. Later there was a tendency to limit the exercise of sovereignty functionally through the multiplication of lawmaking conventions and the development of international unions for economic, cultural, humanitarian, and political purposes. These conventions and unions have ordinarily specified certain limitations and requirements to be observed in the exercise of state functions, but sometimes they go further by creating international agencies with a definite competence to act within the territory of member states.

In recent times, factors militating against the dominance of territorial sovereignty have gained in importance.[33] The rapid increase in foreign trade, travel, and investment has given an increased importance to the responsibilities and powers of states with respect to foreigners in their territory and their nationals abroad, thus shifting emphasis from territory to persons. Definition of the boundary of state domain has become less important than definition of the responsibility for protecting foreigners within that domain.[34]

The same factors, as well as the development of a more destructive war technique, have greatly increased the scope of international organization and legislation. This has correspondingly limited the state's discretion in the exercise within its territory of many functions of external significance such as postal, telegraph, and radio services; land, water, and air transportation; customs, concession, and financial discriminations; health, drug, obscene literature, and prostitution regulation; the conditions of immigration, labor and intellectual work, minority and native protection; the manufacture, trade, possession, and use of armaments and military material; the procedure and principles for settling international disputes; and even the methods and sanctions of national defense.[35]

33 J. W. Garner, "Limitations on National Sovereignty in International Relations," *A.P.S.R.*, XIX (February, 1925), 1–24.

34 Many studies of the latter subject have been made by arbitral tribunals and jurists (see Borchard, *The Diplomatic Protection of Citizens Abroad*, New York, 1915, and Eagleton, *The Responsibility of States in International Law*, New York, 1928).

35 See Reinsch, *Public International Unions*, Boston, 1911; Woolf, *International Government*, New York, 1916; Sayre, *Experiments in International Administration*, New

The multiplication of international contacts and the development of international organization have been accompanied by an increase in the complexity of national constitutions and a steady expansion of the family of nations from the original Christian states of Europe to parts of the world governed by political bodies of widely different conceptions, traditions, and methods. Instead of the simple unitary states of the seventeenth and eighteenth centuries with authority and responsibility vested in an individual or a readily definable body of individuals, there are today Oriental, African, and American as well as European varieties of federations, confederations, empires, protectorates, suzerainties, commonwealths, unions, and leagues of nations, some of which may be as readily classed with international organizations as with states. Apart from these varying degrees of unity and autonomy of political entities, which may or may not be within a single "state," the powers of government within each entity have often been limited or distributed among a variety of organs by relatively permanent constitutions or customs, thus establishing practical if not legal variations in international capacity.[36]

Thus instead of a world of equal, territorially defined, sovereign states we have a world of political entities displaying a tropical luxuriance of political and legal organization, competence, and status. The extent to which the characteristics of these entities are to be regarded as the product of constitutional law or of international law is often a matter of grave doubt in each particular case. Thus the line between states, constitutional circumscriptions within the state, and international organizations is often difficult to define. To which of these classes, for instance, shall we assign Armenia, the British Empire, Canada, Dantzig, the Danube Commission, Egypt, Geneva, Haiti, Iraq, Irish Free State, Johore, the League of

---

York, 1919; Potter, *Introduction to the Study of International Organization*, New York, 1922; Hudson, "The Development of International Law since the War," *A.J.I.L.*, XXII (April, 1928), 330–50, and list of multilateral international instruments of legislative effect (*ibid.*, Supp., pp. 90–108).

[36] Dickinson, *The Equality of States in International Law* (Cambridge, 1920), chaps. vi, vii, viii; and Baty, "Protectorates and Mandates," *B.Y.B.I.L.* (1921–22), pp. 109 ff., for change in character of protectorates from mere contract obligations to limitations of sovereignty.

Nations, Mongolia, Morocco, New Hebrides, the Papacy, Prussia, the Saar Valley, San Marino, the Soudan, and the Union of Soviet Republics?[37] Many other entities could be mentioned whose international status is not obvious. In fact, on examination, difficulties of classification arise with respect to most such entities. As Oppenheim said of the League of Nations, they all have a claim to be considered entities *sui generis*.

b) THE DEFINITION OF SOVEREIGNTY

With these changes in the character of states and their relations wrought by new international contacts, new international organizations, more complex constitutional structures, and the extension of the family of nations to states of widely different culture and situation, the problem of defining sovereignty has become more difficult.

The word "sovereignty" has been used in the preceding discussion to mean legal omnipotence except as limited by applicable international law and treaties or, conversely, freedom from limitation by municipal law. This definition, however, may not correspond to conceptions often implied by the term and may not be sufficiently precise to assist in classifying the diverse political structures of the day, particularly the mandated territories. We must then consider what sovereignty has meant in the past and what we propose to make it mean for present purposes.

Like liberty, democracy, nationality, and most political terms, sovereignty has continually changed its meaning with changes in the typical political structure and the outstanding political problem of the day and in the political objective of the particular writer. It has been a dynamic term whose emotional tone coming from past

[37] The status of some of these is discussed in Willoughby and Fenwick, *Types of Restricted Sovereignty*, 1919, and Hershey, *Essentials of International Public Law and Organization* (New York, 1927), pp. 167–98; Dickinson, *Equality of States in International Law;* Eagleton, *The Responsibility of States*, chap. ii. The status of Great Britain and the dominions was considered at the imperial conferences of 1923 and 1926. See Hurst, Smiddy, Dafoe, *et al.*, *Great Britain and the Dominions*, Chicago, 1928; V. K. Johnston, "Dominion Status in International Law," *A.J.I.L.*, XXI, 481; Report of the Inter-imperial Committee, Imperial Conference, 1926, *G.B.*, *Parl. Pap.* (1926), Cmd. 2768, reprinted in *International Conciliation* (March, 1927), No. 228. The status of the League of Nations is discussed by Oppenheim, *R.G.D.I.P.*, XXVI (1919), 234–44; Corbett, *B.Y.B.I.L.* (1924), p. 119; Voorhees, *A.P.S.R.*, XX, 847; Harriman, *ibid.*, XXI, 137; Sir Herbert Ames, *ibid.*, XXII, 706. See also nn. 96 and 97 and chap. xi, sec. 2*b*.

associations has been persistent, but whose intellectual content, fitted to each particular purpose for which it is employed, has been variable and vague. Thus it has been of more value for purposes of oratory and persuasion than of science and law. Precise definition of its protean meanings is not easy.[38]

It was first used in discussing the relation of government and governed. In the age of absolute monarchs following the disintegration of feudalism writers like Bodin, fearful of disorder, attributed sovereignty to the prince while others like Althusius, fearful of oppression, attributed it to the people, but in either case its relativity was recognized. Bodin called it "the supreme power over citizens and subjects unrestrained by law." Althusius called it "the highest and most general power of administering the affairs which generally concern the safety and welfare of the soul and body of the members of the state." Both, however, recognized its subordination to the law of God and the law of nature, and, in the case of Bodin, the law of nations also. Although these writers used terms like "supreme," "highest," "absolute," it is clear that they meant only that the sovereign part of the state was supreme, relative to the rest of the state.[39]

Sovereignty was later used in discussing the relation of one ruler to another. Grotius defined sovereignty as "that power whose acts are not subject to the control of another, so that they may be made void by the act of any other human will," but the international law of which he wrote flowed from nature and custom, not from human will. Consequently to him sovereignty really meant the status of a prince bound by international law, but not by human commands. He conceived the state as the patrimony of the prince, and since

[38] See illuminating discussion of the "symbolic" and "emotive" use of words (Ogden and Richards, *The Meaning of Meaning*, pp. 149 ff.), and Pollard's statement, "few habits are more fatal to historical understanding than that of assuming that the same word has the same meaning at different periods" (*The Evolution of Parliament* [1920], p. 168). See also Crane, *op. cit.*, chap. ii.

[39] Bodin, *Six Livres de la republique*, I (1576), c. 2, 8; Althusius, *Politica methodica digesta* (1609), c. 9, secs. 122, 125; Merriam, *History of the Theory of Sovereignty since Rousseau* (New York, 1900), pp. 14–20. Brierly states briefly the political situation in which these theories developed (*The Law of Nations* [Oxford, 1928], pp. 7 ff., as does Crane, *op. cit.*, chaps. ii and iii).

in fact princes had varying degrees of control over their lands and peoples, Grotius and his successors of the positive school treated sovereignty like property capable of divided or collective ownership and of limitation by various types of incumbrance.[40]

The relative character of sovereignty was clear enough when the relation of princes to their subjects or to each other was under discussion, but the problem assumed a new character when the state as a whole was personified and the term "sovereignty" was used to define its relation to its parts. For the state was not a concrete thing like the prince but a metaphysical entity difficult to define. It embraced not only government and subjects but also territory, and if one asserted that the state had supreme power over all its parts unrestricted by law, it seemed to mean that it had unlimited control over foreigners within its territory and over its own government agents and subjects abroad, to say nothing of a possible capacity to acquire new subjects and new territory at will. Thus the application of the old definition to the new problem was incompatible with the existence of international law. Such was the conclusion of Hobbes who found "the sovereign power, whether placed in one man, as in monarchy, or in one assembly of men, as in popular and aristocratical commonwealths, is as great as possibly men can be imagined to make it." The only limitation he admitted was natural law, which he interpreted as not law at all but the instinct of self-preservation.[41]

The same conclusion was accepted by Puffendorf and the "naturalist" international lawyers, although they added a moral element to Hobbe's natural law which made it possible to build an international law on the sanctity of agreement held to be a law of nature almost on a parity with self-preservation.[42]

[40] Grotius, *De jure belli ac pacis*, I (1625), c. 3, secs. 7, 16, 17; II, c. 5, sec. 31; Moser, *Beiträge zu dem Neusten europäischen Völkerrecht in Friedenszeiten*, I, sec. 506; Martens, *Précis du droit de gens moderne de l'Europe* (1788), sec. 16; Merriam, *op. cit.*, pp. 21–23, 209–12.

[41] Hobbes, *De Leviathan* (1651), c. 20; Merriam, *op. cit.*, pp. 24–27.

[42] Puffendorf, *De jure naturae et gentium*, VII (1672), c. 6, secs. 2, 10. Locke (*Two Treatises of Government* [1689], secs. 95–99, 129–30, 168) similarly utilized natural law as a limitation upon the power of the sovereign over the subject. By the original contract forming the state, he thought it received from the members only those natural rights

The metaphysical absoluteness of the term gained additional support after sovereignty was identified with will and with law. Rousseau, like Hobbes, personified the state, but instead of gathering it together in the highest governing authority he considered it inalienable by the people as a whole. Sovereignty was the general will. Rousseau himself was not considering the problem of external relations but the relation of the whole to its parts. He compared the power of the body politic over all its members to "the absolute control over all his members which nature gives every man." His successors, however, conceiving the state as a product of nature rather than of art, developed the consequences of its absolute will in other fields, and with the German idealists like Hegel and Treitschke sovereignty became as free from external as from internal limitation.[43]

At the same time John Austin emphasized the legal implications of Hobbe's conception. Agreeing with Bentham that the social contract and natural law had no place in juristic and political thought, he used sovereignty to distinguish law from morality and defined the former as that which the sovereign commands or at least will enforce. For this purpose the sovereign could not be a vague metaphysical entity, but must be a determinate man or group of men unlimited by law because the maker of law. "The power of a monarch properly so called, or the power of a sovereign number in its collegiate and sovereign capacity, is incapable of legal limitation. . . . . Supreme power limited by positive law is a flat contradiction in terms."[44]

---

necessary for the common good. Furthermore, he differed from Hobbes in holding that the state or civil society as a whole retained political sovereignty, conferring on the government by a second contract merely legal sovereignty which it might reassume by "appeal to heaven" if the legal sovereign broke the contract (Merriam, *op. cit.*, pp. 28–32). Vattel (*Le Droit des gens* [1758], Prelim.) utilizes agreement, express, tacit, or presumed, as the basis for a positive law of nations, which, however, rested eventually on the natural law support of agreements.

[43] Rousseau, *Du Contrat social*, I (1762), chap. vi; II, chap. iv. He differs from Locke both in holding that the political sovereign is absolute (I, chap vii) and that it is identical with the legal sovereign (III, chap. v). See Hegel, *Grundlinien der Philosophie des Rechtes* (1821), secs. 258, 278; Treitschke, *Politik*, chap. xxviii; Merriam, *op. cit.*, pp. 33–35, 90–95.

[44] Austin, *Lectures on Jurisprudence* (1832; 3d ed. 1869), I, 270; Bentham, *Fragment on Government* (1776), chap. iv, pp. 152–55; Merriam, *op. cit.*, pp. 130–50. "A

Clearly the political sovereignty of Hobbes and Rousseau, the legal sovereignty of Austin, and the metaphysical sovereignty of Hegel were of no use to the international lawyer, unless indeed he took them as an invitation to commit suicide. Jellinek attempted a reconciliation by defining sovereignty as "the characteristic of a state through which it can be legally bound by its own will," thus permitting a subjective international law, but this was really the same as Austin's "public international morality" and condemned international law to be "anomic." Preuss, Krabbe, Duguit, Figgis, Laski, Cole, Ward, Kelsen, and others in the interest of federalism, internationalism, individual liberty, churches, trade unions, or general social reconstruction, and often using Gierke's *Genossenschaftstheorie* as a weapon, have in recent years emphasized the practical and moral limitations upon the exercise of all authority and urged elimination of the term "sovereignty" altogether or, at least, as a characteristic of the state.[45] While showing the unreality of unified political sovereignty,[46] up to date they have been unable to convince the world that juristic sovereignty is an obsolete conception. The

---

sovereign is exempt from suit not because of any formal conception or obsolete theory, but on the logical and practical ground that there can be no legal right as against the authority that makes the law on which the right depends" (Holmes, in *Kawananako* v. *Polyblank*, 205 U.S. 349, 353 [1907]; see also Gray, *Nature and Sources of the Law* [1909], pp. 77–81; Holland, *Jurisprudence* [11th ed.], pp. 53, 365).

[45] Jellinek, *Die Lehre von den Staatenverbindungen* (1882), p. 34; Preuss, *Gemeinde, Staat, Reich als Gebietskörperschaften, Versuch einer deutschen Staats Konstruktion auf Grundlage der Genossenschaftstheorie* (1889), p. 181; Krabbe, *Modern Idea of the State* (trans. Sabine and Shepard), New York, 1922; Duguit, *Law in the Modern State* (trans. H. and F. Laski), New York, 1919; Figgis, *Churches in the Modern State*, London, 1913; Laski, *Studies in the Problem of Sovereignty*, 1917; *A Grammar of Politics*, 1925; Cole, *Social Theory*, New York, 1920; Ward, *Sovereignty, a Study of a Contemporary Political Notion* (London, 1928), p. 179. Merriam (*op. cit.*, pp. 194, 207–9), Ward (*op. cit.*), and Mattern (*Concepts of State, Sovereignty, and International Law* [1928], chaps. viii–x) review the theories of these writers. Gierke's theory is set forth in *Die deutsche Genossenschaft* (1863–81), and may be studied in Maitland's translation of a portion of Gierke's Althusius, as *Political Theories of the Middle Ages*, Cambridge, 1900; Merriam, *op. cit.*, pp. 114–19, 201; and Ward, *op. cit.*, pp. 86–94.

[46] The conclusion of many contemporary theories is perhaps summed up in Sabine's statement, "For my own part, then, I must reserve the right to be a monist when I can and a pluralist when I must" ("Pluralism, a Point of View," *A.P.S.R.*, XVII, 34 ff.), a conclusion which Ward says shows that the distinction between political monism and pluralism is one of "pure propaganda" (*op. cit.*, p. 176). See also *supra*, sec. 1.

state still seems to exist different from subordinate government agencies and other associations and a term is needed to define it.[47]

If sovereignty is to be useful to international law it must be compatible with the existence of that law, but at the same time its characteristic feature of superiority to municipal law must be preserved. Both can be done if the two types of law are recognized as distinct. One has its source in the family of nations and defines the limits of the sovereign's competence; the other has its source in the sovereign's will acting within his *de facto* competence.[48]

So long as international law and municipal law were both looked upon as imperfect human efforts to embody natural justice, there was no basis for this distinction. As the two approached perfection, they would approach identity on matters involving international relations. International law was or ought to be part of the municipal law of each state, and international law did or ought to accept the universally accepted principles of municipal law.[49] But with the

---

[47] Wilde, *The Ethical Basis of the State* (1924), chap. viii; Willoughby, *Fundamental Conceptions of Public Law*, p. 15; Coker, in Merriam and Barnes, *A History of Political Theories, Recent Times*, p. 917.

[48] International law may be defined as the body of rules, principles, and standards for the violation of which states are habitually held responsible by international processes (see Wright, *Enforcement of International Law through Municipal Law in the United States*, pp. 12–13; *Control of American Foreign Relations*, p. 13). Municipal law, on the other hand, may be defined as the body of rules, principles, and standards which the state controls and enforces. These definitions adequately distinguish the two bodies of law as a whole by their characteristic sanctions, on the assumption that a "body of rules, principles, and standards" exists in each case. Proof of the latter is to be found in the historic existence of the family of nations and national societies and the historic recognition of definite and precise sources of law by each (see *infra*, sec. 3). Triepel emphasizes the distinctiveness of the sources of the two types of law (*Völkerricht und Landesrecht* [1899; French trans., 1920], and brief statement in *Acad.D.I.*, I [1923], 99 ff.).

[49] The idea of the eventual sovereignty of natural law appears in different form in the sovereignty of reason urged by Cousin, Constant, Guizot, and other French writers after the Napoleonic period, in Krabbe's sovereignty of law, and in Duguit's "consciousness of social solidarity" (see Merriam, *op. cit.*, pp. 75 ff.; Ward, *op. cit.*, pp. 127, 158). The British doctrine of supremacy of law means something the same and was at one time invoked to declare even acts of Parliament void (Bonhams case, 8 Coke, 115, 118*a*), as does the doctrine that international law is supreme over municipal law urged by Pillet (*R.G.D.I.P.*, V, 87), Scott (*A.J.I.L.*, I, 831 ff.), Potter (*ibid.*, XIX, 315 ff.), Kelsen (discussed by Mattern, *Concepts of State, Sovereignty and International Law*

view that law is the result of objective sources recognized by the society in which the law operates, the distinction was possible in theory and would be applicable in fact if a family of nations and national societies each existed and in fact each recognized distinct sources of law. The historical development already traced is believed to give ample evidence of these facts.[50]

Thus we may define "sovereignty" as the status of an entity subject to international law and superior to municipal law, but it appears quite different when viewed from one or the other point of view because international law and municipal law are not necessarily consistent.[51]

From the international-law point of view, municipal law lies in the realm not of law but of fact. It may be important for determining the *de facto* legal situation of things, for determining the applicability of rules of international law so far as they depend on recognition or voluntary acceptance, or even as a source for ascertaining what the rule of international law is on a given topic, but it is not international law per se.[52] Thus from the standpoint of international law, every entity has some sovereignty if it has capacity to establish legal relations with other sovereigns, and full sovereignty if it has capacity to establish normal legal relations with all other full sovereigns. Although this capacity is defined by international law, that law in fact utilizes as evidence of capacity the claims asserted by the sovereign's own "municipal law."

On the other hand, from the municipal-law point of view inter-

---

[1928], chap. x), and others (see also Wright, *A.J.I.L.*, XI, 2; XVII, 244). All of these theories seek to subordinate will to reason, holding that the latter is the ultimate source of all authority. For statement of the common-law reluctance to push either sovereignty or natural law too far, see Holdsworth, *Some Lessons from Our Legal History* (New York, 1928), pp. 109 ff.

[50] See *supra*, sec. 2*a*; *infra*, sec. 3. The doctrine of objective sources, sometimes called "positivism" by international law writers, differs both from the "positive" theory which identifies law with the will of a sovereign and from the "naturalist" theory which identifies it with abstract justice (see Brierly, *op. cit.*, pp. 37, 62; *infra*, n. 114).

[51] To similar effect see Fenwick, *International Law* (1924), p. 84. "A state is not, in fact, independent in respect to the rules of international law. It must, however, be independent with respect to the legal control of any other state or states capable of dictating its conduct." See also Garner, *A.P.S.R.*, XIX, 2; Merriam, *op. cit.*, pp. 214–16. Crane emphasizes the inconsistency of the two points of view (*op. cit.*, p. 73).

[52] See *infra*, sec. 3.

national law is not law except in so far as expressly adopted. It is a fact which the political organs of government inevitably consider in judging the expediency of legislation and executive action and which the state may accept as a source of municipal law applicable by the courts so far as its sovereignty has not been expressed to the contrary by competent organs but it is not municipal law per se.[53] From this point of view sovereignty is, therefore, the legally unlimited capacity to create jural relations. But though legally unlimited, the municipal-law sovereign is of course free to act in the light of existing facts and conditions such as the restraints of "international law."

Thus sovereignty as viewed from the two points of view has different sources and different sanctions and may have inconsistent applications. From the standpoint of municipal law, sovereignty springs from the state's existence (as natural rights were said to spring from a man's existence); but from the standpoint of international law, sovereignty springs from international law (as positive legal rights are said to be the creation of law). From the standpoint of municipal law, the claim of a state through its organ with ultimate authority in the matter to a legal right, power, or interest *is* a legal right, power, or interest; but from the standpoint of international law, such a claim is valid only in so far as established through the appropriate international procedure.[54] Thus a municipal law

[53] *Mortensen* v. *Peters*, 14 Scots Q.L.R. 227 (1906); Wright, *Enforcement of International Law, etc.*, p. 16, and "International Law in Its Relation to Constitutional Law," *A.J.I.L.*, XVII, 241, 244; Willoughby, "The Legal Nature of International Law," *ibid.*, II, 357, and *Fundamental Concepts of Public Law*, pp. 284 ff.; Westlake, "Is International Law Part of the Law of England?" *L.Q.R.*, XXII, 14–26; T. E. Holland, *Studies in International Law*, p. 195; C. M. Picciotto, *The Relation of International Law to the Law of England and the United States*, New York, 1919, and Introduction by Oppenheim, p. 10; Triepel, *op. cit.;* and *infra*, chap. xi, n. 33.

[54] This difference is indicated by the fact that national courts accept the legislation or decisions of the political agencies of their state as final on questions of international law, while international courts consider such questions as matters of law (Wright, *Control of American Foreign Relations*, pp. 172–75; "Conflicts of International Law with National Laws and Ordinances," *A.J.I.L.*, XI, 1 ff.). The United States proposed a reservation to its adhesion to the protocol of the Permanent Court of International Justice which would have required the latter to recognize an American "claim of interest" in an advisory opinion as a legal interest, but the parties to the protocol refused to accept it (Wright, "The United States and the Permanent Court of International Justice," *A.J.I.L.*, XXI, 17–19).

sovereign may fail to have any status under international law, while an entity subject in some matters to the municipal law of another may enjoy some sovereignty under international law[54a].

c) THE ANALYSIS OF SOVEREIGNTY

For purposes of legal analysis we shall consider successively the concepts of municipal-law sovereignty, international-law sovereignty, and, under the latter, internal sovereignty and external sovereignty. It is apparent that from the standpoint of municipal law sovereignty cannot be analyzed. It is a unity incapable of division or limitation. A sovereign is controlled only by his own interests, his own procedure, and the circumstances of his environment in asserting legal powers and creating legal rights for himself. Thus by proper enactments he may reorganize himself, extend his sway to the whole universe, or extinguish himself[55] perfectly validly in the light of his own law. The political pressures of his constituents are merely the determiners of his interests, his own constitution is merely a procedure, and other "sovereigns" are merely parts of his environment. They are no more legal limitations than is the presence of wild beasts a legal limitation upon the expansion of his farm by the pioneer.

Sovereign states have in fact usually divided the exercise of their sovereign powers among distinct organs of government or even distinct governments and have sometimes recognized limitations of international law, treaty, or constitutional principle in their fundamental laws. They have sometimes attempted to make such limitations perpetual by constitutional forms and political checks and balances. While the expediency of such measures cannot be easily questioned, it is doubtful whether they have or can effect the unity or scope of sovereignty in the sense of that term in municipal law.[56]

[54a] See *infra*, nn. 99, 100.

[55] Willoughby doubts the possibility of state suicide through the state's consent to its own annexation (*Fundamental Concepts of Public Law*, pp. 173 ff.), but that it has happened cannot be questioned (see Westlake, *International Law*, I, 63–66; Fenwick, *International Law* [1924], p. 116).

[56] "There has been a general tendency to admit the impossibility of placing limitation on the sovereign's power, formally at least" (Merriam, *op. cit.*, p. 223). This is

A constitutional division of power can always be changed so far as municipal law is concerned, either by appropriate action of all the authorities concerned or by constitutional amendment, and constitutional limitations may be swept away by action of the constitutional authority whose function it is to define the limits of the authority in question.[57]

From the standpoint of international law, however, sovereignty is susceptible of analysis, division, and limitation. From that standpoint, sovereignty is the capacity to have jural relations with other sovereigns, and the slightest familiarity with international law shows that its inventiveness in distinguishing varieties of legal capacity has been very great.[58] Thus to define the degree of sovereignty of a given entity, one must investigate its existing jural relations with other entities.[59]

Analytical jurists have struggled with the problem of defining the jural relations about which all systems of law are constructed. Amid much disagreement there seems to be general agreement that the

---

recognized by Dickinson, though he emphasizes the practical importance in international relations of "internal limitations" upon the capacity of governments (*op. cit.*, p. 191). See also Borchard, "The Relation between State and Law," Yale L.J., Vol. XXXVI (1927).

[57] Even such a clause as that in art. 5 of the United States Constitution, which forbids amendments which deprive constituent states of their equal representation in the Senate, would be legally eliminated if the Supreme Court supported an amendment to the article eliminating the clause. Salmond's attempted distinction between the legal control of sovereignty within its own province, which he regards as self-contradictory and the legal appointment of bounds to that province which he considers valid, loses sight of the essential character of municipal-law sovereignty which is to organize and define the limits of its own and all subordinate authority, the Kompetenz-Kompetenz of Meyer, Haenel, and others (see Salmond, *Jurisprudence* [London, 1902], p. 633; Gray, *Nature and Sources of the Law*, sec. 180; Merriam, *op. cit.*, p. 191).

[58] Dickinson, *op. cit.*, chaps. vii, viii. Willoughby and Fenwick, *Types of Restricted Sovereignty and of Colonial Autonomy* (U.S. Department of State, 1919); Fenwick, *Wardship in International Law* (Department of State, 1919); Hyde, *International Law*, I, 20–44.

[59] This point of view is emphasized by Eagleton (*op. cit.*, pp. 41–42), Hyde (*op. cit.*, I, 24), Dickinson (*op. cit.*, pp. 278–79), Fenwick (*International Law*, p. 353). From the subjective point of view sovereignty under international law is the capacity of an entity to have jural relations, but objectively it is the jural relations which the entity actually has. Kocourek recognizes this distinction as applied to persons in general by the terms "personateness" and "personality" (*Jural Relations*, pp. 75–76, 291–92).

right-duty relation and the power-liability relation are fundamental, that from these various other jural relations can be derived by logical processes, and that from such relations and their combinations about common objectives an even wider variety of legal interests can be distinguished.[60] Jural relations exist, like mathematical relations, in a purely conceptual world, between conceptual persons (subjects of law) about conceptual interests (objects of law).[61] These

[60] Salmond (*Jurisprudence* [London], pp. 231–37), Hohfeld ("Some Fundamental Legal Conceptions as Applied in Judicial Reasoning," *Yale L.J.*, XXIII [1913], 16, reprinted in *Fundamental Legal Conceptions*, New Haven, 1923), and Kocourek (*Jural Relations* [Indianapolis, 1927], pp. 7–10) have distinguished four types of legal advantage or of rights in the broad sense—(1) rights or claims, (2) privileges or liberties, (3) powers, and (4) immunities, correlative to which are legal (1) duties, (2) no-rights, liabilities or inabilities, (3) liabilities or responsibilities, and (4) disabilities. A statement of all the rights in a thing or involved in a situation implies all the duties, and it thus is superfluous to state the no-duties (privileges) and no-rights. Similarly, a statement of all the Powers in regard to a thing or involved in a situation implies all the liabilities, and it is superfluous to state the no-liabilities (immunities) and no-powers (disabilities). Usually, however, such a complete statement is not necessary and the legal interests of a single person can be most conveniently expressed by use of the eight terms. Kocourek (*Am. Law School Rev.*, IV, 615, 1921; *Jural Relations*, pp. 378–79) objects to Hohfeld's negative definitions, on the ground that they confuse jural and non-jural relations, but in his constructive exposition he uses the same terms, defined as "reciprocals." By this he appears to mean that a privilege is a power to avoid a duty and an immunity is a claim to avoid a liability. Practically these seem to differ from Hohfeld's conceptions very little but make it possible to express a situation completely even from the standpoint of one person with use merely of the claim-duty and the power-liability relations. "Juristic science," he says, "is able to deal with and completely describe any legal phenomenon in terms of claims and powers" (*Jural Relations*, p. 84; see also pp. 7, 10, 78, 95). As a contribution to Kocourek's quarrel with the Hohfeldians, attention may be drawn to Ogden and Richard's note "On Negative Facts" concluding that "when we dispute as to whether a fact is positive or negative, or whether there are negative facts, we are engaged merely in the criticism of several prose styles" (*The Meaning of Meaning* [1927], p. 294).

[61] Kocourek defines a jural relation as "a situation of fact upon which one may affect (through the existence and exercise of a power) or may claim to affect (because of the existence of a duty), the freedom of another with legal consequences" (*op. cit.*, p. 16). For each jural relation there are two subjects—the person of inherence (or, as Kocourek says, the *dominus*) and the person of incidence (or the *servus*)—and the object or legal interest is analyzable into the things or advantages for which the jural relation exists and the act or abstention by which it is to be accomplished (Salmond, *op. cit.*, pp. 224–25). Kocourek regards the act or abstention as the only object of a jural relation since the advantage aimed at in all is freedom (*op. cit.*, p. 15), but freedom is a purely subjective term and in fact in all systems of law it is defined objectively in terms of some specific thing or function with respect to which the person has freedom as his own body, a

concepts are approximately paralleled by actual persons with actual interests in the physical world, the degree of approximation depending on the development of the law and the efficiency of its administration. Contact between the two worlds occurs mainly through certain observable phenomena which disclose the conceptual world (evidential facts) or which have at some time changed it (operative facts).[62]

The subject or person of law represents an individual (association or community) who is assumed to have real interests which he wants to secure through his own or some other person's act or abstention. He benefits by the law from the dynamic point of view because it enables him to convert his real interests into legal interests and from the static point of view because it secures his legal interests. From the static point of view he is most interested in his rights or claims which imply duties in others to so act or refrain from action as to facilitate his free enjoyment of certain interests. From the dynamic point of view his attention is turned more toward his powers which imply liabilities in others such that by unilateral action he can change their existing legal relations, thus giving him the opportunity to acquire new rights and powers, as well as new duties and liabilities. Thus a plentitude of rights is the paradise of pure reason; a plentitude of powers is the paradise of pure will; and a plentitude of legal interests is the paradise of pure feeling for they would assure a satisfaction of all those real interests which lie outside of law but are its *raison d'être.*[63]

In the absolute sense of municipal law a sovereign has all of these. He can give himself all the rights and powers necessary to secure whatever interests the facts will permit. Under international law, however, he has only such rights and powers as that law has given him and consequently he must be content with the legal in-

---

piece of land, a chattel, etc. In international law the sphere of freedom is usually defined either by the area, the individuals, or the functions with respect to which the state has freedom, i.e., can exercise jurisdiction (see *infra*, n. 67, and chap. xi, n. 59).

[62] Hohfeld, *op. cit.*, p. 32; Salmond, *op. cit.*, p. 368. Kocourek calls the latter "jural facts" (*op. cit.*, p. 17).

[63] See Kocourek, *op. cit.*, pp. 14–16; Salmond, *op. cit.*, p. 335.

terests which these rights and powers secure for him or enable him to acquire.[64]

A state obviously must have a certain minimum of legal interests in order to exist.[65] It must have some subjects, some government, and some territory. From the standpoint of international law the only sense in which it can "have" these things is that it has substantially complete and exclusive legal interests in them, or, in the terminology of private law, that it owns them. This means that it has ultimate rights in them correlative to duties of all or most of the other states in the world together with certain associated powers and responsibilities.[66] The totality of things in which a state has such a complex of legal interests (*jus in re propria*) constitutes its internal sovereignty or independence. According as internal sovereignty is directed toward territory, individuals, or government functions it is called respectively the state's domain, nationality, or domestic jurisdiction.[67]

States, of course, differ in the extent of their domain, in the number of their nationals, and in the scope of their domestic jurisdiction; but a state's freedom is limited, even with respect to what it has, by general principles of international law reconciling claims based respectively on domain, nationality, or jurisdiction, and it

[64] A state can intervene in judicial proceedings between two others only if "it has an interest of a legal nature which may be affected by the decision, and it is for the Court to decide whether an allegation of interest has that character" (Statute, *P.C.I.J.*, arts. 62, 63).

[65] Kocourek discusses the possibility of a person existing without any legal entity (*op. cit.*, p. 292).

[66] See also sec. *d*, *infra*.

[67] These three interests of states are recognized by Crane, *op. cit.*, pp. 45, 65; Willoughby, *Fundamental Conceptions of Public Law*, pp. 51–54, and chap. xvii; Mariattes, *Les Limites actuelles de la competence de la société des nations* (Paris, 1926), pp. 41–57, 198–210; Oppenheim, *op. cit.*, I, 127; Hyde, *International Law*, I, 16; Wilson, *International Law* (2d ed., 1927), p. 17; U.S. Supreme Court, *Texas* v. *White*, 7 Wall. 800 (1868). Westlake (*op. cit.*, I, 3) writes: "We see by reference to our common experience that a state proper is an ideal body, which on the one hand has a certain territory and on the other hand is a society composed of individual men as its members, and having a corporate will distinct from the wills of its members." The frequent confusion of jurisdiction with the possession of territory and that with domain is discussed *infra*, chap. xi, sec. 2*c*.

may be further limited by servitudes or other incumbrances (*jus in re aliena*) attached to the thing, or by contractual, delictual, or other duties owed to a particular state in respect to the thing (*jus in personam*).[68]

Though difficult cases arise, international law generally furnishes the means for defining a state's domain and nationality with precision, but its internal sovereignty with respect to its government or its domestic jurisdiction is more elusive. This exists in so far as the state has a sphere of relatively free action which other states are under a duty to respect and may be defined by reference to the territory or individuals with respect to which the action may be taken or it may be defined by description of the type of action or function itself, irrespective of the territory or person involved, or various combinations may be employed.[68a] Under present international law the domestic jurisdiction of a normal state depends mainly on its domain, yet every state has some such jurisdiction beyond and lacks complete jurisdiction within its domain. For instance, a state ordinarily has complete jurisdiction over its ships at sea, over pirates, over its public forces and legislative but not executive or judicial jurisdiction, over its diplomatic officers, and its nationals abroad.[68b] On the other hand, a state's jurisdiction within its territory is limited with respect to aliens by the duties it owes to the state of which they are nationals. These duties vary with its treaties and the official character of the aliens. Even its jurisdiction over its own nationals and government functions in its own territory is sometimes limited by international servitudes or treaty obligations such as those resulting from minority or disarmament treaties. Matters with respect to which the state's freedom of action is abso-

[68] On distinction between real (*jus in rem*) and personal rights (*jus in personam*) see Salmond, *op. cit.*, pp. 246–53; Hohfeld proposed to substitute the terms "multital" and "paucital" rights (*op. cit.*, pp. 71–72) and Kocourek proposed "unpolarized" and "polarized" rights (*op. cit.*, p. 201). The Roman-law "obligatio" was equivalent to a *jus in personam*. On distinction between ownership (*jus in re propria*) and incumbrance (*jus in re aliena*) see Salmond, *op. cit.*, pp. 257–63.

[68a] All of these methods are used in defining the jurisdiction of the Supreme Court in Art. III of the United States Constitution.

[68b] "The territoriality of criminal law, therefore, is not an absolute principle of international law and by no means coincides with territorial sovereignty" ("The Lotus," *P.C.I.J.* [Ser. A], No. 9, p. 20).

lute are said to be "solely within its domestic jurisdiction (*compe-tence exclusive*)."[69]

External sovereignty or status exists in so far as a state can change, by unilateral action, the jural relations of other states, and must be distinguished from internal sovereignty or independence.[70]

It is thus defined by the powers and liabilities of the state and is sometimes called the "foreign-relations power."[71] In general it lies within the field of the state's jurisdiction but not of its domestic jurisdiction. The latter confers freedom to perform only acts which, apart from special treaty or custom, do not change the jural relations of other states and in which, consequently, such states have no legal interest.

Although in general international law does not permit one sovereign state to exercise authority over another, the jurisdiction of all states under general international law and of many under treaty

[69] See *infra*, n. 79. Jurisdiction may be defined from the standpoint either of municipal law or of international law, from the first by the extent to which the state's municipal law has provided for the exercise of authority, from the second by the extent to which international law gives a state freedom to provide for the exercise of such authority whether the state actually has done so or not. The two do not necessarily coincide. Thus from the standpoint of international law Great Britain had some criminal jurisdiction between the low water-mark and the three-mile limit prior to the Territorial Waters Jurisdiction Act, 1878, but apparently British criminal courts did not have jurisdiction over that area at that time under the common law (*Regina* v. *Keyn*, 2 Ex.D. 63). But, on the other hand, from the standpoint of international law British criminal jurisdiction (apart from treaty) ended at the three-mile limit, though apparently under the Herring Fishery Act, 1889, the courts had some criminal jurisdiction beyond it (*Mortenson* v. *Peters*, 14 Scots, L.T.R. 227 [1906], see also *supra*, n. 53). In practice the two usually do coincide so far as courts are concerned because a state's municipal law ordinarily confers authority on its organs in general terms with the understanding that they will exercise it only in so far as international law permits (*American Banana Co.* v. *United Fruit Co.*, 219 U.S. 347 1909). Municipal law, however, always confers legislative and executive jurisdiction on the political organs of the government far in excess of its jurisdiction under international law (see *infra*, nn. 70, 98). Jurisdiction from the standpoint of municipal law must not be confused with "domestic jurisdiction." The latter is a term of international law.

[70] International-law writers have often recognized this distinction but have frequently failed to define it with precision (Crane, *op. cit.*, pp. 46, 49, 66). From the standpoint of municipal law the distinction does not exist, thus constitutions seldom draw a sharp line between the competence of organs according as they fall in one or the other sphere from the international-law point of view (Wright, *Control of American Foreign Relations*, pp. 135–50, 263).

[71] Wright, *op. cit.*

entitles them to perform some acts which change the jural relations of others. These acts of external sovereignty are usually steps in an international procedure like adjudication or negotiation, but sometimes they finally modify the legal interests of other states without their participation, as by the naturalization of an alien or the denunciation of a treaty according to its terms.

A state must have a certain minimum of powers to be a subject of international law. It must, for instance, have power to appeal to some form of international procedure to remedy violations of its rights, and correlatively it must be responsible to other states for its own delinquencies. Under present international law, diplomatic discussion is the simplest form of such procedure; thus a state can hardly be said to exist unless its government has powers and responsibilities under that process. States, however, usually have many other powers, and in practice a state is not regarded as fully sovereign unless it has substantially all of the powers of normal states at the time. Legal power, manifested through operative facts, is the instrument through which a person may convert his subjective desires into objective legal advantages, and, as in civil societies, normal power is the badge of full status, so in the family of nations normal power is the badge of full sovereignty.[72] Among the powers commonly possessed by states is that to convert a state of peace into a state of war, to defend itself, to recognize new states, to naturalize

[72] "The legal condition of each class is its status, and that status is shared by each member of the class and becomes the measure of each member's capacity for rights. . . . . The equality of states . . . . means, not that all have the same rights, but that all are equally capable of acquiring rights, entering into transactions and performing acts" (Dickinson, *op. cit.*, pp. 3–4). Status in the broadest sense means the sum total of a person's jural relations, including both his legal interests and legal disadvantages (Kocourek, *op. cit.*, pp. 76, 227, who makes it synonymous with "personality" which he considers the objective manifestation of jural capacity while personateness is its subjective side or the capacity to have jural relations (see *supra*, n. 59). Sometimes status is confined to the sum total of legal interests and disadvantages of a personal character in distinction from those of a proprietary character known as "estate" (Salmond, *op. cit.*, pp. 253–54). With either of these two definitions no two people would have the same status. Maine regarded status as the body of jural relations flowing from custom in distinction from the body of jural relations flowing from agreement or contract (*Ancient Law*). Most frequently differences of power and liability rather than of right and duty have been the basis of classifications of status and only "disabilities or exemptions of far reaching character" have been considered (Holland, *Jurisprudence* [12th ed.], pp. 142–43; Salmond, *op. cit.*, pp. 256, 490).

and expatriate individuals, to abandon territory, to occupy *res nullius*, to perform wrongful acts rendering itself responsible, to resort to available international machinery for the redress of wrongs and for reform of the law, and to tender and accept offers in negotiations.

Deprivation of any of these powers is usually considered an impairment of full sovereignty, if exceptional or unequal.[73] The acceptance of neutralization, a protector, or a political servitude[74] have been commonly so regarded. A state not recognized as a member of the family of nations does not have the usual power of diplomatic representation and certainly lacks full sovereignty.[75] On the other hand, inferior voting power or non-participation in international organizations has not usually been considered an impairment of sovereignty though it creates inequality in legal power. Instead of depriving certain states of normal powers, such arrangements give certain states unusual powers and also unusual responsibilities. The same is true where many states transfer certain of their powers to an international organization or reciprocally give each other power to initiate arbitration or judicial settlement by unilateral arraignment. Such mutual sacrifices of power and acceptances of responsibility to promote common interests have become normal in the present state of international relations.[76]

[73] States have been reluctant to sacrifice any powers, and treaties usually limit the exercise of a power not the power itself (see *infra*, n. 75). Compulsory arbitration has often been confined in treaties, to "claims of right" (see Pan-American Arbitration Treaty, 1929, and Locarno treaties, 1926) and the common reservations of "national honor, and vital interests" perhaps exclude questions of the scope of a state's power from arbitration. Liability to arbitration or judicial settlement by unilateral arraignment, of course, limits a state's power to refuse arbitration and exists only on the basis of express agreements (Eastern Carelia Advisory Opinion, *P.C.I.J.* [Ser. B], No. 5).

[74] An ordinary servitude is a mere incumbrance conferring a real right in territory regardless of subsequent changes in its sovereignty, and to be distinguished from "arrangements serving to clothe a foreign grantee with privileges that are more than economic, embracing for example rights of political control" (Hyde, *International Law*, I, 276).

[75] Dickinson discusses many types of limitation upon powers such as protection, supervision of finances, intervention, guaranty, etc. (*op. cit.*, chap. vii and pp. 338–48; see also Hyde, *op. cit.*, I, 24–53).

[76] Dickinson emphasizes "the fundamental distinction between the legal equality of states in their mutual relations and their political equality in whatever pertains to the development of international organization (*op. cit.*, chap. viii, pp. 332, 348–78).

The ultimate test of a state's full sovereignty is its capacity to establish normal jural relations with all other states. If the state lacks the real rights necessary to assure it internal sovereignty of reasonable extent, or the powers necessary to assure it normal external sovereignty, it lacks this capacity and is not fully sovereign. Impairments of full capacity may, of course, exist in fact without sanction of international law, in which case they should properly be described as impairments of the state's political sovereignty but not of its legal sovereignty.[77]

Sovereignty in international law is thus a relative term. Each international person differs to some extent from every other in its capacity in law or in fact to establish normal legal relations with others. The line between a fully sovereign and a partly sovereign state is not precise and is continually changing with the development of international relations. Limitations which were yesterday considered impairments of sovereignty are today normal and vice versa. The tendency to conduct international relations by universal lawmaking conventions rather than by bilateral or limited agreements and to enforce them by peaceful processes of international organization rather than by self-help is tending to promote equality in the practical enjoyment of legal protection and equality in legal power within each of a few recognized classes of international persons. Thus sovereignty is tending to have a more precise meaning as the status of all members of the highest class of international persons.[78]

d) THE SOVEREIGNTY OF THINGS

To ascertain the sovereignty of the mandated territories we must apply our conception of sovereignty in the opposite sense from

---

On international organs with power of local control, see Sayre, *Experiments in International Administration*, pp. 38–97.

[77] On distinction between legal and political sovereignty see Leacock, *Elements of Political Science*, chap. iv; Willoughby, *Fundamental Principles*, p. 112; and *supra*, n. 47.

[78] In view of the great variety in world-conditions, political, cultural, and economic, doubtless numerous special variations of legal powers will long persist and furthermore full equality of sovereigns in the sense here used would not preclude great inequalities in rights and duties, in political influence, and even in political powers in international organizations (see Dickinson, *op. cit.*, pp. 5, 335–36; Crane, *op. cit.*, p. 64).

that considered in the preceding sections. We are not attempting to locate sovereignty within a state nor are we attempting to determine the character of a state's sovereignty in international relations. Our aim is to locate the sovereignty of certain territories, peoples, and governments which apparently are not within any state at all. We wish to locate sovereignty with respect to its objects, not with respect to its subjects.

Law as we have seen expresses itself through establishing jural relations between persons with respect to their interests, and these jural relations are classifiable into the right-duty relation, the power-liability relation, and the legal-interest relation which consists of typical combinations of the others about a definable real interest or thing.

From the standpoint of international law the sovereign of a thing is that legal person (or group of legal persons) who has substantially complete and exclusive rights in it; who has the unlimited and exclusive power to change any of the jural relations directed toward it; and who has complete and exclusive freedom to pursue his interests in respect to it. If any one of these three statements is true in regard to a given thing, all the rest must be. Full and exclusive rights in a thing implies that one can dispose of it at will and enjoy it freely. Unlimited and exclusive power of disposal implies that one owns and is free to enjoy the thing. Complete and exclusive freedom of enjoyment implies that one owns and can dispose of the thing. They are all expressions of the same situation from the standpoints of intelligence, volition, and sentiment, respectively.

However, it is rare that any of these statements accurately characterize the relation of an actual state to an actual object of its interest. While a normal state has very substantial real rights in a portion of the globe known as its domain, other states usually have some rights therein, as that injurious agencies shall not operate from it, that their nationals in it shall receive reasonable protection and remedies, and that their nationals may enter it for purposes of trade. So also a state has, as a rule, very considerable real rights in certain individuals known as its nationals; but these rights are usually greatly diminished if the national is abroad, and they may be limited by the duties imposed by extradition, minority, or other treaties even when the national is at home. While a state's real rights in its government functions are even more extensive, they also are somewhat limited if action is required abroad or if it affects the legal interests of other states. While a state's rights in such intangible things as its reputation, its dignity, and its policy, so far as they exist at all, are doubtless exclusive, completeness can hardly be asserted of things so insusceptible of precise definition. It is true a state has complete freedom in respect to "matters solely within its domestic jurisdiction," but the Permanent Court of International Justice apparently regards it as impossible to define that field in terms of territory, individuals, government functions, or any other tangible thing. A matter upon which a state wishes to exerise jurisdiction, if at issue in a particular controversy, will be held within its exclusive domestic jurisdiction unless some rule or principle of international law or treaty gives the other state a right or a power which will probably be affected, but as the Court said, the question is "essentially relative" and "depends upon the development of international relations," thus definition of the scope of such jurisdiction would seem to require very detailed classification of possible controversies, taking account of all the states legal relations, not only under general international law but under treaties.[79] In looking at any given thing, therefore, whether a territory, an individual, or a government function, we generally find that no state has absolute freedom to deal with it, that many states either permanently or in special situations have some rights and powers in respect to it, and that consequently the question of which state will be called "sovereign" is a matter to be decided either by proving that certain rights and powers have been accepted as an arbitrary criterion of sovereignty or by exercising judgment as to whose rights and powers in the thing are most important under the circumstances.

Practically international law has used the first method to determine the sovereignty of things and has created a concept thereof closely analogous to that of ownership in private law. Ownership is usually associated with extensive rights of enjoyment, use, and possession, but in fact these may be entirely subtracted leaving a

[79] *P.C.I.J.* (Ser. B), No. 4. Though holding that "questions of nationality are in principle within this reserved domain" the Court recognized that they ceased to be, if affected by international law or treaty in the particular controversy (see *supra*, n. 69).

nuda proprietas.[80] Thus the final test of ownership seems to be less in these rights than in the power of ultimate disposition of the thing. In international law this seems to be recognized, in the occasional dissociation of the "sovereignty" and "jurisdiction" of the same territory. Panama, for example, is usually said to be sovereign of the Canal zone though the United States has virtually complete jurisdiction or rights of use and control over it under a permanent lease.[81]

Although the authority competent to dispose of a thing may properly be called its sovereign, it may prove difficult to locate that authority. International law usually anticipates continuance of the *status quo*, especially in regard to territory, and evidence may be lacking as to the legal method by which change can be effected. Furthermore, alternative methods may exist. Territory, for instance, may change sovereignty by prescription or by conquest as well as by abandonment or by cession. Individuals may change nationality by immigration and naturalization as well as by legislative expatriation or by treaty. Jurisdiction may be transferred by revolution, by conquest, or by continued encroachment and general recognition as well as by treaty. Thus, while ordinarily consent of the present sovereign of a thing is a requisite for change of its sovereignty it is not always so. Evidence regarding the ultimate power to dispose of a thing may therefore be supplemented by evidence relating to its present control, which may be examined (1) from the standpoint of other states, or (2) from that of the state exercising such control.

[80] See *infra*, chap. xi, sec. 2*c*. "The right of the owner of a thing may be all but eaten up by the dominant rights of lessees, mortgagees, and other encumbrancers. His ownership may be reduced to a mere name rather than a reality. Yet he none the less remains the owner of the *thing*, while all others own nothing more than *rights* over it. For he still owns that *jus in re propria* which, were all encumbrances removed from it, would straightway expand to its normal dimensions as the *universum jus* of general and permanent use. He, then, is the owner of a material object, who owns a right to the general or residuary uses of it, after the deduction of all special and limited rights of use vested by way of encumbrance in other persons" (Salmond, *op. cit.*, pp. 272–73), Kocourek calls ownership "the most ultimate right of possession and nothing else" (*op. cit.*, p. 328; see also Holland, *op. cit.*, pp. 206–9).

[81] Panama, however, contends that the American rights are limited to the purposes defined in the lease agreement (see *F.P.A., Information Service*, III [June 20, 1928], 354–59; see also chap. xi, n. 69; chap. xii, sec. 1).

Other states are most frequently interested in ascertaining the sovereignty of a thing in order to collect reparation for injuries they have suffered because of the use to which it has been put. International law ordinarily imputes responsibility for international delinquencies to the sovereign of the territory in which the injury occurred. Thus diplomatic demands ordinarily indicate whom the complaining state regards as the sovereign of a given territory. They do not necessarily do so, however. The complaining state may incorrectly attribute sovereignty, and, furthermore, the territorial sovereign is not always responsible for international delinquencies committed within its territory under authority of another sovereign. In such cases complaint should be addressed to the sovereign of the responsible government agent even though the latter was acting in foreign territory.[82] Although a state is not responsible for acts of its nationals unless its government has been negligent, diplomatic claims frequently give evidence of the nationality of individuals. Such claims most commonly arise on the allegation that the claimant state has been injured through an injury to its national, thus the status of the injured person is usually established in such controversies. In certain cases, however, states may protect persons not their nationals, and in some cases they may be precluded from protecting their nationals.[83] Thus while the practice in regard to responsibility does usually involve recognition of sovereignty, this recognition is not conclusive of international status unless general, and, furthermore, recognition of a state's sovereignty of a government function or of an individual is not necessarily recognition of

[82] A state seems to be responsible for injuries to third states due to acts in its territory by the forces of another state engaged in reprisals, intervention, or occupation resulting from its own delinquencies (see American answer to French claims on the bombardment of Greytown, 1852 [Moore, *Digest*, VI, 928 ff.], and British answer to Egyptian note with respect to responsibility for acts during the British military occupation of Egypt ["League of Nations Treaty Series," XVII, 317–18]), but not if such acts are of illegal character and could not be prevented by the territorial sovereign (see Brig. Gen. Armstrong arbitration [Moore, *International Arbitrations*, II, 1096] and Samoan arbitration [Malloy, *Treaties, etc.*, II, 1595]). In these cases the intervening state is responsible (Wright, "The Bombardment of Damascus," *A.J.I.L.*, XX, 276; Eagleton, *op. cit.*, p. 31). Where a state has a recognized jurisdiction in foreign territory, it is responsible for delinquencies arising from its exercise (see *infra*, nn. 89, 90).

[83] Borchard, see *op. cit.*, pp. 463–78, 568–74. A state cannot protect its national if he also has the nationality of the state responsible for his injury.

its sovereignty of the territory in which the jurisdiction is exercised or the individual resides. The generality and the precise intent of the recognition must be ascertained in order to infer from it the sovereignty of a thing.

What evidence of sovereignty can be drawn from the state's *de facto* control or possession of a thing? The state exercising dominant control of a thing is often presumed to be the sovereign, but the extent and intent of that control must be considered if it is to give any evidence of the legal situation. While, as we have seen, a state may have considerable jurisdiction or freedom to control a certain definable thing, it seldom or never has complete freedom in law, and sometimes the state with the most domestic jurisdiction is not considered the sovereign.[84] Consequently, the mere fact that a state exercises domestic jurisdiction in respect to a thing does not prove that it is sovereign of it. If, however, the authority exercising jurisdiction claims to do so by virtue of its sovereignty, i.e., if it has the *animus* as well as the *corpus* of possession, there is a presumption of sovereignty. Municipal law cannot make international law, but its rules are facts of considerable importance which if acquiesced in may acquire the sanction of international law.[85] The authority which asserts competence to change the fundamental municipal law of a territory, the constitution of its government, or the status of its inhabitants proclaims itself the municipal law sovereign of such territory, government, or people, and in so far as it succeeds in exercising such competence it becomes the *de facto* international law sovereign capable of acquiring *de jure* status by recognition on prescription. Thus jurisdiction in respect to a thing, exercised in fact and claimed in virtue of sovereignty by the fundamental municipal law applicable, gives evidence of the sovereignty of the thing.

In summary we may conclude that the best method for determining the sovereignty of a thing under international law is to discover the person or group with ultimate powers to change its status, responsible to other sovereigns with respect to it,[86] and competent in fact to change the fundamental municipal law governing it. If

[84] See *supra*, n. 80. [85] See *infra*, chap. xii, sec. 2.

[86] From the standpoint of the subject, the active aspects of jural relations (duties and powers) should be emphasized (see Kocourek, *op. cit.*, p. 14); but from the standpoint of the object, their passive aspects (rights and liabilities) are equally significant.

these three lines of evidence concur, the conclusion would seem fairly certain.

Difficulties, however, may arise because inquiry discloses that no state or several states appear to be sovereign, or that conclusions from the standpoints of international law and of municipal law differ.

e) DIVIDED AND COLLECTIVE SOVEREIGNTY

While a particular territory, person, or government is usually under the sovereignty of only one state, any one of them may prove to be under the sovereignty of (*a*) no state at all; of more than one state (*b*) severally or (*c*) jointly; or of (*d*) a corporation composed of many states. *Res nullius, heimatlos* persons and unrecognized insurgent or belligerent governments are examples of the first.

Since sovereignty under international law is a relative term, cases in which more than one state have real rights and international responsibilities in the same thing are susceptible of varied interpretations. If, for instance, the world is taken as a unit, its territory, peoples, and governments would seem to be subject to a divided sovereignty of the sixty-odd states of the world.[87] Even within territory under the sovereignty of a single state, however, there are usually many aliens and diplomatic officials subject to the sovereignty of different states,[88] and the governments in leased or administered territories are usually under the sovereignty of a state other than the territorial sovereign.[89] The cases usually discussed as di-

[87] Dante thought a single sovereignty of the world was implicit in the idea of law (*De monarchia*, I, chap. x; Bryce, *The Holy Roman Empire* [ed. 1921], pp. 280 ff.) and some modern writers have concluded that in idea there can be only one sovereign in the world (Burgess, *supra*, n. 12), but these writers spoke of sovereignty from the municipal-law point of view (see *supra*, nn. 54, 56).

[88] A situation which may render the sovereign of the territory responsible to each of these states.

[89] The latter has merely a *nuda proprietas* (see *supra*, n. 80; on United States lease of Panama Canal Zone see *supra*, n. 81). The Powers from the first took the position that the leases of Chinese territory transferred complete jurisdiction to the lessee and that third states could not exercise extraterritorial jurisdiction within them, thus apparently the lessee was alone responsible toward other states for incidents in the territories during the life of the lease (United States, Naval War College, *International Law Situations* [1902], pp. 28–35). In spheres of interest, however, responsibility remains with the local ruler on the theory that the beneficiary of the sphere has merely a "moral claim not a true right" since the sovereign of the area is not a party to the agreement (Hall, *Foreign Powers, etc.*, p. 228; *International Law* [8th ed.], p. 154).

vided sovereignty, however, are those in which the international powers and responsibilities of a community under a single government are divided functionally among two or more sovereigns as in protectorates, suzerainties, confederations, or the British imperial commonwealth.[90] In the last three types the subordinate units are in some relations with the dominant unit governed by the latter's municipal law—a situation to which attention will be given presently.[91]

Apparent divisions of sovereignty have sometimes been interpreted as cases of agency. It has been suggested that a protected state retains full sovereignty, the protector performing certain functions as its agent, although it is difficult to explain all the rights and responsibilities of the protector with respect to third states on this principle. If a subordinate unit, such as a vassal state or a member of a federation, is regarded as the agent of the dominant unit it ceases to have any international status and the relation becomes one of internal law entirely, but this is not the case if the dominant unit is not a state but an international organization.[91a]

[90] Where sovereignty is divided, responsibility is divided, a situation which Eagleton says "is not inconceivable" and which he considers probable of the relations of the British Empire and the Dominions (*op. cit.*, p. 35). Responsibility is undoubtedly divided in the case of a condominium (*ibid.*, p. 38, citing Strupp, *Völkerrechtliche Delikt*, p. 61, n. 1, see n. 89). Great Britain at first refused to exercise any authority in protectorates except over her own subjects or to accept any responsibility toward third states with respect to incidents in the protected territory (Hall, *Foreign Powers, etc.*, p. 206), but gradually on the theory that "as the protecting state interposes voluntarily and for its own selfish objects, it is not morally in a position to demand that foreign governments shall patiently submit to wrongdoing from persons whose natural responsibility it covers with the shield of its own sovereign independence" it has assumed full responsibility and ample power in its protectorates (*ibid.*, p. 219; Lewis, "Mandated Territories," *L.Q.R.*, XXXIX [1923], 466). Other states have always taken the later view (*ibid.*, pp. 207 ff.). The tendency has been similar in respect to the natives of the protectorate. They have tended to come under the allegiance of the protecting power (*ibid.*, pp. 226–27). See also Hall, *International Law* (8th ed.), pp. 150–52; Baty, *supra*, n. 36; and Lewis, *op. cit.*, pp. 458 ff.; Westlake, *International Law*, I, 121 ff., Hyde, *op. cit.*, I, 25, 36, who says with regard to quasi-protectorates of the United States in the Caribbean, "In proportion as the United States by virtue of these conventions exercises rights which they confer as a privilege peculiarly its own, and in which no foreign state is permitted to participate, it appears to assume internationally a certain responsibility for conditions of government within the territories concerned." See *infra*, chap. xii, sec. 1.

[91] See *infra*, n. 100.

[91a] See *supra*, n. 90; *infra*, chap. xi, sec. 3*a*.

Divided sovereignty must be distinguished from joint sovereignty. The latter exists in respect to territory in cases of joint occupation and condominium, in respect to persons in cases of dual nationality, and in respect to governments in some condominiums. In the latter the exercise of sovereignty may be divided, as is true, for example, in the New Hebrides condominium of Great Britain and France; but the sovereignty itself of both the government and the islands seem to be held in joint tenancy. While each state has a defined competence in the government of the islands according to the terms of the treaty which forms its constitution, the interpretation and modification of that instrument are only possible by the united consent of both manifested by some process recognized by international law.[91b]

Joint sovereignty must further be distinguished from the sovereignty of an international corporation. The latter exists where a group of states has created a legal personality different from any or all of them. The League of Nations and perhaps some other international unions are such corporations.[92] Thus the Saar Valley is not under the joint sovereignty of the fifty-six members of the League, but is probably under the sovereignty of the League itself.[93]

The conclusion, however, that entities whose only or main linkage is in the realm of international law may collectively possess the sovereignty of territory suggests a solecism. It means that the internal organization of sovereignty, not merely its scope and the manner of its exercise, may be a question of international law, whereas normally such a question is the typical domestic question, soluble only by internal law. Domestic questions, may, however, as has been pointed out by the Permanent Court of International Justice, become international when affected by treaties,[94] and it

[91b] Lindley, *op. cit.*, pp. 119–20.

[92] See *infra*, chap. xi, sec. 2*b*.

[93] It has been suggested (*infra*, chap. x, n. 61) that sovereignty of the Saar Valley is suspended or retained by Germany pending the plebiscite to be held in 1935, but as that may result in continuance of the present situation it seems necessary to recognize the possibility of League sovereignty; see treaty of Versailles, art. 34, of annex following art. 54 (Lauterpacht, *op. cit.*, p. 202; Corbett, *B.Y.B.I.L.* [1924], pp. 127–28). On the New Hebrides see *A.J.I.L.*, I, 482; Supp. I, 179; and Sayre, *Experiments in International Administration*, pp. 94–104.

[94] "Tunis-Morocco Nationality Decrees Opinion," *P.C.I.J.* (Pub. Ser. B), No. 4.

would seem that this can apply even to the organization of sovereignty.

Sovereignty has been commonly considered an attribute of the state alone, and clearly a group of states, whether acting as several owners of a thing, as a condominium, or as a corporation, cannot be considered a single state. There is, however, as we have noticed, no legal necessity or universal custom which makes it impossible to attribute territorial sovereignty to such groups. They may form a legal community, which, as Oppenheim has pointed out, is a wider conception than the state.[95] "There would appear to be no reason in law why the League of Nations should not acquire and hold territorial sovereignty," writes Lindley.[96] "The particular characteristics which one meets in this association," writes Diena, "do not forbid that it possess in reality an international juridical personality. Without that one could not explain how it could, as trustee, have been charged with the government of the Saar basin, how it could exercise a protectorate of the free city of Dantzig, also a function of tutelage in favor of the minorities, etc."[97] As the municipal law of civilized countries has advanced to the recognition of collective personalities, the creation of law not of nature, so international law is advancing to the recognition of collective personalities, the creation of international law not of municipal law, capable of entering into most of the transactions of states.

We must not forget, however, that this extension of the capacity to acquire sovereignty of things, to groups of states, and collective personalities means that the line between municipal law and international law becomes in many cases difficult to draw. The constitutions of governments under such complex sovereignty are at the same time treaties, interpretable by international processes. They are both the municipal law of the sovereign and international law between states, and our definition of sovereignty as the status of an entity subject to international law and superior to municipal law

[95] *International Law* (3d ed.), I, 8.

[96] *The Acquisition and Government of Backward Territory in International Law*, p. 121.

[97] "Les Mandats internationaux," *Acad.D.I.*, V (1924), 232. Oppenheim, Corbett, Voorhees, Harriman, Sir Herbert Ames, and others though differing in many respects all admit the League's legal personality (see *supra*, n. 37, and *infra*, chap. xi).

requires some modification of the conception of municipal law. Such a collective sovereign, acting through the proper processes, is superior to that part of international law by which it is organized. Thus, for example, though the League of Nations Covenant is international law to which the members of the League are subject, the League as a whole can amend it through the process described in article 26 and thus is superior to it. Though international law from the standpoint of the members, the Covenant resembles municipal law from the standpoint of the League as a whole.

The question of whether a given group of states asserting capacity collectively to possess sovereignty of certain things is entitled to do so under international law is a question of fact and general international recognition precisely as is the claim of a community of individuals to be a sovereign state. If the fact is generally recognized, legal theory must accommodate itself. But the fact may not be so recognized in a given case and probably will not be unless there is a certain unity of responsibility. The claim to collective sovereignty, made by the international law within a group of states, is only valid in universal international law if generally recognized within the family of nations.

Thus sovereignty under international law eventually depends upon international law as recognized by the family of nations as a whole. From that point of view, claims made by the municipal law of a state or by treaties within a limited group of states are merely evidential facts, not operative facts.[98]

We have defined sovereignty as the status of an entity subject to international law and superior to municipal law, but certain en-

[98] See *supra*, n. 62. See Pillet, *R.G.D.I.*, V, 86; Wright, *Control of American Foreign Relations*, pp. 4–5, 15–18; "International Law in Its Relation to Constitutional Law," *A.J.I.L.*, XVII, 240; Borchard, *op. cit.*, pp. 836–60. Although the powers which a state may exercise are defined by international law, the powers which any organ of its government may exercise are defined by its municipal law, consequently the latter is of dominant importance in determining the immediate (though not the eventual) capacity of a state, even in international transactions (Dickinson, *op. cit.*, p. 191); but with respect to responsibilities, trouble is probable if the international-law requirements are not met irrespective of municipal-law limitations. The difficulty which results from the dominance of municipal law in the definition of the powers of government and of international law in the definition of the responsibilities of the state are discussed by the author in *Control of American Foreign Relations*, chap. i; see also *supra*, n. 69.

tities like the British dominions, members of confederations, etc., are subject to international law in some matters but subject to the municipal law of the group as a whole in others. Conversely, certain entities have existed, such, for instance, as the Mexico of Montezuma before the arrival of Cortes which because of a complete absence of relations with the family of nations, then confined to Europe, were not subjects of international law and yet were superior to their own municipal law. Status should properly be determined by international law in both cases. The Aztec empire could not be called a sovereign in the international law sense. Mexican territory from that point of view was *res nullius* and was in fact so treated.[99] On the other hand, the British dominions and constitutent states of the German Reich and the Swiss confederation have some treaties, some powers of diplomatic representation, and some responsibilities under international law, even though their relations with the states of which they are a part are governed by the latter's municipal law. They would thus seem to have a limited sovereignty.[100] Whether in

[99] Some writers have interpreted the acquisition of these territories as conquest rather than as occupation of *res nullius* (see Lindley, *op. cit.*, pp. 11–23, and *supra*, chap. i, n. 10).

[100] Oppenheim attributes some international status to the German states and the Swiss cantons, but not to the states of the United States (*op. cit.*, I, 189). Great Britain has claimed and the Irish Free State has denied that relations of the members of the British commonwealth *inter se* are governed by British constitutional law ("L. of N. Treaty Series," XXVI, 10; XXVII, 449–50; XLIV, 264–69), although apparently the British view was accepted at the Imperial Conference of 1926, where the Interimperial Relations Committee reported: "The making of the treaty in the name of the King as the symbol of the special relationship between the different parts of the Empire will render superfluous the inclusion of any provision that its terms must not be regarded as regulating *inter se* the rights and obligations of the various territories on behalf of which it has been signed in the name of the King. . . . . The Legal Committee [of the Arms Traffic Conference in 1925] laid it down that the principle to which the foregoing sentence gives expression underlies all international conventions. . . . . Where international agreements are to be applied between different parts of the Empire, the form of a treaty between Heads of States should be avoided" (*International Conciliation*, Pamphlet 228, p. 122). Great Britain has also held that the interpretation of the reservations in her recognition of Egyptian independence is a domestic question (note to League of Nations, November 19, 1924, *O.J.*, VI [1925], 302), thus placing Egypt under the suzerainty of Great Britain. This denial of equality of status through a reservation to a recognition of independence may be contrasted with the refusal of the United States Supreme Court to recognize the validity of Congressional reservations to state enabling acts. The power to admit states to the Union, said the latter, "is not to admit

such cases a given thing is under the sovereignty of the whole or the part depends on whether or not it is within the scope of the latter's sovereignty as recognized by general international law. The division of authority recognized by the internal constitution would be merely evidence on this point.[101]

Obviously the difference between such corporations of quasi-sovereigns and corporations or unions of full sovereigns like the League of Nations is not great. The former are theoretically associated by the municipal law of the whole whereas the latter are associated by international law binding only themselves, but in either case eventual appeal has to be made to general international law to determine the status of either the parts or the whole.[102]

International law also determines status where territory is claimed by the internal law of two or more states or where states claim less by their internal law than international law gives them. A colonial protectorate has not usually been considered part of a state's domain by its internal law, but where the protector is solely responsible to third states for conditions of administration within it, as they affect the interests of those states, it has ordinarily been considered part of the protector's domain in international law.[103] Territory has sometimes been annexed by a process giving good title

---

political organizations which are less or greater, or different in dignity or power, from those political entities which constitute the union" (*Coyle* v. *Smith*, 221 U.S. 559 [1911]; for reference on the status of Egypt see Hershey, *op. cit.*, p. 184; see also *supra*, n. 37). Borchard (*Diplomatic Protection of Citizens Abroad*, pp. 17–18) and Wright (*Enforcement, etc.*, p. 18) contend that entities which are not municipal-law sovereigns may have some status in international law, but Crane (*op. cit.*, p. 72) denies it.

[101] Thus from the international-law point of view it would appear that the question whether the interpretation of the British-Irish Free State "treaty" or of the British reservation to its recognition of Egyptian independence (*supra*, n. 100) are domestic questions or international questions is itself an international question (see "Tunis Nationality Decrees Advisory Opinion," *supra*, n. 94).

[102] A number of writers classify the League of Nations as a form of confederation (see *supra*, chap. xi, n. 52).

[103] Hyde, *International Law*, I, 36–38; Lindley, *The Acquisition and Government of Backward Territory in International Law*, pp. 187–88; Baty, *op. cit.; B.Y.B.I.L.*, 1921–22, pp. 112–18. *Rex* v. *Crewe*, L. R. (1910), 2 K.B. 603, 619, in which the court found that Bechuanaland protectorate was not within the dominions of the Crown, though the Crown had in fact complete "power and jurisdiction" there.

in international law but which has not fully conformed to the requirements of the state's own constitution and thus has not constituted it part of the national domain by municipal law.[104]

The same divergence has sometimes existed between municipal law and international law with regard to the status of persons and the functions of government—in fact, they have been more common here than in regard to domain. Divergence in nationality laws resulting in cases of "dual nationality" or of "homelessness" are notorious, and international law having no clear rule for solving them has to recognize such cases as no or joint sovereignty of an individual.[105] Conflicts between national assertions of domestic jurisdiction and the requirements of general international law and treaty are also frequent, as, for instance, in the Calvo doctrine according to which certain states have claimed exclusive jurisdiction over resident aliens[106] and in the occasional claim by states of criminal jurisdiction for offenses committed by foreigners abroad.[107] Even the constitutional laws organizing governmental institutions have sometimes failed to meet the standards required by international law.[108] In all such cases the international status of a thing is determined by international law.

That international status should depend on international law

[104] It has been contended, probably incorrectly, that this is the situation of American Samoa with respect to the United States (see Blakeslee, *F. A.*, VII [October, 1928], 139–40). The Philippines and other American possessions are "unincorporated" territory, not part of the United States in the full constitutional sense though undoubtedly they are part of the national domain under international law (*Fourteen Diamond Rings* v. *U.S.*, 183 U.S. 176 [1901]).

[105] Hyde, *op. cit.*, pp. 653 ff. Natives of the unincorporated insular possessions of the United States are probably not citizens in the constitutional sense, though they are American nationals under international law, and so are not aliens (*Gonzales* v. *Williams*, 192 U.S. 1). The same tends to apply to natives of colonial protectorates of European powers (Hall, *Foreign Powers, etc.*, pp. 226–27, and *infra*, chap. xii.

[106] Borchard, *op. cit.*, pp. 836–60.

[107] Hyde, *op. cit.*, I, 422 ff. See Cuttings case, Moore, *Digest of International Law*, II, 228–42. Under certain circumstances such jurisdiction may be proper (The Lotus, *P.C.I.J.* [Ser. A], No. 10).

[108] Wright, *Control of American Foreign Relations*, pp. 13–20, and "International Law in Its Relation to Constitutional Law," *A.J.I.L.*, XVII, 242–43; Hyde, *International Law*, I, 466, 707–9; Vattel, *Le Droit des gens*, II, c. 12, sec. 196, Carnegie ed., p. 174.

perhaps seems so obvious as to render this discussion superfluous. It has seemed wise to emphasize it, however, because writers in discussing status have often in fact placed great reliance upon national legislation.[109] This is due in part to the fact that international status depends both upon fact and law and municipal law does often furnish important evidence of facts.[110] Furthermore, international law is unfortunately vague on many questions of status and, where more precise sources are lacking, national law may properly be cited as evidence of accepted international doctrine or custom.[111] Thus where international law indicates nothing to the contrary, it may be assumed to recognize the *de facto* status of territories, peoples, and governments as defined by the law of the interested states. Where more than one state is interested, these laws may conflict, in which case the solution must be sought in international law. In-

[109] This is particularly true in discussing the national status of individuals. See the interesting discussion by Westlake, *op. cit.*, I, 220 ff., and Flournoy, in *Proc.*, *A.S.I.L.*, (1928), p. 57. Hyde (*op. cit.*, pp. 610–11), though recognizing the wide freedom of action of states in conferring nationality on or taking it away from individuals, recognizes that "international law limits the right of a state to impress its national character upon an individual or to prevent that character from being lost or transferred." When the Permanent Court of International Justice held in the Tunis-Morocco nationality decrees advisory opinion that questions of nationality are in principle included among matters within the domestic jurisdiction of states (Ser. B, No. 4), it did not deny this principle since it recognized that in so far as rules of customary or conventional international law are applicable they limit this reserved sphere (see report of M. Rundstein of League of Nations Committee on Progressive Codification of International Law and replies of governments to Committee's report [*A.J.I.L.*, Spec. Supp., XX, 23; XXII, 5–7] and schedule of points drawn up by the preparatory commission for the first Codification Conference, February 15, 1928 [*L. of N. Pub.*, *Legal*, I (1928), 1]. Lindley (*loc. cit.*) refers continually to national laws in determining the status of governing organs (Part II) and territories (Part III).

[110] Where, as in the case of nationality, international law leaves the state considerable freedom, the facts (from the international point of view) as determined by national law are of dominating importance.

[111] This is especially true of governmental independence, or, in the phraseology of the League of Nations Covenant, "matters which by international law are solely within the domestic jurisdiction" of states (art. 15, par. 8). Because of the looseness of the treatment of the subject in international documents and juristic writing, international courts have to accept the practice disclosed by the national legislation of states as the main source of international law on the subject. It was on this basis that the Permanent Court of International Justice reached the conclusion referred to in n. 109 *supra*.

ternational law is therefore the ultimate standard for determining status, and we must ask of it who has ultimate powers to dispose of the mandated territories, peoples, and governments; who is ultimately responsible to the states of the world for injuries attributable to them; and who is competent to modify the fundamental law governing them.

3. Sources of International Law

To discover the status of the mandated areas under international law, we must examine the sources of that law, which, as has been noticed, are independent of municipal law. A system of international law can never be built, as some have tried to build one, out of the exercise by individual states of their sovereignty, because an agreement or treaty resting on the individual sovereignty of the parties alone cannot give legal validity to itself. "The fact," writes Oppenheim, "that treaties can stipulate rules of international conduct at all is based on the customary rule of the law that treaties are binding upon the contracting parties."[112] If state sovereignty is taken as the basis, international law proves not to be law at all, but merely morality.[113] Like any other system of law, international law must grow out of the fact of a community whose members generally recognize the existence of externally enforcible rules among them. *Ubi*

[112] *Op. cit.*, I, 23; see also *ibid.*, I, 655.

[113] This was the conclusion of Hobbes and Puffendorf who called it "natural law" (Dickinson, *op. cit.*, pp. 69 ff.; Oppenheim, *op. cit.*, pp. 104–7), of John Austin who called it "positive international morality," and of Jellinek who called it *subjective Recht* (Borchard, in Merriam and Barnes, *op. cit.*, pp. 120–39). Lauterpacht discusses the consequences destructive to international law of this "positivist" doctrine (*Private Law Sources and Analogies of International Law*, chap. ii, esp. p. 56). The term "positivist" is ambiguous, referring, on the one hand, to the theory that law gains its character through enforcement by a determinate political authority and, on the other, to the theory that it gains its character through its manifestation in objective sources, independent of the immediate will of the parties. Oppenheim and Hall are positivists only in the latter sense, both of them recognize the objective existence of international law, and Lauterpacht confuses the issue by classing them with positivists in the first sense (see Oppenheim's discussion of the phrase "common consent," *op. cit.*, pp. 14–17, and Hall, *op. cit.*, pp. 5, 14). The distinction which Oppenheim makes between the "legal" and "diplomatic" schools of international law resembles more closely the distinction between the "positive" and "historical" schools of general jurisprudence which Lauterpacht seems to have in mind (Oppenheim, *op. cit.*, p. 96, and Introduction to Westlake, *Collected Papers;* Wright, *A.J.I.L.*, X [October, 1916], X, 706).

Societas, ibi jus est. "Society and law," writes Westlake, "are mutually dependent." If there is no law recognizing community or family of nations, as some have asserted, then there is no international law. The evidence that there is such a community—for example, the regulation by states of numerous common interests, the practice of foreign offices in appealing to law, the existence of many permanent international organizations—has been convincing to most investigators of the subject, though the frequency of violence and of consequent changes whose only legality is their subsequent recognition demonstrates that the community is a weak one.[114]

Accepting the fact of a law-recognizing family of nations, how may we discover its law? Systems of law though based on historic fact are manifested by their principles, their sanctions, and their sources. Efforts have been made to draw conclusions with respect to the mandated areas from general principles of international law, but no such principles can properly be accepted until proved, and the only proof lies in examination of the sources of that law. There is, however, a danger of specious argument by assuming that principles, such as state sovereignty of territory, are universal without proof. Thus Secretary Lansing wrote, "if the League does not constitute a world state, the sovereignty would have to pass to some national state,"[115] an argument based on the highly questionable hypothesis that no body other than a state is capable of being the sovereign of territory.

Efforts have also been made to draw conclusions as to the status of mandated territories from the sanctions of international law. Thus we may again refer to Secretary Lansing who thought it clear that the great Powers would become the mandatories, and as the League would not be powerful enough to exercise any real restraint on them the transaction was really "the taking of enemy territory as spoils of war." This is but to say that as the sanctions of international law may not prove effective in all cases, the law may be

[114] Westlake, *Principles of International Law* (Cambridge, 1894), p. 3; Oppenheim, *op. cit.*, I, 7–9; Hall, *op. cit.*, p. 1; Brierly, *The Law of Nations*, pp. 37 ff. Lundstedt (*Superstition or Rationality in Action for Peace*, New York, 1925) denies the existence of an international community (pp. 175 ff.).

[115] *Op. cit.*, p. 152.

disregarded, a conclusion which amounts to a denial rather than an application of international law and which rests on an assumption with regard to the League's effectiveness which may or may not prove true.[116]

A system of law cannot survive without sanctions, but this does not mean that it cannot survive an occasional failure of the sanctions either to prevent or remedy wrong. The detailed rules of law cannot be discovered by a calculation in each case of the probabilities of success or failure in an effort at evasion. Sanctions give authority to the recognized sources of law and are in turn supported by general acceptance in the community of the rules and principles of law, but the details of the latter can be discovered neither by a priori reasoning nor by a calculation of the operation of sanctions in particular cases but by a study of the sources.[117]

What are the sources of international law? The most authoritative answer is to be found in article 38 of the statute of the Permanent Court of International Justice which provides:

> The Court shall apply:
>
> 1. International conventions, whether general or particular, establishing rules expressly recognized by the contesting States;
>
> 2. International custom, as evidence of a general practice accepted as law;
>
> 3. The general principles of law recognized by civilized nations;
>
> 4. Subject to the provisions of article 59, judicial decisions and the teachings of the most highly qualified publicists of the various nations, as subsidiary means for the determination of rules of law.

Article 59 provides that "the decision of the Court has no binding force except between the parties and in respect of that particular case," thus denying the compulsory but not necessarily the persuasive authority of such decisions in analogous cases.

This classification of sources which originated in a suggestion of M. Descamps of Belgium in the commission of jurists which framed

[116] *Ibid.*, p. 156.

[117] For conception of sources of law see J. C. Gray, *Nature and Sources of the Law* (New York, 1909), pp. 100, 118–20, 291; Salmond, *Jurisprudence* (London, 1902), pp. 103 ff.; Holland, *Jurisprudence*, chap. v; Amos, *The Science of Law* (New York, 1875), pp. 74–76. These comments attempt to classify the sources of law. The relation of these classes of sources to the sources of international law are discussed by J. P. Hall, "The Force of Precedents in International Law," *I.J.E.*, XXVI, 149, and Wright, *A.J.I.L.*, XI, 3.

the statute was at first opposed by Mr. Root of the United States and Lord Phillimore of Great Britain on the ground that recognition of the last two sources of law would unduly extend the Court's jurisdiction. Agreeing with some English and American writers, these jurists thought treaties and custom should be considered the sole source of international law and that if they furnished no rule for the case the Court should consider itself incompetent. The jurists versed in the Roman-law tradition were unanimously against this contention, and pointed out that there was a difference between the sources of the Court's competence (art. 36) and the sources of its rule of decision (art. 38), that reduction of the latter to treaties and custom might result in requiring the Court either to refuse to give judgment (*non liquet*) where it had jurisdiction which would be a denial of justice or to give a decision without any guidance, and that in fact all tribunals repeatedly drew on "general principles of law." The two common-law jurists then agreed to accept the proposal with a slight modification, Lord Phillimore explaining that the last two sources were really included in the second since it was only by virtue of custom that general principles—"maxims of law" or principles accepted "in foro domestico"—had gained authority as law.[118]

The classification accepted conforms to the view of most text-writers.[119] Under it the most authoritative source of law for the

[118] *P.C.I.J.*, Advisory Committee of Jurists, *Procès verbaux* of the Proceedings of the Committee, June 16–July 24, 1920, pp. 293–97, 306–25, esp. pp. 318, 335. A similar debate took place during the drafting of the French civil code. Art. 4 of this code as finally adopted provides "the judge who shall refuse to give a decision—under pretext of the silence, obscurity, of insufficiency of the law—can be sued as guilty of a denial of justice." Napoleon, himself, seems to have suggested as subsidiary resources for helping a judge in such a dilemma; "(1) *équité naturelle, loi naturelle;* (2) Roman law; (3) ancient customs; (4) *usages, examples, decisions*, jurisprudence; (5) droit commun; (6) *principes généraux, maximes, doctrine, science*" (see Amos, *op. cit.*, p. 74).

[119] It accepts the Grotian view that both reason (*jus naturale*) and practice (*jus gentium*) are sources of law. This was the view generally accepted by jurists in the seventeenth and eighteenth centuries and in the nineteenth century on the continent of Europe. English and American writers of the nineteenth century have tended to be positivists though Wheaton in the United States and Westlake in England were Grotians. See Oppenheim, *op. cit.*, pp. 107 ff.; Westlake, *International Law*, I, 14; Wright, "The Effect of the War on International Law," *Minn.L.R.*, V (May, 1921), 436–39, in which tacit agreement (custom), express agreement (treaty), natural reason (principles),

mandates system is the applicable conventions, i.e., articles 22 and 23 of the Covenant and the mandates. The actual practice of the League organs, the mandatories and other states, is gradually establishing customs which are the source of second importance. After these one must look to the general principles of law recognized by states in past contacts with problems of this character, and to the accepted legal meaning of terms such as "mandate," "tutelage," and "trusteeship" in the documents. Finally, one must examine the opinions of courts and qualified jurists on the institution.

It is proposed to examine these four types of sources in reverse order, thus basing our final conclusions mainly on the documents themselves and their authoritative interpretation. It is worth noting, however, that article 38 of the Court statute does not imply that the authority of the four sources is absolutely in the order named in all cases. The phrase "in the order following" which originally appeared in the first paragraph of the article was stricken out after discussion in the League Council. Such a requirement, writes De Bustamente, one of the jurists, "might not always be possible, and it certainly was dangerous."[120] It is clear that it may sometimes be necessary to resort to custom, general principles, or the opinions of jurists to decide whether a convention which contains applicable rules is valid and to interpret its meaning. Likewise, the opinion of jurists would commonly be invoked to determine the existence of custom or general principles of law. Thus, while the sources later in the list should only be resorted to when the legal problem in hand cannot be fully solved by use of those earlier, it would not often be possible to reach a solution without getting help from all.

---

and formalized reason (authority) are listed as sources. The International Prize Court Convention (XII Hague Convention, 1907, art. VII) defined treaties, rules of international law, general principles of justice and equity, and national enactments as sources of prize law (see also Brierly, *op. cit.*, pp. 39 ff., and *infra*, chap. x, p. 3).

[120] De Bustamente, *The World Court* (New York, 1925), p. 241, and minutes of the Committee of Jurists (*op. cit.*, pp. 332, 337).

CHAPTER X

THE THEORIES OF JURISTS

Jurists enjoy in international law a higher authority than is usual in systems of private law. As has been noted, "the teachings of the most highly qualified publicists of the various nations" is recognized by the statute of the Permanent Court of International Justice as a "subsidiary means for the determination of rules of law" on a parity with "judicial decisions."[1] Perhaps this statement should be interpreted with the limitations voiced by the Supreme Court of the United States that the works of jurists are resorted to primarily for evidence of the customs and usages of nations, "not for the speculations of their authors concerning what the law ought to be, but for trustworthy evidence of what the law really is."[2]

Article 22 of the Covenant clearly leaves room for interpretation, and official organs of the League have thus far been reluctant to commit themselves as to its construction; in fact, the Hymans report adopted by the Council in August, 1920, expressly declined to enter into the interesting controversy "as to where sovereignty actually resided" and declared "legal erudition will decide as to what extent it can apply to this institution the older juridical notions."[3] Examination by jurists is thus officially invited.

Even before the Covenant became effective the jurists recognized

[1] This refers to the decisions of both national and international courts with reference to their value as precedents or sources of law. The doctrine *stare decisis* is limited for the Permanent Court of International Justice by art. 59 of the statute which seems to embody a principle generally applicable to international courts (see Moore, *Digest of International Law*, VII, 38–40; Bustamente, *The World Court*, p. 241). With respect to the specific rights involved in a litigation, the decision of an international court acting within its competence is conclusive on the principle *res adjudicata* (Moore, *op. cit.*, VII, 55 ff.; I Hague [1907], art. 37; L. of N. Covenant, art. 13) but that of a national court is not under international law (Moore, *op. cit.*, VII, 33, 644–52; XII Hague [1907], art 3). For distinction between the "sources of law" and the "sources of rights" or titles see Salmond, *Jurisprudence*, p. 109.

[2] *The Paquette Habana*, 175 U.S. 677, 694 (1899).

[3] *Responsibilities of the League Arising Out of Article 22*, p. 17; reprinted, *O.J.*, I, 339.

in the mandates system a novelty capable of calling forth their highest skill if it was to be fitted into the established frame-work of international law. Some of them indeed gave up the job before attempting it and fancied they had disposed of the matter by asking long lists of questions which they thought impossible to answer.[4] Most of them, however, tackled their problem with enthusiasm, ingenuity, and results, the luxuriance and variety of which are almost baffling. Views that have been set forth with respect to (1) the essential characteristics of the system, (2) the location of sovereignty, and (3) the sources of law applicable will be analyzed.

1. Essential Characteristics of the System

Opinions differ as to the intent of the system. Certain writers, such as former Secretary of State Lansing and former Governor of German East Africa Schnee, look upon it as a veil for annexation which deceived no one but permitted the victorious Powers to allege formal fulfilment of war-time speeches and to refuse Germany reparation credit for her property in these areas.[5] At the other extreme are those who see in the system an important development in public morality and the sense of responsibility for backward peoples.[6] Most of the writers recognize the system as a compromise to which both political and humanitarian motives contributed.[7]

[4] See Lansing, *The Peace Negotiations*, pp. 151 ff.

[5] *Ibid.*, chap. xiii; Schnee, *German Colonization Past and Future* (London, 1926), chap. i; and *supra*, chap. iii, nn. 15–17.

[6] Van Rees describes it as "one of the happiest innovations born of the war and universally recognized as one of the noblest results of the Versailles treaty" (*Les Mandats internationaux*, I, 2); D. Campbell Lee considers it "an open and above board effort to get rid of one of the most potent causes of war" ("Mandates, How They Are Working," *Grotius Soc.*, XII [1926], 31) and M. Van Kol of the Netherlands told the Inter-parliamentary Union in 1922, "As soon as the idea of colonial mandates is generalized and they are fulfilled in good faith in the sole interest of the undeveloped peoples, the first steps in the foundations of the temple of the peace and of the economic development of the human race will be solidly placed" (*Compte rendu de la XX Conférence*, p. 175). See also chap. iii, nn. 20–21.

[7] M. Rappard considers "the administration of the institution of mandates as the most successful achievement of the League to execute the peace treaties," and inquires "by means of what miracle has the League been able to rear to beneficence this child, which though conceived in generosity was undoubtedly born in sin" (*International Relations as Viewed from Geneva* [New Haven, 1925], p. 38). See also *supra*, chap. ii, n. 1.

Opinions also differ as to the essential features of the system and their relative importance. Some see it as a "new method for the transfer of territory." In addition to title by cession, conquest, and prescription, says Lindley, we now have "relinquishment for administration under League of Nations mandate, although this mode would seem to be only a special case of cession."[8]

Others emphasize the co-ordination and legal sanction the system gives to a number of principles for the administration of backward areas, all or most of which had been long growing in favor. Thus, Potter thinks the system embodies seven principles: (1) no annexation, (2) condominium, (3) tutelage by advanced nations, (4) supervision by the League, (5) the open door, (6) no military use of natives, (7) people of area to have a voice in the selection of the mandatory. He admits, however, that all of these are not applied in all the mandated areas.[9] Schneider finds all of these principles in article 22 except the second and transfers the open door to last place. Later he defines the system as "the administration of a defined territory, by a single power in behalf of the actual bearer of sovereignty, in the name of the League of Nations according to principles defined in article 22 of the Covenant and in the mandate in specific terms."[10] With more emphasis upon the moral duty of the mandatory as a trustee, Woolf says, "A mandate is an international trust given to a particular state on behalf of the League, and the mandatory, if it accepts the mandate, thereby undertakes certain duties and obligations in the mandated area both towards the population of that area and towards the League."[11]

Stoyanovsky emphasizes especially the guardianship element of the system, insists that its novelty lies in its recognition that the virtual sovereignty of the undeveloped peoples themselves is "con-

[8] Lindley, *The Acquisition and Government of Backward Territory in International Law*, pp. 2, 247.

[9] Potter, "Origin of the System of Mandates under the League of Nations," *A.P.S.R.*, XVI (1922), 570.

[10] Schneider, *Das völkerrechtliche Mandat* (Stuttgart, 1926), pp. 14, 33.

[11] Woolf, *Scope of Mandates under the League of Nations* (International Law Association, Report of the 29th Conference, 1920), p. 128. Brierly (*The Law of Nations*, Oxford, 1928) says: "The system stands as an international recognition that the relationship with the backward peoples should not be one of mere exploitation" (p. 100).

secrated and guaranteed by the intervention of the international society," and defines "the mandate as an international act by which the League of Nations, the mandant, charges a state called the mandatory with the exercise in its name of the functions of tutelage in the interests of a minor people, until such time as they will be recognized as capable of directing themselves."[12] Van Rees gives the same emphasis when he insists that the "novelty, importance and value" of the system "is the recognition in law of minor peoples, inhabitants of the territories, who enjoy a distinct juridical personality," and the obligation of the mandatory "to guide them toward their majority, to develop the administered territory first toward autonomy, finally toward complete independence." Later M. Van Rees defines the system in terms of the obligation of the mandatory toward the League, other members of the League, and the inhabitants of the territory. Toward the League the mandatory's only obligation is to submit to its supervision. Toward other members it is in general bound to keep the door open for religion and trade, to refrain from military use of the territory, and to submit disputes in reference to the interpretation of the mandate to the Permanent Court. Toward the inhabitants the mandatory is bound to give its services gratuitously, to develop them toward self-government, and to pursue a moral policy along the lines detailed in the mandates.[13]

Most writers emphasize the gratuitous character of the mandatory's mission[14] and many of them, like Lugard, regard its "most distinctive feature" as "the unqualified right of supervision vested in the League," though conceding that this gains significance from the guaranty it gives of a more moral administration of backward peoples.[15] Rappard says, "The originality of the Mandate System con-

[12] Stoyanovsky, *La Théorie générale des mandats internationaux* (Paris, 1925), pp. 48, 84.

[13] Van Rees, *op. cit.*, I, 10, 24; Bentwich succinctly distinguishes the "guardians" of the mandates system who "assume obligations towards the population and towards the society of nations" from the "protectors" of the past who "obtained rights over the population and against the powers" (*B.Y.B.I.L.* [1921–22], p. 49). To same effect see Woolf, *op. cit.*, p. 129.

[14] Lindley, *op. cit.*, p. 248.

[15] Lugard, "The Mandates System and the British Mandates," *J.R.S.A.*, LXXII (June 27, 1924), 538, 547; see also Potter, "Origin of the System of Mandates under the League of Nations, Further Notes," *A.P.S.R.*, XX (November, 1926), 845.

sisted in placing the administration of backward peoples by National governments under a supervision exercised in behalf of the League according to certain principles defined in an international instrument."[16] Thus we find the attention of some writers arrested principally by the implications of the term "trustee," others by the implications of the term "tutelage," and others by the implications of the term "mandate," all of which appear in article 22.

Though some writers regard the mandates system as a modified form of protectorate most of them think it establishes a new institution of international law for controlling the administration of backward territory. "It inaugurated," writes Lindley, "a new species of territorial sovereignty, or, perhaps one should say, a sovereignty to which new incidents or limitations attach."[17] To determine the nature of this novelty the writers have attempted to define the relative rights, powers, duties, and responsibilities of the League, the mandatories, the mandated communities and other authorities concerned with the institution, and to do this generally have considered it necessary to discover the location of sovereignty.[18] They have, however, reached different conclusions.

[16] *P.M.C., Min.*, VI, 123. See also Rappard, *op. cit.*, p. 39; Spiegel, *Das völkerrechtliche Mandat und seine Anwendung auf Palästina* (Wien, 1928), pp. 23–24.

[17] *Op. cit.*, p. 247. To Hershey (*International Law* [1927], p. 188) the system appears to be "a new or modified form of protectorate," the C mandates approximating most closely to "colonial protectorates." See also Baty, *B.Y.B.I.L.* (1921–22), pp. 109 ff.; Lewis, *L.Q.R.*, XXXIX (1923), 458 ff. Diena regards A mandates as "international protectorates" (*op. cit.*, p. 242). Pic, however, distinguishes them from protectorates (*R.G.D.I.*, XXX [1923], 321 ff.) as do Fauchille (*Droit international public*, I, Part II, 820–24), Schneider (*op. cit.*, p. 33), Woolf and Bentwich (*supra*, n. 13). See *infra*, chap. xii, sec. 1. Most writers treat the mandates system as a legal institution (Fauchille, *op. cit.*, I, Part I, 824) though a few regard it as a political device (Millot, *Les Mandats internationaux* [Paris, 1924], p. 90).

[18] Spiegel (*op. cit.*, p. 39) considers acceptance of the proper location of sovereignty the crux of the mandate institution as this institution is in a sense the crux of the League. He distinguishes two principal tendencies in the mandate literature, the state individualistic tendency (*Staatsindividualistische*) which attributes sovereignty to the mandatories and the universal humanity tendency (*Menschheitsuniversalistische*) which attributes it to the League of Nations. "With the juristic principle," he writes, "which here struggles to keep its value uninfluenced by politics, there runs a parallel ethical principle which in the same way seeks to establish itself, the principle of the dominance of objective right over subjective might. One can well say that the outcome of this struggle will determine the ultimate fortune of the international law mandate, even to a certain degree that of the League of Nations itself." See also Lauterpacht, *op. cit.*,

2. The Location of Sovereignty

No less than ten theories of the location of sovereignty have been offered, though many of these have a close-enough affiliation with others to admit of grouping under four heads, which attribute sovereignty to (*a*) the Principal Allied (and Associated) Powers, (*b*) the mandatories, (*c*) the mandated communities, (*d*) the League. Almost every possible combination of these four basic theories has been made, thus joint or sometimes divided sovereignty has been attributed to the Principal Powers and the League, to the mandatories and the mandated communities, to the League and the mandated communities, to the League and the mandatories, or even to the League, the mandatories, and the mandated communities. Some writers distinguish between the statuses defined by different mandates, by attributing partial sovereignty to the A mandated communities, and some to Iraq alone.

a) condominium of the principal powers

The argument for attributing sovereignty to a condominium of the Principal Allied and Associated Powers (the pentarchy) is drawn from the treaty clauses by which the former sovereigns renounced their territories in favor of those Powers, from the absence of any explicit document recording a subsequent transfer, from certain modifications inserted in article 22 in the course of its negotiation, and from statements of some of the statesmen at the conference.[19] Potter, who espouses this view, notes that though President Wilson originally objected to a condominium of the victorious powers over the territory,[20]

---

pp. 191–92. Among some fifty juristic discussions examined the following attempt to discuss the various theories as to sovereignty, existing at the time, with some completeness: Henri Rolin (1920); Fauchille (1922, 1925); Schucking and Wehberg (1921, 1924); Pic (1923); Vallini (1923); Furukaki (1923); Wright (1923, 1924); Van Rees (1923, 1927); Millot (1924); Diena (1924); Stoyanovsky (1925); Schneider (1926); Lindley (1926); Redslob (1926); Francesco (1926); Lauterpacht (1927); Wehberg (1927); H. Rolin (1927); Gsell-Trumpi (1928); Spiegel (1928); Palacios (1928).

[19] See *supra*, chap. ii, nn. 30–32 and sec. 3; chap. iv, nn. 12, 21.

[20] *A.P.S.R.*, XVI (November, 1922), 571–72; Vallini (*I Mandati Internazionali della societa delle nazioni* [Milano, 1923], pp. 80, 88) accepts this view and Fauchille (*op. cit.*, I, Part II, 849) finds it the least objectionable, thus differing from his earlier

in the end Germany was compelled, by article 119 of the treaty of Versailles to cede colonies not to the league but to the allied and associated powers, and from certain corrections which he is reported to have made in the text of his own plan between 10 and 25 January, 1919, after consultation with French and British leaders (striking out "with sovereign right of ultimate disposal" in article I of the "supplementary agreements") the President seems to have been weaned away fairly early from the idea of giving the league ultimate title to the territories in question. This impression is confirmed when we turn to the draft submitted by the American delegates to the Commission on the League of Nations and which may be regarded as the last version of Wilson's own plan; there likewise the idea of reversion of title to the league is conspicuously absent. And whatever its origin, and notwithstanding that it is not found in article XXII of the Covenant, this element of allied condominium—not league title—is an integral part of the mandate system as finally adopted.

Lord Balfour declared in the Council in 1922 that "a mandate is a self-imposed limitation by the conquerors on the sovereignty which they obtained over conquered territory."[21] Sir Frederick Lugard of the Mandates Commission cites this statement with approval and refers to the apparent view of the Allies "that these territories passed to the victors by cession under the treaty of peace" in contrast to the apparent view of the United States "that they passed to the allied and associated powers not by treaty but as a result of war."[22] While director of the mandates section M. Rappard offered some support to the American view. He "did not believe that even the council of the League of Nations had the power to modify the attribution of a mandate. This power, as far as B and C mandates

---

opinion (see *infra*, n. 34). See also Fannie Fern Andrews, *The Mandatory System* (Harvard University, Doctor's thesis), Brief Summary (pub. 1923); Hojer, *Le Pacte de la Société des Nations* (Paris, 1926), p. 374; Luquet, *Le Mandat A, et l'Organization du mandat français en Syrie* (Paris, 1923), pp. 126–27; Levesque, *La Situation internationale de Dantzig* (Paris, 1924), p. 120.

[21] See *supra*, chap. iv, n. 12.

[22] He added the opinion of the South African High Court that "Germany did not cede her colonies to the allies by the treaty of Versailles but placed them at their disposal to be administered under mandate—a status new to international law" (see *infra*, n. 26), thus his own opinion is not clear (*J.R.S.A.*, LXXII [1924], 547). Earlier Sir Frederick had suggested that the mandate system "conferred sovereignty under definite obligations for the fulfillment of which the mandatory is responsible to a constituted authority" (*The Dual Mandate* [1923], p. 53). For official American position see *infra*, chap. ii, sec. 4.

are concerned, appeared to be solely vested in the supreme council of the Allied and Associated Powers including the United States."[23] Miss Freda White's popular exposition of the mandates system probably reflects a common view in England when it asserts that "as the treaties stand the ultimate possession of the mandated territories rests with the Principal Allied and Associated Powers." She regards this situation as both "invidious" and "a little absurd," and suggests that "when the United States enters the league or are more amicably disposed to it, the allies should consign their treaty rights to the League Council."[24]

This theory, especially prominent in England and the United States, is denied by most continental jurists on the ground that annexation by the Principal Allied and Associated Powers would have been contrary to accepted principles of the Peace Conference, is not supported by any of the phraseology of article 22 or of the mandates, and does not follow from a proper interpretation of article 119 of the treaty of Versailles and article 132 of the treaty of Sèvres. President Wilson, Lansing reports, objected to the idea of condominium as strongly as he supported the idea of mandates. Evidently the two notions seemed incompatible to him.[25] "Renounce in favor of," wrote Sir James Ross-Innes of the Supreme Court of South Africa in a careful opinion concurred in by two of his four colleagues, is sometimes equivalent to "cede to" as in articles 83 and 87 of the Versailles Treaty but not so with the overseas territories put under mandate (art. 119) which were distinguished from the

[23] *P.M.C., Min.*, II, 46, and *J.B.I.I.A.* (September, 1925), p. 207. M. Van Rees, in a report presented at the third session of the Mandates Commission, said: "The sovereignty of Germany over her overseas possessions has passed to the Principal Allied and Associated Powers. . . . . The right of supervision appertaining to these powers as grantors of the mandate has automatically passed to the League of Nations" (*P.M.C., Min.*, III, 222). M. Van Rees was primarily concerned to show in this memorandum that the mandatory was not sovereign. He described the opinion that art. 22 "implied the intention of automatically transferring the sovereignty of the Pentarchy to the League" as "a thorny question on which opinions will always differ" (*ibid.*, p. 219). Thus it is not certain that M. Van Rees thought sovereignty was permanently lodged in the Principal Powers as Corbett (*B.Y.B.I.L.* [1924], p. 173) assumes. Certainly that is not his present opinion (see *infra*, n. 30).

[24] Freda White, *Mandates* (London, 1926), pp. 165–66.

[25] Lansing, *The Peace Negotiations*, p. 150.

ceded territories by freedom from German pre-war debt and the allowance of reparation credit for German public property (arts. 120, 257).

> The animus essential to a legal cession was not present on either side. For the signatories must have intended that such possessions should be dealt with as provided by Part I [the League of Nations Covenant] of the treaty and they were placed at the disposal of the Principal Powers merely that the latter might take all necessary steps for their administration on a mandatory basis. . . . . The intention of the signatories seems to have been to place certain overseas possessions relinquished by Germany upon a basis new to international law and regulated primarily by Article 22 of the Treaty.[26]

Stoyanovsky points out that the Principal Allied Powers notified the League of Nations of the appointment of the mandatories and the delimitation of the frontiers of the areas to be placed under mandate. "From the moment of this notification," he continues, "the rôle of the supreme council is terminated, that of the League of Nations begins. It constitutes, then, a sort of disseisin on the part of the supreme council in favor of the League of Nations."[27] Schücking and Wehberg describe the renunciation of the territory in favor of the principal powers as conditioned by the duty to transfer the territories to the League as required by article 22.[28] Lindley and Diena, though believing the mandatories have sovereignty under article 22, have expressed the same opinion.[29]

In the case of A mandates the treaty of Sèvres made the matter perfectly clear. Though Turkey renounced "all rights and titles" to the territories in favor of the Principal Allied Powers by article 132, articles 94 and 95 expressly provided that "Syria and Mesopotamia shall, in accordance with the fourth paragraph of article 22, Part I [Covenant of the League of Nations], be provisionally recognized as

[26] *Rex* v. *Christian*, S.Af.L.R. (1924), App. Div. 106, concurred in by Judges Solomon and Kotz. Judges De Villiers and Wessels thought sovereignty was vested in the mandatory (see *B.Y.B.I.L.* [1925], pp. 211–19, and *A.J.I.L.*, XVIII [1924], 306–8).

[27] Stoyanovsky, *op. cit.*, pp. 65–66.

[28] Schücking and Wehberg, *Die Satzung des Völkerbundes* (2d ed.; Berlin, 1924), pp. 700–702.

[29] Lindley, *op. cit.*, p. 264; Diena, "Les Mandats internationaux," *Acad.D.I.*, V (1924), 238; see also Millot, *Les Mandats internationaux* (Paris, 1924), pp. 113–14; Henri Rolin, *infra*, n. 34.

independent states subject to the rendering of administrative advice and assistance by a mandatory until such time as they are able to stand alone" and "to entrust, by application of the provisions of article 22, the administration of Palestine, within such boundaries as may be determined by the Principal Allied Powers, to a mandatory to be selected by the same powers." This treaty was never ratified, but the treaty of Lausanne which went into effect after the mandates for Syria and Palestine had been confirmed merely affirmed Turkey's renunciation of all rights and titles over the territories, their future "being settled or to be settled by the parties concerned" (art. 16).

The matter is well summarized by M. Van Rees of the Mandates Commission:

The acquisition of sovereignty as a consequence of the renunciation in favor of the principal allied and associated powers constitutes precisely a premise which the adversaries of this theory do not admit. They point out that in effect this same formula of renunciation was employed by the treaty of Versailles for all the European territories detached from Germany and of which the ultimate disposal was submitted to a later decision. It is thus for the territories of Memel (article 99), of Dantzig (article 100), and of Schleswig (article 110). In all these cases, the renunciation by Germany of all her rights and titles in the territories was made in favor of the principal allied and associated powers. Is it necessary to conclude, contrary to the manifest intention of the authors of the treaty, that this group of powers held the right of sovereignty in these territories? To admit it, one would risk at the beginning a misconception of the rôle which is accorded by the treaty to this group of powers; the latter enjoy, so to speak, the rôle of liquidators of the consequences of the war, in particular in regard to provisions bearing on territorial questions, the rôle of provisional administrators charged to accomplish certain acts in the course of a certain transitional period.

It is in pursuance of this rôle—affirm certain of those who oppose the above mentioned thesis—that the supreme council, representing the principal allied and associated powers, proceeded to designate the mandatories, the first act of the entry into force of the mandatory régime. But the intervention of the supreme council is limited to this act. It is to the League of Nations which falls thereafter the right of supervising the execution of this régime in virtue of article 22 of the Covenant. Furthermore, they add, if the German renunciation were to be assimilated to a transfer of sovereign rights of that empire to the principal powers, article 257 of the treaty would be singularly unjust. This article stipulates in effect in its first paragraph that no compensation will be due to Germany from the fact of the loss of her colonies, a clause which can only be explained if one admits that no power was enriched by one or more of these colonies, and consequently that no one is bound to reimburse their value.[30]

As a modification of the theory attributing sovereignty to the principal powers, Schneider suggests that sovereignty is vested in a "co-imperium" (which term he prefers to "condominium") of the Principal Powers and the League of Nations, thus emphasizing the "double title" by which the mandatory administers the territory referred to in the Hymans report of 1920. Giving equal weight to articles 22 and 119 (132 in treaty of Sèvres), he finds that since one seems to vest title in the League and the other in the Principal Powers, and he can find no explicit renunciation of the title by either, it must still be in both.[31]

The objections raised to the simple theory of allied condominium apply to this also. The fact that the mandatory's authority is received from both the Principal Powers and the Council does not indicate that both these groups continue to possess the sovereignty—in fact, the Hymans report rather indicates that the Principal Powers, having assigned the mandates, pass out of the picture. Furthermore, as Schneider, in common with most jurists, eliminates any legal claim of the United States under article 119 of the Versailles Treaty (the United States is not mentioned in the Turkish treaties and was not at war with Turkey) because of its failure to ratify that treaty,[32] this "co-imperium" differs very little from the Council alone which includes all the other Principal Powers as permanent members.[33]

b) The Mandatories

Closely associated with the condominium theory is that of mandatory sovereignty. Though also characteristic of English writers,

[30] *Op. cit.*, pp. 18–19.

[31] Schneider, *op. cit.* (Stuttgart, 1926), p. 41.

[32] *Ibid.*, p. 39, and *infra*, chap. xiii.

[33] There might be a difference in case the mandatory were a party to a dispute before the Council in regard to its mandate. The Council would not then need to count the mandatory's vote to have the unanimity necessary to make a practically binding decision (see *infra*, chap. xiv, 3*b*). Furthermore, the members of the Council appear to be bound in practice so far as the competence of that body goes by the votes of their representatives, while as a member of a condominium doubtless a state would act in important matters only through its constitutional treaty-making power. This, however, is a matter under the control of the state's constitutional law. Any member of the Council could require the consent of its treaty-making power prior to the vote of its representative in the Council if it wished.

its leading juristic exposition has been by M. Henri Rolin, a Belgian. Remarking that our democratic age likes euphemisms, he says, "The colonial mandates appear to us as a convention *sui generis*, different from the civil mandate and implying cessions of a perpetual power in the thing administered. . . . . Article 22, completed by the effective transfer of the mandates, is at bottom in law as it is in fact the equivalent of cession of the German colonies." His argument is drawn from article 119 of the treaty of Versailles, the direct transfer of the territories by the Principal Powers to the mandatories, and the absurdity of holding that these Powers intended to retain any of the sovereignty which would have restored "a sort of feudal system" by making the mandatory a vassal of the Pentarchy with respect to the mandated territory.[34] Others who attribute sovereignty to the mandatory emphasize the actual completeness of the powers of government accorded to the mandatory by the mandates.[35] A number of English writers regard the mandatory as a trustee and point out that under the Anglo-American law of trusts, the trustee has title to the property, though of course his use of it is limited by the terms of the trust.[36] All who maintain the mandatory's sovereignty recognize

[34] Henri Rolin, "Le System des mandats coloniaux," *R.D.I.* (1920), pp. 340, 347–50; see also Fauchille, *op. cit.*, I, Part I (1922), 298. In the second part of his treatise published in 1925 M. Fauchille takes a different view (see *supra*, n. 20, and *infra*, n. 53; Rouard de Card, *Les Mandats français sur le Togoland et le Cameroun* (Paris, 1924), pp. 10, 14, 40–42. Two Italian writers (Diena, *op. cit.*, p. 244, and Mondaini, *L'Assetti coloniale del mondo dope la guerra* [1921], p. 65) and a Polish writer (Makowski, *R.G.D.I.*, XXX [1923], 206), who finds an analogy between the situation of Dantzig and that of the mandated territories, are the only jurists of non-mandatory nationality, who, so far as the present writer's investigations have gone, attribute sovereignty of the mandated territories to the mandatory alone, and in the case of A mandates they consider the mandated communities themselves as sharing in it.

[35] Lindley, *op. cit.*, p. 266; Baty, "Protectorates and Mandates," *B.Y.B.I.L.* (1921–22), pp. 116–19, who writes, "Let us recognize that international law puts facts before phrases," and *Rex* v. *Christian*, S.Af.L.R. (1924), App. Div. 137.

[36] Lee, *The Mandate for Mesopotamia and the Principles of Trusteeship in English Law* (London, 1920), p. 15 (reprinted in *United Empire* [London, N.S., 1922], XIII, 19), and *Grotius Soc.*, XII (1926), 32, 48 (but see *infra*, n. 60); Woolf, *supra*, n. 11; Goudy, "On Mandatory Government in the Law of Nations," *J.C.L.* (3d ser.), I, 182; Keith, "Mandates," *ibid.* (3d ser., 1922), IV, 80; Judge de Villiers, in *Rex* v. *Christian*, S.Af.L.R. (1924), App. Div. 120. Some writers draw from this analogy of a trust of the mandatory that the title of the mandatory is so different from ownership that the latter cannot be regarded as sovereign (Lauterpacht, *op. cit.*, p. 200; Woolf, *loc. cit.;* British League of Nations Union, "A Plan for Government by Mandate in Africa" [1921], p. 7, quoted, *P.M.C., Min.*, III, 218; Brierly, *B.Y.B.I.L.* 1929, p. 219; and *infra*, nn. 60, 77).

that it is limited by the terms of the mandate, a limitation which Rolin prefers to call an "obligation" rather than a "servitude."[37]

Certain statesmen whose attitude may be explained by interest or cynicism, like Lord Milner, General Smuts, M. Barthou, Secretary Lansing, Heinrich Schnee, and Stalin, have on occasions seemed to attribute sovereignty to the mandatory;[38] and, as will be noticed later, expressions carrying this implication have occasionally appeared in official documents.[39] According to this theory, mandates become merely another form for transferring sovereignty and limiting its exercise.[40]

This theory has been continually and emphatically opposed by the Mandates Commission; it has been denied but less explicitly by the Council; and the mandatories have in most cases acquiesced.[41] It runs directly counter to the accepted principles of the Peace Conference, gets little support from article 22 of the Covenant and none from the terms of the mandates.[42] Its critics readily explain the process by which the mandatories acquired administrative authority as a process wholly different from a transfer of sovereignty.[43] It has also been pointed out that other articles of the treaty which refer to the mandatories use such expressions as "government exercising authority" (arts. 120, 122, 127), "mandatory power acting in that capacity" (art. 257), "mandatories" (art. 312), thus distinguishing them

[37] Henri Rolin, *op. cit.*, p. 350, and *infra*, n. 77. Mr. Amery, the British colonial secretary, has suggested that the mandates constitute a servitude (see Brierly, *The Law of Nations*, p. 102).

[38] See *supra*, chap. iii. Fauchille (*op. cit.*, I, Part II, 831) and Antonelli (*L'Afrique et la Paix de Versailles* [Paris, 1921], pp. 227 ff.) point out that French officials appeared to assert at first that Togoland and Cameroons had been annexed while British officials recognized the difference between a mandate and a colony (see *supra*, n. 42).

[39] See *infra*, chap. xii.

[40] Lindley, *op. cit.*, p. 247.

[41] See *infra*, chap. xiii, sec. 2*b*.

[42] See *supra*, chap. ii; *infra*, chap. xiv. Chamberlain, chancellor of the exchequer, said in the House of Commons on May 14, 1919, "None of these territories will become a colony," and Balfour, foreign secretary, in a statement to the French press on February 4, 1919, and Curzon in the House of Lords on February 11, 1919, emphasized the distinction between mandated territories and colonies (Antonelli, *op. cit.*, pp. 222, 223, 227).

[43] See Stoyanovsky, *op. cit.*, p. 69, and *infra*, chap. xiv.

from sovereigns of the territory. The distinction between the treatment of enemy property and pre-war debts in mandated territory and in other former enemy territories has also been noticed.[44] "To hold that the petitioners are British subjects," said Justice Corrie for the Supreme Court of Palestine, "would involve holding that the crown having accepted responsibility to govern Palestine as a mandatory has acquired sovereignty, a view for which no authority has been cited."[45] Though South Africa in the opinion of the Supreme Court had such a "majestas" in Southwest Africa as to found a charge of high treason, it did not have sovereignty in the full sense of that term in the opinion of three of the five judges.[46] M. Van Rees concludes:

> This theory appears not to admit the possibility of the exercise of sovereign rights without the possession of the right of sovereignty in the territory itself. It would lead, furthermore, to the paradoxical consequence that a power, being sovereign in certain territory, nevertheless exercises his sovereignty by delegation and in the name of a third party.[47]

c) The Mandated Communities

Several writers who hold that sovereignty is vested in the mandatories or in the League believe that in the case of A mandates eventual sovereignty, and perhaps a part of or share in the present sovereignty, is vested in the mandated communities.[48] This conclusion seems to be implied from the phraseology of article 22, which declares that these communities "have reached a stage of development where their existence as independent nations may be provisionally recognized subject to the rendering of administrative advice and assistance by a mandatory until such time as they are able to stand alone."[49] A growing school of writers extends this doctrine of self-determination to all the mandated communities, and holds that al-

[44] See *supra*, n. 30.

[45] *Re Ezra Goralshvi*, in *A.J.I.L.*, XX (1926), 771.

[46] See *supra*, n. 26.

[47] *Op. cit.*, I, 19. See also M. Van Rees's elaborate memorandum to the Mandates Commission in 1923, (*P.M.C.*, *Min.*, III, 217–22).

[48] Diena, *op. cit.*, p. 242; Lindley, *op. cit.*, pp. 263, 266; Fauchille, *op. cit.*, I, Part I, 298, but see *supra*, n. 34.

[49] See *infra*, chap. xiv.

though their exercise of sovereign powers is in suspense, "the right of sovereignty itself is recognized implicitly as belonging to the peoples inhabiting the territories under mandate by the Pact which foresees their future constitution as independent unities. In our opinion," continues Stoyanovsky, "it is the peoples submitted to the régime of the mandate which are their own virtual sovereigns according to the spirit of article 22 of the pact and from the moment of its entry into force."[50]

This theory is supported by reference to the intention of the treaty-makers, the spirit of article 22, and the significance of the term "tutelage" which figures in it. It was emphasized by M. Paul Pic, who argued that the principle of no annexation accepted by the Peace Conference would be violated if sovereignty of the former enemy territory were transferred to the Principal Powers, to the League, to the mandatories, or in fact to any one but the communities themselves. "These territories," he said, "belong virtually to the autochthonous populations or communities of which the League of Nations is constituted the defender and in regard to which it enjoys somewhat the rôle of a family council. Thus in internal law, neither a family council nor the tutor whom it designates and whose acts it controls has private rights in the property of the pupil."[51] Developing this theory, Stoyanovsky notes that with the organization of international society the conception of sovereignty in international law is coming to have a meaning similar to that of liberty in internal law. It is a natural right of human groups, and is not destroyed by obstacles of a "personal and material character." Thus, as in internal law, when a community is incapable of properly exercising its sovereignty, a guardian must be supplied which exercises powers for the ward but the latter must still be regarded as possessing its own sovereignty. Thus he believes it is only by applying the principles of tutelage or guardianship in private law that one can solve the problem of the status of mandated territories. To the objection that the communities do not in some cases exercise any appreciable power of government he replies:

[50] *Op. cit.*, pp. 82–83.

[51] "Le Régime du mandat d'après le traité de Versailles," *R.G.D.I.*, XXX (1923), 334.

The exercise of a right does not always imply its possession. The exercise of the attributes of sovereignty by the mandatory is neither more nor less extended according to the arbitrary will of the mandatory or indeed that of the League of Nations, but according to the exigency of the interests of the population under mandate. The exercise of more or less of the attribute of sovereignty is not proof of the possession of more or less sovereignty, for the right of sovereignty, as that of liberty, is one and indivisible; it exists or it does not exist.[52]

Thus he concludes:

The sovereignty of the territories submitted to mandate resides in the peoples of those territories. The exercise of the attributes of sovereignty is provisionally confided to a power acting in the capacity of tutor to these minor peoples. This tutelage is guaranteed by an international control resulting from the mandate confided to the said power by the League of Nations.

This theory is especially favored by French writers,[53] and the French government, with approval of the Mandates Commission, has asserted it as the basis of its policy in Syria, as have the British in Iraq.[54] There are, however, grounds for placing the A territories in a special category.[55] As a general theory of mandates, many jurists do not consider it at all, doubtless because they believe juristic problems are to be solved by the letter rather than the spirit of the law,

[52] *Op. cit.*, pp. 85–86.

[53] Millot concludes that "virtual sovereignty resides in the colony itself and actual sovereignty is exercised in the name and under the supervision of the League of Nations and in the interest of the colony by a mandatory power" (*op. cit.*, p. 118). See also Gsell-Trumpi, *Zur rechtlichen Natur der Völkerbundsmandate* (Glarus, 1928), p. 52; Mendelssohn-Bartholdi, "Kolonialmandate," *M.D.G.V.*, VI (Kiel, 1925), 76. M. Van Rees without actually committing himself seems to favor the theory "which alone takes account of the principle of non-annexation adopted by the peace conference" (*op. cit.*, I, 20) though earlier he seemed to have favored the theory attributing sovereignty to the Principal Powers (see *supra*, n. 23). Some of the French writers who accept the analogy of civil-law tutelage to determine the status of the territory do not conclude from this that the mandated peoples are sovereign. See Fauchille (*op. cit.*, I, Part II, 824) who first inclined to vest sovereignty in the mandatories and later in the Principal Powers (see *supra*, nn. 20, 34) and Ciorceanu who vests sovereignty in the League (*Les Mandats internationaux* [1921], pp. 31–32, 40). Other writers who accept the tutelage analogy are Furukaki, *Les Mandats internationaux et la Société des Nations* (1923), pp. 60 ff.; Larnaude, *La Société des Nations* (1920), p. 44; Rougier, "La Première Assemblée de la Société des Nations. Les mandats," *R.G.D.I.*, XXVIII (1921), 334; Pic, *supra*, n. 51; von Kol, "Union interparliamentaire," *Compte rendu de la XX Conférence, 1922*, p. 168. Bewes finds an analogy to the law of guardianship, the English equivalent of tutelage (*Grotius Soc.*, XII [1926], 48).

[54] See *supra*, chap. vii, n. 43; chap. viii, n. 23.

[55] See *supra*, nn. 48, 49.

and because they attribute a more practical significance to the term "sovereignty."[56] Lindley points out the broad powers of administration given to the mandatory by most of the mandates and concludes, "As regards the native communities, it would appear that, in all cases except that of Iraq, the internal administration, no less than the external sovereignty, is so completely under the control of the mandatory state that there is no room for any sovereignty in any native authority." He admits that the Palestine and Syrian mandates are "contemplated as being of a temporary nature" both in article 22 and in the mandates, "but whatever developments in the direction of self-government and independence may take place in the future, it does not appear possible to trace any sovereignty in the native authorities at present." In Iraq, however, he finds that the king has considerable power, both in form and substance, consequently "it would appear that, at present, the sovereignty over Iraq is divided between His Britannic Majesty and the King of Iraq."[57] Diena also finds a possible claim of self-sovereignty only in case of A mandated territories, and for these he finds the phrase "provisional independence" unhappy. The actual facts, he believes, correspond better to "recognition of independence under conditions of suspense." At present he considers the A communities "international protectorates" which thus divide the sovereignty with the mandatory.[58]

[56] Schücking and Wehberg (*loc. cit.*), who attribute sovereignty to the League, do not refer to it at all, and Lauterpacht, who is of the same opinion, mentions it in a footnote (*op. cit.*, p. 192). Spiegel thinks this theory rests on "a new conception of sovereignty identical with the natural law conception of liberty" and "if the prevailing conception of sovereignty is retained, it is entirely impossible to attribute it to a factor which has none at all or only a more or less limited competence in its territory" (*op. cit.*, p. 37). Wehberg ("Die Pflichten der Mandatarmächte betreffend die Deutschen Schutzgebietsanleihen," *W.A.*, XXV [January, 1927], Chronik und Archivalien, pp. 155–56) thinks this self-determination theory requires that the mandated peoples be permitted to select their mandatories and to free themselves and doubts whether "a sovereignty which never existed at all can be considered as suspended." See also Fauchille, *op. cit.*, I, Part II, 848.

[57] *Op. cit.*, pp. 263–64. Baty ("Protectorates and Mandates," *B.Y.B.I.L.* [1921–22], pp. 111, 118) regards "the loss of control over foreign affairs" as "an almost conclusive criterion of the loss of existence of an international personality," thus "a country which exercises complete control over another can not claim to have it recognized as independent, however much it may wish to have it so."

[58] *Op. cit.*, pp. 239, 243.

In general it may be said of the theory now under consideration that though it may be proper to distinguish sovereignty from the exercise of sovereignty, it is hardly proper to attribute sovereignty to communities which do not exist. Certainly in many of the mandated areas there is no organized community of all the inhabitants. Doubtless the mandatories and the League are both bound to develop such communities if possible and if successful to transfer sovereignty to them, but a possible future sovereignty based on contingent obligations of another to transfer is quite different from either present or "virtual" sovereignty. The two, it may be admitted, approach each other as the contingency becomes more certain and less remote in time as in the case of Syria and especially Iraq.[59]

Similar to this theory is that which holds that not merely the exercise of sovereignty but sovereignty itself over the mandated territories is suspended. "It is highly probable," writes D. Campbell Lee, "that from the view point of international law. . . . the allied powers, by creating the mandatory system, have placed the sovereignty of all mandated territories in suspense during the operation of the respective mandates."[60] The Saar Valley is cited as a similar case.[61] By article 49 of the treaty of Versailles:

> Germany renounces in favor of the League of Nations, in the capacity of trustee, the government of the territory defined above. At the end of fifteen years from the coming into force of the present treaty the inhabitants of the said territory shall be called upon to indicate the sovereignty under which they desire to be placed.

Mr. Smit, the accredited representative of South Africa, adopted this as a "strictly personal" theory in discussion with the Mandates Commission. "The ownership of 'sovereignty,' if such an expression

[59] Wright, *A.J.I.L.*, XVII (October, 1923), 696. Lewis considers mandated territories "international persons *in posse* rather than *in esse*" (*L.Q.B.*, XXXIX [1923], 472).

[60] Lee, *The Mandate for Mesopotamia and the Principle of Trusteeship in English law* (London, 1920), pp. 19. See H. Rolin, "La Pratique des Mandats internationaux," *Acad. D.I.*, XIX (1927), 619; Buza, "Die rechtliche Natur des Mandates," *Z.O.R.*, 1927, p. 242; Margolith, *The International Mandates*, Johns Hopkins University thesis (manuscript), 1929, and *supra*, n. 36, for other writers who adopt this analogy which has been used as a basis for qualified sovereignty of the mandatory as well as for suspended sovereignty.

[61] Stoyanovsky, *op. cit.*, p. 82. This might be interpreted as vesting sovereignty in the League as trustee (see *supra*, chap. ix, n. 93).

were permissible, was dormant, but while that state of affairs continued, the government of the Union of South Africa exercised and possessed that sovereignty on behalf of a third party undefined. That was his position: there could be no question of annexation."[62]

It may be that in both the Saar Valley and the mandated areas sovereignty is suspended in the sense that under the treaty no internal authority has the power radically to change the situation without violating the treaty. If such treaty limitations were held to suspend sovereignty, however, it would seem that nearly all sovereignty would be suspended. Every state is limited in the action it can take by treaties. Thus Diena, though admitting that the exercise of sovereignty may be divided, finds it "impossible not to admit the necessity that in each territory which is not a *res nullius*, there exists from the point of view of international law, a sovereignty" which cannot be suspended.[63] If something is to be done in the future there must be some authority to do it or to decide that under the circumstances it cannot be done, and the source of that authority is the sovereign.

d) The League of Nations

A growing body of writers attributes sovereignty to the League of Nations considering it, as did Smuts in his original proposal, the heir of the defunct empires. Schücking and Wehberg expounded this theory, basing their contention on statements made by President Wilson in the Peace Conference, on the terms of article 22, and particularly on the expression "mandates on behalf of the League of Nations."[64] Redslob explains the process by which the League acquired sovereignty under this theory :

[62] *P.M.C., Min.*, XI, 92.

[63] Diena, *op. cit.*, p. 241; see also Millot, *op. cit.*, p. 114.

[64] *Op. cit.* (2d ed.), pp. 686–89. See also statement by M. Freire d'Andrade of the Mandates Commission, *P.M.C., Min.*, I, 41–42; Woolf, *op. cit.*, pp. 133, 139; Breschi, *La Societa della Nazioni* (Florenz, 1920), p. 72; Ciorceanu, *Les Mandats Internationaux* (Paris, 1921); Fleicher, *L'Analyse juridique du pacte de la Société des Nations* (Paris, 1922), p. 53; Bileski, "Das Mandat des Völkerbundes," *Z.V.*, XII (1923), 66; Fleischmann, "Kolonialmandate," *M.D.G.V.*, VI (1925), 58; Verdross, *Die Verfassung der Völkerrechtsgemeinschaft* (Wien, 1926), p. 215; Redslob, "Le Système des mandats internationaux," *B.I.I.*, XV (1926), 284–85; Wehberg, *op. cit.*, pp. 150–56; Lauterpacht, *op. cit.*, p. 198; Spiegel, *op. cit.*, pp. 29–39.

Since the League of Nations, by its right of recovery and reinvestiture, has the means of disposing of the mandate, in other words, since it belongs to it to depose the authority in the territory and to establish there the master of its choice, in brief since it is the source of all the powers there, it is necessary to conclude that it holds the supreme domination there, the sovereignty. . . .

The principal powers abandoned their sovereign power in the territories under mandate. But this abandonment is double; it is effected in two directions, it is combined with a division. In effect the Great Allies transfer to the League of Nations only the ultimate sovereignty and cede the direct power to the mandatory which they have chosen.[65]

Lauterpacht, in his able analysis of the use of private-law analogies in international law, concludes that the League has sovereignty because there is an increasing tendency to recognize this theory, because the "cumulative effect of the limitations" to which the mandatory is subjected even in C territories "is hardly such as to justify the contention that it is in international law the sovereign of the mandated territories," and because "the ultimate sovereignty of the League is a necessary inference" of the term "mandate."[66]

Germany advanced this theory in a note sent to the League Assembly in 1920, and it has been especially favored by German and Austrian writers. The German note drew from it the implication contrary to the Council's decision of August, 1920, that the League rather than the Principal Powers should designate the original mandatories.[67] Many adherents of this theory accept the procedure adopted for original distribution but regard the League's power as extending to revocation of its mandates in case of a future breach by the mandatory and to appointment of a new mandatory.[68]

Opponents of this theory point out that the excision of the specific clauses conferring sovereignty on the League found in the original drafts of the article prove that the conference did not intend the League to have sovereignty. The inclusion of the article in the Cove-

[65] Redslob, *B.I.I.*, XV, 303, 317.

[66] *Op. cit.*, pp. 193, 195–96.

[67] *L. of N., Assembly, Rec.*, sess. I (1920), Plenary Meetings, pp. 210–13.

[68] See for instance, Woolf, *op. cit.*, p. 133; Lauterpacht, *op. cit.*, pp. 199–21. Corbett, though believing sovereignty is divided between the League and the mandatory, denies any right of revocation by the League (*B.Y.B.I.L.*, 1924, p. 135).

nant rather than another part of the treaties can be explained by its importance and by the fact that it dealt with both German and Turkish territories which were treated in different treaties.[69]

Some writers doubt whether the League is a body capable of possessing sovereignty of territory,[70] though some, like Diena, who think the mandatories are sovereign of these territories, consider the League competent in this respect, and it seems clear from the treaty that it is at least temporary trustee of the Saar Valley.[71]

Others insist that the direct transfer of the territories from the Principal Powers to the mandatories without the League's interposition excluded its claim.[72] "The mandates," said Balfour in the Council, "are neither made by the League nor can they in substance be altered by the League. . . . . The mandatory power is under the supervision not the control of the League. . . . . The League is not the author of the policy but its instrument."[73] As for the term "mandate," many question whether it can be given its technical private-law meaning when used in international law, and Stoyanovsky adds:

> The mandate, properly speaking, exists only in the relations of the League of Nations and the mandatory; it can confer a right of sovereignty, neither to one nor the other, in the administered territory; the latter is not regulated by the principles of mandate, but as we are about to see, by that of tutelage. The mandate, properly speaking, is here only a means to assure the execution of the "sacred mission of civilization," it constitutes the "guaranties for the accomplishment of this mission," of which article 22 (end of paragraph 1) of the pact speaks. It is only a method, an instrument from which one can not in any fashion deduce the solution of the question of sovereignty without falsifying the spirit of the mandates system.[74]

[69] Potter, *supra*, n. 20.

[70] Van Rees, *op. cit.*, I, 17; Lee, *Grotius Soc.*, XII, 48; Stoyanovsky, *op. cit.*, p. 77; Fauchille, *op. cit.*, I, Part II, 847, who however regards the League as an international personality. Baty thinks to regard the mandatory as a mere tool of "the states comprising the League of Nations" would be to "ignore the facts of history, and to press the analogy of private law agency to the verge of the ridiculous" (*op cit.*, 1921–22, p. 119).

[71] See *supra*, chap. ix, nn. 93, 96, 97.

[72] Lindley, *op. cit.*, p. 265; Corbett, *op. cit.*, p. 133.

[73] See *supra*, chap. iv, n. 12.

[74] *Op. cit.*, pp. 76–77, and Gsell-Trumpi, *op. cit.*, pp. 30–35.

A mandate is in fact nothing but an agency which may be established to deal with property belonging to someone else as well as to the principle.

This theory, like that of the mandatory's sovereignty, is sometimes modified in the case of A mandates by admitting these communities to a share of the sovereignty along with the League. Thus Woolf says, tentatively, in A territories "sovereign rights and powers are shared between the new states on the one hand and on the other the League which exercises such powers as it has through its trustee, the mandatory."[75] Some writers combine League sovereignty with self-determination in a somewhat different sense. Spiegel attributes the difficulties of jurists to confusion between the constitutional-law and the international-law conceptions of sovereignty.[76] "Highest competence in the mandated territories" or sovereignty in the first sense he attributes to the League of Nations. But even the League is limited under international law by the objects of article 22, including "no annexation," and consequently does not own the territories except in the sense of trust property. Thus he disagrees with Schücking and Wehberg who consider the areas League territory (*Völkerbundgebiet*). They are, in Spiegel's opinion, territory of their inhabitants (*Gebiet der Bevölkerung der Mandatsländer*) and should not be involved in a war of execution by the League. Spiegel, however, thinks it is a misuse of the term "sovereignty" to attribute that quality to the mandated peoples.[77]

[75] Woolf, *op. cit.*, p. 139.

[76] Spiegel (*op. cit.*, p. 24) accepts the distinction between "two conceptions of sovereignty which lie in entirely different spheres" expounded by Verdross (*Die Einheit des rechtlichen Weltbildes* [Tübingen, 1923], pp. 31–32) as follows: "One is the expression for the quality of that legal sphere which stands in the highest 'sovereign' position in the legal hierarchy, whereas the other indicates the particular competence for the determination of a definite legal situation for which sovereignty in the first sense is invoked." Sovereignty in the first sense, adds Spiegel, "is the expression for the highest complete and real competence in a territory," while in the other it "has as its content the special competence which a state or federation possesses on the basis of international law." See also Gsell-Trumpi (*op. cit.*, pp. 36–40) who emphasizes the relativity of the term "sovereignty" historically and practically.

[77] *Op. cit.*, pp. 29–30, 36, 39. Lindley (*op. cit.*, p. 267) implies the same distinction when he writes, "Even where the whole of such sovereignty as exists over mandated

Some writers have advanced a theory dividing sovereignty between the League and the mandatory. Thus Higgins writes:

> For purposes of international responsibility, the mandatory will doubtless be deemed to be the power from whom redress will be sought, and who will also be able to assert sovereign rights for the protection of the territory in question. This does not of itself carry full sovereignty, which appears to be divided with the League.[78]

To similar effect Corbett writes: "The powers grouped under the term sovereignty have as regards the mandated territories been divided, in general they rest with the mandatory but some of them are reserved to the League of Nations."[79] This theory is based on an examination of the actual exercises of power and attributions of responsibility in respect to the territories, and has been criticized, like the theory of mandatory sovereignty, on the score that it confuses the exercise of sovereignty with sovereignty itself.[80] Many writers have also insisted that divided sovereignty is impossible. Such theories, writes Stoyanovsky, "lead only to a complete confusion of the notion of sovereignty."[81] He continues:

> One can not compromise on a question of law. It is rather a line of conduct which this theory tends to establish between interests: indigenes, League of Nations and Mandatories; but this conception entails danger of constant friction between the different organs of the mandates system of which each is invested with a part (which? or in what measure?) of the sovereignty in question.

In 1923, the writer analyzed the texts and practice to discover what authority was competent to perform such sovereign acts as amending the mandates regarded as constitutions of the territory and alienating or transferring the administrative authority. He

---

territory is in the mandatory that sovereignty is not of the full and complete order which a state possesses over its own territory." See also Lewis (*L.Q.R.*, XXXIX, 463, 467) who thinks the areas are not "within the territorial sovereignty of the mandatories" and Corbett (*op. cit.*, p. 135) who distinguishes between "a man's own property and that of which he is legal owner as trustee," and *supra*, n. 36.

[78] Hall, *International Law* (8th ed.; Higgins), p. 162.

[79] *B.Y.B.I.L.*, 1924, p. 134.

[80] Lauterpacht, *op. cit.*, p. 199; Stoyanovsky, *op. cit.*, p. 85; Van Rees, *op. cit.*, I, 19–20.

[81] Stoyanovsky, *op. cit.*, pp. 80–81. See also Spiegel, *op. cit.*, p. 35; Gsell-Trumpi, *op. cit.*, p. 47; Millot, *op. cit.*, p. 114, and *supra*, chap. ix, sec. 2c.

reached the conclusion that "it would be a close approximation to truth to ascribe sovereignty of the mandated territories to the mandatory acting with consent of the council of the League."[82]

Sovereignty with this theory was considered to be jointly held by the two bodies which in case the mandatory is represented on the Council[83] would not differ materially[84] from the League alone in so far as the Council represents that body[85] and acts by unanimity. Though the exercise of sovereignty may in some cases be divided between the mandatory and local bodies, sovereign acts not expressly delegated to any authority were believed to require the consent of both the League Council and the mandatory, except in the case of continued violation of the mandate determined by the Permanent Court of International Justice in which case the agreement would be broken and sovereignty would vest in the League as principal or mandant which would be obliged under article 22 to appoint a new mandatory.[86] This study approached the question from the standpoint of constitutional law and recognized that the sovereign was limited under international law by treaties, including the Covenant, so "in amending a mandate in any important particular would usually have to get the consent of other states with treaty interests."[87]

This theory did not deny the possibility that the Covenant might require recognition of the independence of the areas in future contingencies, thus foreseeing the future sovereignty of the mandated peoples themselves. It also admitted that prior to recognition of full independence of the mandated communities native governments might be accorded an international status entitling them to share in the sovereignty. Thus it appeared that sovereign acts with respect to Iraq required the consent of the native government of that country as well as that of the mandatory and the League Council. Here

[82] *A.J.I.L.*, XVII, 698; XVIII, 315; *infra*, chap. xiv, sec. 3.

[83] Belgium has not been represented on the Council since September, 1927.

[84] But see *supra*, n. 33.

[85] Gsell-Trumpi (*op. cit.*, p. 47) asks, "If the mandatory must act with consent of the *council* what remains of the rights of the *League?*" The League must act through some organ and in mandate matters; the Council is that organ.

[86] *A.J.I.L.*, XVII, 702.

[87] *Ibid.*, p. 700, and Lindley, *op. cit.*, p. 268.

also there would be a collective but undivided sovereignty, though exercise of sovereignty was in fact divided between the mandatory and the native government.[88]

This theory has usually been confused by writers with a theory of divided sovereignty (for which the writers original exposition gave some justification) and criticized on that basis.[89] Some have pointed out that it differs little from sovereignty of the League.[90]

Our examination of about fifty juristic discussions of the mandates system though affording clear evidence that no doctrine as to the location of sovereignty has been generally accepted does indicate some tendencies. Jurists are inclined to divide on national lines. Americans and Englishmen have often attributed sovereignty to the Principal Allied and Associated Powers though the latter have frequently favored the mandatories. Theories of divided and suspended sovereignty, frequently influenced by the analogy of trusteeship, have been especially prominent among the Anglo-Saxons. Germans and Austrians, impressed by the phrase "mandate in behalf of the League," have nearly always attributed sovereignty to the League; while French jurists, greatly influenced by the analogy of "tutelage," have been inclined to regard the mandated communities themselves as sovereign, though a few French writers are to be found in every group. Italians, like the Anglo-Saxons, have tended to attribute sovereignty to the Principal Powers or to the mandatories. The latter opinion has very seldom been maintained in juristic writings from other non-mandatory nationalities, though publicists of a cynical disposition have done so, especially Americans.[91]

Theories that attribute sovereignty in full or in part to the League of Nations are supported by the largest number of jurists, distributed over the largest number of nationalities, and have steadily gained in adherents. Juristic writings from 1924 to 1928 have more often accorded sovereignty to the League than did those from 1920 to 1924.[92]

[88] *A.J.I.L.*, XVII, 696.

[89] See Stoyanovsky, *op. cit.*, p. 80; Van Rees, *op. cit.*, pp. 19–20; Spiegel, *op. cit.*, p. 35. See also Corbett, *op. cit.*, p. 134.

[90] Lauterpacht, *op. cit.*, p. 199; Gsell-Trumpi, *op. cit.*, p. 47.

[91] See *supra*, n. 35, 38.

[92] See *supra*, n. 64. Lauterpacht (*op. cit.*, p. 193) remarks: "Owing partly to the cautious but vigilant activity of the Permanent Mandates Commission appointed by

Second in number of adherents is the theory vesting at least "virtual" sovereignty in the mandated communities themselves, and this also has increased in relative popularity as the years have passed.[93] The theory attributing sovereignty to the Principal Powers has continued to find supporters, and they are distributed among a large number of nationalities.[94] While at first jurists, especially of mandatory powers, inclined to attribute sovereignty to the mandatories, the definite position against this theory taken officially by the League and the mandatory governments has made it hardly tenable and few have asserted it in recent years.[95] Those that have consider it a qualified sovereignty which does not amount to "annexation" of the territories[96] or partial sovereignty shared with the League[97] or with the native communities.[98] Thus jurists have less and less found it possible to attribute complete sovereignty of a mandated area to a single state. Theories of divided and of suspended sovereignty have also been less frequently advanced, while doctrines of collective[99] and of qualified sovereignty[100] have increased in support.

3. Sources of Law Applicable

These differences of opinion as to the location of sovereignty may no doubt be explained in some cases by differences in the sentiment of the writers toward the system, the treaty in which it was embodied, and the method of its initiation, or in their desires and hopes

---

the Council of the League, as well as to the growing prestige of the League itself, and partly to the circumstance that, morally and psychologically, the claims of the mandatories, so far as they are based on conquest, become less impressive with the passage of years, it appears that the ultimate authority of the League over the mandated territories is becoming generally recognized." Van Rees, however, says (*op. cit.*, I, 16): "This doctrine, abandoned by most of the writers, is at present maintained by only a small number of jurists."

[93] See *supra*, n. 53. Many attribute at least partial sovereignty to the A communities (see *supra*, nn. 49, 57, 58, 75, 88).

[94] See *supra*, nn. 20–24.

[95] See *supra*, nn. 34–36, 41–47.

[96] See *supra*, nn. 36, 37, 77.

[97] See *supra*, nn. 78, 79, 82.

[98] See *supra*, nn. 57, 58.

[99] This would include theories attributing sovereignty to the Allied and Associated Powers, to the League, and to the latter in association with the Principal Powers, the mandatories, or the mandated communities.

[100] All theories admit that the sovereign is limited under international law by art. 22 of the Covenant (see *supra*, nn. 36, 77, 87).

for its future and that of the territories concerned. Germans and League enthusiasts have often found grounds to exalt the legal rôle of the League; statesmen and jurists of the mandatory states have frequently satisfied themselves of the legal dominance of the mandatories in the system; while philanthropists readily convince themselves that the mandated peoples are the center of the system.

From the juristic point of view, however, subjective factors must be neglected,[101] and the writer does not intend to imply that they have in fact influenced the minds of jurists unduly. The ostensible basis for divergence in juristic conclusions must lie in differences of opinion as to the conception of sovereignty or of the sources of law applicable. Unfortunately, jurists frequently have neglected to state their theory of either explicitly. They have argued from undefined premises, which, however, can usually be discovered by analysis.

A few writers have set forth their theory of sovereignty explicitly, usually emphasizing the relativity of the conception historically and its difference when viewed respectively from the standpoints of constitutional law and international law.[102] The latter point of view, which is alone pertinent here, has not been explicitly analyzed, but in fact three quite distinct conceptions seem to have been relied on which emphasize respectively the territorial, governmental, and human aspects of sovereignty.[103] The first regards sovereignty as valid international-law title to territory, locates it by narrating the history of past transactions, and usually attributes it to the Principal Allied and Associated Powers by reference to article 119 of the treaty of Versailles.[104] The second regards sovereignty as ultimate competence in governing a territorial community, locates it by citing present law and practice, and usually attributes it to the League, the mandatory, or both by reference to the texts of article 22 and the

[101] "Of course the motives of a judge's opinion may be almost anything—a bribe, a woman's blandishments, the desire to favor the administration or his political party or to gain popular favor or influence—but these are not sources which jurisprudence can recognize as legitimate" (J. C. Grey, *Nature and Sources of the Law*, p. 274).

[102] See Spiegel, *op. cit.*, pp. 24 ff.; Gsell-Trumpi, *op. cit.*, pp. 36 ff.; Stoyanovsky, *op. cit.*, pp. 83 ff.

[103] See *supra*, chap. ix, sec. 2*d*.

[104] See, for example, Schneider, who uses the term *Gebietshoheit* (*supra*, n. 31).

mandates and to the actual authority governing the areas.[105] The third regards sovereignty as the eventual right of recognized peoples to self-determination, locates it by construing the eventual purpose of the institution, and attributes it to the mandated communities themselves by reference to the recognition given their aspirations in the letter and spirit of the Covenant.[106]

Historical and philosophical support can be found for each of these conceptions. In law, however, it is important to know the support given them by recognized sources of law.[107] The writers have thus (more often implicitly than explicitly) looked back of their conceptions to the sources of law by which they may be justified.[108]

Some have gone on the theory that the intention of those who created the system and drew up the documents should control interpretation and construction, and that this intention is to be found in "authentic" statements of the creating bodies or, in their absence, in "preliminary material"—records of Peace Conference and Supreme Council debates, or even in statements of important statesmen and political groups and the general historical milieu from which the institution arose. Because of the variety of opinions entertained and expressed before and at the Conference this method lacks precision. It can be used to support imperialisic or idealistic interpretations at will. It has in fact been relied on especially by cynics like Lansing and Schnee who assume that the interests of the victors indicate the intent of the instruments and by jurists like Henri Rolin and Schneider who record the history of the transfers of the mandated territories in detail and attach importance to their original renunciation—in favor of the Principal Allied and Associated Powers and their subsequent allocation to mandatories by those Powers.[109]

That international law sanctions the use of "preliminary mate-

[105] See, for example, Spiegel who uses the term *Souverainität*, and Lindley, *supra*, n. 77.

[106] See especially Stoyanovsky, *supra*, n. 52.

[107] See *supra*, chap. ix, sec. 3.

[108] Gsell-Trumpi (*op. cit.*, pp. 7 ff.) has done this most explicitly.

[109] For criticism of this method see *ibid*.

rial" for the interpretation of treaties no one can deny,[110] but many of the writers find it impossible to discover from the historical data any definite intention on which all agreed, and resort to "the science of international law." Lauterpacht notes that the Council and the Mandates Commission have repeatedly expressed the opinion that it is for this science to supply a correct construction of article 22, and submits:

> International jurists, while discarding all attempts at the interpretation of mandates in terms of the wishes or the expectations of one group of the signatories of the covenant, will have to base their construction: (*a*) on the provisions of article 22, on the mandate agreements concluded between the mandatories and the council of the League, and on the relevant pronouncements of the mandates commission, of the council and the assembly of the League; (*b*) on a juristic analysis of the controversial term "mandate" used in the covenant."[111]

Gsell-Trumpi, a Swiss writer, has discussed the appropriate sources at greater length. On the ground that all the members of the League are equally interested in the interpretation of the Covenant, he rejects interpretations preceding from the opinion of particular statesmen or political groups before the going into effect of the treaty or even of the Supreme Council, the League Council, or the Permanent Mandates Commission afterward. Though admitting that the intention of the parties must prevail in treaty interpretation, he insists that it must be the intention upon which all the parties have agreed and of this there is no evidence except the text itself. Thus a self-consistent system built upon the text will alone furnish a satisfactory interpretation. Furthermore, the League of Nations Covenant is a lawmaking treaty for which principles of statutory rather than contract interpretation are applicable. Practical considerations also militate against reliance on historic materials, which would too much limit the development of the law. "If the same form," he writes, "could never be filled with a new content so long as it lasted, new circumstances and conditions could be taken into consideration only with difficulty and the development of new ideas would be thwarted." Gsell-Trumpi and other writers who resort to scientific analyses of

[110] Hyde, *International Law,* II, 61; Westlake, *ibid.*, I 293; Oppenheim, *ibid.* (3d ed.), I, 700, 703; Wright, *A.J.I.L.*, XVII, 694.

[111] Lauterpacht, *op. cit.*, pp. 193–94.

the texts actually apply private-law analogies, reaching different conclusions according as they emphasize the terms "trust," "mandate," or "tutelage."[112]

Writers whose opinion is formed by study of the practical operation of the system since it began functioning usually assume the propriety of that method of interpretation without discussion, or, like Lindley, with a general reference to the recognized importance of custom as a source of international law.[113] Such writers, however, are likely to reach different conclusions according as their attention has been attracted by the activities in the mandated territories or at Geneva. Lindley, Rouard de Card, Baty, and others observing the dominance of the mandatory in the territories regard it as the sovereign, while others like Schücking, Wehberg, Redslob, and Van Rees, impressed by the importance of the League's rôle in the system, find such a conclusion impossible.

Some of the latter class of writers, especially those whose official position suggests caution, rely less on practice than on authentic interpretation. They often cite the conclusions of the League organs on a parity with conclusions of the Peace Conference and the Principal Allied Powers, though admitting that they still leave many problems unsolved.[114]

It will be observed that the three sources of interpretation which jurists have actually used correspond to the civilian's well-known classification into authentic, usual, and doctrinal interpretation,[115] and furthermore that these resemble the first three sources of international law listed in article 38 of the statute of the Permanent Court of International Justice, treaties, custom, and general principles of

[112] Gsell-Trumpi, *op. cit.*, pp. 7–13. In spite of the fact that the original text of art. 22 was in English, he insists that for purposes of legal interpretation English can have no priority over French which is expressly made equally authentic (Versailles Treaty, art. 440, par. 3; St. Germain Treaty, art. 381, par. 2). This makes it possible to argue against the technical use of the term "trust" in art. 22.

[113] Lindley, *op. cit.*, p. vii.

[114] See Van Rees, *op. cit.*, I, 21.

[115] Bouvier, "Interpretation," *Law Dictionary*. Holland (*Jurisprudence* [11th ed.], pp. 418–19) classifies "authentic" and "usual" interpretation as two types of "legal interpretation," and divides "doctrinal interpretation" into "grammatical" and "logical," the latter of which may be "extensive" or "restrictive." See also Amos, *The Science of Law*, pp. 205–7, and chap. v, also *infra*, chap. xi, sec. 2*a*.

law.[116] There obviously has not developed as yet a sufficient consensus of juristic opinion to permit of reliance upon that source for determining either the location of sovereignty or the proper method of interpretation, though most of the jurists agree that the essential characteristic of the system is the assurance, through gratuitous activity of a mandatory acting under supervision of the League, of certain defined rights in the territories.

[116] See *supra*, chap. ix, sec. 3.

CHAPTER XI

GENERAL PRINCIPLES OF LAW

The statute of the Permanent Court of International Justice recognizes as a source of international law, after conventions and customs, "the general principles of law recognized by civilized nations." The phrase, as originally introduced by Baron Descamps of Belgium in the Commission of Jurists, read; "the rules of international law as recognized by the legal conscience of civilized nations." This was opposed by the Anglo-Saxon jurists (Root and Lord Phillimore) who, in common with many Anglo-American international-law writers, thought conventions and customs were the only sources of positive international law and that such a phrase as this would open the way for decision on the basis of subjective conceptions.

The continental jurists who constituted a majority of the Commission insisted that there was a body of objective principles of justice which courts whether municipal or international always resorted to, and in view of the incompleteness of conventional and customary international law "a rule must be established . . . . to avoid the possibility of the court declaring itself incompetent (*non liquet*) through lack of applicable rules." Baron Descamps called attention to article 7 of the International Prize Court Convention of 1907 which authorized that Court in the absence of a treaty to "apply the rules of international law" and "if no generally recognized rule exists" to "give judgment in accordance with the general principles of justice and equity." He also referred to the preamble of the Hague Convention on rules of land warfare by which the Powers declared that in cases not included in the regulations "the inhabitants and the belligerents remain under the protection and the rule of the principles of the law of nations as they result from the usages established among civilized peoples, from the laws of humanity and the dictates of the public conscience." "It is impossible," said Baron Descamps, "to disregard a fundamental principle of justice in the application of law, if this principle clearly indicates certain rules necessary for the system of international relations and applicable to the various circumstances arising in international affairs." To this argument the Anglo-Saxon jurists yielded, and Mr. Root introduced a revision in the phraseology finally accepted.[1]

1. Evidence of General Principles of Law

a) *Jus naturale and jus gentium*

What is the evidence for these "general principles of law recognized by civilized nations?" This clause must point to evidences other than conventions, customs, judicial decisions, and the teachings of publicists which are referred to in other clauses of the article. Descamps refers to "necessity for the system of international relations," a phrase suggestive of the "natural law" posited by seventeenth- and eighteenth-century jurists[2] or the "reason" which Westlake says "is a source of international law" and in practice means Roman law often called "written reason" and accepted as a source of international law, especially by British jurists.[3]

Phillimore, the British member of the Commission, interpreted the phrase as permitting resort to "maxims of law," "accepted by

[1] *P.C.I.J.* (Advisory Committee of Jurists, *Procès-verbaux* of the proceedings of the Committee, June 16–July 24, 1920), pp. 296, 324, 331, 344, and *supra*, chap. ix, sec. 3.

[2] Grotius considered natural law "the dictate of right reason indicating that an act from its agreement or disagreement with the rational nature has in it a moral turpitude or a moral necessity" (I, 1, 10, 1). Puffendorf thought natural law was "so exactly congruous with the rational and social nature of man that human kind can not maintain an honest and peaceful society without it" (*De jure naturae et gentium*, I, 6, 13, and 18; see also *ibid.*, II, 3, and Dickinson, *Equality of States*, pp. 40, 77). Vattel used "the term necessary law of nations for that law which results from applying the natural law to nations" (*Prelim.*, sec. 7).

[3] Westlake, *International Law*, I, 14–15, and Lauterpacht (*op. cit.*, p. 24) who after discussing the views of numerous international law writers finds that the classical writers relied greatly on Roman law as a source of international law and that British and American writers adopt "Roman private law not only as a source of international law in the historical sense; i.e. as evidence of the part played by Roman law in the formation of the law of nations, but also as a living source from which its numerous gaps may be filled. Unlike the continental writers, they never discarded the idea that Roman law is the source most likely to contain the 'reason of the thing' on many a question of international law" (see Wright, *Minn.L.R.*, V, 437, and Dickinson on the use of natural law in the development of international law, *op. cit.*, pp. 33, 40, 76, and on the use of Roman law as a source, *ibid.*, p. 50, and *Yale L.J.*, XXVI, 578).

all nations in *foro domestico*, such as certain principles of procedure, the principle of good faith, and the principle of *res judicata*," while De Lapradelle thought the only evidence of these "general principles" would be the "doctrine" of publicists and the "jurisprudence" of courts referred to in the next clause.[4] Bustamente says, "This is the field for the intervention of national rules applicable to international life,"[5] and Lauterpacht, in an illuminating book which he considers a commentary on this clause, thinks it follows Holland's suggestion that "international law is private law writ large" and gives "formal approval on the part of practically the whole international community" to the application of "private law sources and analogies" in international law. He, however, recognizes that the use of such sources and analogies is limited by four considerations: (1) the private law rule must be "recognized by the main systems of jurisprudence," (2) there must be a real analogy between the private and the international situation, (3) there must be no rule established by or easily deducible from international conventions or customs, (4) there must be sufficient international procedure to make application of the rule practicable. Often the absence of a court with compulsory jurisdiction prevents the practical recognition of the correct legal principle. With the development of international organization and procedure, however, this obstacle to the use of private law analogies will gradually be removed.[6]

With these limitations, the internal law analogies of Lauterpacht recall the *jus gentium* by which the *praetor perigrinus* supplemented

[4] *P.C.I.J.* (Advisory Committee of Jurists, *op. cit.*), pp. 335, 336.

[5] Bustamente, *The World Court*, p. 242.

[6] Lauterpacht, *op. cit.*, pp. viii, xxv, 84–86. See also Holland, *Studies in International Law*, p. 152; Dickinson, discussion of the use of the analogy between states and individuals, in the development of international law, *op. cit.*, chaps. i-iii, and *Yale L.J.*, XXVI, 574 ff. Willoughby emphasizes the first limitation upon the use of private law sources as follows: "That municipal acts may often have a strongly persuasive international force is granted, but that they may be determinative of the rights of other states is never conceded. It may, indeed, be pointed out that, were the doctrine once established that municipal law could create international law, the doom of international law as a fixed and generally binding body of principles would be at once pronounced. For not only would it thus be within the recognized right of each state to escape from the application of previously acknowledged rules of international law, but that law itself would lose its generality and have a content that would vary for each state" (*Fundamental Concepts of Public Law* [New York, 1924], p. 284).

and developed the law of Rome in the late republic by discovering the common element in the various laws which aliens brought with them. On the other hand, the necessary law of Descamps recalls the *jus naturale* by which Cicero and later Roman jurisconsults introduced ethical principles of Greek philosophy into the law. The two were frequently confused in later Roman legal development though careful writers recognized a substantial difference in the fact that slavery existed under the *jus gentium* but not under the *jus naturale*.[7]

Both conceptions were used by Grotius and his successors in developing international law, sometimes with the Roman law meanings, sometimes with derivative meanings. Thus one might consider that the universal practice of men embodied in the Roman *jus gentium* gave evidence of principles of justice which should be applied to states in analogous situations, or one might ascertain the common elements in the practice of states in conducting international relations and call this *jus gentium*. Similarly one might hold that the philosophic principles of Roman *jus naturale* were applicable to state as well as individual relations, or in studying the nature of states and their relations, one of philosophic disposition might be led to posit certain necessary principles from which a new *jus naturale* could be deduced. In one sense *jus gentium* and *jus naturale* meant to Grotius respectively the generally accepted and the ideal rules of individual conduct assumed to be applicable to the relations of all legal personalities including states. In the other sense they meant the actual and the reasonable conduct of states. In the latter sense *jus gentium* is found by comparing state treaties and customs and *jus naturale* by comparing the opinions of qualified jurists, publicists, and philosophers on international problems. It is in the former sense that the *jus gentium* and *jus naturale* resemble the "general principles of law" with which we are now concerned, and their applicability to relations between states depends upon the validity of the analogy between situations internal and external to the state.[8]

[7] Sherman, *Roman Law in the Modern World* (Boston, 1917), I, 38, 54–62; Dickinson, *op. cit.*, pp. 9–16.

[8] Lauterpacht, *op. cit.*, pp. 12 ff.; Dickinson, *op. cit.*, pp. 40 ff. Vattel clearly discerned the distinction and thought the analogy of states to men could be used but sparingly. "A civil society or a state is a very different subject from an individual per-

b) THE ARGUMENT FROM ANALOGY

Do such analogies exist in fact? Can Lauterpacht's requirement that there be a "real analogy" ever be fulfilled in relations between entities so different as the state and the individual? Practically all writers have admitted that it can. In an illuminating discussion of the subject Dickinson preceded Lauterpacht in pointing out the almost universal resort to the analogy by international jurists of all schools, and though he emphasized the differences between states and individuals, though he believed that indiscriminate use of the analogy had often confused thinking, and though he deplored its influence in maintaining doctrines of international law ill suited to the world in which we live, nevertheless he did not wish to "belittle the usefulness of municipal law in the development of the international system" and did not doubt that there are "principles of jurisprudence that are fundamental to all legal systems whatever the nature of their subjects."[9]

The problem, therefore, is to distinguish a "real" from an "unreal" analogy. Historically the analogy has been used in three quite different ways. Among the founders of international law it was often employed to determine the characteristics of international persons and to indicate which of their interests should be protected by law. Thus assuming that states in the family of nations resembled men in a state of nature, the former were attributed fundamental or natural rights identical with those which contemporary philosophers attributed to individuals. Some writers, however, have not sought analogies to the state but to the family of nations and have found them in primitive societies of individuals. Such analogies, however, are used, not to discover general principles of law or to justify their application in international relations, but to account for pecu-

---

son, and therefore, by virtue of the natural law, very different obligations and rights belong to it in most cases" (*Prelim.* sec. 6). To same effect see Wolff, Introduction, *Jus gentium methodo scientifica pertractatum* (1764); Dickinson, "The Analogy between Natural Persons and International Persons in the Law of Nations," *Yale L.J.*, XXVI (1917), 574, and Vinogradoff, *Outlines of Historical Jurisprudence*, I, 90–91.

[9] Dickinson, *Yale L.J.*, XXVI, 590–91, and *Equality of States*, p. 50. Westlake considers it "a logical error to assume, because states are moral persons and therefore capable of rights equally with natural individuals, that they must have the same rights as natural individuals" (*International Law*, I, 307).

liarities in international practice, such as the recognition of self-help and the protection of forcible acquisitions, and to suggest the course of development by which they will gradually be eliminated. Finally, among a number of recent writers, in international tribunals and in the writings of some of the founders, especially of the Grotian school, the analogy has been used to assist in developing the consequences of relations, recognized by customary international law or treaty as similar to internal relations. Such writers, on discovering for example, that customary international law recognizes the validity of agreements between states, have resorted to the law of agreements between individuals (contracts) to ascertain the consequences of this relationship in circumstances not covered by international precedents, or authority. While the three uses of analogy differ perhaps in degree rather than kind, it is believed that the shift of emphasis from a resemblance of persons or of societies to a resemblance of relations is important.[10]

Analogy in logic is a form of argument which assumes that because two situations are alike in certain elements which have been observed they will also be alike in other elements which have not been observed in one of the situations. A true analogy exists where the latter elements of the situation can be reasonably expected to follow from the former, and such expectation seems to be warranted only when the two aspects are related by customary observation or by logical necessity. Experience shows that the probability of two things or persons resembling each other in aspects unknown for one is slight, unless they are alike in a very large number of known characteristics. Certainly in most observable characteristics a state and an individual are very unlike, thus conclusions based on a direct analogy between them is likely to be false. There is perhaps more resemblance between the family of nations today and certain primitive societies, thus suggestive analogies may be discovered.

If, however, two situations present relations which precisely correspond to the same abstract proposition, any logical deductions from that proposition would inevitably be true of both. Thus, for example, if two situations, however different, are each analyzable into six identical parts, we may with considerable assurance assert that each is also analyzable into either two or three identical parts

[10] See nn. 8, 23, 64.

because it is a property of the concept six to be thus divisible. Law may be looked upon as a logical system flowing from defined relations between persons; and if the same relation exists in each of two sets of persons, however different the persons may be, all the logical implications of the relation will be true of both situations.

Unfortunately, however, there is not such universal agreement upon the logical properties of legal relations as there is upon those of mathematical relations. Even though one discover an internal law situation really analogous to an international law situation, one cannot, thus, be secure in applying the legal consequences of the former to the latter unless assured that the legal argument appeals to universal human reason. Thus analogies should be sought in the most highly developed systems of law, systems which will presumably most completely incorporate both the generally accepted and the ideal rationalizations of human relations. The almost universal acceptance of either Roman law or English law by modern nations seems to make these systems with their modern national adaptations most important.[11] No reason appears, however, why analogies should be taken only from private law. If any principles of internal public law fulfilled the requirements of general acceptance, true analogy, harmony with existing international treaties and custom, and practicability in the international situation, they would seem equally available as evidence of "general principles of law recognized by civilized nations."[12]

[11] Bryce, *Studies in History and Jurisprudence*, Vol. I, Essay 2. Sherman considers the common law, as well as most other modern legal systems, derivative from Roman law (*op. cit.*, I, 344). Sir John Fischer Williams argues that since international society is in a primitive state of organization analogies should be sought in primitive internal-law systems (see *infra*, n. 64). He however uses analogy to ascertain the extent to which the international community by custom and treaty or because of procedural difficulties fails to apply "general principles of law," in short to explain the peculiarities of international law, recognized in Lauterpacht's third and fourth points, not to discover "general principles of law" themselves. One might, for instance, get some light on the scientific opinions of the Hottentots by analogy with the scientific opinions of the Iroquois, but if one wanted to learn science he would go to neither but to the best scientific opinions of the most civilized nations. And a knowledge of science would undoubtedly be of value to the anthropologist in interpreting the opinions of the savages so far as they were based on actual observation and reason rather than on blind tradition.

[12] See Textor, *Synopsis juri gentium* (1680; Carnegie ed., 1916), chap. viii, p. 41; chap. ii, pp. 14, 15, cited by Lauterpacht, *op. cit.*, p. 14. Books on jurisprudence by writers of the analytical school like Holland and Salmond purport to set forth the

There appear to be three sorts of internal law which may throw light on the mandatory system: (1) law applied to constitutional or private relations and situations analogous to those involved in the mandates system, (2) law applicable to internal-law institutions and conceptions suggested by certain terms in article 22 and the mandates, and (3) law which states have laid down for the guidance of their own officials, nationals, and protégés in the actual application of the mandates system.

While the latter type of law may give evidence of some "general principles of law," even where it does not, it constitutes a practical interpretation of specific aspects of the mandates system by those applying it and thus is evidence of the customary international law of mandates. Internal legislation directly relating to the mandates system will therefore be considered in the next chapter. Attention will here be given to the first two types of internal law which are significant for this study only in so far as they give evidence of "general principles of law" applicable, so far as tradition and the state of political organization permits, to legal relations, whatever may be the characteristics of the personalities concerned.

2. The Internal Law of Analogous Situations

Historically a large part of international law was undoubtedly derived from private law analogies, and a re-examination of many of these foundations might assist in interpreting the mandates system. We will, however, content ourselves with consideration of certain analogies which may assist (*a*) in interpreting the documents establishing the mandates system, (*b*) in defining the legal character of

---

common essence of developed private law systems, thus recalling the Roman *jus gentium* (but see Holland, *Jurisprudence*, pp. 7–9) while those by writers of the sociological school like Ihering (*The Ends of Law*) and Pound (*Introduction to the Philosophy of Law*) attempt to deduce rules from the nature of existing social relations recalling the Roman *jus naturale*. Such efforts have resulted in definite and authoritative systems which courts can readily utilize in seeking the "general principles of law" applicable to a given situation. The more ambitious efforts of the historical school (Maine, *Ancient Law*) to discover universal principles by comparing law in communities of every stage of development and of the modern law of nature school (Lorimer, *The Institutes of Law, a Treatise of the Principles of Jurisprudence as Determined by Nature*) to deduce universal principles from human nature have been less successful in producing applicable bodies of law.

the League of Nations, (*c*) in explaining the relation of the mandated territory to its sovereign, and (*d*) the relation of the mandated community to the mandatory.

a) THE INTERPRETATION OF DOCUMENTS

Though article 22 of the Covenant and the mandates are not documents of the kind ordinarily before national courts, still they are documents expressing the intention of legal personalities, and the principles of internal law developed for determining the true meaning of statutes, contracts, wills, and other documents may be in part applicable.

Internal law systems have recognized two methods for the interpretation of documents.[13] The first utilizes concrete acts and utterances applicable to that particular document and has been variously called "historical"[14] or "legal"[15] interpretation. It includes the "authentic" and "usual" interpretation of the civilians which designate, respectively, express statements of the authority responsible for the instrument and their practice in applying it. The second method of interpretation utilizes generally accepted definitions and principles of law, language, logic, and reason and was called "doctrinal interpretation" by the civilians.[16] Doctrinal interpretation is usually divided into "grammatical" which looks to the literal meaning of words and phrases[17] and "logical" which construes them so as to give effect to the spirit or general intention of the document as disclosed by its content as a whole, by its preamble or even by extrinsic evidence.[18] Logical interpretation may be restrictive or extensive according as it narrows or broadens the literal meaning of terms.[19]

[13] Holland, *Jurisprudence* (11th ed.), pp. 418–19.

[14] Gsell-Trumpi, *Zur rechtlichen Natur der Völkerbundsmandate* (Glarus, 1928), p. 11.

[15] Holland, *loc. cit.*

[16] *Ibid.*, Lieber, *Legal and Political Hermeneutics* (3d ed., 1880), p. 239; Phillimore, *International Law* (3d ed.), II, 97 ff.

[17] Called by Lieber merely "interpretation."

[18] See Lieber, *op. cit.*, pp. 11, 44, and Wharton, *Commentaries on American Law*, pp. 739–41, who call this "construction" to be distinguished from "interpretation" as a question of law rather than of fact.

[19] Holland, *loc. cit.;* Salmond, *Jurisprudence* (London, 1902), pp. 126 ff. Wigmore (*The Law of Evidence*, Vol. IV, sec. 2458) distinguishes "the standard of interpretation"

The written instruments most commonly before national courts are contracts and statutes, and systems of internal law commonly look mainly to concrete evidences of meaning in interpreting the former and to general principles in interpreting the latter. Express statements of the legislature which passed the statute if made in the form of a new statute would of course be an "authentic" interpretation cognizable by the courts and official commentaries considered by the legislature when it acted would usually be considered important. But statements of intention or meaning in legislative debate, committee, or correspondence have little weight.[20] The meaning must be found by applying law, grammar, and logic to the text itself.[21] In the

---

or sense in which the terms are employed from the "sources of interpretation" or materials for ascertaining the tenor of the standard. He recognizes four commonly used standards: the popular (usage in the community at large), the local (usage in a special class of the community), the mutual (usage by the parties to a bilateral act), and the individual (usage by a particular person). A special type of the local standard might be the legal or technical usage among lawyers.

Doctrinal interpretation assumes the legal or the popular standard, i.e., that terms are used according to the dictates of law, grammar, logic, and reason generally accepted in the community in question. Historic investigation is thus of value only to discover what their dictates were at the time, though in organic and constitutional documents they are frequently avoided even for that purpose, thus making it possible for the meaning of the instrument to evolve with the natural evolution of law, language, logic, and ideas (Wright, *A.J.I.L.*, XIV, 579).

Historic interpretation makes no such assumption and utilizes historic material to ascertain whether a local, mutual, or even individual standard was not employed in the particular document rather than the legal or popular standard and if so what that particular standard dictated. Thus A and B may have agreed that in cable orders for the purchase of stock the word "not" shall be used or omitted contrary to the usual sense. The results of doctrinal and historic interpretation with respect to a contract based on such understanding would be opposite. Clearly in the case of contracts the possibility of such a convention should be recognized and sought for, if the agreement of the parties is to be given effect, but in the case of a statute the legal or ordinary meaning of terms can be assumed (see *infra*, nn. 21 and 22).

[20] Wharton, *American Law*, pp. 749–50, citing *Rex* v. *Whittaker*, 2C. and K. 640; *Barbot* v. *Allen*, 7 Ex. 616; *U.S.* v. *Union Pacific R.R.*, 91 U.S. 72; *et al.* See also Wilberforce, *Statute Law* (London, 1881), pp. 105–6; Maxwell, *On the Interpretation of Statutes* (6th ed.; London, 1920), p. 5; English, *Interpretation of Statutes* (1888), sec. 30.

[21] "The first and most elementary rule of construction [of statutes] is that it is to be assumed that the words and phrases are used in their technical meaning if they have acquired one, and in their popular meaning if they have not, and that the phrases and sentences are to be construed according to the rules of grammar and from this presumption it is not allowable to depart unless adequate grounds are found either in the con-

case of contracts, however, written or oral communications between the parties or other evidence of peculiar usages of terms by the parties in the business involved or in the locality, and historic data on the entire setting of the contract are of importance.[22]

Are treaties analogous to statutes or contracts? Text-writers and courts noting that treaties register at least formal agreement of the parties and bind no one but the parties have generally accepted the latter analogy. "The legal nature of private law contracts and international law treaties is essentially the same," writes Lauterpacht.[23] He adds that the analogy is not carried out completely, especially in the lesser effect which international law attributes to duress in the invalidating of agreements and the greater influence it allows to changed circumstances in justifying unilateral termination under the

---

text or in the consequences which would result from the literal interpretation for concluding that that interpretation does not give the real intention of the legislature" (Maxwell, *op. cit.*, p. 3). See also Salmond, *op. cit.*, pp. 126 ff. Wharton allows considerable weight to "national antecedents and conditions" at the time the statute or written constitution is made (*op. cit.*, pp. 411–12, 750–52), in which he is supported by most writers. They distinguish the general history of legislation and common law on the subject, which can properly be utilized to establish the legal meaning of terms and the general intent of the legislature (by the mischief-and-remedy rule, Heydon's case, 3 Rep. 7*b*), from the parliamentary history of the act, which cannot ordinarily be used (Wilberforce, *op. cit.*, p. 107; Maxwell, *op. cit.*, p. 51; English, *op. cit.*, secs. 29–30).

[22] Such evidence can be used only to discover the meaning or sense of the words and phrases used, i.e., the fixed association between the symbol and some external object, not to discover directly the will or intention of the parties. "The question . . . . is not what was the intention of the parties, but what is the meaning of the words they have used" (Denman, *L.C.J.*, *Riches* v. *Carstairs*, 5 B. and Ad. 663 [1833]). With this limitation, however, the tendency of the law has been to allow continually wider latitude in the use of extrinsic evidence. The old rules against disturbing the clear meaning of terms and construction within the four corners of the instrument have tended to become obsolete, i.e., the original tendency to insist upon the legal or the popular standard as against the local or mutual is becoming modified in the case of contracts. The legal or popular standard is still assumed for statutes while the individual standard is valuable only for wills or other unilateral documents (Wigmore, *op. cit.*, Vol. IV, secs. 2458, 2459, 2462, 2465, 2470, and *supra*, n. 19; see also Wharton, *op. cit.*, p. 750, citing 1 Serg. and R. [Pa.] 27, 464; 11 Mass. 30; 12 Johns. [N.Y.] 77).

[23] Lauterpacht, *op. cit.*, p. 156. See also *U.S.* v. *D'Auterive*, 11 How. 609 Wharton (*A Digest of the International Law of the United States*, II, 36) outlines the respects in which treaties resemble and differ from contracts. See also Moore, *A Digest of International Law*, I, 250, 252. A treaty "possesses in ordinary the same essential qualities as a contract between individuals" (*France* v. *Venezuela*, 1902, Ralston, *Report*, p. 44, cited in Ralston, *The Law and Procedure of International Tribunals* [1926], p. 6).

implied *clausula rebus sic stantibus*. These divergencies, however, he attributes to the undeveloped character of international organization and suggests that they will tend to disappear as the international legal order evolves. From this analogy writers have emphasized the importance of preliminary material for the interpretation of treaties. Hyde, for example, writes:

> As the sense which contracting states have attached to the terms of their agreement is controlling in the estimation of those to whom are entrusted the duty of interpreting treaties, as all circumstances probative of that fact are admissible for the purpose of its establishment, the formation of rules of interpretation can hardly serve a useful purpose. Times when proof is not to be had are rare. Even when it is wholly lacking, it is dangerous to impute to a state assent to a particular significance of the word of a treaty.[24]

It has however been urged that some treaties at least bear a closer resemblance to statutes than to contracts in their objects, in the methods by which they are made, and in their legal effects.

The distinction which Oppenheim considers of "the greatest importance" is that between "lawmaking" and other treaties.[25] The lawmaking character of some treaties is recognized by most text-writers and by the statute of the Permanent Court of International

[24] Hyde, "Concerning the Interpretation of Treaties," *A.J.I.L.*, III (1909), 46, and *International Law*, II, 64, 68; Crandall, *Treaties, Their Making and Enforcement* (2d ed., 1916), sec. 166; Ralston, *op. cit.*, pp. 192, where numerous instances from the practice of arbitral tribunals are cited. See also Oppenheim, *International Law*, p. 700. Miller (*Reservations to Treaties* [1919], pp. 89, 171; *The Peace Pact of Paris* [1928], pp. 119–22) considers the difference between explanatory notes and reservations merely formal. "Considering that the evidence seems to show that the intention of the parties to the treaty of 1919, *as indicated by the records of the negotiation*, and by the subsequent attitude of the governments, was to admit the United States to such fishery, the tribunal is of opinion, etc." (North Atlantic Fisheries arbitration, Wilson, *The Hague Arbitration Cases*, p. 189). "The official preliminaries recited are to be considered as part of the treaty" (*Chile* v. *Peru*, 1875; Moore, *International Arbitrations*, II, 2092). In support of this the arbitrator cites statements from Wheaton (Lawrence, 6th Amer. ed., p. 318; Dana ed., p. 329) and Field (*Outlines of an International Code*) to the effect that "all communications, written or verbal, between the parties to a treaty, preceding its signature and relating to the subject thereof, are merged in the treaty"; but the doctrine of merger would rather exclude consideration of such preliminary material on the theory that "the final and common intention of the parties which may have undergone change during the progress of the negotiations" is recorded by the written instrument alone (Crandall, *op. cit.*, sec. 166).

[25] Oppenheim, *op. cit.*, I, 654.

Justice which names as the first source of law for the court "international conventions, whether general or particular, establishing rules expressly recognized by the contracting states." Oppenheim defines lawmaking treaties as those "concluded for the purpose of confirming, defining or abolishing existing customary rules, and of establishing new rules for the law of nations." Triepel says they record a "realization of identical aims" while contractual treaties record a compromise "on different and opposing ends."[26] Scelle writes that while contractual treaties are made "to realize a particular juridical operation" and "disappear as soon as that operation is realized" lawmaking treaties present an entirely different interest of stability and of generality. They aim to establish a rule of law and are true legislative acts.[27] Though none of these definitions is perhaps capable of precise application, they indicate a type of treaty which has been growing in importance, as indicated by a recently published list of 394 "multipartite international instruments of legislative effect" between 1864 and 1928.[28]

These treaties tend to resemble statutes as much in the methods by which they are made as in their objects. Hudson writes:

> The quarter of a century between 1850 and 1875 saw the launching of an attempt to deal with the needs of the new world society by means of international conferences engaged in legislative activities, the results of which were embodied in multipartite international conventions. Such conferences became increasingly frequent before 1914 and their legislation was embodied in numerous instruments. They effected a big extension of our international legal order, and filled some of the gaps in our customary law.

With the creation of new agencies under the League of Nations and the international labor organization there has been "a great quick-

[26] Triepel, *Völkerrecht und Landesrecht* (1899), p. 53; cited by Lauterpacht, *op. cit.*, p. 158. See also W. Kaufmann, *Die Rechtskraft des internationalen Rechtes und das Verhältniss des Staatsorgan zu demselben* (Stuttgart, 1899), p. 31. Jellinek (*System des subjectiven Rechtes*, pp. 195–96) says, "Such unions are not in the character of contracts for they shape no *jus intra partes* but a *jus supra partes*."

[27] Scelle, *Le Pacte des nations et sa liaison avec la traité de paix* (Paris, 1919), p. 49, cited by Gsell-Trumpi, *op. cit.*, p. 10.

[28] Hudson, *A.J.I.L.*, Supp., XXII (April, 1928), 90–108. See also Hudson, *Cornell L.Q.*, X (1925), 433; Gsell-Trumpi, *op. cit.*, p. 10, and Lauterpacht, *op. cit.*, pp. 35, 157–69, who somewhat questions this distinction.

ening of this legislative process in international affairs."[29] Though the principles of unanimity and ratification are usually, but not always, adhered to in this procedure, and though such instruments generally bind only the parties to them, in practice the procedure tends to resemble that of a legislative body, with its secretarial staff, committees, debates, and votes.[30]

The legal effects of such treaties are also worth noting. While contractual treaties of the older type usually called for such things as military assistance, payments of money, withdrawal from territory, observance of rules of capture at sea, or other action of an executive character, lawmaking treaties frequently govern the day-to-day conduct of individuals and a wide range of administrative officials. Thus their proper execution requires the continuous action of internal law, and states have tended to follow the example of the United States in giving them automatic effect as internal law within the territory.[31] In that case, for the domestic courts and administrative officials they appear in the same light as statutes.[32] Strictly

[29] Hudson, "The Development of International Law since the War," *A.J.I.L.*, XXII (April, 1928), 340–41.

[30] Hill, "Unanimous Consent in International Organization," *A.J.I.L.*, XXII, 319 ff.; Knudson, *Methods of International Legislation* (Geneva, 1928). The principle that only parties are bound tends to give interpretive statements by single parties the character of conditions and so to increase their importance, but this effect is less in a conference than in a diplomatic negotiation and less still where unanimity is not observed in the preparation of a draft convention.

[31] Wright, "The Legal Nature of Treaties," *A.J.I.L.*, X (October, 1916), 708, 717; Picciotto, *The Relation of International Law to the Law of England and of the United States of America* (1915), chap. iv.

[32] "All treaties made or which shall be made under the authority of the United States shall be the supreme law of the land" (U.S. Constitution, art. vi, sec. 2). "It is a rule in construing treaties as well as laws, to give reasonable meaning to all their provisions, if that be practicable" (*Geofroy* v. *Riggs*, 133 U.S. 258, 270 [1890]; Moore, *Digest*, V, 249). There is danger that the habit of looking upon treaties as national legislation will cause them to be looked upon as nothing else, as noted by John Jay. "Some insist and profess to believe that treaties, like acts of assembly, should be repealed at pleasure. This idea seems to be new and peculiar to this country, but new errors as well as new truths often appear. Those gentlemen would do well to reflect that a treaty is only another name for a bargain, and that it would be impossible to find a nation who would make any bargain with us which should be binding on them absolutely but on us only so long and so far as we may think proper to be bound by it" (*The Federalist*, No. 64 [Ford. ed.], p. 431).

speaking, treaties as such bind states and only states, and each state can use its own methods for carrying out their terms in its territory.[33] But practically the task of carrying out complicated multilateral treaties would be almost insuperable unless the courts and administrative officials whose co-operation is essential have authority to apply them and to interpret them like statutes by uniform principles.[34]

The general and permanent objects aimed at by lawmaking treaties, the complicated procedure by which they are made, and the internal law effect often attributed to them all suggest an analogy to statutes. This suggests resort to interpretive materials which all states can be presumed to have accepted in advance, which will assure uniformity of application, and which will permit of adaptation to changing conditions. Reliance on preliminary material or on national rules of interpretation would probably result in applications contrary to the intent of some of the parties, would certainly interfere with the generality, uniformity, and permanence of the instrument's applicability, and would militate against effective administration of the instrument by courts and officials in the various countries. It has thus been urged that such treaties must be interpreted by doctrine rather than history.[35] Some writers have even urged

[33] Oppenheim, *International Law* (3d ed.), I, 577; Wright, "International Law in Its Relation to Constitutional Law, *A.J.I.L.*, XVII (1923), 240–41. The Japanese jurist, Hozumi, devotes a chapter to treaties in his "Principles of the Constitution" (*Kempo Taiyo*, Part V, chap. viii [1910], pp. 763–86), in which he argues that treaties are contracts between states and not commands of the state to its subjects. While the state ought to assure obedience to its treaties by its subjects, the act giving this assurance is juridically distinct from that making the treaty, though they may be formally the same. (The writer was supplied a translation of this chapter by Mr. Sterling T. Takeuchi.)

[34] For this reason some writers hold that lawmaking treaties necessarily are law within the states united by that legal order, in the same way as national law is law within all the states of a federation (Kaufmann, *op. cit.*, p. 31). The same seems to flow from the Declaration of Rights of Nations of the American Institute of International Law (1916) that "International Law is at one and the same time both national and international." Even states like England which do not automatically attribute to treaties internal legal effect usually provide for such effect by special legislation, and Kaufmann (*loc. cit.*) regards this as the final step in making the treaty. After exchange of ratifications the treaty is concluded (*abgeschlossen*), but not until this final act is it in force (*vollziehbar*).

[35] Gsell-Trumpi, *op. cit.*, p. 11.

such a standard for the interpretation of all treaties. "What," writes Sir Robert Phillimore, "is meant by the term 'interpretation'? The meaning which any party may choose to affix?—or a meaning governed by settled rules and fixed principles, originally deduced from right reason and rational equity and subsequently formed into laws? Clearly the latter."[36]

The line between contractual treaties and lawmaking treaties is not a sharp one any more than is that between internal contracts and statutes.[37] The use of internal law analogies in their interpretation is not, however, precluded. After all, the object of both contract and statute interpretation is to find the real meaning which those who made the instrument put into it. The differences in method ultimately result from the fact that contracts are usually made by two or a small number of persons to fit special circumstances while statutes are made by a large body to fit a wide variety of circumstances. Consequently, preliminary conversations and subsequent actions usually furnish sufficient evidence of the intention of all the makers of a contract while legislative debates seldom indicate the full intention of all the makers of a statute. It cannot be assumed that an exposition of a bill by one legislator discloses his full intention with respect to it, much less that it indicates the intention of all other members of the legislature. Even those who heard such an exposition without protest and then voted for the bill cannot be presumed to have indorsed the arguments. Furthermore, contracts are often drafted by persons unused to the precise expression of their meaning, thus the prospect of correctly discovering the latter by the application of general rules is not good. Statutes, on the other hand, are more likely to be drawn with deliberation and knowledge of the purport of legal phraseology. In general it would seem that instruments made by many persons through an elaborate procedure to cover a wide range of circumstances, some of them only dimly or not at all foreseen, can most reasonably be interpreted by general rules developed by experience, utilizing historic evidence with respect to the specific document only when "authentic" in the sense of having been formally approved by the makers of the document, when necessary to disclose

[36] Phillimore, *International Law* (3d ed.), II, 95.

[37] The constitutions of corporations have in private law characteristics of both statutes and contracts (see Lauterpacht, *op. cit.*, p. 157).

its general purport and the contemporary use of terms, or when ambiguities, inconsistencies, or manifest errors cannot be resolved by a thorough consideration of the whole text.[38]

The practice in regard to treaty interpretation seems to follow this distinction. Courts, arbitrators, and diplomats have given great weight to preliminary material in the interpretation of bilateral treaties.[39] Thus in spite of its established practice of interpreting most favored nation clauses conditionally, in 1900 the United States admitted the unconditional interpretation of such a clause in the Swiss treaty of 1850 on the basis of correspondence of the negotiators. "Both justice and honor," wrote the Secretary of State, "require that the common understanding of the high contracting parties at the time of the execution of the treaty should be carried into effect."[40] But that such materials do not have the weight of formal reservations is indicated by discussion in regard to the effect of notes interpreting the American treaties with Mexico (1848) and Great Britain (1850) exchanged at the time of exchange of ratifications. These notes had not been before the Senate when it consented to ratification of the treaties, and though Mexico and Great Britain considered them binding interpretations, the United States refused to do so.[41]

With respect to multilateral lawmaking treaties, however, it is

[38] This in general follows the accepted view of statutory interpretation (see *supra*, nn. 15, 16). Salmond insists on keeping close to the text of statutes to avoid substituting the will of the interpreter for the will of the legislature. He thinks it would be improper to say that the legislature "did not say what it meant or mean what it said" (*op. cit.*, p. 127). Gsell-Trumpi urges an avoidance of historic materials which would limit an instrument intended to be permanent and general by particular circumstances (*op. cit.*, p. 11). Wharton says, "Laws are evolved in large measure unconsciously from the conditions in which the community is placed" and consequently what the makers say about it is not necessarily "equally authoritative with what they did and what caused their action" (*American Law*, pp. 410, 750).

[39] See *supra*, n. 24; *infra*, n. 44.

[40] Moore, *Digest*, V, 284; Wright, "Amendments and Reservations to the Treaty," *Minn.L.R.*, December, 1919, p. 28. All of the cases cited by Crandall on the use of preliminary material relate to bilateral treaties (*op. cit.*, sec. 166).

[41] Moore, *Digest*, III, 138; V, 205–6; Crandall, *op. cit.*, pp. 85, 381. Bigelow (*Breaches of Anglo-American Treaties*, pp. 116–49) discusses at length the effectiveness of these and other documents alleged to be explanatory of the Clayton-Bulwer Treaty. The Mexican agreement is printed in Malloy, *Treaties, etc.*, p. 1119. See Wright, *Minn. L.R.*, December, 1919, pp. 16, 22.

not common to utilize preliminary materials except in so far as incorporated in reservations formally attached to the instrument on signature or ratification, and accepted by the other parties to the convention.[42] During the World War the French prize court even refused to accept the report of the drafting committee as a conclusive interpretation of the Declaration of London. "The clear and precise provisions of an article which the state had adopted, though the declaration itself had not been ratified, could not be weakened by any extraneous document."[43] In the Tunis nationality decrees case the Permanent Court of International Justice paid no attention to Peace Conference discussion introduced by France in support of a particular interpretation of paragraph 8, article 15, of the League of Nations Covenant. Instead the paragraph was interpreted by textual analysis and general principles of law. The same was true with respect to the Roumanian effort to interpret the definitive statute of the Danube by preliminary material. The Court recalled that "preparatory work should not be used for the purpose of changing the plain meaning of a text," and refused to consider confidential preparatory material at all.[44] This has been the usual basis for Cove-

[42] Reservations and interpretations of the Hague conventions were in all cases formally submitted at signature or exchange of ratifications (see Scott, *Reports to the Hague Conferences of 1899 and 1907*, pp. xxv–xxviii; Wright, *Minn.L.R.*, December, 1919, pp. 21–25; Miller, *Reservations to Treaties*, p. 154).

[43] The Federico, *Conseil d'Etat*, July 18, 1916; Hall, *International Law* (Higgins, 8th ed.), p. 823; Garner, *Prize Law during the World War*, pp. 614–16.

[44] *P.C.I.J.* (Ser. B), No. 4, pp. 23–25; No. 14, pp. 31–35; *ibid.* (Ser. C.), No. 2, pp. 75–82. In general the Permanent Court of International Justice has relied on textual analysis and legal principle for interpreting treaties (*ibid.* [Ser. B], Nos. 2 and 3, p. 41; No. 6, p. 37; No. 7, p. 20; No. 13, p. 14) though it has sometimes cited preliminary material in interpreting provisions of bilateral treaties or provisions of multilateral treaties affecting only two states (*ibid.* [Ser. B], No. 10, pp. 10, 22; No. 11, pp. 37, 40; No. 12, p. 22). As an exception may be noted the reference to an earlier draft of the mandate for Palestine to confirm a conclusion reached from the text itself (*ibid.* [Ser. A], No. 2, p. 24). In the case of the Muscat Dhows the Hague Arbitration Tribunal held that terms of the general act of Brussels, 1890, if not expressly defined "must be understood in the sense which corresponds best as well to the elevated aims of the conference and its Final Act, as to the principles of the law of nations, as they have been expressed in the treaties existing at that time, in internationally recognized legislation and in international practice" (Crandall, *op. cit.*, p. 395). Only rarely have Peace Conference debates been cited in discussion by the League organs of the meaning of the articles of the Covenant. For such exceptional case see *infra*, n. 64.

nant interpretation. The League Council has expressly ruled that reservations to multilateral treaties must be made at signature and cannot be attached to accessions. The International Labor Office has similarly ruled that labor conventions, resulting as they do from a process assuring proper consideration of the interests not only of states but of industrial classes, must be considered as *ne varietur documents*.[45] Multilateral treaties have sometimes by their own terms prohibited reservations[46] or permitted them only for specified articles.[47] The misunderstandings which would result from reservations or interpretations of such treaties made in any but the most formal manner and with full opportunity for consideration by the ratifying authority in all the states has been fully appreciated.

Thus with respect to interpretation it seems both reasonable and in accord with practice to regard treaties between two or a small number of states as analogous to contracts, while multilateral law-making treaties bear more resemblance to statutes. The latter analogy seems especially applicable to multilateral treaties open to general accession since the acceding states are usually officially cognizant only of the text and formal reservations and cannot be supposed to have accepted interpretations suggested in the preliminary conversations of the original negotiators. In this class is the League of Nations Covenant to which states are continually becoming bound without official knowledge of the discussions at Paris which led to the text. The meaning of article 22 should thus be ascertained from intrinsic rather than extrinsic evidence. The same is true of the texts of the individual mandates. Though having some resemblance to agreements between the Principal Allied and Associated Powers, the mandatories, and the League of Nations it can not be said that the discussions over their formulation were known by all the Principal Powers, or by all members of the League. Furthermore, some of the phraseology suggests that they have the character of resolutions or leg-

[45] L. of N., Council, 1927, Min., sess. XLV, *O.J.*, VIII, 770, 800, 880–84.

[46] Declaration of London, art. 65, and Renault's report thereon; Protocol 24 of the Paris Congress, 1856, with reference to the Declaration of Paris, Naval War College, *International Law Topics* (1909), p. 155; *ibid.* (1905), p. 110; Wright, *Minn.L.R.*, December, 1919, p. 20.

[47] See Convention protocol and declaration concerning import and export prohibitions and restrictions (*O.J.*, XIII, 1653).

islation by the League.[48] It would thus be unreasonable to control interpretation by preliminary discussions. Grammar, logic, general principles of law, and customary international law would be more important.

b) THE LEGAL NATURE OF THE LEAGUE OF NATIONS

The League of Nations, though undoubtedly different from any private law institution, is a legal entity composed of many legal personalities, and the relation of the parts to the whole and of the whole to third parties may be in some respects identical with such relations known to internal law. Three theories may be distinguished which look upon the League as (1) not a personality at all but merely a machinery for conducting international relations, (2) a partnership or purely contractual association, (3) a corporation or legal personality.

With the first theory the Covenant is simply a contract by which the members have accepted certain obligations and agreed to follow certain procedures but have not given any organ authority to represent them, contract for them, or bind them in the future.[49] The partnerships (*societas*) of Roman law where there was no doctrine of

[48] The term "mandate" is used in two senses: (1) as the legal authority to administer the territory and (2) as the document defining the terms of that administration. According to the preambles of these documents the mandate in the first sense was "conferred" ("selected" in the case of Palestine) by the principal powers and "accepted" by the mandatory, thus suggesting the form of agreement known as a grant, which was, however, "confirmed" by the League of Nations. In the second sense the mandate was "formulated" by the Principal Powers, "defined" by the League, and "undertaken" by the mandatories, suggesting either an executory agreement between the Principal Powers, the League, and the mandatory or a quasi-legislative action by the League. In the case of Iraq, as the terms were already specified by the Anglo-Iraq Treaty, the League Council resolution of September 27, 1924, merely "accepted" the British "undertaking" set forth in their communication, the terms of which it "affirmed." Although these documents have many characteristics of international agreements it does not appear that they have been ratified according to the usual formality of treaties by any of the interested powers. Nevertheless they are regarded by the Permanent Court of International Justice as valid instruments for the purpose of subjecting the mandatories to its jurisdiction (see collection of texts governing the jurisdiction of the court, *P.C.I.J.* [Ser. D], No. 5, pp. 125–66, and Mavromatis Palestine concession case, *ibid.* [Ser. A], No. 2, p. 11, and dissent by Judge Moose, p. 69).

[49] This seems to be implied by Manley O. Hudson's statement: "I do not attribute a personality to the League of Nations. I do not say that it is to do things of its own accord and out of its own will. It is not a superstate. . . . . It is a mere machinery for conference, for bringing men together about a table to discuss the common problems of the world" (*U. of Calif., Chronicle*, October, 1924, p. 438).

implied agency were practically in this class. They were merely contractually defined relations between the partners, and did not furnish a means of unified action in respect to third parties.[50] With this theory the League would have no legal existence except as a collective name for the totality of its members, and consequently as all the members did not ratify the mandates the League would be in no sense a party to them. Although the Council confirmed and defined them, its members did not do so by individual ratification and many of the present members of the Council, which is a changing body, never confirmed them even through representatives. This view of the League, however, is extremely difficult to reconcile with the important powers given to various organs in respect to the League's budget, disarmament, settlement of disputes with outside states and certain territories such as the Saar Valley and Dantzig, not to mention the mandated areas themselves. By these provisions the members seem to have recognized in advance the legal value of decisions by League organs on certain matters.

Thus the League is thought by some to be a partnership in the sense of most systems of modern law whereby within the terms of the contract one of the partners or a group of them is made agent of the others.[51] With this theory the League itself would not be a personal-

[50] Sherman, *Roman Law in the Modern World* (Boston, 1917), II, 355, citing *Dig.*, xvii. 2, frag. 82; xxviii. 63, sec. 3.

[51] Discussing the title to and control of the League's physical property, Sir Herbert Ames, first financial director of the League, said informally that the League was not "a nation, nor a state nor a superstate nor a corporation" but "a holding partnership of fifty-six states each with an equal voice in the management of $7,000,000 worth of assets, but with property rights in proportion to contributions" (*Chicago Tribune*, February 9, 1927). Perhaps in relation to its political activity he would not have used the word "partnership" and in a carefully written statement made later he avoided use of that term, describing the League "as a voluntary association of self-governing states, bound together by treaty to forego certain rights and employ certain methods for the preservation of the peace of the world and for cooperation in the mutual interest. . . . . The physical instruments necessary to the functioning of this enterprise—lands, building, monies in bank, etc.—are the property of each of the fifty states, in the exact proportion in which their several contributions have made its acquisition possible. Any state withdrawing from the group may take out whatever it has paid in, minus such portion as has been actually used in meeting current expenses." In the same article he asks, after noting the diplomatic privileges of the League agencies, "Is the institution at Geneva, then, anything more than a combination of embassies, the aggregation enjoying the same privileges and immunities as would be granted to a recognized embassy?" (*A.P.S.R.*, XXII [August, 1928], 709, 710).

ity but each of its members would be liable for the acts of every other provided they were in pursuance of the Covenant, and it would follow that by confirming the mandates as therein authorized, the Council made each member of the League responsible for the acts of the mandatory. Such a doctrine goes too far. The limits of responsibility of the members seem to be carefully defined by the Covenant. There is no evidence that a principle of implied agency was intended, and in view of the rule against implying encroachments on sovereignty it would be difficult to read it into the Covenant.[52]

There remains the possibility that the League is itself a personality capable of contracting obligations and acquiring rights, apart from its members. This is the most generally accepted theory[52a] and seems to present the fewest difficulties, perhaps the major one is that which rests on the conception of all private law systems that a corporation cannot be a creature of contract but only of legislation. It must be created from above not from below.[53] To conform to the private law analogy it would thus be necessary to consider the Covenant an act of international legislation not a mere contract. How-

[52] League members do of course have rights and duties defined by the mandates and other decisions of League organs within the powers expressly given them by the Covenant. See *supra*, chap. xiii, n. 3, and sec. 4.

[52a] Voorhees, "The League of Nations, a Corporation, Not a Superstate," *ibid.*, XX (November, 1926), 847; E. A. Harriman, "The League of Nations, a Rudimentary Superstate," *ibid.*, XXI (February, 1927), 137; P. E. Corbett, "What Is the League of Nations?" *B.Y.B.I.L.*, 1924, pp. 119–48, who regards the League as a loose species of confederation, with which A. P. Higgins (Hall, *International Law* [8th ed.], p. 32) agrees; Sir John Fischer Williams, *The Status of the League of Nations in International Law* (I.L.A., 1926), XXXIV, 675, who submits that "the authors of the League, consciously or unconsciously . . . . were making a step forward in international law; they were constructing for the first time on any great scale, a thing in international law analogous to the body corporate in municipal law"; Oppenheim, *International law* (3d ed.), I, 269, who regards the League as an international person *sui generis;* Sir Herbert Ames, who in spite of his preference for the word "partnership" or "association" to describe the League, points out that it possesses "international personality and legal capacity" under Swiss law (*A.P.S.R.*, XXII [August, 1928], 709). Though differing in details, all of these writers agree that the League is an artificial legal personality which seems the essence of the corporation or *universitas* of Roman and modern law (Sherman, *op. cit.*, II, 122; Salmond, *op. cit.*, pp. 346 ff.). It is interesting to note that English law requires partnerships of over twenty to incorporate (Holland, *op. cit.*, p. 341), a rule based on practical expediency which suggests that an association of so large a number as fifty-six states should do likewise.

[53] Holland, *op. cit.*, p. 338.

ever, in view of the theories of the real nature of the corporation,[54] the fact that public corporations like the United States of America have sprung up spontaneously by an act of their own people, if not by agreement between member states; the possibility of discovering authority from the international community if that is necessary in subsequent recognition as well as prior enactment; not to mention the arguments for attributing to lawmaking treaties the character of international legislation—in view of all these considerations the difficulty does not seem insuperable. The universally admitted capacity of the League to acquire and own property as a corporation in Geneva, Paris, and elsewhere, the limited liability of the members, and the various continuing powers given to the Council and Assembly by the Covenant seem sufficient support for this theory. The corporate capacity of the League is doubtless limited,[55] but writers who admit it all recognize that it exists in the matter of mandates, if not as a right of sovereignty at least as a right of supervision.

The Covenant clearly gives the Council power to act for the League in regard to mandates; thus we may consider that the confirmation and definition of the mandates by the Council made the League, as a corporate personality, a party to these acts along with the Principal Powers and the mandatories.

Doubts have been expressed as to the capacity of the League to acquire territorial sovereignty. Some who recognize it as a corporate personality deny it this capacity, thus distinguishing it from a state or a confederation. Corporate persons are denied many of the legal perquisites of natural persons under most systems of private law, so such a situation is not inconceivable.[56] In fact, however, the League seems to be given power of a territorial character. Article 49 of the treaty of Versailles by which Germany renounced in favor of the

[54] *Ibid.;* Salmond, *op. cit.*, p. 350; Maitland, Introduction to translation of Gierke, *Political Theories of the Middle Ages;* Freund, *The Legal Nature of the Corporation*, Chicago, 1897.

[55] Systems of private law usually recognize that acts of a corporation beyond capacity are *ultra vires* even though unanimously agreed to by the corporators (Holland, *op. cit.*, p. 345, quoting Lord Hatherley in *Riche* v. *Asbury Carriage Co.*, L.R. 7, E and I, App. 684).

[56] Corporations have particularly been precluded from landownership at times as in the British statute of mortmain (Holland, *op. cit.*, p. 342).

League in the capacity of trustee the government of the Saar basin, indicates its capacity to exercise the most important part of sovereignty. Such facts support the corporation analogy, and some writers, while not admitting that the League has or shares in the sovereignty of the mandated territories, admit that it is a legal personality juridically capable of possessing sovereignty.[57]

The recognition by international law of corporations formed of many states is a development which the history of law might lead one to anticipate. All systems of private law on reaching a certain stage of maturity have recognized the corporate status of groups of persons which according to one authority "perhaps more than any other human device has contributed to the civilization of Europe." Perhaps with the development of international corporations the civilization of international relations will begin.[58]

c) TITLES TO TERRITORY

However much the subjects of international law may differ from individuals, they are both legal personalities and their rights in material things like land in relation to other legal personalities may be susceptible of identical classification. Sovereignty has been the leading conception of international law and in its internal aspect comprises the sphere of freedom defined by rights available against the world[59]—not only with respect to its territory but also with respect to

[57] See views of Lindley and Diena, *supra*, chap. ix, nn. 96, 97.

[58] Holland, *op. cit.*, p. 338, quoting Grant on *Corporations*, p. 4. See also Sir John Fischer Williams, *op. cit.*, n. 37.

[59] A jural relation involves a person of inherence (*dominus*), a person of incidence (*servus*), and an act (or abstention) (see *supra*, chap. ix, n. 61). Each one of these elements has been made the basis for fundamental classification of law. With reference to the person of inherence, the distinction has been made between "personal" rights which cannot be separated from him (right to life, liberty, reputation, etc.) and "proprietary" rights which can (rights in land, chattels, negotiable instruments, etc.). This was the basis of the fundamental Roman law distinction between the law of persons (*jus quod ad persones pertinet*) and the law of things (*jus quod ad res pertinet*). With reference to the person of incidence the distinction has been made between "real" rights good against anyone (rights to property, personal security, etc.) and "personal" rights good only against specified persons (rights arising from contract, tort, quasi-contract, etc.). Roman law recognized this distinction in its classification of things as *dominium* (*jus in rem*) or *obligatio* (*jus in personam*). It will be observed that the term "personal right" is used in two different senses. With reference to the act, the distinction has been made

its nationals and with respect to its government. Can this conception be analyzed as are the real rights known to internal law?[60]

Writers have assimilated one aspect of internal sovereignty to the individual's right of liberty and another aspect to the individual's right of life, but the most common analogy views sovereignty from its territorial aspect and identifies it with either possession or ownership.[61]

---

between "rights" where the act (or abstention) is from the person of incidence to the person of inherence and "powers" where the act (or abstention) is in the opposite direction. In private law the most obvious powers are procedural, and Roman law treated of these in its final main division of the law, cognate with the law of persons and the law of things called the law of actions (*jus quod ad actiones pertinet*). Broader applications of the distinction have been suggested by recent analytical jurists (see *supra*, chap. ix, n. 60). Sovereignty from the standpoint of international law has been used in this book to include all the "real" legal advantages of the state, its real "powers" constituting its external sovereignty or status and its real "rights" its internal sovereignty or independence (see *supra*, chap. ix, sec. 2*c*). Possibly the state's rights with respect to government (domestic jurisdiction) might be denominated "personal" sovereignty in distinction from "proprietary" sovereignty in respect to territory (domain) and individuals (nationality).

[60] Perhaps the best-known classification of real rights is that which figures in the United States Constitution (Amendments 5 and 14), as rights to life, liberty, and property. The distinction between rights of body, mind, and estate suggested by Justice Cave (*Allen* v. *Flood*, L.R. [1890], A.C. 1) is similar. All of these have been called "fundamental," "inalienable," or "natural" rights in distinction from "accidental," "alienable," or "artificial" rights (Holland, *Jurisprudence*, p. 166). Real rights have also been distinguished according as they are "personal" or "proprietary" (see *supra*, n. 59), and nearly all systems of private law have distinguished, in the latter category, ownership from possession. Ownership in turn has been analyzed into numerous categories which need not be noted here (see Salmond, *op. cit.*, p. 270). Holland suggests a rather empirical classification of real rights in six heads: (1) personal safety and freedom, (2) family and dependents, (3) reputation, (4) advantages open to the community generally, (5) possession and ownership, (6) immunity from damage by fraud (*op. cit.*, p. 167).

[61] Former Secretary of State Lansing wrote: "If the analogy between a community of persons and the community of nations is even in a measure complete, then a state must possess fundamental rights analogous to the personal rights of life, liberty and property. That it does, I think, may be asserted without hesitation, the analogous fundamental rights being those of existence, independence, and the acquisition and control of possessions" (Amer. Soc. for Judicial Settlement of International Disputes, *Proc.* [1912], p. 232). A similar analogy is implied by the classification of the fundamental rights of states found in most treatises on international law and set forth notably in the Declaration of the rights of nations of the American Institute of International Law (1916) as rights of existence, independence, equality, and territory. Stoyanovsky (*op.*

As between nations the proprietary character of the possession enjoyed by a state is logically a necessary consequence of the undisputed facts that a state community has a right to the exclusive use and disposal of its territory as against other states. . . . . When a person in law holds an object with an unlimited right of use and alienation as against all other persons, it is idle to say that he does not legally possess complete property in it.[61a]

Hall here draws an analogy between territorial sovereignty and ownership though he does not distinguish the latter conception clearly from possession.

In Roman law and modern civil law the distinction between ownership and possession is fundamental. "*Nihil commune habet proprietas cum possessione,*" says the *Digest.*[62] While the Anglo-American common law recognizes this distinction, it has abandoned that between possessory and proprietory actions and is more inclined to infer ownership from possession. "Possession," according to an English adage, "is nine points of the law."[63] It is perhaps partly for this reason that Anglo-American jurists have been inclined to assimilate territorial sovereignty to occupation,[64] and to argue from

---

cit., p. 83) finds sovereignty analogous to the private-law conception of liberty (see *supra*, chap. x, nn. 52, 106).

[61a] Hall, *op. cit.*, p. 53; see also Lauterpacht, *op. cit.*, p. 92. Sir John Fischer Williams regards sovereignty as properly meaning *imperium*, a relation of superior to inferior persons, but in the secondary sense of authority over territory (*dominium*) he considers it analogous to possession rather than to ownership ("Sovereignty, Seisin and the League," *B.Y.B.I.L.*, 1926, p. 29). Grotius regarded full sovereignty as ownership of both the land and its inhabitants though partial sovereignty was possible as are limited property rights (*op. cit.*, I, 3, sec. 12).

[62] *Digest* xli. 2. 12. 1; Sherman, *op. cit.*, II, 153.

[63] Salmond, *op. cit.*, pp. 327–30; Holdsworth, *History of English Law*, VII, 459; Williams, *infra*, n. 64.

[64] See, for instance, Sir John Fischer Williams's interesting article cited *supra*, n. 61a, in which he argues against the proposition set forth by the Mosul boundary commission that "a district of which a state has lost actual possession remains in international law an integral part of the territory of that state and subject to that state's 'legal sovereignty' until that state renounces its rights" (p. 25). He warns against the application of analogies from developed private law systems (p. 32) on the ground that international law is primitive, and it would "only administer a little opium to our mental and moral vigour, to say that war and conquest while we allow them to take place produce results which are invalid in law" (p. 42). Consequently for analogies he looks to primitive law, particularly to Henry II's assize of novel disseisin aimed to discourage self-help as "in not dissimilar conditions" does art. 10 of the League Covenant. He is clear that the

the mandatory's wide powers of government in the mandated areas and its right to administer them "as integral portions of its territory" that they are within its sovereignty. Civil-law writers have been less inclined to make this inference.[65]

Possession in private law implies "some actual power over the object possessed (*corpus*) and some amount of will to avail oneself of that power (*animus*)."[66] Ownership, on the other hand, which has been described as "a right over a determinate thing, indefinite in point of user, unrestricted in point of disposition and unlimited in

---

"territorial integrity" protected by that article is not "an imaginary integrity defined by a jurist or moralist" but "the actual seisin," because "in primitive societies, such as the international society of the present day, possession must be protected, even the possession of the disseisor." In such societies "there is no room for the conception of ownership distinct from seisin. If this is right, international law, while resembling English law, does not follow Roman jurisprudence. For English law what is important in tracing title to land is that possession or seisin which is older in origin, and, therefore, better, than that of any known claimant; ownership is not a new conception different from seisin. Roman law, on the other hand, representing the mature product of a long elaborated and regulated civilization—'regarded *dominium* and *possessio* as quite distinct conceptions. *Dominium* denoted primarily a right, and might or might not connote the fact of physical control. *Possessio* denoted primarily the fact of physical control. It had, as such, no legal consequences, and was therefore totally distinct from *dominium*,' " (pp. 37–38, quoting Holdsworth, *History of English Law*, VII, 459). Sir John believes the Mosul commission was making a direct application to international affairs of the conception of Roman law "far removed from the true theory of international jurisprudence." He might also have noted the divergence of continental interpretations of art. 10 of the Covenant from that which he set forth. Far from agreeing that it "consecrates definitive possession" continental jurists have been inclined to hold that it consecrates *legal* titles and forbids League members from recognizing mere conquest as giving any title. "The aim in view," wrote Belgium in response to the Canadian proposal for amendment of art. 10, "is to render it impossible for the states to increase their territory by acts of violence," pointing out that Peace Conference debates showed a distinction between "integrity" protected from all external aggression under art. 10 and "inviolability" protected only from unlawful aggression in arts. 15 ff. The aim of art. 10 was thus not to prevent invasions but to prevent violence resulting in a transfer of title, an interpretation supported by art. 15, par. 2, of the Geneva protocol of 1924 (see League of Nations, Doc. A 17 [1923], v; and Wright, *A.P.S.R.*, XIII [November, 1919], 559).

[65] See *supra*, chap. x, n. 91. The issue is not only whether possession of the territory is equivalent to ownership of it, but whether the former can be inferred from ownership of the use (in this case the government or jurisdiction). It would seem that the animus necessary for possession leading to ownership of the territory would be lacking (see *infra*, n. 69).

[66] Holland, *op. cit.*, p. 190.

point of duration," may exist without any physical control of the thing whatever.[67] Systems of law have advanced from mere holding by force to legally protected possession and then to legally protected ownership.[68]

Though international law theoretically has long recognized occupation which may ripen into title as a legal relation distinct from mere physical holding, it has not always succeeded in maintaining the distinction practically and can hardly do so while wars recur. It has also difficulty in giving practical effect to its clearly recognized distinction between occupation whether as *de facto* territorial sovereignty or as *de jure* governmental sovereignty (jurisdiction), and *de jure* territorial sovereignty and the difficulty will continue so long as military occupation can readily turn into completed conquest. International law, however, is gaining sanctions as international organization develops, and these legal distinctions are acquiring greater practical importance. While before the war it was customary to refer to Chinese leases as veiled annexations, few would so consider them today. The possibility of divorcing territorial sovereignty from occupations and comprehensive jurisdictions in time of peace has been shown by leased territories, administered territories, in-

[67] John Austin, *Jurisprudence*, II, 477; Holland, *op. cit.*, p. 205; Salmond, *op. cit.* pp. 268, 505.

[68] Holland, *op. cit.*, p. 204, and Williams, *supra*, n. 64. The law seeks to defend right from might by constructing a series of concepts like breastworks around it. Justice demands that right be based on the relative desire of individuals (*animus*) irrespective of their relative power (*corpus*), but the weak law of primitive societies is forced to recognize situations created by unjust power which it cannot control. In crude systems of law might is right, he who can control can enjoy, but as the power of the law increases the power of the individual loses in influence. With respect to the individual's relation to things, the law first protects physical possession, seisin, or detention, a low and easily taken breastwork but one which somewhat tempers the assaults of the would-be disseisor. With increasing strength the law protects possession, a higher breastwork, nearer to justice, and finally it erects ownership, a fortification in which he with much right but little might can safely enjoy his property. All of these structures have been recognized only by the Roman law. With it physical control was the *corpus* of detention, which was the *corpus* of possession which was the *corpus* of ownership which was the *corpus* of enjoyment. Reciprocally enjoyment was the *animus* of ownership which was the *animus* of possession which was the *animus* of detention which was the *animus* of physical control. The common law seems never to have clearly distinguished possession from seisin or detention and modern civil-law systems tend to assimilate them. International law is just beginning to distinguish ownership from possession.

trusted territories—all of which resemble familiar divorces of ownership from possession in private law.[69] It is possible that mandated territories furnish another such illustration.

d) PERSONS OF LIMITED STATUS

Different as are organized communities and individuals, both may be legal personalities, and if they are, the relation of superior and inferior may suggest analogies in the fields of private, public, and international law. Colonies formed by migration from the mother-country are often spoken of as "daughter-states," implying thus a relation analogous to that of parent and child. Similarly, there is both psychological and juristic authority for calling politically backward peoples without such a "mother" country, "adolescent," and to refer to relations established over them by more developed peoples as "protection," "guardianship," or "tutelage."[70] There are certain respects in which the analogy to a minor is not accurate, since there is not the same presumption that with the mere passage of time the backward people will reach majority. Perhaps in some cases, as Lorimer suggests,[71] the analogy is closer to persons *non compos mentis* or incorrigible, or to patron and client, as Lawrence suggests.[72] Since some such analogy is implied by the use of the term "tutelage" in article 22 itself, the matter will be dealt with later in discussing the

[69] See *supra*, chap. i, secs. 3, 4; chap. ix, sec. 2*c*. According to the theory supported by Savigny and most modern civil-law codes (Holland, *op. cit.*, pp. 195–98) in such cases, A both owns and possesses the thing, B's physical possession being in the name of A; or, according to Salmond (*op. cit.*, p. 325), B both owns and possesses the incumbrance, thus a divorce of possession and ownership of the same right occurs only in case of adverse possession. But according to the usage favored by Ihering and the common law (Holland, pp. 199–200), B, having the *corpus*, is said to possess the thing even though his *animus* is directed only to the incumbrance (see Salmond, p. 325 n.). Roman law distinguished detention or natural possession, which clearly followed the *corpus*, from possession properly so called, protected by the interdicts, on the interpretation of which Savigny and Ihering differ, though Savigny's view is more generally accepted (Holland, *op. cit.*, pp. 194 ff.; Sherman, *op. cit.*, II, 153 ff.). International law seems to distinguish between ownership of the land (domain) and ownership of the government functioning on it (jurisdiction) (*supra*, chap. ix, sec. 2*c*) though the latter is sometimes regarded as possession of the land (*supra*, nn. 61*a*, 64).

[70] G. Stanley Hall, *Adolescence, Its Psychology* (1904), chap. xviii on "Adolescent Races"; Buell, *International Relations*, p. 328.

[71] Lorimer, *Institutes of the Law of Nations*, I, 156 ff.

[72] Lawrence, *Principles of International Law* (7th ed.), p. 56.

significance of internal law analogies for the interpretation of words of the Covenant. The private law conception of slavery, though recognized by the Roman *jus gentium*, has been abandoned by practically all modern private law systems, so could not be regarded as a "general principle of law."

A closer analogy is suggested to the internal public law principle by which imperial powers have governed in the past peoples at a state of development similar to that of the mandated communities whether as a colony or a colonial protectorate. Such principles have sometimes been referred to in mandate discussions. Thus Great Britain has cited her colonial practice in regard to the refusal of the central authority to give oral hearings to natives and to the wisdom of leaving details to the administration on the spot.[73] Writers have also referred to the supervisory function which the government of Great Britain exercises over the native administration of some of the autonomous dominions as analogous to the function of the League in relation to the mandatories.[74] It may also be noted that examples exist of native areas entirely administered by a power though they lie outside of its constitutional domain.[75]

Nearly all colonial powers have accepted the theory that native races deserve a certain humanitarian consideration and have legislated in their colonies to give effect to this principle. Some have applied the open door in colonies even when not required by treaties. Such practices, however, are not uniform among colonial powers, and could hardly furnish rules of law.[76] Clearly they throw no light on the problem of locating sovereignty over the areas.

This examination has illustrated a wealth of analogy between internal law situations and those found in the mandates system. Instances examined suggest that the mandate documents should be interpreted like statutes by textual criticism rather than historic evidence; that the League of Nations is a corporate international

[73] Letter of November 8, 1926, *O.J.*, VII, 1651.

[74] See *supra*, chap. i, nn. 47, 48.

[75] "The Bechuanaland Protectorate is under His Majesty's dominion in the sense of Power and jurisdiction but is not under his dominion in the sense of territorial dominion" (*Rex* v. *Crewe* [1910], 2 K.B. 603; Lindley, *op. cit.*, p. 188.

[76] See *supra*, chap. i.

personality capable of acquiring territory; that territorial sovereignty like ownership can be divorced from possession, occupation, or administration of the territory; and that while private and public law systems recognize relations of superior to inferior persons, real analogy between such situations and those involved in the mandates system is dubious.

3. The Private Law Meaning of Certain Terms

We must now turn to analogies suggested by the use of familiar internal law terms in the documents. In the absence of more express evidence terms in international documents would be presumed to have the meaning commonly understood in international law. Only in case customary international law offers no help may internal law analogies be invoked. "As treaties are contracts between independent nations," said the Supreme Court of the United States, "in their construction words are to be taken in their ordinary meaning, as understood in the public law of nations, and not in any artificial or special sense impressed upon them by local law, unless such restricted sense is clearly intended."[77]

Thus in deciding whether the terms "mandate," "tutelage," and "trust"—all of which appear in article 22 of the Covenant—can be interpreted in the light of private law institutions of the same name, we must first inquire whether customary international law or the preliminary papers of the negotiators do not furnish materials adequate for their interpretation. Apparently they do not. Though the word "mandate" has been used in diplomacy it is not a term of art in international law. Tutelage and trust are even less familiar to that law.[78] Furthermore, the records of the Peace Conference and other preliminary material are not only of doubtful value for the interpretation of such an instrument but furnish most meager information on the precise intention of the parties in this regard. Such evidence as there is in the Conference itself shows divergence rather than unanimity—a situation which in the interest of compromise formulas discouraged probing into the precise meaning of terms at the time.[79]

[77] *Geofroy* v. *Riggs*, 133 U.S. 258, 271 (1890); Moore, *Digest*, V, 251; "Exchange of Greek and Turkish Populations," *P.C.I.J.* (Ser. B), No. 10, pp. 20–21.

[78] See *supra*, chap. i, and *infra*, chap. xii.

[79] See *supra*, chap. ii.

We may, however, consider what preliminary evidence there is on this matter.

The term "mandate" was introduced to the Peace Conference by General Smuts who was familiar with the term in the technical sense attributed to it by the Roman Dutch law of South Africa. The usages of the terms "mandatory" and "mandate" in both the English and the French texts of article 22 are wholly consistent with this technical significance, and this is even more evident from their initial appearance in General Smuts' memorandum. He writes:

> The League should . . . . nominate a particular state to act for and in behalf of it in the matter, so that subject to the supervision and ultimate control of the League, the appointment of the necessary officials and the carrying on of the necessary administration should be done by the mandatory state.[80]

The term "mandate" does of course have a more popular usage as equivalent to a command or a commission, but in this sense there is no cognate noun "mandatary" or "mandatory" though the adjective "mandatory" is in current usage.[81] However, as the word is a *terminus technicus* of both the civil law and the common law, writers have usually assumed that the treaty-drafters had this usage in mind though many have doubted whether all the implications of the private law institution could be applied to the international law institution.[82]

The terms "tutelage" and "trust" have also each been made the basis for an analysis of the system set up by article 22 of the Covenant through the use of private law analogies, but others have assumed that these terms were used in a popular rather than a technical sense. Both of them, especially "trust," are common terms of non-technical discourse in English, and the connection in which the word "trust" appears in article 22 raises a doubt whether a technical use was intended. Thus the phrases "well being and development of such peoples form a sacred *trust* of civilization" and "the securities for the performance of this *trust* should be embodied in the covenant" suggest that the League of Nations, as the embodiment of civilization is the trustee, while the later phrase "the tutelage of

[80] Smuts memorandum of 1918 (see *infra*, chap. i, n. 54).

[81] See Story, *Commentaries on the Law of Bailments* (Boston, 1878), p. 141; *infra*, chap. xii, n. 12a.

[82] See *supra*, chap. x.

such peoples should be *entrusted* to advanced nations" suggests that the mandatory is the trustee. Both phrases indicate that the "peoples not yet able to stand by themselves" are the beneficiaries of the trust. In the French text, the term "trust" is rendered "mission" while "entrusted" appears as "confier" words which do not suggest a technical institution of private law.[83]

There seems to be nothing inconsistent with the term *tutelle* in the French version having a technical meaning. In fact, it is mainly French writers who have so read it, while in England, where "tutelage" is not a technical term of law, more attention has been given to possible analogies of the word "trust." The word "tutelage" does not appear in the Smuts draft which merely refers to the "authority, control or administration exercised by the mandatory," and the word "trust" appears only incidentally in the descriptive material, not in the proposed articles. "The mandatary," writes Smuts, "should look upon its function as a great *trust* and honor not as an office of profit or a position of private advantage for its nationals."

Thus the evidence that the word "mandate" was used in a technical sense seems considerable. With regard to the word "tutelage" the evidence is less satisfactory and least of all for the word "trust."

Bearing in mind the conditions previously considered under which private law analogies may be used in international law, we may now inquire: To what extent do the legal institutions designated by the terms "mandate," "tutelage," and "trust" have common characteristics in the law of modern states? How far is it possible to apply those characteristics by analogy to the international institution? Because of the great importance of Roman law as a source of international law and to some extent of all developed systems of modern private law, it will be considered first, followed by consideration of modern civil law and common law.[84]

a) MANDATE

Mandatum was a consensual contract in Roman law described by most writers as a gratuitous agency. In his original proposal General

[83] Although this article was originally drafted in English, art. 440 of the treaty of Versailles, art. 381 of the treaty of St. Germain, and art. 364 of the treaty of Trianon make the French text equally authoritative (see also Gsell-Trumpi, *op. cit.*, pp. 12–13, 26–30). Brierly, however, thinks the language points to the trust as the governing principle of the new institution. *B.Y.B.I.L.*, 1929, p. 217.

[84] On the importance of Roman law see Sherman, *op. cit.*

Smuts used the words "agent" and "mandatary" as synonymous. Some writers have translated the term into English as "commission," and some have simply taken it over as "mandate." The principal was known in Rome as the *mandans* or *mandator*, and for the agent the term *mandatarius* was introduced by the medieval commentators.[85]

The contract could not be *contra bona mores;* the *mandatarius* must have voluntarily accepted and must not exceed the limits of the *mandatum*. The *mandans* could renounce the contract before it had begun to be executed and his death or that of the *mandatarius* in such circumstances extinguished it, but if the *mandatarius* had begun execution (even after the *mandans* death in case he was ignorant of that fact) he had an action. The *mandatarius*, having accepted, could not renounce the contract if it would cause the *mandans* inconvenience unless there was a compelling reason such as illness, a deadly enmity, or insolvency of the *mandans*. He was responsible to third parties for acts under the *mandatum*, and to the *mandans* he was responsible for its faithful execution, extraordinary diligence being required under penalty of infamy.[86]

Mandatum was the only consensual contract of Roman law that was gratuitous and thus differed from *locatio et conductio* or letting to hire of things or services (*operae*).[87]

An attorney or *procurator* was a type of *mandatarius*. Though the rule still existed that the service was gratuitous, *honoraria* were often given but even in later Roman law could be recovered only by extraordinary process.[88] Roman law considered a *mandans* closely analogous to a surety (*fidejussor*); in fact, the two are treated under the same head in the Digest and the Code. Although the *mandatarius* was immediately responsible, the *mandans*, in the later law, was ultimately so. Thus existence of the contract *mandatum* depended upon proof of the *mandans* intention to accept this responsibility, and there was a presumption of law against such intention where the *mandatarius* was the sole beneficiary. Thus *mandatum*

[85] *Ibid.*, II, 356.

[86] Justinian *Inst.* iii. 26. 7; 27. 11; *Dig.* iii. 2. 1; xvii. 1. 23–25; Sandars, *The Institutes of Justinian* (London, 1900), pp. xliv, 378.

[87] *Inst.* iii. 24. 4; 26. 13.

[88] *Ibid.*, iv. 10; *Dig.* iii. 3. 1–2; Sandars, *op. cit.*, p. 384; Holland, *op. cit.*, p. 298.

might be for the benefit of the *mandans*, of the *mandans* and the *mandatarius*, of a third party, of a third party and the *mandatarius*, but an apparent *mandatum* where the *mandatarius* alone benefited was considered mere advice and not actionable.[89]

To recapitulate we may analyze the Roman law *mandatum* into the following thirteen characteristics:

1. Its object must be *pro bona mores*.
2. It must be intended to benefit some one other than the *mandatarius*.
3. It terminates by death of either *mandatarius* or *mandans* and revocation by the latter before execution is begun.
4. The *mandans* must have accepted the responsibility of the contract.
5. He may not revoke after execution has begun.
6. He is responsible within defined limits to third parties for acts of the *mandatarius*.
7. He is responsible to the *mandatarius* for expenses and losses under the contract and so is his estate in case execution had begun before his death or in ignorance of his death.
8. The *mandatarius* must have voluntarily accepted.
9. His service must be gratuitous with exception of *honoraria* recognized by the later law.
10. He cannot renounce the contract except in extraordinary circumstances.
11. He is bound to keep within the terms of the *mandatum* and employ extraordinary diligence under penalty of infamy.
12. He is responsible to third parties for acts under the *mandatum*.
13. He is responsible to the *mandans* for an accounting and for faithful execution and so is his estate if execution had begun before his death.

To what extent are these characteristics found in the mandate of modern private law systems? According to Sherman, this contract "underlies the modern law of agency."[90] Modern civil law systems use the term "mandate" and the institution conforms quite closely to the Roman law *mandatum* except that compensation to the mandatory is allowed though usually not presumed; the *mandans* is responsible for acts of the mandatory in all cases. The mandatory is not held to such a high degree of diligence and is not ordinarily responsible to third parties.[91]

[89] *Inst.* iii. 26. 1–6; Sanders, *op. cit.*, pp. 381, 572.

[90] Sherman, *op. cit.*, II, 356.

[91] *Ibid.*, pp. 357 (n. 132), 358. Art. 1984 of the French civil code says, "The mandate or procuration is an act by which one person gives another the power to do something for the mandant and in his name."

The Anglo-American law of agency corresponds closely to the modern civil law of mandate though compensation of the agent is presumed. The term "mandate" is not used in the common law in the general sense but survives in the special case of a gratuitous bailment of personal property upon which some act is to be performed by the bailee. In *Coggs v. Bernard* (1763),[92] Lord Holt was confronted by a case in which defendant, though not a common carrier and acting without remuneration, negligently stove in some hogsheads of brandy which he was transporting from one wine cellar to another. Lord Holt found in the gratuitous character of the Roman *mandatum*, as transmitted to England by Bracton, a ground for holding the defendant liable and incidentally expounded his opinion with a treatise on bailments in which he insisted that the degree of responsibility of the bailee varied inversely with the extent of his benefit. In the case of mandate, where he benefited slightly if at all, he could only be liable for gross negligence which existed in this case. In this respect the Roman law was not followed. Lord Holt's recognition of this type of bailment was taken over by Sir William Jones and Story in their commentaries on the subject, though, as they both remark, actions on this contract "are very uncommon for a reason not extremely flattering to human nature, because it is very uncommon to undertake any office of trouble without compensation."[93] In a recent opinion, the Judicial Committee of the Privy Council used the word in its broader civil law sense and said it was "incident to the relationship that he [the Mandatory] is entitled to look to his principal and employer for reimbursement" of expenses in discharge of his "mandate."[93a]

It appears that private law systems quite generally recognize the institution of mandate, though in a number of characteristics such as the compensation of the mandatory the degree of diligence expected of him and the relative responsibility of *mandans* and mandatory to third parties there are important differences. In the common law mandate the *mandans* has title to the property bailed, but this is not necessarily true in the Roman or modern civil law contract. A man-

[92] 2 Ld. Raym. 909.

[93] Jones on *Bailments*, p. 57; Story, *Commentaries on the Law of Bailments*, p. 200.

[93a] *In re Southern Rhodesia*, L.R. (1919), A.C. 244-45.

date may be given with respect to property of the mandatory or of a third party.

With respect to such a broad relationship as agency, analogy between nations and individuals seems possible. In fact, the cases where a nation has acted as agent or mandatory of another nation or a group of nations are so numerous that applicability of the analogy can hardly be denied. Apart from such cases as the French mandate in behalf of the Powers to restore order in the Lebanon in 1860, mention may be made of the numerous cases where states have undertaken the diplomatic representation of one belligerent in the capital of another and the provisions in the first Hague (art. 8) convention for mutual representation of two litigating states by third states as agents to facilitate pacific settlement.

It is doubtless proper to hold with Lauterpacht that if the words "mandate" and "mandatory" "are taken in their usual meaning, then it is clear that along side of the 'mandatory' there exists a corresponding 'mandant,' who is logically and legally the 'principal,' and from whom the authority of the mandatory is derived, no matter how nominal the authority of the mandant may be." But the writer cannot agree that "in this case the ultimate sovereignty of the League of Nations over the mandated territories is a necessary inference."[94] A mandate might be given under Roman law for any purpose whatever provided it was not immoral and not solely for the mandatory's benefit. There was not necessarily any property at all involved, and if there was there was no necessary implication that it belonged to the *mandans*. Although the restricted common law usage of the term does imply ownership of the property by the *mandans* or bailor, this usage applies only to personal property and is adopted by no other legal system. Modern mandates and agencies do not imply the principal's ownership of the property though doubtless such is most commonly the case.

Thus beyond the implication that the League is a principal and the mandatory an agent and as such bound to keep within the limitations of the mandate, few legal conclusions seem necessarily to flow from the term in respect to the status of the territories.[95] The Roman law

[94] Lauterpacht, *op. cit.*, p. 196.

[95] Stoyanovsky, *op. cit.*, p. 42; Ormsby-Gore, *The League of Nations Starts*, pp. 106–7.

mandatum seems to be followed in making the mandatory's service gratuitous and in holding him rather than the *mandans* primarily responsible to third parties. Justinian recognized a type of *mandatum* where a third party was the beneficiary, thus the term is not inconsistent with the mandated communities having this position. The connotations of the Roman *mandatum* as drawn from its history, however, suggest that the real party at interest is the *mandans* and that the mandatory has a fiduciary relation to him. The gratuitous character of Roman agency arose from the theory that one person could not represent another. Sandars says:

> The person who actually made the contract, who uttered the binding words, or went through the binding formalities, was the only legal contractor; he alone could sue and be sued. The law would not take notice that it was really in behalf of another that he made the contract.
>
> But a friend on whom reliance could be placed might be persuaded to make the contract in his own name. Honor and friendship would then effect what the law would not compel. This friend would give up all that he gained by the contract to the person at whose request he entered into it. The promise to perform this act of friendship was given, in the old times of Roman manners, with an appropriate formality. The person really interested took the friend by the right hand, and told him that he placed in his hand the trust he was anxious to have discharged. The trust, or commission itself, was hence called *mandatum* (*manu datum*).
>
> The execution of a mandatum was thus a discharge of an office of friendship. And it never lost the traces of its origin. It was always necessarily gratuitous; the mandatarius . . . . was obliged to bestow on it the care of the most diligent paterfamilias and if he failed to discharge the trust, and was condemned in an *actio mandati*, he was stamped with infamy.

The responsibility of the mandatory to the League was considered a moral rather than a legal one by the Hymans report, thus accentuating the analogy to the early Roman *mandatum*. The process whereby the *mandans*, ordinarily the real party at interest in the Roman *mandatum*, from being protected only by the honor of his friend, gradually acquired legal rights even against third parties, is instructive and suggests a possible evolution of the League's position in the international mandate. Sandars continues:

> When the introduction of the praetorian system furnished a method by which every equitable claim could be enforced, friends who entered into such an agreement were obliged to discharge their reciprocal duties. The praetor, by

the *actio mandati directa* given to the mandator, compelled the mandatarius to account for all he received, and to pay over the profits, and, by the *actio mandati contrario* given to the mandatarius, compelled the mandator (i.e. the person who requested the favor) to reimburse, with interest, the mandatarius for all expenses incurred, to indemnify him for all losses, and to free him from all obligations contracted in the execution of the mandate. . . . .

The praetorian law went a great step further, by allowing the mandator to bring equitable actions against, and to be sued by, the third party, with whom the mandatarius contracted. First as to actions brought by the mandator. Whatever direct actions the mandatarius would properly have brought or was liable to, the mandator was allowed to bring in the shape of *actiones utiles;* and if the mandator sued or intended to sue, the mandatarius could not sue. . . . .

Secondly as to actions brought against the mandator. There were some acts, of a solemn character, in which one citizen could at no time of Roman law act for another. . . . . Nor did the civil law ever permit any one except a son or a slave to contract for another so as to make the person for whom he contracted directly responsible or directly able to sue on the obligation. But the praetorian system gradually recognized the intervention of an agent. . . . . Thus ultimately, obligations were acquired by or against the mandator through the agent, and not for him by the agent.[96]

b) TUTELAGE

Tutela in Roman law was a guardianship of children under fourteen and distinguished from *curatio*, a less extensive guardianship established at a later date over children fourteen to twenty-five or over idiots, insane, spendthrifts, or other incompetent persons. *Tutela* was recognized by the twelve tables and was a sort of artificial *patria potestas*. It implied a fiduciary relation between tutor and pupil though its evolution in Roman times was marked by a gradual increase in the court's supervision of the tutor. This, however, never became very extensive. Its characteristics may be indicated as follows:[97]

1. Its object is protection of the pupil or minor.
2. It may exist in one of five types, (*a*) tutelage over pupils 1 to 7, (*b*) tutelage over pupils 7 to 14 (12 for girls), (*c*) general curatorship over minors 14 to 25, (*d*) general curatorship over interdicted persons (insane, idiots, spendthrifts), (*e*) special curatorship for single transactions.
3. Tutors and curators are appointed by magistrates and tutors for children by will, or operation of law.

[96] Sandars, *op. cit.*, pp. 378–79.

[97] *Inst.* i. 13. 1; Sherman, *op. cit.*, II, 105.

4. Tutelage or curatorship terminated by death or degradation of the tutor or curator, the pupil or minor, by the latter's coming of age, reduction to slavery, deportation, capture, ingratitude upon demand of patron, fulfillment of conditions or court removal.

5. A tutor or curator must be a man (or woman for her own children or grandchildren) over 25, not lunatic, spendthrift, deaf and dumb, bishop, monk, soldier, person guilty of corruption to obtain the office, Jew (for a Christian) and a qualified person must accept unless over 70, already burdened with three children or three pupils, holder of certain public offices, ill, illiterate or poor.

6. A tutor or curator has a right of action against anyone who interferes with his tutorship or curatorship and against pupil or minor for expenses and losses but by curator only after his mission has ceased.

7. A tutor or curator must submit to limited court supervision, and give security in most cases and if the magistrate does not ask this or it proves insufficient the magistrate may be liable to action by the pupil.[98]

8. A tutor can not alienate the pupil's property except with consent of the court. A curator of an interdicted person has full control of the estate. A curator of a minor can consent to alienations.

9. A tutor or curator is liable for fraud, neglect or waste of pupil's, minor's or interdicted person's property, to restitution, double fine, or removal by court. In such a case the pupil gets a curator *ad hoc* to sue the tutor. On termination of the relation the tutor or curator must give a full accounting. A tutor or curator removed for fraud is infamous.

10. A pupil must submit to the tutor both as to property and personal acts. A minor or interdicted must submit to the curator only as to property.

11. A pupil under 7 can perform no legal act even with the tutor's consent. The tutor acts in his own name for the pupil. The acts of a pupil under 14 and over 7 are invalid unless the tutor acted also except for release from obligations, acquisitions or inheritance or succession and contracts for his own benefit. A minor could act legally without curator's consent but subject to restoration of previous conditions by the court if the act was to his disadvantage. Practically this had the effect of compelling minors to get curators as no one would transact with them alone. An interdicted person could not act. His curator acted for him.

According to Gaius, the institution of tutelage for children was "agreeable to the law of nature"[99] and the institution is found in all private law systems. Modern civil law uses the same name and the institution is very similar though usually tutelage applies up to the pupil's attainment of majority, the tutor is not obliged to accept appointment, and closer supervision by a family council or the court is

[98] *Inst.* i. 24. 23.

[99] Gaius *Inst.* i. 189.

provided. The Anglo-American law of guardianship is similar. Courts of chancery have power to appoint guardians.[100]

The institution of tutelage thus seems to exist with considerable uniformity in legal systems, though not always with the same details, but is there sufficient analogy between a minor and the "peoples unable to stand by themselves" mentioned in article 22 to warrant the precise application of the legal conception? Clearly the rule as to termination of the relation upon the pupil's reaching majority cannot be literally applied. All private law systems do not agree on this age, and it can hardly be assumed that the peoples under mandate will reach full competence at any predeterminable time. The extent of the mandatories' power in A, B, and C mandated territories, however, suggests the distinction between the powers of the curator over adolescents, of the tutor over children seven to fourteen, and of the tutor over infants one to seven.

Application of the analogy would mean that the mandated community would eventually acquire independence and sovereignty of its territory, that the mandatory must act for the benefit of that community, may be removed by the League for malfeasance, and may be held to an accounting by the mandated community on termination of the relation or even before. An action for the latter purpose could be brought by the pupil acting through a curator *ad hoc*. Analogy would suggest that in addition to the process of petition the community should be entitled to bring action in the Permanent Court through a mandatory *ad hoc* appointed by the League Council. The mandatory applying the analogy would be entitled to recoup expenses and losses and to object to any interference by outside states with the performance of his mission.

c) TRUST

A trust is an institution of Anglo-American law whereby property is held or duties are undertaken by a person for the benefit of another. It differs from a mere contractual obligation to use property for the benefit of another in that the beneficiary has a right in the property itself, not merely a personal right against the trustee,

[100] Sherman, *op. cit.*, II, 113–14.

and from an agency in that the trustee has a right in the property itself. In short,

trust property is that which is owned by two persons at the same time, the relation between the two owners being such that one of them is under an obligation to use his ownership for the benefit of the other. The former is called the trustee and his ownership is trust (or legal) ownership. The latter is called the beneficiary and his ownership is beneficial (or equitable) ownership.[101]

Trusts originated in the practice of granting the legal estate in land to a friend "to the use" of a monastery in order to evade the statute of mortmain which sought to prevent alienations to the dead hand of the church with consequent loss of customary feudal perquisites on transfer. In spite of several adverse statutes the ecclesiastical chancellors favored such "uses" which according to Lord Hardwicke implied "such a confidence between parties that no action at law will lie, but there is merely a case for the consideration of courts of equity."[102] The institution seems to combine the following characteristics:

1. The object of a trust is the use or employment of property by the trustee for the benefit of some one else.

2. A trust may be created expressly in deed, writing or will, or impliedly by the nature of the transaction or by presumption of law.

3. A trust is terminated only by the fulfillment of its purpose as interpreted by the court of chancery.

4. The trustee, in accepting legal title to the property, must accept the conditions of the trust.

5. If the trustee is not named by the grantor or if he dies, fails or refuses to accept or execute the trust, the court of chancery supplies a trustee, even though the power to do so is not expressly given in the instrument.

6. A trustee cannot resign but may procure discharge by provisions of the instrument of appointment, by consent of all interested or by court order.

7. A trustee may not delegate his powers (unless this power is expressly given him), may not retain profit, or become purchaser at a sale. In some jurisdictions he is now allowed compensation for his efforts.

8. Joint trustees must generally act together in all transactions and on the death of one, the trust passes to the survivor.

9. All actions for or against third parties in respect to the property are brought in the name of the trustee.

[101] Salmond, *op. cit.*, pp. 278–82. Lepaulle contends that a trust is not a species of ownership but an institution to be contrasted with ownership. *Cornell L. Q.*, XIV, 52, and *B.Y.B.I.L.*, 1929, p. 218.

[102] 2 Atk. 612; Holland, *op. cit.*, pp. 246 ff.

10. The trustee is liable in equity to the beneficiary (*cestui que trust*) for any breach of trust, all losses due to negligence, all actual profits and all profits which might have been made by good management.

11. The beneficiary is entitled to rents and profits; may, subject to terms of the trust, transfer or encumbrance his interest; and may defend his title in the name of the trustee.

The English trust was to some extent a descendant of the Roman *fideicommissa* which was known to the ecclesiastical chancellors, but the latter never attained a similar importance nor has it in modern systems of civil law. The *fideicommissa* differed from the English trust in being the product only of a testamentary act, in being terminated by a single transaction, in "establishing no permanent relationship of trustee and beneficiary," in becoming unenforcible if the heir failed, and in being enforcible only by extraordinary process.[103]

Thus the trust enforcible by judicial process, though appearing in limited application in all systems of law, has nowhere else received the development it has in the Anglo-American equity system. Trusts are under most systems of law moral rather than legal obligations. In Anglo-American law, however, the protection of equity has shown an extraordinary tendency to extend not only to strict trusts and recognized "fiduciary" relations like agency and guardianship, but to other relations of an inherently "confidential" character.[104] Thus Bogert has written:

> In strict trusts equity has two fundamental doctrines, namely, (1) the trustee must act solely in the interest of the *cestui que trust*, and never in the trust administration accept a personal benefit aside from his commissions; (2) when the trustee and the *cestui que trust* contract or the *cestui* conveys property to the trustee, the burden is on the trustee to show the fairness of the contract or transfer.
>
> The former rule arises from knowledge that if the interests competing for the trustee's attention are those of the *cestui* and of the trustee personally, the trustee will often, out of the weakness of human nature, prefer his own advan-

[103] *Ulp. Reg.*, xxv; Sandars, *op. cit.*, p. 251; Sherman, *op. cit.*, II, 277.

[104] On distinction between "fiduciary" relations which, having "distinct names and compartments in law," emphasize the "intimacy arising from the innate character of certain fixed institutions," and "confidential" relations where "actual trust or confidence of a high type creates a corresponding duty but where no tag or label can be given to the relationship except the broad term confidential relationship" see Bogert, "Confidential Relations and Unenforceable Express Trusts," *Cornell L. Q.*, XIII (February, 1928, 248).

tage to that of the beneficiary. It is a rule of policy to force the trustee to single-minded loyalty to his trust. The penalty for its violation is that the *cestui que trust* may, at his option, treat the trustee as a constructive trustee of the private gain the trustee has made in administering the trust, irrespective of proof by the trustee of his good faith or the lack of injury to the cestui.

The second rule is designed to prevent imposition on the *cestui* by the trustee. The former is generally superior in knowledge as to value of the *cestui que trust's* interest. The *cestui que trust* naturally expects that he may confide in the trustee and rely on his honesty. These advantages which the trustee has over the *cestui* make it easy for him to defraud the *cestui*. History shows many cases of actual imposition. To guard the *cestui que trust* against this danger, equity places a burden on the trustee to show the fairness of the transaction between himself and the beneficiary. Equity does not declare the transaction void, or voidable in all events by the *cestui*. It makes the trustee a constructive trustee of the property received from the *cestui que trust*, unless the trustee sustains the burden of proving the transfer fair.

It is common knowledge that equity has applied these two doctrines to situations outside the realm of strict trusts where analogous circumstances exist and the same results are to be accomplished.

The no-profit-in-trust-administration rule has been applied to agents, executors, administrators, attorneys, directors of corporations, guardians, and others who are not strict trustees but whose functions are like those of the trustee in that they act for others and are entrusted with power over, and title to or possession of, things to be used for the advantage of another. These quasi-trustees have well recognized distinct names and classifications in the law. There are also many transactions, situations and dealings which can not be tagged or placed in a particular compartment of the law, but which nevertheless show a status of reliance on the integrity and skill of another. The one trusted has received communications and information, rendered services and given advice in a way analogous to the transactions which occur in trusts and agencies. The one trusted in a loose way acts for the other and has the power to affect the latter's financial interests. Equity applies this no-profit rule to all these fiduciaries from the strict trustee down to the most remote quasi-trustee in order to encourage fidelity and loyalty.

The presumed-fraud-in-superior-to-inferior transaction rule is likewise administered where the relation is a quasi-trust having a distinct name in the law as, for example, agency and guardianship; and in the looser, vaguer relationships without a separate tag or pigeon-hole in the analysis of legal relations. So long as there is trust reposed on the one side and superiority of influence on the other, there is need for scrutiny of transactions between the two parties, no matter what names the parties may bear in digest or dictionary.[105]

[105] *Ibid.*

In view of this tendency it is not surprising that British lawyers have found it natural to apply the doctrine of trusts to the mandates, which clearly indicate a relation of confidence between the mandatory and the mandated community. The duty of the mandatory to refrain from making any profit from the administration is perhaps the most notable example though comments of the Mandates Commission on the Nauru phosphates monopoly and the proposed British loan to Tanganyika suggest care for the "presumed-fraud-in-superior-to-inferior transaction rule."[106]

That the analogy is sufficiently close to warrant the conclusion that the mandatory has legal title to the territory may be doubted. As the French text indicates, the terms "trust" and "intrusted" were used to emphasize the fiduciary character of the relations of both League and mandatory to the mandated peoples rather than to import into the institution the English law of strict trusts.[107]

There is, however, a historical characteristic which the mandatory system has in common with all trusts, namely, it marks an effort to adjust the law to new conditions—in fact, to evade the existing law. Maitland writes:

> The chancellor's willingness to enforce these honorable understandings, these "uses, trusts or confidences," is an exceedingly curious episode. The whole nation seems to enter into one large conspiracy to evade its own laws, to evade laws which it has not the courage to reform. The chancellor, the judges, and the parliament seem all to be in the conspiracy. And yet, there is really no conspiracy: men are but living hand-to-mouth, arguing from one case to the next case, and they do not see what is going to happen. Too late the king, the one person who had steadily been losing by the process, saw what had happened. Henry VIII put into the mouth of a reluctant parliament a statute which did its best—a clumsy best it was—to undo the work. But past history was too strong even for that high and mighty prince.[108]

Trusts were in fact a means of eliminating from the law feudal restrictions unsuited to the rising mercantile society as in Roman times the *fidiecommissa* were means of evading the strict laws of inheritance likewise unsuited to the business activity of imperial Rome. So in more recent times in the United States, in spite of Congressional

[106] See *infra*, chap. xiii, nn. 135, 143. [107] See *supra*, n. 83.

[108] Maitland and Montague, *A Sketch of English Legal History*, p. 123.

Sherman acts, trusts have been found the means of creating great business organizations suitable to the large-scale capitalistic production of twentieth-century America against the opposition of eighteenth-century notions of individual competition which had grown into constitutional law. Trusts have been a means whereby the pioneers of a changing society have been able to get the law back of plans and intentions in which they are interested but which the law in the past has failed to recognize or has even opposed.[109]

Thus the mandate trust may likewise prove a means for evading the theory of absolute and exclusive territorial sovereignty unsuited to present international society and for giving legal protection to interests newly arisen. But just whose interests are these that have come to the front? All three words—"mandate," "tutelage," and "trust"—suggest interests originally protected only by good faith but which were gradually taken under the wing of the law. The term "mandate," however, suggests that the interests involved are those of the League of Nations, while the term "tutelage" suggests that they are the interests of the mandated communities. The uses of the term "trust" in article 22 are more ambiguous but perhaps suggest the latter conclusion. The various schools of writers fall into two major groups on this distinction. Perhaps we do not need to make a choice. Perhaps the very object of this new status was to assure protection to the interests of both the world at large as represented by the League and the mandated peoples, and while by application of the analogies the mandatory, tutor, or trustee has duties rather than rights, perhaps it was assumed that his actual if not his legal position would assure that his interests would not be entirely neglected.

[109] The confidential-relation principle has been a means of evading applications of the statute of frauds in oral transfers of land (Bogert, *op. cit.*, XIII, 245–46; see also Holland, *op. cit.*, p. 246). Brierly thinks it as "idle to attempt to force the mandate, which is a social institution, into the individualist concept of sovereignty, as it is to force the trust into a scheme based only on private property. . . . . For the mandatory's rights, like the trustees have their foundation in his obligations; they are tools given to him in order to achieve the work assigned to him; he has 'all the tools necessary for such end, but only those.' " (*B.Y.B.I.L.*, 1929, p. 219.)

CHAPTER XII

THE PRACTICE OF STATES

"International custom" is looked upon by the statute of the Permanent Court of International Justice as a source of international law if it "evidences a general practice accepted as law." To create a custom there must be not only uniform practice over a considerable time but also acceptance of the practice as obligatory by the states bound. Such acceptance may be implied from the absence of protest.[1]

Three sorts of international practice may throw light on the mandates system. Uniform practice of the interested parties establishes a practical or usual construction of the texts and may form the basis for a customary international law of mandates. This and the following chapter will be mainly devoted to consideration of the practice of the mandatories and the League of Nations so far as it throws light on the legal status of the mandated territories. Brief consideration must be given, however, to international practice, not in administering the mandates system itself, but in dealing with similar situations which, in two ways, may be a source for the law of mandates.

1. The Practice of States in Similar Situations

Has the practice of states established rules of customary international law controlling international situations analogous to the mandates system or controlling the interpretation of certain terms employed in the mandate documents? Analogous institutions and identical terms in private law have been considered. Here we are inquiring whether customary international law itself has dealt with analogous institutions or identical terms.

The evolution of the practices and the ethical and legal concepts of states in dealing with backward peoples has been traced in the

[1] Westlake, *International Law*, I, 14–17; Oppenheim uses the word "usage" instead of "practice" (*International Law*, I, 15–16, 21–22).

first chapter of this volume. These data are perhaps of some value in indicating the spirit of the mandates system but are of little assistance in determining its legal character. These conceptions have not been applied uniformly or universally and, apart from particular treaties, have been regarded as ethical rather than legal obligations, consequently do not give sufficient evidence of international custom. Furthermore, as no such institution as the League of Nations has been involved in these situations in the past, it may be doubted whether any of them presented a real analogy to the mandates system. Attention may, however, be directed for a moment to the international institutions of state protectorate, colonial protectorate, and territorial lease.

Some writers have inferred from an assumed analogy between mandates and state protectorates that sovereignty is vested in the mandated communities and is exercisable by them except in so far as its exercise has been expressly delegated to the mandatory by the mandate or other document.[2] The phrase "provisionally recognized as independent" in article 22 gives especial support to this doctrine as applied to a mandatory.

However, it seems that there is little customary law on the subject of protectorates whether "state" or "colonial." They have been essentially institutions of treaty, the terms and conditions of which have varied greatly.[3] Some writers have insisted on implying from the protectorate relationship sufficient power in the protecting state to meet the responsibilities which flow from its assumption of the protected state's foreign relations, especially sufficient internal administrative power to assure aliens the degree of protection required by international law.[3a] Practice has been by no means uniform.

[2] See Diena, *Acad. D.I.*, V, 239, 243; Baty, "Protectorates and Mandates," *B.Y.B.I.L.* (1921–22), pp. 109 ff.; Lewis, *L.Q.R.*, XXXIX (1923), 458 ff., and *supra*, chap. x, n. 17.

[3] Lindley, *The Acquisition and Government of Backward Territories in International Law*, pp. 186, 206; "The Tunis Nationality Decrees," *P.C.I.J.* (Ser. B), No. 4.

[3a] The Judicial Committee of the Privy Council defined a British protectorate as follows, citing Sir Henry Jenkyns, *British Rule and Jurisdiction beyond the Sea*, p. 165: "Although the protected country is not a British dominion, its foreign relations are under the exclusive control of the crown so that its government can not hold direct communication with any other foreign power, nor a foreign power with its government" (Haldane, P.C., in *Sobhuza II* v. *Miller*, L.R. [1926], A.C. 523). See also Anson, *The*

The United States and Great Britain in their protectorates and spheres of influence have been more reluctant to assume continuous power of internal control than have France and Germany. Hall, however, suggested in 1894 that international law requires Great Britain to increase its powers in such areas:

The mark of a protected state or people, whether civilized or uncivilized, is that it cannot maintain political intercourse with foreign powers except through or by permission of the protecting state. Whatever results from this fact is necessary to the relation created by a protectorate; whatever is independent of it descends from some other source. Starting from this point, it becomes at once evident that the interposition of the protecting state between the protected country and foreign powers deprives the latter of the means of exacting redress for themselves for wrongs which their subjects may suffer at the hands of the native rulers or people; and that as the protecting state interposes vountarily and for its own selfish objects, it is not morally in a position to demand that foreign governments shall patiently submit to wrongdoing from persons whose natural responsibility it covers with the shield of its own sovereign independence. A state must be bound to see that a reasonable measure of security is afforded to foreign subjects and property within the protected territory, and to prevent acts of depredation or hostility being done by its inhabitants. It must consequently exercise whatever amount of control may be found necessary for the purpose.[4]

President Roosevelt set forth a similar doctrine ten years later in asserting that the United States might by its adherence to the Monroe Doctrine be forced "however, reluctantly, in flagrant cases of . . . . wrongdoing or impotence, to the exercise of an international police power" in the Western hemisphere.[5] The United States, however, does not have a protectorate over all the American countries and has not set up a continuous administration over those

---

Law and Custom of the Constitution (3d ed.; Oxford, 1908), II, Part II, 59–63, 90–91; Hall, *infra*, n. 4.

[4] Hall, *Foreign Powers and Jurisdiction of the British Crown*, p. 218; see also Anson, *op. cit.*, II, Part II, 92, and *supra*, chap. ix, n. 90.

[5] Message, December 6, 1904, and letter of May, 1904, quoted in Moore, *Principles of American Diplomacy*, p. 262. Hyde suggests that because of its privileges in certain Caribbean countries, the United States "appears to assume internationally a certain responsibility for conditions of government within the territories concerned" *International Law*, I, 36). While as a practical matter responsibility ought to carry with it commensurate power, it hardly furnishes a satisfactory legal basis for the assumption of power (see Wright, *Control of American Foreign Relations*, pp. 154 ff.).

whose foreign relations it has limited by treaty, though perhaps there has been a tendency in this direction. Hall admits that the amount of internal control must "vary greatly with the degree to which a people is advanced toward civilization, with the readiness with which it lends itself to guidance, with the number and character of the Europeans who visit or reside in the country." With qualifications of such a vague character the principle can hardly be called one of law though in fact it has been applied to the mandated territories. Both the documents and practice indicate that international responsibility rests primarily on the mandatory and that it has sufficient internal control to meet this responsibility, in all cases,[6] though the extent of this control varies among the three classes of mandate "according to the stage of the development of the people, the geographical situation of the territory, its economic conditions and other similar circumstances."[7]

The B and C mandated territories, the people of which are less civilized than those in A territories and the mandatory of which is given more extensive control, have been compared to "colonial" protectorates, such protectorates, differing from "state" protectorates, have frequently evolved toward annexation, though not always. Thus Great Britain considers all "protectorates" as foreign territory under her own law though it appears that international law usually considers "colonial" protectorates as within the protector's domain.[8] In view of the express terms of the documents and decisions of the Council no such conclusion would seem applicable to the mandated territories of any class.[9]

Leases under international law either for a term of years or in perpetuity give clear evidence of the customary recognition of the possibility of dissociating sovereignty from its exercise. Although the Chinese leases were looked upon by some as veiled cessions, it now seems recognized, especially since the return of some of them

[6] See *supra*, chap. xiv.

[7] L. of N. Covenant, art. 22, par. 3. The "readiness with which a people lends itself to guidance" may well have a relation to the "geographical situation" of the territory and "the number and character of Europeans who visit or reside in the country" would certainly have a relation to its "economic condition."

[8] Lindley, *op. cit.*, pp. 182–88; Anson, *op. cit.*, II, Part II, 59, 93; *Rex* v. *Crewe*, L.R. (1910), 2 K.B. 603, 619; *Sobhuza II* v. *Miller*, L.R. (1926), A. C. 523; *infra*, n. 26.

[9] See *infra*, chap. xiii, sec. 2*b;* chap. xiv.

to China, that Chinese sovereignty in the areas continued in spite of her lease of full powers of administration for a term of years.[9a] An even more striking case is that of the Panama Canal Zone, "the use, occupation and control" of which was granted by Panama to the United States "in perpetuity . . . . for the construction, maintenance, operation, sanitation and protection" of the canal and with "all the rights, power and authority within the zone . . . . which the United States would possess and exercise if it were the sovereign of the territory . . . . to the entire exclusion of the exercise" by Panama of "any such sovereign rights, power or authority." A controversy has arisen over the right of the United States to engage in commerce within the zone for purposes other than the "control, maintenance, etc." of the canal. Panama contends that the grant is limited by those objects. This contention seems to have been admitted by Secretary of War Taft in 1904 though practice since has not wholly conformed to it.[10]

So far as any deduction can be drawn from these analogies it would be against the existence of sovereignty in the mandatory, but it is doubtful whether the conceptions of protectorate and lease in international law sufficiently resemble that of mandate to be made the basis of any legal deduction. The novelty arising from the relation of the League of Nations to the mandatory, and the absence in article 22 of the terms commonly used to describe the older institutions, suggests that a wholly new international institution was created. These older international institutions are of interest in this connection only in showing that international law is familiar with the dissociation of sovereignty from its partial or entire exercise temporarily or permanently.[11]

[9a] "The general position assumed by the powers is not that sovereignty has passed, but that the jurisdiction to the extent named in the treaty of cession has passed to the leasing power" (G. G. Wilson, citing the texts and diplomatic correspondence in regard to various Chinese leased territories, Naval War College, *International Law Situations* [1902], p. 32).

[10] F.P.A., Information Service, January 20, 1928, III, 354 ff., and Lindley, *op. cit.*, pp. 237–44, who discusses territorial leases of Zanzibar, China, Great Britain, the Congo Free State, and Turkey. Others are discussed by Lauterpacht, *Private Law Analogies*, pp. 183 ff.

[11] The same is true of rights of control and administration as exercised by Austria-Hungary under the treaty of Berlin from 1878 to 1908 in Bosnia and Herzegovina and by Great Britain in Egypt (Lindley, *op. cit.*, pp. 244–46). See also *supra*, chap. ix, sec. 2*e*.

Does customary international law furnish an interpretation of the terms "mandate," "tutelage," and "trust"? Apparently it does not. The term "mandatory" has been applied to both individuals and states acting as agents of groups of powers in international relations, but the cases are relatively few and indicate little consistency or effort at precision in usage.[12] Examination of these cases gives little if any evidence that customary international law has defined the rights and duties of a mandans and a mandatory as such.[12a] The terms "tutelage" and "trust" have also been used before in reference to international situations but in a descriptive rather than a technical sense.[13] These terms have long had technical meanings in various systems of private law,[14] but international practice had not

[12] See *supra,* chap. i, nn. 43–45; chap. ix, n. 91*a;* chap. xi, sec. 3.

[12a] The term "mandatory" was so unfamiliar in international law that during the Peace Conference there was doubt whether it should be spelled "mandat*o*ry" or "mandat*a*ry." General Smuts used the latter spelling in his memorandum of December 16, 1918, and Manley O. Hudson, one of the American legal advisers, favored this spelling as preferred in the technical sense by the dictionaries (D. H. Miller, *My Diary at the Conference of Paris* [with documents privately printed, 1928], V, 275). David Hunter Miller, the principal American legal adviser, favored "mandat*a*ry" as a noun and "mandat*o*ry" as an adjective since the latter word though of frequent use as an adjective "was uncommon as a noun before 1919 in ordinary writing," but he was overruled in the final text, "the choice being perhaps one of fancy" (Miller, *The Drafting of the Covenant,* I, 223, 504, and *Diary,* I, 366; V, 287, 457).

[13] Lindley, *op. cit.,* pp. 327–36. The word "trusteeship" was used by the British government in 1923 to express its relation to Kenya (*Parl. Pap.* [1923], Cmd. 1922), and by the United States Supreme Court to express American relations with Cuba during the occupation (*Neeley* v. *Henkel,* 180 U.S. 109 [1901]). Chief Justice Marshall spoke of the relation of the Indians to the United States as one of "pupilage" (*Cherokee Nation* v. *Georgia,* 5 Pet. 17). President McKinley in his message of 1900 spoke of the United States as "guardian" of the Philippines; Secretary Frelinghuysen spoke of the United States as having a "relation of quasi-parentage" to Liberia (Moore, *Digest,* V, 778), and President Taft referred to the American "Moral Guardianship" of that country (Message, December 3, 1912, *U.S. Foreign Relations* [1912], p. xxi). The Berlin conference said it had assumed toward the natives the position of "guardian (*tuteur officieux*)" (*Parl. Pap.* [1885], Cmd. 4361, p. 65; Lindley, *op. cit.,* p. 327). Lorimer developed a theory of international guardianship of immature nations (*Institutes of the Law of Nations,* I, 101, 157, 161), and a number of writers have contended that differences in domestic institutions and governing capacity affect international status (Dickinson, *Equality of States in International Law,* pp. 131 ff., 233 ff.), but these differences have not been defined with legal precision (Wright, "The Bombardment of Damascus," *A.J.I.L.,* XX, 265–66, and *supra,* chap. i, n. 35).

[14] See *supra,* chap. xi.

made them terms of art in international law prior to their use in article 22 of the Covenant.

2. Practice of the Interested States in Applying the Mandates

The mandatories and the League of Nations are the recognized international entities most interested in the mandates system, and their practice is of most significance as evidence of the international law of mandates. The mandated communities have a major interest but it may be questioned whether their practice can have an international lawmaking character. International custom may arise from the practice of international persons in their relations with each other. It cannot arise from the practice of entities which enjoy no international status or which have no international relations.[15]

While the mandated territories and communities undoubtedly enjoy a status under international law recognized by the League of Nations, the mandatories, and other states, they have not as yet participated as persons in international relations—in fact, the mandates expressly or impliedly confide the conduct of their foreign relations to the mandatory in each case.[16] In only four of the communities—Iraq, Transjordan, Syria, and Lebanon—are there governments distinct from that of the mandatory, which could in any

[15] Westlake, *op. cit.*, I, 16.

[16] By art. 5 of the Iraq treaty of alliance with Great Britain "His Majesty the King of Iraq shall have the right of representation in London and in such other capitals and places as may be agreed upon by the High Contracting Parties. Where His Majesty the King of Iraq is not represented he agrees to entrust the protection of Iraq nationals to His Britannic Majesty. His Majesty the King of Iraq shall himself issue exequaturs to representatives of foreign powers in Iraq after His Britannic Majesty has agreed to their appointment." The British mandate for Palestine, art. 12, provides: "The mandatory shall be entrusted with the control of the foreign relations of Palestine and the rights to issue exequaturs to consuls appointed by foreign powers. He shall also be entitled to afford diplomatic and consular protection to citizens of Palestine when outside its territorial limits." The French mandate for Syria and the Lebanon (art. 3) is similar with addition of the word "exclusive" before "control." Diplomatic representation of the B and C areas is not expressly mentioned in the mandates but can readily be inferred from the mandatory's "full powers of administration and legislation in the area," and from art. 127 of the treaty of Versailles entitling the "native inhabitants" to its "diplomatic protection." See *infra*, chap. xiii, sec. 3*a*.

sense be said to represent the entire local community.[17] Even in these areas, the native government lacks complete control of internal affairs, and has almost no control of foreign affairs. Iraq alone has made treaties under the authority of the native government. While the mandate suggests that this government can send diplomatic representatives and negotiate with other states on subjects not reserved to the mandatory,[18] in fact her international relations up to date have been exclusively with Great Britain, the mandatory, and the latter has represented her in other international transactions. The proposal made at one time that a representative of the Iraq government appear with the British representative during League consideration of the mandate was withdrawn, and the League has made it clear that it looks upon the mandatory in this case and in all others as responsible for the territories.[19] Thus the practice of the native governments would not as yet appear to be of significance in international law.

The practice of states other than the mandatories in their transactions relating to the mandated territories may be of international lawmaking value and will be dealt with in connection with the practice of the mandatories and the league. Suffice it to say here that while such states have negotiated and made treaties with the mandatory alone to define and protect their interests in mandated territories, they have generally recognized that the territory was held as a mandate without further indication of the significance they attached to the relation.[20] While correspondence of the United States has sometimes suggested that that country regards mandated territories as having been annexed by the mandatories, the treaties

[17] See *supra*, chap. vii, sec. 3*d*. The native kings, chiefs, or councils in Ruanda-Urundi, Samoa, and other mandated areas have been treated as administrative agencies of the mandatory rather than as governments with independent authority in certain matters, and the legislative assembly in Southwest Africa elected by the white minority cannot be said to represent the entire local community.

[18] See *supra*, n. 16.

[19] See *infra*, chap. xiii. The situation of Transjordan is somewhat similar under the treaty of 1928 with the Emir Abdullah (see *infra*, n. 50*a*).

[20] For discussion of the Portuguese–South African treaty defining the Angola–Southwest Africa boundary and referring to South Africa as possessing "sovereignty" of the area see *infra*, chap. xiii, sec. 2*b*.

concluded by the United States on the subject all recite the terms of the mandate and recognize the mandatory's administration only in so far as pursuant to that document.[21] Members of the League in the Assembly and Council have often insisted that the distinction between mandatory administration and annexation is vital.[22]

The mandatories undoubtedly have more practical influence on the development of the areas than any other states. What is the importance for international law of their legislation and official acts? A state as such acts only through law. The conduct of officials in excess of their legal authority or contrary to principles of the state's law cannot ordinarily be regarded as action of the state. Thus to ascertain the practice of the mandatories we look to their laws and the acts of officials in applying them.[22a]

Clearly one state cannot legislate for others, thus the laws and official acts of the mandatories are not per se international law.[22b] Such laws may however enjoy or acquire international validity in three ways. They may be merely declaratory of or supplementary to existing international law or treaty on the subject. They may be acquiesced in or followed by other states for a time sufficiently long and with a sufficient sense of obligation to establish an international custom or prescription or a customary interpretation of a treaty. They may be formally accepted or recognized by other states, or by an international authority competent to decide the question under international law.[22c]

It should be presumed that the legislation of the mandatory states is in accord with the international law of the subject, on the

[21] The United States note of May 17, 1920, in regard to Mesopotamian oil referred to the conditions on which the United States had been "willing to agree that the acquisition of certain enemy territory by the victorious powers would be consistent with the best interests of the world." See *supra*, chap. ii, sec. 4.

[22] See *supra*, chap. iii.

[22a] The condition under which action of different types of officials is regarded as acts of the state under international law is discussed in Wright, *Control of American Foreign Relations*, chap. iv, and Borchard, *Diplomatic Protection of Citizens Abroad*, chap. iv.

[22b] See *supra*, chap. xi, n. 6.

[22c] Hall, *International Law* (8th ed.), pp. 12–13; Wilson and Tucker, *International Law* (8th ed.), p. 44; Hyde, *International Law*, I, 7–8; Lawrence, *Principles of International Law* (7th ed.), secs. 54, 55.

principle that bad faith ought not to be imputed to states until proved. It is fair to presume that the mandatories have acted to meet their international responsibilities rather than to violate them.[22d]

In any case unless promptly contested the mandatory's legislation may become the basis of a customary or practical interpretation of the documents. "Whether or not," said the Spanish-American Treaty Claims Commission, "the clause [of the treaty of 1795] was originally intended to embrace real estate and personal property on land as well as vessels and their cargoes, the same has been so construed by the United States and this construction has been concurred in by Spain; and therefore the commission will adhere to such construction in making its decisions."[23] Going even farther the Supreme Court of the United States held in the case of the Scotia that the British maritime regulations of 1863 to prevent collisions had been generally accepted before 1872 and so had become the international law of the sea. "This is not giving to the statutes of any nation extraterritorial effect," said the Court. "It is not treating them as general maritime laws, but it is recognition of the historical fact that, by common consent of mankind, these rules have been acquiesced in as of general obligation. Of that fact we think we may take judicial notice."[24]

The Mandates Commission's repeated request for all mandatory legislation and its meticulous criticism of phrases which do not accord with its interpretation of the legal status of the territories indicates its anxiety to avoid any claim of customary interpretation through acquiescence on its part. Acceptance of a national view by the Commission, on the other hand, would go a considerable distance toward confirming it, and approval by the Council would appear to establish its international validity beyond question.[25]

[22d] This principle is applied by courts in the usual rule that statutes should be interpreted in accord with international law if possible (*Murray* v. *The Charming Betsey*, 2 Cranch 64, 118 [1804]; Wright, *Control of American Foreign Relations*, chap. xi; Oppenheim, *op. cit.*, secs. 23, 24).

[23] Fuller's *Report* (Washington, 1907), p. 23. On "usual" interpretation see *supra*, chap. xi, n. 15.

[24] *The Scotia*, 14 Wall. 170 (1872). See also Hall, *op. cit.*, pp. 12–13; *supra*, chap. ix, nn. 109–11.

[25] See *infra*, chap. xiii.

The authority exercised by representatives of the mandatory in each of the areas will be examined from the standpoint of its source in national law, and the legal limitations to which it is subject in legal theory and in judicial practice. Such an examination indicates that the mandatories have usually recognized, in the form of their legislation, that their authority flows not from territorial sovereignty but from jurisdictional rights in foreign territory and consequently that the mandated areas are not within the national domain as defined by national law. This is not conclusive evidence that the mandatories regard the areas as outside the national domain in the sense of international law. Numerous examples might be cited of territories which from the standpoint of national law are foreign but from that of international law are national. The "colonial" protectorates of the European powers[26] and the unincorporated insular possessions of the United States[27] seem to have this status. The possibility of such an anomalous status renders it important to consider the limitations which the mandatories have recognized in their own law as applicable to the administration of the mandated areas.

All civilized states have incorporated in their constitutions, whether written or customary, certain limitations upon political and administrative tyranny or caprice in the interests of the inhabitants of their territories. The character of these guaranties and the method by which they are applied differ from state to state, and the same state may recognize differences in different parts of its territory;[28] but some such guaranties are generally applied throughout the territory

[26] See *supra*, n. 8, and chap. ix, n. 103.

[27] *Downes* v. *Bidwell*, 182 U.S. 244, 288, in which Justice Brown suggested that although the insular possessions were not a part of the United States entitled to the constitutional guaranties, they might be entitled to certain of these guaranties in so far as they reflected "natural" rights. See also chap. ix, n. 104, and *Dorr* v. *U.S.*, 195 U.S. 138.

[28] Thus in the United States certain constitutional guaranties apply in the states and the District of Columbia while others apply to the incorporated territories also (*Rassmussen* v. *U.S.*, 197 U.S. 516; *Callan* v. *Wilson*, 127 U.S. 540; *Downes* v. *Bidwell*, 182 U.S. 244, 261; J. P. Hall, *Constitutional Law* [1910], pp. 266 ff.), and in the British Empire the United Kingdom and settlement colonies are entitled to British law modifiable only by act of Parliament or act of a local legislature (*Phillip* v. *Eyre*, L.R. [1867] 4 Q.B. 225), while other colonies and the empire of India are governed by the prerogative—limited, however, by "fundamental principles" (*Campbell* v. *Hall*, 20 State Trials 239 [1774]; *Sprigg* v. *Sigcau*, L.R. [1897], A.C. 238; Anson, *op. cit.*, II, Part II, 61, 76).

and have become so imbedded in the system of law, in the practice of the administration, in the traditions of the legislature and other political bodies, and in the mores of the people that departure from them is unlikely except in times of great emergency.

The exercise of authority by a state in the territory of another state is not checked by such constitutional provisions, but it is ordinarily checked by international law which limits the conduct of states toward the inhabitants of foreign territory in war as well as in peace and which, at least in the relations of states of similar civilization and power, is sanctioned by the possibility of retaliation by the state whose nationals are injured or of intervention by others, by the diplomatic habit of respect for international law, and by general public opinion, as well as by special sanctions which may be provided by particular treaties or international organizations.

The natives of regions which are neither in the national domain nor in the domain of a foreign state enjoy neither of these protections. In holding that the high commissioner of Bechuanaland protectorate could detain a former chief, Sekgome, through the issue of a proclamation which had the character of an act of attainder, the British Judicial Committee of the Privy Council admitted that it was maintaining the "startling proposition" that the British government there was a "despotism." Yet in finding that the territory was not in the national domain and its native inhabitants were not British subjects, it was driven to this conclusion and was obliged to deny to the appellant the writ of habeas corpus or any other guaranty of British law not expressly provided for in the orders in Council providing for the government of the territory.[29] At the same time as the Bechuanaland protectorate was not within the territory of any recognized state, but was entirely administered under British authority, it appeared that under international law it was British territory and thus no foreign state was entitled to protest against the conduct of this "despotism."[29a] With this case may be contrasted one involv-

[29] *Rex* v. *Crewe* (*Ex parte Sekgome*) L.R. (1910); 2 K.B. 576, 612. The court held that Mansfield's dicta (*Campbell* v. *Hall*, I Cowp. 208; 20 State Trials 239) that in exercising the prerogative in British territory the crown was limited by "fundamental principles" did not apply to exercises of the prerogative under the Foreign Jurisdiction Act.

[29a] This situation resembles that of possible independent states outside the family of nations. It has been contended that such states and their nationals are not entitled

ing an almost identical state of facts arising from Nigeria, which was British territory.[30] The Judicial Committee insisted that the deposed chief in question be given all the privileges of the writ of habeas corpus recognized by British law, thus carrying out the principle set forth in a recent case from the Gold Coast that "in cases coming before them from the dominions of the crown, their lordships first consideration always is to secure, if possible, that substantial justice is done."[31]

These curious situations have doubtless arisen because of the awkwardness of applying a system of constitutional guaranties to a people wholly unhabituated to them. This doubtless was the practical reason back of the American Supreme Court's definition of American Indian tribes as "domestic dependent nations,"[32] and of the islands acquired from Spain in 1898 as "territory appurtenant and belonging to the United States but not a part of the United States,"[33] as it was back of the continued recognition by the European states of some of their African territories as "colonial protectorates."[34] Such a status has the advantage that it leaves the government free to organize a system of law and administration without regard to either constitutional or international law. The corresponding danger that the native inhabitants will be oppressed is evident both in theory and practice.[35]

---

to any rights under international law (Oppenheim, *op. cit.*, sec. 29; *Hearn* v. *Bridault*, Scott, *Cases on International Law*, p. 1). Others take the position that native races, whether in protectorates or annexed territories, enjoy certain rights by "express international agreement" or by "general usage" (Lindley, *op. cit.*, p. 323), but this does not mean that they are entitled to the standard of treatment from the governing states which is due the nationals of a recognized state abroad (see authorities cited in Wright, "The Bombardment of Damascus," *A.J.I.L.*, XX, 265–67, and *supra*, chap. i, nn. 33–37).

[30] *Eshugbcgi Eleka* v. *Officer Administering the Government of Nigeria*, L.R. (1928), A.C. 459.

[31] *Kojo Pon* v. *Atta Fona*, L.R. (1927), A.C. 693, 696. See also *Campbell* v. *Hall* and *Sprigg* v. *Sigcau* (*supra*, n. 28).

[32] *Cherokee Nation* v. *Georgia*, 5 Pet. 1 (1831).

[33] *Downes* v. *Bidwell*, 182 U.S. 284; J. P. Hall, *Constitutional Law*, p. 268.

[34] *In re Southern Rhodesia*, L.R. (1919), A.C. 211; Lindley, *op. cit.*, p. 188.

[35] To quiet the fear "lest an unrestrained possession of power on the part of Congress may lead to unjust and oppressive legislation in which the natural rights of territories or their inhabitants may be engulfed in a centralized despotism," Justice Brown

If the mandates system were to leave the areas in question in this situation the native inhabitants would be unlikely to benefit from it. In fact, it has been suggested that the insistence by the League organs that the territories may not be annexed by the mandatories constitutes a real danger for the inhabitants. Belgian representatives at one time pointed out the advantages which the natives would gain by becoming Belgium nationals. Members of the Mandates Commission, however, have taken the view that any loss of constitutional protection would be more than compensated by the greater assurance of international protection if the territories were not annexed and the natives were not nationals of the mandatory.[36]

If these international guaranties are to be really effective they must be fully incorporated into the law applied by the mandatory's officials and courts in the areas. The League organs do not administer the areas and they cannot act as a court of appeal in every individual case of alleged abuse. They must necessarily deal with the mandatory's policy in a more general way and particularly with the recognition it gives to the mandate principles in its laws applicable to the areas. The following examination indicates that the mandatories have in most cases enacted the mandate texts as fundamental law in the areas, governing the conduct of officials and applicable by the courts irrespective of contrary provisions in local legislation or ordinances. It must be added, however, that the mandates have not usually been given a legal status superior to ordinances by the central executive authority of the mandatory.[36a] Furthermore the texts con-

---

in *Downes* v. *Bidwell*, 182 U.S. 244, 282, though holding that the insular possessions were not part of the United States in the meaning of the Constitution, denied that the people were subject to "the merely arbitrary" or "unrestrained" control of Congress and suggested that even if regarded as aliens they were entitled to certain "natural rights" recognized in the Constitution including fundamental protection to life, liberty, and property. The Judicial Committee of the Privy Council was perhaps more realistic in admitting that the British government in the Bechuanaland protectorate was a "despotism" (see *supra*, n. 29). M. Matsuda of Japan pointed out that while it would be contrary to the spirit of art. 22 of the Covenant to assimilate native inhabitants of the mandated territories to subjects of the mandatory power, "having in mind their interests, they should be accorded every advantage guaranteed to such subjects" (*O.J.*, III, 592).

[36] *Ibid.*, III, 594, 600–607.

[36a] The mandates are expressly recognized by statute only in Belgium and the British dominion mandatories.

tain many general principles, susceptible of wide differences of interpretation, and in such cases a national court is inclined to accept the interpretation by its own political authorities as conclusive. The results of the application of the mandates, and the conformity of national interpretations with its own, has concerned the League Council and its advisory commission and is dealt with elsewhere.[37] Suffice it to say here that but few cases have been found of legislative or administrative activity on the part of a mandatory's representatives which was clearly in conflict with a fair interpretation of the mandate, and where such cases have occurred remedy has been available through petition to the Council or action in the Permanent Court of International Justice. At present we are concerned with the state of the law of each mandatory with respect to the source of its authority in the areas, the limitations upon the exercise of that authority, and the competence of the courts to compel the observance of such limitations.

3. The Practice of Great Britain as Mandatory

The British Empire, which through four of its governments is mandatory of nine of the fourteen mandated areas, has developed an elaborate system for exercising jurisdiction outside of its national domain. Authority to exercise such jurisiction may flow from the royal prerogative, from act of a British Parliament, or from the common law. The latter can apply only in relations between British subjects abroad and seems practically to be limited to the power of clergymen in episcopal orders to perform marriages between British subjects abroad.[38]

The prerogative was the sole source of foreign jurisdiction over aliens up to the passage of the first foreign jurisdiction act by Parliament in 1843, and Hall thinks enough of it still remains "to cure any error of excess committed through overstepping the power delegated by parliament into which an order in council issued under authority

[37] See *supra*, chaps. vii, viii, xiii.

[38] Hall, *A Treatise of the Foreign Powers and Jurisdiction of the British Crown* (Oxford, 1894), pp. 12, 110, 194. "At common law the crown had no power of territorial legislation outside the domain of the crown. There might be power to make certain laws binding on British subjects abroad but there was no power to make territorial law outside the crown's dominions" (*Rex* v. *Crewe*, L.R. [1910], 2 K.B. 57).

of an act might possibly fall."[39] It seems to be still the source of the crown's authority to charter companies with a jurisdiction in territories not within the domain of any recognized state; to instruct diplomatic, consular, naval, military, and other officers abroad to influence foreign governments by agreement, advice, protests, threats, or coercion; and to exercise military jurisdiction by reprisals, intervention, and war.[40]

On the other hand, the civil jurisdiction exercised by consuls, commissioners, courts, and other officials in foreign states, British protectorates, and other regions not in the British domain (as defined by British law) flows mainly from the Foreign Jurisdiction Act of 1890.[41] This act recites:

> WHEREAS, By treaty, capitulations, grant, usage, sufferance, and other lawful means, Her Majesty the Queen has jurisdiction within divers foreign countries, ...
>
> *Be it therefore enacted, etc.*
>
> 1. It is and shall be lawful for Her Majesty the Queen to hold, exercise, and enjoy any jurisdiction which Her Majesty now has or may at any time hereafter have within a foreign country in the same and as ample a manner as if Her Majesty had acquired that jurisdiction by the cession or conquest of territory. . . . .
>
> 3. Every act and thing done in pursuance of any jurisdiction of Her Majesty in a foreign country shall be as valid as if it had been done according to the local law then in force in that country.
>
> 4. If in any proceeding, civil or criminal, in a court in Her Majesty's dominions or held under the authority of Her Majesty any question arises as to the existence or extent of any jurisdiction of Her Majesty in a foreign country, a Secretary of State shall, on the application of the court, send to the court within a reasonable time his decision on the question, and his decision shall for the purposes of the proceeding be final.

Certain acts are then scheduled which may be applied to such regions. The jurisdiction conferred by the act may be extended to regions within its terms by order in council.

[39] Hall, *Foreign Powers*, p. 10; Anson, *op. cit.*, II, Part II, 93. The Judicial Committee thought it indifferent whether the Swaziland orders in council flowed from the foreign Jurisdiction Act or from an act of state untraversable in a court of justice (*Sobhuza II* v. *Miller*, L.R. [1926], A.C. 523).

[40] Hall, *Foreign Powers*, p. 9; Anson, *op. cit.*, II, Part II, 94 (n. 3). This includes most acts in the field of external sovereignty (see *supra*, chap. ix, nn. 70–72).

[41] 53–54 Vict. 57 (printed in Hall, *Foreign Powers*, pp. 287–88).

The authority of the British agents flows from this act in the mandated areas of Palestine, Tanganyika, British Cameroons, British Togoland, and Western Samoa. In the cases of Southwest Africa and New Guinea authority flows from acts of the South African and Australian parliaments, respectively, and in Western Samoa the New Zealand Parliament had conferred authority on the government to accept a mandate prior to the issuance of the British order in council under the Foreign Jurisdiction Act. In the case of Nauru authority flows from an act of the Parliament of Great Britain giving effect to an agreement between the governments of Great Britain, Australia, and New Zealand. In Iraq no legislative authority to exercise civil jurisdiction has been given.[42] The powers of the British high commissioner are thus based on the Anglo-Iraq Treaty and instructions issued under the prerogative.

In so far as British authority in mandated areas flows from the Foreign Jurisdiction Act it is clear that in British law the territories are not within the national domain, and the same conclusion can be reached from the legislation or orders affecting the other areas. It must be noticed, however, that with respect to the application of several statutes territory "in respect of which a mandate is being exercised by the government of any part of His Majesty's dominions" has been assimilated to "His Majesty's Dominions."[43] In re-

[42] Unless it could be found in the various treaty of peace acts (Germany, 9–10 Geo. V [1919], p. 90; Austria and Bulgaria [1920]; Hungary [1921] giving general authority to execute the treaties of peace which included the mandates article (22) or the Treaty of Peace (Turkey) Act, 1924, for the execution of the Lausanne Treaty by which Turkey renounced the Arab territories. This treaty did not contain the League Covenant, nor did it, like the abortive treaty of Sèvres, expressly provide for mandatory administration of the renounced areas. MacNair suggests that the other treaty of peace acts authorize orders in council in execution of art. 16 of the Covenant (economic blockade) (*B.Y.B.I.L.* [1928], p. 62).

[43] Teachers (Superannuation Act), 15–16 Geo. V, c. 59 (1925), art. 21 (*c*), p. 1431; *ibid.*, Scotland, art. 4, sec. 2(*a*), p. 1351; Importation of Pedigree Animals Act (1922), p. 1020; Origin of Trade Mark Goods Act (1926), 16–17 Geo. 5, c. 53, p. 470. See also Finance Act (1919), 9–10 Geo. V, c. 32, sec. 8, authorizing preferences on goods from the empire and protectorates or mandated territories included by order in council, and imperial preference orders (No. 184), 1922 (Stat. Rules and Orders [1922], pp. 167, 168) declaring that for purposes of the act Southwest Africa, New Guinea, Western Samoa, Tanganyika, British Cameroons and Togoland, "shall as from the first of February 1922 be included within the definition of the British Empire" for the purposes of sec. 8 of the act. Various fugitive offenders orders in council have treated mandated territories

spect of other acts, however, mandated territories are assimilated to "protectorates"[44] to "places outside His Majesty's Dominions,"[45] or to "foreign states."[46] No implication as to the status of the territories can be drawn from such phraseology. The assimilation to national territory in certain cases is merely a convenient device to bring the mandated territory within the terms of a statute which may be applied thereto.[47] Let us now consider the actual basis of authority in each of these areas.

In Iraq, as has been noted, there is no legislation or executive order giving authority. The British high commissioner's powers rest on the Anglo-Iraq Treaty and his instructions, and are limited to advising the native government under which the treaty must in certain matters follow this advice. The instructions are however issued not from the foreign office but from the colonial office, which also receives reports, and is responsible for representing Great Britain in respect of this as of all other British mandated areas before the League of Nations. This practice has been criticized in Parliament on the ground that it seems to "assume that the mandates became *ipso facto* parts of the British Empire," and the suggestion has been made that their affairs should be transferred to the Foreign Office.[48] In spite of this, legislative, administrative, and judicial au-

"as if British possessions" (S.R. and O., I [1920], 754, 756; [1924], p. 465; [1925], pp. 505, 507).

[44] Army Annual Act, 13 Geo. V (1923), c. 3, pp. 17–18; Copyright order in council, S.R. and O. (1924), pp. 183, 184.

[45] Merchant-shipping (administration in mandated territories) order in council based on sec. 737, Merchant Shipping Act, 1894, S.R. and O. (1923), pp. 553, 555; (1922), p. 376, art. 36; (1920), p. 692, art. 15.

[46] The Finance Act (1923), 14–15 Geo. V (1924), c. 21, p. 64, which granted relief where profits of shipping were charged to both British and foreign income tax, was applied as if "references therein to any foreign state included references to any British dominion, any territory which is under His Majesty's protection, and any territory in respect of which a mandate is being exercised by any part of His Majesty's dominions."

[47] The same is of course true of the occasional assimilation of mandated territory to territory of the mandatory in international conventions as in art. 40 of the convention for the regulation of aerial navigation of October 13, 1919, though Diena seems to imply some judicial significance from this assimilation (*Acad. D.I.*, V [1924], 247, 258).

[48] Ponsonby, M.P., *Great Britain, House of Commons Debates*, Vol. CXCI (February 18, 1926), col. 2231. It may be noticed that France exercises the Syrian mandate through her foreign office.

thority are exercised only in the name of the king of Iraq. Though under the treaty the king of Iraq must appoint British subjects as advisers in certain departments, they are his officials, and though he must appoint British subjects as judges on some of the courts, especially those in which foreigners may be tried, they are his courts and appeal does not lie to the Judicial Committee of the Privy Council as it does, for instance, from British consular courts in China.[49] It would thus seem that in British law Great Britain has diplomatic influence but no jurisdiction in Iraq, consequently the latter is to be considered an independent state.

The Palestine order in council of 1922[50] by which civil government was established there recites the agreement of the Principal Allied Powers, "for the purpose of giving effect to the provisions of article 22 of the Covenant of the League of Nations," to intrust the administration to a mandatory; the Balfour declaration; and the selection by the Principal Powers of His Majesty as mandatory. It then continues:

WHEREAS, By treaty, capitulation, grant, usage, sufferance and other lawful means, His Majesty has power and jurisdiction within Palestine, now therefore, His Majesty by virtue and in exercise of the power in this behalf of the Foreign Jurisdiction Act, 1890, or otherwise in His Majesty vested, is pleased, by and with the advice of His Privy Council to order, and it is hereby ordered, as follows:

The order then proceeds to define the territory, authorizing the exclusion of Transjordania (art. 86)[50a] and to organize the government under a high commissioner, provision being expressly made that "no ordinance shall be passed [by the legislative council] which shall be in any way repugnant to or inconsistent with the provisions

[49] Bentwich, *The Practice of the Privy Council in Judicial Matters* (2d ed.; London, 1926), pp. 100, 102.

[50] S.R. and O. (1922), p. 362. See also Stoyanovsky, *The Mandate for Palestine* (London, 1928), where this and the Palestine (amendment) order in council, 1923, are reprinted, and Bentwich, *op. cit.*, pp. 100–101.

[50a] An agreement of February 20, 1928, between Great Britain and the Emir Abdullah recognized the latter's government in Transjordan. The Permanent Mandates Commission questioned the compatibility of this with the Palestine mandate which vested "full powers of legislation and administration" in the mandatory save as limited by the mandate. The British accredited representative recognized the Palestine mandate as still in effect in Transjordan, which was thus in a somewhat different status from Iraq (*P.M.C., Min.*, XIII, 42–45, 225–26).

of the mandate" (art. 18). Appeal from the Supreme Court of Palestine to the Judicial Committee of the Privy Council is permitted where more than £500 is in dispute (art. 44). Ordinances of the preceding military government are validated and petitions to the high commissioner are authorized by way of the legislative council. "Any memorandum so submitted shall be dealt with in such manner as may be described by His Majesty in conformity with the procedure recommended by the council of the League of Nations" (art. 85).

A subsequent order in council[51] authorized elections, and on the failure of these another[52] authorized the high commissioner to promulgate ordinances but with the same requirement of conformity to the mandate and in addition the provision that ordinances "which concern matters dealt with specifically by the provisions of the mandate shall not be promulgated until a draft thereof has been communicated to a Secretary of State and approved by him, with or without amendment." Subsequent orders in council also based on the Foreign Jurisdiction Act have excluded controversies respecting holy places from the civil courts, regulated appeals to the Privy Council, and defined Palestinian citizenship and its acquisition. The naturalization oath requires that the citizen be "faithful and loyal to the government of Palestine."[53]

The scope of the ordinance power of the high commissioner was tested in the Urtas Spring case. The Arab inhabitants of Urtas claimed that the ordinance permitting the diversion of water from this spring to Jerusalem took their property without adequate compensation and so was repugnant to article 2 of the mandate which made the mandatory responsible for "safeguarding the civil . . . . rights of all the inhabitants of Palestine irrespective of race and religion." Pursuant to the Palestine order in council and to "the general rule that the validity of laws made by a legislature which is not sovereign but the creature of some instrument of government, may be questioned by the local courts on the ground that they are repugnant to some provision to be found in that instrument," the Supreme Court of Palestine brought the ordinance to the test of the mandate in spite of some reluctance springing from the vagueness of the man-

[51] S.R. and O. (1922), p. 382. [52] *Ibid.* (1923), No. 619, art. 17(*c*).

[53] *Ibid.* (1924), p. 453; (1924), p. 614; (1924), pp. 474, 481.

date article in question. "The mandate," said Chief Justice Haycroft, "is a political and not a legal document and likely to contain expressions of good intention which are more easy to write than to read. We are, however, bound to read them and give them a practical value." The Court thus found the ordinance void because it violated the "principles of sound legislation" which required adequate compensation for property taken for public purposes.[54] On appeal, the Judicial Committee of the Privy Council agreed that by the terms of the order in council "it was the right and duty of the court to examine the terms of the mandate and to consider whether the ordinance was in any way repugnant to those terms," but on the issue of such repugnancy they differed.

> Their Lordships agree that in such a case, and in the absence of exceptional circumstances, justice requires that fair provision shall be made for compensation, but this depends, not upon any civil right, but (as the Chief Justice said) upon principles of sound legislation; and it cannot be the duty of the court to examine (at the instance of every litigant) the legislative and administrative acts of the administration, and to consider in every case whether they are in accordance with the view held by the court as to the requirements of natural justice.[55]

In another case decided by the Supreme Court of Palestine soon after the Urtas Spring case, the court adopted practically the view subsequently taken by the Judicial Committee. The word Palestine was printed on the postage stamps in the three official languages—English, Arabic, and Hebrew—but after the Hebrew text appeared the initials "E.I." (Alef Yod), signifying "Eretz Israel" or the "Land of Israel." This aroused intense feeling among the Arabs who saw a veiled recognition of the most extreme Zionist aspirations, and an effort was made to enjoin the use of these initials on the ground of incompatibility with the mandate provision that "any statement or inscription in Arabic on stamps or money in Palestine shall be repeated in Hebrew, and any statement or inscription in Hebrew shall be repeated in Arabic." The Supreme Court, however, refused to

[54] *Murrah* v. *District Governor of Jerusalem*, June 25, 1925. Not reported but opinion seen in manuscript (Wright, "Some Recent Cases on the Status of Mandated Areas," *A.J.I.L.*, XX [October, 1926], 769).

[55] *Jerusalem–Jaffa District Governor* v. *Murra*, L.R. (1926), A.C. 327.

grant the injunction on the ground that the form of the word Palestine in each language was a matter of administrative discretion.[56]

From these cases it appears that the Palestine order in council recognizes the mandate as a limitation enforcible by the courts against the mandatory's government in Palestine but that, in accord with the British traditions, the courts will presume that that government in performing political and administrative acts has correctly interpreted the rather vague terms of that instrument. In other words, interpretation of the mandate is largely intrusted to the political rather than the judicial arm of the mandatory.[57] It may be noted however, that the interpretive authority given to the Permanent Court of International Justice indicates that the mandates were intended to be documents susceptible of judicial interpretation. The Judicial Committee, in fact, appears to have had some doubt of the major grounds for its decision, because it thought it advisable to buttress it by an argument showing that the ordinance did in fact make all the provisions for compensation that justice required.

Civil government was established in Tanganyika under an order in council of July 22, 1920, before the mandate had been confirmed.[58] The preamble of this document recited Germany's renunciation of overseas territory in favor of the Principal Allied and Associated Powers by the treaty of Versailles, the ratification of the treaty, the agreement of the powers that this territory "be administered by His Majesty the king subject to and in accordance with the provisions of the said treaty," and the conditions justifying application of the Foreign Jurisdiction Act as in the Palestine mandate. It then defines the territory, organizes a government under a "governor and commander in chief" whom it authorizes to make ordinances of legislation but with due "respect for existing native laws and customs except so far as the same may be opposed to justice and morality." A

[56] Not reported (see *A.J.I.L.*, XX, 770, and *P.M.C.*, *Min.*, IX, 163, 223). These cases are discussed by Stoyanovsky, *The Mandate for Palestine*, pp. 236–61 and by *Bentwick zeitschrift für auslandisches öffentliches Recht und Völkerrecht*, 1929.

[57] Under the Foreign Jurisdiction Act, art. 4, the interpretation of the extent of British jurisdiction under the mandate by a secretary of state is conclusive in all British courts (*Rex* v. *Crewe*, L.R. [1910], 2 K.B. 585). But see Stoyanovsky, *op. cit.*, pp. 242–43; see also *supra*, n. 41, and *infra*, nn. 77, 78.

[58] S.R. and O. (1920), sec. 685.

high court of Tanganyika is established, and the law of the territory is defined as the codes of India, common law and equity and proclamations, orders in council and statutes, "provided always that the said common law doctrines and equity and statutes of general application shall be in force in the territory so far only as the circumstance of the territory and its inhabitants and the limits of His Majesty's jurisdiction permit, and subject to such qualification as local circumstances may render necessary" (art. 17).

This order clearly recognized the limitations of British authority imposed by the treaty though less assurance of judicial enforcement of these limitations is offered than in the case of Palestine. This may have been due to the fact that the mandate was not yet confirmed, but the order in council of March 19, 1926,[59] organizing a legislative council pays even less respect to the limitations of the mandate—in fact, as was pointed out by the Mandates Commission,[60] it does not mention that document either in the preamble or the text. It recites the order in council of 1920, and the Foreign Jurisdiction Act by which "it is among other things communicated that it shall be lawful for His Majesty to hold, exercise and enjoy any jurisdiction which His Majesty now has, or may at any time hereafter have, within a foreign country in the same and as ample a manner as if His Majesty had acquired that jurisdiction by the cession or conquest of territory." This is a direct quotation from the Foreign Jurisdiction Act (art. 1), but the fact that it is put before rather than after the recital that "by treaty, grant, usage, sufferance, and other lawful means, His Majesty has power and jurisdiction within the Tanganyika territory" might lead to the assumption that Great Britain claimed as much jurisdiction as she would have in "ceded or conquered territory." The incorrectness of such an assumption is indicated by Hall's comments on article 1 of the Foreign Jurisdiction Act.

[59] *Ibid.* (1926), p. 576, supplemented by another Tankanyika order in council (*ibid.* [1926], p. 583).

[60] *P.M.C.*, *Min.*, XI, 67, 202. This document seems to have been drafted with a view to quieting the fears of capitalists who hesitated to invest in Tanganyika because of doubt of the permanence of its status. The colonial secretary and the governor of the territory made statements at about the same time describing the territory as "within the framework of the empire" and as "part of the British Empire" criticized by the Mandates Commission (*ibid.*, IX, 135; XI, 65–67; Buell, *The Native Problem in Africa* [New York, 1928], I, 432).

It is unnecessary to say that this language does not assimilate the jurisdiction exercised in a foreign country, either in nature or degree, to that which belongs to the crown in conquered territory. Its object is simply to provide that such jurisdiction as may have been acquired by express consent or sufferance of the foreign state shall be exercised by the crown precisely as if it were exercised by sole virtue of the prerogative. The position of the crown relatively both to parliament and to individuals is declared to be identical with that which it holds in a country which has been conquered or ceded.[61]

The order in council provides for a legislative council of thirteen official and ten unofficial members appointed by the governor and required to make an oath or affirmation to "be faithful and bear true allegiance to His Majesty King George, his heirs and successors according to law." Respect for native laws and customs in the making of ordinances is required and ordinances varying or affecting any order in council relating to the territory are not in force without previous approval by a secretary of state. Instructions must be observed, but failure to do so does not invalidate the ordinance if made with advice and consent of the legislative council. There thus appears to be little explicit guaranty that the mandate will be observed.

Much more explicit recognition of the mandates system is to be found in the orders in council of 1923 establishing civil government in Togoland and the Cameroons. The first of these[62] recites article 119 of the treaty of Versailles, the agreement of the Principal Allied and Associated Powers that France and Great Britain make a joint recommendation, the joint recommendation made by them to the Council of the League proposing the mandates, His Majesty's agreement to accept the mandate and "exercise it on behalf of the League of Nations in accordance with the terms of the mandate," the Council's confirmation of the mandate, the provision in article 9 of the latter that "the mandatory shall have full powers of administration and legislation in the area" and may administer it "as an integral part of his territory and subject to the above provisions," the expediency of uniting the territory for customs, fiscal, and administrative purposes with the neighboring Gold Coast and the Foreign Jurisdiction Act of 1890. The order in council then divides the area into a northern and southern sphere integrated respectively with the Gold Coast colony and the Gold Coast protectorate, "provided always

[61] Hall, *Foreign Powers*, p. 11.

[62] Togoland, order in council, October 11, 1923, S.R. and O. (1923), p. 330.

that should any such law so applied as aforesaid or any ordinances enacted by the governor as aforesaid be repugnant to any provision of the mandate, such law or ordinance shall, to the extent of such repugnancy but not otherwise, be and remain absolutely void and inoperative" (secs. 5 and 6).

The Cameroons order in council,[63] enacted a few months earlier, has the same preamble substituting Nigeria for the Gold Coast. The governor is required to legislate in accord with the Nigeria protectorate order in council, 1922,[64] which provides that:

all ordinances whether passed by the legislative council or by the governor as aforesaid shall be subject to the following conditions or provisions: (1) nothing in any such ordinance or ordinances contained shall take away or affect any right secured to any native in the protectorate by any treaties or agreements made on behalf of or with the same by Her Majesty Queen Victoria, His Late Majesty King Edward 7th or of His Majesty and all such treaties and agreements shall remain operative and in force and all pledges and undertakings therein contained shall remain mutually binding on all parties to the same. . . . . If any ordinance to which the provisions of this article apply shall be in any respect repugnant to any provisions of this order or of any other order made by His Majesty in Council such ordinance shall be read subject to such order and shall to the extent of such repugnancy be absolutely void.

In view of the express recognition by the Cameroons order in council of the mandate which is in effect "an agreement on behalf" of the natives, this article seems sufficiently broad to nullify ordinances conflicting with the mandate.

Though no cases involving the judicial cognizability of the British B mandates seem to have been before the Judicial Committee of the Privy Council, that body has occasionally had to consider the limitations upon the power of the crown or its local representatives to deal arbitrarily with natives in African colonies and protectorates. In a number of cases arising from the West African colonies of Nigeria and the Gold Coast it has recognized that communal occupation of land sanctioned by native custom is entitled to legal protection, though it has considered that ultimate title to the land vested in the crown.[65] Natives have also been protected from arbitrary de-

[63] S.R. and O. (1923), p. 325. [64] *Ibid.* (1922), p. 301.

[65] *Att. Gen. of Southern Nigeria* v. *John Holt* (Foreshore case), L.R. (1915), A.C. 599; *Amodu Tijani* v. *The Secretary, Southern Nigeria* (Appapa land case), L.R. (1921), 2 A.C., 399; *Summonu* v. *Disu Raphael*, L.R. (1927), A.C. 881.

tention in these colonies by full opportunity for judicial hearing.[66] On the other hand, the opinion in several important cases from South African territories have been less considerate of native rights. Thus detention of an ex-chief without judicial hearing was permitted in the Bechuanaland protectorate,[67] and the government was permitted to alienate land to white settlers without consideration for native interests in the Swaziland protectorate[68] and Southern Rhodesia.[69]

The latter was a protectorate in 1891 governed by orders in council and the chartered South African company. The native chieftain, Lobengula, died in 1893 and the territory was conquered by the British, becoming a colony sometime during the next five years. During this period orders in council provided for land alienations to settlers by the British South Africa Company without consideration for native claims. The Judicial Committee advised that these alienations were valid and that title to unalienated lands vested in the crown, which, however, was obliged to reimburse the South Africa Company to the amount of its adverse balance resulting from legitimate expenses in carrying out its "mandate." The "respectable but slender" argument on behalf of the natives was held insufficient on the grounds (1) that the British object of white land settlement must not be interfered with, (2) that the native conceptions of communal land tenure were so vague as to be unrecognizable at law, and (3) that in conquered territory the crown can extinguish land titles by manifesting an intention to do so. It is true that during most of this period the territory was actually governed under the Foreign Jurisdiction Act, orders in council in pursuance thereof, and the companies charter, and that in 1894 the colonial secretary had found objection to establishing a crown colony; but the Judicial Committee considered these facts no bar to recognition that conquest had actually taken place even though there was no formal act of annexation. Such an act

is a well understood mode in which a conquering power announces its will *urbi et orbi*. It has all the advantages (and the disadvantages) of publicity and pre-

[66] *Eshugbogi Eleka* v. *Officer Administering the Government of Nigeria*, L.R. (1928), A.C. 459.

[67] *Rex* v. *Crewe* (*Ex parte Sekgome*), L.R. (1910), 2 K.B. 576.

[68] *Sobhuza II* v. *Miller*, L.R. (1926), A.C. 518, 523, 529.

[69] *In re Southern Rhodesia* (1919), A.C. 211, 225, 232–34, 241–42.

cision. But it is only declaratory of a state of fact. . . . . As between state and state special authority may attach to this formal manner of announcing the exercise of sovereign rights, but the present question does not arise between state and state. It is one between sovereign and subject.

Thus the company's claim to title of the land was ousted and, as for the natives, "in 1894 the field was clear, for the native sovereignty was gone," and "the exercise of the powers given by the foreign jurisdiction act did not operate as a negation of the exercise of other powers in the present still less as a renunciation of the right to resort to them in the future."

It thus appears that the crown was free from the usual international limitations in protected territory and the usual constitutional limitations in conquered territory though the opinion suggests that the old principles that in protectorates the crown cannot alienate domain land[69a] and that in conquered territory the prerogative is limited by "fundamental principles"[70] had both become obsolete, at least in the case of territory occupied by natives "so low in the scale of social organization that their usages and conceptions of rights and duties are not to be reconciled with the institutions or the legal ideas of civilized society."[70a] Lord Sumner said:

[69a] *Ibid.*, at p. 241, citing statements by Lords Derby (1885) and Ripon (1895) that land titles cannot issue in the name of the queen in a protectorate; see also Lindley, *op. cit.*, p. 321. Anson (*op. cit.*, II, Part II, 93), citing Uganda and East African orders in council (S.R. and O. [1898], pp. 381, 382), remarks that the crown can acquire land in protectorates and exercise general control over land where the native concepts of ownership are vague, thus "the rights exercised over these protectorates may be said to differ from territorial sovereignty in little but name."

[70] *Campbell* v. *Hall*, I Cowp. 208–9; 20 State Trials 239 (1774), in which Lord Mansfield said: "If the king has a power to alter the old and to introduce new laws in a conquered country, this legislation being subordinate, that is subordinate to his own authority in parliament, he can not make any new change contrary to fundamental principles; he can not exempt an inhabitant from that particular dominion; as for instance from the laws of trade or from the power of parliament, or give him privileges exclusive of his other subjects; and so in many other instances which might be put." The Judicial Committee pointed out in *Rex* v. *Crewe*, L.R. (1910), 2 K.B. 612, that this limitation had probably been rendered obsolete by *Phillips* v. *Eyre*, L.R. (1867), 4 Q.B. 225; 6 Q.B. 1, and in any case was not applicable to protectorates governed under the Foreign Jurisdiction Act.

[70a] *In re Southern Rhodesia* (1919), A.C. 233, 234. The Judicial Committee admitted that "there are indigenous peoples whose legal conceptions, though differently developed, are hardly less precise than our own. When they once have been studied and understood they are no less enforceable than rights arising under English law."

According to the argument, the natives before 1893 were owners of the whole of these vast regions in such a sense that, without their permission or that of their king and trustee, no traveler, still less a settler, could so much as enter without committing a trespass. If so, the maintenance of their rights was fatally inconsistent with white settlement of the country, and yet white settlement was the object of the whole forward movement, pursued by the company and controlled by the crown, and that object was successfully accomplished, with the result that the aboriginal system gave place to another prescribed by the Order in Council. This fact makes further inquiry into the nature of the natives' rights unnecessary. If they were not in the nature of private rights, they were at the disposal of the crown when Lobengula fled and his dominions were conquered; if they were, any actual disposition of them by the crown upon a conquest, whether immediately in 1894 or four years later, would suffice to extinguish them as manifesting an intention expressly to exercise the right to do so.

In the Swaziland case the native king claimed on the basis of an article in the treaty of 1894 between Great Britain and the South African Republic which "guaranteed the natives in the continual use and occupation of land now in their possession." But, advised the Judicial Committee:

The limitation in the convention of 1894 on interference with the rights and laws and customs of the natives can not legally interfere with a subsequent exercise of the sovereign powers of the crown, or invalidate subsequent orders in council. . . . . The power of the crown to alienate land was exercised either under the Foreign Jurisdiction Act or as an act of state which cannot be questioned in a court of law. The crown could not, except by statute, deprive itself of freedom to make orders in council, even when these were inconsistent with previous orders.

Swaziland was clearly a protectorate at the time, but the protecting state's powers had become so great as to be hardly distinguishable from "possession," thus apparently it enjoyed the advantages of both positions and was subject to the limitations of neither.[70b]

Apart from possible differences in the degree of native civilization and of white anxiety for land, these cases may be distinguished from those arising from West Africa in that British orders in council were held to have extinguished native rights, while in Nigeria and the Gold Coast the only acts alleged to have had this effect were those of local authorities. Furthermore the former territories were protector-

[70b] *Sobhuza II* v. *Miller*, L.R. (1926), A.C. 518, 529; Lindley, *op. cit.*, p. 350.

ates or had just been conquered, which apparently under British law gives the crown more extensive powers than it has in colonies of long standing.[71]

All of the cases are consistent with the Palestine cases discussed,[72] indicating that in British law local legislation repugnant to orders in council organizing the local government are void, but that one order in council may ordinarily be overruled by a later, and of course by an act of the imperial Parliament.[72a] Since treaties are not ordinarily per se sources of law in British courts,[73] it appears that the mandate texts are British law applicable by the courts only in so far as they have been expressly made so by orders in council or other legislation. They appear to be adequately recognized in the present orders in council with exception of those dealing with Tanganyika, but since the power of the crown to legislate by orders in council under the Foreign Jurisdiction Act is practically unlimited, the continued ap-

[71] See Anson, *op. cit.*, II, Part II, 62, 76. Buell (*The Native Problem in Africa*, I, 200, 209–12, 755–56) distinguishes the cases by the differences in precision of native land-tenure conceptions (as interpreted by the court) and by the differences in the length of time during which the native interests had been respected under the British régime. Lindley takes the optimistic view that "the establishment merely of a protectorate does not entitle the protecting power to deal with private rights to land in the protected territory, and any such power must be based upon express grant or acquiescence on the part of the local government" and furthermore that international law sets limits to the right of alienating native communal land even in annexed territory for which he cites examples from the legislation of a number of colonial powers "securing natives in the possession of a sufficient quantity of land to enable them to obtain an adequate subsistence in the circumstances of their condition as modified by the presence of a white population" (*op. cit.*, pp. 321, 350). It may be questioned whether the latter statement really recognizes native communal rights in land and whether it or any other principle is judicially enforcible against orders in council (see *supra*, n. 70). Lindley indicates that the degree of protection given natives has been largely a matter of executive discretion and that there has often been injustice. The statement in regard to protectorates clearly needs qualification (see *supra*, n. 69a).

[72] See *supra*, nn. 54–56.

[72a] *Att. Gen.* v. *Bishop of Manchester*, L.R. 3 Eq. 436; *The Zamora*, L.R. (1916), 2 A.C. 77; Wright, "Conflicts of International Law with National Laws and Ordinances," *A.J.I.L.*, XI, 2, 14; Goodnow, *Comparative Administrative Law*, I, 101.

[73] *Walker* v. *Baird*, L.R. (1892), A.C. 491; Anson, *op. cit.*, II, Part II, 109–10; Picciotto, *The Relation of International Law to the Law of England and of the United States of America* (New York, 1915), p. 71; MacNair, "When Do British Treaties Involve Legislation?" *B.Y.B.I.L.*, 1928, pp. 67–68.

plicability of the mandates is not in any sense guaranteed by the courts as against subsequent acts of the crown in council.

The prerogative of the crown to legislate for a British colony by orders in council has been held to be limited for the future, by a grant of powers of local legislation to a representative assembly.[74] It is not certain that this principle applies to representative assemblies organized by order in council in territory governed under the Foreign Jurisdiction Act. In view of the greater proclivity of local white representative assemblies, as compared with distant imperial authorities, to pass legislation oppressive to natives, it seems expedient that powers should never be given to such bodies inconsistent with native rights. Once given they cannot be taken back by the crown in British territory except by act of Parliament. Since the same position might be taken with regard to mandated territories it would seem wise expressly to limit the powers of any local representative body by the mandate text itself in the order in council constituting such body.[75] This actually has been done in the order providing for an assembly in Palestine though the order has never gone into effect.[76] Furthermore, since the crown and all other British authorities are subject to acts of Parliament, the mandate texts would acquire an improved status in British law if they were expressly designated by act of Parliament as the fundamental law of the areas. If that were done the courts could regard even orders in council conflicting with them as void, thus giving greater assurance to the continuous fulfilment of British mandatory responsibilities.

It must be recalled, however, that even where the mandate text is cognizable by the courts and there is no conflicting legislation of superior validity in British law, the courts are often obliged to accept executive construction of them as conclusive. Under the Foreign Jurisdiction Act the opinion of a secretary of state is made conclusive on the courts as to the "existence or extent of any jurisdiction of Her Majesty in a foreign country,"[77] and it seems to be a recognized prin-

[74] *Campbell* v. *Hall* (cited in n. 70); Anson, *op. cit.*, II, Part II, 77.

[75] The Permanent Mandates Commission has expressed some concern at the setting-up of a white legislative authority in South West Africa (*P.M.C.*, *Min.*, VI, 58–61, 177; *supra*, chap. vii, n. 57), though this act expressly subjected the local legislature to the provisions of the mandate (see *infra*, n. 93).

[76] See *supra*, nn. 50–52.

[77] See *supra*, n. 41.

ciple of British law that political conditions are matters of state on which courts must follow the opinion of the executive.[78] On this principle executive officials have sometimes been held immune from suit for acts violative of private right on the ground of some special fact, necessity, or political situation.[79] Closely related to this principle is the tendency of the courts, illustrated in the Judicial Committee's opinion in the Urtas Spring case, to accept executive interpretation of texts prescribing vague principles of "natural justice," "legislation," or "policy."[80] In view of the importance of such provisions in the mandates, it is clear that their execution can never be completely guaranteed by the law and the courts alone. Carrying out of their spirit will inevitably be in large measure a problem for executive and administrative discretion.

4. Practice of the Dominions as Mandatories

The Nauru mandate, like those just considered, was confirmed to His Majesty, without specifying his government which should be responsible for it, but an agreement was made between "His Majesty's government in London, His Majesty's government of the Commonwealth of Australia and His Majesty's government of the Dominion of New Zealand" for joint administration of the government under the direction, during the first five years, of an administrator appointed by Australia. The administrator was given power to make ordinances, which, however, do not constitute statutory rules and orders.[81] After the first five-year term, the three governments may agree on the future administrator. The phosphate deposits were to be administered by these three governments through a board of commissioners which should defray the expenses of government. This agreement was confirmed by an act of the British Parliament in 1920 before confirmation of the mandate "subject to the provisions of article 22 of the covenant of the League of Nations."[82]

[78] *Mighell* v. *Sultan of Johore*, L.R. (1894), 1 Q.B. 149; W. Harrison Moore, *Act of State in English Law* (New York, 1906), chap. iii. The same doctrine of political questions is recognized in the United States (*Luther* v. *Borden*, 7 How. 1 [1848]; Wright, *Control of American Foreign Relations*, p. 172) and in France (see *infra*, n. 109).

[79] *Cook* v. *Sprigg*, L.R. (1899), A.C. 572; Moore, *Act of State*, chap. vii.

[80] See *supra*, n. 55.

[81] S.R. and O., Index (1924), p. 532.

[82] 10–11 Geo. V (1920), c. 27.

On October 29, 1919, the New Zealand Parliament passed the treaties of peace act which authorized the acceptance of "any mandate for the government of the said islands of Western Samoa which his majesty may be pleased to accept from the League of Nations in pursuance of the aforesaid treaty of peace with Germany."[83] On March 11, 1920, before confirmation of the mandate, the British government approved an order in council reciting article 119 of the peace treaty, the agreement of the Principal Allied and Associated Powers "that the said islands shall be administered by His Majesty in his government of his dominion of New Zealand, subject to and in accordance with the provisions of the said treaty," the existence of His Majesty's jurisdiction in the islands, and the Foreign Jurisdiction Act of 1890. The order defines the territorial limits and vests the Parliament and executive government of New Zealand with full power to make laws for the peace, order, and good government of the islands "subject to and in accordance with the provisions of the treaty of peace."[84]

The governments in New Guinea and Southwest Africa are based solely on legislation of the parliaments of Australia and South Africa. No British order in council based on the Foreign Jurisdiction Act was issued as in the case of Western Samoa. In view of the colonial laws validity act and the constitutional limitation of the legislative power of the dominions to the peace, order, and good government of the country, question might be raised of the legality of this extraterri-

[83] New Zealand Statutes, 10 Geo. V (1919), No. 20, p. 105. The government was organized by the Samoa constitution order, 1919; later incorporated in the Samoa act, 1921. The Samoa amendment act, 1923, extended the representative character of the legislative council.

[84] S. R. and O., I (1920), 745. In *Tagaloa* v. *Inspector of Police* (1927), N.Z.L.R. 883, four of five judges supported the authority of New Zealand based on this order made in pursuance of two imperial statutes, the Foreign Jurisdiction Act, 1890, and the Treaty of Peace Act, 1919. The fifth judge thought New Zealand had ample authority "given by the League of Nations directly to the Dominion as a member of the League." The latter basis of authority was supported by the supreme court of New Zealand in *In re Tamasase* (*Gazette L. R.*, 1929, p. 149) in which habeas corpus was denied a Samoan on the ground that since "New Zealand in administering the affairs of Samoa, is a mere servant bound to obey the directions of its master, the Council of the League of Nations" the British Habeas Corpus act did not apply. See W. H. Coker, in *New Zealand Affairs*, 1929, pp. 185–94.

torial legislation by the dominions.[85] Apparently it was felt that the recognition of the independent status of the dominions by the peace treaty and the League Covenant, and the express attribution of mandates to them in the conference, gave them the necessary authority. "South Africa," said Judge de Villiers in the South African Supreme Court, "in respect to the mandate is not in any respect subject to the British parliament."[86] At any rate, the exercise of authority by these dominions on their own responsibility has been acquiesced in by Great Britain.

The Australian New Guinea Act was passed on September 30, 1920, before confirmation of the mandate.[87] It recites the conquest of the territory on September 17, 1914, the surrender to the naval and military forces of the commonwealth, the German renunciation by the treaty of Versailles, the present occupation by the commonwealth, the agreement of the Principal Allied and Associated Powers to confer the mandate according to the Covenant, and the expediency of providing for its acceptance when issued and also of providing for civil government. The Act then declares the "territory under the authority of the Commonwealth," authorizes the governor-general to accept the mandate when issued and organizes the administration. Commonwealth legislation does not extend unless so expressed and the governor-general may make ordinances. The express guaranties of the Covenant in respect to C territories are then inserted, and the governor-general is required to make an annual report to the League Council "containing full information as to the measures taken to carry out the requirements" of these guaranties and as to "the well-being and progress of the native inhabitants of the territory." The administrator is required to take an oath "well and truly to serve our sovereign lord the king in the office of administrator of the territory of New Guinea."[88] This Act gives very ex-

[85] 28–29 Vict. (1865), c. 63. Removal of this limitation was suggested at the Imperial Conference of 1926 (Hurst, *Great Britain and the Dominions*, p. 47).

[86] *Rex* v. *Christian*, S.Af.L.R. (1924), App. Div. 101, 120. The Australian constitution authorizes the commonwealth to legislate for any territory placed under its authority by the Crown "or otherwise acquired by the commonwealth." The High Court treated the mandate as accepted by the Imperial Treaty of Peace Act in *Mainka* v. *Custodian of Expropriated Territory*, 34 C.L.R. 297. See New Zealand cases, *supra*, n. 84.

[87] Commonwealth Acts (1920), pp. 75–76.

[88] *Ibid.* (1926), p. 40.

plicit recognition both in form and substance to the limitations of the mandate even though passed before confirmation of the latter.

Governing authority in Southwest Africa flows from the Peace Treaty Act passed in 1919 by the Union Parliament which recites:

> WHEREAS, At Versailles on the 28th day of June 1919 a treaty of peace, a copy of which has been laid before parliament, was signed in behalf of His Majesty and it is expedient that the governor general should have power to do all such things as may be proper and expedient for giving effect in so far as concerns the Union to the treaty or to any mandate issued in pursuance of the treaty with reference to the territory of Southwest Africa. . . . .[89]

The governor-general is then authorized to make appointments, establish offices, issue proclamations and regulations as appear to him necessary to give effect to the treaty or mandate. Certain Union laws may be applied in the territory, and the grant of interest in "state lands or minerals" is prohibited except by Parliament. Originally in effect for a year, the Act was made permanent in 1921.[90] An act of 1922 transferred the railways and harbors of Southwest Africa as of June 10, 1920, "in full dominion" to the Union and vested them in the governor-general "to be controlled and managed by the railway administration as part of the system of the Union." Another act of this year provided that Walvis Bay, an enclave in Southwest Africa but long a part of Cape Colony, should be administered as part of the "mandated territory" and as if its inhabitants were a part of the latter.[91] The Southwest African Naturalization of Aliens Act passed in 1924 extended the South African Naturalization Act of 1910 with the provision that every adult European subject of the late enemy power and domiciled in the territory on January 1, 1924, or therafter until the act goes into effect shall be deemed a British subject after six months unless he declares himself not desirous of doing so, in which case he remains in the territory without loss of privilege.[92]

An act of 1925 organized a representative government in Southwest Africa.[93] It recites the issuance of the mandate by the League Council in pursuance of article 22 under which the government of

[89] Statutes of the Union of South Africa (1919), p. 492.

[90] *Ibid.* (1921), p. 172.

[91] *Ibid.* (1922), p. 62.

[92] *Ibid.* (1924), p. 124.

[93] *Ibid.* (1925), p. 734.

the union possesses "full power of administration and legislation as an integral part of the union," the Treaty of Peace Act of 1919, the expediency of giving further authority for the welfare of the people and of admitting European inhabitants to representation in the administration and legislation of the territory, "subject always to the provision of the mandate." It then provides for an executive committee, an advisory council, and a legislative assembly. An act of 1926 extends the South African Mental Disorder Act of 1916 to the mandated territory and "for the purpose of the said act, the mandated territory shall be regarded as a province of the union."[94]

This legislation gives explicit recognition of the limitation of the mandate, though occasionally expressions have been used which might imply sovereign rights in the territory. The term "state lands" and "full dominion" of the railways and harbors have been criticized by the Mandates Commission as has the term "possess sovereignty" which appears in the preamble to the treaty of 1925 between South Africa and Portugal regarding the Angola boundary.[95]

The South African Supreme Court had occasion to interpret the mandatory's authority in the area in a treason prosecution which arose out of the Bondelzwart rebellion of 1923.[96] The sole question before the Supreme Court was whether South Africa had such a degree of authority in the territory as to justify a prosecution for treason. The Court held that it did but the judges differed somewhat in their reasons. Chief Justice Innis discussed the nature of sovereignty as conceived by medieval and modern jurists with the conclusion that it was susceptible of limitation and division as instanced by protectorates and confederations. Turning then to the treaty, he concluded that the phrase "renounce in favor of the principal allied and associated powers" in article 119 of the treaty was not equivalent to "cede to" in this instance in view of the pledge of article 22 and the differences in the treatment of enemy property from that accorded in actually ceded territory (arts. 254, 257). "The animus essential to a legal cession was not present on either side." The League

[94] *Ibid.* (1926), p. 198.

[95] See *supra*, chap. vii, n. 48. The administrative separation of the Caprivi Zipfel from Southwest Africa and its administrative union with Bechuanaland protectorate has also been commented on (*ibid.*, n. 49).

[96] *Rex* v. *Christian*, S.Af.L.R. (1924), App. Div. 101, 112, 120, 122, 129, 137.

of Nations, however, was not a state capable of enjoying sovereignty. Analyzing article 22 he continued:

> The main features are these:—There was no cession of the German possession to the principal powers: there was merely a renunciation in their favor in order that such possessions might be dealt with in terms of the covenant. And the principal powers became bound, as signatories to the treaty, to do everything necessary on their part to give effect to the arrangement. This they did by selecting a mandatory as contemplated by article 118, and thereby conferring a mandate upon him. The matter then passed under the cognizance of the League and it became the duty of the council to settle the terms of the mandate in conformity with the provisions of the covenant. The mandate having been accepted the mandatory became obliged to report annually to the council. No limit was placed on the duration of the mandate and no sanction was provided for a breach of its terms. It was probably considered that the force of public opinion, and in case of dispute the authority of the Court of International Justice would ensure a due observance of the mandate. It is not necessary to enquire whether the mandate once given could be cancelled either by the council which did not appoint the mandatory or by the principal powers which having made the appointment passed the matter on to the council, because the status of the mandatory during the existence of the mandate can be sufficiently determined for the purpose of this case by reference to the treaty and the document itself. And assuming that the terms of the mandate do not exceed the limits of the covenant, I have come to a definite conclusion upon the contention of the appellant. It can not be said that the government of Southwest Africa is possessed of Majestas in the full sense of that term; in other words it is not a sovereign and independent state. But Majestas operating internally may by our law be sufficient to found a charge of high treason, in spite of the fact that its external operation is considerably contracted, and where the internal characteristics of sovereignty are present; where a community is organized under a government which has the power of making laws and enforcing them, this Majestas adequate for the above purpose must reside either in the government of the community or in some other government to which it is subject.

With this opinion that the mandatory was not sovereign of the area Judge Salomon concurred without opinion as did Judge Kotze, who compared a mandate to a charter giving authority to govern. Power to punish for treason, he thought, flowed from the mandatory's duty of maintaining order.

Two judges, De Villiers and Wessels, seemed to attribute sovereignty of the territory to the mandatory, though recognizing that such sovereignty was limited. The first began by insisting that in respect to the mandate South Africa was not in any respect subject to the British Parliament. The League of Nations was not a state capable of possessing sovereignty of territory. "Southwest Africa," he said, "was transferred to the people of the Union not by way of absolute property but in the same way as a trustee is in the possession of the property of the *cestui que trust* or a guardian of the property of the ward." Though "the legal terms in article 22, trust, tutelage and mandate, cannot be taken literally as expressing the definite conception for which they stand in law," they at least indicate the "spirit" in which the territory should be administered and "the use of the terms shows that in so far as those legal principles are reasonably applicable to these novel institutions they should loyally be applied. . . . . In municipal law the principal can, e.g., revoke his authority at his own mere pleasure. Such is the rule. Could this be done in the case of South Africa when the Union government, if there is a principal at all, must be considered as joint principal together with all the high contracting parties?" He thus concludes that "Majestas or sovereignty in Southwest Africa resides neither in the principal allied and associated powers nor in the League of Nations nor in the British Empire but in the government of the Union of South Africa which has full power of administration and legislation (only limited in certain definite respects by the mandate) and does not recognize the sovereignty of any person or body in the territory."

Judge Wessels argued in similar manner, that though the term "mandate" implied that South Africa was an agent of the League or the Principal Allied and Associated Powers, yet as neither of the latter was a state capable of sovereignty this implication could not be made. "There is no question here of *respondeat superior*. Once having elected to hand over Southwest Africa to the Union of South Africa, the League of Nations as such has no right or power to dictate to the mandatory power what laws are to be established in Southwest Africa and how it has to be governed." The duty to respect the mandate he considered a "mere treaty obligation" which does not affect sovereignty.

In South Africa there thus seems to be a tendency greater than elsewhere for the legislature, the executive, and the courts to regard the mandated territory as under the mandatory's sovereignty, but neither legislative, executive, nor judicial authorities have been unanimously or even in a majority of that opinion, and there has been unusual recognition of the limitations imposed by the mandate.

In general, the British dominions have formally recognized in their legislation that their authority to administer the territories flows not from sovereignty but from their designation as mandatories and have enacted the mandate limitations as law applicable by their courts.

5. The Practice of France, Belgium, and Japan as Mandatories

France, which has three of the fourteen mandates, has exhibited considerable uniformity in the form of conferring governing authority in these areas. French law has never drawn such a sharp distinction as has British law between colonies within the national domain and protectorates outside of it. France has been more inclined than Britain to exercise full jurisdiction even over foreigners in protectorates.[97] Furthermore, the constitution recognizes a broad executive ordinance power on matters not covered by parliamentary legislation.[98] Since in fact the French Parliament has legislated very little in regard to colonies and foreign jurisdiction, the French executive is competent to legislate for the mandated areas by decree and is not obliged to motivate such decrees by reference to parliamentary legislation. The treaties and mandates themselves, when in effect at the time, have been cited as adequate legal bases for the decrees.

A number of such decrees, still in effect, were issued during the period of military occupation, and are unmotivated or cite merely the fact of occupation and sometimes the Hague Convention on Rules of Land Warfare as the basis of authority.

Thus the first decree authorizing French authority in Syria was issued on October 8, 1919, and that establishing civil government on November 23, 1920,[99] before ratification of the peace treaty with Turkey or confirmation of the mandate, but after the latter had been conferred on France by the Principal Allied Powers. Like all decrees relating to Syria, it was issued on the proposal of the minister of foreign affairs, thus according a certain recognition to the status of

[97] Hall, *Foreign Power*, pp. 207–8.

[98] Goodnow, *Comparative Administrative Law*, I, 85. This power flows from a broad construction of art. 3 of the French constitutional law of February 25, 1875, requiring the president of the republic to "look after and secure the execution" of the laws.

[99] *J.O.*, November 27, 1920, p. 19254.

Syria as a foreign state.[100] This decree declares that the representative of the republic in Syria shall be a high commissioner responsible to the ministry of foreign affairs. He is empowered to exercise the powers of the Republic in Syria and to "assure the execution of the mandate conferred on the French government." A decree of December 12, 1920,[101] creates a body of *conseillers-controlleurs* under the authority of the high commissioner to advise and supervise the native administration and "to assure the exercise of the mandate conferred on the French government in Syria and the Lebanon." Syrian legislation, apart from that promulgated by the native parliaments, has been in the form of *arrêté* issued under authority of the high commissioner. Such *arrêté* have in fact constituted the bulk of important legislation and usually recite the decrees of October 8, 1919, and November 23, 1920, and, since its confirmation, the relevant article of the mandate.[102]

Apparently the Syrian mandate enjoys such a legal status under these decrees that repugnant local legislation is void. Article 90 of the Lebanon constitution of 1926 provided: "The power established by the present constitution shall be exercised subject to the rights and duties of the mandatory power as they result from article 22 of the Covenant of the League of Nations and from the mandate." In explaining this to the Permanent Mandates Commission the accredited representative of France said: "It would be superfluous to restrict the rights of government of a mandated territory by special articles in a constitution, since nothing which exceeded the terms of the mandate could legally be done in that territory."[103]

Civil government was established in the French Cameroons on March 23, 1921, before confirmation of the mandate by a decree based on a report of the minister of colonies which read:

[100] Great Britain governs even her A mandates through the colonial office.

[101] *J.O.*, 1920, p. 20815.

[102] *Republique française, Haut Commissariat en Syrie et au Liban, Recueil des actes administratifs du Haut-Commissariat de la Republique française en Syrie et au Liban, 1919–1924* (Beirut, 1925). The most important *arrêté* are published in the annual reports of France to the League of Nations.

[103] *P.M.C., Min.*, XI, 143. France refused to accept several articles of the proposed Syrian constitution in August, 1928, on the ground of conflict with the mandate (*F.P.A., Inf. Ser.*, V [May 1, 1929], 74).

As the conditions of the mandate of the League of Nations under which these territories must be administered by France conformably to articles 22 and 119 of the treaty of Versailles of June 28, 1919, will be fixed only by later decisions, it seems to me convenient, in the interests, indeed of the indigenous populations, not to delay the advantage of a more precise determination of the powers of our representatives.

The decree itself recited earlier decrees establishing military occupation, and established the Cameroons as a "special territory" under the authority of a commissar of the republic, with a council of administration to assist him. "The territory enjoys administrative and financial autonomy" and "possesses a budget of its own supplied by receipts of every kind taken in the territory." "Commercial equality is assured in the Cameroons under the conditions provided by article 22 of the treaty of June 28, 1919."[104]

French Togoland was also organized by a decree of March 23, 1921, identic with that of the Cameroons except for the omission of the article dealing with commercial equality.[105] Decrees for both these territories since confirmation of the mandates have recited "the mandate confirmed to France by the council of the League of Nations in execution of articles 22 and 119 of the treaty of Versailles of June 28, 1919."[106] The decrees of May 22, 1924, and May 5, 1926, which rendered applicable in these territories the laws and decrees of adjacent African territories of France promulgated before January 1, 1924, expressly excepted provisions "contrary to the decrees made specially for the Cameroons (or Togoland) and to the French mandate in the Cameroons (or Togoland) of July 20, 1922."[107] Under the authority of these decrees the local commissars have issued numerous *arrêté*.[108]

In view of the general immunity of the French administration

[104] *J.O.*, March 25, 1921, p. 3722.

[105] *Ibid.*, p. 3723. See also Rouard de Card, *Les Mandats français sur le Togoland et le Cameroun* (Paris, 1924), p. 63, who makes no mention of the difference between the decrees but assumes that commercial equality is provided in both.

[106] *J.O.*, February 26, 1925, pp. 2058–59.

[107] *Recueil général de jurisprudence, de doctrine et de legislation coloniales et maritime. La tribune des colonies et des protectorats* (D. Penant, *directeur*) (Paris, 1924), III, 201; *ibid.* (1926), III, 218.

[108] These are regularly published in the French annual reports to the League of Nations.

from the ordinary courts the duty of annuling *ultra vires* ordinances normally rests in France with the administration itself or the administrative courts. The highest administrative court, the Conseil d' Etat, has a broad competence to annul such ordinances on the initiative of interested individuals.[109] In fact, criticism of the terms of ordinances by the Mandates Commission or the League Council have usually resulted in prompt remedy. Thus the term *domaine de l'état* used in some of the early decrees and ordinances seemed objectionable to the Mandates Commission because it implied something other than public lands of the mandated territory, and this was changed to *domaine du territoire du Togo* by decree of March 13, 1926.[110] So also when the Commission pointed out that the terms of certain customs regulations of the adjacent territories in customs union with the mandated areas implied a preference, changes were promptly made.[111]

In addition to such administrative remedies local courts may refuse to enforce in criminal prosecutions *arrêté* issued by the French commissars in the mandated territories on the ground of excess of power, or conflict with superior legislation.[112] Thus in 1923 the court of first instance of Douala, Cameroons, refused to apply to a resident

[109] A civil action can be maintained against an officer who "raises the conflict" only if the tribunal of conflicts decides that his act is a personal fault clearly beyond his competence (*Affaire Peletier*, Arrêt 26 [Juillet, 1873]; Goodnow, *op. cit.*, II, 174). Actions, however, lie against the state itself, occasionally in the civil courts (Goodnow, II, 161–62), but ordinarily by the *contentieux administratif* in the administrative courts for administrative acts of non-political character and of special application, which directly violate the rights of an individual (*ibid.*, pp. 226–29). The courts may refuse to proceed in a criminal prosecution if they find the ordinance creating the liability was *ultra vires* (*ibid.*, p. 178), but the most important means for testing the validity of administrative ordinances is by the very inexpensive action before the highest administrative court, the Council of State, open to all individuals whose interests (not necessarily rights) are affected, for annulment of acts in excess of power or in violation of law (*Affaire Lesbats*, *Arrêts du Conseil d'Etat*, February 25, 1864, June 7, 1865; Lois, May 24, 1872). This applies to all administrative acts whether of specific or general application provided they are of non-political character. Acts of Parliament may not be tested by this process but non-political decrees of the president of the republic may (Goodnow, *op. cit.*, II, 229–36).

[110] *P.M.C.*, *Rep.*, IV, *O.J.*, V (1924), 1404, 1407–8; Min., IV, 157, 166; Min., VI, 173; Min., XI, 202.

[111] *P.M.C.*, Min. III, 314; Rep., IV, *O.J.*, V (1924), 1407–8.

[112] See *supra*, n. 109.

European an *arrêté* imposing heavy penalties on the sale of liquor to the indigenes on the ground that by a decree of 1877 administrative authorities cannot apply more severe penalties than those provided by the general law without express approval of the authorities in Paris.[113]

Under French practice the courts may consider treaties of non-political character as direct sources of law, but ordinarily they regard such instruments as political in character and look to the laws and decrees of the political departments for authority to apply them.[114] The French Parliament has not expressly provided for the application of the mandate texts as fundamental law in the areas, but in view of the express recital of the mandates in the decrees since their confirmation and the recognition of the obligatory character of these instruments in the decrees of 1924 and 1926 relating to the African mandates, it would appear that local courts may refuse to enforce penalties provided by *arrêté* conflicting with the mandate texts and that the Council of State on appeal by an interested person may annul any *arrêté* conflicting with such texts and not regarded as of a political character.

The Belgian system of conferring authority resembles the French, though the basic legislation for the mandated territory has been in the form of a law passed by the Belgian Parliament rather than that of executive decree. The law of August 21, 1925, giving final organization to Ruanda-Urundi, was vigorously assailed by the German press on the ground that it amounted to a complete incorporation of the territory with the Belgian Congo and of its inhabitants with the natives of the latter. The German government protested to the League, and the Mandates Commission found that certain expressions in article 1 and 5 of the law might give rise to "unfortunate interpretations." These articles provided:

ARTICLE 1.—The territory of Ruanda-Urundi shall be united for purposes of administration with the colony of the Belgian Congo, of which it shall form a Vice Governor-General's province. It shall be subject to the laws of the Belgian Congo, except as hereinafter provided.

ART. 5.—The rights conferred on the Congolese by the laws of the Belgian

[113] *Recueil général, Penant*, XXXIV, Part I (1924), 291; *ibid.*, XXXVI, Part II (1926), 1.

[114] Wright, "The Legal Nature of Treaties," *A.J.I.L.*, X (1916), 714–15.

Congo shall apply subject to the distinctions specified in the said laws to the nationals of Ruanda-Urundi.

The Belgian accredited representative insisted that these articles did not amount to annexation of the territory or naturalization of its inhabitants and were in accord with the mandate which permitted the mandatory "to administer the territory in accordance with its laws as integral parts of its territory and subject to the preceding provisions."[115]

This law[116] contained no preamble, though it declared "Ruanda-Urundi a distinct juridical personality" with "its own patrimony" (art. 2). It requires special laws for recruiting natives and specifies that the indigenes can be enlisted only for "local police and the defense of their territory" (art. 4). There is also an express provision that "the provisions of Congolese law contrary to the stipulations of the mandate and the agreement approved by the law of October 20, 1924" do not apply to Ruanda-Urundi.

Prior to this law the authority of the Belgian Royal Commissaire was exercised under the *arrêté-loi* of December 5, 1916, providing for military occupation and the *arrêté royal* of July 16, 1922, providing civil government. Both of these are recited in the many *ordinance-loi* issued by the Royal Commissaire. Under the present law it seems clear that the courts can refuse to apply local ordinances or even decrees of the central government if considered contrary to the mandate.

Japan created an organ known as the South Seas Bureau to govern her seven hundred small mandated islands by an imperial ordinance of March 30, 1922.[117] It is not the Japanese custom to recite in a preamble the authority under which laws and ordinances are issued, and neither this nor any subsequent imperial ordinance, law, or South Seas Bureau order contains any preamble nor any mention of the text of the mandate nor of the limitations it imposes.[118]

[115] *P.M.C., Min.*, VII, 53, 55, 215.

[116] *Rapport presenté par le gouvernment belge au Conseil de la Société des Nations au sujet de l'administration du Ruanda-Urundi pendant l'année* (1925), p. 111.

[117] *Annual Report to the League of Nations on the Administration of the South Sea Islands under Japanese Mandate* (1925), p. 129.

[118] All of the important laws, ordinances, and orders to date are printed in the 1925 *Report*.

The director of the South Seas Bureau, who resides at Koral, one of the Pelew islands in the West Caroline group, is authorized to issue ordinances, but for those with penal sanctions of over one year's imprisonment or two hundred *yen* fine he must get the sanction of the prime minister unless there is an emergency (arts. 4, 5). In practice important matters are often dealt with by imperial ordinances. The South Seas Bureau is also authorized to establish branch offices whose chiefs may issue ordinances subject, however, to suspension or cancellation by the director if "at variance with fixed regulations, or injurious to the public benefit or in excess of its authority" (art. 8). The director may summon the assistance of senior naval commanders in the neighborhood "when he consider it necessary for the preservation of peace and good order within his jurisdiction" (art. 6).

Ordinances have provided for judicial administration in the islands with courts or first instance and appeal.[119] Japanese laws are in general applicable, but "civil cases in which natives of the islands alone are concerned are dealt with in accord with precedents and usages," unless to do so would be contrary to "public order and good customs" (art. 2). Provision was made for protecting native land rights during the military occupation by an ordinance of January 20, 1916, forbidding native land transfers except to the administration.[120] The judicial ordinance of January 26, 1923, provided that land rights should be dealt with for the time being in accordance with precedents and usage,[121] but a South Seas Bureau order of October 25, 1925, authorized a land survey and registration.[122] Prior to the last act the suggestion was made in the Permanent Mandates Commission that the land law was inadequate to protect native rights and contrasted unfavorably with the situation under Germany before the war.[123] The Commission has definitely criticized the financial regulations as failing adequately to separate the finances of the mandated territory from those of Japan.[124]

Observance of this mandate appears to be in the hands of the

[119] Imperial Ordinance No. 26, January 26, 1923 (*Annual Report* [1925], p. 304).

[120] Civil Administration Station Order No. 3, January 20, 1916 (*ibid.*, p. 346).

[121] *Ibid.*, p. 305. [122] *Ibid.*, p. 347. [123] *P.M.C., Min.*, V, 44.

[124] *Ibid.*, V, 47, 195. See *supra*, chap. vii, n. 67.

administration rather than the judiciary. The director of the South Seas Bureau, like the governor-general of Korea and Formosa, is under the control of the prime minister through the intermediary of the colonial department of Japan, and in turn controls his own subordinates.[125] Through this administrative control the laws and imperial ordinances are doubtless assured superior validity to local ordinances but it does not appear that the courts can set aside ordinances of any kind on grounds of conflict with the mandate.

We conclude that in applying the system the mandatories have in general given full recognition to the mandatory régime and have taken care to preserve it from inadvertent encroachment. The Tanganyika order in council of 1926, the Belgian law of 1925, some of the South African legislation, and the Japanese ordinances, however, seem to give hardly sufficient recognition to the status of the territory in form and exhibit some points of possible repugnancy in substance. This legislation might thus be cited as evidence of mandatory sovereignty of the areas. The vigorous protests made by the Commission, and in most cases accepted by the Council and the mandatory, would seem sufficient to prevent such a claim developing.

[125] *Ibid.*, X, 37–38.

CHAPTER XIII

THE PRACTICE OF INTERNATIONAL INSTITUTIONS

Public international institutions are often obliged to interpret the rights and duties of their members as well as their own competence. Such practice will undoubtedly create customary international law if acquiesced in for a sufficient period of time. The League of Nations is the international institution of most importance with reference to the mandates system, and certain writers have attributed an immediate juridical significance to its formal resolutions. Thus Fauchille writes:

> The League of Nations created by the covenant of April 28, 1919, constitutes a juridical person, invested with its own juridical authority distinct from that of the governments which are parties to it. Its organs, the council and the assembly, can vote resolutions capable of producing juridical effects by themselves, without the need of ratification by the governments of the League members. In this it differs from congresses and conferences, the decisions of which must be ratified in order to become obligatory as conventions. The resolutions of the League of Nations are juridical acts creative of international obligations: they constitute thus a particular source of positive international law. This follows from the provisions of the covenant itself. There are, at the same time, certain matters on which by exception the League has only the rôle of facilitating the conclusion of agreements between the members as would a congress or conference (art. 23 of the covenant).[1]

This goes rather far. The text of the Covenant and the practice under it suggests that what is here stated as an exception is the rule. While all League practice may contribute to the growth of customary international law, it would seem that it can have legislative effect only where the Covenant or other treaties expressly so declare, and then only with respect to the parties to such treaties. There appear to be comparatively few matters on which it has been given this competence, but the mandates question is one of them.[2] Since the Covenant expressly authorizes the Council "explicitly to define" for

[1] Fauchille, *Traité de droit international public* (Paris, 1922), I, Part I, 48.

[2] See Wright, *Control of American Foreign Relations*, p. 114, and *supra*, chap. xi, n. 52a.

each area "the degree of authority control or administration to be exercised by the mandatory if not previously agreed upon by the members of the league," it would appear that Council resolutions making such definitions are law on the subject, at least for the League members.[3] While formal opinions of the Permanent Mandates Commission and resolutions of the Assembly do not have this status they are of considerable weight in developing a practical interpretation of the system. Decisions of the Permanent Court of International Justice are undoubtedly law with respect to any controversy within its jurisdiction, and the mandatories have accepted this jurisdiction for disputes with members of the League in respect to the interpretation and application of the mandates after diplomacy has failed to settle them. Furthermore, in spite of article 59 of the court statute, which confines the legal effect of a decision to the immediate controversy, such decisions have had and will continue to have great importance as precedents.[4]

Attention has been given in the second part of this book to the activity of League organs in formulating a policy in regard to the mandates system and in supervising its administration. Here attention will be devoted to their conclusions on the law protecting interests (1) of the League, (2) of the mandatories, (3) of the mandated peoples, and (4) of the third states. The system is designed primarily in the interests of the mandated peoples and third states, thus the documents and the League organs have been mainly concerned with defining their rights and the corresponding duties of the mandatories. This has led some writers to define the law in terms of the duties of the mandatories respectively toward the League, toward third states, and toward the mandated peoples.[5] The League and the

[3] Art. 22, par. 8. Statement by Sir Frederick Lugard, *P.M.C., Min.*, VII, 38. In fact, the Council usually gets express consent of the mandatories before passing a formal resolution on a point of law (see *supra*, chap. viii, sec. 1).

[4] On the competence of these organs see chap. v *supra*.

[5] Van Rees, *Les Mandats internationaux*, I, 23–24. Stoyanovsky (*La Théorie générale des mandats internationaux*) follows much the same classification though he groups the duties of the mandatory to the League and to third states as two classes of obligations among those resulting from the "mandate" and designates the duties of the mandatory to the inhabitants of the area as obligations resulting from the "tutelage." Both of these writers classify non-militarization of the areas as duties owed to third states, and Van Rees but not Stoyanovsky thus classes freedom of conscience and reli-

mandatories do, however, enjoy some rights under the system involving duties on the part of others, and they enjoy many powers involving responsibilities on the part of others, consequently it is believed a more comprehensive treatment will result by considering in succession the rights belonging to each of these four interests. The term "rights" is here used in the broadest sense to include powers, privileges, and immunities as well as rights in the narrow sense, and the existence of corresponding duties, responsibilities, and disabilities in the person of incidence is understood.[6]

While the decisions reached on some of these questions bear on the problem of sovereignty in a negative sense, there has been no authoritative positive statement locating sovereignty of the areas. Implications may, however, be drawn from the interpretations thus far made.

1. Rights of the League

The League has certain rights strictly so called, under the mandates system, as, for instance, its right to receive annual reports from the mandatories and to be consulted on any proposed change in the mandate texts,[6a] but as its interest is to see that others enjoy the benefits accorded them by the system rather than to benefit itself directly its legal relation to the system is mainly defined in terms of powers with respect (*a*) to the tenure of the mandatories, (*b*) to the mandated areas, (*c*) to the mandate texts, and (*d*) to the mandatories' activities.

a) Appointment and dismissal of mandatories

There has been more or less academic discussion of the original power of the League with respect to the appointment of manda-

gion though the phraseology of art. 22 suggests that both are "safeguards in the interest of the indigenous population." Stoyanovsky elsewhere suggests that the freedom of conscience guaranty is primarily in the interests of the natives in A territories but in the interests of third states in the B and C territories (*Mandate for Palestine*, p. 249).

[6] For useful definitions of these terms see Salmond, *Jurisprudence* (London, 1902), pp. 231–37. See *supra*, chap. ix, n. 60.

[6a] These rights are specified in all the mandates. Some of the duties of the mandatories are doubtless owed to the League as well as to its members and to the inhabitants of the area (see *supra*, sec. 4), and certain of them, such as that to co-operate with the League in promoting health work, specified in the Iraq (art. 13), Palestine (art. 20), Syria (art. 13), and Tanganyika (art. 9) mandates seem to be owed primarily to the League.

tories. Germany early contended that the League had this power but practice and the Hymans report accepted by the Council decided it did not. The fact that the former sovereigns renounced the territories in favor of the Principal Allied (and Associated) Powers by the peace treaties was considered to give those powers the original authority to select the mandatories, an authority which they exercised during the Peace Conference.[7]

The Covenant provides that the mandatories must be "advanced nations who by reason of their resources, their experience or their geographical position can best undertake the responsibility and who are willing to accept it." There is no indication that the League on receiving notification from the Principal Powers selecting the mandatories made an investigation to discover whether they conformed to these conditions, although it would seem in principle that the League is as much obliged to scrutinize the qualifications of the mandatory as to scrutinize the terms of the draft mandate. The query has been raised whether the term "nations" qualified to become mandatories is to be taken in the sense of "states" under international law. Apparently not since some British dominions have been made mandatories.[8] It is also interesting to recall that at one time the Armenian mandate was offered by the Supreme Council of the Allied Powers to the League of Nations itself. The League Council recognized that the League could not conform to the description of "an advanced nation" and could not properly become a mandatory in its own behalf, consequently it declined the offer.[9]

The question has also been asked whether a mandatory need be a member of the League. In most cases in the Covenant the term "member of the League" has been used instead of such a word as "state" or "nation" which might exclude the British dominions. In this case, however, the phrase "advanced nation" is used, consequently there seems to be no theoretical reason why a non-member could not be a mandatory. The League Council in refusing to accept

[7] See Hymans report, adopted by the Council, August 8, 1920 (*Responsibilities of the League Arising out of Article 22*, p. 14), and Council note to the United States, March 1, 1921 (*O.J.*, II, No. 2, 143). A mandates were assigned at the San Remo conference which occurred before signature of the treaty of Sèvres with Turkey (see *supra*, chap. ii, sec. 3; chap. iv, sec. 3).

[8] See Stoyanovsky, *op. cit.*, pp. 55–58.

[9] *O.J.*, I, No. 3, 85–87; I, No. 8, 89 ff.

a mandate for Armenia itself expressed the hope that "a member of the League or some other power could be found," and the United States after rejecting the covenant was offered this mandate. Paragraph 5 of article 22, however, refers to the trade and commerce of *other* members of the League," the submission article in all the Mandatories refers to disputes "between the mandatory and *another* member of the League," and the practical difficulties of supervising a non-member mandatory would certainly be almost insuperable.[10]

Whether the League can appoint a new mandatory in case one of the present mandatories should cease to function has not been determined. Nor has it been decided whether the League can dismiss a mandatory though both powers may be implied from the Covenant assertion that the mandatories act "on behalf of the League," and members of the Permanent Mandates Commission have assumed that they exist.[11] Furthermore, it would seem that the mandate of a given nation would automatically come to an end in case the mandatory ceased to meet the qualifications stated in the Covenant and that the League would be the competent authority to recognize such a fact.[12] Australia, however, has declared that the League has no power to dismiss a mandatory, and in reply to the question of her representative the Council's *rapporteur* said the decision with regard

[10] *Ibid.;* see also Stoyanovsky, *op. cit.*, p. 55.

[11] It has seldom been contended that the League could dismiss a mandatory as a matter of political or administrative discretion, but it has often been contended that it could do so as a quasi-judicial function after the mandatory had been found guilty of violating its duties under the mandate by the proper procedure. Sir Frederick Lugard wrote in a report to the Commission in 1923, "Theoretically the mandate may be revoked," and in 1924, "Wherever the power of revocation (in consequence of breach of contract by mal-administration) may exist, there can be no doubt that in this almost inconceivable contingency the international court of justice would be the agency employed" (*P.M.C., Min.*, III, 286; V, 177). In 1925 Mme Bugge Wicksell wrote to similar effect (*ibid.*, VI, 154) and M. Rappard, although admitting that the probability of revocation was remote, "did not think the Permanent Mandates Commission should refuse to admit the theoretical possibility of such revocation. To state that, however unworthy in theory a mandatory power might be, its misdeeds could never in any conceivable circumstance lead to revocation would be to weaken, before public opinion, that sentiment which gives its special value to the institution of which we are the recognized defenders" (*ibid.*, p. 157). See also *infra*, chap. xiv, sec. 2*b*.

[12] Stoyanovsky (*op. cit.*, p. 55) suggests that a mandatory which withdrew or was expelled from the League would automatically lose its mandate. If this is true the Council could dismiss a mandatory which had violated art. 22 or any other Covenant of the League by expelling it from the League under art. 16, par. 4, of the Covenant.

to the guaranty of loans in case of transfer of mandate carried no implication in regard to the way in which that might take place.[13] Since the areas subject to mandate are defined in article 22 of the Covenant it would seem that the League, whose competence is defined by the Covenant, could not withdraw a territory from the status of mandated territory unless through recognition that the conditions there defined no longer exist in the territory.[14] Its power to recognize such a fact is considered in the next paragraph.

b) DETERMINATION OF MANDATED AREAS

The Hymans report held that the League had no original authority to define the mandated areas. This was also to be done by the Principal Powers though the Council has subsequently recommended minor modifications.[15] The Covenant requires that these territories shall include all of and only those "which as a consequence of the late war have ceased to be under the sovereignty of the state which formerly governed them" and "which are inhabited by peoples not yet able to stand by themselves in the strenuous conditions of the modern world." In principle it would seem that the League should have scrutinized the areas submitted to them but it did not. In fact, some areas conforming to the description such as the Kionga triangle, the part of the Cameroons ceded by France to Germany in 1911, Cilicia, and Armenia were not submitted to mandate.[16] It does not appear that they were excluded by the second qualification regarding the characteristics of the inhabitants. The people of none of the areas are actually standing by themselves today. According to this provision, it would seem that when any of them are able so to stand the mandate should cease. Is the League competent to recognize this condition? It has been often so interpreted, and the Iraq Treaty seems to support this view. The League Assembly by admitting one of these communities to that body would under article I, paragraph 2, of the Covenant recognize its attainment of that qualification.[17]

13 L. of N., Council, Min., sess. XXIX, *O.J.*, V, 1076; sess. XXXV, *ibid.*, VI, 1364.

14 Lindley, *The Acquisition and Government of Backward Territories*, pp. 268–69.

15 See *supra*, chap. iv, secs. 4, 5.

16 See *supra*, chap. ii. The latter two were in fact reabsorbed by Turkey before peace was finally made with that power.

17 *O.J.*, III, 1506, 1509; *Monthly Summary*, III, 107; Lindley, *op. cit.*, pp. 268–69.

May the League extend the mandates system to new territory? It has been assumed that it may, provided the present sovereign of the territory consents.[18] Clearly the Covenant does not expressly apply the system to areas beyond those in the definition cited. The provisions in article 23 with regard to "fair and humane conditions of labor," "just treatment of natives," "arms trade," and "equitable treatment of commerce," however, would seem to permit the League to extend its functions in relation to the mandates system to areas "not yet able to stand by themselves" in case such action would promote these conditions. In such an emergency and with consent of the former sovereign it would probably be for the League to select the mandatory, define the area, and draft the mandate.

c) DRAFTING OF MANDATE TEXTS

Is the original power of drafting mandates vested in the League? Lord Robert Cecil and Germany early claimed that it was on the ground that the expression "members of the League" in article 22, paragraph 8, of the Covenant meant the Assembly, but the Council in accepting the Hymans report in 1920 definitely answered no. As to just who "the members of the League" were is not entirely clear though in practice the Principal Allied Powers have acted.[19]

It has also been decided that the League may not by itself amend the mandate texts, though its confirmation is necessary for amendments proposed by the mandatory in question as it is for the original texts. Furthermore, article 22 of the Covenant authorizes the Council to interpret and supplement the mandate texts so far as "not previously agreed upon by the members of the League."[20]

d) SUPERVISION OF MANDATORIES

The League's powers of supervision have given rise to problems in connection with reports, oral hearing of mandatories, petitions, and commissions of inquiry. These questions are mainly of a procedural nature and have been considered in Part II of this book. Only

[18] See *supra*, chap. iv, sec. 5. The official British commentary on the Covenant foresaw extension of the system to other areas (*G.B.*, *Parl. Pap.*, Misc. 3 [1919], Cmd. 151, p. 18).

[19] See *supra*, chap. iv, sec. 3.

[20] See *supra*, chap. iv, secs. 4, 5.

the important powers of the League in this regard will be considered here.

An annual report from the mandatories is required by the Covenant, but questions of the League's capacity to control its scope have been debated. The Council, after getting the opinion of the mandatories, refused to recommend a questionnaire presented by the Commission with its ninth report apparently on the ground that it called for details of administration beyond the scope of League supervision.[21]

The Council has provided for annual oral hearings by the Commission of an accredited representative from each mandatory, and the Commission has held that it is obliged to give opportunity for such hearing though the mandatory is not obliged to take advantage thereof. If it does not the Commission must advise on the basis of the written report alone.[22]

The Council decided in January, 1923, that the League may receive petitions in respect to mandated territories from the inhabitants if transmitted through the mandatory and from outside persons. The rules also permit the mandatory to submit comments on all petitions, and the Council has urged that this privilege be utilized in order to assist the Commission. At its sixth session the Commission agreed upon an interpretation, holding that petitions were only receivable if they alleged a violation of the mandate and if local remedies had been exhausted. The Commission has drafted regulations approved by the Council providing that petitions based on an alleged inconsistency of the terms of the mandate with those of the Covenant, anonymous petitions, and those repeating the allegations and information of earlier petitions be not received.[23]

May the League hear petitions orally? The Commission considered the question at its fourth, seventh, and eighth session and in its ninth report suggested such action, with considerable hesitation, but the Council, supported by a majority of the mandatories who had been especially consulted, refused to acquiesce. This seems to apply to the Commission only. Presumably the Council itself could, if it

[21] See *supra*, chap. vi, sec. 1.

[22] See *supra*, chap. vi, sec. 2.

[23] See *supra*, chap. vi, sec. 3. The procedure in respect to petitions is summarized in *P.M.C.*, *Min.*, XII, 176–78.

desired, hear petitioners. On September, 1925, the Council provided that answers to petitions be communicated to the petitioners and the mandatory. The Commission with approval of the Council has reserved discretion to recommend that the answer to petitioners go either direct or through the mandatory.[24]

The Council sent a commission of inquiry to the Mosul area in 1925 but this was in connection with the Anglo-Turkish boundary dispute submitted to it by treaty and at the request of the parties. Its power to send commissions for investigating conditions in mandate areas has not been decided. The Mandates Commission has frequently discussed the subject, and though doubting its own power to send such a commission has assumed that the Council had the power though no recommendation has been made.[25]

2. Rights of the Mandatories

A mandatory's major interest in the system like that of the League is to secure advantages to others rather than to itself, thus its legal relation to the system is also mainly defined by powers rather than by rights, strictly so called. The mandatories, however, do have certain rights, ancillary to efficient administration, as, for instance, the right to receive petitions from the areas before transmission to the League, the right to sit in the Council during discussion of their mandates, and the right to exclude direct relations of other states with the mandated peoples.[26] Their legal powers are more important and relate (*a*) to their assumption and continuance of the mandates, to their control of the mandated areas themselves, and to their government within those areas. As their powers over the areas and administrations are very extensive, it is often easiest to define them in terms of disabilities or exceptions from complete power. With respect to the areas themselves such disabilities exist with respect (*b*) to sovereignty, (*c*) to land titles, and (*d*) to territorial incumbrances. With respect to powers of administration (*e*) certain disabilities are specified in the mandate texts, and others

[24] *Ibid.* [25] See *supra*, chap. vi, sec. 4.

[26] Even in Iraq, where the mandatory's powers are the most limited, the native government cannot appoint foreign advisers or establish diplomatic missions without the mandatory's consent (Anglo-Iraq Treaty [October 10, 1922], arts. 2, 5).

exist generally, especially with respect to (*f*) direct profits and (*g*) expenses of administration. The mandatories are of course bound to exercise their powers in such a way as to meet their responsibilities and to perform their duties correlative to the powers and rights of the League, the mandated peoples, and third states.

a) ACCEPTANCE, RESIGNATION, TRANSFER, AND AMENDMENT OF MANDATES

The Covenant, by virtue of an amendment introduced after the first draft was published, makes it clear that nations are free to refuse a tendered mandate,[27] but can they resign after accepting? The question has arisen in connection with the provision in the Anglo-Iraq Treaty terminating the mandate in a period of years, but the Council in confirming this arrangement required that its consent to any agreement defining the future relations of the countries must be obtained at that time.[28] The Commission has also expressed the opinion in the cases of Nauru and Transjordan that a mandatory cannot transfer its responsibility without Council consent,[29] and in connection with the loan problem the Council on recommendation of the Commission declared that a mandate could not terminate or be transferred without its approval.[30] Each mandate requires, and the Council has insisted, that a mandatory cannot amend its mandate without the Council's consent.[31]

b) SOVEREIGNTY OF MANDATED AREAS

If a mandatory cannot resign, transfer, or amend its mandate, without the consent of an outside authority the question of its sovereignty of the area would seem to be answered in the negative. There is, however, even more specific evidence. The Hymans report

[27] The United States refused the mandate for Armenia and France that for Cilicia.

[28] Council resolution (September 27, 1924), art. 7 (Appendix II, 1), and discussion on British proposal to admit Iraq to the League in 1932. *P.M.C.*, XVI, 203; L. of N. Council, January 13, 1930, sess. LVIII, item 2553). The occasional suggestions in the Commission that the mandatory might resign (see Sir F. Lugard, *P.M.C.*, *Min.*, III, 286) probably contemplated a resignation with Council consent, and the Commission has formally accepted that interpretation (see *infra*, n. 30).

[29] *P.M.C.*, *Rep.*, II, 4; observations on the report relating to C mandates (1922), p. 4; *Min.*, XIII, 226.

[30] *Ibid.*, V, 176, 177; VI, 172.

[31] See *supra*, chap. iv, sec. 5.

accepted by the Council implies that the mandatory is not the sovereign of the territory.[32] Several reports written by members of the Commission have drawn deductions from the hypothesis of non-sovereignty;[33] the Commission with indorsement of the Council has recommended the modification of passages in laws, decrees, and treaties which might be interpreted as implying sovereign powers,[34] and courts, both national and international, have assumed that the mandatory is not sovereign.[34a] At its tenth session the Commission sharply denounced the apparent assumption of sovereignty over Southwest Africa by the union of South Africa implied in the preamble of its treaty with Portugal fixing the Angola boundary.[35] The Commission's position was acquiesced in, but because of certain declarations which had been made in the South African Parliament, the Commission felt obliged to revert to the matter in its eleventh ses-

[32] "I shall not enter into a controversy—though this would certainly be very interesting—as to where the sovereignty actually resides. We are face to face with a new institution. Legal erudition will decide as to the extent to which the older juridical notions can apply to the institution" (*Responsibilities of the League Arising out of Article 22*, p. 17).

[33] See especially M. Van Rees, memorandum on system of state lands (*P.M.C., Min.*, III, 216, 221, 222), who writes, "If these provisions of the covenant are examined as a whole, it will be seen that under the mandate system the mandatory state is merely the governor of a territory which does not belong to it. . . . . This supervision [by the League]—which affects the entire fabric and not merely certain given parts, of the administration of the mandatory, who in any case acts merely on behalf of the League of Nations—excludes any supposition that the sovereignty over the territory is vested in the mandatory." Sir Frederick Lugard said that the mandated territories were at an economic disadvantage because the mandatory's title was considered precarious and that this opinion existed "because theoretically the mandate may be revoked—or it may be resigned by the mandatory without serious loss or prestige, or the mandatory may prematurely consider the country ripe for self government" (*P.M.C., Min.*, III, 286). Ormsby-Gore as a member of the Permanent Mandates Commission said in the second session that "the ultimate sovereignty over the mandated territories must either belong to the Principal Allied and Associated Powers or to the League of Nations (*ibid.*, II, 24), and elsewhere he wrote, "One of the chief objects of the mandates is to prevent a mandated territory from becoming an annexed territory or protectorate or even a sphere of influence" (*The League of Nations Starts*, p. 112).

[34] See *supra*, chap. vii, sec. 3.

[34a] "The international obligations of the mandatory are not, *ipso facto*, international obligations of Palestine" (*P.C.I.J.* [Ser. A], No. 2, p. 23); "To hold that the crown having accepted the responsibility of governing Palestine as a mandatory has thereby acquired sovereignty is to hold a view for which no authority has been cited" (*Re Ezra Goralshvih* [Supreme Court of Palestine], *A.J.I.L.*, XX, 771).

[35] *P.M.C., Min.*, X, 182.

sion,[36] and at its meeting on September 8, 1927, the Council indorsed the Commission's position in accepting the report of M. van Blokland of the Netherlands, the *rapporteur*.

The commission considers that on one aspect of this question, namely, the legal relationship between the mandatory Power and the mandated territory, certain expressions used by the Government of the Union might lead to misunderstandings, and has therefore again brought the matter to the attention of the council. I appreciate the scrupulous care with which the mandates commission has continued its efforts to remove any doubts on a point of this importance.

It seems to me that, from all practical points of view, the situation is quite clear. The Covenant, as well as other articles of the treaty of Versailles, the mandates themselves, and the decisions already adopted by the Council on such points as the national status of the native inhabitants of mandated territories, the extension to mandated territories of international conventions which were applicable to the neighboring colonies of the mandatory powers, the question of loans and the investment of public and private capital in mandated territories, and that of State lands formerly belonging to the German Government, all have had their part in determining or in giving precision to the legal relationship between the mandatories and the territories under their mandate. This relationship, to my mind, is clearly a new one in international law, and for this reason the use of some of the time-honored terminology in the same way as previously is perhaps sometimes inappropriate to the new conditions.

Under these circumstances, the situation seems clear, except perhaps from the formal point of view.[37]

c) TITLE TO LAND

On this as on other occasions the League organs systematically refrained from attempting to locate sovereignty, but their opinion that the mandatory does not have it seems conclusive. From this assumption the Commission early drew the conclusion that the mandatory could not have any title to public or domain lands in mandated territory except in its capacity as mandatory, thus in case of transfer or termination of the mandate such lands would go with the territory. A formal recommendation to this effect at its fourth session was submitted to the mandatories, and with their consent formally adopted by the Council in June, 1926.[38]

[36] *Ibid.*, XI, 204–5.

[37] *O.J.*, VIII, 1120. South Africa acquiesced in this statement (*ibid.*, IX, 709 and L. of N. Council, sess. LVIII, item 2552). See also statement in the Council in March, 1926, by the French and the Italian representatives (*O.J.*, VII, 524, 526).

[38] P.M.C., Rep., IV, *O.J.*, V, 1404; Council, Min., sess. XL, *O.J.*, VII, 946. See also discussion (*P.M.C.*, *Min.*, II, 23, 74) and memorandum by M. Van Rees (*ibid.*, XII,

This principle clearly applied to public property of the former sovereign in the areas transferred to the mandatory by the treaties, but estates of ex-enemy subjects sequestered under provisions of the treaties were in a different category. If sold the proceeds belonged to the mandatory government not in its mandatory capacity but as an owner of private property, and were credited to reparations account, the land of course being wholly subject to the mandatory administration.[39] In some of the mandated areas, however, very extensive estates of this character had not been sold. They were either retained pending sale or permanently retained by the mandatory government, their value having been placed to reparation account. What was their status with reference to the mandatory's administration? The Commission first discussed the question at its third session, and at its seventh session decided that in neither case were they to be regarded as public domain of the mandatory in that capacity. They should be treated as private property subject to the usual taxation and enjoying no preference in respect to recruiting labor. Their maintenance and operation cost must be kept in a separate account to the benefit or loss of the mandatory government considered as a private entrepreneur and must impose no burden on the budget of the territory. At the request of the Commission the Council asked the mandatories for precise information to assure that these principles were being observed.[40]

---

216 ff.). Art. 257 of the Versailles Treaty, according to which Germany received no reparation credit for public property in mandated territories as she did in other ceded territories (art. 256), strengthened this conclusion.

[39] Art. 297 of the Versailles Treaty authorized the allied governments to liquidate and credit to reparations German property, rights, and interests in their territories including ceded territories, and Germany agreed to compensate her own nationals. By art. 121 the same provision applied to mandated territories (see interpretation by Sir Cecil Hurst, *L. of N., Council, Min.*, XI, 38). As a result of German representations during the peace negotiations, art. 438 provided for the transfer of German missionary properties in the mandated territories to boards of trustees of the faith of the mission, the allied and associated governments retaining control of the personnel of the mission (see German note, May 18, and allied reply, June 16, 1919, *Conditions of Peace with Germany* (U.S. 60th Cong.; 1st sess.), *Sen. Doc. 149*, pp. 74, 120).

[40] *P.M.C.*, *Min.*, III, 40; Memoranda by Sir F. Lugard, *ibid.*, p. 286, and VII, 159, 211. The replies received were summarized with a memorandum by Sir F. Lugard indicating that they were somewhat unsatisfactory in 1928 (*ibid.*, XII, 178–81).

d) INCUMBRANCES UPON THE TERRITORY

The right of the mandatory to mortgage mandated territory for loans has also been discussed. After investigation of the question by the Commission,[41] a recommendation was submitted to the mandatories some of whom gave answers based on extended analyses of the legal notion of mandates.[42] The Council recommitted the question to the Commission which recommended at its sixth session that the mandatory could contract loans in behalf of the territory and hypothecate its resources and that in case of transfer the territory or a new mandatory would remain obligated.[43] It was expected that this decision, which was formally accepted by the Council,[44] would encourage capital to aid in the economic development of the territories.

Though recognizing that loans or mortgages might burden the territory for purposes or under circumstances contrary to the principles of the mandate, the Council has not insisted on prior scrutiny of such transactions but has regarded primary responsibility as resting with the mandatory. Such a view is perhaps reasonable with regard to loans since the League can always hold that if improper the mandatory and not the territory is responsible. In the case of mortgages, however, the burden may not so easily be taken from the territory,[45] and the same is true of treaties.

The Council has recognized as a consequence of the mandatory's want of sovereignty that the latter's treaties do not automatically extend to mandated territory,[46] and it has insisted that treaties affecting the boundaries of the areas, which would necessarily amend the mandates, must receive its approval before ratification, though

[41] See recommendation of the Permanent Mandates Commission (*ibid.*, III, 311–12) and report by Sir F. Lugard (*ibid.*, V, 176–80).

[42] *O.J.*, V, 1076–80, 1224, 1596; VI, 495–601.

[43] *P.M.C.*, *Min.*, VI, 171–72; discussion (*ibid.*, pp. 52–54) and memoranda by M. Van Rees, Mme Bugge-Wicksell, and M. Rappard (*ibid.*, pp. 151–58).

[44] *O.J.*, VI, 510.

[45] Sir F. Lugard proposed a resolution prohibiting "the hypothecation of specific works or undertakings" for loans in mandated territory (*P.M.C.*, *Min.*, V, 178), but the majority of the Commission thought the probability of such a proceeding was remote and of its abuse even more so (*ibid.*, VI, 52–54, 152, 155, 158).

[46] *Report of P.M.C.*, *Min.*, III, 309–10, considered by Council, Min., sess. XXVII, *O.J.*, IV, 336, and *P.M.C.*, *Min.*, VI, 172; XI, 148. See also *infra*, n. 95.

on several occasions it has urged that such treaties be made in order to prevent the dismemberment of a tribe or for some other reason beneficial to the inhabitants.[47]

Most of the mandatories have made treaties with the United States admitting the latter to equality with League members in the benefits but not the burdens of the mandates. These treaties were made by the mandatories on their own responsibility without obtaining the Council's express consent before ratification, though in some cases they were concluded before the mandate had received Council confirmation.[48] The B mandates require the extension by the mandatory of general conventions applicable to their contiguous territories, and the Council has urged a similar extension of bilateral conventions without requiring its own prior consent though it has recognized that in the latter case there is danger that the principle of equal commercial opportunity for all members of the League may be impaired.[49] It thus appears that the mandatory may make treaties respecting or extend existing treaties to mandated territory without prior Council consent, and the responsibility for seeing that they do not violate the mandates rests primarily with it. Treaties modifying the boundary of a mandated territory are an exception to this rule, and possibly other treaties creating a real right such as a servitude or other permanent burden on the territory would be similarly regarded. However, all treaties, as well as mortgages and hypothecations, differ from legislation, administrative decrees, and ordinary loans in that they burden the territory in a way which cannot be easily modified by the unilateral act of the mandatory. Thus there would seem to be an argument for distinguishing between the two and insisting on prior Council scrutiny for all international incumbrances of the territory.[50]

e) POWERS OF ADMINISTRATION

The extent of the mandatory's governmental powers in the mandated territory varies with the terms of the particular mandate. The B and C mandates give the mandatory full powers of legislation and

[47] See *supra*, chap. iv, sec. 5.

[48] See *supra*, chap. ii, sec. 4.

[49] See *supra*, n. 46, and *infra*, sec. 3*h*.

[50] Wright, *Mich.L.R.*, May, 1925, pp. 746–47.

administration subject only to the express and implied limitations of the document. The C mandates and all of the B mandates but Tanganyika permit the mandatory to administer the territory as an integral part of its own territory. The Tanganyika mandate, however, as well as the other B mandates, permits the mandatory to "constitute the territory into a customs, fiscal and administrative union or federation with adjacent territories under his own sovereignty or control; provided always that the measures adopted to that end do not infringe the provisions of this mandate" (art. 10). The A mandates require the mandatory to establish local constitutions and to encourage self-government. The Palestine mandate, however, gives the mandatory full powers of legislation and administration as do the B and C mandates, and the Permanent Mandates Commission questioned the compatibility with this of the British agreement of February 20, 1928, with the emir of Transjordan intrusting him with the exercise of these powers in that area.[51] France has insisted that local constitutions cannot impair her authority to intervene at any time to enforce her mandate in Syria and the Lebanon.[52] In the case of Iraq, however, Great Britain seems to possess only such authority as is expressly given her by the Anglo-Iraq Treaty, accepted by the League as defining the mandate, and this is largely confined to advice to the native government.[53]

Article 127 of the treaty of Versailles and the texts of the A mandates authorize the mandatory to extend diplomatic protection to the inhabitants of the mandated territories. By express statement or implication from its legislative, administrative, and protective powers the mandatories have authority to represent the mandated territories diplomatically, and to conclude treaties in regard to them[54] though under the Anglo-Iraq Treaty (art. 5) the mandatory may permit the native government to establish its own foreign representatives.

[51] *P.M.C., Min.*, XIII, 226.

[52] *Ibid.*, XI, 143–44.

[53] The king of Iraq agrees to follow this advice "in all important matters affecting the international and financial obligations and interests of his Britannic Majesty for the whole period of this treaty" (art. 4).

[54] See *supra*, n. 48.

f) PROFITS OF ADMINISTRATION

It has been recognized that the conception of mandates in the Covenant requires that the mandatory receive no direct profit from its administration of the territory. Thus upon the German delegation's protest at the Peace Conference the Allies replied, "The mandatory powers in so far as they may be appointed trustees by the League of Nations will derive no benefit from such trusteeship."[55] The same principle has been emphasized by the Assembly and by the Council of the League.[56]

This principle, however, has not been held to forbid all economic discrimination in favor of the mandatory's nationals. Since such discrimination may be beneficial to the mandatory, the United States has contended that the open door is inherent in the conception of a mandate.[57] Nevertheless the Peace Conference negotiations, the text

[55] Allied note, June 16, 1919, *Conditions of Peace with Germany* (U.S. 66th Cong.; 1st sess.), *Sen. Doc. 149*, p. 119. This was thought to justify the denial of reparation credit to Germany for public property in the mandated areas.

[56] "The mandatory should not be allowed to make use of its position to increase its military strength . . . . or to use its power under the mandate to exploit for itself or its friends the natural resources of the mandated territory" (recommendations to the Council adopted by the first Assembly, December 18, 1920, with especial reference to A mandates). "It is essential that the accounts submitted should clearly show that the powers do not draw any pecuniary profit from their administration" (report of M. Branting, adopted by the Council, December 12, 1923, Min., sess. XXVII, *O.J.*, IV, 337, 389; see also *P.M.C., Min.*, III, 167).

[57] Nevertheless the United States seems to have recognized that the open door does not apply in full to C mandated areas by its treaty with Japan of 1921 (*U.S. Treaties, etc.*, III, 2723–28). This assures the United States and its nationals the privileges enjoyed by members of the League under the mandate, freedom of entry and prosecution of their calling to missionaries, and treatment equal to that of Japanese with respect to electrical communications in Yap. It also provides for the application of existing treaties with Japan to the islands, but the treaty of 1911 (*ibid.*, pp. 2712–18), while assuring to Americans national treatment in regard to entry and residence for commercial purposes, taxation, transit, shipping, and tonnage dues (arts. 1, 2, 6, 8, 9, 11), accords only most-favored-nation treatment with respect to commerce, navigation, and customs duties (arts. 4, 5). An exchange of notes at the time of the 1921 treaty assured to "the nationals and vessels of the United States" the "usual comity" on "visiting the harbors and waters of those islands," and by another exchange of notes the United States agreed to seek the extension to the mandated islands of the South Pacific of any commercial treaties it might make applicable to the mandatory dominions. All of these provisions together do not assure the open door in the sense of full equality of treatment between Americans and Japanese in respect to trade and investment in the islands.

of article 22, and the League's practice make it clear that the open door is not required in C mandated territories.[58] There is also some variation in the degree to which it is applicable to the A mandated areas. A distinction has in fact been drawn between direct profits to the mandatory government, which is prohibited, and advantage to its citizens, which is not in all cases.

The principle of gratuitous administration does, however, require independent accounting for the mandated areas, even for those financially incorporated with adjacent colonies. The Commission insisted in its third report on sufficient financial autonomy to make it clear that all revenues from the mandated territory are used for that territory's benefit, and this was indorsed by the Council.[59] The Commission has expressed some concern at the accumulation of reserve funds by some of the mandatory administrations through budgetary surpluses. Through depreciation in some cases the mandated area has in this way suffered considerable losses. The Commission has insisted that surpluses can be used only for the mandated territory,[60] and that the funds of the territory can be devoted to institutions or works only in case they "benefit the territory materially or morally."[60a]

Does the principle of gratuitous administration prohibit the mandatory from engaging in business for profit in the mandated area? Apparently not. The Commission has distinguished between the mandatory government in that capacity and in the capacity of a private entrepreneur. We have noted that the mandatory's right in the latter capacity to operate ex-enemy estates for profit was recognized provided in this activity it was subject to the general laws and control of the administration.[61] The same issue was raised in the case of Nauru. The main resource of this island is phosphates, the exploitation of which is conducted as a monopoly by a commission repre-

[58] See *supra*, chap. ii, sec. 2, and chap. iv, sec. 4.

[59] *P.M.C.*, *Min.*, III, 310; comments on financial administration under each of the areas examined in this report, especially British Togo and Cameroons, pp. 318, 319, and Council Min., sess. XXVII, *O.J.*, IV, 337, 389. See also *P.M.C.*, IX, 79 ff.

[60] See comment on French Togoland, *P.M.C.*, *Min.*, III, 38, 181, 316; XV, 292, and Buell, *The Native Problem in Africa*, II, 284 ff.

[60a] *P.M.C.*, *Min.*, XIII, 191.

[61] See *supra*, n. 39.

senting Great Britain, Australia, and New Zealand who are the mandatories. The Mandates Commission in its second report expressed concern as to the relations of the administration and the phosphate commissioners but were assured that the latter had the powers only of business management and were subject in labor and other matters to the control of the administration. As the open door is not required for C mandates the fact that this business was a monopoly could not be protested though the Commission "desired to know whether the establishment" by the mandatory governments of a "state organization enjoying the sole rights of development of the only natural resources of the area is fully in keeping with the disinterested spirit which should characterise the mission of a mandatory state." The mandatories replied that they had merely taken over an existing private monopoly and that in any case the production of the island was but a small proportion of the world's supply of phosphates.[62]

Somewhat similar was the case of the Bank of Syria established by the mandatory with a monopoly of note issue based on the French franc at a fixed ratio of twenty to the Syrian pound. The Permanent Mandates Commission found nothing directly contrary to the mandate in this arrangement but pointed out its two-fold disadvantage for the mandated territories.

> For the fluctuations of the French franc must necessarily produce unfortunate effects on the economic state of Syria and the Lebanon; and it may be asked whether the mandatory Power, by closely relating the Syrian pound with a currency foreign to the country, does not run the risk of impeding the development of its own policy, which, as we have seen, aims at preparing the mandated territories for the full exercise of their independence, a result which would be inconceivable without autonomy in financial and monetary matters.[63]

g) EXPENSES OF ADMINISTRATION

Although the mandatory is prohibited from making a profit, is it bound to shoulder losses? The question was discussed at length in

[62] *P.M.C., Rep.*, II, 4; observations on reports relating to the territories under C mandate (p. 3) and comments on these observations (p. 4). See also comments of Commission on profits of the commercial agency organized by Australia in New Guinea (*ibid.*, III, 167, 321).

[63] *Ibid.*, VIII, 205. The Commission approved the principle of financial independence for mandated territories generally in 1921 (*ibid.*, I, 23; Stoyanovsky, *Mandate for Palestine*, p. 219).

the Commission during its eleventh session in connection with a report by M. Van Rees on the financial obligations of the mandated territories to the mandatory powers. While recognizing that expenses incurred by the mandatory owing to war should not burden the territory, the Commission seemed to agree that advances granted by the mandatory for administrative needs during the period of military occupation might justifiably be charged to the mandated territories. From this M. Van Rees was convinced that

> neither the responsibilities [undertaken by the mandatory to advance the territory and its inhabitants] nor the fact that [it] was chosen—among other reasons—"by reason of its resources" nor the disinterestedness which it should display in administering the territory, should result in part of the normal expenses of administration being borne by the mandatory state. The mandate, although it should not be a source of profit, should not necessarily become a burden.

M. Van Rees, however, went further and expressed the opinion that grants or loans made by the mandatory which resulted in a development of the territory's resources creating a surplus should be repayable provided "the administration cannot be criticized on any point with regard to the way in which it has accomplished its duties."[64] Most of the members agreed with this though M. Rappard felt that if funds were originally contributed by the mandatory as grants without any indication that they were repayable the mandatory could not later demand payment. M. Van Rees pointed out that Belgium had already stated that it regarded all sums expended in Ruanda-Urundi as repayable, even those not at the time so described. Sir Frederick Lugard thought observations should be made by the Commission in case the interest rate was too high or in case the local population had protested a loan, and agreed with M. Rappard that the mandatories should state at the time whether the advance was a grant or a loan and stick to it. These suggestions met general ap-

[64] *P.M.C., Min.*, XI, 192. See also remarks of A. J. Balfour, *L. of N., Assembly, Rec.*, sess. I, Plenary Meetings, p. 721; Sir J. Cook, accredited representative of Australia, *P.M.C., Min.*, III, 167; and M. Orts, member of the Commission, *ibid.*, XII, 165. The Judicial Committee of the Privy Council has held that reimbursement is inherent in the idea of a "mandate" using the term in the broadest sense without specific reference to the mandates under the League of Nations (*In re Southern Rhodesia*, L.R. [1919], A.C. 244–45). The principle of financial independence (*supra*, n. 63) suggests reimbursement for advances and defense expenditures (see Palestine mandate, art. 17, par. 2), though in fact the latter have been largely borne by the mandatory.

proval, but M. Freire d'Andrade still felt it inadmissible to establish any definite principle at the present time. He pointed out:

> If there were a question of transferring the mandate, the mandatory power might have expended sums so large as to prevent that transfer. Again, the mandatory might have administered the territory badly or have spent considerable sums without consulting the population. In such a case, would the mandated territory be called upon to repay such expenditure as might have been incurred in consequence of maladministration?[65]

It would seem possible to distinguish loans which are really for local benefit from those which are not. Such a distinction, implied by M. Van Rees, has often been made in determining the burdens of transferred territory,[66] but the Commission decided to make no formal recommendation to the Council.

3. Rights of Mandated Peoples

The great majority of the provisions of the mandates are for the benefit of the inhabitants of the areas. Care for their interests may doubtless be implied from the terms "trusteeship" and "tutelage" of the Covenant. The Commission has discussed at length the meaning of the phrase "welfare and development" of the peoples of the area especially in reference to labor, land, health, and educational policy; the definition of "peoples" to whom the guaranties apply (whether all inhabitants of the area or only the "natives"); and the significance of the requirements of "local autonomy" and "agreement with native authorities" all of which occur in certain mandates, but it has concluded that such broad phrases were hardly susceptible of exact legal definition. Consequently these discussions throw light on the policy recommended by the Commission rather than on its interpretation of the duties of the mandatories for the benefit of the mandated peoples.[67]

There are, however, certain provisions of the Covenant and other documents which have admitted of more precise definition. Some of

[65] *P.M.C., Min.*, XI, 173–74.

[66] Griggs, Att. Gen., in Manilla Ry. Case, 23 op. 181, Moore, *Digest of International Law*, I, 396–406. See also A. N. Sack (*Les Effets des transformations des états sur leur dettes publiques et autres obligations financières* [Paris, 1927], pp. 76–78), who notes the practical difficulties of accurately making such allocations.

[67] See *supra*, chap. viii.

these define legal powers, as, for instance, the power of A mandated communities to express a preference for the mandatory, and the power of the inhabitants of mandated territories to petition the League. Collectively these powers constitute the status either (*a*) of the mandated communities or (*b*) of the individual inhabitants of the areas. (*c*) Other provisions are designed to guarantee certain benefits to the inhabitants, especially the native inhabitants, by imposing express duties upon the mandatories. Some of these duties seem to vest correlative rights primarily in the mandated peoples. While ordinarily rights under international law vest only in states,[68] it appears that the mandated peoples have a status, withdrawing them from the sovereignty of any state and giving them the opportunity to invoke the direct protection of the League, which makes it not inappropriate to speak of them as enjoying rights under international law correlative to the duties imposed by the mandates upon the mandatories for their benefit. Of such duties, those relating to (*d*) forced labor, (*e*) slavery, and (*f*) native land titles are most important. Other duties of the mandatory, though also, according to the Covenant, "in the interests of the indigenous population" undoubtedly interest third states as well. The most important of these deal with (*g*) liquor traffic, (*h*) extension of international conventions to the areas, (*i*) religious liberty, and (*j*) military exploitation.

a) STATUS OF THE NATIVE COMMUNITIES

While the League regards the mandated territories, their inhabitants, and their governments as under a special status in international law, it does not seem to have recognized any of the native communities as states with the exception of Iraq. The "right" of petition is a personal right of each inhabitant, and denies rather than implies the statehood of the community. Utilization by the mandatory of native councils, chiefs, or representative organs with a quasi-independence in internal administration has not been held to make

[68] Oppenheim, *International Law*, Vol. I, secs. 288–92; Holland, *Jurisprudence* (11th ed.), p. 388; Lindley, *op. cit.*, p. 327; Borchard, *Diplomatic Protection of Citizens Abroad*, sec. 9. A few writers think the individual is, or is tending to become, a subject of international law (see Westlake, *Chapters on the Principles of International Law* [1894], p. 2; W. Kauffmann, *Die Rechtskraft des internationalen Rechtes* [1899], pp. 3 ff.; Eagleton, *Responsibility of States in International Law*, pp. 220–29).

the native communities they represent states. The League has held that the mandatory is alone responsible for the internal order and the international relations of the territories and that it is competent to modify such local arrangements at discretion subject only to the terms of the mandate.

This has been held specifically, not only in regard to the native kingdoms of Ruanda and Urundi under B mandate,[69] but also with regard to the emirate of Transjordan and the republics of Lebanon and of Syria under A mandate.[70] This has been true in spite of the frequent reference to the A mandated territories as "states" in the treaties of Sèvres and Lausanne, of the "provisional recognition of these communities as independent nations" by the Covenant and of the "principal consideration" which the Covenant assured to their "wishes . . . . in the selection of the mandatory."[70a] In considering the agreement of February 20, 1928, by which Great Britain transferred the exercise of administration in Transjordan to the Emir Abdullah, the Permanent Mandates Commission questioned whether such an agreement could be effective without Council consent and whether it did not conflict with the mandate for Palestine which gave full powers of legislation and administration to the mandatory.[71] The British representative on the Council explained that Great Britain still regarded itself as responsible for the application of the mandate in Transjordan and the Council was satisfied. M. Paul

[69] *P.M.C., Min.*, II, 70; VII, 63; IX, 102; *supra*, chap. viii, sec. 3*d*.

[70] In Palestine west of the Jordan the mandatory has administered directly, nevertheless the postal agreement between Great Britain and Palestine of October, 1922, was registered in the League of Nations Secretariat (*L. of N.*, *Treaty Series*, XIII, 10–24).

[70a] Since the A mandated communities were not parties to the peace treaties they could not acquire rights from them. Thus the Permanent Mandates Commission has properly refused to consider petitions from the inhabitants of the areas based on an alleged incompatibility of the mandate with art. 22 (see *supra*, chap. vi, sec. 3). But although the Principal Powers owed no duty to the mandated communities to give weight to their wishes in selecting the mandatory, it does seem that in ratifying art. 22 they recognized the capacity of these communities to express a preference. See treaty of Sèvres, arts. 94, 123; treaty of Lausanne, art. 30, referring to the "state to which such territory is transferred." This evidently refers to the territory itself not the mandatory, though the same is not true of art. 257, par. 2, of the treaty of Versailles with reference to B and C territories (Stoyanovsky, *op. cit.*, p. 264).

[71] *P.M.C., Min.*, sess. XIII, pp. 42–45, 225–26.

Boncour thus explained the French position in Syria at the same session of the Council:

> We are agreed that the final aim was the emancipation of the peoples under administration when they have shown themselves capable of carrying out their own administration. We agree that subject to the reservations in connection with which Lord Cushendon has just given the council such an interesting basis for discussion, this final aim, which releases a mandatory from the mandate it has accepted, can only be attained in full agreement with the League. Thirdly, we recognize that, until this desire, which is the aim laid down in Article 22 of the Covenant, has been realized, the mandatory power has definite responsibilities toward the League, which, like all responsibilities, imply the powers by which they are assumed.[72]

Thus it appears that the statement in the Covenant that "certain communities formerly belonging to the Turkish Empire have reached a stage of development where their existence as independent nations can be provisionally recognized" has not been literally applied to the communities covered by the Palestine and Syrian mandates if the word "nation" is considered equivalent to "state." The statement has been construed to mean, not that these communities have been recognized as states "provisionally" but that they will be so recognized "ultimately." Possibly, in fact, the latter construction is justified by the Covenant's qualification of this provisional recognition as "subject to the rendering of administrative advice and assistance by a Mandatory until such time as they are able to stand alone."[73]

In the case of Iraq, however, there appears to be an exception because the mandate itself recognizes the British-Iraq Treaty of alliance as the operative instrument defining the mandate, and by this instrument Great Britain seems to have recognized Iraq as a state and to have permitted international representation and treaty-mak-

[72] *L. of N.*, *Monthly Summary*, VIII (October, 1928), 270. This was in reply to the statement in the Commission's thirteenth report that "while recognizing that the country must be prepared for that emancipation which is the aim of the mandate by a policy that will gradually accustom it to self government, the commission hopes that, until that moment has arrived, the mandatory power will retain such a measure of authority as will fully enable it to continue to direct and superintend this evolution, and to fulfill all its obligations to the League of Nations" (*P.M.C.*, *Min.*, XIII, 226, and remarks of Marquis Theodoli, *ibid.*, pp. 197–98). On Syria see also *ibid.*, XI, 143. See also F.P.A., *Inf. Ser.*, V, 74.

[73] Diena suggests that the phrase means in fact "a recognition of independence in a condition of suspense" (*Acad. D.I.*, V, 239).

ing by the native government under certain conditions. Nevertheless, the League holds Great Britain alone responsible for the enforcement of the mandate in Iraq. Iraq has not actually established diplomatic representation except at London,[73a] and the British proposal that a representative of the Iraq government appear before the Permanent Mandates Commission along with the British accredited representative was declined by Iraq.[74] Thus though Iraq is a state, it is a state whose international relations are conducted almost entirely by the mandatory.

But, it has been suggested, if the native communities have not been recognized as "states" the A communities, at least, have been recognized as "nations." According to this theory, the peace treaties and the League of Nations have given a legal meaning to the term "nation" which hitherto has had merely an ethnographic and political meaning. International law, according to this contention, which formerly began with states, now begins with nations and any fairly considerable population with a desire for autonomy may be recognized as of that status. Such recognition of nationhood implies a right of the community to further recognition as a state only when it has a level of culture and a capacity for government rendering it "able to stand alone." If those conditions are not fulfilled, recognition of nationhood entitles the community to special international protection, taking the form of minority protection in case the incapacity results from the geographic distribution or inadequate size of the community, or the form of mandate protection in case the incapacity results only from the social or political immaturity of the community.[75]

This theory renders the "provisional recognition as independent

[73a] *P.M.C., Min.*, X, 65. There were in 1926 consuls from France, Persia, Italy, Norway, Germany, and the United States in Iraq, and all except Persia and the United States had formal exequaturs accepted under the Iraq government's interpretation, that since these consuls exercised some diplomatic functions their formal application for an exequatur constituted an act of recognition. Though Persia and the United States had not recognized Iraq their consuls were permitted to remain and act informally. The treaties made by Iraq and the relation of Great Britain to such transactions are explained (*ibid.*, p. 66).

[74] *Ibid.*, VII, 94, 212; X, 54. See Q. Wright, "The Government of Iraq," *A.P.S.R.*, XX, 766.

[75] Stoyanovsky, *The Mandate for Palestine* (London, 1928), p. 53.

nations" of the A communities consistent with the practice, and particularly it renders the provision of a "national home" for the Jewish people in Palestine consistent with the mandates system on the assumption that the general recognition of the nationhood of this people by the Balfour declaration entitled them to the protection of the mandates system, for their "national home" which because of "historical connection" could only be in Palestine.[75a] Although it is not clear that the drafters of article 22 had clearly in mind the sharp distinction between state and nation drawn by this theory, some support may doubtless be found for it in the "national home" provision in the Palestine mandate and in a resolution of the second Assembly calling for a "national home" for the Armenians entirely independent of Turkish rule.[76]

b) STATUS OF THE INHABITANTS

If mandated areas are not under the sovereignty of the mandatory and are not states, what is the status of the inhabitants individually? The question was considered by some of the prospective mandatories even before the mandates were confirmed[77] and the Commission raised the problem in its first report.[78] The chairman of the Commission was instructed by the Council to form a subcommittee to get the view of the mandatories.[79] This was done, and on request of the Council the Commission framed a recommendation at its second session, holding that the native inhabitants of B and C mandated territories were not nationals of the mandatory though they might be naturalized individually. They were to be regarded as nationals of the territory itself, and it was desirable that they be designated by some form of descriptive title which would specify their status under the mandate.[80] After an extensive debate in the Coun-

[75a] *Ibid.*, pp. 61 ff. and Bentwich, *B.Y.B.I.L.*, 1929, p. 138.

[76] *L. of N., Assembly, Rec.*, II, Plenary Meetings, p. 299.

[77] Opinions of Sir John Salmond of New Zealand, May 11, 1920 (*P.M.C., Min.*, II, 67–68) and of General Smuts of South Africa, September 18, 1920 (*ibid.*, p. 92).

[78] *Ibid.*, I, 41; Rep., I. *O.J.*, II, 1126. See also *infra*, chap. xiv, sec. 3*c*.

[79] *L. of N., Council, Min.*, XIV, 125.

[80] *P.M.C., Min.*, II, 16–19, 65–68, 73. See also *O.J.*, III, 524, 589–608. The action taken to give effect to these requirements was found fairly satisfactory by the commission at its fifteenth session. (*P.M.C.*, XII, 198; XV, 276, 289 and *infra*, chap. xiv, n. 105.

cil in April, 1923, this was adopted but with special permission to South Africa to naturalize the Germans in Southwest Africa *en masse* giving individuals an option to refuse.[81] Article 127 of the treaty of Versailles entitles native inhabitants of the former German territory to diplomatic protection by the mandatory when abroad.[82] M. Yanaghita in a memorandum presented during the third session of the Commission raised the question of what protection they were entitled to when in the colonial or home territory of the mandatory, but it seems not to have been answered directly.[83] While in the mandated territory itself they are entitled to petition the League according to the procedure established by the Council, and while this procedure has been designed with the primary object of supplying the Council with information it also assures the petitioner that grievances will receive careful consideration by the League and, if violation of the mandate is shown, such remedies as the League's supervisory powers afford.[84] The question of just who are the "inhabitants," "native inhabitants," and "indigenous population" of the areas has not been decided.[84a]

[81] *O.J.*, IV, 568–72, 603–4, 659. Though the League has given no formal opinion in respect to nationals of A territories, it has been held by the Supreme Court of Palestine that they are not nationals of the mandatory (*Re Ezra Goralshvi, A.J.I.L.*, XX, 771), and in fact their situation is further removed from that of mandatory nationals than is that of the B and C natives (Stoyanovsky, *op. cit.*, p. 261). *Infra*, chap. xiv, nn. 104, 105.

[82] *O.J.*, III, 594, 608; IV, 658; *P.M.C., Min.*, II, 19, 67; III, 310. States have often protected abroad persons who are not their nationals, as, for instance, inhabitants of protectorates (*P.M.C., Min.*, II, 69). The United States protected Cubans during the military occupation (*U.S. Foreign Relations* [1900], p. 864; Moore, *Digest of International Law*, III, 295–96; Borchard, *op. cit.*, pp. 463–78, 568–74). The treaty of Lausanne had no similar provision but the A mandates expressly "entitle" the mandatories to protect citizens of the mandated territories. In spite of this phraseology Stoyanovsky considers this protection a duty rather than a right of the mandatory (*op. cit.*, p. 276).

[83] *P.M.C., Min.*, III, 281; Stoyanovsky, *op. cit.*, p. 278.

[84] See *supra*, chap. vi, sec. 3; chap. vii, sec. 4.

[84a] See *supra*, chap. viii, sec. 3*a*. The procedure on petitions distinguishes between petitions from "inhabitants of the mandated territory" and from "other sources." In practice, the first category includes not only petitions from the "native inhabitants" residing in the territory, but from anyone else residing there. Thus the Commission has approved a memorandum written by M. Van Rees holding that the "*de facto* situation" of the petitioner rather than his "*de jure* situation" was decisive with respect to the procedure to be followed (*P.M.C., Min.*, XIII, 95, 214–16). Whether the *de facto* residence or the *de jure* domicile of nationals of the former sovereign of the territory at the

c) GUARANTIES FOR THE BENEFIT OF THE INHABITANTS

All of the mandates contain certain specific guaranties limiting the power of the mandatory in the interest of the inhabitants, though the precise terms vary among the mandates. The B and C mandates, applying provisions of the Covenant, require the mandatory to regulate slave, arms, and liquor trade, to limit military preparations, and to permit freedom of religion subject to the preservation of public order. These mandates even go beyond the Covenant in prohibiting forced labor, and the B mandates provide for the elimination of all forms of slavery, for the protection of native land titles, for strict regulations against usury, and for the application of general international conventions applicable to contiguous territories. The A mandates are less explicit though equal protection of all classes of native inhabitants and respect for their vested rights is, in general, required. Most of these guaranties have raised legal problems.

d) FORCED LABOR

"Forced labor" has proved a very difficult term to define. All of the B and C mandates prohibit "forced labor except for essential public works and services and then only for adequate remuneration," and the B mandates in addition require the mandatory "to protect the natives from abuse and measures of fraud and force by the careful supervision of labor contracts and the recruiting of labor." In its first report the Permanent Mandates Commission recognized "the obligation to work" as "the foundation of all civilized society,"[85] but members of the Commission have manifested considerable difference of opinion in memoranda submitted on the subject. M. Van Rees expressed the opinion that by the terms of the mandates natives could not be compelled to work at all except on public works and services and that then they must be remunerated, though he admitted that this standard could not be lived up to in practice.

---

time of transfer determines their acquisition of the status of "inhabitant of mandated territory," apart from special privileges of option has been extensively discussed in connection with art. 30, treaty of Lausanne (identical with art. 123, treaty of Sèvres). See Bentwich, *B.Y.B.I.L.* (1926), p. 97. Stoyanovsky, *op. cit.*, pp. 265 ff.

[85] *L. of N., Council, Min.*, XIV, 180; *O.J.*, II, 1126, 1127; see also *P.M.C., Min.*, I, 37, 43; *supra*, chap. viii, sec. 4*a*.

Mr. Grimshaw, on the other hand, preferred an interpretation which would confine the expression "forced labor" to work for an employer, i.e., for the benefit of someone other than the laborer himself. Thus compulsory local road-making, sanitation, education for which the worker himself benefits is not "forced labor" and need not be remunerated. M. d'Andrade based his opinion on the obligation to work, thus sanctioning vagrancy laws which practically force all natives to find work.[86] At the tenth session M. Van Rees and Mr. Grimshaw suggested in a joint report that whatever might be the words the intention of the mandates was that the conditions of labor should be the best existing at the time in any colonies. They proposed later to submit recommendations in this sense. M. Orts feared that this standard might be interpreted as a policy of overbidding by the Commission. What was intended was a generous application of the terms of the mandates.[87] The definition of forced labor has also been considered by the Temporary Commission on Slavery set up by the Council in 1924 and by the Committee on Native Labor set up by the governing body of the International Labor Office in 1927. Article 5 of the slavery convention of 1926 imposes limitations upon resort to force labor but does not define the term.[88]

e) SLAVERY

The clauses in the B and C mandates prohibiting slave trade and those in the B mandates providing "for the eventual emancipation of all slaves and for as speedy an elimination of domestic and other slavery as social conditions will allow" have not been defined by the

[86] *P.M.C., Min.*, VI, 18–20, and memoranda, VII, 154; X, 164–68.

[87] *Ibid.*, X, 119.

[88] *L. of N.*, *Treaty Series*, VI, 253. The text with a commentary is printed in *International Conciliation*, No. 236 (January, 1928), pp. 16–17. See also *supra*, chap. viii, sec. 4*a*. The work of the Labor Office Committee is discussed in a memorandum by Mr. Grimshaw from which he foresaw "the gradual conclusion of a series of international conventions which will, in time, amount to that native labour charter the necessity of which had been urged so frequently and so ably by some members of the Mandates Commission, and notably by M. Freire d'Andrade. It is impossible, however, in my opinion, to draft such a charter immediately as a single document comprising all aspects of native labour. It can only be approached in stages, and the Office, with the concurrence of the expert committee, has decided to concentrate at the outset upon the most urgent problems" (*P.M.C., Min.*, XII, 189).

Mandates Commission, but have been discussed by various League organs during the preparation of the slavery convention. This document, approved by the Assembly in 1926, defines slavery as "the status or condition of a person over whom any or all of the powers attaching to the right of ownership are exercised."[89]

f) NATIVE LAND TITLES

The B mandates require consideration for native law and custom and respect for native rights and interests in legislation on landholding and transfer; consent of public authority for transfers of land except between natives or creation of real rights over land in favor of non-natives; and strict regulations against usury. The application of these provisions has caused much discussion, but in regard to proper native land policy rather than in regard to the precise definition of native land titles.[90]

g) LIQUOR CONTROL

What regulation of the liquor traffic is required? The Council early had certain inconsistencies in the texts of the Covenant, the mandates, and certain international conventions drawn to its attention by private societies, and the *rapporteur* drew attention to this before confirmation of the mandates. He noted that opinions differed whether all alcoholic beverages must be prohibited in the territory, whether they must be prohibited only to "natives," or whether only dangerously intoxicating spirits need be prohibited. The Council passed a resolution in July, 1922, asking the Commission to investigate the matter.[91] Definitions which prohibited only "trade spirits," i.e., cheap distilled spirits, were recommended by the British Colonial Office, and the Council asked the opinion of the mandatories, receiving various answers from all after the fifth Assembly had urged action. In June, 1926, the Council resubmitted the matter to the Commission, which at its tenth session interpreted the phrase "shall exercise a strict control over . . . . the sale of spirituous li-

[89] See *supra*, n. 88.

[90] See *supra*, chap. viii, sec. 4*b*. For discussion of native land titles in British courts see *supra*, chap. xii, sec. 3. Certain cases in respect to the provisions of the Palestine mandate (art. 2) for "safeguarding the civil . . . . rights of all the inhabitants of Palestine, irrespective of race and religion," are there considered.

[91] *O.J.*, III, 793, 850.

quors" in B mandates to apply to all distilled beverages and fermented beverages with over 20 per cent alcohol. The C mandates provide that "the supply of intoxicating spirits and beverages to the natives shall be prohibited." This was held applicable to all beverages with over 3 per cent pure alcohol. This was referred by the Council to the mandatory powers on December 6, 1927, and after acceptance by all of them and another indorsement by the Assembly and the Commission was approved by the Council on March 4, 1929.[92]

At its third session the Commission recommended that in order to prevent smuggling, powers with colonies contiguous to mandated areas maintain uniform customs rates on liquor.[93] After resolutions by the Council and Assembly had requested the Commission to consider why liquor traffic was increasing in some of the B mandated areas,[93a] the Commission at its thirteenth session summarized its work to date on liquor traffic, recommended the submission by the mandatories of more complete statistical compilations on the subject, and also of information as to their application of the liquor-traffic provisions of the St. Germain convention of 1919 in the mandated areas.[93b] The latter prohibits the importation, distribution, sale, and possession of spirituous liquors in those regions of the Central African zone where their use had not been developed (art. 4, par. 2), and with respect to the signatories, which include all the mandatories, supersedes the liquor-traffic articles (90–95) of the Brussels Act of 1890.[93c] The bureau set up by the latter at Brussels was, however, continued and put under the control of the League by the treaty of St. Germain, and at its tenth session the Mandates Commission accepted the offer of this bureau for the annual trans-

[92] *P.M.C., Min.*, X, 181–82; XIII, 13, 213; XIV, 14, 269. See also discussion, *ibid.*, VII, 87–91, and memoranda, IV, 180; VII, 152 (Van Rees); and X, 175 (Lugard). For Council action, sessions XL and LIV, see Min., *O.J.*, VII, 867, 946, IX, 126 and (*Monthly Summary*, IX, 91). For resolution of Assembly session VIII and IX see *ibid.*, VII, 317; VIII, 294.

[93] *P.M.C., Min.*, III, 309.

[93a] *L. of N., Assembly, Monthly Summary*, VII, 317; Council, Min., sess. XLVIII, *O.J.*, IX, 126.

[93b] *P.M.C., Min.*, XIII, 224. See memoranda (*ibid.*, XII, 189–93; XIII, 89–93, 189) and summary of work on liquor traffic (*ibid.*, XIII, 208–14).

[93c] For texts of these conventions and comment on their operation see Buell, *op. cit.*, II, 932–34, 942–53.

mission of information.[94] Recommendations made by the Commission at its fourteenth session for increase and unification of customs duties and strengthening of the license systems were accepted by the Council in March, 1919.[94a]

h) EXTENSION OF INTERNATIONAL CONVENTIONS

The B mandates require the mandatory "to apply to the territory any general international conventions applicable to contiguous territories,"[94b] and many such conventions have been extended. The mandates for Syria (art. 12) and Palestine (art. 19) require the mandatory to adhere in behalf of the mandated area to such conventions on specified topics. The Commission has frequently urged the more rapid extension to the areas of labor and other conventions in the interests of the natives. Certain general conventions, such as that on air navigation (1919), have been expressly extended to mandated territory by assimilating such territory and its inhabitants to the domain and nationals of the mandatory (art. 40). In such cases third states might benefit more than the natives, although the provision was doubtless inserted in the mandates with the latter in view.[95]

Should the mandatory extend bilateral conventions in the interest of the area? The Commission recognized that neither such conventions nor multilateral conventions apply automatically, but recommended that they should be applied for the benefit of the area where not inconsistent with the open door or other provision of the mandate.[96] It was evident, however, that the mandatory was not

[94] *P.M.C., Min.*, VII, 209; X, 119, 179.

[94a] *Ibid.*, XIV, 269, and *Monthly Summary*, IX, 91.

[94b] Art. 9 of the Tanganyika mandate differs from the corresponding article on the subject in other B mandates and resembles the provision in the Palestine and Syrian mandates.

[95] M. Palacios wrote in 1925, "General treaties have always applied *ipso facto* and *de jure* to mandated territory" (*P.M.C., Min.*, VI, 170), nevertheless the Commission in its third report had requested the mandatories to inform it "as to which of these conventions applicable to their contiguous territories have been extended to the territories under their mandates," thus indicating that a special act of the mandatories was necessary (*ibid.*, III, 310). For British note explaining reason for not applying white-slave convention to certain B mandated territories see *O.J.*, V, 1081. The C mandates do not provide for extension of general conventions (see *P.M.C., Min.*, VII, 136).

[96] See *supra*, n. 46.

able to apply such treaties to mandated territory without consent of the other party to the treaty, and the other party might have no interest in giving its consent in the case of commercial conventions since if a member of the League or the United States, it would enjoy equality of treatment in the mandated area anyway. To rectify this inequality of bargaining power with which the mandatories were confronted the Commission's recommendation was addressed not only to the mandatories but "to all states whether members or not of the League." After getting the opinion of the mandatories, the Council indorsed this recommendation and it was approved by the sixth Assembly.[97] A number of such conventions have been extended though apparently the anticipated difficulties because of inequality of the mandatories' bargaining power have arisen. The French have protested to Liberia that Syrian traders have been discriminated against in the latter's territory, and on the Liberian delay in making a treaty on the subject the matter was discussed in the thirteenth and fourteenth sessions of the Permanent Mandates Commission. The Council in September, 1928, renewed its resolution of 1925 and attempted to promote agreement between Liberia and France.[98]

Apart from the difficulty of extending such treaties, doubt has been raised as to the applicability of their benefits to inhabitants of the mandated areas. The Supreme Court of Palestine held that although the Anglo-Italian extradition treaty had been extended to Palestine and contained an exemption in favor of nationals of the contracting parties, this could not extend to Palestinians as they were not British nationals. Since typical articles of commercial treaties usually benefit only nationals of the contracting parties this interpretation would seem to nullify in part the very object of extending such treaties to the mandated territories. Unless the terms of such articles were expressly modified to assimilate the mandated people to nationals of the mandatory, the treaty would operate only to the benefit of nationals of the other contracting party and such nationals of the mandatory as happened to reside in the mandated territory. No League organ has passed on the question, but it would

[97] *P.M.C., Min.*, III, 309–10; VI, 100, 169, 172; VII, 6–7; IX, 10; XI, 148.

[98] *Ibid.*, XIII, 169; XIV, 157, 219, 229; reports by Van Rees and Rappard (*ibid.*, pp. 236, 241). See also *ibid.*, XI, 149; XV, 289, and *L. of N., Monthly Summary*, VIII, 269.

seem reasonable to hold that, with respect to the benefits of treaties extended to mandated areas, the inhabitants of the areas should be assimilated to nationals of the mandatory.[99]

i) RELIGIOUS LIBERTY

The Permanent Mandates Commission has found itself obliged to interpret the article in all the mandates which guarantees inhabitants "complete freedom of conscience and the free exercise of all forms of worship, subject only to the maintenance of public order and morals," and requires the open door for the activity of missionaries, nationals of states members of the League, subject to the "control necessary for the maintenance of public order and good government."[100] A recommendation admitting the claims of order "as the first duty of the governor" and the "necessary condition for the full development of all freedom, not excepting freedom of religion," was passed by the Commission though it intimated that it should look upon segregation of missionary bodies into defined spheres of influence as an extreme measure. This was approved by the Council. One of the mandatories had drawn the Commission's attention to the difficulty of keeping the peace between rival missionary organizations.[101]

The Commission has often had to consider the problem of keeping peace between the various religious groups of Palestine. This mandate contains special provisions for the protection of holy places and maintenance of free access to and worship in them, and makes the mandatory "responsible solely to the League of Nations" in all matters connected therewith (art. 13). The mandatory is also required to constitute with approval of the League of Nations a commission to define rights in regard to holy places, but this commission has not yet been constituted (art. 14).[102] The provisions of this man-

[99] *Re Ezra Goralshvi* (1925) *A.J.I.L.*, XX, 772, and Stoyanovsky, *op. cit.*, pp. 287 ff.

[100] The article in A mandates on this subject is not limited to missionaries of League members. A proposal at the Peace Conference for a general provision in art. 23 of the Covenant on religious liberty was dropped (Miller, *The Drafting of the Covenant*, I, 269).

[101] *P.M.C.*, *Min.*, III, 311. German missionary establishments were given some protection by art. 438 of the Versailles Treaty (see *supra*, n. 39).

[102] The difficulties in regard to it were illustrated by the Council's discussion on confirmation of the mandate (see *supra*, chap. ii, n. 103).

date to facilitate the establishment of a Jewish national home in Palestine (arts. 2, 4, 6, 7, 11) and to permit the exclusion of Trans-jordan from their operation (art. 25) may also be mentioned as related to religious interests. There has been a great deal of discussion of these articles in the Commission and of their compatibility with the basic principle of the mandates system,[103] but neither the Commission nor the Council has attempted to define with greater precision the rights of the Jews under them. The mandatory, however, has issued a white paper defining the national home policy and has passed laws and rendered judicial decisions in respect to the matter.[104] The League has contented itself with carefully observing these efforts "to reconcile the two principles laid down in the mandate," and when legal problems have arisen as they did in the Kabbara lands petition in regard to the mandatories duty "on the one hand to facilitate close settlement of the Jews on the land, and, on the other hand, to respect in every way the rights of the native inhabitants of the country," it has preferred to let the local courts settle it.[105]

Somewhat related to the religious interest in A mandated areas is the archaeological interest, and all of these mandates contain a detailed statute with regard to excavations and antiquities and a provision assuring equality of treatment to nationals of League members in such matters. The Commission has discussed proposals of the Committee on Intellectual Co-operation and others for co-operative study of archaeological problems in these areas but has made no recommendation.[106] A list of permits granted and refused in Syria was requested of the mandatory in 1926.[107]

In agreeing to the French and British mandates in Syria and Palestine the United States has gained the right for its nationals by treaty "to establish and maintain educational, philanthropic and religious institutions in the mandated territory, to receive voluntary applicants and to teach in the English language," subject to the pro-

[103] See *supra*, chap. viii, sec. 3*a*.

[104] *G.B.*, *Parl. Pap.* (June 3, 1922), Cmd. 1700; Stoyanovsky, *The Mandate for Palestine*, Part I, and *supra*, chap. xii, sec. 3.

[105] *P.M.C.*, *Min.*, XI, 211–12.

[106] *Ibid.*, V, 126; VI, 54; VII, 117.

[107] *Ibid.*, IV, 33–34; V, 109, 187; VIII, 198.

visions of any local laws "for the maintenance of public order and public morals."[108] A similar provision appears in the American treaty with Japan with reference to the North Pacific islands.

j) MILITARY EXPLOITATION

The B and C mandates require a strict control of traffic in arms and ammunition, prohibit the establishment of military or naval bases or the erection of fortifications, and permit natives to be recruited only for police and the defense of territory. The French African mandates, however, add, "The troops thus raised may, in the event of general war, be utilized to repel attack or for defence of the territory outside that subject to the mandate."[109] The Council, in confirming the mandate, and the Commission have expressed doubt of the compatibility of this provision with the Covenant.[110] Several members of the Commission have written memoranda on the question with the conclusion that in C areas natives can only be used within the territory and that in B areas natives can be recruited only for police and defense, and ordinarily can be used only in the territory and for its defense. Opinions differed, however, as to whether the French mandates merely specified what was understood in the other B mandates, that in case of general war the troops already recruited could be used outside of the mandated territory but only for its defense, or whether they meant that these troops could in such an event be used by the mandatory at discretion. When this divergence developed during the ninth session, the Chairman noted the "delicacy" of the question, called attention to the statement of the Council's *rapporteur* when the mandates were confirmed, and said:

> The origin of this would be found in a declaration of M. Clemenceau during the negotiations in connection with the Treaty of Versailles. France had stated that she reserved the right to use troops raised in Togoland and the Cameroon for the defence of her frontiers on the Rhine, since, if she lost the Rhine, she would lose also the Cameroons and the Togoland.

[108] American missionaries would have enjoyed equal treatment under the mandate itself, though doubtless without the special treaty the United States would not have had a legal basis for demanding such treatment (see *supra*, n. 100).

[109] For discussion of this provision in the Peace Conference, see *supra* chap. ii, secs. 2, 3.

[110] See *supra*, chap. iv, secs. 3, 4.

M. Rappard then emphasized the practical uselessness of the discussion since in case of general war involving France any definition now made would be of little avail,

> accordingly it did not seem to him that it was useful again to raise these questions of interpretation which were of so delicate a character and of so dubious a utility. It was enough that it should be understood that the forces referred to in the second paragraph of article 3 of the mandate were only the troops raised for local police purposes and for the defence of the mandated territory.[111]

At the third session of the Commission the question was raised whether natives of a mandated territory could be voluntarily enlisted by the mandatory in case they applied outside the territory. The Commission thought this practice would be contrary to the spirit of the mandates, and all the mandatories whose opinion was asked by the Council agreed except South Africa, who said it was contrary to her policy to enlist native troops but she could not agree not to do so in her own territory. France accepted the principle with reservation of the exceptional paragraph in her mandates. The Council therefore formally indorsed the Commission's recommendation on June 6, 1926.[112] Though these requirements assure the natives against military exploitation in the interest of the mandatory, doubtless the interest of third states in the disarmament of the mandated areas was an even more important reason for their inclusion in the Covenant and the mandates. This is less true of the military provisions in A mandates. While the mandatories for Palestine (art. 17) and Syria (art. 2) are permitted to organize local military units only for police and defense of the territory, they are not forbidden to secure local financial assistance and transportation for their own forces in the territories. The Iraq treaty (art. 7) contemplates British assistance to Iraq military forces.

4. Rights of Third States

Third states, if members of the League of Nations, have two sorts of legal advantages in mandated territory which they do not enjoy in other foreign territory. They have power to invoke special international processes for protecting their interests and they also enjoy certain special rights expressly accorded them by the Cove-

[111] *P.M.C., Min.*, IX, 132; see also memoranda (*ibid.*, VII, 150–58; IX, 193–94).

[112] *Ibid.*, III, 311; IX, 9; see also memoranda (*ibid.*, IV, 179, 182).

nant and the mandates. These documents impose duties upon the mandatories, but they do not always make it clear to whom the duty is owed, i.e., who enjoys the correlative right.

The traditional theory has been that duties of states, even if for the benefit of individuals, are owed under international law not to the individuals but to other states. Ordinarily the state to which the duty is owed is the state of which the individual is a national, but if the individual benefited is a national of the state which owes the duty, as is true under various treaties protecting natives and minorities, the duty is owed to the other parties to the treaty.[113] Under the peculiar conditions of the mandatory system, the inhabitants of the territory, themselves, have a special status under international law which accords them rights against the mandatory, but this does not prevent the states, members of the League, from also having rights corresponding to all of the duties imposed upon the mandatories by the Covenant and the mandates.[114]

This conclusion is justified not only by the traditional view with respect to treaties for the protection of natives and minorities but by the theory back of such treaties as well as article 22 that all the contracting states have a real interest in the protection of backward peoples and minorities.[115] While the interest of League members in some of the mandate guaranties, such as those prohibiting forced labor, slavery, and disregard of native land titles, is mainly of a humanitarian character, their interest in others, such as those requiring religious toleration and demilitarization, may be definitely related to their own missionaries or their own national defense. Nevertheless, the Covenant (art. 22, par. 6) regards all these safeguards as "in the interests of the indigenous population," and they are included in all the B and C mandates, thus entitling the inhabitants of those territories to petition in regard to them.[116] Consequently they have been

[113] See *supra*, n. 68. [114] See *supra*, sec. 3*b;* chap. v, n. 71; chap. xi, n. 52a.

[115] See *supra*, chap. i. "The well being and development of such peoples form a sacred trust of civilization" (Covenant, art. 22, par. 1). "The Members of the League undertake to secure just treatment of the native inhabitants of territories under their control" (art. 23*a*). See also arts. 11, pars. 2 and 19.

[116] The Permanent Mandates Commission has ruled that petitions from the inhabitants alleging incompatibility of the mandate with art. 22 will not be received but petitions alleging violation of the mandate will, thus apparently recognizing that the inhabitants acquired rights only through the latter document (see *supra*, n. 70a).

treated in the preceding chapter as vesting rights primarily in the inhabitants of the areas. Thus, although they confer rights also on the members of the League, they need not be again considered here.

The only Covenant guaranty which has not been considered in this class is the requirement that the B mandatories "secure equal opportunities for the trade and commerce of other members of the league" (art. 22, par. 5). While in fact the interests of the native may be profoundly affected by the presence or absence of the open door,[117] the Peace Conference found it politically necessary to exclude this guaranty from the C territories and deemed such a course more reasonable if the native interest in the matter were not admitted.[118] Thus the mandatories' duties in pursuance of this requirement have been considered peculiarly in the interest of League members.

In addition to these (*a*) procedural powers and (*b*) economic rights enjoyed by League members, all states have the usual rights with respect to their own interests and those of their nationals enjoyed under general international law in all foreign territory. Such rights always give rise to problems upon a change of sovereignty, and in view of the complexity of the mandates system, there has been discussion over certain rights of third states in the areas under (*c*) general international law and (*d*) applicable treaties. States not members of the League have not always been content with recognition merely of these rights, but have claimed on various grounds some of the powers and rights accorded by the documents only to members of the League. Certain claims of this character advanced (*e*) by the United States, a participant in the war on the allied side, and (*f*) by Germany and Turkey, parties to the treaties ceding the territory, have been considered by League organs.

a) INVOCATION OF INTERNATIONAL PROCESSES

Since the mandates system is an institution of international law and not of national sovereignty, third states are entitled to invoke appropriate international processes for the protection of their interests and the enforcement of their rights with respect to it, and the mandatory cannot regard any such question as a "domestic ques-

[117] *P.M.C., Min.*, I, 47, and *supra*, chap. viii, sec. 5, and chap. xiii, sec. 2*f*.

[118] See *supra*, chap. ii, secs. 1, 2.

tion" exempt from international jurisdiction. While states outside the League can resort only to diplomatic negotiations as has the United States, or to such conciliatory or arbitral processes as their treaties may provide, states in the League can raise all phases of mandatory administration in the League Council or Assembly.[119] They have done so freely, and on one occasion the French representative remarked that since his country did not have sovereignty of Syria "no susceptibilities could be prejudiced" by the close scrutiny to which its administration had been subjected.[120]

The members of the League are also entitled to invoke the jurisdiction of the Permanent Court of International Justice for any dispute with the mandatory involving the interpretation or application of the mandate which diplomacy has failed to settle.[121] Thus League members have a better opportunity to protect their interests and secure their rights in mandated territory than they would in the domain of another state. Furthermore, opportunities to utilize these powers are likely to rise more frequently than in similarly situated foreign territory because League members have rights in the mandated territories not only for the protection of their national interests, and the interests of their nationals, but also for the protection of the interests of the inhabitants of the area.[122]

Every member of the League can regard its rights as infringed by every violation by the mandatory of its duties under the mandate, even those primarily for the benefit of natives, and can make representations which if not effective will precipitate a dispute referable to the Permanent Court of International Justice if negotiation fails to settle it. The additional paragraph in the submission article of the Tanganyika mandate may seem to cast doubt on this conclusion.

[119] Domestic questions are excluded from the competence of the League by art. 15, par. 8 (except in so far as a threat of war may be involved under art. 11), and from the scope of many arbitration treaties including those negotiated by the United States since 1927. The elimination of this plea on mandate questions would seem to mean that the scope of the mandatory's powers in mandated territory, as well as its duties toward other states, can be raised in the international forum.

[120] L. of N., Council, Min., sess. XXXIX, *O.J.*, VII, 524.

[121] For interpretation of this provision, which is identical in all the mandates, see Palestine Mavromatis concession case, *P.C.I.J.* (Ser. A), No. 2.

[122] See *supra*, nn. 113, 114.

This paragraph provides that "states members of the League of Nations may likewise bring any claims on behalf of their nationals for infraction of their rights under the mandate before the court for decision." However, the Court's opinion in the Mavromatis case suggested that this paragraph added nothing to the article in all the mandates providing for submission of "any dispute whatever" with the mandatory by another member of the League "relating to the interpretation or the application of the provisions of the mandate" which negotiations have failed to settle. On the principle that a state has a right to just treatment of its nationals abroad, this article was found broad enough to cover claims presented by a member of the League on behalf of its national. But League members have a right that natives of the areas be treated as prescribed by the mandates, thus the article would seem broad enough to cover claims presented by League members in behalf of such natives.[123]

b) EQUALITY OF ECONOMIC OPPORTUNITY

The principle of trusteeship suggests that the mandatories should make no profit from administering the areas, and it is clear that they are precluded from gaining a direct financial profit or a direct military advantage.[124] It would seem that a mandatory should also be prohibited from giving its own or its friends' nationals special advantages of any kind in the areas.[125] This of course would not preclude special advantages for the inhabitants of the mandated territory, but would require equality as between all others. This principle has been applied in the cultural and economic field but with certain important exceptions. Equality generally applies only as between nationals of League members. Outside states can claim the privilege only on the basis of special treaties.[126] Furthermore, in certain matters and in certain of the areas discrimination is permitted. That favorable to the immigration and settlement of Jews in Palestine is perhaps most notable though this discrimination is not in

[123] See *supra*, chap. v, sec. 5. The British government admitted in the Mavromatis case that it was "open to any member of the League to question" acts "which infringed the international obligations which His Britannic Majesty as mandatory for Palestine has accepted" (*P.C.I.J.* [Ser. A], No. 2, p. 22; [Ser. C], No. 5, Part I, p. 445, and Stoyanovsky, *op. cit.*, p. 145).

[124] See *supra*, secs. 2*f*, 3*j*.

[125] See *supra*, n. 56.

[126] See *infra*, secs. *d*, *e*, *f*.

favor of a particular state but of a particular cultural group, dispersed through nearly all nations.[127] Equal opportunity for missionary enterprise is required in all the areas, and in the A areas this is not restricted to nationals of League members. In the A areas equal opportunity is especially required for archaeological enterprise though only for nationals of League members.[128] The open door, however, has not given rise to so much discussion in religious, philanthropic, and scientific matters as in economic matters, and especial attention must be given to the latter subject.

Article 22 of the Covenant provides that in B mandated areas the mandatory "will also secure equal opportunities for the trade and commerce of other members of the league," and the six mandates for these areas contain identical provisions assuring to nationals of members of the League the same treatment as it accords to its own nationals in respect to protection and acquisition of property, exercise of trades or professions, navigation, transit, trade, and acquisition of concessions. Concessions having a character of general monopoly or giving preferential advantage "inconsistent with economic, commercial and industrial equality" are prohibited, though government organization of "essential public works and services," government grant of concessions for "monopolies of a purely fiscal character," or government operation or control of agencies for developing natural resources form an exception.

The League Assembly and the United States insisted that the economic open door must apply in A mandated areas also, though there is no such requirement in the Covenant, and this desire was complied with in all three of these mandates.[129] In the Syrian mandate the provision seems to be as extensive as in the B mandates except for the permission to make special customs arrangements with adjoining countries on grounds of contiguity (art. 11). The Palestine mandate contains this exception (art. 18), and also permits the mandatory to prefer the Jewish agency in the grant of concessions for public services and the development of natural resources (art. 11). The Iraq Treaty permits that country to form customs or other

[127] See *supra*, nn. 75a, 103–5; chap. viii, sec. 3*a*.

[128] See *supra*, sec. 3*i*.

[129] See *supra*, n. 56, and chap. ii, secs. 4, 5.

unions with neighboring Arab states (art. 16), and the open-door article (art. 11) makes no mention of concessions or investments. Discussion in the Mandates Commission have made it clear that practical discriminations resulting from the action of subordinate officials are prohibited by the mandate as well as discrimination in the laws,[130] and that subsidies or contributions to institutions are not permissible if they attack the principle of economic equality.[130a] Prior to the entry of Germany into the League her trade was quite generally discriminated against in mandated areas, but after her entry in 1926 the Commission took pains to see that these discriminations were removed.[131]

The Covenant permits the mandatory to administer C mandated territories "as integral portions of its territory, subject to the safeguards above mentioned in the interests of the indigenous population." Japan contended before confirmation of the mandates that the open-door requirement for B mandates was in the interests of the indigenous population and consequently applied to the C areas, but she was unable to get this contention accepted and eventually accepted C mandates without such a provision, contenting herself with the expression of her own attitude in a reservation.[132] The United States has contended that the open door should continue to apply in Samoa as required under the tripartite convention of 1899, but this contention has not been accepted,[133] nor has her contention that the gratuitous character of the mandatory's mission implies the open door in all of the areas.[134]

Thus the open door is not legally required in C mandated areas, but the Commission has included the heading "Economic Equality"

[130] *P.M.C., Min.*, XI, 150. The matter was discussed at length in the thirteenth session and the Commission asked for information in regard to the application of the principle of economic equality in regard to public works, concessions, coasting trade, and price estimations on which ad valorem duties were based (*ibid.*, XIII, 172–75, 227).

[130a] *Ibid.*, XIII, 191.

[131] *Ibid.*, XI, 29, 150. Prior to Germany's entry into the League, the discriminations against her applied also in some cases to her neighbors who were members of the League. The Permanent Mandates Commission considered this contrary to the mandate (*ibid.*, V, 187).

[132] See *supra*, chap. ii, sec. 1; chap. iv, sec. 4.

[133] See *infra*, n. 160.

[134] See *supra*, n. 57, and U.S. notes, May 12 and November 20, 1920 (U.S. Department of State, *Mandate for Palestine* [1927], pp. 27, 38, 39).

in the C questionnaires and has not hesitated to draw attention to particular economic discriminations that seemed contrary to the interests of the indigenous population. Thus a reference to the phosphate monopoly in Nauru called forth elaborate explanations from the mandatory;[135] a reference to an alleged phosphate monopoly in the Japanese mandated islands brought forth the information that there was no such monopoly;[136] and a reference to the Australian law restricting trade with New Guinea to Australian vessels brought about a prompt repeal of the law.[137]

Do the open-door requirements prohibit customs incorporation of mandated areas with neighboring colonies? Clearly not in the case of the A mandates, which expressly permit customs agreements with neighboring states. In confirming the B mandates, which permit the territory to be administered as integral parts of neighboring territories, the Council insisted on the addition of a clause that this should not infringe the provisions of the mandate.[138] When the colony with which a mandated area is incorporated lies within the open-door zone of the Congo the Commission has held that customs incorporation is proper,[139] but at its first and third sessions it reached the conclusion that such incorporation with a colony giving preferences should not be permitted.[140] During the eleventh session the accredited representative from Tanganyika recognized that if Uganda and Kenya colonies formed a customs union with Tanganyika they would have to abandon their preferential duties.[141]

Is a mandatory prohibited from attaching the requirement to loans to B mandated territories that purchases from the proceeds be made from its territory? Discussion in the eleventh and twelfth ses-

[135] See *supra*, n. 62, and chap. vii, sec. 3.

[136] *P.M.C.*, *Min.*, III, 303; and Japanese reports on her mandated territories (1923), p. 8; (1924), p. 51.

[137] *P.M.C.*, *Min.*, VI, 180; VII, 8.

[138] See *supra*, chap. iv, sec. 4, and *P.M.C.*, *Min.*, XII, 68.

[139] The Berlin act of 1885 required free trade in this zone, but the St. Germain convention of 1919 modified this to a requirement of the open door as among League members (Beer, *African Questions at the Peace Conference*, pp. 85–86; Buell, *op. cit.*, 405; II, 893, 936).

[140] P.M.C., Rep., I, *O.J.*, II, 1126; *P.M.C.*, *Min.*, I, 21; III, 27, 314.

[141] *Ibid.*, XI, 86.

sions of the Mandates Commission in connection with Tanganyika indicates that it is. The loan here in question, however, was intended to be used for public works, which were expressly excepted from the open-door provision, so the mandatory was not criticized. Nevertheless, in its thirteenth report the Commission asked for information on the subject from all the A and B mandatories.[142]

The bearing of the open-door provisions upon discriminatory postal rates, upon concession tenders, and upon various customs schedules has also been discussed. At its ninth session the Commission drew attention to the postal discrimination in favor of letters going from Tanganyika to British possessions, and although discussion disclosed differences of opinion in the Commission on the compatibility of this practice with the mandates, a formal request for information was made in the Commission's twelfth report.[143] Concession questions have been raised in regard to Syria and Iraq, and information has been asked, though in the case of Iraq the Commission appreciated that the open-door article did not refer specifically to concessions.[144] The Commission has several times drawn attention to tariff schedules not in accord with economic equality.[145]

The question has been raised in the Commission whether the privileges accorded to "all nationals of states members of the league apply to natives as well as white people," but has not been decided. Though the term "citizen" is often restricted to subjects with certain political privileges, the term "national" is applied to all persons owing the state allegiance, thus native subjects would seem to enjoy that status.

c) RIGHTS VESTED UNDER GENERAL INTERNATIONAL LAW

The treaties gave the mandatories the right to sequestrate property of ex-enemy nationals though the proceeds were credited on

[142] *Ibid.*, XIII, 224; see also *ibid.*, XI, 79; XII, 64–67, 164–69; XIII, 94–95; XVI, 200.

[143] *Ibid.*, XII, 198; see also *ibid.*, IX, 148, 219; XII, 67–69, 160–62, 170; XIII, 93; XVI, 201.

[144] On Iraq see *ibid.*, XII, 38, 70, 200. M. Orts of the Commission "thought that people would learn with surprise that the clause referring to economic equality did not apply to Iraq's principal industry [oil]" (p. 38). On Syria see *ibid.*, XIII, 172–75, 227.

[145] See, e.g., objection to the Cameroons decree of September 14, 1925, exempting only French-language books from import duty (*ibid.*, XIII, 227).

reparations account.[146] Apart from this, provisions of varying character with regard to private property rights exist in different mandates. C mandates contain nothing except the general duty of the mandatory to promote the material and moral well-being of the natives. B mandates require the mandatory to respect native rights and interests in land and to accord equal treatment in the protection of rights of all nationals of states members of the League. The A mandates require the mandatory to provide courts assuring protection to the rights of natives and foreigners. The Palestine mandate in addition requires the mandatory to respect the civil rights of all the inhabitants and, in providing for public ownership or control of natural resources and public works, services, or utilities, to respect international obligations which it has accepted (art. 11). Apparently the last clause only applies to a concession in case it has been recognized by the mandatory in an international agreement and in case its impairment can be attributed to an assumption by the mandatory of public ownership or control of public works, services, or utilities. Such an impairment was discovered where the government had subsequently granted a conflicting public-service concession in which it retained unusual powers of regulation.[147]

Apart from the terms of the mandates, the mandatories are undoubtedly bound to accord the respect for vested rights of third states and their nationals required under general principles of international law. Those principles require that the new sovereign respect rights of individuals which have become vested under the present or some previous sovereign of the area, but under the mandate clauses the court does not have compulsory jurisdiction over controversies involving such rights, except in so far as they are expressly recognized by the mandates. The American treaties with mandatories expressly stipulate that "vested American property rights shall be respected and in no way impaired." Though the United States is placed by the treaties on a parity with members of the League and consequently has the right to sue the mandatory in the Permanent Court of International Justice on a question of interpretation or ap-

[146] See *supra*, n. 39.

[147] Palestine Mavromatis concession case (*P.C.I.J.* [Ser. A], No. 2); *supra*, chap. v, sec. 5.

plication of the mandate, it would appear that this provision in the treaty, going as it does beyond the guaranties of the mandate, could not be so submitted without special agreement.

The A mandates, in case of termination, impose certain responsibilities upon the League for obligations entered into by the mandatory in behalf of the territory.[148] In discussing loans the Commission and Council recognized that legally acquired rights would have to be respected by a subsequent administration in case of transfer or termination of any of the mandates.[149]

d) RIGHTS UNDER APPLICABLE TREATIES

Attention has been given to the rights of the mandatories and of the natives with regard to the extension of conventions to the areas.[150] Foreigners, of course, enjoy the benefit in the areas of multilateral or bilateral treaties to which their state is a party and which have been extended to the areas. As has been noted, many extradition, commercial, and other treaties have been so extended. The United States treaty in regard to the North Pacific islands provides that all treaties between the United States and Japan shall apply to these islands, and its treaties with regard to African mandated areas provide that extradition conventions between the parties shall apply. No such provision is in the treaties relating to Syria and Palestine.

The Council has held the mandatory competent to make such treaties on its own responsibility, though the Commission has made it clear that no treaty provision can be extended so as to give a particular state any privilege contrary to the open door or other requirement of the mandate.[151] As the mandatory is incompetent to act in respect to mandated territory beyond the scope of the mandate, a treaty which violated that instrument would be void[152] al-

[148] Palestine mandate, art. 28; Syria, art. 19; Iraq, decision of the Council, September 27, 1924, art. 7.

[149] See *supra*, n. 43.

[150] See *supra*, sec. 3*d*.

[151] See *supra*, n. 49, and sec. 3*h*.

[152] It is recognized that if a state has made two treaties with different states the earlier prevails under international law (*Costa Rica* v. *Nicaragua*, Central American Court of Justice, *A.J.I.L.*, XI, 181; Wright, "Conflicts between International Law and Treaties," *ibid.*, pp. 576–79; Wilson and Tucker, *International Law* [8th ed.], p. 216; Oppenheim, *International Law* [3d ed.], I, 662; Hall, *International Law* [8th ed.], pp. 396–97).

though doubtless the mandatory would be responsible to the other party for any damage which it might have suffered through that fact.[153]

Controversy has arisen as to the status of rights enjoyed under treaties previously applicable to the mandated areas. In general, treaties are obligations of the state treated as a juristic personality, and when the state ceases to exist[154] or parts with territory the treaties cease to be applicable to that territory.[155] Thus a treaty of the United States or other states with Germany or Turkey, formerly applicable to a territory now under mandate, would normally cease to be so upon relinquishment of the territory by that power. But an exception to this rule is recognized in the case of treaties intended to establish a permanent condition in a territory such as a boundary, a servitude, or a status. Rights of individuals which have become vested in a territory do not terminate even though the treaty on which they were originally founded does, and in the same way treaties intended to establish a permanent condition would seem to create vested rights in states, perhaps sometimes even in states not a party to them.[156]

The United States has contended that its extraterritorial privileges in the former Turkish territories continue until expressly renounced, apparently on the theory that the capitulations constituted a sort of servitude permanently attached to the territory. This theory seems to be accepted in the mandates of Palestine (art. 8) and Syria (art. 5), which recognize that extraterritorial privileges are merely suspended for the period of the mandate and shall be "immediately re-established" upon its expiration. In treaties with Great Britain and France in regard to these areas the United States ac-

[153] The United States recognized that it owed reparation to France for injury resulting to the latter from its inability to execute a treaty considered beyond its constitutional competence (the Dillon case, in Moore, *Digest of International Law*, V, 80; Wright, *Control of American Foreign Relations*, pp. 81–82).

[154] A state does not necessarily cease to exist when it places itself under a protectorate (Lindley, *op. cit.*, p. 310) or joins a federation (*Terlinden* v. *Ames*, 184 U.S. 270).

[155] Oppenheim, *op. cit.*, Vol. I, sec. 82.

[156] On the principle *res transit cum suo onere* (*ibid.*, secs. 82, 84; Westlake, *International Law* [2d ed.], I, 67; Phillipson, *Termination of War and Treaties of Peace*, pp. 34, 305; Roxburgh, *International Conventions and Third States* [London, 1917], pp. 57, 103; and *infra*, nn. 171–73).

cepted the mandates including this provision on condition that it enjoy within the territories all rights secured to members of the League, that vested American property rights in the territory be respected, that a duplicate of the mandatory's reports be sent it, that Americans be permitted to establish and maintain educational, philanthropic, and religious institutions in the territory and to teach the English language, and that modifications of the terms of the mandates shall not affect American rights unless it has consented.[157]

By the Iraq Treaty with Great Britain the king of Iraq agrees to give effect to reasonable provisions considered necessary by Great Britain for "safeguarding the interests of foreigners in consequence of the non-application of the immunities and privileges enjoyed by them under capitulation or usage," such provisions to be embodied in a separate agreement communicated to the League. The latter agreement was concluded on March 25, 1924, and provided special safeguards in cases involving foreigners defined as meaning "the nationals of any European or American State which formerly benefited by capitulations in Turkey and did not renounce the same by an agreement signed before the 24th of July, 1923, and of any Asiatic State which is now permanently represented on the Council of the League of Nations." Persia protested to the Council that she was the only state with interests in Iraq excluded by this definition. Great Britain replied that Iraq was willing to negotiate an agreement with Persia on the subject.[158] The United States has not yet concluded a treaty accepting the mandate in Iraq nor has she recognized Iraq, and she continues to insist that extraterritorial rights may still be exercised there.[159]

The United States has contended that under the convention of 1899 between Great Britain, Germany, and the United States by

[157] U.S. memorandum to Great Britain, August 24, 1921 (Department of State, *Mandate for Palestine* [1927], p. 51) and text of treaty (*ibid.*, p. 107 ff.). The U.S.-French treaty on Syria is printed in *U.S. Treaty Series*, No. 695.

[158] *P.M.C.*, *Min.*, XII, 25; XIV, 176. See also *L. of N.*, *Assembly*, *Rec.*, sess. IX (sixth committee), September 14, 15, 1928, and *F.P.A.*, *Inf. Ser.*, V, 69.

[159] The British accredited representative reported to the Permanent Mandates Commission in October, 1927, that the negotiation of a treaty with the United States in regard to Iraq was approaching completion (*P.M.C.*, *Min.*, XII, 31, 200).

which the Samoan group was divided between Germany and the United States it is entitled to continued enjoyment of the open door though the mandate does not require such treatment even for League members.[160] This convention provided "that each of the three signatory powers shall continue to enjoy, in respect to their commerce and commercial vessels, in all the islands of the Samoan group privileges and conditions equal to those enjoyed by the sovereign powers, in all ports which may be open to the commerce of either of them." It is understood that New Zealand has pointed out that the United States has itself failed to observe this provision by treating trade between American Samoa and any other American port as coastwise trade to which only American vessels are admitted.[161] It would appear that the convention of 1899 intended to establish a permanent condition and consequently should continue in effect in spite of the war, except in so far as expressly renounced.[162] New Zealand clearly could acquire no rights under this treaty as successor to Germany since the latter's rights were considered by the treaty of Versailles (art. 288) "to have terminated on August 4, 1914," but as a part of the British Empire she would be entitled to the privileges of the treaty. The United States might contend that this discrimination against foreign vessels is within the exception in the final clause of the article, though this interpretation would be doubtful because the ports of American Samoa are not closed to foreign commerce but merely to the entry of goods and passengers coming from the United States on foreign vessels.

[160] U.S. Tariff Commission, *Colonial Tariff Policies* (1922), p. 277. It was reported at the sixth session of the Permanent Mandates Commission that conversations between the United States and Great Britain were proceeding in regard to this treaty (*P.M.C., Min.*, VI, 10). For a brief statement of American protests in regard to these mandated areas and existing tariff practices therein see U.S. Tariff Commission, *op. cit.*, pp. 265–78.

[161] The Merchant Marine Act of July 5, 1920 (sec. 21) applied the coast shipping restrictions to American Samoa (see U.S. Tariff Commission Tariff, *op. cit.*, pp. 21, 580, 616).

[162] See *supra*, n. 156. The accredited representative of New Zealand expressed doubt whether this treaty was still in effect, but the chairman of the Mandates Commission thought it still in force (*P.M.C., Min.*, VII, 24). The report of the United States Tariff Commission on Colonial Tariff Policies (1922) considers this treaty still in effect between the United States and Great Britain (*op. cit.*, pp. 277, 576–77).

e) BASIS OF AMERICAN CLAIMS

The United States put forth a claim to participation in the assignment and formulation of the terms of mandates soon after rejecting the peace treaty and the Covenant. The Council acquiesced in this claim and invited the United States to participate in the work of confirming mandates, though it did not reply until the C mandates had been confirmed. The United States refused the offer but during the next few years made treaties with most of the mandatory powers which assured it the rights but not the duties of members of the League in those areas. The Council has acquiesced in the conclusion of these treaties though no occasion has arisen which required positive recognition of them.[163]

The American claim was based on three distinct grounds. The first rests on the express inclusion of the United States among the Powers in whose favor Germany renounced the territories by article 119 of the treaty of Versailles. This article is recited in the preamble of all the treaties made by the United States in regard to former German territories. "The United States," wrote Secretary Colby on February 21, 1921, "which is distinctly included in the very definite and constantly used descriptive phrase 'the allied and associated powers,' has not agreed to the terms or provisions of the mandate which is embodied in this text."[164] Clearly, this argument cannot apply to former Turkish territory since the word "associated" is omitted in both the treaty of Sèvres and the treaty of Lausanne.[165] Even with respect to German territory, in view of the failure of the United States to ratify the treaty of Versailles, the argument runs counter to the usually accepted principle, *pacta tertiis nec nocent nec prosunt*. "Neither rights nor duties," writes Oppenheim, "as a rule, arise under a treaty for third States which are not parties to the treaty." It has been suggested that treaties establishing an international settlement or permanent condition of things have a different

[163] See *supra*, chap. ii, secs. 4 and 5.

[164] *O.J.*, II, No. 2, 138; *Council, Min.*, XII, 70. See also U.S. notes, April 2, 1921 (Levermore, *L. of N.*, *Y.B.*, II, 59).

[165] Nevertheless it is referred to in the memorandum to the British Foreign Office of August 24, 1921, in regard to A mandates as additional support to other arguments (*Mandate for Palestine*, p. 50).

character, and third states may acquire vested rights under them immediately upon "giving express or implicit consent to the stipulations of such treaties." Oppenheim accepts this in case sufficient time has elapsed to enable the third states to acquire a customary right or in case the contracting states "really intended to offer such a right to third states," which, however, is not to be presumed.[166] It may be questioned whether the parties to the treaty of Versailles intended that the United States share in the territories unless it ratified the treaty and thus accepted its burdens as well as benefits. Both the Allied and Associated Powers and Germany seem to have regarded the Principal Powers to whom the territory was originally transferred as trustees whose sole duty was to institute the régime of article 22—a function which clearly implied their membership in the League of Nations.[167]

[166] Oppenheim, *op. cit.* (3d ed.), I, 678; Roxburgh, *International Conventions and Third States*, pp. 42–44, 111–13. Denmark acquired no rights under the treaty of 1866 between Prussia and Austria for a plebiscite in Schleswig-Holstein; for facts of this case see Wambaugh, *A Monograph in Plebiscites* (New York, 1920), pp. 145–47.

[167] "[The Treaty of Versailles] was entered into by the Allied powers upon the assumption that it represented the common views of all those who had taken part in its preparation after their combined efforts to achieve the victory. It was upon the faith of this assumption that the Allied powers undertook obligations not only towards Germany, but also towards each other, and from which it is now impossible for them to escape. The decision of one of the Allied and Associated powers not to ratify the treaty does not modify the obligations which that treaty imposed upon those who have ratified it, nor release them from the pledges it contains; nor can they now enter into new engagements which would be inconsistent with its terms. What is said above is pre-eminently true with regard to the overseas territories which formerly belonged to Germany. By the Treaty of Versailles Germany renounced all her sovereignty over them; that renunciation was intended, as pointed out in the American note, to be indivisible; no part of that sovereignty remains to Germany today. But Germany parted with her sovereignty upon the terms laid down in the treaty. Among the conditions so laid down was the assurance that these territories would in future be administered by mandatories on behalf of, and subject to, the general control of the League of Nations. By that engagement the Allied powers are bound to stand; they are pledged not only to Germany but to their own peoples to recognize and to accept the special rôle and function of the League of Nations in connection with the mandates over these territories; they can consent to no arrangement with any power which is inconsistent with the pledges they have given" (British note to United States, December 22, 1921, *Mandate for Palestine*, pp. 53–54). See also the Hymans report adopted by the Council, August, 1920, *Responsibilities of the League under Article 22*, p. 14; *L. of N. Assembly, Rec.*, sess. I, sixth committee, p. 382; German note to League, November 23, 1920, *ibid.*,

The weakness of this first argument probably accounts for the further recital in the preamble to the American treaties referring to former German territories that "the benefits accruing under the aforesaid article 119 of the treaty of Versailles were confirmed to the United States by the treaty between the United States and Germany signed August 25, 1921." This confirmation, however, assists the United States' claim only to a limited extent. The treaty of Versailles provided in article 440 that it shall go into effect between the contracting parties as soon as ratifications are deposited by Germany and three of the Principal Allied and Associated Powers. This happened at 4:15 P.M., January 10, 1920.[168] At that moment, therefore, Germany had renounced all her rights and titles over her overseas possessions.[169] Thus it would seem that when she made the treaty of Berlin with the United States a year and a half later (August 25, 1921) she had no power to grant or to confirm to the United States any rights in her former territories.

It may be said that Germany renounced the territories specifically to the Principal Allied and Associated Powers and thus is entitled, as long as the treaty of Versailles lasts, to see that they all share in the benefits. Such an argument would clearly have little weight in regard to an ordinary treaty of cession. With the presumption of exclusive sovereignty of territory, a state cannot exercise a future control over territory it has renounced. Thus Spain could not invoke clauses or understandings of the treaty of St. Ildefonsa to prevent France ceding Louisiana to the United States.[170] International titles to territory are less complicated than private titles to

---

Plenary Meetings, pp. 204, 210–13; and opinion of South African Supreme Court in *Rex* v. *Christian*, *supra*, chap. xii).

[168] *U.S. Treaties, etc.*, III, 3329.

[169] This is admitted in the United States note of August 24, 1921. "In providing as stated in article 440, for the coming into force of that treaty when it had been ratified by Germany and three of the principal Allied and Associated powers it was manifestly not the intention that on such ratification by three powers there should still remain in Germany any undivided share of title or sovereignty in the overseas possessions described" (*Mandate for Palestine*, p. 50). Great Britain accepted this in her note of December 22, 1921 (see *supra*, n. 167).

[170] *Amer. State Papers, For. Rel.*, II, 569; Adams, *History of the United States*, II, 56, 252; Fish, *American Diplomacy*, p. 150.

real property. While the state annexing territory is bound to respect certain rights of the inhabitants, it is not burdened by past treaties relating to the territory[171] unless they constitute an international settlement or establish a servitude intended to burden the territory permanently,[172] which, however, will not be implied.[173]

It appears that the present case is within that exception. The League Council and the Supreme Court of the Union of South Africa as well as the allied and the German governments have recognized that this was not an ordinary cession.[174] Article 119 is to be read with article 22. Germany did not cede the territory—she renounced it that it might be administered by "mandatories on behalf of the League of Nations." Thus Germany argued before her entry into the League that as a party to the treaty she had a right to object whenever the régime set up for these territories by the treaty was not observed.

The German argument was not accepted by the Allied Powers and was not acted on by the League, and the wide discretion given to the Principal Powers over the renounced territory by article 118 of the treaty renders it somewhat doubtful.[175] In any case it would contribute support to the American claim only with respect to the B mandated areas. Germany never had any title to the A mandated territories, and the C mandates had been confirmed by the League prior to her treaty with the United States. With this confirmation the function of the Principal Allied and Associated Powers under ar-

[171] The United States refused to be bound by treaties covering Hawaii and the Spanish islands prior to their annexation in 1898 (Moore, *Digest of International Law*, V, 348–53). Japan refused to be bound by Korean treaties (Oppenheim, *op. cit.* [3d ed.], Vol. 1, sec. 82). For other instances see Phillipson, *Termination of War and Treaties of Peace*, p. 303, and *supra*, n. 155.

[172] See *supra*, n. 156.

[173] The doctrine of servitude "could in the general interest of the community of nations, and of the parties to this treaty, be affirmed by this tribunal only on the express evidence of an international contract (North Atlantic Fisheries Arbitration, Wilson, *Hague Arbitration Cases*, pp. 159). "The grave consequences attaching to the construction of an international obligation as a servitude require that it should be resorted to only when there is no doubt that the parties intended it to be a permanent relation independently of who is the sovereign of the entitled or encumbered territory" (Lauterpacht, *Private Law Sources and Analogies of International Law*, p. 123; Roxburgh, *op. cit.*, pp. 103 ff.).

[174] See *supra*, n. 167.

[175] See *infra*, sec. *f*.

ticle 119 was executed,[176] and Germany's only possible claim would be to the proper fulfilment of article 22. In view of article 118 she certainly could not go back to alleged irregularities in the allocation of the mandates by the Principal Powers. Even if, prior to her admission to the League, Germany was entitled to insist that article 22 be carried out, she could hardly give the United States, which was neither a mandatory nor a member of the League, any powers in that regard.

The final claim by the United States rests on its participation in the war against Germany which, according to the treaties relating to Palestine and Syria, "contributed to her defeat and the defeat of her allies and to the renunciation of the rights and titles of her allies in the territory transferred by them." This recital appears in modified form in all the treaties relating to former German territory except that with Japan, and is the only justification for the American claim in the treaties dealing with former Turkish territory. From the legal point of view the argument, which was in fact the main one advanced in the correspondence,[177] rests on the doctrine of conquest; but as the United States was not at war with Turkey and never occupied any of her territory its applicability in a legal sense to her territory seems questionable. With respect to German territory the argument, if applied in the broad sense of the correspondence, would prove too much as it would give the United States and all the rest of Germany's enemies a share in Alsace-Lorraine and other "conquered" territory. If applied in the usual sense, it would confer a title only on the ally in actual occupation when the war ended, which would not give the United States any claim to any of the mandated territories.

Furthermore, the sufficiency of title by conquest alone has been questioned. One school of writers holds that peace automatically gives title to the occupant of enemy territory (*uti possidetis*) while another holds that military occupation has no effect on title and that the *status quo ante bellum* returns with peace except in so far as expressly changed by treaty.[178] The latter view is more in accord with

[176] See *supra*, chap. x, sec. 2*a*; *infra*, chap. xiv.

[177] See *infra*, n. 185; see also comments (*A.J.I.L.*, XV, 424, 426).

[178] Unless there is a complete subjugation of one belligerent, in which case title changes by the victor's proclamation of annexation (Oppenheim, *op. cit.*, secs. 264, 265). "The date of change of sovereignty is that on which the annexation was proclaimed, or

the spirit of the times and particularly with the past pronouncements of the United States.[179] It has never favored title by conquest. In practice it has not only had title to territories acquired by war validated by treaty but has generally paid money to the defeated state.[180] The Supreme Court has said that aggrandizement cannot be assumed as the intent of a war under the Constitution, and therefore the president cannot annex occupied territory without authorization by treaty or act of Congress.[181] At the first Pan-American Congress in 1890 the United States sponsored a proposal for the abolition of title by conquest in the Americas,[182] and on entering the World War the president repudiated all intention of material gain.[183] The terms of the treaty itself are clearly based on the assumption that the war had no legal effect on German titles to territory, and the Permanent Court of International Justice has held that Poland did not acquire title to former German territory until the peace treaty came into effect.[184] It can hardly be contended that the United States contributed toward putting the treaty into effect since her own refusal to ratify considerably delayed that result. Any contribution, military or diplomatic, which the United States may have made toward inducing Germany to sign the treaty hardly supports a legal claim

---

that on which the treaty of peace was concluded" (Phillipson, *op. cit.*, p. 33). See also *ibid.*, pp. 6–7, and Cobbett, *Leading Cases on International Law*, II (1913), 245. Hyde (*International Law*, II, 854) supports the doctrine of *uti possiditis*.

179 Moore, *Digest*, I, 290–92; Wright, "Effects of the League of Nations Covenant," *A.P.S.R.*, XIII, 558–59.

180 See treaty of Guadeloupe Hidalgo (1848), art. 12, and treaty of Paris (1898), art. 3.

181 *Fleming* v. *Page*, 9 How. 603 (1850). "The holding of a conquered territory is regarded as a mere military occupation until its fate shall be determined by the treaty of peace" (Chief Justice Marshall in *American Insurance Co.* v. *Canter*, 1 Pet. 511 (1828).

182 *Minutes of the International American Conference* (1889–90), pp. 798–806; Moore, *Digest*, I, 922.

183 "We have no selfish ends to serve. We desire no conquest, no domination. We seek no indemnities for ourselves, no material compensation for the sacrifices we shall freely make" (President Wilson, address to Congress, April 2, 1917).

184 In its advisory opinion regarding German settlers in Poland, the Permanent Court of International Justice held, September 10, 1923, that German title to her former territory did not pass until the treaty of Versailles went into effect on January 10, 1920 (*P.C.I.J.* [Ser. B], No. 6, pp. 27, 28).

though perhaps it deserved moral or political consideration from the Allies, and in fact such consideration seems to be all the United States was actually contending for,[185] and both the League Council[186] and the mandatories[187] were entirely willing to accord it.

Thus the American claim to a voice in the disposition of the mandated territories rested in reality upon a moral or political rather than a legal basis. In any case the claim was limited to participation in the original establishment of the régime of article 22. The United

[185] "Such powers as the Allied and Associated nations may enjoy or wield in the determination of the governmental status of the mandated areas accrued to them as a direct result of the war against the Central powers. The United States as a participant in that conflict and as a contributor to its successful issue can not consider any of the Associated powers, the smallest not less than itself, debarred from the discussion of any of its consequences, or from participation in the rights and privileges secured under the mandates provided for in the treaties of peace" (U.S. note, November 20, 1920, *Mandate for Palestine,* p. 39; *O.J.,* II, No. 2, 140). "The Government of the United States adheres to the position already stated that the right to dispose of the overseas possessions of Germany was acquired only through the victory of the allied and associated powers, and that there can be no valid or effective disposition of these territories without the assent of the United States as one of the participants in that victory. . . . . With respect to mandated territories other than those which were formerly possessions of Germany, while it is true that the United States did not declare war against Turkey, still the opportunity of the Allied powers to secure the allocation of mandates and the administration of territories formerly under Turkish rule was made possible only through the victory over Germany" (note, August 24, 1921, *Mandate for Palestine,* pp. 49, 50). "This government has made clear its position that the changed situation is a consequence of the common victory of the allied and associated powers over Germany, and that in view of its relation to this victory the United States is entitled to insist that no measure could properly be taken which would subject the United States to discrimination or deprive its nationals within these territories of equality of treatment with the nationals of any other power" (Secretary Hughes's address, January 23, 1924, *A.J.I.L.,* XVIII, 243), but see Hyde, in *The American Secretaries of State and Their Diplomacy* (Bemis ed.), X, 238–40, 433–35.

[186] "The United States was one of the leading actors both in the war and in the negotiations for peace. The rights which it acquired are not likely to be challenged in any quarter. But the American Government will itself recognize that the situation is complicated by the fact that the United States, for reasons which the Council would be the last to question, has so far abstained from ratifying the Peace Treaty and has not taken her seat in the Council of the League of Nations" (note of the Council to U.S., March 1, 1921, *Mandate for Palestine,* p. 44).

[187] "His Majesty's government have the honour to state that they have never desired to deprive the United States of the fruits of a victory to which it contributed so generously. . . . . The co-operation of the United States in the making of peace was a necessary corollary of their co-operation in the war and in the victory" (British note to U.S., December 22, 1921, *Mandate for Palestine,* p. 53).

States, having by its treaties recognized that régime, has renounced any original claim it may have had to the territories. Its future rights are limited to the provisions of its treaties with the mandatories. Possible conflicts of these treaties with future amendments or interpretation of the mandates made by proper authorities would be a diplomatic problem for the mandatory to wrestle with. These treaties, it may be noticed, do not give the United States a veto on future changes of the mandates but merely provide "nothing contained in the present convention shall be affected by any modification which may be made in the terms of the mandate as recited above unless such modification shall have been assented to by the United States."[188]

f) BASIS OF GERMAN, TURKISH, AND OTHER CLAIMS

Germany's claim to a voice in mandate matters was first put forward in her note of November, 1920, to the League of Nations insisting that the Assembly rather than the Principal Allied and Associated Powers should appoint the mandatories. "If this appeal should be unsuccessful," the note concluded, "the German government desires, at once, to protest solemnly against this violation of the Covenant and, as regards the future, reserves its rights concerning this question."[189] A note of September 16, 1925, also to the League protested that the Belgian law organizing Ruanda-Urundi as a part of the Congo was contrary to the Covenant and stated "as a signatory of the treaty of Versailles, the German government may claim the proper application of article 22."[190]

A Belgian memorandum of October 16, 1925, states that this note was unacceptable for the following reasons:

> Under articles 118 and 119 of the Treaty of Versailles, Germany surrendered her former overseas colonies and protectorates and accepted in advance the régime to which these territories might be subjected by the principal allied and associated powers. She is therefore precluded from criticizing the conditions of the mandate for Ruanda-Urundi which has been duly conferred upon Belgium. The German objections to the status laid down for Ruanda-Urundi amount, when all things are considered, to a condemnation of article 10 of the Belgian mandate which was approved by the League of Nations.

[188] On the right of the mandatory to make such treaties see *supra*, sec. 2*d*.

[189] *L. of N., Assembly, Rec.*, I, Plenary Meetings, 213.

[190] *O.J.*, VIII, 316.

Moreover, all questions relating to the application of article 22 of the Covenant are within the exclusive competence of the League of Nations, and so long as Germany is not a member of the League she has no right or title to intervene in such questions. It is useless for her to claim that, as a signatory of the Treaty of Versailles, with which the Covenant is incorporated, she is entitled to supervise the application of the provisions of the Covenant. The latter holds a separate place in the Treaty of Versailles. It confers rights only upon States which are members of the League of Nations. . . . .

The Royal government continues to hold the view that, until Germany is a member of the League of Nations, she has no title to intervene, especially in the question which she has raised. It respectfully submits this view for the consideration of the council, persuaded that the latter cannot but accept it.[191]

Germany appreciated in both notes that her claim to a voice could depend on article 22 of the Covenant alone. The renouncing articles seemed to leave the Allied and Associated Powers full discretion as to the setting-up of that régime. By article 118 Germany not only renounced "all rights, titles and privileges whatever in or over territory" outside her European frontiers as fixed by the treaty, but she "undertook to recognize and to conform to the measures which may be taken now or in the future by the Principal Allied and Associated Powers in agreement where necessary with third powers, in order to carry the above stipulation into effect." By article 119 she renounced "her oversea possessions" in favor of the Principal Allied and Associated Powers.

The extent of German rights under article 22 are more doubtful. As a party to the treaty Germany would seem entitled to a fair application of all its terms. Yet the text of the Covenant as well as the allied exchanges of notes with Germany before its signature suggest that only members of the League are entitled to the benefits of the Covenant which appears as Part I of the treaty, except where nonmembers are expressly mentioned as in article 17, or other entities such as the mandated peoples in article 22, or international bureaus as in article 24. The German complaint in regard to unequal economic treatment before signature of the treaty was answered by the statement that "as soon as Germany is admitted to the league she would enjoy the benefit of these provisions" (art. 23).[192] With refer-

[191] *Ibid.*, p. 317.

[192] Allied reply to Germany, June 16, 1919 (U.S. 66th Cong.; 1st sess.), *Sen. Doc. 149*, p. 109.

ence to mandates Germany was informed in that correspondence that "the control to be exercised by the League of Nations will provide the necessary guarantees."[193] There is no suggestion that she had a right of protest on the basis of this or any other article of the Covenant until she became a member.[194]

The League seems to have given no decision on the point, except as such may be implied from its refusal officially to answer the German complaints, and since Germany is now a member of the League the question has become academic.

Turkey would clearly have even less claim than Germany to a voice in the disposition of her former territory. Though the Covenant appeared as Part I of the treaty of Sèvres and stipulations in the body of that treaty expressly asserted that Palestine, Syria, and Mesopotamia were to be placed under mandate, the treaty was never ratified. The treaty of Lausanne does not contain the Covenant, and Turkey expressly renounced all claim to the territories outside her boundaries as defined in that instrument. During the Mosul controversy she refused to recognize the proposal that the British mandate of Iraq be continued twenty five years longer as in any way strengthening the claim of either Iraq or Great Britain to that area.

> As Turkey has not recognized in the territories detached from the former Ottoman Empire the Mandatory system, how, in these conditions, can one speak to her of the establishment of a mandate, not in some casual district, but in a territory which now forms an integral part of her own territory; for, according to the report of the commission, the first condition for detaching from Turkey the contested territory is the establishment of a mandate over that territory? . . . .

[193] *Ibid.*, p. 119.

[194] Great Britain, however, in correspondence with the United States asserted that the Allied Powers "are pledged not only to Germany but to their own peoples to recognize and to accept the special rôle and function of the League of Nations in connection with the mandates over these territories" (see *supra*, n. 167). Perhaps the German contention can receive some support from the legal opinion on which the Emperor Francis Joseph based his award in the British-Nicaraguan arbitration of July 2, 1881. This stated that Great Britain, in insisting on Nicaraguan observance of the treaty of 1860 by which Great Britain resigned the protectorate of the Mosquito territory and specified certain rights for the natives, was not "intermeddling with the internal affairs" of Nicaragua and was not claiming a continued exercise of the relinquished protectorate" but was merely claiming "a right of its own" to insist upon the fulfilment of the treaty clauses assuring "certain political and pecuniary advantages for the Mosquitoes" (Moore, *Digest of International Arbitrations*, V, 4965).

In these conditions, it is certainly not for the Turkish republic whose attitude and feelings toward the mandatory system are known to all the world, to recommend to the Iraq nation to make sacrifices of its right of sovereignty and independence.

I should add that Turkey refused categorically to accept articles 94–99 of the draft treaty of Sèvres relating to the mandate as also all the other clauses of that draft. The treaty of Lausanne makes no allusion whatever to the mandate."[195]

Austria, Hungary, and Bulgaria were parties to peace treaties each of which contained the Covenant as Part 1, but none of these states made any claim in respect to mandated areas on the basis of that fact and all are now members of the League of Nations.

The Hedjaz and Ecuador were named in the annex of the Covenant as original members of the League though neither of them has in fact become a member. The first protested to the League in August, 1920, against certain activities of the French in the Lebanon, holding that "the League is morally responsible for this injustice." The protest, however, did not refer specifically to article 22 but to the League as "the only protector of the rights and liberties of both individuals and nations." In replying the Council referred to the absence of any specific reference to a Covenant article in the protest and drew attention to the fact that the mandate had not been confirmed, that Syria was still enemy territory, and consequently that it was beyond their province to intervene "where the new system to be established by the peace is not yet in operation."[196]

There is perhaps in this letter a certain implication that the League has some responsibility to all third states for a proper execution of article 22. The legal basis for such a responsibility would rest on the supposition that article 22 had created a settlement or status recognized by all states, sanctioned by customary international law, and entitling all states—apart from any special treaty to which they might be parties—to continued enjoyment of its benefits until modified by a legal procedure.[197] Such a contention has been put forward with regard to states or areas neutralized by convention among a

[195] L. of N., Council, Min., sess. XXXV, September 3, 1925, *O.J.*, VI, 1326–27.

[196] L. of N., Council, Min., sess. VIII, pp. 53, 177, 239–41, *O.J.*, I, No. 6, 342–43. See also protest from the King, March 28, 1921 (*ibid.*, II, No. 3, 281).

[197] See *supra*, n. 166.

limited number of states,[198] and it would perhaps justify third states, not members of the League, in protesting against a departure from the fundamental principles of the mandates system, as would occur, for instance, if a mandatory should exploit a mandated area for profit or convert it into a military base. It is doubtful, however, whether states without special treaty rights and not members of the League of Nations can claim specific rights under the mandates system. The latter according to the documents extend only to members of the League. Such states are of course entitled to protection for the persons and property of their citizens in mandated territories and to security against military expeditions or other noxious influences proceeding from such territories according to universally recognized standards of international law.

This examination of authoritative interpretations of the law of mandates indicates that in theory the natives of the mandated territories and the members of the League are intended to be the main beneficiaries of the mandates system and that they enjoy exceptional rights and powers under it. The mandatory is not sovereign of the area, although no authoritative utterance has attempted to define who is.

[198] De Visscher, *Belgian's Case* (London, 1916), pp. 142–43; von Liszt, *Das Völkerrecht* (1915), p. 63; Hagerup, "La Neutralité permanente," *R.G.D.I.P.* (1905), p. 590; Lawrence, *Principles of International Law* (7th ed.), p. 591; Roxburgh, *op. cit.*, pp. 58–60.

CHAPTER XIV

INTERPRETATION OF THE DOCUMENTS

"International conventions, whether general or particular" are mentioned by the Court statute as the first source of international law in so far as they "establish rules expressly recognized by the contending states." The peace treaties, the League of Nations Covenant, and the mandates made in pursuance of it are international conventions binding members of the League, and most of the latter have been expressly recognized by the United States in special treaties with the mandatories. These documents are thus the fundamental law of the mandates system but what do they mean?

Among them article 22 of the League Covenant is the most important. It has been considered "the unique foundation of the mandatory régime" but also a document of singular obscurity.[1] "Drafted hastily," says Van Rees, "by authors inspired by essentially political considerations, it escaped attentive examination by a competent drafting body" with resulting "lapses from precision and obscurities." Henri Rolin writes:

> No one will pretend that this text is a model of juridical drafting. The lack of precision of certain phrases, the clumsy circumlocutions, the absence of that simplicity and directness which enables us to see in the expressions what is really meant, causes us obvious embarrassment as soon as we read it. . . . The thread suggests the plan of a dissertation rather than the stipulations of a convention. It seems that to this first sketch, written by an author imbued with humanitarian ideas, corrections were made by spirits of another temper. But the author is obstinate: he has demanded the maintenance at least of his "principles"; he has indicated as from a high pulpit "the best method of giving practical effect" to them; he has classed doctorally in three categories the territories according to their geographic situation, their economic conditions and "other similar circumstances." To justify the evident lack of logic, reasons have been added, good or bad.

M. Rolin adds that "officially one knows nothing of the origins of article 22."[2]

[1] Van Rees, *Les Mandats internationaux*, I, 12; see also *P.M.C., Min.*, VII, 153.

[2] *R.D.I.* (1920), p. 332; see also Baty, *B.Y.B.I.L.* (1921–22), pp. 119.

Other writers are more specific in accounting for infelicities of the text. Stoyanovsky notes that article 22 was not scrutinized by the League of Nations commission of the Peace Conference like all other articles of the Covenant but was inserted as drafted by the Council of Ten because of the political complications involved in the secret treaties. This, he says, has given it a

> special character as to form and in a certain measure as to the substance itself. It is not the work of experts and contains less of principle than of general direction. Its intentional vagueness is explained by the desire of the drafters to conceal divergencies of view among the different powers and to leave to the future and to experience the task of deciding certain fundamental principles.[3]

Millot finds ample evidence in the text that the article "did not have in the thought of the authors the meaning which it has received. It foresaw the creation of an institution; it traced the body which should receive the institution; it did not itself proceed to create it."[4] Furukaki comments that though extremely long this article "expresses itself in language, not only lacking in precision, but which leaves a multitude of questions without answer."[5]

With such difficulties in the text it is not surprising that opinions have differed as to its meaning and that commentators have found it necessary to resort to various sources of interpretation. The contributions of jurists, of general principles of law, and of practice, both by the mandatories and by the League, have been considered in the preceding chapters. It is now proposed to focus the results of this investigation upon certain questions resulting from our analysis of sovereignty under international law,[6] the answer to which may define the status which article 22 and the other documents have given these territories.

Article 22, however, seeks not so much to define a status as to guide an evolution. It attempts not merely to provide for the transfer of the territories and for the government of their inhabitants, but for the evolution in them of communities eventually capable of self-determination. Perhaps it is primarily this attempt which ac-

[3] *La Théorie générale des mandats internationaux*, p. 19.

[4] *Les Mandats internationaux*, p. 33.

[5] *Nature juridique des mandats internationaux de la Société des Nations*, p. 382.

[6] See *supra*, chap. ix, sec. 2*d*.

counts for the criticism which jurists have showered upon its phraseology. Law is a logical system which strives to express itself by propositions which are true regardless of time and space. Thus it has some difficulty to account for processes and to allow for development, and this difficulty increases with its logical perfection. However, article 22 has made that attempt and we cannot define the status of the mandated territories in its spirit if we neglect evolution. We must attempt to define the status of these territories in terms of the future as well as of the present and the past.

Thus we propose to seek the answer to four questions: (1) Who has title to mandated territories in the sense of ultimate power to change their status? (2) Who has ultimate responsibility for injuries to other states arising from the acts or omissions of the governments of the territories? (3) Who has authority to change the fundamental law binding the inhabitants of each area? (4) Whom does the policy of the system contemplate as the eventual sovereign?

1. Title to Mandated Territory

International law has treated territorial sovereignty like real property the title to which can be determined by tracing back valid transfers as far as the memory of man or to original acquisition. It recognizes certain legitimate modes of acquisition and transfer and assumes that sovereignty of territory can only exist by virtue of proper original acquisition of *res nullius* or proper transfer from the former sovereign. As a rule only he who has title can give title. Sovereignty of a territory thus involves ultimate power of disposal under international law and so is distinguished from jurisdiction or *de jure* control of the administration in whole or part, permanently or temporarily as in leases, protectorates, and foreign administrations and also from merely *de facto* control as in military occupation. Occupation not only original but also adverse may in time develop into sovereignty as by prescription or by completed conquest, consequently it gives some evidence of sovereignty in the absence of other data. But we may regard title in the sense of ultimate power of disposal established by the final instrument in a chain of valid transfers from a former sovereign as the best evidence for determining the sovereignty of the mandated territories.[7]

[7] See *supra*, chap. ix, sec. 2*d*; chap. xi, sec. 2*c*. Although international law resembles Roman law in emphasizing that occupation (possession) is not sovereignty (ownership),

Germany was undoubtedly the sovereign of the African and Pacific territories before 1914,[8] and by article 119 of the peace treaty she renounced them in favor of the Principal Allied and Associated Powers. Was this a transfer of sovereignty to those Powers? Since the same phrase was used as to Dantzig, the Saar, Memel, and other places which were clearly given a different ultimate disposition by other clauses of the treaty and since a different ultimate disposition was specified for the mandated territories themselves in article 22 we must answer in the negative. The Principal Allied and Associated Powers were not given sovereignty of the territory in the sense of discretion to keep it or alienate it. They were merely, as emphasized by the Supreme Court of South Africa, given a commission to dispose of it in a specified manner.[9] This disposition was described by article 22 of the Covenant which prescribed that all of these territories should be administered by "mandatories in behalf of the League."

The Principal Powers performed this commission through resolutions assigning the territories to mandatories on May 7, 1919, and May 20, 1920, through subsequent agreement on the boundaries, and through notification of these decisions to the League Council.[10] All of this is recorded in the preambles of the mandates, which are in the form of grants by the League of Nations reciting article 119 of the treaty; the agreement of the Principal Powers to intrust the administration of the territory to the named mandatory "for the purpose of giving effect to the provisions of article 22 of the Covenant"; the acceptance by the mandatory, and also the provision of article 22, that "the degree of authority, control or administration to be exercised by the mandatory not having been previously agreed upon by the members of the League shall be explicitly defined by the council of the League of Nations."[11]

---

it recognizes that occupation may become sovereignty, in time, consequently in result this method of proving territorial sovereignty differs little from what has been called the "best evidence of title" in English law: "that possession or seisin which is older in origin, and therefore better, than that of any known claimant" (see *supra*, chap. xi, n. 64).

[8] Germany called them *Schutzgebiete*, or "protectorates," but her laws assimilating them to national territory seem to have been recognized (Lindley, *The Acquisition and Government of Backward Territories in International Law*, pp. 205–6).

[9] See *supra*, chap. xii, sec. 4; *infra*, n. 115.

[10] See *supra*, chap. ii, sec. 3.

[11] See *supra*, chap. iv, sec. 3.

To the writer the reasonable interpretation of these documents is that the Principal Powers, having performed the mission intrusted to them by the treaties, passed out of the picture. It is true the evidence of definitive transfer from the Principal Powers is not as satisfactory as it might be. There is no formal treaty signed and ratified by them, merely the record of their resolutions, of their notifications to the League, and the preambles of the mandates. In view, however, of the duty laid upon them by fair implication from the terms of article 22 which they had ratified formally, further formal ratification seemed unnecessary. They did what they had agreed to do and the territories came under the régime established by article 22.[12]

In the case of the mandates of Palestine and Syria, there is merely the recital that the Principal Allied Powers have agreed to intrust the territory "which formerly belonged to the Turkish Empire" to the mandatory in accord with article 22, with no indication of the method by which Turkey lost her sovereignty. The treaty of Sèvres by which she renounced these territories in favor of the Principal Allied Powers was never ratified, and the treaty of Lausanne by which she renounced them was not made at the time the mandates were assigned. It would thus appear that the transfer from Turkey at the time the mandates were assigned could be accounted for only on the principle of successful revolution or completed conquest. The United States argued for the latter—in fact, it asserted that the Principal Allied Powers gained title to the German colonies by conquest and, since it assisted in the defeat of the central Powers, although never at war with Turkey, it was entitled to a share in all the spoils of victory.[13]

It does not appear, however, that the mode by which the Principal Allied Powers got a transitory title makes any present difference. Turkey expressly renounced her title by the subsequent treaty of Lausanne, and the Principal Allies were bound by their previous ratification of the Covenant which specifically refers to former Turkish territories, if not by articles 94–97 of the treaty of Sèvres, to consign all the former territories of Turkey as well as the non-European territories of Germany to the régime of article 22.

[12] See *supra*, chap. x, sec. 2*a*.

[13] *Ibid.* and chap. ii, sec. 4; chap. xiii, sec. 4*e*.

In the case of Iraq, the treaty of 1922 between Great Britain and that country recites, "His Britiannic Majesty has recognized Feisal Ibn Hussein as constitutional king of Iraq," and makes no mention of the mandate. This seems to assume a British recognition of the independence of Iraq. The Council's decision of September, 1924, defining the Iraq mandate, however, recites article 16 of the treaty of Lausanne by which Turkey renounced the territory, article 22 of the Covenant, and a British statement asserting that Iraq had passed under British occupation, that the Principal Allied Powers had intended to confer on her a mandate, that she had accepted, but in view of the rapid progress of Iraq had concluded the treaty of alliance "to ensure the complete observance and execution in Iraq of the principles which the acceptance of the mandate was intended to secure." Although the term "mandate" does not appear in the Anglo-Iraq Treaty it seems that Iraq agreed in that document to the British exercise of power adequate to fulfil the mandate.[14]

It is to be noted that the Mosul controversy was settled on the basis that Turkey did not lose territory by conquest but by the Lausanne Treaty and the subsequent interpretation of it by the League Council as authorized in its second article.[15] Nevertheless, the recognition of Iraq in 1922 before the Lausanne Treaty was signed indicates that for Great Britain, at least, Iraq became independent as a result of allied conquest and Iraq revolt. Part of this independence she then gave up by the treaty of alliance with Great Britain, and this part Great Britain then submitted to the régime of article 22.

Thus a study of the transfers indicates that for all the mandated areas except Iraq title passed from Germany or Turkey to the Principal Powers, who, however, never had full sovereignty but merely a transitional title of which they divested themselves in transferring title to the régime set up by the Covenant. Consequently, for all the areas except Iraq full sovereignty is located as defined in that instrument, and for Iraq, which has been recognized as independent, it is so vested except for a portion of sovereignty retained by the government of that country itself.

[14] See *supra*, chap. ii, sec. 5.

[15] Wright, "The Mosul Controversy," *A.J.I.L.*, XX, 455.

This is as far as a study of the history of transfers will take us. No subsequent transactions have modified the legal status of the areas. The various emendations of the Iraq Treaty merely relate to the time when a modification of the latter's status will be considered, and while amendments of other mandates and recognition of other native governments have rectified boundaries or forms of government, they have not affected international status.[16]

The status set up by article 22 will be discussed from the standpoints of responsibility, *de facto* control, and policy in subsequent sections. Here we shall assume that the territories now have the status of mandated territory as defined in article 22 of the Covenant, and ask what authority or combination of authorities has power to change that status. Such a change would seem possible through (1) modification of the article, (2) performance of the article, or (3) an act which was legally effective though in violation of the article.

Article 22 is part of the Covenant, which is a treaty between the fifty-six members of the League. In general, a treaty can be modified only in accord with its own terms or by consent of all the parties. The possibilities of article 22 terminating by conclusion of a new treaty among all the parties, by obsolescence or by application of the rule *rebus sic stantibus*, may be neglected. A war does not ordinarily affect multilateral treaties in law.[17] Thus the only practical way to modify article 22 is by the amending process defined in article 26 of the Covenant, i.e., by ratification of an amendment by the members of the League whose representatives compose the Council and a majority of those whose representatives compose the Assembly.

Article 22 in terms applies to "certain territories which are inhabited by peoples not yet able to stand by themselves under the strenuous conditions of the modern world," thus it would appear that if the inhabitants of one of the territories evolved out of that stage, article 22 would be performed, and the status it prescribes would no longer be applicable to that territory. This conclusion is fortified by use of the word "tutelage," by reference to "the stage of the development of the people," and by the express assertion that some of these communities "have reached a stage of development

[16] See *supra*, chap. iv, sec. 5.

[17] On methods of terminating treaties see Oppenheim, *op. cit.*, Vol. I, secs. 534-49.

where their existence as independent nations can be provisionally recognized subject to the rendering of administrative advice and assistance by a mandatory until such time as they are able to stand alone."[18] Who is competent to recognize the achievement of that evolution? Admission of one of these communities to the League would imply that it had become "fully self governing" (Covenant, art. 1) and thus apparently beyond the stage contemplated in article 22. This has been recognized in the case of Iraq.[19] Such admission can be effected by a vote of two-thirds of the Assembly. In international law, however, political claims may always become legal rights through general recognition. Thus if one of these communities asserted that it no longer needed tutelage and the states of the world expressly recognized that claim, the status of the community would seem to be legally changed. Such a general recognition, however, is hardly conceivable without formal action by the League.

There is finally the possibility of annexation or other change of the status of an area by the mandatory, conquest by some other power or revolution, and ousting of the mandatory by the inhabitants, any of which would be in violation of article 22. Such violent changes might acquire *de jure* character through subsequent general recognition or long acquiescence in the changed situation. A change of this character may, of course, come about with reference to any territory in the world, whether under mandate or not, but the mandate status, sanctioned as it is by all the members of the League, is perhaps less liable than others to such a change.[20]

Thus it appears that the only probable manner of changing the status of mandated territory is through action of the League by

[18] Lindley agrees with regard to A mandates but says, "In the cases of B mandates and C mandate territory, article 22 does not appear to contemplate the termination of the status of territory under mandate" (*op. cit.*, p. 269).

[19] See L. of N. Council, sess. LVIII, item 2553, *supra*, chap. ii, sec. 5. Woolf seems to think that a mandated community might become a member of the League without changing its status (International Law Association, *Report of the 29th Conference* [1920], p. 136).

[20] The Russian repudiation of the Black Sea clauses of the treaty of Paris in 1870 and the Austrian annexation of Bosnia and Herzegovina in 1908 in violation of the Berlin Treaty of 1878 are examples of action which gained general recognition in time of peace though the consequences of the latter were not such as to commend the practice.

amending article 22, by admitting a mandated community to its membership, or by otherwise recognizing the latter's independence. Thus the League of Nations seems competent and alone competent to change the status of territory now under article 22.

2. Responsibility for Mandatory Administration

Some writers pay less attention to past and possible future transfers of territory than to present control in determining the sovereignty of territory. Holding that possession is nine if not ten points of the law, they tend to regard the *de facto* ruler as the sovereign—a procedure which may seem supported by the fact that conquest has been deemed a legitimate mode of transfer.[21] Mere military occupation, however, has never been regarded as equivalent to sovereignty. It can only acquire that status through subsequent acts or events.[22] In fact, to hold that violence could immediately become the foundation for legal rights would seem to deny a legal order altogether. Nevertheless, all systems of law recognize the influence of long acquiescence, not only as a source of law (custom), but as a source of particular jural relations (prescription).[23] Titles may be lost through long abandonment or acquired through long possession. Actions may be barred by the passage of time. The status of individuals may change through long residence. While possession is different from ownership, it is considered in all systems of law to give a presumption of ownership and to be entitled to some legal protection.[24] In public law the legal recognition of *de facto* authority is even stronger. A general *de facto* government has but to manifest its intention and ability to stay in power to become a *de jure* government so far as the

[21] See *supra*, chap. x, n. 35; chap. xi, nn. 63, 64.

[22] Effect of the League of Nations Covenant, *A.P.S.R.*, XIII, 559. Military occupation has been said to suspend the sovereignty of the *de jure* sovereign and to give temporary rights of sovereignty (*U.S.* v. *Rice*, 4 Wheat. 246 [1819]).

[23] Salmond, *Jurisprudence*, pp. 109, 155–56, 534–35.

[24] *Ibid.*, p. 324; *supra*, chap. xi, sec. 2*c*. The Roman law of *usucapion* required that possession, to enjoy legal protection, must have been taken bona fide and *ex justa causa* (Justinian *Inst.* ii. 6). International law does not go so far (Lindley, *op. cit.*, p. 178) though it does not minimize the distinction between possession and ownership so much as does English law, which protects possession against anyone except he with a possession older in origin (see *supra*, chap. xi, sec. 2).

state's own courts are concerned.[25] While international law requires that *de facto* political changes achieved by revolution, insurrection, or conquest secure general recognition from the states of the world to become *de jure*, the fact that tacit recognition will be assumed from acquiescence through a reasonable time renders the transition easy. "It is a settled principle of the law of nations," said the Hague tribunal of arbitration in 1909, "that a state of things which actually exists and has existed for a long time should be changed as little as possible."[26] Thus even if the sovereignty of a mandated territory were clearly defined by the record of transfers, that sovereignty might gradually change through general acquiescence in a different practice.

Who is the *de facto* sovereign of a territory? From the international law point of view it is the authority which other states hold responsible for injuries which they receive in the territory, and from the municipal law point of view it is the authority competent in fact to change the fundamental law of the territory.[27] Neither of these is necessarily the *de jure* sovereign. States may hold a particular authority responsible for injuries in a given territory without intending to recognize the latter as sovereign of the territory, but merely of the administration. The lessee, for instance, is held responsible for international delinquencies in leased territory, and the protector is usually held responsible for such incidents in a protectorate.[28] Thus the practice in regard to responsibility is not conclusive evidence of recognition of sovereignty.

The same is true with regard to ascriptions of sovereignty by the operative internal law of the territory. Municipal law cannot overrule international law in determining international status. If, however, the authority accorded sovereignty by the internal law is at the same time recognized by foreign states as responsible, that authority

[25] *Luther* v. *Borden*, 7 How 1, 40; Dodd, *The Revision and Amendment of State Constitutions* (1910), p. 101; Noel-Henry, *Les Gouvernements de fait devant le juge* (Paris, 1927), pp. 5, 237.

[26] Norway-Sweden maritime frontier arbitration, Scott, *Hague Court Reports*, p. 130; see also Lindley, *op. cit.*, p. 178. A general *de facto* government has been held competent to bind the state (Great Britain–Costa Rica arbitration [1923], *A.J.I.L.*, XVIII, 155).

[27] See *supra*, chap. ix, sec. 2*d*.

[28] See *supra*, chap. ix, nn. 82, 89, 90.

would seem to be both superior to municipal law and subject to international law with respect to the territory, and so sovereign of it. The *de facto* sovereign would have become the *de jure* sovereign. The *animus* and *corpus* necessary to establish possession would be present, and this would have received the general acquiescence necessary to convert it into ownership.[29]

We shall, then, attempt to locate the authorities responsible for the acts of mandatory governments and the authorities accorded sovereignty of the mandated peoples by the fundamental law of the regions, with the clear understanding that the conclusions reached on either point are not in themselves conclusive, but only contributing, evidence of the sovereignty of the areas.

International law requires that every state provide within its government some definite representative authority before which foreign states may make complaints. Clearly, division of responsibility in this regard would make international relations exceedingly difficult.[30] It appears that the mandatory's home governments have actually been held responsible by foreign states with respect to mandated territory.[31] Does this practice conform to the provisions of article 22 and the mandates?

International responsibility only becomes manifest upon the complaint of another state that international law has been violated to its injury. Such international delinquencies may arise from (*a*) wrongful acts of officials or agencies of the government resulting in injury to foreign governments, their territory, or their citizens; (*b*)

[29] Salmond, *op. cit.*, pp. 294, 325; *supra*, chap. xi, sec. 2*c*.

[30] Wright, *Control of American Foreign Relations*, pp. 15–20. Eagleton discusses the possibility of divided responsibility (*op. cit.*, p. 35). See *supra*, chap. ix, n. 90.

[31] Great Britain, for instance, was hailed before the Permanent Court of International Justice by Greece on the allegation that the Mavromatis Palestine concession had been violated and Turkey negotiated with Great Britain in regard to the Mosul boundary. Stoyanovsky discusses possible differences in the responsibility of "the mandatory" and "the administration of Palestine," both of which expressions appear in the mandate, concluding that the mandatory alone is responsible in international law but that it is proper to recognize the distinction internally in order to prepare the administration of Palestine for eventual autonomy. Several international agreements have been made by Palestine by authority of the high commissioner, one of them with the mandatory (*The Mandate for Palestine*, pp. 199–200, 283; *L. of N. Treaty Series*, XIII, 10–24).

from inadequate administrative or judicial processes within the territory resulting in such injury; (*c*) from repudiation or non-fulfilment of contracts, loans, agreements, treaties, arbitral awards, or other obligations due to another state. A state is bound to control its agents, to govern its territory, and to fulfil its obligations, and is responsible if its failure to do so results in injury to other states.[32] For the acts of their private nationals abroad states do not seem to be responsible.[33]

a) WRONGFUL ACTS OF OFFICERS

It is believed that responsibility for acts of the first type belongs to the mandatory alone in B and C territories. The mandatory is in charge of the area's foreign affairs, is intrusted by the mandate with "full powers of administration," and the officials in the B and C territories are its officials acting under its laws.[34] States injured as a result of their official acts would seem entitled to hold the mandatory responsible, even though the official is not a national of the mandatory but a native of the territory and probably even if the act is committed outside the mandated territory. In the case of A mandated territories the administration acts to some extent under native governments accorded a certain degree of recognition, but in each case the mandatory is mainly or entirely responsible for the conduct of foreign relations.

If foreign nations established definite relations with Iraq, as is possible, with British consent, under article 5 of the treaty, they could undoubtedly hold Iraq responsible for torts by its official agents. In the absence of such recognition, however, foreign governments can undoubtedly hold Great Britain responsible. By the treaty of alliance, the king of Iraq agrees to appoint no gazetted official of other than Iraq nationality without British consent (art. 2) and to be guided by British advice in all important matters affecting the latter's international and financial obligations and interests (art. 4) and not to establish diplomatic relations with any foreign capital without British consent (art. 5). Under the League decision

[32] Wright, *Control of American Foreign Relations*, pp. 151–53.

[33] Though it may acquire rights from their acts (Lindley, *op. cit.*, pp. 84–90).

[34] The Tanganyika order in council, 1926, requires members of the legislative council to make an oath of allegiance to the British crown (see *supra*, chap. xii, sec. 3).

putting the mandate in effect Great Britain declared that the purpose of the treaty "is to ensure complete observance and execution in Iraq of the principles which the acceptance of the mandate was tended to secure," and "assumes towards all members of the League of Nations who accept the provisions of this arrangement and the benefits of the said treaty, responsibility for the fulfillment by Iraq of the provisions of the said treaty of alliance." These provisions seem to make Great Britain responsible for tortious acts of Iraq officials. Although responsibility is expressly assumed only toward members of the League, it is believed that under general international law other states could hold Great Britain responsible if they have not recognized Iraq.[35]

In Palestine, the administration is entirely under British control and responsibility,[36] and in Syria and the Lebanon, France seems to assume full responsibility. In granting a constitution to the latter in 1927 provision was made in article 90 that "the powers established by the present constitution shall be exercised subject to the right and duty of the mandatory as they result from article 22 of the covenant of the League of Nations and from the mandate." Her accredited representative explained at the eleventh session of the Commission that this gave the mandatory full control. "If these populations really require a guardian," he said, "it could not be admitted that they were entitled to take decisions which could be legally opposed to those of their guardian, and which would annul the mandate itself." M. Orts of the Commission approved this because it showed that "the mandatory did not consider itself discharged from the point of view of the League of Nations from the responsibility for the execution of the provisions of the mandate as a result of the powers conferred on the local governments by the constitutional laws."[37]

[35] See *supra*, chap. xiii, sec. 3*b*.

[36] Mandate, art. 12. The Permanent Mandates Commission questioned the British recognition of the Emir Abdullah's government in Transjordan on this account (see *supra*, chap. xiii, sec. 3*b;* see also Stoyanovsky, *The Mandate for Palestine*, p. 199).

[37] See Mandate, art. 3; *P.M.C.*, *Min.*, XI, 144. On account of this responsibility France refused to accept a provision in the proposed Syrian constitution of 1929 conferring certain foreign-relations powers on the native government, and her position was approved by the Permanent Mandates Commission (*Min.*, XIII, 183, 217; see also *F.P.A.*, *Inf. Ser.*, V, 74, and *supra*, chap. xiii, sec. 3*b*).

b) INADEQUATE GOVERNMENT IN THE TERRITORY

In regard to the inadequacy of legislative, administrative, or judicial processes within mandated territories resulting in injury to foreign states or their citizens, the primary responsibility has also been with the mandatory, though it seems that in this case the League may have some eventual responsibility. The mandatory administers the B and C areas except Tanganyika as integral parts of its own territory, and the mandates declare it responsible for the peace, order, and good government of the territory.

In Palestine and Syria, the mandatory assumes full responsibility for internal conditions. In the former, clauses specifically impose sole responsibility upon it in connection with the holy places (art. 13). The United States would have to claim from France in behalf of its citizens damaged by the bombardment of Damascus, and the same seems to be true in Iraq under the provisions of the treaty and the Council's decisions referred to, in spite of the presence of the native government. The Iraq Treaty, as well as the Syrian and Palestine mandates, provide for the suspension of extraterritoriality, but in each case the mandatory expressly assumes responsibility for the maintenance of an adequate judicial system for cases involving foreigners.[38]

The mandatory is primarily responsible, but in case he fails to meet that responsibility, may recourse be had to the League? The mandatory administers the territory in "behalf of the League," and under principles of private law the *mandans* is responsible like a principal for acts of his agent.[38a] If, however, we applied the concepts of tutelage and trusts, a different conclusion would follow. The trustee or tutor alone would be responsible. The court or chancellor would never be responsible for the malfeasance or negligence of the trustee or the tutor except in the sense of a duty to compel such person to make reparation and perhaps to transfer the trust or tutelage to another.[39] The League is clearly burdened with at least this latter type of responsibility. Its entire activity indicates its sense of a duty

[38] Palestine Mandate, art. 9; Syrian Mandate, art. 6.

[38a] Though this was not originally true of the Roman Mandatories (see *supra*, chap. xi, n. 96).

[39] See *supra*, chap. xi, sec. 3.

to see that the mandates are observed. The provisions in all the mandates for appeal in case of alleged infractions injurious to foreign states, to the Permanent Court of International Justice, is an important assistance to the League in meeting this responsibility.[39a]

To say that the League is bound to exert every effort to induce the mandatory to meet its responsibilities with respect to the government of the territory is not to say that it becomes itself responsible if these efforts fail. The League may receive petitions, make recommendations, and after a decision of the Permanent Court may even transfer the mandate; but it is difficult to state a definite ground, except the analogy to the private law of *mandatum*, for holding it obligated to make financial or other reparation itself if, in spite of these measures, third states suffer because of the inadequacy of the local governments.[40]

c) OBLIGATIONS OF MANDATED COMMUNITIES

Treaties, agreements, contracts, loans, or other obligations contracted or assumed in behalf of mandated countries and due to third states can only be made by the mandatory, which, except in the case of Iraq, has sole charge of the foreign relations of the territory.[41] Iraq has agreed by treaty to accept British advice on all important matters "affecting the international and financial obligations" of Great Britain (art. 4) and to conclude separate agreements to be communicated to the League of Nations "to secure the execution of any treaties, agreements or understandings which His Britannic Majesty is under obligations to see carried out in respect to Iraq "

[39a] Stoyanovsky points out that the League is bound to intervene to preserve the territorial integrity of mandated territory, peace within them, and fulfilment of the mandate, not under art. 10 of the Covenant, but under art. 22 (*op. cit.*, pp. 209–10, and Wright, "The Bombardment of Domascus," *A.J.I.L.*, XX, 276–80).

[40] The texts furnish less basis for League responsibility in this case than in that of contract obligations discussed in the next section. If the responsibility on account of a tort were liquidated by a decision of the Permanent Court of International Justice or an agreement with the mandatory, it would seem to be a personal obligation of the latter rather than an obligation of the territory for which the League might be responsible. That international law recognizes no succession to tortious liability was decided by the Robert E. Brown claim (*U.S.* v. *Great Britain*, *B.Y.B.I.L.*, 1924, pp. 163 ff., Lauterpacht, *op. cit.*, p. 283).

[41] See *supra*, nn. 36, 37.

(art. 10). In the Council decision confirming the mandate Great Britain assumed responsibility for the execution of this treaty toward members of the League who accepted it.

Thus it appears that in all the areas the mandatory is primarily responsible for the execution of agreements, including the mandates themselves made in behalf of the territory. Under the terms of some of the mandates this responsibility applies to certain agreements made by earlier governments. Thus Greece was able to hold Great Britain responsible when its citizen Mavromatis claimed that his concession granted by Turkey was impaired.[42] Turkey dealt with Great Britain in reference to the treaty for determining the Mosul boundary. The United States dealt with the mandatories alone when it felt its cable interests in Yap and its commercial interests in the Near East were impaired, and eventually made treaties with them. Such agreements, however, bind the mandatory only in that capacity. In case of transfer the successor to the mandate is bound. This is expressly provided in the A mandates, and the Council has held the same for B and C mandates.[43]

Is the League eventually responsible for the execution of such agreements? The mandate for Palestine (art. 28) provides that in the event of the termination of the mandate the Council of the League "shall use its influence for securing, under guarantee of the League," that the successor will honor the financial obligations legitimately incurred by the administration of the territory. The Syrian mandate (art. 19) is similar, omitting the phrase "under guarantee of the League." The Council's decision on Iraq provides that on termination it "shall be invited to decide what further measures are required to give effect to article 22 of the covenant." The term "guarantee" in the Palestine mandate seems to indicate that the League would be financially responsible if the successor failed to meet obligations of the previous administration.[43a]

[42] See *supra*, chap. v, sec. 5; chap. xiii, n. 147.

[43] See *supra*, chap. xiii, secs. *2d* and *4c, d*.

[43a] It is surprising that the word "guarantee" was not omitted since the words "shall use its influence for securing" were substituted for "shall use such arrangements as may be deemed necessary .... for securing" after the Secretary-General had suggested that the latter phraseology might "impose on the League a new guarantee which was of a

The same question has arisen with regard to other mandates. Australia submitted a proposed loan to New Guinea to the League for confirmation. After considerable discussion the original proposal in the Council to do this was abandoned, apparently because the Council feared it might involve the League in responsibility for the loan, so the Australian statement was merely noted.[44]

The lack of confidence of investors in the mandatory régime led mandatories to raise the question of the possibility of mortgaging specific revenues or land for loans and the consequences of transfer of the mandate upon such transactions. The Commission gave extensive study to the matter, and the opinions of the mandatories were elicited, some of which involved extensive expositions of the legal theory of the system. Australia thought that so far as possible the mandatory should get express sanction of the Council before hypothecating revenues for loans.[45] France and Japan, on the other hand, insisted it would be contrary to the system to do so. The mandatory, they insisted, was alone responsible for such a transaction, and Japan feared that Council sanction would involve the League in serious responsibilities.[46] Belgium developed an elaborate analogy to the private law tutelage and asked, "What, then, in modern law is the effect of tutelage on the property of the ward?" . . . . "All acts," the note concluded, "carried out by the guardian in behalf of the ward are valid and irrevocable and the estate is still liable in respect of all engagements, debts and mortages regularly contracted" after termination of the relation or change of guardian.[47] All agreed that the successor was liable, and the general sentiment was against express Council sanction of such agreements. These conclusions were eventually embodied in a formal Council resolution.[48]

The question of the League's eventual responsibility, however, does not seem to be finally solved. In the opinion of the present writer the Council might well have taken the view that loans, contracts, or treaties which impose fairly permanent burdens on the ter-

---

financial character," and that the League "had not hitherto accepted a guarantee of that kind" (*O.J.*, III [1922], 822; Stoyanovsky, *op. cit.*, p. 228).

[44] L. of N. Council, Min., sess. XXX, *O.J.*, V, 1334, 1596.

[45] *Ibid.*, p. 1076.

[46] *Ibid.*, VI, 335; V, 1813.

[47] *Ibid.*, V, 1078.

[48] *Ibid.*, VI, 510.

ritory should receive its sanction before ratification by the mandatory, both because they might involve an eventual responsibility even if not expressly sanctioned and because the Council's scrutiny would be an additional security against violations of the mandate which might occur in such agreements and which would be more difficult to eliminate than infractions occurring in ordinary legislative or administrative decisions.[49]

The Council has insisted that any agreements modifying the boundaries of mandated territories be approved by it, and it originally suggested that the United States meet with it to discuss its claims to most favored nation treatment in mandated territory. The United States, however, declined to do so and made treaties with the mandatories individually, which were not submitted to the League for approval.[50] In the light of practice we must conclude that the mandatory can impose obligations upon mandated communities without express Council consent but that the League is bound to see that rights accruing to foreigners under them are respected by the successor in case of transfer, and possibly is, in some cases, under financial responsibility itself in case of default.

Responsibility to outside states with respect to mandated territory thus seems to vest, both according to practice and according to the documents, primarily in the mandatory, though in Iraq the native government seems to assume responsibility for its acts toward states which have recognized and exchanged diplomatic officers with it. The League is bound to use every effort to induce the mandatory to meet its responsibilities in regard to the territory, to see that a successor fulfils contract obligations made in behalf of it and possibly in certain cases itself to meet such obligations in case the mandatory defaults.[51]

3. Jurisdiction over Mandated Peoples

De facto internal sovereignty of a thing may be said to reside in the authority competent in fact to change the fundamental munici-

[49] See *supra*, chap. xiii, sec. 2*d*.

[50] *Ibid.*

[51] The Hymans report of August, 1920, referred to the League responsibility as of a moral rather than a legal character (see *infra*, n. 119; see also Ormsby-Gore, in *The League of Nations Starts*, p. 113).

pal law governing it. Let us then attempt to locate the authority competent under the existing fundamental law of each mandated territory (*a*) to modify that law, (*b*) to alienate or transfer the governing authority, and (*c*) to determine the status of the inhabitants.

a) AMENDMENT OF MANDATE TEXTS

Any one of four documents might be considered fundamental law of each mandated area: the treaty article ceding the territory, article 22 of the Covenant, the mandate, or the local constitution. The first was apparently transient and ceased to have effect after the régime of article 22 was established.[52] Article 22 is undoubtedly the basic document establishing the régime under international law, but it has not been considered law within the areas. Although it attempted to bring the mandate texts into conformity with this article before original confirmation, the League has refused to consider subsequent petitions alleging action in conflict with article 22, and local authorities have never looked beyond the mandate to the Covenant. From the standpoint of the municipal law of the areas article 22 appears to be a political not a legal document.[53]

The mandate texts or charters have been regarded by the League and the mandatories as the fundamental law for the areas. Legislation contrary to their terms has been criticized by the League Council and usually considered void by the mandatory's own courts. They are, it is true, documents of international law, resting on international agreement and interpretable by the Permanent Court of International Justice, but they are also the fundamental constitution from which internal governing authority in the areas derives.[54] In each of the areas there is also a local constitution. In Iraq this was formed by a native constitutional convention, and the same is true in some of the other A territories. In other cases the local constitution is in the form of a decree or a statute of the mandatory. These docu-

[52] See *supra*, sec. 1.

[53] The authority of the Permanent Mandates Commission under the Covenant extends only to advising on "all matters relating to the observance of the mandates," and the jurisdiction of the Permanent Court of International Justice only extends to disputes "relating to the interpretation or the application of the provisions of the mandate" (see *supra*, chap. iv, sec. 4).

[54] See *supra*, n. 53, chap. xii, sec. 2; chap. xiii, sec. 2*e*.

ments, however, are considered subordinate to the mandate texts, by the League organs and also in most cases by the mandatories' courts. They usually recite that document as the basis of authority, are interpreted in accord with it, and are void if in violation of it.[55]

Legal validity was originally given to the mandates through the authority of three bodies: the Principal Allied (and Associated) Powers, the mandatory, and the Council of the League. The preamble of each mandate indicates the approval of all of these bodies although the A mandates omit the term "associated powers" in consideration of the official non-participation of the United States in the war against Turkey and in the treaties of Sèvres and Lausanne. A mandates also indicate no participation of the Principal Allied Powers in the drawing of the mandate but only in the selection of the mandatory. None of the mandates except that for Iraq indicates any acceptance of the mandate or the mandatory by the mandated community, though article 22 says with regard to A mandates: "The wishes of these communities must be a principal consideration in the selection of the mandatory." The Iraq mandate, based on a treaty between Great Britain and Iraq, alone fulfils this condition.[56]

Is not approval by the same three authorities necessary to amend the mandate? In practice the Principal Allied (and Associated) Powers seem to have exercised no authority in respect to the matter since allocation of the mandates. From that time the government of the territories has been determined entirely by article 22 and the mandates. The eighth paragraph of this article says: "The degree of authority, control or administration to be exercised by the mandatory shall, if not previously agreed upon by the Members of the League, be explicitly defined in each case by the council." It was contended in the first Assembly meeting that the expression "members of the League" referred to all the members of the League, consequently the Assembly was the body for defining the terms of the mandates. The Council, however, has held that this expression refers only to the members of the League parties to the peace treaties.[57] This paragraph is recited in the preamble of all but C mandates and apparently refers to the power of the "members of the League" in

[55] See *supra*, chaps. xii, xiii.

[56] See *supra*, chap. ii, sec. 3.

[57] See *supra*, chap. iv, sec. 3; chap. xiii, sec. 1*c*.

drawing the original mandates—a power which they seem not to have exercised in the case of A mandates—but has not implied any control over subsequent mandates. This paragraph does, however, indicate a necessity for Council consent to all amendments or interpretations, a necessity stipulated in each mandate and recognized in practice. Since the mandate records an "agreement," no one party should be entitled to change it at discretion and practice indicates that the Council alone cannot amend a mandate, nor can the mandatory. It appears, however, that within the limits of the Covenant the two together may do so. Modification of the Palestine mandate, excluding the provisions relating to a Jewish national home from Transjordan, were actually proposed by the mandatory and became effective on approval by the Council. The modifications of various mandate boundaries such as that between Ruanda and Tanganyika were effected by a similar procedure.[58] Where, as in the case of Iraq, the mandate accepts an agreement between the mandatory and the local government as the mandate text, consent of that local government as well as of the Council seems necessary for an amendment, and this procedure has actually been followed on several occasions.[59]

Any amendment, even if accepted by the mandatory and the Council, would violate international law if contrary to article 22, and any member of the League would be entitled to complain and to hold the mandatory responsible. It also appears that the United States, although not a member of the League, has gained under special treaties with most of the mandatories the power to protest modifications of the present mandates, at least as affects itself.[60] But, although the mandatory together with the Council (and in some cases the native government) in amending a mandate in any important particular would be responsible under international law if they failed to get the consent of other states with such treaty interests, this limitation does not seem different from that upon the international capacity of any sovereign state to modify its own constitution in derogation of the

[58] See *supra*, chap. iv, sec. 5; chap. xiii, secs. 1*c*, 2*d*.

[59] See Council resolution on Iraq, March 11, 1926, and British proposal to change the judicial system in Iraq, approved in principle by the Council (54th sess., March 9, 1929).

[60] See *supra*, chap. ii, sec. 4.

treaty rights of other states.[61] It does not militate against the possession of sovereignty by those authorities so far as the municipal law of the area is concerned.

b). ALIENATION AND TRANSFER OF MANDATES

The mandate of a particular mandatory would of course be terminated by termination of the mandate status of a territory, through modification or fulfilment of article 22 of the Covenant.[62] Without changing that status it is conceivable that the mandate of a particular power might terminate through resignation, revocation, or transfer of its mandate. The A mandates expressly provide that "on the termination of the mandate, the council of the League of Nations shall use its influence" to assure the fulfilment of financial obligations by the mandated territory and, in the case of Palestine, the security of holy places. The method of such termination is not stated, nor have any mandates actually been terminated.[63]

If the mandatory acting with consent of the Council can amend the mandate text, the same authorities would seem competent to change the mandatory, subject, in international law, to the limitations of article 22 and other relevant treaties. This, of course, means that while the particular mandate might be revoked, the territory would remain under article 22 of the Covenant until there was general recognition of its independence or annexation or until the League as a whole had given its consent in the proper manner.

It has been contended, on analogy to the Roman law of *mandatum*, that the mandatory may, on finding the burden too heavy, resign the responsibility, or that the League, represented by the Council as *mandans*, may revoke the mandate.[64] Some writers have interpreted the article referred to in A mandates as authority for resignation by the mandatory with assurance of reimbursement of administrative expenses in such an event.[65] The general principle of international law which forbids the unilateral termination of international agreements in the absence of breach of duty or express provision is,

[61] Wright, *Control of American Foreign Relations*, p. 58; "International Law in Relation to Constitutional Law," *A.J.I.L.*, XVII, 242.

[62] See *supra*, sec. 1.

[63] See *supra*, chap. xiii, secs. 1*a*, 2*a*.

[64] Goudy, *Journ. C.L.* (3d ser.), I, 180–81.

[65] Keith, *ibid.*, IV, 80.

however, opposed to this interpretation.[66] The mandate, while the constitution of the area, is also an international agreement between the League represented by the Council and the mandatory and can normally be terminated only by agreement of the two.[67]

The same statement would also apply to the transfer of a mandate under normal conditions. The discussion in the Permanent Mandate Commission and the Council over the assumed transfer of the mandate of Nauru from the British Empire to Australia indicates that the mandatory cannot voluntarily transfer a mandate. It appears also and has been expressly stated by Australia that so long as the mandatory meets the terms of the mandate the League has no authority to transfer the mandate to another state.[68]

The mandatory is undoubtedly under a duty, both as a member of the League bound by article 22 and as a party to the particular mandate to observe the latter. The League has provided an elaborate system of informal advice, administrative recommendation, and judicial decision backed by full publicity to induce such observance. If these means fail—if a mandatory persists in violating the mandate or proves incapable of meeting responsibilities under it—what is the result? Under general principles of international law breach of agreement by one party justifies denunciation by the other.[69] Thus breach of a mandate by the mandatory would justify the League in considering the agreement at an end, in which case there would be no internal constitution of the area but article 22 of the Covenant would remain in effect. Would the League be competent to appoint a new mandatory?

Though given originally by the Principal Allied (and Associated) Powers, the mandates once given are exercised "on behalf of the League." Under the Roman law of *mandatum* the right of revocation and transfer in case of breach of agreement rested in the *mandans*.

[66] See declaration of London conference of 1871 (Satow, *Diplomatic Practice*, II, 131). In fact, neither party to a private law mandate or agency has a right to terminate the contract at discretion after execution has begun (see *supra*, chap. xi, sec. 3*a*).

[67] As has been noticed, the Principal Powers, though also parties to the mandates, seemed to have ceased to exist as a corporate body.

[68] See *supra*, chap. xiii, secs. 1*a*, 2*a*.

[69] Vattel, *Droit des gens*, Vol. II, chap. xiii, sec. 202.

Henry Goudy, writing in 1919, though admitting that the analogy of international mandates to mandates in private Roman law is rather vague, says: "Undoubtedly on legal principles failure by the mandatory state to carry out its instructions will warrant revocation." Later he remarks: "Nor is it clear what remedy the mandant will have if the mandatory state neglects its duty under the contract though probably withdrawal of the mandate would follow."[70] D. Campbell Lee, lecturing on the Cecil Rhodes Foundation at London University in 1921, found a close analogy between the obligations of a mandatory and those of a trustee from which he implied "the duty [of the mandatory] to retire whenever requested so to do by the parties interested."[71] A. B. Keith, on the other hand, writes: "The commission, of course, has no authority over the mandatory and the council and assembly alike have no means of enforcing their views on the mandatories other than through the general procedure of the League of Nations which normally implies unanimity of opinion."[72] The members of the Permanent Mandates Commission have generally assumed that power of revocation exists in case the mandatory violates his agreement, but recognize that the general procedure of the League would have to be resorted to.[73] Articles 13 and 14 of the Covenant, in connection with the compromissary article in each of the mandates, would require decision by the Permanent Court of International Justice before action could be taken. If the Court decided that the mandatory had violated the mandate, and its decision were not observed, then the final paragraph of article 13 of the Covenant would become applicable. "The members of the league agree that they will carry out in full good faith any award or decision that may be rendered and that they will not resort to war against a member of the League which complies therewith. In the event of any failure to carry out such an award or decision, the council shall propose what steps should be taken to give effect thereto." The Council un-

[70] *Loc. cit.* See also remarks by Sir Sivaswamy Aiyer of India, in third Assembly (Levermore, *L. of N.*, *Y.B.*, III, 278) and *Round Table* (December, 1918, IX), 27, 97.

[71] *The Mandate for Mesopotamia and the Principle of Trusteeship in English Law* (L. of N. Union, 1921), p. 15.

[72] *Loc. cit.*

[73] See *supra*, chap. xiii, n. 11; see also Ormsby-Gore, *op. cit.*, p. 110.

der this article and under its specific supervisory powers over mandatories would seem competent to transfer the mandate.

Would it have to act unanimously in such a matter? The general requirement of unanimity in article 5 of the Covenant is modified in article 15 by giving weight to a recommendation of the Council on a dispute even though the representatives of the litigants fail to concur. This principle of excluding the parties from being judges in their own case was given a wider application by the Permanent Court of International Justice in the Mosul advisory opinion.[74] It seems highly probable that the issue presented by breach of mandate by the mandatory would arise in a dispute, and thus the vote of the delinquent mandatory would be excluded.[74a] Furthermore under the final paragraph of article 16, which provides for expulsion from the League for "violation of any covenant of the League," the Council could expel the delinquent mandatory from the League by a vote of "all the other members" of the Council, which suggests that dismissal of a mandatory would be possible by the same vote.[75]

c) DETERMINATION OF STATUS OF MANDATED PEOPLES

Where is the power to determine the status of the inhabitants of mandated territory? It was generally recognized that the inhabitants of mandated territory whether of native or European origin did not automatically become nationals of the mandatory, but it was not clear what status they had or who could define it. The manda-

[74] *P.C.I.J.* (Ser. B), No. 12, pp. 31–32.

[74a] The Council has held in respect to minority matters that once they have come before it, "they become an affair between the Council and the state to which the minority belongs, nationally, not a question between that state and the state with which the minority is racially connected" (*O.J.*, IX, 942). But this was because the system was "intended to prevent that questions concerning minority protection should acquire the character of a dispute between nations," and "to insure that states with a minority within their borders should be protected from the danger of interference by other powers in their internal affairs." These reasons hardly apply to the mandated areas and also the compromissory clauses of the mandates evidently foresee the possibility of disputes between a mandatory and a League member in respect to the mandatory's application of his mandate (see *supra*, chap. v, n. 71; chap. xiii, nn. 114, 123).

[75] Stoyanovsky (*La Théorie générale des mandates internationaux*, p. 55) suggested that expulsion of a mandatory from the League would automatically terminate its mandate and that a non-member of the League cannot be a mandatory (see *supra*, chap. xiii, nn. 10, 12).

tory acting with consent of the League Council has assumed the power to determine within the limits of the Covenant the status of such persons even to the extent of permitting mass naturalization of ex-Germans in Southwest Africa by the mandatory with permission for individual declination.[76]

The status of the inhabitants has not yet been precisely defined, though the terms "administered or protected persons under mandate" has been suggested.[77] However, the terms of the treaty of Versailles, the Covenant, and the mandates make it clear that persons under B and C mandates cannot be drafted for military service outside the mandated territory, except for necessary defense;[78] that they are entitled to freedom of conscience and religion and to protection from slave, arms, and liquor trade;[79] that they have a power to petition the League of Nations for redress of grievances;[80] and that they can enjoy the diplomatic protection of the mandatory while abroad.[81] The Supreme Court of South Africa has held that inhabitants of C mandated territory, at least, owe a certain allegiance to the mandatory which may render them liable for treason.[82] Though nationality is often spoken of as "the reciprocal relation of allegiance and protection on the part of the person and the state,"[83] states often extend diplomatic protection to persons not nationals,[84] and persons

[76] See *supra*, chap. xiii, sec. 3*b*. In the B and C mandated areas other than Southwest Africa the "German subjects of European origin" were expelled by the military administration prior to confirmation of the mandates as permitted by art. 122 of the treaty of Versailles.

[77] *P.M.C.*, *Min.*, II, 20, 66, 68; XIV, 15; XV, 276–79; *O.J.*, IV, 568.

[78] See *supra*, chap. xiii, sec. 3*j*.

[79] See *supra*, chap. xiii, sec. 3*e*, *g*, *i*.

[80] See *supra*, chap. vi, sec. 3; xiii, sec. 3*b*.

[81] Treaty of Versailles, art. 127; *supra*, chap. xiii, n. 82.

[82] *Rex* v. *Christian*, S.Af.L.R. (1924), App. Div., 101 ff.; *supra*, chap. xii, n. 96.

[83] Wilson and Tucker, *International Law* (8th ed.), p. 131; Hyde, *International Law*, I, 610; *Luria* v. *U.S.*, 231 U.S. 9 (1913); Tunis nationality decrees advisory opinion, *P.C.I.J.* (Ser. C), II, 116. Strictly speaking, nationality in international law is a legal relation between states of which individuals are the object. It involves a right of a state to the allegiance and protection of an individual even when abroad correlative with the duty of all other states to acquiesce.

[84] As to inhabitants of protectorates see opinion of Sir John Salmond of New Zealand, May 11, 1920, *P.M.C.*, *Min.*, II, 69. For other classes of non-nationals who have

not nationals may be prosecuted for treason.[85] Thus there is no contradiction between the subjection of the inhabitant of mandated territory to those relations and his want of mandatory nationality.[86]

The question of the status of inhabitants of the mandated areas arose even before the mandates were confirmed. Sir John Salmond, solicitor-general of New Zealand, gave his government an opinion on September 30, 1919, that inhabitants of Western Samoa had not acquired New Zealand nationality by the assignment of the mandate; that under New Zealand laws they could not acquire it while resident in Samoa; and that under British imperial law it was doubtful whether New Zealand could provide for their naturalization.[87] On September 18, 1920, General Smuts, prime minister of South Africa, told the German inhabitants of Southwest Africa that, "in effect, the relations between the Southwest protectorate and the Union amount to annexation in all but name"; that the mandatory provisions were designed to offer protection to the "indigenous population"; that the inhabitants of German origin who had not been expelled as they might have been under the treaty (art. 122) could not look to Germany for protection; that they were not nationals of South Africa; that the Union was anxious to have them become citizens, but would bring no pressure to bear.[88] Later General Smuts expressed the conviction that the only solution would be to make these Germans Union citizens by general act, giving an opportunity of individual refusal.[89] In both of these instances the question had arisen with regard to persons of German origin who had not been repatriated, and in

---

been given protection see Borchard, *Diplomatic Protection of Citizens Abroad*, pp. 463–78; 568–74.

[85] In the United States treason laws may be applied against domiciled aliens (Pomeroy, *Constitutional Law*, sec. 432).

[86] This was expressly stated in regard to protection in the Council resolution (see *infra*, n. 101).

[87] *P.M.C.*, *Min.*, II, 67. See also opinion of Sir John Salmond, May 11, 1920, including statement that the Samoans had the right under the peace treaty "to become incorporated in the British Empire if they so desire." The Permanent Mandates Commission put itself on record as unable to understand this (*ibid.*, p. 68).

[88] *Ibid.*, p. 92.

[89] Letter of July 4, 1922, to M. Rappard (*ibid.*, p. 91).

neither case did the mandatory evince any intention of considering that such persons had automatically become nationals of the mandatory.

During the first session of the Permanent Mandates Commission, on October 7, 1921, while the Southwest African report was under discussion, M. Rappard, director of the mandates section of the Secretariat, drew the attention of the Commission to the difference of opinion between those who held that the mandatory could impose its nationality upon inhabitants of the mandated territory and those who held that the mandatory's nationality could only be acquired by voluntary naturalization, remarking that the former view "appeared to strengthen the argument of those who maintained that a C mandate amounted to disguised annexation." The members of the Commission expressed very diverse opinions on the subject, and it was decided to draw the Council's attention to the matter.[90]

At its meeting on October 10, 1921, the Council, in accordance with this suggestion, appointed a subcommittee of the Permanent Mandates Commission to examine the question.[91] This subcommittee obtained the views of the mandatories, in most cases by personal interviews, disclosing a considerable divergence of opinion.[92] M. Matsuda of Japan thought it "contrary to the spirit of Article 22 of the Covenant to assimilate the native inhabitants of mandated territory to the subjects of the mandatory Power. On the other hand, having in mind the interests of these peoples, they should be accorded every advantage granted to subjects of the mandatory Power." Consequently, "they occupied a new position in international law and ought to receive a new legal status." Inhabitants other than native should, however, preserve their original nationality, in his opinion.[93] Representatives of New Zealand and Australia took a similar position. They regarded the natives as "British protected persons" and contemplated naturalization of the Germans, if difficulties of the kind suggested by Sir John Salmond could be

[90] *Ibid.*, I, 41.

[91] *Ibid.*, II, 85; *L. of N., Council, Min.*, XIV, 125.

[92] Report, *O.J.*, III, 589–608.

[93] *Ibid.*, p. 592.

avoided by British imperial legislation.[94] The representative of South Africa, Sir Edgar Walton, pointed out that Southwest Africa was the only mandated territory with a large German population, and experience had proved that it was impossible to govern unless the Germans were naturalized, in which case they could participate in the government on equal terms with the resident South Africans and could also be represented in the Union Parliament. South Africa, therefore, hoped to obtain British and League consent to the naturalization of these people. The subcommittee raised the question whether this procedure would not "risk destroying a distinction essential for the maintenance of the system of mandates."[95] The British and French representatives considered the native inhabitants of mandated territory as protected persons whose naturalization they did not contemplate. Germans had all been repatriated in the territories under their mandates.[96] The Belgian colonial ministers who were interviewed at first developed an elaborate argument for extending Belgian nationality to the native inhabitants as a privilege necessary to assure them the protection contemplated by the treaty and the mandate. After M. Rappard had drawn their attention to the limitation this might impose upon the right of native inhabitants to petition the League and of the League to supervise their protection as required by the Covenant, the Belgians presented a written opinion similar to that given by the British and French representatives.[97] At its meeting, May 12, 1922, the Council considered this report and requested the Permanent Mandates Commission to submit definite proposals on the basis of it.[98]

The Permanent Mandates Commission considered the question at its second session, August 1–11, 1922. The special situation in Southwest Africa was considered, but the Commission was unable to reconcile collective naturalization with the separate status of mandatories contemplated by the Covenant.[99] Consequently, it drafted a

[94] *Ibid.* Such legislation was discussed at the imperial conferences of 1923 and 1926 and was still under consideration by the British mandatory governments in 1928 (*P.M.C.*, XIV, 15).

[95] *O.J.*, III, 593, 598.

[96] *Ibid.*, pp. 593–95.

[97] *Ibid.*, pp. 594, 600–607.

[98] *Ibid.*, p. 524.

[99] *P.M.C.*, *Min.*, II, 16–19, 86. The Commission also reached the conclusion that under general principles of international law Germans in the mandated areas did not automatically lose their German nationality (*ibid.*, p. 17).

resolution proposing that native inhabitants be given a distinct status, that the mandatory define this status, and that the mandatory be entitled to provide by law for "the individual and purely voluntary naturalization of any inhabitants of the mandated area."[100] These resolutions were accepted with slight modifications by the Council in its meeting of April 23, 1923, as follows:

The Council of the League of Nations,

Having considered the report of the Permanent Mandates Commission on the national status of the inhabitants of territories under B and C mandates.

In accordance with the principles laid down in article 22 of the Covenant:

Resolves as follows:

(1) The status of the native inhabitants of a mandated territory is distinct from that of the nationals of the Mandatory Power and cannot be identified therewith by any process having general application.

(2) The native inhabitants of a mandated territory are not invested with the nationality of the Mandatory Power by reason of the protection extended to them.

(3) It is not inconsistent with (1) and (2) above that individual inhabitants of the mandated territory should voluntarily obtain naturalization from the Mandatory Power in accordance with arrangements which it is open to such Power to make, with this object under its own law.

(4) It is desirable that native inhabitants who receive the protection of the Mandatory Power should in each case be designated by some form of descriptive title which will specify their status under the mandate.[101]

While vote on this resolution was still pending, an extended debate took place on the question of recognizing the right of South Africa to provide for collective naturalization of the persons of German origin in her mandated territory.[102] The South African delegate called attention to Article 122 of the treaty of Versailles by which a mandatory which did not repatriate German subjects of European origin might provide conditions upon which they "shall or shall not be allowed to reside, hold property, trade or exercise a profession" in the mandated area, and proposed that South Africa be authorized to confer British nationality on the Germans of Southwest Africa, with the proviso that every such inhabitant might decline, and those

[100] *Ibid.*, pp. 19, 85–86, 73; *O.J.*, IV, 659.

[101] *O.J.*, IV, 604. The distinct status which the United States accords the natives of the Philippines was referred to as a precedent for the proposed status of the inhabitants of the mandated territories (*ibid.*, p. 569).

[102] *Ibid.*, pp. 508–72.

who did so might remain and would not be disturbed or molested in any way.[103] The Council then voted, with M. Branting of Sweden abstaining:

> The Council of the League of Nations, taking into consideration the special case presented to it and the fact that only the inhabitants of Southwest Africa alluded to in Article 122 of the Treaty of Versailles are concerned, takes note of the declaration made by the representative of South Africa and sees no objection to the proposed action.[104]

Although the substance is in general terms, the preamble of the Council resolution suggests that B and C mandates alone were under consideration. There has been no special Council decision with reference to the status of inhabitants of A mandated territories, but inasmuch as these territories by article 22 are provisionally recognized as independent nations, it seems clear that their inhabitants cannot be considered nationals of the mandatory. The Palestine mandate expressly provides for "Palestinian citizenship" (art. 7), and the Supreme Court of Palestine has held that Palestinians are not subjects of the mandatory.[105]

Thus we conclude that municipal law sovereignty in the areas is exercised, under the limitations of article 22 and other treaties, by the mandatory acting with consent of the League Council, but in case of established breach of duty the League might remove a mandatory and appoint a new one. Responsibility to other states with respect to the territories is vested immediately in the mandatory, and with respect to certain matters, eventually in the League. If we consider this *de facto* situation in connection with the strong evidence that present sovereignty is not vested in the Principal Powers, in the mandated communities, or in the mandatories, and that the League has ultimate power to change the régime through the Covenant

[103] *Ibid.*, p. 659.

[104] *Ibid.*, p. 603. Act 30 of 1924 (South West Africa Naturalisation of Aliens Act) in conformity with this conferred British nationality on all adult Germans domiciled in the territory who did not decline by declaration in six months. Act 40 of 1927 (Union Nationality and Flags Act) conferred South African nationality on all British subjects (with certain exceptions) born or domiciled in Southwest Africa and was questioned by the commission (*P.M.C., Min.*, XVI, 187–94, 203).

[105] *Re Ezra Goralshvi*, *A.J.I.L.*, XX, 771; see also Stoyanovsky, *The Mandate for Palestine*, pp. 149 ff., 286. British subjects, however, do not lose that status on acquiring

amending process we conclude that it is not far from the truth to say that sovereignty under international law is vested in the League of Nations. This conclusion seems to command the support of a larger number of writers than any other theory,[106] and is also suggested by the term "mandate" as used in private law.[107] It can hardly be said that vesting of sovereignty in the League violates the no-annexationist formula of the Peace Conference, especially in view of the transitional purpose of this sovereignty to be indicated in the next section.

4. The Destiny of Mandated Communities

Though law is distinguished from policy, wise judges, especially in the field of public law, know that the two are not very far apart. "We must consider," wrote Justice Holmes, sustaining the power of Congress to enforce a treaty to protect migratory birds, "what the country has become in deciding what that amendment (x) has secured..... Here a national interest of very nearly the first magnitude is involved. It can be protected only by mutual action in concert with that of another power."[108] The law cannot live unless it adequately serves and guides the interests of those bound by it. Thus this ultimate purpose should be considered in the day-to-day application of the law. Where the law is clear and precise the court and the jurist can only accept it. But opportunity for judgment is seldom entirely excluded, and where it exists the judge must be guided by the

---

Palestinian nationality. *B.Y.B.I.L.*, 1929, p. 141. In response to the commissions request at its twelfth session for the descriptive title given to natives of mandated territories as required by the fourth resolution of 1923 the following information was published: Great Britain—"British protected persons, native of the mandated territory of British Togoland (British Cameroons, or Tanganyika)." France—"Natives of Togoland (or the Cameroons) protected under French mandate." Belgium—"Nationals (*ressortissants*) of Ruanda-Urundi." South Africa—"Native inhabitant of Southwest Africa under the protection of the Union of South Africa in its capacity as mandatory of Southwest Africa." Australia—"British protected person, native of the mandated territory of New Guinea (or Nauru)." Japan—"Inhabitants of the (mandated) islands." The laws of most of the mandatories permit individual naturalization of these natives (*P.M.C., Min.*, XII, 198; XV, 278).

[106] See *supra*, chap. x, sec. 2*d*.

[107] See *supra*, chap. xi, sec. 3*a*.

[108] *Missouri* v. *Holland*, 252 U.S. 416 (1920). "Coke's observation that many things have been introduced into the common law because of 'convenience' .... remained profoundly true" (Pound, *Interpretations of Legal History* [New York, 1923], p. 161, citing Coke on Littleton, pp. 66*a*, 97*a*, 97*b*, 152*b*, 279*a*, 379*a*).

general policy of the law. In this way the law will continually develop so as to serve more adequately the interests for which it exists. Article 22, as we have seen, has furnished the basis for the development by the Mandates Commission of certain policies for developing the territories and their peoples while in the condition of tutelage.[109] It is clear that this policy goes further and contemplates an eventual change of that status. The essence of the system is in the very phrases, so shocking to legal purists, "not *yet* able to stand by themselves," "well being and *development* of such peoples form a sacred trust of civilization," "tutelage," "stage of development," "provisionally recognized."

These can only be interpreted to mean that in all classes of mandates the people must have the opportunity to advance toward independence, and that this must be granted if and when achieved. The machinery for making this decision is not specified. It is guaranteed merely by the good faith of the League. It is a pledge that eventually sovereignty shall be vested in the communities themselves, though with exception of the A "communities" there is every evidence that the time was considered remote. The B "peoples" and the C "territories" are not even "communities" as yet, thus the day of their self-determination is not on the horizon.[110]

Thus perhaps our tentative statement might be completed by stating that sovereignty of the areas is vested in the League acting through the Covenant amending process, and is exercised by the mandatory with consent of the Council for eventual transfer to the mandated communities themselves. In the case of Iraq and possibly other A communities, it appears that the native community already shares in the sovereignty. With this interpretation, sovereignty is in some cases held jointly by the League and the mandated community, the exercise of sovereignty being in those cases divided between them and the mandatory in proportions which vary according to the terms of the particular mandate.

What legal deductions can be drawn from the acceptance of this

[109] See *supra*, chap. viii.

[110] See *supra*, chap. viii, sec. 2, especially statement by Sir Frederick Lugard (n. 26). Lindley thinks that the A but not the B and C mandates contemplate eventual termination by the independence of the areas (*op. cit.*, p. 269).

theory? Mainly that there is no legal presumption in favor of the exercise of unspecified powers by the mandatory, the mandated community, or even the Council, but that the power and responsibility of each must be determined from the nature of the institution as found in the relevant documents, principles, and precedents, or if that is not possible, by action of the League through amendment of article 22. The sovereign authority is in the background and acts infrequently. The government is one of limited powers, kept from usurpation by checks and balances. Its practicability, like that of the government of the United States or of the British commonwealth of nations, depends on a spirit of co-operation between independent bodies, not upon the existence of ultimate authority in one.

Experience has shown that complex political structures of this kind are likely to be unstable. Federations tend either to become national states or to break up.[111] Protectorates and states under suzerainty usually move toward annexation or toward independence. Condominiums have usually resulted eventually in a division of the territory. A study of the mandates system discloses tendencies in some of these areas toward annexation by the mandatory and in some toward independence, while the actual authority of the League of Nations has varied but on the whole has tended to increase.

To secure permanence in such complex systems two devices have been used: (1) a political balance of power and responsibility and (2) a judicially enforced division of power and responsibility. The first is characteristic of British institutions; the second, of American.[112] Both are utilized in the mandates system.

The complex distribution of actual power and responsibility in respect to each area between the mandatory, the Council, and the mandated peoples gives each a certain control over the others and correspondingly renders extension of its functions by any one somewhat difficult. The mandatory's extensive powers over the mandated people are checked by its responsibility toward the League, sanctioned by extensive publicity and the eventual power of the League to transfer a mandate in case of persistent breach of obliga-

[111] See Freeman, *History of Federal Governments*, chap. i.

[112] See J. B. Moore in *Proc.*, *American Philosophical Society*, XL (1921), No. 3; xiv, and Wright, *Control of American Foreign Relations*, p. 376.

tion by the mandatory. The Council's extensive powers of supervising the mandatory are checked by the latter's representation upon it and by its responsibilities toward the mandated community and the members of the League defined in the mandates and sanctioned by the Assembly's power to criticize and to terminate the mandates by admitting the mandated communities to the League. The mandated communities are undoubtedly in the weakest position. They have the power to petition the League for redress of grievances and to ask for recognition of independence and admission to the League when they are "able to stand by themselves." These powers are sanctioned by publicity through the Assembly and the reports of the Mandates Commission, and by the possibility of resort to violence and revolution, but undue use of these sanctions is checked by the actual responsibility of the mandated peoples to the mandatory whose authority dominates their government.

Political checks and balances if alone relied on produce an exceedingly unstable equilibrium. When control is purely political, the equilibrium can be so radically disturbed before reaction sets in that violence results. On the other hand, efforts to eliminate political forces altogether and to maintain government by law alone has proved equally disastrous. Law alone cannot keep pace with social changes while politics alone are likely to outstrip them. Thus in successful governments political checks and balances have been supplemented by legal definitions and distributions of power and responsibility administered by established organs and procedures. Progress by evolution rather than revolution seems to depend upon a proper co-ordination of political and legal controls. Too much politics suggests the effort to balance scales by successively casting heavy weights in one pan and then the other. Too much law suggests the apparently simple device of clamping the scales, with the danger, however, that one pan will become so overloaded that the cross-bar will break. Equilibrium can only be indefinitely maintained by the assurance that weights will only be added to either pan in very small increments. Perhaps a more perfect analogy could be made to the culture of a plant which requires that successive increments of sun, water, heat, and fertilizer be administered neither in too large nor too small amounts, if the plant is to grow.

Political forces must play on the body politic, but within defined limits. In the family of nations, where political checks and balances have been too little regulated by law, the equilibrium has been frequently disturbed by violence. Progress has come through a series of catastrophes. Today the League of Nations and the Permanent Court of International Justice are trying to regulate the hitherto dominantly political balance of power by the restraining influence of law and established procedures. On the other hand, the Roman Empire may be cited as a structure where law came to limit the natural development and adjustment of political forces so much that adaptation to the barbarian migrations proved impossible.

Among modern states the British Empire has succeeded in maintaining a workable balance of political forces both among the dominions and within each of them, but even in this dominantly political structure, as Dicey has pointed out, the conventions of the constitution operate within limits set by law. Too radical a departure from the conventions will prove to be illegal.[113] In the United States the emphasis has been the other way. Governmental powers and responsibilities are defined and distributed by judicially enforcible constitutions, but commentators agree that the structure has only stood because in practice the law has been interpreted and applied with sufficient breadth to allow considerable play for political forces guided only by the "understandings" of the constitution.[114]

Thus in the mandates system the political checks and balances are regulated by the precise legal definition of the field within which each of the various authorities is free to act. The legal element of the system has an importance more comparable to that in the American than in the British constitution. This legalistic character is clearly evidenced by the attitude assumed by the Mandates Commission; by the express provision in every mandate for ultimate interpretation of its terms by the Permanent Court of International Justice; and by the legislation and judicial decisions of the mandatories themselves. The Supreme Court of South Africa undertook to examine the legal position of the South African government in South-

[113] *The Law of the Constitution.*

[114] Wright, "The Understandings of International Law," *A.J.I.L.*, XIV, 578–79; *Control of American Foreign Relations*, pp. 7–9, 339 ff., 376.

west Africa with special reference to its power to punish an inhabitant of the latter for treason. It found that this "situation was new to international law," and the powers of the various organs could only be discovered by reference to the terms of article 22 of the Covenant and the mandate which subject to certain explicit limitations gave the mandatory "full power of administration and legislation" within the territory. Consequently, though South Africa's exercise of sovereignty over the area "was considerably curtailed" it could exercise sufficient internal sovereignty "to support a charge of high treason."[115] Implicit in the whole argument was the assumption that all governing authority in the area was legally limited by the mandate. This position has been more definitely taken by the Supreme Court of Palestine, which applied "the general rule that the validity of laws made by a legislature which is not sovereign but the creature of some instrument of government [in this case the mandate] may be questioned by the local courts on the ground that they are repugnant to some provision to be found in that instrument." This argument, which strongly suggests that by which the courts of the United States declare unconstitutional legislation void, was supported by the Judicial Committee of the Privy Council on appeal although the decision on the particular issue was reversed.[116] In other areas legislation and instructions seem to give full recognition to the mandates as judicially enforcible limitations upon the exercise of power by the mandatory.

The legal relationships between the mandatory, the League, and the mandated communities as set forth in the Covenant and the mandates seem to correspond rather closely to the conceptions of mandate, trust, and tutelage in private law, although, as has been pointed out, the analogies cannot be pushed too far.[117]

With this qualification the relation of the League and the mandatory is analogous to the Roman law conception of *mandatum*. The League as principal or *mandans* is entitled to supervise the mandatory's administration, while the mandatory as agent is bound to per-

[115] *Rex* v. *Christian,* S.Af.L.R. (1924), App. Div. 101 ff.; *supra,* chap. xii, n. 96.

[116] *Murrah* v. *District Governor of Jerusalem, A.J.I.L.,* XX, 769, and *Jerusalem-Jaffa District Governor* v. *Murra,* L.R. (1926), A.C. 327; *supra,* chap. xii, nn. 54–55.

[117] See *supra,* chap. xi, sec. 3.

form the services specified in the mandate and to submit to the League's supervision by reporting, answering to cross-examination, and observing resolutions of the Council. This system of international supervision for the administration of backward people is the major novelty of article 22, although, as we have noticed, there are precedents.[118] Its practical value depends on the adequacy of the procedure of reports, hearings, petitions, investigations, and publicity to keep the League *en rapport* with the conditions in mandated areas, to enable it to develop superior standards, and to assure their actual application in the areas.

The relation of the mandatory to the mandated community is analogous to the conception of tutelage or guardianship in private law. The mandatory as guardian is bound to exercise its powers in accordance with its responsibility toward the League and the terms of the trust which it has accepted jointly with the latter, so as to promote the "well-being and development" of the mandated peoples. This people or community as ward is bound to submit to this administration until "it is able to stand by itself." The value of this tutelage depends on the extent to which the mandates and their authoritative interpretations embody rules, principles, and standards actually adapted to the mandated peoples and to the development of their capacity for self-government. The mutual confidence implied by tutelage is impossible unless these basic instructions are fundamentally sound for each area.

The relation of the League in collaboration with the mandatory toward the mandated community and the members of the League is analogous to the conception of trust in Anglo-American law. The League and the mandatory are joint trustees of the areas and as such are bound to fulfil in good faith the "sacred trust of civilization" for the "well-being and development" of the peoples of these areas, while the mandated communities and the members of the League as beneficiaries have rights merely of an equitable character. They must rely primarily on the good faith of the trustees, but breach of this trust is not without remedy. Regular procedures of petitions to the Council and, for members of the League, appeal to the Permanent

[118] See *supra*, chap. i, sec. 4.

Court of International Justice have been established, and if these prove inadequate interested League members may give publicity to abuses in the Assembly—a method which has proved effective. Normally, however, the assurance that the trust will be fulfilled depends on the precision with which its terms and conditions are defined in the documents. A trustee is more likely to fulfil his duties satisfactorily if he knows precisely what is expected of him than if he does not.

The Hymans report accepted by the Council in 1920 expressed the opinion that the responsibility of the League under its trust was moral rather than legal in character. The report said:

There is no legal responsibility except in respect of another person. Now, the responsibility of the League of Nations could only occur in respect of the populations who are under mandatory rule. But it is difficult to see in what way this responsibility could be organized or what measures could enforce it. *Qui custodiat custodies?* The responsibility of the League before the public opinion of the civilized world will in point of fact be a moral one.[119]

Nevertheless, the procedures of petition and appeal to the Permanent Court of International Justice do seem to be at least a beginning toward organizing the League's responsibility, which clearly would normally be met by inducing the mandatory to observe the joint trust rather than by any direct action of the League. Remedies given to individuals against the state by such processes as petition of right, courts of claims, or administrative courts would seem to give them claims of a legal character even though such decisions are not ordinarily enforcible if opposed by political organs of the government. Thus the obligations of the trustees to the *cestui que trust* in this case illustrate the transition from purely moral to strictly legal obligations, and may be appropriately denominated "equitable."

Putting together these complex relations we find an institution of distinct novelty. Advanced states administering backward areas have long professed a moral duty to respect the interests and aid in the advancement of the natives, but in the mandates system the moral duty has been converted into a legal or at least equitable duty. Furukaki writes:

Heretofore certain powerful states of superior civilization have attributed to themselves a civilizing mission among backward peoples. France, for ex-

[119] *O.J.*, I, 338–39.

ample, admits and practices the theory of the colonization-tutelage. But this is a purely moral duty, voluntarily accepted by the colonizing state as a politic means of justifying in the name of civilization the conquest and the administration of colonial territories difficult to justify from the democratic point of view. This duty has been envisaged as the consequence of the suzerainty over the colony. It allows sovereignty in its full integrity to remain in the colonizing government which has to render account to no one for its action.

Very different appears the situation of the mandatory power. The territories which it administers are not placed under its sovereignty. It is in the name and as mandatory of the League of Nations that it assumes the administration. One cannot say that these territories belong to it as do colonies. They are confided to it in the expectation of an administration conformable to the interests of the inhabitants.

. . . . Tutelage, in this conception embodied in the covenant, is no longer a simple moral duty, purely voluntary. The power which exercises it is the mandatory of the League of Nations. In accepting the mandate, it contracts an obligation as tutor; in accepting the tutelage, it accepts obligations and responsibilities. In occupying or in organizing colonies, the powers acquired rights over the territories and populations. They were sovereigns of them, under a practical and moral duty of protection. Today, it is no longer rights which they acquire with the mandate, it is obligations which they assume. And these obligations are juristically sanctioned. The mandatory, as the tutor, must render account. A permanent commission examines the annual reports and the Council of the League of Nations takes the necessary measures.[120]

"One could not define more clearly," comments The Vice-Chairman of the Mandates Commission, "the profound difference between the colonization-tutelage founded on sovereignty, the action and effects of which may be appreciated only by the colonizing nation itself, and the tutelage under the régime of the mandates, regulated by a mass of prescriptions and prohibitions and submitted to the permanent and effective control of an international organization."[121]

[120] *Op. cit.*, p. 385.

[121] Van Rees, *op. cit.*, I, 11.

PART IV

THE VALUE OF THE MANDATES SYSTEM

CHAPTER XV

THE ACHIEVEMENTS OF MANDATORY ADMINISTRATION

1. Methods of Measuring Administrative Achievement

The mandates system may be an episode for the historian to record, an experiment for the administrator to observe, and a novelty for the jurist to rationalize, but has it, or is it likely to have, much effect on human life and activity in the areas to which it applies or in the world at large? An estimate of its value should doubtless be based on its actual accomplishments. How can we appraise them? Four methods suggest themselves which may be designated (*a*) the judicial, (*b*) the technological, (*c*) the statistical, and (*d*) the historical methods.

a) the judicial method

The Covenant and the mandates lay down certain rules, principles, and standards which have been interpreted and supplemented by the Commission and the Council. We might judge the system by the extent to which these rules, principles, and standards have actually been observed in the areas as determined by a detailed examination of alleged abuses. For such a judgment the records of the Mandates Commission furnish the best material. It is the Commission's primary duty to advise the Council on any departure from the prescriptions of the mandates. The character of these comments, based largely on the evidence received from the mandatory's report, the oral hearing of its accredited representatives, and written petitions, has already been indicated.[1] The Commission, though choosing its phraseology with care, has found much to criticize. In its opinion financial accounts have not always been satisfactory especially in the B areas, policies have been adopted hardly compatible with the open door, liquor-traffic regulations have not had the result contemplated in all cases, administrative mistakes

[1] See *supra*, chap. vi, sec. 3; chap. vii, sec. 3.

by the mandatory have been considered in part accountable for the revolts in Southwest Africa, Syria, and Western Samoa, education and public health have not always received adequate attention, labor and land policy has not always been wholly in the spirit of the mandates. Doubtless the Mandates Commission will continue to find details to criticize, but on the whole it has expressed itself as satisfied with the action and attitude of the mandatories. While the bulk of its discussion has tended to increase rather than decrease, this has not been true of its formal reports. It appears that the Commission is acquiring better understanding of the problem of the areas and the mandatories a better understanding of its point of view.

While the Mandates Commission is impartial and doubtless its opinion would usually be better evidence as to the observance of the mandates than would that of commissions set up by the mandatory, of members of the opposition in the mandatory's parliament, of publicists, reporters, or natives of the area, still the Commission labors under difficulties which cannot be overlooked. It does not have the power to summon and hear witnesses, and its sources of information, mainly dependent on the good faith of the mandatories, hardly guarantee that it will have cognizance of all abuses which exist or of all the facts with respect to incidents or conditions which come to its attention. Evidence exists that mandatory officials may suppress information when they think they can do so without detection.[2] Thus for deciding whether the law of the mandates is being observed evidence from other sources should be considered, especially from impartial observers who have visited the areas. The opinion of the Permanent Court of International Justice is

[2] Buell notes some omissions in the French reports on Togoland and the Cameroons, particularly the elimination of adverse comments by natives in the minutes of the councils of notables printed in the annexes to the Togoland report (*The Native Problem in Africa*, II, 372–73, 410–11). The Permanent Mandates Commission has noted a few cases where it has failed to receive from the mandatories petitions which they were known to have received (*P.M.C.*, *Min.*, XII, 62). The hearings of the Joint Samoa Committee of the New Zealand Parliament have not been published though they are said to differ in some respects from the Royal Commission's report on the 1927 disturbances and the minority members have tried to get them published (H. E. Holland, *The Revolt of the Samoans* [1928], pp. 11, 16). The Commission found the information submitted to it by the South African government in regard to the Bondelzwart uprising of 1922 so unsatisfactory that it could not express a final opinion (*P.M.C.*, *Min.*, III, 293, 296).

doubtless the best evidence as to the facts of alleged abuses. The Court has the power which the Commission lacks to hear evidence from both sides. But thus far only one case of alleged infraction of a mandate, the Palestine Mavromatis concession case, has been before it, and it is not likely that such cases will ever become very frequent.

b) THE TECHNOLOGICAL METHOD

The Covenant and the mandates are brief documents. Their most significant clauses assert broad standards susceptible of varied application. We might judge the system by the extent to which the application given these formal instruments by the combined efforts of the League and the mandatories has been adjusted to actual conditions in these varied areas. Are mandatory policies and regulations developing capable of guiding and instructing the administrator on the spot in a direction approved by the best expert knowledge with reference to the particular matter?

Attention has been given elsewhere to the standards of policy which the League has developed.[3] While there has been an effort in the Council to direct the Commission's activity to judgment on things done rather than suggestion of things to do, and while the Commission has on the whole conformed to that view and has been cautious of generalization,[4] yet the very limitations which the Council imposes upon its effective performance of a judicial task have led it to interpret its mission as one of co-operation with rather than criticism of the mandatories.[5] That function requires the approach of the scientist rather than of the lawyer, and in fact the Commission has utilized scientific materials and the work of technical commissions especially on native labor problems.[6] The policies which have developed from this process, such as use of native institutions and indirect government; protection of native interests in the land and minimizing of forced labor; priority of native welfare over economic development and economic self-determination; ample appropriation for health, agricultural development, education of a practical character, and employment of trained anthropologists in the

[3] See *supra*, chap. viii; chap. vii, n. 31.

[4] See *supra*, chap. v, n. 58; chap. viii, sec. 1*b*.

[5] See *supra*, chap. vii, nn. 4, 5, and sec. 2.

[6] See *supra*, chap. v, nn. 1–4.

native administration as well as the elimination of abuses specifically referred to in the mandates have in the main been approved by impartial investigators and experienced administrators.[7] All agree on the virtue of caution in introducing any reform in native life. Measures for the improvement of health, agriculture, and education, or even for the elimination of customs shocking to the Western mind—such as native slavery, witch-doctoring, head-hunting, and tribal warfare—are likely to have unexpected consequences. Anthropologists emphasize the interrelation of culture traits and realize that the native culture must be fully understood before any part of it is tampered with.[8]

[7] See *supra*, chap. iii, nn. 11–14. These policies in general conform to those applied in British West Africa (see Lugard, *The Dual Mandate in British Tropical Africa;* McPhee, *The Economic Revolution in British West Africa* [London, 1926], esp. chap. vii; Buell, *op. cit.*, esp. Vol. I, chap. xliii, on indirect rule; Vol. I, sec. 5, on Tanganyika; and Vol. II, sec. 12, on the French mandates).

[8] "The commandments of law and custom are always organically connected and not isolated; their very nature consists in the many tentacles which they throw out into the context of social life; they only exist in the chain of social transactions in which they are but a link" (Malinowski, *Crime and Custom in Savage Society* [New York, 1926], p. 125; see also p. 67). "In contemplating the legal institutions of all negro peoples, we are again reminded of the intimate bond connecting departments of primitive culture that are largely, though not wholly, separated in our own" (Lowie, *Primitive Society* [New York, 1920], pp. 418–19). "Primitive civilization is stiff-jointed and the number and kind of movements and adjustments it can make at short notice are strictly limited" (Goldenweiser, *Early Civilization* [New York, 1923], p. 402). "The resistance to change is largely due to emotional sources and in primitive culture emotional associations are the prevailing type" (Boaz, *The Mind of Primitive Man* [New York, 1911], pp. 239–40). "It is not possible to change them [the mores] by any artifice or device, to a great extent, or suddenly, or in any essential element; it is possible to modify them by slow and long continued effort if the ritual is changed by minute variations" (Sumner, *Folkways* [Boston, 1906], p. 87). "It is evident that native institutions, evil as they may seem to us, are often too closely bound up with the whole framework of society for a hasty attack upon them to be likely to succeed. The good in them may not be apparent, but it is obvious that no peoples could perpetuate from generation to generation social practices that were unqualifiedly evil. Even though some harmful mores do exist they are believed to be necessary for societal welfare, and often may have served a useful purpose in the past. The civilization of savage man has a consistency as a whole, and we cannot easily eliminate certain parts and substitute for them those of our own civilization without dislocating the whole" (Muntz, *Race Contact* [New York, 1927], p. 315, quoting Alston, *White Man's Work in Asia and Africa*, p. 72). See also Rivers (*Essays on the Depopulation of Melanesia* [Cambridge, 1922], pp. 93, 101, 107) on the unfortunate consequences of eliminating head-hunting in the Solomon Islands without substituting something in its place.

Methods and purposes of administration in the mandated areas have been commended by experts. Observers find British methods in Tanganyika preferable to those in Kenya and French methods in Cameroons and Togoland preferable to those in West and Equatorial Africa.[9] Precipitancy in introducing certain reforms in land tenure in the Jebel Druse seems, however, to have been one cause of the Syrian insurrection of 1925, and similar overzeal in health efforts may have contributed to the Samoan disturbances of 1927. The tactlessness of officials in the latter case have been vigorously assailed by experts on Polynesian culture.[10]

c) THE STATISTICAL METHOD

Let us turn from the incident before the judge and the method before the expert to the general results of the system upon the areas and upon the world. How can these results be measured? There seems to be general agreement that the aims of the system are threefold: betterment of the inhabitants, economic development of the areas, and elimination of international friction in regard to them. Are the inhabitants of the areas really better off on account of the system? Are the areas really producing more on account of it? Is there actually less danger of international friction because it exists? Although the answer to the first question would be affected by the answer to the other two, since eventually the welfare of a people depends on the productiveness and political stability of their country, yet this relation may not be very immediate. The interests of the inhabitants of the area may for a long time be quite diverse from the economic or the political interests of the world in general.[11]

The difficulty in formulating precise answers to these questions is obvious. Comparisons are necessary but to indicate the effective-

[9] Buell, *op. cit.*, I, 539–40; II, 371–73; Roberts, *History of French Colonial Policy*, I, 372.

[10] *P.M.C., Min.*, VIII, 205; MacCallum, *The Nationalist Crusade in Syria*, pp. 233, 240. "The very rapidity with which reforms have been effected has caused dissatisfaction. Attachment to old and harmful customs dies hard among Pacific Natives and much tact must be brought to bear in the handling of them" (Editorial, *Sydney Morning Herald*, December 14, 1927). See also speech of Sir Maui Pomare, minister for the Cook Islands and a Moari, *New Zealand Parliamentary Debates* (2d sess,. 1927), No. 10, pp. 928–31; Condliffe, *New Zealand in the Making*, 1930, chap. xiii; Rivers, *loc. cit.*

[11] See *supra*, chap. viii, sec. 2.

ness of the mandates system they should generally be made in terms of rates of change or progress. A comparison of the present condition of the inhabitants, the degree of utilization of resources, or the international rivalries in a mandated area with those in another area of the world, or even with those in the same area under the earlier régime, would perhaps indicate the relative backwardness of the mandated area, but it would give little evidence of the effects of the mandates system. To declare the mandates system a failure because the Iraqi are worse off than the Irish would be as nonsensical as to declare it a success because they are better off than the Iroquois. We must attempt to compare the rate of change in the mandated areas with the rate of change elsewhere, and for this the data are inadequate.

Furthermore, it is difficult to express such conceptions as "better off," "producing more," and "danger of international friction" in statistical data. "Better off," for instance, seems to have a relation to population, health, education, property, and consumption statistics, though clearly elements such as self-expression and enjoyment of traditional values, the most vital to individual happiness, are difficult to express statistically. "Producing more" can perhaps be more adequately expressed in statistics of trade, investment, and public finance, though if one considers long-run production, the imponderable factors effecting the happiness of the population cannot be neglected, nor can those effecting the "danger of international friction." The latter seems impossible to express statistically, unless possibly by some universal questionnaire scheme indicating world public opinion.

Thus the most perfect statistics could not tell all we want to know, but the statistics available are far from perfect. Backward areas are not encouraging places to hunt for accurate and comparable statistics. No one has reduced the consumption of a Ruanda native to terms comparable to those of a Rhodesian farmer or a Rhode Island laborer. Even the elementary statistics of population are usually estimates throwing no light upon rates of change. The trade and financial statistics are better but less important from the natives' point of view.

Even if we could compare the statistical progress of the mandated areas with other areas, would it tell us much about the efficiency of the mandates system? Every area differs from every other in many respects besides the presence or absence of the mandates system, and furthermore it is to be anticipated that sound methods initiated by the mandates system will soon be utilized in colonies and protectorates. Thus it might seem more reasonable to compare progress in the same areas before and after the system was established. Have the Syrians, for instance, progressed more rapidly under the mandate than under Turkish rule? Even such comparisons would, however, be of doubtful value. Many of the mandated areas had been overrun by war, all had suffered a profound disturbance of their economic life, most had been subjected to a radical change in administrative method during the period of military occupation preceding the establishment of the mandatory régime. The mandatories, just emerging from war, were less able to devote funds to the mandated areas than they would have been in normal times. They had to build up new administrative organizations. They were assured of opposition from some elements of the population. The world, recently divided by war, was not reunited by peace. The former sovereigns of the areas were disappointed. The system was new and its stability uncertain. Because of these unfavorable conditions in the inauguration of the system it is doubtful whether progress less rapid than in long-established colonies, even ten years after the war, should be considered discreditable to the new régime. The United States was probably worse off in most respects ten years after the Declaration of Independence than before it, but that is not conclusive that it was a mistake. The effect of government systems is slow. Sound judgment must be based on achievement not through years or even decades but through centuries.

Finally, we must note the difficulty of distinguishing the effect of the mandates system as such from that of other conditions of the administration. Full supervision by the League of Nations, definition of the mandatory's duties in an international document, and an administrative policy giving primary consideration to the interests of the inhabitants, secondary consideration to the interests of the world in general, and no special advantages to the mandatory government seem to be the essential features of the system;[12] but perhaps the traditions of the particular mandatory and the customs of the particular mandated people have more effect on the progress of the area. French Cameroons and French West Africa, for instance, are under a more similar régime than are French Cameroons and British Cameroons. The régimes in all three of them, however, are probably more alike than is that in any one of them with the régime of Palestine or Syria. Furthermore, the unfavorable circumstances referred to affect the areas in very varying degrees. Tanganyika was more disturbed by the war than were the North Pacific islands. There is, then, a serious danger in attributing the results of statistical comparisons to the mandates system as such without more refined statistical methods than the data permit of.

While it cannot be denied that the test of the system must be in its results, the present prospect of applying that test does not seem very bright. Nevertheless, some figures have been collected, though perhaps no more can be said of them than that on the whole they seem not unfavorable to the system.

d) THE HISTORICAL METHOD

The historian as a technician attempts to state events of the past with precision, but as an historian he attempts to relate their

[12] The latter seems to flow from the idea of gratuitous administration (see *supra*, chap. xiii, sec. 2*f*). The "dual mandate" is a British expression for the conception that "Europe is in Africa for the mutual benefit of her own industrial classes and of the native races in their progress to a higher plane." It rests on the supposition that "European brains, capital and energy have not been and never will be expended in developing the resources of Africa from motives of pure philanthropy," "that the benefit can be made reciprocal," and "that it is the aim and desire of civilized administration" to make it so (Lugard, *op. cit.*, p. 617). Apparently it does not deny that the administering people is entitled to special advantages beyond those which it shares with the world in general. Thus Mr. Amery, secretary of state for the colonies, defined the policy in June, 1926, as "a policy which recognizes our trusteeship both to the native population—whom we had found on the spot and whom it was our duty to bring forward and develop in every possible way—but also our trusteeship to humanity at large for the fullest development of those territories and towards those in particular of our own race who had undertaken the task of helping forward that development" (*London Times*, June 12, 1926, p. 13). Thus the policy differs from the mandates system in its objects as well as in its legal and administrative characteristics, and is likely to prove much less satisfactory to the native (Buell, *op. cit.*, I, 527 ff.).

antecedents to their consequences by something more than mere chronology, which he calls "historical causation." He does not rely on legal formula, on technical knowledge, or on statistical tabulations, though he may make use of all of them, but on common sense, weighing all the materials he can find in the light of his own experience. Dependent as such a method is upon the common sense, the experience, and the honesty of the particular historian, perhaps it still is the best we have for judging the effects of complex institutions and situations. Precise objective methods continually make inroads upon the historian's field, but for a long time there will be a residuum left for him, and perhaps our present problem is within that residuum. Because of the difficulties of statistical analysis and the presence of many imponderable factors, perhaps the subjective judgment of competent historians and observers in the areas is as reliable as the results of more refined methods.

Attention has been given to the attitudes of different groups and classes with respect to the mandates system in general.[13] Numerous volumes and articles have been written, dealing specifically with conditions in certain of the mandated areas as seen by travelers and publicists, sometimes in comparison with adjacent colonies. For the detailed opinions of these writers and the data on which they rely the reader must go to the books themselves. The opinions of disinterested observers, as has been noted, has generally been favorable to the system.[14]

All four of these methods will be used, but particularly the last two, in considering the effect of the system upon native welfare, economic development of the areas, and international harmony.

2. Native Welfare in Mandated Areas

Improvement of the conditions of the inhabitants of the areas is generally recognized as the first aim of the mandates system.[15] Changes in (*a*) population, (*b*) health, (*c*) land tenure and wages, (*d*) education, (*e*) security, and (*f*) freedom may be assumed to have a rather direct bearing upon native welfare. The earlier give more

[13] See *supra*, chap. iii. [14] *Ibid.* and *supra*, n. 9.

[15] See *supra*, chap. viii. There may be some doubt of this in the special conditions of the Palestine mandate (*ibid.*, nn. 24, 25).

prospect of statistical statement than the later in the list. For purposes of study and comparison the areas fall into three definite groups: the Near East, the African, and the Pacific territories. These conform to the legal classification except that Southwest Africa is legally classified with the Pacific territories.

a) POPULATION

After noting the tendency of native populations to die out from contact with civilization, G. Stanley Hall suggests that "the best test of the success of the method of treating subject races is fertility."[16] M. Rappard of the Mandates Commission has insisted that "if the native races were dying out, it was clear that their moral and material welfare were being sacrificed."[17] The statistics available, however, do not permit of any computation of the changes in fertility of the peoples in the mandated areas.[18] Even the population figures available are so incomplete and inaccurate as to be almost useless for purposes of comparison.

The League of Nations compilation of mandates statistics,[19] based on reports of the mandatories, contains for Iraq only the census of 1919 classified by religion and race and none at all for Syria, though the mandatory report for 1926 contained a census classified by sixteen religious groups. For Palestine the estimated figures indicate an increase of over 20 per cent from 1921 to 1926. The bulk of this increase was due to Jewish immigration, but apparently there was a natural increase of over 8 per cent. Vital statistics show that in spite of very heavy infant mortality there is an excess of births over deaths of 2.20 per cent in the whole settled population, 2.34 per cent among the Moslems, 1.81 per cent among the Jews, and 1.83 per cent among the Christians.[20]

[16] Adolescence, II, 718. See also Muntz (*op. cit.*) on native population tendencies in America, Polynesia, and Africa, and Rivers (*op. cit.*).

[17] *P.M.C.*, *Min.*, VI, 48, and *supra*, chap. viii, n. 58.

[18] For discussion of fertility indices see Kuczynski, *The Balance of Births and Deaths*, 1929.

[19] Statistical information concerning territories under mandate, *Pub. of L. N.*, *Mandates*, VI (1928), A4, and *infra*, Appendix V.

[20] Joint Palestine Survey Commission, *Report of the Experts* (Boston, 1928), p. 574.

In the African territories the data are no more satisfactory. French Cameroons shows a population decrease of over 30 per cent from 1921 to 1927—probably an error. French Togoland shows an increase of 7 per cent from 1921 to 1927 and Southwest Africa an increase of 5 per cent in the native population from 1921 to 1925. British Cameroons shows a 3 per cent increase from 1921 to 1926, but suspicion is aroused through the fact that a 15 per cent decrease appears in the 1922 figures. Some French investigations in Togoland indicate that each woman on an average gave birth to 4.03 children during her life, of which 3.02 live after fifteen years—a fertility rate small for a backward area but considerably higher than that common in Europe or America today.[21] British Togoland, Tanganyika, and Ruanda-Urundi give population figures only for one year and those estimates. The disparity between the native population statistics published by Germany in 1913 and those published by the mandatories is so great as to preclude any use of the former.[22]

In most of these territories an increase in the non-native population is noticed from 1921 to 1927: French Cameroons, 200 per cent; French Togoland, 100 per cent; British Cameroons, 300 per cent; Ruanda-Urundi, 350 per cent; Southwest Africa, 24 per cent. Only in the latter and Tanganyika does the non-native population include many more than the administrative officials. Some of the reports state that the native population is increasing slowly and the non-native rapidly—an impression generally borne out by the figures and one which probably reflects the situation of Africa as a whole today. Impartial investigators are fairly unanimous that white settlement is disastrous for the native, and it appears that the British proposals for an East African federation including Tanganyika has the object of stimulating white settlement. While there appear to be no formal grounds in the mandate by which such a federation can be opposed by the League, it would undoubtedly

[21] Buell, *op. cit.*, II, 349.

[22] The German figures of 1913, for instance, show only about half the native population in Southwest Africa, shown by the South African figures of 1921 (see *infra*, Appendixes IV and V).

give a great influence in Tanganyika to the white settlers of Kenya and would make observance of the mandate principles more difficult.[23]

Among the Pacific territories Nauru shows a 10 per cent increase of native population and a 5 per cent decrease of non-native (mostly Chinese contract laborers) from 1922 to 1926. New Guinea's native population was not completely enumerated and her non-native population decreased 7 per cent from 1920 to 1925. Western Samoa showed a 7 per cent increase of natives from 1920 to 1924,[24] and a 20 per cent decrease of non-natives (Chinese contract laborers). The Japanese islands show a 2 per cent native increase in the same period and a 37 per cent non-native increase. Apart from the New Guinea natives, these figures probably are fairly reliable and indicate a gradual increase in the Polynesian and Micronesian races in the mandated islands. This condition appears to have existed among them in all the Pacific islands except the Marquesas since about 1900, in contrast to the steady decline of the race before that time after contact with the whites began.[25]

b) HEALTH

Health is undoubtedly an important element in human welfare, and the Mandates Commission has often drawn attention to conditions such as recruiting of labor for work at a distance which might militate against it. The Commission has also requested an explanation of heavy mortality in certain types of labor and suggested increases in medical staffs, adequate health expenditures, and instruction in hygiene in the schools.[26] It must be noticed, however, that health measures sometimes interfere with tribal custom and may cause resentment. The very efficiency of New Zealand's health ad-

[23] See *infra*, sec. *c*. See Buell (*op. cit.*, I, 511) for details of the proposal, and W. Regendanz for denunciation of it as contrary to the mandates' principle (*British Policy in Mandated Colonies*, Berlin, 1929). He sees an ominous significance in the substitution of King George's head for that of a giraffe on the Tanganyika stamps. See also Leonard Stein, *Nation and Atheneum*, July 7, 1928, and discussion of the Hilton Young report in the Mandates Commission especially by M. Kastl, the German member. *P. M. C.*, XV, 105, 292; XVI, 202.

[24] This has about compensated for the severe losses of the 1921 influenza epidemic.

[25] Condliffe (ed.), *Problems of the Pacific* (Chicago, 1928), p. 194; Roberts, *Population Problems in the Pacific*. The situation among the Melanesians is apparently less satisfactory (see Rivers, *op. cit.*).

[26] See *supra*, chap. vii, sec. 3; chap. viii, sec. 4*d*.

ministration in Western Samoa has been cited as one cause of the native disturbances of 1927, while her inefficiency in handling the disastrous influenza epidemic of 1918 has been cited as another.[27]

There has been some co-operation between the Mandates Commission and the health organization of the League, and the Commission has drawn attention to the spread of venereal disease in certain areas, as the Assembly has to the increased import of spirits in some;[28] but accurate health statistics for these areas do not exist. The attention devoted to the matter may be roughly judged from the expenditures budgeted to that account.

In Iraq, health expenditures decreased 20 and in Palestine 10 per cent from 1921 to 1926, while in the African areas they more than doubled during that period except in Southwest Africa where they were practically stationary from 1921 to 1925. In the Pacific areas there has been a rapid increase, except in the Japanese mandated islands.[29]

In 1926 the health expenditures in African areas compared favorably with those in neighboring colonies of the mandatory. Thus France devoted over 11 per cent of the budget in the Cameroons and Togoland to sanitation and medicine while she devoted only 4 per cent to those purposes in West Africa and 10 per cent in Equatorial Africa. Her per capita health expenditures were about $0.07 in Togoland, $0.06 in Cameroons and West Africa, and $0.04 in Equatorial Africa. Great Britain devoted 9 per cent of the Tanganyika and Cameroons budgets to these purposes, and 13 per cent of the Togoland budget compared with 11 per cent in Uganda, 9 per cent in Zanzibar, and 8 per cent in Kenya. This, however, meant only about $0.16 per capita in Tanganyika, $0.13 in Togoland, and $0.08 in Cameroons, compared with $0.21 in Uganda, but $0.37 in Kenya, and $1.03 in Zanzibar. Belgium devoted 5 per cent of the Ruanda budget, or $0.02 per capita, to health, and South Africa 2 per cent of the Southwest Africa budget, which amounted, however, to $0.35 per capita.[30] It will be observed that the per capita health expenditure is highest in the regions where there is a considerable white

[27] See *supra*, n. 10; Holland, *The Revolt of the Samoans*, *op. cit.*, 1928.

[28] See *supra*, chap. V, n. 2; chap. xiii, sec. 3*i*.

[29] See *infra*, Appendixes VI, VII.

[30] Most of these figures are tabulated by Buell (*op. cit.*, II, 980).

population and that the general British standard is considerably above that of France. This is partly due to the higher professional standard required for doctors in British West Africa. It has been suggested, however, that the less expensive native dispensers used by the French, the Belgians, and by the British in Uganda bring a greater social return for the same money.[31]

These statistics give a far from adequate picture of health activity in the mandated areas. Private investigators report steady improvement of health conditions in Palestine under the mandate administration,[32] and the work in Tanganyika and the French West African mandates has been commended for its emphasis upon preventive measures against sleeping sickness, training of native dispensers, and maternity work.[33] It seems probable that the mandates system has induced the mandatories to devote especial attention to health problems in the mandated territories though at present the revenues are inadequate and conditions in some cases compare unfavorably to those under German rule.

c) LAND TENURE AND WAGES

A statistical measure of the changes in native wealth or income in the African and Pacific mandated areas which lack a wage system seems unattainable. The statistics of trade, investment, and taxation would clearly have little relation to native wealth. In fact, over a brief period of time increases in these may result from a milking of the country and indicate that the natives are getting poorer. If, however, the productiveness of the country to foreign traders, concessionaires, and the government steadily increases over a long period of time, and there is little emigration or immigration, the explanation is probably to be found in a Europeanization of the native and an increase in his wealth by the European standard.

Where a wage labor system exists, it is possible, with adequate statistics, to determine the changes in real wages, but a comparatively small percentage of the population lives on wages in even the most advanced of these areas. In the near eastern areas, where the wage system is most advanced, the bulk of the population farms on

[31] *Ibid.*, I, 608–9, 657; II, 37–40.

[32] Joint Palestine Survey Commission, *op. cit.*, pp. 460, 709.

[33] Buell, *op. cit.*, I, 471; II, 349.

shares or is nomadic.[34] The wage system is progressing in Africa and the Pacific but is still resorted to by the native mainly for the payment of taxes and the purchase of luxuries.[35] He gets his living from the forest or from agriculture. In any case, statistics do not exist for ascertaining the progress of wages in the mandated areas.[36]

The wealth of the natives in most of these areas is land, which in Africa and the Pacific is for the most part communally owned, though individual native ownership is developing. While land cannot increase in amount, it may increase in value through better utilization. Most of the mandatory administrations devote portions of the budget to agricultural development, and as the accepted mandate policy favors the retention of native ownership, this should increase the value of native land. In Iraq and Palestine the amount of public revenue devoted to agriculture has increased from 1921 to 1926 but has been only about one-third of that devoted to health. In Palestine, however, land values have risen greatly because of Jewish immigration. The latter is also generally admitted to have raised the native "fellaheen in efficiency and manner of living rather than lowering the Jew."[37] The British devoted less than half as much to agriculture as to health in their mandated territories of Cameroons, Togoland, and Tanganyika though in the latter two the agricultural expenditures have steadily increased since 1920. The French have somewhat increased their agricultural expenditures in Cameroons and Togoland, more in the latter where it has been about a half as large as the health expenditures. The agricultural expenditures in

[34] This is not true of the Jews in Palestine, three-fourths of whom are industrialized (Joint Palestine Survey Commission, *op. cit.*, p. 495).

[35] Lugard, *op. cit.*, pp. 402–4.

[36] There are more data on Palestine than elsewhere, owing to the Jewish investigations. There appears to have been a substantial rise in both Jewish and Arab wages during the boom period, 1924–26, the Jewish unskilled labor being almost three times as expensive (Jewish, $100–$125, and Arab, $30–$50 per month) which may be compared with native wages in East Africa of $2–$5 a month [Lugard, p. 396]). With the depression of 1926 Jewish wages fell more rapidly than Arab, and in 1928 the margin between the two was slight (Joint Palestine Survey Commission, *op. cit.* [Wolman], pp. 497–98), but the Jewish immigration is said to have "favorably affected the prevailing standard of living among both the old and new population of the country, Jews and Arabs" (*ibid.*, p. 494).

[37] *Ibid.*, p. 38.

Ruanda-Urundi declined from 1922 to 1924 to a point one-sixth of the health budget. In Southwest Africa alone, where much of the land is in the hands of white planters, does agriculture exceed health expenditures. The former increased by 75 per cent from 1921 to 1925, at which date they were nearly ten times as large as the health expenditures and constituted 23 per cent of the total expenditures of the country. These expenditures compare favorably with those in adjacent colonies. Agriculture forms a larger proportion of the Tanganyika expenditures than it does in any British East African colony, and a larger proportion of the French Togoland expenditures than it does in French West or Equatorial Africa.[38] Furthermore, land alienations to non-natives have been less in Tanganyika than in any British or East or South African colony except Uganda.[39]

Of the Pacific territories Nauru indicates no expenditure for agriculture. New Guinea shows a steady increase amounting to about one-fifth of the health expenditures in 1926. Samoa has tended to decrease its agricultural expenditures which in 1924 were only one-eighth as large as the health expenditures, while Japan devotes almost as much to each in her mandated islands. The per capita expenditures for agriculture vary enormously among the mandated areas, from almost three dollars in Southwest Africa to less than one-tenth of a cent in Ruanda-Urundi, but they generally exceed those in adjacent colonies of the mandatory.[40]

In most of the mandated areas the real income of the native is mainly his food and his leisure. Statistics of changes in native consumption in the areas would be most interesting but they do not exist.[41] "In the strenuous conditions of the modern world" the native will doubtless steadily lose leisure. That is inevitable if the countries are to be developed by his labor.[41a] The ease of the transi-

[38] Buell, *op. cit.*, II, 980.

[39] *Ibid.*, I, 513; but see *infra*, n. 47.

[40] *Ibid.*, II, 980.

[41] A few observations in the Joint Palestine Survey Commission's report on the diet of Arabs and Jews in Palestine indicates that the latter are the better off, though they have not fully adapted their habits of consumption to the country (pp. 500, 549).

[41a] Industrialization, the substitution of machines for hand labor, may eventually decrease the demand for labor but an increased application of labor is necessary if economic progress is to begin.

tion will be measured by the extent to which he acquires from contacts with the world new wants for the satisfaction of which he will voluntarily part with his leisure.[42] Experience indicates that if white settlers or concessionaires are permitted to acquire large areas of land for agricultural development or mines, the rate of transition will be increased beyond this with the result of forced labor or slavery, a development which some think justified by the experience of the Dutch in Java but which is contrary to the mandates system. "European ownership on a large scale," writes Sir Frederick Lugard, "has in all cases resulted in the demand for alien or for compulsory labor by which alone large foreign owned interests can be kept going."[43]

Undoubtedly land and labor statistics are most important for tracing the progress of native welfare in the areas. At present, however, the situation can be studied only by a detailed description of the policy pursued in each area which cannot be undertaken here. As has been noticed, the mandates require and the League of Nations has insisted upon respect for native land titles and prohibition of slavery and forced labor. The League has recognized that these principles may retard the rate of economic development.[44] It seems probable that in Southwest Africa, which has a considerable white population and where the mandatory's policy appears to be devoted to white rather than native interests, it will be most difficult to enforce these principles. Here economic progress has been rapid but the natives have been restless.[45] In the other African and Pacific

[42] Lugard emphasizes the natural industry of the native and his willingness to work if under satisfactory conditions and for a suitable reward (*op. cit.*, pp. 401 ff.).

[43] *Ibid.*, p. 419. Lugard also says: "The requirements of the settlers, to put it bluntly, are incompatible with the interests and advancement of the agricultural tribes" (p. 397). For his opinion of the argument justifying forced labor as of educational value to the native see *ibid.*, p. 412. Buell says, after a detailed examination of the conditions in native Africa, "Wherever this principle [dual development for the white settler and the natives] has been admitted in East Africa, the native has been deprived of land which he has regarded as his own and because of land shortage created in these various territories (except in Southern Rhodesia) he has been obliged to work for the European employers" (*op. cit.*, I, 527). See also *supra*, chap. viii, sec. 3*b*.

[44] See *supra*, chap. viii, sec. 4*a*.

[45] See *supra*, chap. vii, sec. 3. Judged by the statistics of railroads per square mile, per capita trade, and per capita revenue, Southwest Africa is the most developed of the African mandated territories (see *infra*, Appendix VIII).

areas the mandatories appear to have been developing the mandates policy with some success, though labor exactions for railway construction in the French Cameroons have led to extensive emigration[46] and the non-native element in Tanganyika presses for land alienation to white settlers.[47] In the near eastern areas native welfare is more directly dependent upon industrialization and the economic development of the country to be considered in a later section.[48] There the problem is first to increase the country's wealth, then to distribute it so that the people can satisfy wants they have. In Africa and the Pacific the problem is to delay the economic development of the country until the native has wants which make him willing to aid voluntarily in that development.

d) EDUCATION

The least civilized native is likely to reckon declining population, a high death-rate, ill health, and losses of land and the things he

[46] See Buell (*op. cit.*, II, 330), who, however, commends the French mandate administration for the elimination of labor-recruiting for private employers, recognized in French West Africa, and for better legal protection of land tenures (*ibid.*, p. 372).

[47] The Tanganyika government seems to have yielded to the pressure engineered mainly from Kenya, and on December 11, 1926, the Governor announced a policy of encouraging non-native settlement where possible without depriving the native of sufficient land for his use (*ibid.*, I, 495). Commenting on this, Buell remarks, "It is significant that the German Government in East Africa before the War, realizing the effect of extensive European development, restricted the alienation of land in order to reduce the demand for labor. It is significant that the Belgian Congo is imposing similar restrictions today. In contrast to the policies of these territories, the Tanganyika Government, which unlike the German and Belgian governments is subject to specific obligations imposed by the Treaty of Versailles to advance the welfare of the native, is employing a land and labor policy which will accentuate rather than restrict the evils which the uncontrolled introduction of European industry into Africa involves" (p. 510). The antagonism between white settlement and the mandates policy seems to be recognized by the white settlers whose paper, the *Tanganyika Times*, frankly hopes that the territory will become a Crown Colony. "It would be much more honest," wrote this sheet on September 11, 1926, "if the Allied Powers were to drop the mandate pretence and the other pretence that Germany's Colonies were taken from her because *she lost.* Why not, then, tell her so in plain language and drop *pretence and hypocrisy?* It would be far better and would put an end to the matter, at least until Germany felt she was fit enough to attempt to re-take them. By no other method will they ever return to her" (Buell, *op. cit.*, I, 492–93). Buell emphasizes the danger that this white settlement policy would be promoted by federation of Tanganyika with the East African colonies of Great Britain (*ibid.*, pp. 511 ff. and *supra*, n. 23).

[48] Apparently the industrialization which has gone with Jewish immigration to Palestine has benefited the native Arabs (see *supra*, n. 36).

consumes as bad, and thus would probably reckon increasing population, better health, and more land and wages as good, even though he might not like some of the means necessary for obtaining them, and some of the consequences which they bring. But imported brands of education, security, and freedom seem to him of more doubtful value. Others may think these things are good for the native but does the native want them? He may like leisure more than learning, excitement more than security, folk ways more than freedom. He has his own types of education, security, and freedom adapted to the life he knows. Imported varieties seem to have no relevancy to that life, but only to a new life which it takes him time to imagine and which may not appeal to him if he does imagine it. Thus if the native's welfare is measured by progress in these processes it is only on the assumption that his transition to more "civilized standards" is eventually inevitable. The native policy of Western administrators, arising from the contact of aggressive industrial civilization with passive native folk ways, inevitably proceeds on that assumption.[49]

Even with this assumption it is clear that native education cannot succeed unless it enlists a certain minimum of native co-operation. Mere exposure to education does not educate. The first new ideas must be relevant to the natives' present life if they are to stick. Gradually new ones can be added. The three first gifts of white

[49] "The practical man recognizes the futility of theoretical disputations as to whether or not civilization is a benefit. Though the Allies in their reply to the German demand for the restitution of her colonies stated that a Mandatory Power will derive no benefit from the exercise of his trusteeship, it would be absurd to deny that the initial motive for the penetration of Africa by Western civilization was (with the exception of the religious missions) the satisfaction of its material necessities, and not pure altruism" (Lugard, *op. cit.*, p. 92). With this "practical" attitude may be contrasted the attitude of J. B. S. Haldane ("Science and Ethics," *Harper's Magazine*, June, 1928, p. 2): "As long as my services to my neighbor are confined to feeding him when hungry or helping him to raise his wages, and tending him when sick or preventing future sickness, and so forth, I am probably following the golden rule, for I do not want to be hungry, poor or sick, and few of my neighbors are good enough Christians to do so. But if I soar above the mere claims of the body, I shall try to educate my neighbor against his will, convert him to my particular brand of religion or irreligion, or even to psychoanalyze him. As I do not personally want to admire Gertrude Stein, worship a biscuit, or remember the moral lapses of my infancy, these forms of charity are very liable to be breaches of the golden rule; and if they are carried too far they may well develop into missions to the heathen or even crusades."

civilization to natives have usually been guns, gin, and Bibles. The first has an immediate educative effect. The natives can see that a gun is an improvement on means he already uses for ends he understands. The second he very soon begins to value for itself, but it is much more difficult for him to see the relevancy of Bibles. Successful missionaries have learned that they must gradually lead him to appreciate this relevancy.[50] The Mandates Commission has emphasized the importance of practical rather than literary education, carried on in the vernacular, and devoted especially to character-training, to agriculture, crafts, and hygiene as the means by which the native himself will be led to wish for an economic development of the region.[51] It does not appear that this policy has been fully accepted in the French territories where education seems to be directed toward the creation of a Frenchified native élite. The favoritism toward Catholic missions is, however, less marked in the mandated areas than in French colonies.[52]

The quality of educational effort cannot be considered here. A number of valuable reports on African education exist, and they are generally commendatory of results in the mandated territories.[53] The quantity of this effort (the value of which, of course, depends entirely upon the quality) can, however, be indicated to some extent by educational expenditures which have tended to increase in the mandated areas. In Iraq these expenditures doubled from 1920 to 1926 and at the latter date ran slightly ahead of health expenditure. The native government took a genuine interest in education, which it appeared to be developing successfully in view of its limited

[50] Lugard commends missionary educational activity but blames them for "having set too slight a value on discipline and concentrated too much on the acquisition of such knowledge as would enable their pupils to do creditably in the government examinations, and the training of a specialized class for evangelical work" (*op. cit.*, pp. 429–30).

[51] See *supra*, chap. viii, sec. 4*c*.

[52] Buell, *op. cit.*, II, 353.

[53] See Buell, *op. cit.;* T. J. Jones, *Education in Africa* (study of West, South, and Equatorial Africa by the African Education Commission under the auspices of the Phelps Stokes Fund and foreign-mission societies of North America and Europe), New York, 1922; *Education in East Africa* (a study of East, Central, and South Africa by the second African Education Commission under the Phelps Stokes Fund, in co-operation with the International Education Board), New York, 1925; and various reports by Mme Bugge Wicksell to the Permanent Mandates Commission (see *supra*, chap. viii, sec. 4*c*).

financial resources. About 2 per cent of the population were in schools in 1925, about equally divided between public and private schools. This may be compared with 7 per cent in Mexico and 22 per cent in the United States.[54] Palestine also increased her educational expenditures in these years, and on the latter date spent nearly one-fifth more for education than for health. The Jewish education is largely self-supported.[55]

All of the African mandated areas showed rapid progress in education, the results comparing very favorably with those in the neighboring colonies. The British expenditures in her three Central African mandate areas tripled from 1921 to 1926. Tanganyika, after an initial setback because of inadequate appropriations, discontinuance of mission subsidies, and expulsion of the German missions, made rapid progress after 1922 until the number of children in the schools in 1925 was about equal to that under Germany in 1914—about 2.4 per cent of the population. This may be compared with 1.7 per cent for Kenya and an estimate of 5.5 per cent in Uganda, though the latter figure represented almost entirely missionary enrolments.[56] The Tanganyika per capita expenditures were in fact greater than those in Uganda but less than in Kenya where, however, much of the money goes to the education of the considerable white population. Among the British Central African mandates in 1926 Cameroons was spending half as much on education as on health, Togoland a little more, and Tanganyika less than one-fifth as much.

The French progress in education in Togoland and Cameroons was particularly notable. The expenditures doubled from 1920 to 1927, though at the end they were only one-third of the health expenditures. In Togoland on the latter date the expenditures were more than four times those of Germany in 1914 and in Cameroons twice as much, while the number of pupils in the schools was 25 per cent greater. The proportion of the population in the schools, 2.2 per cent in French Togoland and 2 per cent in French Cam-

[54] Wright, "The Government of Iraq," *A.P.S.R.*, XX (1926), 754.

[55] The Jews have devoted especial attention to agricultural education (Joint Palestine Survey Commission, *op. cit.*, pp. 421 ff.).

[56] Buell, *op. cit.*, I, 387, 481.

eroons, was far beyond the average in West African colonies: .24 per cent in French West Africa, 1.3 per cent in the Gold Coast, 1.4 per cent in Southern Nigeria, 1.8 per cent in Congo, and only .1 per cent in Liberia.[57] The per capita expenditures, however, in Togo were no greater than those in French West Africa though the Cameroons expenditures were double those in French Equatorial Africa. The greater number of children accommodated was probably due to the encouragement of mission schools contrary to the French policy in its colonies. Though difficulties had arisen with the American missionaries in Cameroons because of the rule requiring the French language in the schools, this rule is not enforced and actually native language is more used in instruction than in the French colonies.[58]

The Ruanda-Urundi educational expenditures were stable from 1921 to 1926. On the latter date they were about two-thirds of the health expenditures. Southwest Africa developed her educational expenditures during this period. They became over five times the health expenditures, but the larger part went to education of the white population.[59]

Of the Pacific mandated territories, Nauru and Western Samoa more than doubled their educational expenditures from 1923 to 1926, at which time the figure was a third those for health. New Guinea expenditures, after rising until 1924, sank and were 12 per cent those for public health in 1926. Japan's educational expenditures for her mandated islands varied, amounting to about two-thirds the health expenditures. The variations in the ratio of educational to health expenditure is very great, ranging from one-eighth in New Guinea to five times in Southwest Africa. In general, the greater the absolute per capita expenditures of a government the larger the proportion devoted to education. The same relation generally applies to the proportion of the expenditures devoted to native welfare as a whole. Until a certain minimum is done for government, order, and communications, little can be devoted to native welfare, but health is the first consideration in the latter. Only after a necessary minimum of effort has been devoted to health can education receive

[57] *Ibid.*, II, 54, 352, 591, 731, 846.

[58] *Ibid.*, pp. 353, 372.

[59] See *infra*, Appendix VII.

very much attention. On the whole it appears that the mandates system has stimulated educational effort in the mandated areas.

e) SECURITY

Security from the European's point of view means adequate protection of life and property, including the prevention of invasions, rebellion, tribal war, head-hunting, and other forms of violence. It exists when order and justice are regularly maintained and will be discussed later.[60]

From the native point of view, security means continuance of traditional customs, and these are frequently opposed to economic and political development. The Arabs of Palestine have felt that the Zionist movement menaced this kind of security,[61] and the Syrians felt that the progress of Frenchification similarly menaced their security.[62] The changed conditions of Southwest Africa eliminated the German settler's sense of security, and the action of the mandatory government to reassure them made the native and colored population less secure, leading to the Bondelzwart and Rehoboth uprisings.[63] The rapid reform in Samoa seems to have similarly interfered with the sense of security of both the half-bloods and the natives, who combined in the Mau against the administration leading to the deportation of three half-blood leaders in 1927.[64]

The existence of general security is hardly susceptible of statistical measurement, but the Mandates Commission's policy, urging prior consideration to and conciliation of local interests; respect for native institutions, and land titles; prohibition of forced labor and labor recruiting at a distance; and elimination of conscription except for police purposes, would seem to promote it. In the latter respect a marked contrast seems to exist between the French man-

[60] See *infra*, sec. 3*e*.

[61] See Wright, "The Palestine Problem," *P.S.Q.*, XLI (September, 1926), 384 ff.

[62] See Wright, "The Bombardment of Damascus," *A.J.I.L.*, XX (1926), 362 ff.; "Syrian Grievances," *Current History*, XXIII (February, 1926), 687–93; MacCallum, *P.M.C., Min.*, VIII.

[63] *P.M.C., Min.*, III; see *supra*, chap. vii, sec. 3.

[64] Holland, *The Revolt of the Samoans*, 1928; Cocker, "The Mandate for Western Samoa," *New Zealand Affairs*, 1929, pp. 198–206; Condliffe, *New Zealand in the Making*, 1930, chap. xiii; *P.M.C., Min.*, XIII, 97–138, 229–30.

dated territories and the French colonies of West Africa. The cost of the local militia in Togoland and Cameroons is much less than was the military cost under German rule, and even less than the British military expenses in Tanganyika.[65]

In Palestine, the opposition of a large proportion of the population to the Zionist program incorporated in the mandate placed difficulties in the way of the normal mandatory duty to serve local interests first, and the overrapid Jewish immigration in 1925 brought about an economic crisis in 1926. Order was, however, maintained until 1929 and the apparent abatement of antagonism between the racial and religious elements led Stoyanovsky to write:

> If the Mandatory has succeeded, as he undoubtedly has, in bringing the various communities in Palestine nearer to each other and making future co-operation between them much more probable than could at one time have been reasonably anticipated, his success is largely due to the intervention of the Permanent Mandates Commission and its influence as an institution of the League on world public opinion and on such local public opinion as is gradually developing in Palestine.[66]

f) FREEDOM

Freedom from the European point of view means for the individual capacity to have and satisfy wants and for the community independence or self-determination. Achievement of either would require considerable modification of native life in the mandated areas, and it is undoubtedly the mandates' policy to work toward both. Reference has been made to the practice with respect to native education and participation in government in the areas.[67] The carrying-out of these policies doubtless depends on the absence of important foreign interests in the areas. Self-determination means

[65] Buell, *op. cit.*, II, 372, 383.

[66] *The Mandate for Palestine*, p. 354. "Substantial progress has been made in introducing order into the country and thus making possible the conduct of the peaceful pursuits of business. In view of the feelings between the Arabs and the Jews which at one time ran high, the establishment of an orderly and peaceable state of affairs is no mean accomplishment. Slow but measurable advance is also being made by the government in health and educational measures, in which the interests of the Arabs as well as of the Jews must be consulted" (Joint Palestine Survey Commission, *op. cit.* [Wolman], p. 512; see also Wright, "The Palestine Problem," *P.S.Q.*, XLI, 411). The serious incidents which arose in the summer of 1929 undoubtedly retarded this progress.

[67] See *supra*, chap. viii.

that local are to be preferred to foreign interests, and this becomes difficult if the latter are more powerful. Thus backward areas dominated by foreign capital or controlled by foreign governments seldom develop according to the interests of the natives and seldom get out of such control except by violence. Charles Francis Adams wrote:

> A dependency is not merely a possession but a trust, to be dealt with in a large altruistic spirit. I submit that there is not an instance in all recorded history, from the first precedent to that now making [referring to the Philippines] where a so-called inferior race or community has been elevated in its character or made self sustaining and self governing or even put on the way to that result, through a condition of dependency or tutelage.[68]

This is perhaps extreme but it certainly expresses general experience.

In each of the territories the mandatory government is a foreign interest, which, however, is pledged to the mandates principle and supervised by the League. Have the governments actually advanced the local communities toward independence? In Africa and the Pacific progress toward native self-determination must admittedly be slow.[69] In Southwest Africa there are Europeans who have been given a representative government in the area. They will unquestionably make it difficult for South Africa to live up to her obligations to the natives. "The settlers, not the natives, have the ear of the public at home," wrote J. S. Mill[70]—an observation amply justified by experience in Kenya, Rhodesia, and other African white settlement colonies, not to mention earlier illustrations from America, Australia, and New Zealand. Proposals have been made for extension of white settlement and white representation in government in Tanganyika, a move which would probably tend toward a similar subversion of native interests.[71] In Palestine the Zionist pledge renders representative institutions impossible so long as the majority of the population are irreconcilably opposed to Jewish immigration. Efforts at partial representation have failed in national affairs but progress has been made in local self-government through institutions based on religious community represen-

[68] *A.H.R.*, January, 1902, quoted in Hall, *Adolescence*, II, 712.

[69] Lugard, *op. cit.*, pp. 86, 194 ff.; Buell, *op. cit.*, I, 722.

[70] Quoted in Hall, *loc. cit.*

[71] See *supra*, n. 47.

tation.[72] In Iraq progress has been the most rapid. The native community has been recognized as a state with representative institutions and a limited international status.[73] Transjordan seems to be moving in the same direction though the native government is more primitive in structure. In Syria there seems to be general agreement that the Mandates Commission has contributed toward making the Syrian demand for more self-government, expressed by violence in 1925, partially effective.

As a mere colony of France, Syria could not have hoped for that degree of success in its recent rebellion which it appears actually to have achieved. Without the Permanent Mandates Commission the Syrian rebellion, which was destined from the beginning to meet military defeat, might have been as barren of achievement as the Moroccan rebellion. But with the publicity attendant upon the work of the Commission serving to intensify the public demand for fulfillment of the spirit of the mandate, France has not cared to force Syrian Nationalists to renounce the chief principles for which they fought. Military defeat was not accompanied by moral defeat.[74]

Economic concessions constitute another type of foreign interest. The oil concessions of Mosul and various economic concessions in Syria and Palestine may eventually give an influence to interests hostile to those of the local population. The phosphate concession in Nauru is virtually the government itself, which may render its influence all the more dangerous, and the same is true of the government-operated ex-enemy estates in New Guinea and Western Samoa.[75] Such concessions, unless carefully regulated, instead of developing the country may milk it, and instead of benefiting the native may enslave him. The experience of the Congo and French Equatorial Africa is one which the Mandates Commission has evinced every desire to avoid.[76]

Religious missions are a foreign interest which may interfere with native interests although the mandatory has ample power to

[72] Wright, "The Palestine Problem," *P.S.Q.*, XLI, 394.

[73] Wright, "The Government of Iraq," *A.P.S.R.*, XX, 143 ff.

[74] MacCallum, *op. cit.*, p. 248.

[75] See *supra*, chap. vii, sec. 3. Delisle Burns thinks the complete separation of government and business should be the first principle in administering backward areas (International Politics [1920], p. 63).

[76] Buell, *op. cit.*, II, 229 ff., 415 ff.

deal with them in the interests of public order. Experience has shown that missions in Africa tend to devote themselves to practical education with a genuine regard for the natives though trouble has sometimes arisen through their rivalries.[77] It is only in Palestine that religious interests are likely to prove more determining than the interests of the local inhabitants. The right of the Jews to establish a national home in Palestine is recognized in the mandate, but powerful Christian and Moslem organizations outside Palestine also have important interests there. Thus it seems not unlikely that Palestine will develop into a religious preserve in which the Jews, the Moslems, and the Christians will each have an assured privilege to visit their religious shrines and to establish cultural institutions connected with them.[78] In the other countries, however, there seems at least a reasonable prospect that development will be guided more by internal than by external interests.

From the natives' point of view, freedom means to be let alone, an aspiration which seems doomed to disappointment in the "strenuous conditions of the modern world." Economic penetration can hardly be stopped, and if the native cannot adjust his own culture to meet it, that culture is likely to disappear altogether, possibly carrying the native stock with it, as happened in Tasmania, Australia, and parts of America.[79] The only freedom which the inhabitants of the areas can hope to enjoy is a freedom sustainable in continuous contact with the modern world, and the freedom to pursue their age-old folk ways is not of that type. Nevertheless, if they are to enjoy the "new freedom," the transition must not be too rapid and roots of the "old freedom" must be used in its growth. The Commission has urged and the mandatories have agreed that native customs and institutions be utilized as much as possible and developed to meet new conditions rather than destroyed.[80]

While strict statistical demonstration is impossible, it appears that the mandates system has developed policies favorable to native health, agriculture, education, and security. While the native may not enjoy the application of all these policies at the moment, if

[77] Lugard, *op. cit.*, pp. 586 ff.

[78] Wright, "The Palestine Problem," *P.S.Q.*, XLI, 411.

[79] See *supra*, n. 16.

[80] See *supra*, chap. viii and n. 69.

carried out, they will increase his ability to make his own wishes effective, especially through use of the mandate institutions.

3. Economic Development in Mandated Areas

The population of the world has steadily increased during the past century and the economic wants of individuals have increased even more rapidly, thus the demand for an efficient utilization of all parts of the earth's surface has become more insistent.[81] The development of backward areas helps to meet this world demand for economic goods, and if one assume that it is better for people to have what they want than to want only what they have, such development may be considered for the good of the world. This assumption is challenged in many quarters[82] but it will probably remain valid unless schemes of education and propaganda which seek to modify the wants of people according to an external ideal gain ascendancy over business, technology, and inventiveness which profit by controlling nature in order to supply wants which exist. Men curb their appetites when confronted by necessity or conflicts in their own desires, but not for much else. There seems to be historic as well as psychologic ground for supposing that so long as he can man will prefer to bend circumstances to his will rather than bow before them. When scientific conquests cease, and the resources to be utilized by those already made are exhausted, the latter expedient may again come into vogue.

While increase in productiveness of the areas will inevitably modify the habits of the natives and if not carefully regulated may lead to their oppression or even extermination, yet on the assumption that native isolation from world-contacts is impossible, and that such contacts will gradually convert them to the modern attitude, their welfare, unless they migrate, is eventually bound up with

[81] Lugard, *op. cit.*, pp. 498 ff., 614–15.

[82] As, for instance, by Gandhi in India and similar spirits elsewhere characterized by Toynbee as "zealots" in contradistinction to "Herodians" (Toynbee and Kirkwood, *Turkey* [New York, 1927], p. 300). Hu Shih, who represents an important school of Chinese thought, accepts industrialization as do most of the other writers in *Whither Mankind?* (New York, 1928), C. A. Beard, editor. Goldenweiser (*op. cit.*, p. 404) considers control of nature, or at least belief in such control, a characteristic of advanced civilizations. Primitive civilizations adapt themselves to nature.

an increase in economic productiveness of the areas. We need not, on the other hand, go to the extreme of those who hold that better utilization of the areas should be the first aim of the mandates system on the assumption that humanitarian considerations are not practical and that the places of natives who cannot adjust themselves sufficiently rapidly will be filled by immigrants or contract laborers. We may then recognize that economic development is a second aim of the mandates system, to be pursued as rapidly as native welfare will permit.[83] Changes in (*a*) external trade, (*b*) investments and loans, (*c*) public revenues, (*d*) public works and services, and (*e*) order and justice may be assumed to indicate economic progress or decline and to give some prospect of statistical statement, the earlier more than the later in the list. Other indices, such as the total internal trade, the total wealth of the country, or the total annual income, might be better, but these conceptions are difficult to apply even in countries with the most highly developed statistics and could not be determined in any of the mandated areas.[84]

a) EXTERNAL TRADE

Trade has, in the main, developed satisfactorily in the near eastern areas. The trade of Iraq has been over half re-export trade, which on account of the break-up of the Turkish Empire and the creation of customs barriers declined 50 per cent from 1921 to 1926. Both net import and net exports, however, almost doubled during that period. The imports were over twice the exports.

Syria also has had a considerable transit and re-export trade. Her gross imports rose about 20 per cent from 1923 to 1925, but the insurrection of the latter year brought a reduction to the former figure in 1926. In the same way her gross exports, which rose 35 per cent from 1923 to 1925, sank in 1926. Like Iraq, Syria imports considerably more than she exports.

Palestine's re-export and transit business, like Iraq's, declined 50 per cent from 1922 to 1926. Her total imports, however, rose

[83] See *supra*, chap. viii.

[84] Wolman, in the Joint Palestine Survey Commission reports, finds it impossible to determine the internal trade even of Palestine (*op. cit.*, p. 505).

33 per cent from 1920 to 1925, a slight decline appearing in 1926. Her total exports were only a quarter as large and remained comparatively stable during this period. The per capita foreign trade of these countries in 1926 was: Iraq, $38; Syria, $28; Palestine, $43, which may be compared with the neighboring countries: Turkey, $16; Egypt, $36; and Persia, $16.[85]

All the African mandated areas showed trade increases from 1921 to 1926, and the exports and imports nearly balanced with the exception of British Togoland whose exports were four times her imports. In per capita foreign trade these territories varied greatly; Southwest Africa ranked near the top of Africa south of the Sahara, $100, compared with $103 for South Africa, $83 for Zanzibar, and $54 for Southern Rhodesia. Ruanda-Urundi, on the other hand, had the lowest, $0.18, compared with $2.50 for Liberia and $2.70 for French Equatorial Africa. Tanganyika with $7 was considerably below Kenya with $19 and Uganda with $13 but above Mozambique with $6, Nyassaland and Northern Rhodesia with $5. West Africa, with the exception of the Gold Coast, is generally below East Africa in foreign trade. French Togoland, the highest of these mandates, was $8; British Togoland, $5; French Cameroons, $5; and British Cameroons, $3.50, compared with $40 for the Gold Coast, $11 for Sierra Leone, $9 for Nigeria, $8 for French West Africa, $7 for Belgian Congo, and $6 for Angola. The average trade for Africa south of the Sahara was $17 per capita; thus all of the mandated areas are relatively undeveloped for Africa except Southwest Africa.[86]

The mandatories have been no more successful in developing these African territories than was Germany from 1907 to 1913. In that period Germany increased their total trade about 130 per cent. In 1920 due to the war the combined trade of the colonies was about

[85] These figures are computed from those in the *Statesman's Yearbook*, 1927.

[86] Buell, *op. cit.*, II, 977. If exports instead of total trade were used, Tanganyika would be considerably above Kenya. The latter's imports are almost three times its exports. Buell assumes from this that Kenya is less productive than either Tanganyika or Uganda and urges it as an argument against the economic value of white settlers (*ibid.*, I, 357).

the same as it had been in 1907, and by 1926 the mandatories had only brought it back to the 1913 figure.[87]

The Pacific mandated territories, with the exception of Western Samoa, showed substantial increases of trade between 1920 and 1925. Nauru and New Guinea each increased its exports by 80 per cent though the imports were fairly constant while the Japanese mandated islands more than tripled their imports, the exports increasing about 50 per cent. Western Samoa's exports remained constant, but its imports declined by nearly a half. The per capita foreign trade of these islands was similar to that of the near eastern territories and more than the African on the average. Nauru, with its valuable phosphate deposits and small population, had a per capita trade of $1,100, Western Samoa followed with $74, the Northern Pacific islands with $46, and New Guinea with $19. With these may be compared the per capita foreign trade of American Samoa, $38; Hawaii, $734; Fiji, $109; the Cook Islands, $113; and Papua, $22.[88]

Here, as in the African territories, the effort of the mandatories is comparable with that of Germany, though the rate of development has fallen off. Germany more than doubled the trade of the Pacific islands from 1907 to 1913. In this area the war did not cause such a setback as in Africa, and by 1920 the total trade of these islands had increased 40 per cent over the 1913 figure. In the six following years the trade has again increased 40 per cent.

b) INVESTMENTS, LOANS, AND SUBSIDIES

It is difficult to determine the amount of productive capital which has entered the territories under mandate, but there apparently has not been very much apart from the loans and grants made by the mandatories, except in Palestine. The mandatories have complained that capital was reluctant to enter the territories because of want of confidence in the mandates system, and in 1925 the Council, on recommendation of the Permanent Mandates Com-

[87] The German figures are given in United States Tariff Commission, *Colonial Tariff Policies* (Washington, 1922), p. 231. See also *infra*, Appendix IV.

[88] *Statesman's Yearbook*, 1927.

mission, asserted that a future mandatory would be responsible for loans and mortgages in case of transfer.[89] Members of the Commission have indicated that there is no objection to a mandatory recovering advances made to an area over which it exercises a mandate but such loans should be designated at the time and only a fair rate of interest required.[90] Though no formal resolution has been passed, this attitude may encourage such loans by the mandatories, and a number have in fact been made as well as a number of non-recoverable grants, usually to balance budgetary deficits.

Among the near eastern territories Iraq has given an oil concession to the Turkish Petroleum Company and an agricultural concession which it is hoped will result in irrigation projects and cotton culture, but no large sums seem yet to have been invested in either.[91] The mandatory made non-recoverable grants to the Iraq government in 1920 of about $3,000,000 and in 1925 of about $400,000, but these were for the cost of the military administration and to assist the army so aided little in economic development. A number of concessions for public works have been given in Syria mostly to Frenchmen but a few to natives.[92] In Palestine the mandatory made non-recoverable grants of over $4,000,000 from 1923 to 1926. There have been large investments by the Zionist organization and the Jewish immigrants, which have been a major factor in offsetting the unfavorable trade balance of $20,000,000 to $30,000,000 a year. These investments have gone to the development of the Jewish agricultural colonies as well as to cement, silicate brick, soap, and other factories said to employ an aggregate of about six thousand persons. Several concessions have been given, some of them on the suggestion of the Zionist organization, of which the Rutenberg, Jordan power and irrigation concessions are the most important.[93]

In the African areas before the war the only important investments were German agricultural estates which were expropriated

[89] See *supra*, chap. xiii, sec. 2*d*. See also Lugard, *op. cit.*, p. 55; Stoyanovsky, *op. cit.*, p. 229.

[90] See *supra*, chap. xiii, sec. 2*g*.

[91] Wright, "The Government of Iraq," *A.P.S.R.*, XX, 753.

[92] *Report on Syria* (1926), pp. 175–76.

[93] Joint Palestine Survey Commission, *op. cit.*, pp. 501, 506.

under the terms of the Versailles Treaty except in Southwest Africa where many of the German settlers still live. There was considerable difficulty in selling these expropriated estates, but most have been sold or leased by the mandatory governments, some to their former German owners; others, to Frenchmen, Englishmen, and natives. In general they seem to have realized less than a proper value, and in French Cameroons and Togoland some of the sales and concessions made by the government savored of graft which was eventually aired in the French Parliament.[94] The receipts from these ex-enemy estates, however, are not property of the mandated territory but of the mandatory to be credited to German reparations account. In New Guinea and Western Samoa the mandatories have retained and operate some of these ex-enemy estates.[95]

In Tanganyika the mandatory made non-recoverable grants in 1920–21 totaling about $1,500,000, and had made loans of over $11,000,000 before 1925. The Belgian government has made loans of $60,000 a year to Ruanda-Urundi. The British have covered the annual deficit of the Cameroons and Togoland mandates by non-recoverable grants. There have been no other loans or grants by the mandatories to West or Southwest African mandated areas; French Togoland, in fact, developed such a surplus that in 1927 she loaned $250,000 to the French Cameroons.

In the Pacific territories Australia has loaned $135,000 and granted $100,000 to New Guinea from 1923 to 1926; New Zealand has loaned about $450,000 to Western Samoa in varying annual amounts and has made non-recoverable grants of about $100,000 a year. There have been no government subsidies or loans to Nauru, but the phosphate monopoly operated by a joint British-Australian–New Zealand commission contributes to the support of the government. The South Seas Bureau is really a branch of the Japanese government, and both governs and exploits the North Pacific islands. The government has granted $4,500,000 to these islands. The mandatory governments have been much less generous in contributing to the territories than was Germany before the war. The total grants to former German territory since the war has been only about $20,000,000 with about half as much in recoverable loans.

[94] Buell, *op. cit.*, II, 295.

[95] See *supra*, chap. xiii, sec. 2*c*.

Germany contributed about $7,500,000 annually to these possessions, and although her policy was to make them self-sufficient, this was achieved only in the cases of Togo and Samoa, and in 1914 the subsidies constituted 28 per cent of the total colonial expenditures.[96]

Economic development of all the mandated areas undoubtedly depends upon the inflow of capital as well as upon the development of a labor supply to utilize it. As yet external capital has come mainly from the mandatory powers with exception of the Zionist investments in Palestine, and the mandatories exhausted by war have not had large sums to invest. Great Britain and Japan have invested the most, while Belgium and the British dominions have put more into their mandated areas than France.

c) PUBLIC REVENUES

Public revenues perhaps give rough evidence of the people's capacity to pay taxes and so of the development of the country, although for a considerable period backward areas may be taxed beyond their capacity with resulting depopulation.

In Iraq the annual revenue has increased 50 per cent while in Palestine it doubled from 1920 to 1926. In Syria the revenue has been fairly constant, and has for the most part developed a surplus which in 1924 was as much as $3,300,000. In these territories the per capita revenue in 1926 was Iraq, $7.41; Palestine, $13.92; and Syria, $5.65.

Among the African territories revenues have tended to increase greatly. The revenue of Tanganyika rose nearly 300 per cent from 1919 to 1925, that of Ruanda-Urundi, 5 per cent; British Cameroons, 240 per cent; and British Togoland, 2,000 per cent. The French have developed a surplus in both their West African mandates as they have in Syria and the revenues on a gold basis have been about constant. The Southwest African revenue alone has declined, about 15 per cent, in spite of which the territory has accumulated a surplus. The per capita revenue in these territories showed a wide range in 1926, from $13 in Southwest Africa to $0.05 in Ruanda-Urundi. The others were Tanganyika, $1.75; British Togoland, $1.05; French Togoland, $0.64; British Cameroons, $0.90; French Cameroons,

[96] United States Tariff Commission, *op. cit.*, pp. 235–36.

$0.45. These may be compared with per capita revenues of other African territories as follows: South Africa, $19.50; Gold Coast, $6.00; Kenya, $4.50; Nigeria, $1.50; French West Africa, $1.40; and Belgian Congo, $1.30; French Equatorial Africa and Liberia, $0.50. The average for all Africa south of the Sahara is $3.30, thus indicating that the mandated areas are relatively backward for Africa.

A comparison of the revenue of these territories now and under the German régime indicates striking similarity with exception of Southwest Africa, whose population was probably greatly underestimated by the Germans. The Germans, however, added a subsidy to all but Togo which averaged 28 per cent of the expenditures. East Africa, whose population has been equally divided between Tanganyika and Ruanda-Urundi, had a per capita revenue in 1914 of $0.50; Kamerun, $1.25; Togo, $0.87; and Southwest Africa, $60.

In the Pacific islands the tendency of revenue has been similar to that in the African territories. Nauru's revenue increased 60 per cent from 1922 to 1926 and New Guinea's about the same. The Japanese increased the revenues of the North Pacific islands 230 per cent. Western Samoa alone has shown a decline, about 10 per cent. The per capita revenues in these in 1926 was Japanese islands, $26.36; Western Samoa, $13.05; Nauru, $36.09; New Guinea, $3.12. The average is considerably higher than in the African territories and also than in these islands under the German régime. Thus the per capita revenue of Samoa in 1914 was $8 and of the others, $0.87.

d) PUBLIC WORKS AND SERVICES

It is recognized that public buildings, ports, roads, railroads, bridges, telegraph lines, are essential for development of backward areas, and the mandates permit the use of forced labor, with pay however, for such necessary public works and services. Only second in importance to these essentials for government, conveyance, and communication are irrigation, drainage, afforestation, and other agricultural projects.[97] Programs of construction have been undertaken in all the areas. The territories were of course supplied with many of these public works when the mandates system began. In

[97] Lord Lugard puts railroads first and after them research of both a laboratory and experimental character and agricultural propaganda and education (*op. cit.*, pp. 498 ff.).

1925 Palestine had 55 miles of railroad per thousand square miles of area; Transjordan, 14; Syria, 9; Iraq, 6; French Togoland, 10; Southwest Africa, 4; Tanganyika, 3; and French Cameroons, 2.[98] British Togoland, Cameroons, and the Pacific mandated territories seem to have had no railways.

The part of the budget devoted to public works roughly indicates the progress in supplying the essentials for economic development although some may be supplied by concessions or private enterprise. Of the A mandated areas Iraq reduced her public-work expenditures 40 per cent from 1921 to 1925. Palestine, on the other hand, increased hers by 80 per cent in the same period, and a considerable extension of roads and railroads has taken place. The African mandated territories generally show an increase of such expenditures during this period; Tanganyika, 100 per cent; Ruanda-Urundi, 70 per cent; French Cameroons, 15 per cent; French Togoland, 30 per cent; and British Cameroons, 25 per cent. British Togoland and Southwest Africa each kept this budget about constant. The French have devoted the surpluses from their West African mandates to public works. The Pacific mandated territories have also devoted extensive sums to public works, the amounts varying from year to year but showing a tendency to increase. Japan especially enlarged her expenditures in this field from $125,000 to $189,000 a year. The public-works expenditures were considerably larger than the health expenditures in all the mandated territories except New Guinea, Western Samoa, the Nauru.

e) ORDER AND JUSTICE

The maintenance of order including the prevention or suppression of invasion, insurrection, and violence, the protection of life and property, and the regular administration of justice are recognized as a first essential of economic development. The investment of money and the prosecution of long-time enterprises are only possible when there is confidence that order will continue. The preservation of order might be measured by analysis of the statistics of crime, violent death, property losses by violence, etc.; by questionnaire studies designed to indicate a sense of security in different classes

[98] *Statesman's Yearbook*, 1927, and *infra*, Appendix VIII.

and regions; or by economic statistics indicating the confidence of investors. As has been noted, the League of Nations has attempted to increase confidence in the mandatory régime by assurances of the permanent responsibility of the areas for loans, but capital has not moved into most of the areas very rapidly. Economic factors, as well as political hazards, of course, are important in determining the flow of capital, though in backward areas the latter is usually important. None of these types of statistics is available for the mandated areas, and space does not permit of a detailed history of incidents in each area.

Iraq had an insurrection in 1920 and has been menaced by border raids and tribal invasion, but her frontier has been preserved and the government has operated effectively for eight years.[99] Palestine had rioting in 1920, many of the Arabs have remained irreconcilable with the Zionist program, and serious disturbances occurred in the summer of 1929 as a result of Arab-Jewish disputes over the use of the "Wailing Wall."[100] Syria has had the most violence of any mandated area. Beginning with the French war against Feisal in 1920 and the loss of Cilicia before the Turkish advance in 1921, Syria had an insurrection almost every year until 1927. To the Syrian desire for independence and opposition to the French, who were least popular as the prospective mandatory at the time of the Peace Conference, economic, cultural, and personal grievances were added, until the climax was reached in the Arab Druse revolt of 1925 culminating in the bombardment and destruction of the central area of Damascus. The multiplicity of sects, the breach in trade conditions, and the original unpopularity of France among the Moslems and Druses were underlying factors, but the Mandates Commission found the French administration was not without blame, especially for its frequent territorial changes of the "states" within the mandated area, for the neglect of an earlier agreement with the Jebel Druse, and for precipitancy in reform and the tactlessness of General Sarrail under whose administration the revolt broke out. Since 1928 the situation has improved with the develop-

[99] Wright, "The Government of Iraq," *A.P.S.R.*, November, 1926; "The Mosul Dispute," *A.J.I.L.*, July, 1926.

[100] See *supra*, nn. 61, 66.

ment of self-governing constitutions in the Lebanon and Syria.[101]

In the African territories there has been no important disturbance except in Southwest Africa, where the Bondelzwart revolt of 1921 and the Rehoboth disturbances of 1923 occurred. Both were the subject of extensive League investigation, and the majority of the Permanent Mandates Commission found fault with the South African conduct in the first case. The situation in Southwest Africa with a small white population of mixed Boers and ex-Germans controlling the natives and the colored (half-breeds) in this large thinly populated area is one of great difficulty, augmented by the traditional color cleavage in South Africa.[102]

The Pacific islands have been quiet except for the Samoan disturbances of 1927, which arose partly from the anxiety of New Zealand to fulfil her mandatory duties strictly and partly from tactlessness of the administration but mainly from the ambition of certain half-blood leaders. The Samoans early showed a lack of confidence in New Zealand by asking that the mandate be transferred to Great Britain, and the feeling was increased by inefficiency in handling the serious influenza epidemic which struck the islands in 1921. New Zealand antagonized the white and half-blood settlers by prohibiting all alcolohic beverages and interfering with the marketing of native copra, while she antagonized the natives by too rigorous sanitary regulations, and by creating an expectation of native representation in the legislative council without fulfilment. The military administrator evidently failed to understand native psychology, and New Zealanders, some of them Maoris, have criticized the administration for not using Maoris or persons familiar with the Polynesian race in handling Western Samoa.[103]

In general, order seems to have been maintained in mandated areas as well as in most colonial areas which have just undergone a transition of government. Occasional disturbances and punitive expeditions occur in all such contacts of advanced and backward peoples, but it has been the preoccupation of the Mandates Commission to reduce them to a minimum.

While the evidence indicates that the mandated areas are back-

[101] See *supra*, n. 62.

[102] See *supra*, chap. vii, sec. 3.

[103] See *supra*, nn. 10, 64.

ward—the African among the most backward on that continent—the economic productiveness of the areas seems to have advanced at a rate which, if not above normal, is equal to that of colonies and perhaps as much as could be expected in the difficult post-war situation.

4. International Harmony in Respect to Mandated Areas

The mandates system seeks to benefit the world outside the areas, not only by increasing the supply of economic goods available to it, but also by reducing the probability of international unfriendliness, rivalry, and hostility. While it is difficult to measure the extent to which backward areas have contributed to the causation of wars, there can be little doubt but that, because of the common uncertainty or instability of their status, they have stimulated rivalries more frequently than have fully developed areas. One might cite as example the Anglo-Russian contests over "the sick man of Europe"; the Anglo-American maneuvers over Oregon, Texas, and Hawaii; the Anglo-American-German transactions in regard to Samoa; the Anglo-French relations over Egypt and the Sudan culminating in Fashoda; the Russo-Japanese-Chinese rivalries over Korea and Manchuria; the French-German relations over Morocco; and the Anglo-German negotiations over the routes from the cape to Cairo and from Berlin to Bagdad, not to mention sixteenth- and seventeenth-century rivalries over the American continents and the East Indies.[104]

There also appears little doubt that, whether annexed or not, commercial discriminations in such areas have often led to irritation, as witness the German protest in regard to Morocco in 1911, and the American protests in regard to China and Mesopotamia at various times. Doubtless such protests are sometimes a pretext to veil political maneuvers, but the fact that backward areas are often looked upon as political prey makes it all the more important that such pretexts should not be available.

While statistical measurement of the effect of the mandates system in international political relations in regard to the areas is not at present possible, we may assume that (*a*) full legal recogni-

[104] Most of them are discussed in Moon, *Imperialism and World Politics.*

tion, (*b*) an effective open door, and (*c*) general confidence in the stability of the system would give evidence that such relations are satisfactory.

a) RECOGNITION OF THE MANDATES SYSTEM

We have noticed that the opinion of states as formally expressed in the League of Nations Assembly has been uniformly favorable to the system, and in fact there seem to have been no formal complaints in regard to it except from Germany and the United States though Turkey and Russia have evinced little enthusiasm for it.[105] The United States has at this writing indicated its satisfaction with respect to most of the territories by making treaties with the mandatory recognizing their status, and Turkey has made a treaty recognizing the present Iraq boundary.[106] Germany protested against the original assignment of mandates by the Principal Powers rather than the League, and later against some of the legislation for Tanganyika and Ruanda-Urundi.[107] Now, however, as a member of the League of Nations she has accepted the system and is entitled to assist in supervising it to the same extent as other members of the Council. Thus it appears that substantially all the states have fully accepted the system in law and in fact with the exception of soviet Russia.

b) THE OPEN DOOR

The law relating to the open door in the mandated territories has been discussed, and it appears that the Mandates Commission has been taking an increasingly meticulous view of its duty to enforce it, as witness the Tanganyika loan and postage questions, and the careful scrutiny of tariffs and concessions in Syria and Iraq.

The mandates, however, do not require the open door in the C areas, though the gratuitous character of the mandatory's mission and consideration for the welfare of the inhabitants may require it in some circumstances. The special situation of the C territories was considered a derogation from principle at the Peace Conference and has not been recognized by the United States, which has not made treaties accepting the status of any of the C areas except the North

[105] See *supra*, chap. iii.

[106] See *supra*, chap. ii; chap. xiii, sec. 4*e*.

[107] See *supra*, chap. xiii, sec. 4*f*.

Pacific islands. This treaty practically assures the open door though it does not do so formally. Japan has also registered her dissatisfaction with the non-application of the open door in the C areas in a reservation to her approval in the council of the C mandates.[108] It thus appears that in so far as the open door is not applicable there is an element of weakness in the system. In fact, with respect to the C areas it is a retrogression from the previous situation since Germany applied the open door uniformly in her colonies, both in law and in fact.[109]

c) GENERAL CONFIDENCE

Although the mandates system has been very generally recognized in law and in principle, has it been accepted in policy and sentiment? Has Germany given up the ambition to reacquire her former colonies? Does she want a mandate? Does Italy want a mandate? Do any of the mandatories want to annex the territories? Some of these possibilities may at one time have deterred investors from putting money into the areas but at present there seems to be general confidence in the system's stability. The legal sanction of the system seems considerably superior to that of most protectorates and colonies as all the members of the League are directly interested in its maintenance. Thus it seems unlikely that any individual state will attempt to upset the system by illegal conduct. The status of the areas may change—in fact, the mandates and the Covenant contemplate that they shall—but it is to be anticipated that any such change will be by the orderly processes of the League of Nations.

While the period of its operation has been short and the available data incomplete, it seems fair to say that the mandates system has proved a practical method for administering backward areas, more satisfactory than others that have been tried from the standpoint of the natives and from the standpoint of the world in general. Whether or not it has been as advantageous to the administering state as have the traditional systems of colonies, protectorates, and spheres of interest, at least none of the mandatory powers has offered to resign.

[108] See *supra*, chap. xiii, sec. 4*b*.

[109] United States Tariff Commission, *op. cit.*, p. 244.

CHAPTER XVI

THE FURTHER DEVELOPMENT OF THE MANDATES SYSTEM

There is undoubtedly a problem of backward areas. Psychologists,[1] biologists,[2] anthropologists,[3] sociologists,[4] economists,[5] political scientists,[6] international lawyers,[7] historians,[8] geographers,[9] administrators,[10] publicists,[11] and humanitarians[12] have written about

[1] G. Stanley Hall, *Adolescence* (New York, 1904), chap. xviii on "Adolescent Races."

[2] Grant, *The Passing of the Great Race* (New York, 1923), pp. 76 ff.; East, *Mankind at the Cross Roads* (New York, 1923), chap. v.

[3] Rivers, *Essays on the Depopulation of Melanesia*, Cambridge, 1922.

[4] Keller, *Colonization*, New York, 1908; Ross, *Report on Employment of Native Labor in Portuguese Africa*, New York, 1925.

[5] Muntz, *Race Contact*, New York, 1927; Woolf, *Empire and Commerce in Africa, a Study in Economic Imperialism*, London, 1919; Nearing and Freeman, *Dollar Diplomacy*, New York, 1925; McPhee, *The Economic Revolution in British West Africa*, London, 1926.

[6] Reinsch, *World Politics*, New York, 1900; *Colonial Government*, New York; Buell, *International Relations*, New York, 1925; *The Native Problem in Africa*, New York, 1928; Ram, *Comparative Colonial Policy*, London, 1926; Delisle Burns, *International Politics*, London, 1920.

[7] Snow, *The Question of the Aborigines*, New York, 1921; Lindley, *The Acquisition and Government of Backward Territory in International Law*, London, 1926.

[8] Beer, *African Questions at the Paris Peace Conference*, New York, 1923; Moon, *Imperialism and World Politics*, New York, 1926; Johnston, *A History of the Colonization of Africa by Alien Races*, Cambridge, 1899; *The Backward Peoples and Our Relation with Them*, Oxford, 1926; Bryce, *The Relations of the Advance and the Backward Races of Mankind*, Oxford, 1902; Paul Leroy Beaulieu, *De la Colonization chez les peuples modernes* (6th ed.), Paris, 1908; Marvin (ed.), *The Western Races and the World*, London, 1922; Lucas, *The Partition and Colonization of Africa*, Oxford, 1922; Chirol, *The Occident and the Orient*, Chicago, 1924; Edgerton, *British Colonial Policy in the 20th Century* (London, 1922), Part II.

[9] Demangeon, *The British Empire*, New York, 1925; Bowman, *The New World*.

[10] Lugard, *The Dual Mandate in British Tropical Africa*, London, 1923; Olivier, *White Capital and Coloured Labor*, London, 1906; Cromer, *Ancient and Modern Imperialism;* Schnee, *German Colonization, Past and Future*, London, 1926.

[11] Stoddard, *The Rising Tide of Color*, New York, 1920, Leo Chiozza Money, *The Peril of the White*, London, 1925; Norton, in Cassel *et al.*, *Foreign Investments*, Chicago, 1928; Peffer, *The White Man's Dilemma*, New York, 1927.

[12] Morel, *The Black Man's Burden*, London, 1920; Harris, *Dawn in Darkest Africa*, London, 1914; *Slavery or Sacred Trust*, London, 1926.

it though few have attempted to define the concept. The term may be applied in a cultural, political, or an economic sense but in none does it seem susceptible of very precise definition. Cultures differ in kind but the anthropologist hesitates to classify them as higher or lower. Everyone regards his own as the best.[13] Political differences, whether in the sense of governmental structure or in the sense of degree of external sovereignty, depend in large measure on historical accidents and fail to correspond with the other connotations of the term. Canada, lacking full sovereignty, would hardly be regarded as more backward than Costa Rica. Morocco, a protectorate, is not more backward than Abyssinia, an independent state. Economic backwardness is also difficult to define but perhaps a country with relatively slight international trade and industrial production in proportion to its population and relatively slight communications in proportion to its area would usually be called backward.[14]

[13] Sumner, *Folkways* (Boston, 1906), p. 13; Lowie, *Primitive Society* (New York, 1920), p. 439; Faris, *The Superiority of Race* (data paper), Institute of Pacific Relations, 1927. Dr. Felix Speiser, however, "cannot picture an intercourse where the lower people would not be forced to compare their own organizations with those of the superior people, with the consequent contempt for their own" (in Rivers, *op. cit.*, p. 37). Lindley apparently has this cultural sense of the term primarily in mind when he writes: "The term 'Backward Territory' is not one that is known to international law, nor is it possible or desirable to give it any exact definition or denotation for our present purpose. At the one extreme, it may perhaps be said to be marked by territory which is entirely uninhabited; and it clearly includes territory inhabited by natives as low in the scale of civilization as those of Central Africa. On the other hand, all that can be said as to its upper limits probably is that it is obviously intended to exclude territory which has reached the level of what is sometimes known as European or Western civilization. The term is a relative one, and as civilization advances it may cease to apply to territory which would today be said to be included within it; or it may conceivably become applicable to countries which would not in the circumstances of the present time be called 'backward' " (*op. cit.*, Preface).

[14] Backward in this sense is the opposite of industrialized. Art. 393 of the treaty of Versailles requires eight members of the governing body of the International Labor Office to be nominated by "the members [of the international labor organization] which are of the chief industrial importance." To determine this the League of Nations Council (following in the main a decision of the organizing committee of the first session [1919] of the labor conference) decided in 1922 on seven criteria. Four were absolute (total wage-earning industrial population, total horse-power [steam- and water-power] not including locomotives and vessels, total length of railways, and development of the merchant marine), but the remaining three were relative (proportion which the wage-earning industrial population bears to the whole population, horse-power per head of

All three points of view are likely to be present, in fact, when the problem is discussed, and for this very reason the conception lacks precision. An economically developed country whose inhabitants own its capital and control its policy is usually considered more advanced than one whose capital is owned or policy controlled from abroad. Furthermore, countries of European or Western civilization are considered most advanced by Western writers. Thus lack of Europeanization, lack of self-determination, and lack of industrialization perhaps contribute about equally to the usual notion of a backward area, and probably there is a causal relation between the three. In recent history, however, the economic sense of the term has been most significant, the others tending to follow as consequences.

The problem of backward areas in this sense has arisen as a by-product of the industrialization of Europe. This has induced a search for markets, raw materials, and opportunities for investment and the application of industrial techniques in new areas. The effort to develop these backward areas has led to exploitation of natives unable to adjust themselves rapidly, and to political rivalries, especially when the economic motive has been supplemented by political, strategic, and cultural motives for expansion. Some states have sought to annex or otherwise gain exclusive control of a given backward area (imperialism), and others have sought to prevent such action, often with pleas of native self-determination and hopes that fortune may favor their own claims later. With the increase in the proportion of the earth's surface which is developed and a corresponding decrease in the backward areas remaining, the problem has become more acute, the policy of imperialism has become more dangerous, and that of self-determination by inexperienced or incompetent natives more impracticable.

The mandates system, as we have seen, clearly visualizes these three phases of the problem: economic backwardness, native exploitation, and international friction. The League and the mandatories have been developing a policy in regard to each, which has in the past ten years achieved tolerable success in the regions where applied. It is

---

population, length of railways per thousand square kilometers of territory) and could perhaps be taken as a measure of economic backwardness or advancement (see *O.J.*, II [1922], 1339 ff.; Behrens, *The International Labor Office* [London, 1924], pp. 41, 185).

believed that the system has advantages from the standpoint of the inhabitants of the area and of the world in general over the system of imperial control (whether under the form of colonies, protectorates, or spheres of interest) which has characterized the relation of advanced and backward peoples in the Eastern hemisphere, and also over the less precise system of self-determination qualified by the Monroe Doctrine, sporadic interventions, quasi-protectorates, receiverships, and occasional annexations by the United States which has characterized those relations in the Western hemisphere. While the systems of the two hemispheres approach the problem from different theoretic positions, the only differences which exist in practice are those which spring from the fact that one "great power" has gained a recognized dominance in the new world. As a consequence that power has not been pressed to assume such continuous responsibility for and to exercise such continuous power over the backward areas which it wished to keep within its sphere as has been true of powers whose spheres closely trenched upon each other in the delicate balance of power situation of the Eastern hemisphere. The supervision of the League of Nations makes it possible for the mandates system to accept the theoretic position of both hemispheres, the one insisting on the technical superiority of advanced nations and the other on the legitimate aspirations of backward peoples.

Continuous international supervision is the essence of the mandates system. It focuses attention upon the problem of backward areas as concretely presented by the mandated area from the native and the world points of view. Anyone is a poor judge in his own case, and however it may try, a state has always found it difficult to visualize a subject people except from the standpoint of its own interests. The backward native has had neither the knowledge to formulate his own needs nor the power to achieve them, and the world in general has been too disorganized to find out what its interests were or to act upon them if it was told. When, as has occasionally happened, the inhabitants of a one-time backward area have acquired capacity to formulate their interests and to act together efficiently, the ruling state has seldom realized or been willing to acknowledge the situation until forced to by violence. The mandates system introduces the novelty of a disinterested body, the Permanent Mandates Commission, to examine the situation impartially as it develops in each area from the native and world points of view, appraising particularly the evolution of a capacity for self-government. The novelty of the system as well as the mass of data it has made public has encouraged a greater degree of attention to the problem from technical commissions and private jurists than it had ever received before.

Attention is the first step in control,[15] and from this attention to the problem of particular backward areas by the common instrument of most of the states of the world definite policies for protecting the interests involved are developing, and the machinery of the League is ready to give them practical effect. The opportunity exists for international science to guide national policy in handling problems as they arise, and the full supervisory authority of the League assures that the opportunity will be utilized. Science, it is true, has had a part before in the development of colonies, but mainly as a handmaid of national interest. Under the League the administration of mandated areas may become the "white man's burden" in the opinion of the black man as well as of the white, in the opinion of the non-colonial state as well as the colonial empire.[16]

Finally, as a by-product of the League's supervisory control of mandatory administration, rules, principles, and standards of broader application are being formulated. An international code of native rights and of the open door is developing. The territories under mandate include three important types of backward areas—the Moslem, the Negro, and the Oceanic (Polynesian, Melanesian, Micronesian)—each of which includes other areas, now governed for the most part

[15] Thomas, *Source Books for Social Origins* (Chicago, 1909), pp. 14–19. The significance of the concentration of attention on colonial problems is emphasized in the memorandum prepared inofficially by members of the League Secretariat for the Institute of Pacific Relations in 1927 (Condliffe, *Problems of the Pacific*, pp. 519 ff.).

[16] The importance of scrupulous good faith in mandatory administration is thus emphasized by Lord Olivier: "It is not wise to tell an African you are exercising 'trusteeship' (a conception he quite understands) 'in his interests' when, for example, you are taking away land that belongs by his tribal law to some of his families, and giving it to white planters. He will only smile appreciatively at your artistry in palaver, smile still more if it appears that you suppose he believes you, and despise you if it dawns on him that you really believe it yourself" (*The Nation*, New York, June 6, 1928, p. 639).

as colonies or protectorates. Thus principles found satisfactory in mandated territories will in most cases have a broader application. Lord Lugard, one of its members, after twenty years' administrative experience in Africa writes:

The commission will gradually acquire a unique experience of the methods of administration and development adopted by the different mandatories, and by placing this at the common service, it may become an invaluable instrument of international co-operation even beyond the limits of Mandated territories. To achieve this object it must earn for itself the character of a useful ally rather than that of a censorious critic.[17]

The success of the system depends on full understanding of the facts by the League organs in order that their supervision may be wise. The Commission must recommend practically, not doctrinally, if it is to be of value, and no matter how able and experienced its members it can do this only if it knows the entire situation.

Better sources of information are needed, and it is believed informal visits by Secretariat officials or members of the Commission to the areas would be useful. Personal contact adds greatly to the information supplied by documents. Formal visits which might impair the mandatory's prestige in the area should take place only in case of grave emergency on special Council resolution. In such cases, however, a formal investigation on the spot would increase native confidence and world-confidence in the system. The procedure of petition also seems susceptible of improvement by occasional hearing of petitioners, not as a litigation but for information.[18]

Better standards are also needed, and they should be scientific and not dogmatic. The Permanent Mandates Commission should co-operate, as it has with the Labor Office, the health organization, the economic and financial organizations of the League, and with private scientific agencies, in order to bring all the wisdom available to the problems of native welfare, economic development, and international harmony in relation to the mandated areas.[19]

Finally better publicity should be given, both to assure observance of recommendations by the mandatories and to encourage the understanding and application of the accepted principles in colonial areas of similar type. The process of formulation is gradual, but

[17] *Op. cit.*, p. 57. [18] See *supra*, chap. vi. [19] See *supra*, chap. viii.

eventually the Committee of Experts for the Progressive Codification of International Law, the labor organization, or other bodies might develop conventions covering certain accepted principles of native administration for ratification by all colonial powers, but since backward areas differ greatly such a code could not be too rigid.[20]

The question of extending the system to other areas in the administrative sense is of less importance than the extension of its principles. The system has already resulted in wider recognition of the principle of trusteeship, that dependencies should be administered in the interests of their inhabitants; in the principle of tutelage, that the cultivation of a capacity for self-government is such an interest; of the principle of international mandate, that states are responsible to the international community for the exercise of power over backward peoples even if that responsibility is not fully organized. The system now embraces typical areas—if more were added the Commission's administrative duties might swamp its scientific and investigatory functions. Nevertheless the advantages of the League's supervision will doubtless be considered in the event of a future political exigency suggesting a change in the status of a dependency. The League's major work however is to focus attention on the problem, to co-ordinate investigations and experiments toward its solution, and to see that the mandated areas are administered in the interests of the natives and the world according to the best learning and experience in the world, thus setting examples for the administration of backward areas everywhere.

[20] See *supra*, chap. vii, sec. 4.

APPENDIXES

APPENDIX I

MANDATE ARTICLES OF THE LEAGUE OF NATIONS COVENANT

ARTICLE 22

1. To those colonies and territories which as a consequence of the late war have ceased to be under the sovereignty of the States which formerly governed them and which are inhabited by peoples not yet able to stand by themselves under the strenuous conditions of the modern world, there should be applied the principle that the well-being and development of such peoples form a sacred trust of civilization and that securities for the performance of this trust should be embodied in this Covenant.

2. The best method of giving practical effect to this principle is that the tutelage of such peoples should be intrusted to advanced nations who, by reason of their resources, their experience or their geographical position, can best undertake this responsibility, and who are willing to accept it, and that this tutelage should be exercised by them as Mandatories on behalf of the League.

3. The character of the mandate must differ according to the stage of the development of the people, the geographical situation of the territory, its economic conditions and other similar circumstances.

4. Certain communities formerly belonging to the Turkish Empire have reached a stage of development where their existence as independent nations can be provisionally recognized subject to the rendering of administrative advice and assistance by a Mandatory until such time as they are able to stand alone. The wishes of these communities must be a principal consideration in the selection of the Mandatory.

5. Other peoples, especially those of Central Africa, are at such a stage that the Mandatory must be responsible for the administration of the territory under conditions which will guarantee freedom of conscience and religion, subject only to the maintenance of public order and morals, the prohibition of abuses such as the slave trade, the arms traffic and the liquor traffic, and the prevention of the establishment of fortifications or military and naval bases and of military training of the natives for other than police purposes and the defense of territory, and will also secure equal opportunities for the trade and commerce of other Members of the League.

6. There are territories, such as Southwest Africa and certain of the South Pacific islands, which, owing to the sparseness of their population or their small size, or their remoteness from the centers of civilization, or their geographical contiguity to the territory of the Mandatory, and other circumstances, can

be best administered under the laws of the Mandatory as integral portions of its territory, subject to the safeguards above mentioned in the interests of the indigenous population.

7. In every case of mandate, the Mandatory shall render to the Council an annual report in reference to the territory committed to its charge.

8. The degree of authority, control or administration to be exercised by the Mandatory shall, if not previously agreed upon by the Members of the League, be explicitly defined in each case by the Council.

9. A permanent Commission shall be constituted to receive and examine the annual reports of the Mandatories, and to advise the Council on all matters relating to the observance of the mandates.

ARTICLE 23

Subject to and in accordance with the provisions of international conventions existing or hereafter to be agreed upon, the Members of the League:

a) will endeavor to secure and maintain fair and humane conditions of labor for men, women, and children, both in their own countries and in all countries to which their commercial and industrial relations extend, and for that purpose will establish and maintain the necessary international organizations;

b) undertake to secure just treatment of the native inhabitants of territories under their control;

c) will entrust the League with the general supervision over the execution of agreements with regard to the traffic in women and children and the traffic in opium and other dangerous drugs;

d) will entrust the League with the general supervision of the trade in arms and ammunition with the countries in which the control of this traffic is necessary in the common interest;

e) will make provision to secure and maintain freedom of communications and of transit and equitable treatment for the commerce of all Members of the League. In this connection, the special necessities of the regions devastated during the war of 1914–1918 shall be borne in mind;

f) will endeavor to take steps in matters of international concern for the prevention and control of disease.

APPENDIX II

THE MANDATES

I. IRAQ

a) DECISION OF THE COUNCIL OF THE LEAGUE OF NATIONS RELATING TO THE APPLICATION OF THE PRINCIPLES OF ARTICLE 22 OF THE COVENANT TO IRAQ

The Council of the League of Nations:

Having regard to Article 16 of the Treaty of Peace signed at Lausanne on July 24th, 1923;

Having regard to Article 22 of the Covenant of the League of Nations:

In view of the communication which has been made by the Government of His Britannic Majesty to the Council of the League of Nations on September 27th, 1924, in the following terms:

"WHEREAS, The territory of Iraq, which formerly constituted a part of the Turkish Empire passed into the occupation of the military forces of His Britannic Majesty in the course of the recent war, and

"WHEREAS, It was intended by the Principal Allied Powers that the territory of Iraq should until such time as it might be able to stand alone be entrusted to a Mandatory charged with the duty of rendering administrative advice and assistance to the population in accordance with the provisions of Article 22 (paragraph 4) of the Covenant and that this Mandate should be conferred on His Britannic Majesty; and

"WHEREAS, His Britannic Majesty agreed to accept the Mandate for Iraq; and

WHEREAS, His Britannic Majesty has, in view of the rapid progress of Iraq, recognised an independent Government therein and has concluded with the King of Iraq a treaty with Protocol and subsidiary agreements, as set forth in the Schedule hereto, and hereinafter referred to as the Treaty of Alliance; and

"WHEREAS, The purpose of the said Treaty of Alliance is to ensure the complete observance and execution in Iraq of the principles which the acceptance of the Mandate was intended to secure:

"The Government of His Britannic Majesty is willing to agree as follows:

"I. So long as the Treaty of Alliance is in force, His Majesty's Government will assume, towards all Members of the League of Nations who accept the provisions of this arrangement and the benefits of the said Treaty, responsibility for the fulfilment by Iraq of the provisions of the said Treaty of Alliance.

"II. During the currency of the Treaty of Alliance, the Government of

His Britannic Majesty, in consultation with His Majesty the King of Iraq, will take such steps as may be necessary for the conclusion of special extradition agreements on behalf of Iraq. Copies of all such agreements shall be communicated to the Council of the League.

"III. An annual report, to the satisfaction of the Council of the League, will be made to the Council as to the measures taken in Iraq during the year to carry out the provisions of the Treaty of Alliance. Copies of all laws and regulations promulgated in Iraq during the year will be attached to the said report.

"IV. No modifications of the terms of the Treaty of Alliance will be agreed to by His Britannic Majesty's Government without the consent of the Council of the League.

"V. If any dispute should arise between the Government of His Britannic Majesty and that of another Member of the League as to whether the provisions of the Treaty of Alliance or of the present decision are being fulfilled in Iraq, or as to their interpretation or application, such dispute, if it cannot be settled by negotiation, shall be submitted to the Permanent Court of International Justice provided for by Article 14 of the Covenant of the League.

"VI. In the event of Iraq being admitted to the League of Nations, the obligations hereby assumed by His Britannic Majesty's Government shall terminate.

"VII. On the conclusion of the period for which the Treaty of Alliance has been concluded, the Council of the League of Nations shall, if Iraq has not been admitted to the League, be invited to decide what further measures are required to give effect to Article 22 of the Covenant."

ACCEPTS the undertakings of the Government of His Britannic Majesty; and

APPROVES the terms of the above communication as giving effect to the provisions of Article 22 of the Covenant; and

DECIDES that the privileges and immunities, including the benefits of consular jurisdiction and protection formerly enjoyed by capitulation or usage in the Ottoman Empire, will not be required for the protection of foreigners in Iraq so long as the Treaty of Alliance is in force.

The present instrument shall be deposited in original in the archives of the League of Nations and certified copies shall be forwarded by the Secretary-General of the League of Nations to all Members of the League.

DONE at Geneva, on the twenty-seventh day of September, one thousand nine hundred and twenty-four.

Certified true copy:

For the Secretary-General:

J. A. VAN HAMEL

b) TREATY BETWEEN HIS BRITANNIC MAJESTY AND HIS MAJESTY THE KING OF IRAK

(Signed at Bagdad, October 10, 1922)

(Ratifications Exchanged at Bagdad, December 19, 1924)

His Britannic Majesty of the one part, and His Majesty the King of Irak of the other part;

WHEREAS, His Britannic Majesty has recognised Feisal Ibn Hussein as constitutional King of Irak; and

WHEREAS, His Majesty the King of Irak considers that it is to the interests of Irak and will conduce to its rapid advancement that he should conclude a treaty with His Britannic Majesty on the basis of alliance; and

WHEREAS, His Britannic Majesty is satisfied that the relations between himself and His Majesty the King of Irak can now be better defined by such a treaty of alliance than by any other means:

For this purpose the High Contracting Parties have appointed as their plenipotentiaries:—

His Majesty the King of the United Kingdom of Great Britain and Ireland and of the British Dominions beyond the Seas, Emperor of India:

SIR PERCY ZACHARIAH COX, G.C.M.G., G.C.I.E., K.C.S.I., High Commissioner and Consul-General of His Britannic Majesty in Irak;

His Majesty the King of Irak:

HIS HIGHNESS SIR SAIYID 'ABD-UR-RAHMAN, G.B.E., Prime Minister and Naquib-al-Ashraf, Bagdad;

Who, having communicated their full powers, found in good and due order, have agreed as follows:—

ARTICLE 1. At the request of His Majesty the King of Irak, His Britannic Majesty undertakes subject to the provisions of this treaty to provide the State of Irak with such advice and assistance as may be required during the period of the present treaty, without prejudice to her national sovereignty. His Britannic Majesty shall be represented in Irak by a High Commissioner and Consul-General assisted by the necessary staff.

ART. 2. His Majesty the King of Irak undertakes that for the period of the present treaty no gazetted official of other than Irak nationality shall be appointed in Irak without the concurrence of His Britannic Majesty. A separate agreement shall regulate the numbers and conditions of employment of British officials so appointed in the Irak Government.[1]

ART. 3. His Majesty the King of Irak agrees to frame an Organic Law for presentation to the Constituent Assembly of Irak and to give effect to the said law, which shall contain nothing contrary to the provisions of the present treaty and shall take account of the rights, wishes and interests of all populations in-

[1] A "British Officials Agreement" in accordance with this article was signed on March 25, 1924, and ratifications were exchanged December 19, 1924 (*G.B., Treaty Series*, No. 17 [1925], p. 9).

habiting Irak. This Organic Law shall ensure to all complete freedom of conscience and the free exercise of all forms of worship, subject only to the maintenance of public order and morals. It shall provide that no discrimination of any kind shall be made between the inhabitants of Irak on the ground of race, religion or language, and shall secure that the right of each community to maintain its own schools for the education of its own members in its own language, while conforming to such educational requirements of a general nature as the Government of Irak may impose, shall not be denied or impaired. It shall prescribe the constitutional procedure, whether legislative or executive, by which decisions will be taken on all matters of importance, including those involving questions of fiscal, financial and military policy.

ART. 4. Without prejudice to the provisions of articles 17 and 18 of this treaty, His Majesty the King of Irak agrees to be guided by the advice of His Britannic Majesty tendered through the High Commissioner on all important matters affecting the international and financial obligations and interests of His Britannic Majesty for the whole period of this treaty. His Majesty the King of Irak will fully consult the High Commissioner on what is conducive to a sound financial and fiscal policy and will ensure the stability and good organisation of the finances of the Irak Government so long as that Government is under financial obligations to the Government of His Britannic Majesty.

ART. 5. His Majesty the King of Irak shall have the right of representation in London and in such other capitals and places as may be agreed upon by the High Contracting Parties. Where His Majesty the King of Irak is not represented he agrees to entrust the protection of Irak nationals to His Britannic Majesty. His Majesty the King of Irak shall himself issue exequators to representatives of foreign Powers in Irak after His Britannic Majesty has agreed to their appointment.

ART. 6. His Britannic Majesty undertakes to use his good offices to secure the admission of Irak to membership of the League of Nations as soon as possible.

ART. 7. His Britannic Majesty undertakes to provide such support and assistance to the armed forces of His Majesty the King of Irak as may from time to time be agreed by the High Contracting Parties. A separate agreement regulating the extent and conditions of such support and assistance shall be concluded between the High Contracting Parties and communicated to the Council of the League of Nations.[2]

ART. 8. No territory in Irak shall be ceded or leased or in any way placed under the control of any foreign Power; this shall not prevent His Majesty the King of Irak from making such arrangements as may be necessary for the accommodation of foreign representatives and for the fulfilment of the provisions of the preceding article.

[2] A "Military Agreement" in accordance with this article was signed on March 25, 1924, and ratifications were exchanged December 19, 1924 (*ibid.*, p. 27).

ART. 9. His Majesty the King of Irak undertakes that he will accept and give effect to such reasonable provisions as His Britannic Majesty may consider necessary in judicial matters to safeguard the interests of foreigners in consequence of the non-application of the immunities and privileges enjoyed by them under capitulation or usage. These provisions shall be embodied in a separate agreement, which shall be communicated to the Council of the League of Nations.[3]

ART. 10. The High Contracting Parties agree to conclude separate agreements to secure the execution of any treaties, agreements or undertakings which His Britannic Majesty is under obligation to see carried out in respect to Irak. His Majesty the King of Irak undertakes to bring in any legislation necessary to ensure the execution of these agreements. Such agreements shall be communicated to the Council of the League of Nations.

ART. 11. There shall be no discrimination in Irak against the nationals of any State, member of the League of Nations, or of any State to which His Britannic Majesty has agreed by treaty that the same rights should be ensured as it would enjoy if it were a member of the said League (including companies incorporated under the laws of such State), as compared with British nationals or those of any foreign State in matters concerning taxation, commerce or navigation, the exercise of industries or professions, or in the treatment of merchant vessels or civil aircraft. Nor shall there be any discrimination in Irak against goods originating in or destined for any of the said States. There shall be freedom of transit under equitable conditions across Irak territory.

ART. 12. No measure shall be taken in Irak to obstruct or interfere with missionary enterprise or to discriminate against any missionary on the ground of his religious belief or nationality, provided that such enterprise is not prejudicial to public order and good government.

ART. 13. His Majesty the King of Irak undertakes to co-operate, in so far as social, religious and other conditions may permit, in the execution of any common policy adopted by the League of Nations for preventing and combating disease, including disease of plants and animals.

ART. 14. His Majesty the King of Irak undertakes to secure the enactment, within twelve months of the coming into force of this treaty, and to ensure the execution of a Law of Antiquities based on the rules annexed to article 421 of the Treaty of Peace signed at Sèvres on the 10th August, 1920. This law shall replace the former Ottoman Law of Antiquities, and shall ensure equality of treatment in the matter of archaeological research to the nationals of all States members of the League of Nations, and of any State to which His Britannic Majesty has agreed by treaty that the same rights should be ensured as it would enjoy it if were a member of the said League.

ART. 15. A separate agreement shall regulate the financial relations between the High Contracting Parties. It shall provide, on the one hand, for the transfer

[3] A "Judicial Agreement" in accordance with this article was signed on March 25, 1924, and ratifications were exchanged December 19, 1924 (*ibid.*, p. 34).

by His Britannic Majesty's Government to the Government of Irak of such works of Public utility as may be agreed upon and for the rendering by His Britannic Majesty's Government of such financial assistance as may from time to time be considered necessary for Irak, and, on the other hand, for the progressive liquidation by the Government of Irak of all liabilities thus incurred. Such agreement shall be communicated to the Council of the League of Nations.[4]

ART. 16. So far as is consistent with his international obligations His Britannic Majesty undertakes to place no obstacle in the way of the association of the State of Irak for customs or other purposes with such neighbouring Arab States as may desire it.

ART. 17. Any difference that may arise between the High Contracting Parties as to the interpretation of the provisions of this treaty shall be referred to the Permanent Court of International Justice provided for by article 14 of the Covenant of the League of Nations. In such case, should there be any discrepancy between the English and Arabic texts of this treaty, the English shall be taken as the authoritative version.

ART. 18. This treaty shall come into force as soon as it has been ratified by the High Contracting Parties after its acceptance by the Constituent Assembly, and shall remain in force for twenty years,[5] at the end of which period

[4] A "Financial Agreement" in accordance with this article was signed on March 25, 1924, and ratifications were exchanged December 19, 1924 (*ibid.*, p. 37).

[5] The following protocol signed April 30, 1923, and ratifications exchanged December 19, 1924, were submitted to and approved by the League of Nations Council at the same time as the principal treaty:

"It is understood between the High Contracting Parties that, notwithstanding the provisions of article 18, the present treaty shall terminate upon Irak becoming a member of the League of Nations and in any case not later than four years from the ratification of peace with Turkey. Nothing in this protocol shall prevent a fresh agreement from being concluded with a view to regulate the subsequent relations between the High Contracting Parties; and negotiations for that object shall be entered into between them before the expiration of the above period."

As a result of the League Council's resolution of December 16, 1925, on the Mosul boundary dispute, Great Britain and Iraq concluded a treaty on January 13, 1926, abrogating this protocol, as follows:

"ARTICLE 1. The provisions contained in Article XVIII of the Treaty between the High Contracting Parties signed at Baghdad on the 10th day of October 1922, of the Christian Era, corresponding with the 19th day of Safar, 1340, Hijrah, and in the Protocol signed on the 30th day of April, 1923, of the Christian Era, corresponding with the 14th day of Ramazan, 1341, Hijrah, in so far as they relate to the duration of the said Treaty are hereby abrogated, and the said Treaty shall remain in force for a period of twenty-five years from the 16th day of December, 1925, unless before the expiration of that period 'Iraq shall have become a Member of the League of Nations.

"The Various agreements between the High Contracting Parties subsidiary to the said Treaty of the 10th day of October, 1922, shall in so far as their duration is made dependent on that of the said Treaty, likewise remain in force for the period laid down in the present Treaty, but in other respects their provisions shall not be affected.

the situation shall be examined, and if the High Contracting Parties are of opinion that the treaty is no longer required, it shall be terminated. Termination shall be subject to confirmation by the League of Nations unless before that date article 6 of this treaty has come into effect, in which case notice of termination shall be communicated to the Council of the League of Nations. Nothing shall prevent the High Contracting Parties from reviewing from time to time the provisions of this treaty, and those of the separate agreements arising out of articles 7, 10, and 15, with a view to any revision which may seem desirable in the circumstances then existing, and any modification which may be agreed upon by the High Contracting Parties shall be communicated to the Council of the League of Nations.[6]

"Art. II. The High Contracting Parties agree, immediately after the ratification of the Present Treaty and its approval by the Council of the League of Nations, to continue active consideration of the questions which have already been under discussion between them in regard to the revision of the agreements arising out of Articles VII and XV of the Treaty of October 10th, 1922."

"Art. III. Without prejudice to the provisions of Article VI of the Treaty of October 10th, 1922, in regard to the admission of 'Iraq into the League of Nations or the provisions of Article XVIII of the said Treaty which permit the revision at any time, subject to the consent of the Council of the League of Nations, of the provisions of the said Treaty or of certain of the agreements subsidiary thereto, His Britannic Majesty undertakes that, at the time when the Treaty of October 10th, 1922, would have expired under the protocol of April 30th, 1923, and at subsequent successive intervals of four years until the expiry of the period of twenty-five years mentioned in the present Treaty or until the admission of 'Iraq into the League of Nations, he will take into active consideration the following two questions, namely:

"(1) The question whether it is possible for him to press for the admission of 'Iraq into the League of Nations;

"(2) If it is not so possible, the question of the amendment, on account of the progress made by the Kingdom of 'Iraq or for any other reason, of the agreements referred to in Article XVIII of the Treaty of October 10th, 1922.

"The present Treaty, in English and Arabic, of which in case of divergence the English text will prevail, shall be ratified and ratifications shall be exchanged as soon as possible" (*O.J.*, VII, 551).

On March 2, 1926, after this treaty had been approved by the British House of Commons and the Chamber of Deputies and Senate of Iraq, Great Britain submitted it to the League Council (*ibid.*, p. 550), which approved it on March 11, 1926, as follows:

"The Council of the League of Nations supplementing its decision of September 27th, 1924, approves the terms of the letter from the British Government dated March 2nd, 1926, to which the text of the Treaty between Great Britain and Iraq dated January 13th, 1926, is annexed as giving effect to the provisions of Article 22 of the Covenant" (*ibid.*, p. 502).

[6] Great Britain submitted to the Mandates Commission a draft treaty signed with Iraq on December 14, 1927, which limited British control. The Commission discussed it at its fourteenth session but "refrained from formulating any observations or recommendations on it until expressly invited to do so by the Council." The British ac-

The ratifications shall be exchanged at Bagdad.

The present treaty has been drawn up in English and Arabic. One copy in each language will remain deposited in the archives of the Irak Government, and one copy in each language in those of the Government of His Britannic Majesty.

In witness of which the respective plenipotentiaries have signed the present treaty and have affixed thereto their seals. Done at Bagdad in duplicate this tenth day of October, one thousand nine hundred and twenty-two of the Christian Era, corresponding with the nineteenth day of Sa'far, one thousand three hundred and forty-one, Hijrah.

P. Z. COX
His Britannic Majesty's High Commissioner in Irak

ʾABD-UR-RAHMAN
Naqib-al-Ashraf of Bagdad and Prime Minister of the Irak Government

II. PALESTINE (AND TRANSJORDAN)

The Council of the League of Nations:

WHEREAS, The Principal Allied Powers have agreed, for the purpose of giving effect to the provisions of Article 22 of the Covenant of the League of Nations, to entrust to a Mandatory selected by the said Powers the administration of the territory of Palestine, which formerly belonged to the Turkish Empire, within such boundaries as may be fixed by them; and

WHEREAS, The Principal Allied Powers have also agreed that the Mandatory should be responsible for putting into effect the declaration originally made on November 2, 1917, by the Government of His Britannic Majesty, and adopted by the said Powers, in favor of the establishment in Palestine of a national home for the Jewish people, it being clearly understood that nothing should be done which might prejudice the civil and religious rights of existing non-Jewish communities in Palestine, or the rights and political status enjoyed by Jews in any other country; and

WHEREAS, Recognition has thereby been given to the historical connection of the Jewish people with Palestine and to the grounds for reconstituting their national home in that country; and

WHEREAS, The Principal Allied Powers have selected His Britannic Majesty as the Mandatory for Palestine; and

WHEREAS, The mandate in respect of Palestine has been formulated in the following terms and submitted to the Council of the League for approval; and

---

credited representative emphasized that the treaty might never be ratified (*P.M.C., Min.*, XIV, 192, 270) and on November 4, 1929, the British government communicated to the Secretary General of the League of Nations their decision not to proceed with it and in accordance with article 3 (1) of the treaty of January 13, 1926, to recommend Iraq for admission to membership in the League of Nations in 1932 (*ibid.*, XVI, 183, 203).

WHEREAS, His Britannic Majesty has accepted the mandate in respect of Palestine and undertaken to exercise it on behalf of the League of Nations in conformity with the following provisions; and

WHEREAS, By the aforementioned Article 22 (paragraph 8), it is provided that the degree of authority, control or administration to be exercised by the Mandatory, not having been previously agreed upon by the members of the League, shall be explicitly defined by the Council of the League of Nations;

Confirming the said mandate, defines its terms as follows:

ARTICLE 1. The Mandatory shall have full powers of legislation and of administration, save as they may be limited by the terms of this mandate.

ART. 2. The Mandatory shall be responsible for placing the country under such political, administrative and economic conditions as will secure the establishment of the Jewish national home, as laid down in the preamble, and the development of self-governing institutions, and also for safeguarding the civil and religious rights of all the inhabitants of Palestine, irrespective of race and religion.

ART. 3. The Mandatory shall, so far as circumstances permit, encourage local autonomy.

ART. 4. An appropriate Jewish agency shall be recognized as a public body for the purpose of advising and co-operating with the administration of Palestine in such economic, social and other matters as may affect the establishment of the Jewish national home and the interests of the Jewish population in Palestine, and, subject always to the control of the administration, to assist and take part in the development of the country.

The Zionist organization, so long as its organization and constitution are in the opinion of the Mandatory appropriate, shall be recognized as such agency. It shall take steps in consultation with His Britannic Majesty's Government to secure the co-operation of all Jews who are willing to assist in the establishment of the Jewish national home.

ART. 5. The Mandatory shall be responsible for seeing that no Palestine territory shall be ceded or leased to, or in any way placed under the control of, the government of any foreign Power.

ART. 6. The administration of Palestine, while ensuring that the rights and position of other sections of the population are not prejudiced, shall facilitate Jewish immigration under suitable conditions and shall encourage, in co-operation with the Jewish agency referred to in Article 4, close settlement by Jews on the land, including state lands and waste lands not required for public purposes.

ART. 7. The administration of Palestine shall be responsible for enacting a nationality law. There shall be included in this law provisions framed so as to facilitate the acquisition of Palestinian citizenship by Jews who take up their permanent residence in Palestine.

ART. 8. The privileges and immunities of foreigners, including the benefits of consular jurisdiction and protection as formerly enjoyed by capitulation or usage in the Ottoman Empire, shall not be applicable in Palestine.

Unless the Powers whose nationals enjoyed the aforementioned privileges and immunities on August 1, 1914, shall have previously renounced the right to their re-establishment, or shall have agreed to their non-application for a specified period, these privileges and immunities shall, at the expiration of the mandate, be immediately re-established in their entirety or with such modifications as may have been agreed upon between the Powers concerned.

ART. 9. The Mandatory shall be responsible for seeing that the judicial system established in Palestine shall assure to foreigners, as well as to natives, a complete guarantee of their rights.

Respect for the personal status of the various peoples and communities and for their religious interests shall be fully guaranteed. In particular, the control and administration of Wakfs shall be exercised in accordance with religious law and the dispositions of the founders.

ART. 10. Pending the making of special extradition agreements relating to Palestine, the extradition treaties in force between the Mandatory and other foreign Powers shall apply to Palestine.

ART. 11. The administration of Palestine shall take all necessary measures to safeguard the interests of the community in connection with the development of the country, and, subject to any international obligations accepted by the Mandatory, shall have full power to provide for public ownership or control of any of the natural resources of the country or of the public works, services and utilities established or to be established therein. It shall introduce a land system appropriate to the needs of the country, having regard, among other things, to the desirability of promoting the close settlement and intensive cultivation of the land.

The administration may arrange with the Jewish agency mentioned in Article 4 to construct or operate, upon fair and equitable terms, any public works, services and utilities, and to develop any of the natural resources of the country, in so far as these matters are not directly undertaken by the administration. Any such arrangements shall provide that no profits distributed by such agency, directly or indirectly, shall exceed a reasonable rate of interest on the capital, and any further profits shall be utilized by it for the benefit of the country in a manner approved by the administration.

ART. 12. The Mandatory shall be entrusted with the control of the foreign relations of Palestine and the right to issue exequaturs to consuls appointed by foreign Powers. He shall also be entitled to afford diplomatic and consular protection to citizens of Palestine when outside its territorial limits.

ART. 13. All responsibility in connection with the Holy Places and religious buildings or sites in Palestine, including that of preserving existing rights and of securing free access to the Holy Places, religious buildings and sites and the free exercise of worship, while ensuring the requirements of public order and decorum, is assumed by the Mandatory, who shall be responsible solely to the League of Nations in all matters connected herewith, provided that nothing in this article shall prevent the Mandatory from entering into such arrangements as he may deem reasonable with the administration for the purpose of carrying the provisions of this article into effect; and provided also that nothing in this mandate shall be construed as conferring upon the Mandatory authority to interfere with the fabric or the management of purely Moslem sacred shrines, the immunities of which are guaranteed.

ART. 14. A special commission shall be appointed by the Mandatory to study, define and determine the rights and claims in connection with the Holy Places and the rights and claims relating to the different religious communities in Palestine. The method of nomination, the composition and the functions of this commission shall be submitted to the Council of the League for its approval, and the commission shall not be appointed or enter upon its functions without the approval of the Council.[7]

ART. 15. The Mandatory shall see that complete freedom of conscience and the free exercise of all forms of worship, subject only to the maintenance of public order and morals, are ensured to all. No discrimination of any kind shall be made between the inhabitants of Palestine on the ground of race, religion or language. No person shall be excluded from Palestine on the sole ground of his religious belief.

The right of each community to maintain its own schools for the education of its own members in its own language, while conforming to such educational requirements of a general nature as the administration may impose, shall not be denied or impaired.

ART. 16. The Mandatory shall be responsible for exercising such supervision over religious or eleemosynary bodies of all faiths in Palestine as may be required for the maintenance of public order and good government. Subject to such supervision, no measures shall be taken in Palestine to obstruct or interfere with the enterprise of such bodies or to discriminate against any representative or member of them on the ground of his religion or nationality.

ART. 17. The administration of Palestine may organize on a voluntary basis the forces necessary for the preservation of peace and order, and also for the defence of the country, subject, however, to the supervision of the Mandatory, but shall not use them for purposes other than those above specified save with the consent of the Mandatory. Except for such purposes, no military, naval or air forces shall be raised or maintained by the administration of Palestine.

Nothing in this article shall preclude the administration of Palestine from

[7] The British government, on August 31, 1922, submitted to the Council of the League of Nations a scheme for the Holy Places Commission provided for in Article 14 of the mandate (*O.J.*, III, 1150, 1153). At the meeting of the Council on October 4, 1922, the question was adjourned for study by and agreement among the interested powers (*ibid.*, p. 1152).

contributing to the cost of the maintenance of the forces of the Mandatory in Palestine.

The Mandatory shall be entitled at all times to use the roads, railways and ports of Palestine for the movement of armed forces and the carriage of fuel and supplies.

ART. 18. The Mandatory shall see that there is no discrimination in Palestine against the nationals of any state member of the League of Nations (including companies incorporated under its laws) as compared with those of the Mandatory or of any foreign state in matters concerning taxation, commerce or navigation, the exercise of industries or professions, or in the treatment of merchant vessels or civil aircraft. Similarly, there shall be no discrimination in Palestine against goods originating in or destined for any of the said states, and there shall be freedom of transit under equitable conditions across the mandated area.

Subject as aforesaid and to the other provisions of this mandate, the administration of Palestine may, on the advice of the Mandatory, impose such taxes and customs duties as it may consider necessary, and take such steps as it may think best to promote the development of the natural resources of the country and to safeguard the interests of the population. It may also, on the advice of the Mandatory, conclude a special customs agreement with any state the territory of which in 1914 was wholly included in Asiatic Turkey or Arabia.

ART. 19. The Mandatory shall adhere on behalf of the administration of Palestine to any general international conventions already existing, or which may be concluded hereafter with the approval of the League of Nations, respecting the slave traffic, the traffic in arms and ammunition, or the traffic in drugs, or relating to commercial equality, freedom of transit and navigation, aerial navigation and postal, telegraphic and wireless communication or literary, artistic or industrial property.

ART. 20. The Mandatory shall co-operate on behalf of the administration of Palestine, so far as religious, social and other conditions may permit, in the execution of any common policy adopted by the League of Nations for preventing and combating disease, including diseases of plants and animals.

ART. 21. The Mandatory shall secure the enactment within twelve months from this date, and shall ensure the execution of a law of antiquities based on the following rules. This law shall ensure equality of treatment in the matter of excavations and archaeological research to the nationals of all states members of the League of Nations.

(1) "Antiquity" means any construction or any product of human activity earlier than the year 1700 A.D.

(2) The law for the protection of antiquities shall proceed by encouragement rather than by threat.

Any person who, having discovered an antiquity without being furnished with the authorization referred to in paragraph 5, reports the same to an official of the competent department, shall be rewarded according to the value of the discovery.

(3) No antiquity may be disposed of except to the competent department, unless this department renounces the acquisition of any such antiquity.

No antiquity may leave the country without an export licence from the said department.

(4) Any person who maliciously or negligently destroys or damages an antiquity shall be liable to a penalty to be fixed.

(5) No clearing of ground or digging with the object of finding antiquities shall be permitted, under penalty of fine, except to persons authorized by the competent department.

(6) Equitable terms shall be fixed for expropriation, temporary or permanent of lands which might be of historical or archaeological interest.

(7) Authorization to excavate shall only be granted to persons who show sufficient guarantees of archaeological experience. The administration of Palestine shall not, in granting these authorizations, act in such a way as to exclude scholars of any nation without good grounds.

(8) The proceeds of excavations may be divided between the excavator and the competent department in a proportion fixed by that department. If division seems impossible for scientific reasons, the excavator shall receive a fair indemnity in lieu of a part of the find.

ART. 22. English, Arabic and Hebrew shall be the official languages of Palestine. Any statement or inscription in Arabic on stamps or money in Palestine shall be repeated in Hebrew and any statement or inscription in Hebrew shall be repeated in Arabic.

ART. 23. The administration of Palestine shall recognize the holy days of the respective communities in Palestine as legal days of rest for the members of such communities.

ART. 24. The Mandatory shall make to the Council of the League of Nations an annual report to the satisfaction of the Council as to the measures taken during the year to carry out the provisions of the mandate. Copies of all laws and regulations promulgated or issued during the year shall be communicated with the report.

ART. 25. In the territories lying between the Jordan and the eastern boundary of Palestine as ultimately determined, the Mandatory shall be entitled, with the consent of the Council of the League of Nations, to postpone or withhold application of such provisions of this mandate as he may consider inapplicable to the existing local conditions, and to make such provision for the administration of the territories as he may consider suitable to those conditions, provided that no action shall be taken which is inconsistent with the provisions of Articles 15, 16 and 18.[8]

[8] On September 16, 1922, the British government submitted the following memorandum to the League Council which the latter approved:

"1. ARTICLE 25 of the mandate for Palestine provides as follows: . . . .

ART. 26. The Mandatory agrees that, if any dispute whatever should arise between the Mandatory and another Member of the League of Nations relating to the interpretation or the application of the provisions of the mandate, such dispute, if it cannot be settled by negotiation, shall be submitted to the Permanent Court of International Justice provided for by Article 14 of the Covenant of the League of Nations.

ART. 27. The consent of the Council of the League of Nations is required for any modification of the terms of this mandate.

ART. 28. In the event of the termination of the mandate hereby conferred upon the Mandatory, the Council of the League of Nations shall make such arrangements as may be deemed necessary for safeguarding in perpetuity, under guarantee of the League, the rights secured by Articles 13 and 14, and shall use its influence for securing, under the guarantee of the League, that the Government of Palestine will fully honor the financial obligations legitimately incurred by the administration of Palestine during the period of the mandate, including the rights of public servants to pensions or gratuities.

"2. In pursuance of the provisions of this Article, His Majesty's Government invite the Council to pass the following resolution:—

"The following provisions of the mandate for Palestine are not applicable to the territory known as Trans-Jordan, which comprises all territory lying to the east of a line drawn from a point two miles west of the town of Akaba on the Gulf of that name up the centre of the Wady Araba, Dead Sea and River Jordan to its junction with the River Yarmuk; thence up the centre of that river to the Syrian frontier.

"PREAMBLE,—Recitals 2 and 3.

"ART. 2.—The words "placing the country under such political administration and economic conditions as will secure the establishment of the Jewish national home, as laid down in the preamble, and

"ART. 4.

"ART. 6.

"ART. 7.—The sentence "There shall be included in this law provisions framed so as to facilitate the acquisition of Palestinan citizenship by Jews who take up their permanent residence in Palestine.

"ART. 11.—The second sentence of the first paragraph and the second paragraph.

"ART. 13.

"ART. 14.

"ART. 22.

"ART. 23.

"In the application of the Mandate to Trans-Jordan, the action which, in Palestine, is taken by the administration of the latter country, will be taken by the administration of Trans-Jordan under the general supervision of the Mandatory.

"3. His Majesty's Government accept full responsibility as Mandatory for Trans-Jordan, and undertake that such provision as may be made for the administration of that territory in accordance with Article 25 of the mandate shall be in no way inconsistent with those provisions of the mandate which are not by this resolution declared inapplicable" (*O.J.*, III, 1390).

The present instrument shall be deposited in original in the archives of the League of Nations and certified copies shall be forwarded by the Secretary-General of the League of Nations to all members of the League.

Done at London the twenty-fourth day of July, one thousand nine hundred and twenty-two.[9]

III. SYRIA AND THE LEBANON

The Council of the League of Nations:

WHEREAS, The Principal Allied Powers have agreed that the territory of Syria and the Lebanon, which formerly belonged to the Turkish Empire shall, within such boundaries as may be fixed by the said Powers, be entrusted to a Mandatory charged with the duty of rendering administrative advice and assistance to the population, in accordance with the provisions of Article 22 (paragraph 4) of the Covenant of the League of Nations; and

WHEREAS, The Principal Allied Powers have decided that the mandate for the territory referred to above should be conferred on the Government of the French Republic, which has accepted it; and

WHEREAS, The terms of this mandate, which are defined in the articles below, have also been accepted by the Government of the French Republic and submitted to the Council of the League for approval; and

WHEREAS, The Government of the French Republic has undertaken to exercise this mandate on behalf of the League of Nations, in conformity with the following provisions; and

WHEREAS, By the aforementioned Article 22 (paragraph 8), it is provided that the degree of authority, control or administration to be exercised by the Mandatory, not having been previously agreed upon by the members of the League, shall be explicitly defined by the Council of the League of Nations;

Confirming the said mandate, defines its terms as follows:

ARTICLE 1. The Mandatory shall frame, within a period of three years from the coming into force of this mandate, an organic law for Syria and the Lebanon.

[9] On this date the Council passed the following resolution:

"In view of the declarations which have just been made, and of the agreement reached by all the members of the Council, the articles of the mandates for Palestine and Syria are approved. The mandates will enter into force automatically and at the same time as soon as the Governments of France and Italy have notified the President of the Council of the League of Nations that they have reached an agreement on certain particular points in regard to the latter of these mandates.

"The present negotiations will be resumed at Geneva on August 30, before the meeting of the next Assembly, expressly to solve the questions submitted for its decision under Article 14 of the mandate for Palestine" (*ibid.*, p. 825).

The notification referred to in the first paragraph was received and the mandates went into effect on September 29, 1923 (*ibid.*, IV, 1355). The negotiations referred to in the second paragraph have not been completed (see *supra*, n. 7).

This organic law shall be framed in agreement with the native authorities and shall take into account the rights, interests, and wishes of all the population inhabiting the said territory. The Mandatory shall further enact measures to facilitate the progressive development of Syria and the Lebanon as independent states. Pending the coming into effect of the organic law, the Government of Syria and the Lebanon shall be conducted in accordance with the spirit of this mandate.

The Mandatory shall, as far as circumstances permit, encourage local autonomy.

ART. 2. The Mandatory may maintain its troops in the said territory for its defence. It shall further be empowered, until the entry into force of the organic law and the re-establishment of public security, to organize such local militia as may be necessary for the defence of the territory and to employ this militia for defence and also for the maintenance of order. These local forces may only be recruited from the inhabitants of the said territory.

The said militia shall thereafter be under the local authorities, subject to the authority and the control which the Mandatory shall retain over these forces. It shall not be used for purposes other than those above specified save with the consent of the Mandatory.

Nothing shall preclude Syria and the Lebanon from contributing to the cost of the maintenance of the forces of the Mandatory stationed in the territory.

The Mandatory shall at all times possess the right to make use of the ports, railways and means of communication of Syria and the Lebanon for the passage of its troops and of all materials, supplies and fuel.

ART. 3. The Mandatory shall be entrusted with the exclusive control of the foreign relations of Syria and the Lebanon and with the right to issue exequaturs to the consuls appointed by foreign Powers. Nationals of Syria and the Lebanon living outside the limits of the territory shall be under the diplomatic and consular protection of the Mandatory.

ART. 4. The Mandatory shall be responsible for seeing that no part of the territory of Syria and the Lebanon is ceded or leased or in any way placed under the control of a foreign Power.

ART. 5. The privileges and immunities of foreigners, including the benefits of consular jurisdiction and protection as formerly enjoyed by capitulation or usage in the Ottoman Empire, shall not be applicable in Syria and the Lebanon. Foreign consular tribunals shall, however, continue to perform their duties until the coming into force of the new legal organization provided for in Article 6.

Unless the Powers whose nationals enjoyed the aforementioned privileges and immunities on August 1, 1924, shall have previously renounced the right to their re-establishment, or shall have agreed to their non-application during a specified period, these privileges and immunities shall at the expiration of the mandate be immediately re-established in their entirety or with such modifications as may have been agreed upon between the Powers concerned.

ART. 6. The Mandatory shall establish in Syria and the Lebanon a judicial system which shall assure to natives as well as to foreigners a complete guarantee of their rights.

Respect for the personal status of the various peoples and for their religious interests shall be fully guaranteed. In particular, the control and administration of Wakfs shall be exercised in complete accordance with religious law and the dispositions of the founders.

ART. 7. Pending the conclusion of special extradition agreements, the extradition treaties at present in force between foreign Powers and the Mandatory shall apply within the territory of Syria and the Lebanon.

ART. 8. The Mandatory shall ensure to all complete freedom of conscience and the free exercise of all forms of worship which are consonant with public order and morality. No discrimination of any kind shall be made between the inhabitants of Syria and the Lebanon on the ground of differences in race, religion or language.

The Mandatory shall encourage public instruction, which shall be given through the medium of the native languages in use in the territory of Syria and the Lebanon.

The right of each community to maintain its own schools for the instruction and education of its own members in its own language, while conforming to such educational requirements of a general nature as the administration may impose, shall not be denied or impaired.

ART. 9. The Mandatory shall refrain from all interference in the administration of the Councils of management (*Conseils de fabrique*) or in the management of religious communities and sacred shrines belonging to the various religions, the immunity of which has been expressly guaranteed.

ART. 10. The supervision exercised by the Mandatory over the religious missions in Syria and the Lebanon shall be limited to the maintenance of public order and good government; the activities of these religious missions shall in no way be restricted, nor shall their members be subjected to any restrictive measures on the ground of nationality, provided that their activities are confined to the domain of religion.

The religious missions may also concern themselves with education and relief, subject to the general right of regulation and control by the Mandatory or of the local government, in regard to education, public instruction and charitable relief.

ART. 11. The Mandatory shall see that there is no discrimination in Syria or the Lebanon against the nationals, including societies and associations, of any state member of the League of Nations as compared with its own nationals, including societies and associations, or with the nationals of any other foreign state in matters concerning taxation or commerce, the exercise of professions or industries, or navigation, or in the treatment of ships or aircraft. Similarly, there shall be no discrimination in Syria or the Lebanon against goods originating in or destined for any of the said states; there shall be freedom of transit, under equitable conditions, across the said territory.

Subject to the above, the Mandatory may impose or cause to be imposed by the local governments such taxes and customs duties as it may consider necessary. The Mandatory, or the local governments acting under its advice, may also conclude on grounds of contiguity any special customs arrangements with an adjoining country.

The Mandatory may take or cause to be taken, subject to the provisions of paragraph 1 of this article, such steps as it may think best to ensure the development of the natural resources of the said territory and to safeguard the interests of the local population.

Concessions for the development of these natural resources shall be granted without distinction of nationality between the nationals of all states members of the League of Nations, but on condition that they do not infringe upon the authority of the local government. Concessions in the nature of a general monopoly shall not be granted. This clause shall in no way limit the right of the Mandatory to create monopolies of a purely fiscal character in the interest of the territory of Syria and the Lebanon, and with a view to assuring to the territory the fiscal resources which would appear best adapted to the local needs, or, in certain cases, with a view to developing the natural resources either directly by the state or through an organization under its control, provided that this does not involve either directly or indirectly the creation of a monopoly of the natural resources in favor of the Mandatory or its nationals, nor involve any preferential treatment which would be incompatible with the economic, commercial and industrial equality guaranteed above.

ART. 12. The Mandatory shall adhere, on behalf of Syria and the Lebanon, to any general international agreements already existing, or which may be concluded hereafter with the approval of the League of Nations, in respect of the following: the slave trade, the traffic in drugs, the traffic in arms and ammunition, commercial equality, freedom of transit and navigation, aerial navigation, postal, telegraphic or wireless communications, and measures for the protection of literature, art or industries.

ART. 13. The Mandatory shall secure the adhesion of Syria and the Lebanon, so far as social, religious and other conditions permit, to such measures of common utility as may be adopted by the League of Nations for preventing and combating disease, including diseases of animals and plants.

ART. 14. The Mandatory shall draw up and put into force within twelve months from this date a law of antiquities in conformity with the following provisions. [Remainder identical with Palestine, Art. 21.]

ART. 15. Upon the coming into force of the organic law referred to in Article 1, an arrangement shall be made between the Mandatory and the local governments for reimbursement by the latter of all expenses incurred by the Mandatory in organizing the administration, developing local resources, and carrying out permanent public works, of which the country retains the benefit. Such arrangement shall be communicated to the Council of the League of Nations.

ART. 16. French and Arabic shall be the official languages of Syria and the Lebanon.

ART. 17. The Mandatory shall make to the Council of the League of Nations an annual report to the satisfaction of the Council as to the measures taken during the year to carry out the provisions of this mandate. Copies of all laws and regulations promulgated during the year shall be attached to the said report.

ART. 18. [Identical with Palestine, Art. 27.]

ART. 19. On the termination of the mandate, the Council of the League of Nations shall use its influence to safeguard for the future the fufillment by the Government of Syria and the Lebanon of the financial obligations, including pensions and allowances, regularly assumed by the administration of Syria or of the Lebanon during the period of the mandate.

ART. 20. The Mandatory agrees . . . . [identical with Palestine, Art. 26].

The present instrument shall be deposited in original in the archives of the League of Nations and certified copies shall be forwarded by the Secretary-General of the League of Nations to all members of the League.

Done at London on the twenty-fourth day of July, one thousand nine hundred and twenty-two.[10]

IV. TANGANYIKA (AND RUANDA-URUNDI)

The Council of the League of Nations:

WHEREAS, By Article 119 of the Treaty of Peace with Germany signed at Versailles on June 28, 1919, Germany renounced in favor of the Principal Allied and Associated Powers all her rights over her oversea possessions, including therein German East Africa; and

WHEREAS, In accordance with the treaty of June 11, 1891, between Her Britannic Majesty and His Majesty the King of Portugal, the River Rovuma is recognized as forming the northern boundary of the Portuguese possessions in East Africa from its mouth up to the confluence of the River M'Sinje; and[11]

WHEREAS, The Principal Allied and Associated Powers agreed that, in accordance with Article 22, Part I (Covenant of the League of Nations), of the said treaty, a mandate should be conferred upon His Britannic Majesty[12] to administer part of the former colony of German East Africa, and have proposed that the mandate should be formulated in the following terms; and

WHEREAS, His Britannic Majesty[12] has agreed to accept the mandate in

[10] See *supra*, n. 9.

[11] This paragraph is omitted from the Ruanda-Urundi mandate.

[12] "His Majesty the King of the Belgians" is substituted in the Ruanda-Urundi mandate.

respect of the said territory, and has undertaken to exercise it on behalf of the League of Nations in accordance with the following provisions; and

WHEREAS, By the forementioned Article 22, paragraph 8, it is provided that the degree of authority, control or administration to be exercised by the Mandatory, not having been previously agreed upon by the members of the League, shall be explicitly defined by the Council of the League of Nations;

Confirming the said mandate, defines its terms as follows:

ARTICLE 1. The territory over which a mandate is conferred upon His Britannic Majesty (hereinafter called the Mandatory)[12a] comprises that part of the territory of the former colony of German East Africa situated to the east[12b] of the following line:

From the point where the frontier between the Uganda Protectorate and German East Africa cuts the River Mavumba, a straight line in a southeasterly direction to point 1640, about 15 kilometres south-southwest of Mount Gabiro;

Thence a straight line in a southerly direction to the north shore of Lake Mohazi, where it terminates at the confluence of a river situated about 2½ kilometres west of the confluence of the River Msilala;

If the trace of the railway on the west of the River Kagera between Bugufi and Uganda approaches within 16 kilometres of the line defined above, the boundary will be carried to the west, following a minimum distance of 16 kilometres from the trace, without, however, passing to the west of the straight line joining the terminal point of Lake Mohazi and the top of Mount Kivisa, point 2100, situated on the Uganda-German East Africa frontier about 5 kilometres southwest of the point where the River Mavumba cuts this frontier;

Thence a line southeastwards to meet the southern shore of Lake Mohazi;

Thence the watershed between the Taruka and the Mkarange and continuing southwards to the north-eastern end of Lake Mugesera;

Thence the median line of this lake and continuing southwards across Lake Ssake to meet the Kagera;

Thence the course of the Kagera downstream to meet the western boundary of Bugufi;[13]

Thence this boundary to its junction with the eastern boundary of Urundi;

Thence the eastern and southern boundary of Urundi to Lake Tanganyika.

The line described above is shown on the attached British 1:1,000,000 map, G.S. G.S. 2932, sheet Ruanda and Urundi. The boundaries of Bugufi and Urundi are drawn as shown in the *Deutscher Kolonialatlas* (Dietrich-Reimer), scale 1:1,000,000 dated 1906.

ART. 2. Boundary commissioners shall be appointed by His Britannic Maj-

[12a] See *supra*, n. 12.

[12b] "west" is substituted in the Ruanda-Urundi mandate.

[13] This boundary was modified in an agreement between Great Britain and Belgium transferring the Kissaka district to the Belgian mandate, submitted to the Council on August 3, 1923, and approved by that body on August 31, 1923 (*O.J.*, IV, 1273).

esty and His Majesty the King of the Belgians to trace on the spot the line described in Article 1 above.[14]

In case any dispute should arise in connection with the work of these commissioners, the question shall be referred to the Council of the League of Nations, whose decision shall be final.

The final report by the boundary commission shall give the precise description of this boundary as actually demarcated on the ground; the necessary maps shall be annexed thereto and signed by the commissioners. The report, with its annexes, shall be made in triplicate; one copy shall be deposited in the archives of the League of Nations, one shall be kept by the Government of His Majesty the King of the Belgians and one by the Government of His Britannic Majesty.

ART. 3. The Mandatory shall be responsible for the peace, order and good government of the territory, and shall undertake to promote to the utmost the material and moral well-being and the social progress of its inhabitants. The Mandatory shall have full powers of legislation and administration.[15]

ART. 4. The Mandatory shall not establish any military or naval bases, nor erect any fortifications, nor organize any native military force in the territory except for local police purposes and for the defence of the territory.

ART. 5. The Mandatory:

(1) shall provide for the eventual emancipation of all slaves and for as speedy an elimination of domestic and other slavery as social conditions will allow;

(2) shall suppress all forms of slave trade;

(3) shall prohibit all forms of forced or compulsory labor, except for essential public works and services,[16] and then only in return for adequate remuneration;

(4) shall protect the natives from abuse and measures of fraud and force by the careful supervision of labor contracts and the recruiting of labor;

(5) shall exercise a strict control over the traffic in arms and ammunition and the sale of spirituous liquors.

ART. 6. In the framing of laws relating to the holding or transfer of land, the Mandatory shall take into consideration native laws and customs, and shall respect the rights and safeguard the interests of the native population.

No native land may be transferred, except between natives, without the previous consent of the public authorities, and[17] no real rights over native land in favor of non-natives may be created except with the same consent.

[14] In the Ruanda-Urundi mandate the first words are "A boundary Commission" and the order of the two parties is reversed.

[15] The last sentence is omitted in the Ruanda-Urundi mandate.

[16] This reads "public works and essential services" in the Ruanda-Urundi mandate.

[17] The word "and" is omitted and "No" begins a new sentence in the Ruanda-Urundi mandate.

The Mandatory will promulgate strict regulations against usury.

ART. 7. The Mandatory shall secure to all nationals of states members of the League of Nations the same rights as are enjoyed in the territory[18] by his own nationals in respect of entry into and residence in the territory, the protection afforded to their person and property, the acquisition of property, movable and immovable, and the exercise of their professon or trade, subject only to the requirements of public order, and on condition of compliance with the local law.

Further, the Mandatory shall ensure to all nationals of states members of the League of Nations, on the same footing as to his own nationals, freedom of transit and navigation, and complete economic, commercial and industrial equality; provided that the Mandatory shall be free to organize essential public works and services[19] on such terms and conditions as he thinks just.

Concessions for the development of the natural resources of the territory shall be granted by the Mandatory without distinction on grounds of nationality between the nationals of all states members of the League of Nations, but on such conditions as will maintain intact the authority of the local government.

Concessions having the character of a general monopoly shall not be granted. This provision does not affect the right of the Mandatory to create monopolies of a purely fiscal character in the interest of the territory under mandate, and in order to provide the territory with fiscal resources which seem best suited to the local requirements; or, in certain cases, to carry out the development of natural resources for the benefit of the Mandatory or his nationals, directly or indirectly, nor any preferential advantages which shall be inconsistent with the economic, commercial and industrial equality hereinbefore guaranteed.

The rights conferred by this article extend equally to companies and associations organized in accordance with the law of any of the members of the League of Nations, subject only to the requirements of public order, and on condition of compliance with the local law.

ART. 8. The Mandatory shall ensure in the territory complete freedom of conscience and the free exercise of all forms of worship which are consonant with public order and morality; missionaries who are nationals of states members of the League of Nations shall be free to enter the territory and to travel and reside therein, to acquire and possess property, to erect religious buildings and to open schools throughout the territory, it being understood, however, that the Mandatory shall have the right to exercise such control as may be necessary for the maintenance of public order and good government, and to take all measures required for such control.

ART. 9. The Mandatory shall apply to the territory any general interna-

[18] The words "in the territory" are omitted in the Ruanda-Urundi mandate.

[19] See *supra*, n. 16.

tional conventions[20] already existing, or which may be concluded hereafter, with the approval of the League of Nations, respecting the slave trade, the traffic in arms and ammunition, the liquor traffic, and the traffic in drugs, or relating to commercial equality, freedom of transit and navigation, aerial navigation, railways, postal, telegraphic, and wireless communication, and industrial, literary and artistic property.

The Mandatory shall co-operate in the execution of any common policy adopted by the League of Nations for preventing and combating disease, including diseases of plants and animals.

ART. 10. The Mandatory shall be authorized to constitute the territory into a customs fiscal and administrative union or federation with the adjacent territories under his own sovereignty or control; provided always that the measures adopted to that end do not infringe the provisions of this mandate.[21]

ART. 11. The Mandatory shall make to the Council of the League of Nations an annual report to the satisfaction of the Council,[22] containing full information concerning the measures taken to apply the provisions of this[23] mandate.

A copy of all laws and regulations made in the course of the year and affecting property, commerce, navigation or the moral and material well-being of the natives shall be annexed to this report.[24]

ART. 12. The consent of the Council of the League of Nations is required for any modification of the terms of this mandate.[25]

ART. 13. The Mandatory agrees that if any dispute whatever should arise between the Mandatory and another member of the League of Nations relating to the interpretation or the application of the provisions of the mandate, such

[20] In the Ruanda-Urundi mandate the words "applicable to contiguous territories" are added after "conventions" and the rest of the article is omitted.

[21] In the Ruanda-Urundi mandate the following article is substituted:

"ARTICLE 10. The Mandatory shall have full powers of administration and legislation in the area subject to the mandate: this area shall be administered in accordance with the laws of the Mandatory as an integral part of his territory and subject to the preceding provisions.

"The Mandatory shall therefore be at liberty to apply his laws to the territory under the mandate subject to the modifications required by local conditions, and to constitute the territory into a customs, fiscal or administrative union or federation with the adjacent possessions under his own sovereignty or control; provided always that the measures adopted to that end do not infringe the provisions of this mandate."

[22] In the Ruanda-Urundi mandate the sentence ends here and the next sentence begins "This report shall contain. . . ."

[23] In the Ruanda-Urundi mandate "the present" is substituted for "this."

[24] This paragraph is omitted in the Ruanda-Urundi mandate.

[25] This is identical with art. 27 of the Palestine mandate.

dispute, if it cannot be settled by negotiation, shall be submitted to the Permanent Court of International Justice provided for by Article 14 of the Covenant of the League of Nations.

States members of the League of Nations may likewise bring any claims on behalf of their nationals for infractions of their rights under this mandate before the said Court for decision.[26]

The present instrument shall be deposited in original in the archives of the League of Nations. Certified copies shall be forwarded by the Secretary-General of the League of Nations to all members of the League.

Done at London, the twentieth day of July one thousand nine hundred and twenty-two.

V. BRITISH CAMEROONS, BRITISH TOGO (FRENCH CAMEROONS AND FRENCH TOGO)

The Council of the League of Nations:

WHEREAS, By Article 119 of the treaty of peace with Germany signed at Versailles on June 28, 1919, Germany renounced in favor of the Principal Allied and Associated Powers all her rights over her oversea possessions, including therein the Cameroons [Togoland]; and

WHEREAS, The Principal Allied and Associated Powers agreed that the Governments of France and Great Britain should make a joint recommendation to the League of Nations as to the future of the said territory; and

WHEREAS, The Governments of France and Great Britain have made a joint recommendation to the Council of the League of Nations that a mandate to administer in accordance with Article 22 of the Covenant of the League of Nations that part of the Cameroons [Togoland] lying to the west of the line agreed upon in the declaration of July 10, 1919, annexed hereto [these two words omitted in Togoland mandate], referred to in Article 1,[27] should be conferred upon His Britannic Majesty;[28] and

WHEREAS, The Governments of France and Great Britain have proposed that the mandate should be formulated in the following terms; and

WHEREAS, His Britannic Majesty[28] has agreed to accept the mandate in respect of the said territory, and has undertaken to exercise it on behalf of the League of Nations[29] in accordance with the following provisions;

Confirming the said mandate, defines its terms as follows:

[26] This paragraph is omitted in the Ruanda-Urundi mandate and all the other mandates. The preceding paragraph is identical with art. 26 of the Palestine mandate and the corresponding article in all the other mandates.

[27] In the French mandates "east" occurs instead of "west," the words "annexed hereto" are omitted and the words "of which mention is made in article I below" are substituted.

[28] In the French mandates "the French Republic" is substituted.

[29] The remainder of the sentence is omitted in the French mandates.

ARTICLE 1. The territory for which a mandate is conferred upon His Britannic Majesty[30] comprises that part of the Cameroons [Togoland] which lies to the west[31] of the line laid down in the declaration signed on July 10, 1919, of which a[32] copy is annexed hereto.[33]

Art. 1 describes the boundary in detail. Art. 2 authorizes the boundary commission to make minor modifications subject to approval of the two governments "to avoid separating villages from their agricultural lands" and to permit natives living near the border to cross over within a period of six months. Art. 3 describes the maps used, a copy of which is included in the original (*O.J.*, III, 872 ff.).

This line may however, be slightly modified by mutual agreement between His Britannic Majesty's Government and the Government of the French Republic where an examination of the localities shows that it is undesirable, either in the interests of the inhabitants or by reason of any inaccuracies in the map, Moisel 1:300,000 [Sprigade 1:200,000], annexed to the declaration, to adhere strictly to the line laid down therein.

The delimitation on the spot of this line shall be carried out in accordance with the provisions of the said declaration.

The final report of the mixed commission shall give the exact description of the boundary line as traced on the spot; maps signed by the commissioners shall be annexed to the report. This report with its annexes shall be drawn up in triplicate: one of these shall be deposited in the archives of the League of Nations, one shall be kept by His Britannic Majesty's Government, and one by the Government of the French Republic.[34]

ART. 2. The Mandatory shall be responsible for the peace, order and good government of the territory, and for the promotion to the utmost of the material and moral well-being and the social progress of its inhabitants.

ART. 3. [Identical with Tanganyika, Art. 4.][35]

[30] In the French mandates "France" is substituted.

[31] In the French mandates "east" is substituted.

[32] The word "a" is omitted in the French mandates.

[33] This declaration reads:

"The undersigned:

"Viscount Milner, Secretary of State for the Colonies of the British Empire.

"M. Henry Simon, Minister for the Colonies of the French Republic, have agreed to determine the frontier, separating the territories of the Cameroons [Togoland], placed respectively under the authority of their governments, as it is traced on the map, Moisel 1:300,000 [Sprigade 1:200,000], annexed to the present declaration, and defined in the description in three articles also annexed hereto.

MILNER
HENRY SIMON"

London, July 10, 1919

[34] In the French mandates the order is reversed and the word "French" is omitted.

[35] In the French mandates the words "in the territory" are transferred to the first line between "establish" and "any" and the following paragraph is added:

ART. 4. [Identical with Tanganyika, Art. 5.]

ART. 5. [Identical with Tanganyika, Art. 6.]

ART. 6. [Identical with Tanganyika, Art. 7.]

ART. 7. [Identical with Tanganyika, Art. 8.]

ART. 8. [Identical with Ruanda-Urundi, Art. 9.]

ART. 9. [Identical with Ruanda-Urundi, Art. 10, except that the word "above" is substituted for "preceding" in paragraph 1, last line.]

ART. 10. [Identical with Tanganyika, Art. 11, first paragraph.][36]

ART. 11. [Identical with Tanganyika, Art. 12; also Palestine, Art. 27.]

ART. 12. [Identical with Ruanda-Urundi, Art. 13; first paragraph identical with Palestine, Art. 26.]

VI. NAURU (NEW GUINEA, WESTERN SAMOA, SOUTHWEST AFRICA, AND THE NORTH PACIFIC ISLANDS)[37]

The Council of the League of Nations:

WHEREAS, By Article 119 of the treaty of peace with Germany signed at Versailles on June 28, 1919, Germany renounced in favor of the Principal Allied and Associated Powers all her rights over her overseas possessions, including therein Nauru[38]; and

---

"It is understood, however, that the troops thus raised may, in the event of general war, be utilized to repel an attack or for defence of the territory outside that subject to the mandate."

[36] In the French mandates the words "containing full" are omitted and a new sentence begins, "This report shall contain. . . ."

[37] Viscount Ishii of Japan read the following declaration in regard to these mandates at the Council meeting of December 17, 1920, at which they were confirmed:

"From the fundamental spirit of the League of Nations, and as the question of interpretation of the Covenant, His Imperial Majesty's Government have a firm conviction in the justice of the claim they have hitherto made for the inclusion of a clause concerning the assurance of equal opportunities for trade and commerce in 'C' mandates. But from the spirit of conciliation and co-operation and their reluctance to see the question unsettled any longer, they have decided to agree to the issue of the mandate in its present form. That decision, however, should not be considered as an acquiescence on the part of His Imperial Japanese Majesty's Government in the submission of Japanese subjects to a discriminatory and disadvantageous treatment in the mandated territories; nor have they thereby discarded their claim that the rights and interests enjoyed by Japanese subjects in these territories in the past should be fully respected" (*O.J.*, II, 95).

[38] In the other C mandates the following substitutions occur:

"German New Guinea and the group of islands in the Pacific Ocean lying south of the Equator other than German Samoa and Nauru."

"German Samoa."

"German Southwest Africa."

"The group of islands in the Pacific Ocean lying north of the equator."

WHEREAS, The Principal Allied and Associated Powers agreed that, in accordance with Article 22, Part I (Covenant of the League of Nations), of the said treaty a mandate should be conferred upon His Britannic Majesty to administer Nauru,[39] and have proposed that the mandate should be formulated in the following terms; and

WHEREAS, His Britannic Majesty has agreed to accept a mandate in respect of Nauru[40] and has undertaken to exercise it on behalf of the League of Nations in accordance with the following provisions; and

WHEREAS, By the aforementioned Article 22, paragraph 8, it is provided that the degree of authority, control or administration to be exercised by the Mandatory not having been previously agreed upon by the members of the League, shall be explicitly defined by the Council of the League of Nations;

Confirming the said mandate, defines its terms as follows:

ARTICLE 1. The territory over which a mandate is conferred upon His Britannic Majesty (hereinafter called the Mandatory) is the former German island of Nauru (Pleasant Island, situated in about 167° longitude East and 0° 25′ latitude South).[41]

[39] In the other C mandates the following substitutions occur:

"His Britannic Majesty to be exercised on his behalf by the government of the Commonwealth of Australia to administer New Guinea and the said islands."

"His Britannic Majesty to be exercised on his behalf by the Government of the Dominion of New Zealand to administer German Samoa."

"His Britannic Majesty to be exercised on his behalf by the Government of the Union of South Africa to administer the territory aforementioned."

"His Majesty the Emperor of Japan to administer the said islands."

[40] In the other C mandates the following substitutions occur:

"His Britannic Majesty, for and on behalf of the Government of the Commonwealth of Australia . . . . in respect of the said territory."

"His Britannic Majesty, for and on behalf of the Government of the Dominion of New Zealand . . . . in respect of the said territory."

"His Britannic Majesty for and on behalf of the Government of the Union of South Africa . . . . in respect of the said territory."

"His Majesty the Emperor of Japan . . . . in respect of the said islands."

[41] In the other C mandates the following substitutions occur:

"Upon his Britannic Majesty for and on behalf of the Government of the Commonwealth of Australia (hereinafter called the mandatory) comprises the former German colony of New Guinea and the former German islands situated in the Pacific Ocean and lying south of the equator other than the islands of the Samoan group and the island of Nauru."

"Upon his Britannic Majesty for and on behalf of the Government of the Dominion of New Zealand (hereinafter called the mandatory) is the former German colony of Samoa."

"Upon his Britannic Majesty for and on behalf of the Government of the Union of South Africa (hereinafter called the mandatory) comprises the territory which formerly constituted the German protectorate of Southwest Africa."

"Upon His Majesty the Emperor of Japan (hereinafter called the mandatory)

ART. 2. The Mandatory shall have full power of administration and legislation over the territory subject to the present mandate as an integral portion[42] of his territory.

The Mandatory shall promote to the utmost the material and moral well-being and the social progress of the inhabitants of the territory subject to the present mandate.

ART. 3. The Mandatory shall see that the slave trade is prohibited, and that no forced labor is permitted, except for essential public works and services, and then only for adequate remuneration.

The Mandatory shall also see that the traffic in arms and ammunition is controlled in accordance with principles analogous to those laid down in the convention relating to the control of the arms traffic, signed on September 10, 1919, or in any convention amending the same.

The supply of intoxicating spirits and beverages to the natives shall be prohibited.

ART. 4. The military training of the natives, otherwise than for purposes of internal police and the local defense of the territory, shall be prohibited. Furthermore, no military or naval bases shall be established or fortification erected in the territory.

ART. 5. Subject to the provisions of any local law for the maintenance of public order and public morals, the Mandatory shall ensure in the territory freedom of conscience and the free exercise of all forms of worship, and shall allow all missionaries, nationals of any state member of the League of Nations, to enter into, travel and reside in the territory for the purpose of prosecuting their calling.

ART. 6. The Mandatory shall make to the Council of the League of Nations an annual report to the satisfaction of the Council, containing full information with regard to the territory, and indicating the measures taken to carry out the obligations assumed under Articles 2, 3, 4 and 5.

ART. 7. The consent of the Council of the League of Nations is required for any modification of the terms of the present mandate.

The Mandatory agrees that, if any dispute whatever should arise between the Mandatory and another member of the League of Nations relating to the interpretation or the application of the provisions of the mandate, such dispute, if it cannot be settled by negotiation, shall be submitted to the Permanent

---

comprises all the former German islands situated in the Pacific Ocean and lying north of the equator."

[42] In the other C mandates the concluding words of the paragraph are:

"Of the [Commonwealth of Australia] [Dominion of New Zealand] [Union of South Africa] [Empire of Japan] and may apply the laws of the [Commonwealth of Australia] [Dominion of New Zealand] [Union of South Africa] [Empire of Japan] to the territory, subject to such local modifications as circumstances may require."

Court of International Justice provided for by Article 14 of the Covenant of the League of Nations.

The present declaration shall be deposited in the archives of the League of Nations. Certified copies shall be forwarded by the Secretary-General of the League of Nations to all Powers signatories of the treaty of peace with Germany.

Certified true copy.

SECRETARY-GENERAL

Made at Geneva the 17th day of December, 1920

APPENDIX III

ORGANIZATION OF THE COMMISSION

I. CONSTITUTION OF PERMANENT MANDATES COMMISSION

(Approved by the Council, December 1, 1920)

The Council of the League of Nations in accordance with paragraphs 7 and 9 of Article 22 of the Covenant, namely:

"In every case of Mandate, the Mandatory shall render to the Council an Annual Report in reference to the territory committed to its charge.

"A Permanent Commission shall be constituted to receive and examine the Annual Reports of the Mandatories, and to advise the Council on all matters relating to the observance of the Mandates."

has decided as follows:—

a) The Permanent Mandates Commission provided for in paragraph 9 of Article 22 of the Covenant, shall consist of nine Members.[1] The majority of the Commission shall be nationals of non-Mandatory Powers.

All the Members of the Commission shall be appointed by the Council and selected for their personal merits and competence. They shall not hold any office which puts them in a position of direct dependence on their Governments while Members of the Commission.

The International Labour Organisation shall have the privilege of appointing to the Permanent Commission an expert chosen by itself. This expert shall have the right of attending in an advisory capacity all meetings of the Permanent Commission at which questions relating to labour are discussed.

b) The Mandatory Powers should send their annual report provided for in paragraph 7 of Article 22 of the Covenant to the Commission through duly authorised representatives who would be prepared to offer any supplementary explanations or supplementary information which the Commission may request.

c) The Commission shall examine each individual report in the presence of the duly authorised representative of the Mandatory Power from which it comes. This representative shall participate with absolute freedom in the discussion of this report.

d) After this discussion has ended and the representative of the Manda-

[1] By resolution of September 8, 1927, the Council increased this to ten members to permit of appointing a member of German nationality, Germany having just been admitted to the League (*O.J.*, VIII, 1120). By resolution of December 11, 1924, on suggestion of the Commission, the Council had appointed M. W. E. Rappard, who had just retired as director of the mandates section, an "extraordinary member" because of his "special qualifications" and without "constituting a precedent" (*ibid.*, V, 143).

tory Power has withdrawn the Commission shall decide on the wording of the observations which are to be submitted to the Council of the League.

e) The observations made by the Commission upon each report shall be communicated to the duly authorised representative of the Mandatory Power from which the report comes. This representative shall be entitled to accompany it with any comments which he desires to make.

f) The Commission shall forward the reports of Mandatory Powers to the Council. It shall annex to each report its own observations as well as the observations of the duly authorised representative of the Power which issued the report, if the representative so desires.

g) When the Council publishes the reports of the Mandatory Powers and the observations of the Permanent Commission, it shall also publish the observations of the duly authorised representatives of those Mandatory Powers which have expressed such a desire.

h) The Commission, acting in concert with all the duly authorised representatives of the Mandatory Powers, shall hold a Plenary Meeting to consider all the reports as a whole and any general conclusions to be drawn from them. The Commission may also utilise such a meeting of the representatives of the Mandatory Powers to lay before them any other matters connected with Mandates which in their opinion should be submitted by the Council to the Mandatory Powers and to the other States Members of the League. This Plenary Meeting shall take place either before or after the presentation of the annual report as the Commission may think fit.

i) The Commission shall regulate its own procedure subject to the approval of the Council.

j) The Commission shall sit at Geneva. It may summon technical experts to act in an advisory capacity for all questions relating to the application of the system of Mandates.

k) The Members of the Commission shall receive an allowance of 100 gold francs per day during their meetings.[2] Their travelling expenses shall be paid. Expenses of the Commission shall be borne by the League of Nations.

II. RULES OF PROCEDURE OF THE PERMANENT MANDATES COMMISSION

(Approved by the Council, January 10, 1922, with Amendments Approved, December 12, 1923, and March 5, 1928)

Whereas, In conformity with Article 22 of the Covenant, the Permanent Mandates Commission is entrusted with the duty of receiving and examining the annual reports which the Mandatory Powers shall render to the Council in

[2] By the Council resolution of January 10, 1922, this was reduced to 70 gold francs *per diem* but by resolution of the Council on June 7, 1926, approved by the Assembly, it was increased to 2,000 gold francs a year (*ibid.*, VII, 856).

reference to the territories committed to their charge, and of advising the Council on all matters relating to the observance of the mandates;

AND WHEREAS, By the provisions of the Constitution of the Permanent Mandates Commission, which was approved by the Council on December 1st, 1920, the Commission is instructed to draw up its own Rules of Procedure, subject to the approval of the Council;

Now therefore the Commission adopts the following provisions for its Rules of Procedure, subject to the above-mentioned reservation:

RULE 1. The Permanent Mandate Commission will assemble in ordinary session at least once a year at the seat of the League of Nations, as a rule in the second half of June.

It will meet for extraordinary sessions at the request of one of its members, on condition that this request, which should be addressed to the Secretary-General and submitted by him to the other members of the Commission, be approved by the majority of these members and by the President of the Council of the League.

The Mandatory Powers and the President of the Council shall be informed, at least one month in advance, of the dates of sessions.

RULE 2. The Permanent Mandates Commission shall consist of nine[3] members, as laid down by paragraph (*a*) of its Constitution.

The International Labour Organisation may detail an expert, selected by itself, to sit on the Permanent Commission. This expert shall be entitled to attend, in an advisory capacity, all the meetings of the Permanent Commission at which questions connected with the labour system are discussed.

RULE 3. At any meeting six members shall constitute a quorum.

All decisions of the Commission shall be adopted by a majority of the votes of the members present at the meeting. In a case of equality of votes, the Chairman shall have a casting vote. Any statement of views by a minority consisting of one or more members of the Commission shall be transmitted to the Council at the request of the minority.

RULE 4. At the beginning of the first ordinary session of each year, the Commission shall elect from among its members, by secret ballot, a Chairman and a Vice-Chairman for the period of one year. The Mandates Section of the Secretariat of the League will constitute the permanent Secretariat of the Commission.

RULE 5. The Commission shall be put in possession of the annual reports concerning Palestine, Syria, Cameroons and Togoland under French mandate, Tanganyika, Southwest Africa, New Guinea and Nauru, before May 20th, and those concerning Iraq, Cameroons and Togoland under British mandate, Ruanda-Urundi, Pacific Islands under Japanese mandate, and Western Samoa before September 1st of each year.

The Mandatory Powers shall be requested to send one hundred copies of

[3] See *supra*, n. 1.

these reports to the Secretariat of the League, and one copy each, at the same time, to the members of the Permanent Mandates Commission, whose names and addresses shall be communicated, with this object in view, to the Governments of these Powers.

RULE 6. The Agenda for each session shall be prepared by the Secretariat of the League, submitted for the approval of the Chairman of the Commission, and communicated to the members, together with the notice convening the Commission.

The Commission may decide, during the course of a session, by a two-thirds majority of the members present, to add any question to the Agenda.

RULE 7. The Chairman shall convene the Commission through the agency of the Secretariat; he shall direct the work at the meetings, ensure that the provisions of the Rules of Procedure are observed, and announce the results of ballots.

The Secretariat shall draw up the minutes of each meeting. These minutes, after being approved by the Commission, shall be kept in a special file. Copies shall be communicated to the Council and to the Mandatory Powers.

The Secretariat shall, as a rule, make all the necessary arrangements for meetings of the Commission. It shall keep the Chairman informed of all questions which may be brought before the Commission for consideration, and shall supply, in due course, all the Members of the Commission with the documents required for the study of the problems on the agenda.

RULE 8. During the ordinary sessions, the Commission shall undertake a separate examination and discussion of each of the annual reports submitted by the Mandatory Powers. The examination and the discussion shall take place, in each case, in the presence of the accredited representative of the Mandatory Power which issued the report.

After this examination, the Commission shall decide upon the form to be given to the observations to be transmitted to the Council of the League. If the Commission is not unanimous, it may present its observations in the form of majority and minority reports. These observations shall be, in every case, communicated to the accredited representative of the Power which issued the report to which they refer. The representative concerned may attach his own remarks.

The Commission shall forward the reports of the Mandatory Powers to the Council. It shall annex to each report its own observations as well as the observations of the duly authorised representative of the Power which issued the report, if the representative so desires.

If a majority of the members of the Commission should express the desire, the Commission shall hold a plenary meeting in the presence of the duly authorised representatives, when it has adopted the final terms of its observations on all the reports which it has examined. The Commission may take advantage of the presence of the duly authorised representatives of the Mandatory Powers to bring before them all matters connected with the Mandates which, in its opinion, should be submitted by the Council to the Mandatory Powers and to the other Members of the League.

The meetings, as well as the plenary meeting, shall be public if it be so decided by a majority of the Commission.

RULE 9. French and English shall be the official languages of the Commission.

If a member of the Commission should express the desire, the Secretariat will cause all written documents emanating from the Commission, together with the annual reports of the Mandatory Powers and the remarks of the duly authorised representatives of the latter, to be translated into French when they have been submitted in English, and *vice versa*.

Members of the Commission may speak in French or in English. On the request of a member of the Commission, speeches in French will be summarised in English, and *vice versa*, by an interpreter on the staff of the Secretariat.

RULE 10. Subject to the approval of the Council, these Rules of Procedure may be modified if at least five members of the Commission so decide.

III. MEMBERS OF THE PERMANENT MANDATES COMMISSION

NATIONALS OF NON-MANDATORY STATES[4]

ITALIAN—1921 to date. MARQUIS THEODOLI, chairman, former undersecretary of state to the ministry of colonies

DUTCH—1921 to date. M. D. F. W. VAN REES, vice-chairman, former vice-president of the Council of the Dutch East Indies

SPANISH—1921–22. M. RAMON PINA, former undersecretary of state to the minister of foreign affairs and ambassador of Spain at Rome

1922–24. COUNT DE BALLOBAR, former consul at Jerusalem

1924 to date. M. LEOPOLDO PALACIOS, professor at the University of Madrid

PORTUGUESE—1921–29. M. FREIRE D'ANDRADE, former governor of Lorenzo Marques, former governor-general of Mozambique, former minister of foreign affairs

1929 to date. COUNT DE PENHA GARCIA

SWEDISH—1921–28. MME ANNA BUGGE-WICKSELL, LL.D.

NORWEGIAN—1928 to date. MLLE VALENTINE DANNEVIG, educator

GERMAN—1927 to date.[5] DR. LUDWIG KASTL, former senior official in the colonial administration, former chief of the reparation section of the finance ministry

[4] In its original nominations of February 22, 1921, the Council included Mr. Cameron Forbes (American), former governor-general of the Philippines, but he declined to serve.

[5] See *supra*, n. 1.

NATIONALS OF MANDATORY STATES

BRITISH—1921–23. MR. W. G. ORMSBY-GORE, member of the House of Commons

1923 to date. LORD (SIR FREDERICK) LUGARD, former governor of Nigeria

FRENCH—1921–26. M. J. B. P. BEAU, former governor-general of French Indo-China, former ambassador of France at Berne

1926 (substitute in eighth session). M. H. ROUME, honorary governor-general of the colonies

1926 to date. M. MARTIAL MERLIN, former governor-general of French Indo-China

JAPANESE—1921–24. M. KUNIO YANAGHITA, former secretary-general to the House of Peers

1924–28. M. H. CHIYUKI YAMANAKA, former counselor of embassy

1928 to date. M. NOBUMICHI SAKENOBE, former minister to Chile

BELGIAN—1921 to date. M. PIERRE ORTS, former secretary-general of the ministry of foreign affairs

EXTRAORDINARY MEMBER[6]

SWISS—1925 to date. M. WILLIAM E. RAPPARD, professor at University of Geneva, former director of the mandates section of the Secretariat

REPRESENTATIVE OF THE INTERNATIONAL LABOR ORGANIZATION

BRITISH—1922–29. MR. HAROLD A. GRIMSHAW

1929 to date. MR. C. W. H. WEAVER

SECRETARY TO THE COMMISSION

1921–25. M. WILLIAM E. RAPPARD, director of the mandates section

1925 to date. M. VITA CATASTINI, chief of the mandates section

[6] See *supra*, n. 1.

APPENDIX IV

AREA, POPULATION, AND TRADE OF GERMAN COLONIES BEFORE THE WORLD WAR*

	Area	Population, 1913				
		Per Sq.Mi.	Total	Native	European†	Other
East Africa‡....	384,000	20.0	7,666,336	7,646,000	5,336	15,000 §
Togoland‖......	34,000	30.0	1,032,368	1,032,000	368	.......¶
Kamerun**.....	298,000	9.0	2,652,871	2,649,000	1,871	2,000
Southwest Africa	322,000	0.3	98,830	81,000	14,830	3,000
Total Africa	1,038,000	11.0	11,450,405	11,408,000	22,405	20,000
Samoa.........	1,000	38.0	38,544	35,000	544	3,000
New Guinea††..	95,000	6.0	603,427	600,000	1,427	2,000
Total Pacific	96,000	7.0	641,971	635,000	1,971	5,000‡‡

Trade
(in Thousands of Dollars)

	Total			Exports			Imports		
	1907	1913	Per Capita 1913	1907	1913	Per Capita 1913	1907	1913	Per Capita 1913
East Africa‡....	9,076	22,224	2.90	3,125	8,887	1.15	5,951	13,337	1.75
Togoland‖......	3,154	4,942	4.79	1,479	2,284	2.21	1,675	2,658	2.58
Kamerun**.....	8,297	16,042	6.05	3,973	7,388	2.80	4,324	8,654	3.25
Southwest Africa	8,503	28,431	287.18	404	17,575	177.53	8,099	10,856	109.65
Total Africa	29,030	71,639	6.26	8,981	36,134	3.16	20,049	35,505	3.10
Samoa.........	1,151	2,754	70.62	443	1,335	34.23	708	1,419	36.39
New Guinea††..	2,297	5,324	8.83	867	3,022§§	5.01	1,430	2,302§§	3.82
Total Pacific	3,448	8,078	12.58	1,310	4,357	6.78	2,138	3,721	5.80

* From U.S. Tariff Commission, *Colonial Tariff Policies*, pp. 230–31, based on figures in *Statistisches Jahrbuch für das Deutsche Reich* (1915), p. 457, and Statesman's *Year Book* (1914). For somewhat different figures and more details, see the *Peace Handbooks of the British Foreign Office*, Nos. 110–13 and 146.

† Some of these figures include the German garrisons.

‡ Includes present Tanganyika and Ruanda-Urundi.

§ Chiefly East Indians who controlled the retail trade.

‖ Includes Togoland at present under British and French mandates.

¶ Not determined.

** Includes Cameroons at present under British and French mandates and (for 1913) part of French Equatorial Africa ceded to Germany in 1911 and retroceded in 1919.

†† Includes Nauru and the North Pacific Islands which though only 1 per cent of the area of New Guinea (Kaiser Wilhelm's land and Bismarck Archipelago) had about as large a white population.

‡‡ Chiefly Chinese indentured laborers.

§§ The statistics for New Guinea for 1913 not being available, the 1912 figures for that colony have been given. Imports were divided as follows: Kaiser Wilhelm's land, 1468; East Caroline and Marshall Islands, 491; West Caroline, Pelew, and Marianne Islands, 343. Exports were 1,260, 1,291, and 471, respectively.

APPENDIX V

AREA, POPULATION, AND RAILROADS OF MANDATED TERRITORIES[1]

	Area	Population							Miles Railway
		Per Sq. Mi.	Total		Native		Non-native		
		1926	1921	1926	1921	1926	1921	1926	1926
Iraq	116,511	24	2,849,282*	(2,849,282)	....	....	....	....	754
Palestine	9,010	99	761,796†	887,000‡	....	....	....	....	492
Transjordan	20,000§	12	(240,000)	240,000‖	....	....	....	....	283
Syria	52,000¶	27	(1,416,954)	1,416,954 } **	....	....	....	....	492
Greater Lebanon	8,000	79	(623,863)	623,863 }					
Total Near East	205,521	29	5,896,895	6,022,099	....	....	....	....	2,021
Tanganyika	373,494	12	(4,336,438)	4,336,438	(4,319,000)	4,319,000††	17,438‡‡	(17,438)	1,140
Ruanda-Urundi	21,429	238	5,000,172	5,000,605	(5,000,000)	5,000,000§§	172	605	00
Togoland (Br.)	13,240	14	187,959	(187,959)	187,939‖‖	(187,939)	20	(20)	00
Togoland (Fr.)	20,077	37	698,340	742,808	698,130¶¶	742,428	210	380	204
Cameroon (Br.)	34,236	20	645,229	667,061	645,174	666,841	55	220	00
Cameroon (Fr.)	164,094	13	2,830,722	1,878,683***	2,830,000	1,877,113***	722	1,570	369
Southwest Africa	322,393	00.7	227,739	235,804	208,307†††	211,336‡‡‡	19,432	24,468	1,431
Total Africa	948,963	14	13,926,599	13,049,358***	13,888,550	13,004,657***	38,049	44,701	3,144
Western Samoa	1,133	35	36,422	37,865	32,601	34,817	3,821	3,048	00
Nauru	9	266	2,129	2,217	1,113	1,251	1,016	966	00
New Guinea	91,300	4	254,190	421,050	251,017	417,918	3,173	3,132	00
North Pacific Islands	830	64	52,222	54,421	48,505	49,324	3,717	5,097	00
Total Pacific	93,271	5	344,963	515,553	333,236	503,310	11,727§§§	12,243§§§	00
Grand total	1,247,755	16	20,168,457	19,587,010***	....	....	....	....	5,165

[1] Unless otherwise indicated, the data is from League of Nations, *Statistical Information concerning Territories under Mandate*, 1928.

APPENDIX V—*Continued*

* Iraq: According to the 1919 census the population was divided by race and religion as follows:

Moslems:		Arab	2,206,192
Sunnite	1,146,685	Kurdish	499,336
Shia	1,494,015	Persian	79,908
Jewish	87,488	Turkish	60,493
Christians	78,792	Indian	3,061
Other	42,302	European	292
Total	2,849,282	Total	2,849,282

† Palestine: According to the 1922 census the population was divided as follows (*Statesman's Year Book* [1927], p. 190):

Moslems	590,890
Jews	83,794
Christian	73,024
Druzes	7,028
Samaritans	163
Other	6,632
Total	761,796

‡ Palestine: Estimate, 1927, divided as follows (*Joint Palestine Survey Commission Report*):

		Moslems	633,000
		Jews	158,000
Settled	783,161	Christians	87,726
Nomadic	103,839	Other	8,274
Total	887,000	Total	887,000

§ Estimated.

|| Transjordan: Estimate (*Statesman's Year Book* [1927], p. 195) divided as follows:

Arab Moslems	220,000
Arab Christians	10,000
Caucasians	10,000
Total	240,000

¶ Including West Syria and the Jebel Druze.

** Syria and Lebanon, census, 1926 (*Annual Report* [1926], pp. 190–94), divided as follows (the division by countries is from the *Statesman's Year Book* [1927], p. 890):

Moslems	1,185,818		
Christians	505,419	Syria	1,198,829
Post Islamic (Druze)	328,937	Lebanon	628,863
Jews	16,526	West Syria	261,062
Others	10,157	Jebel Druze	50,328
Total	2,046,857	Total	2,139,072

†† Estimated.

‡‡ Census.

§§ Estimated.

|| || Census, 1921.

¶¶ Census, 1921.

*** The apparent decrease is attributed to an error in the 1921 figure based on the German estimate. See French Cameroons, *Annual Report* (1926), p. 49.

††† Divided: Native, 177,462; colored, 30,845.

‡‡‡ Divided: native, 186,175; colored, 25,161.

APPENDIX VI

TRADE AND FINANCIAL STATISTICS OF THE MANDATED TERRITORIES°

Foreign Trade (in Thousands of Dollars)

	Total Trade		Exports		Imports	
	1921	1926	1921	1926	1921	1926
Iraq	89,380	108,480	27,740	43,920	61,640	64,560
Palestine*	28,496	38,153	5,536	6,363	22,960	31,790
Syria†	50,261	57,983	5,137	17,434	45,124	40,599
Total Near East	168,137	204,616	38,413	67,717	129,724	136,899
Tanganyika‡	13,763	28,356	7,406	14,526	6,357	13,830
Ruanda-Urundi§	125	919	46	442	79	477
Togoland (Br.)||	578	942	435	760	143	182
Togoland (Fr.)	1,362	5,788	523	2,575	839	3,213
Cameroons (Br.)	464	2,410	154	1,072	310	1,338
Cameroon (Fr.)	4,107	9,640	1,603	5,037	2,504	4,603
Southwest Africa¶	10,772	23,566	6,110	12,990	4,662	10,576
Total Africa	31,171	71,621	16,277	37,402	14,894	34,219
Western Samoa**	3,473	2,811	1,417	1,597	2,056	1,214
Nauru††	1,566	2,510	1,219	2,004	347	506
New Guinea	5,140	8,131	2,594	5,369	2,546	2,762
North Pacific Islands‡‡	1,352	2,491	1,019	1,456	333	1,035
Total Pacific	11,531	15,943	6,249	10,426	5,282	5,517
Grand total	210,839	292,180	60,939	115,545	149,900	176,635

Public Finance (in Thousands of Dollars)

	Revenue				Amount Spent On							
	External Sources		Other than External Sources		Education		Agriculture		Public Health		Public Works	
	Loans and advances, Average, 1921–26	Non-recoverable Grants, Average, 1921–26	1921	1926	1921	1926	1921	1926	1921	1926	1921	1926
Iraq	00	633	14,760	21,110	327	827	177	213	877	708	2,790	1,415
Palestine*	00	896	7,700	12,349	339	493	254	310	550	403	593	1,030
Syria†	2,720|| ||	00	7,161	11,537	622	680	181	193	350	293	997	2,081
Total Near East	2,720	1,529	29,621	44,996	1,288	2,000	612	716	1,777	1,404	4,380	4,526
Tanganyika‡	2,822	310	2,891	7,586	11	138	40	223	333	714	607	1,241
Ruanda-Urundi§	82	00	225	236	8	8	25	2	6	12	33	51
Togoland (Br.)||	00	00¶¶	7	198	11	28	2	16	6	25	63	68
Togoland (Fr.)	4	00	353	478	16	23	7	27	27	53	70	92
Cameroons (Br.)	00	175¶¶	283	602	8	39	19	6	32	56	84	105
Cameroons (Fr.)	30	00	990	851	18	30	8	15	66	117	770	862***
Southwest Africa¶	00	00	6,163	3,149	134	412	410	710	64	74	604	526
Total Africa	2,938	485	10,915	13,100	206	678	511	999	534	1,051	2,231	2,945
Western Samoa**	92	89	546	494	12	34	20	13	58	108	51	109
Nauru††	00	00	50	80	2	4	00	00	5	15	6	9
New Guinea	27	19	1,008	1,312	0	32	27	47	115	257	112	111
North Pacific Islands‡‡	00	908	622	1,434	72	68	108	103	112	104	125	189
Total Pacific	119	1,016	2,226	3,320	86	138	155	163	290	484	294	418
Grand total	5,777	3,030	42,762	61,416	1,580	2,816	1,278	1,878	2,601	2,939	6,905	7,889

* Excluding Transjordan. † The public finance data are for 1924 and 1926. ‡ The data are for 1920 and 1925. § The data are for 1920 and 1924. || The data are for 1922 and 1925. ¶ Excluding the Caprivi Zipfel. The data are for 1921 and 1925. ** The data are for 1920 and 1924. †† The data are for 1922 and 1926. ‡‡ The data are for 1921 and 1924. || || France appears to contemplate recovery of advances made during the military occupations. See Syria, Report, 1922–23, p. 55; 1924, p. 90. ¶¶ The budget deficits of British Togoland and Cameroons were at first made up by unaccounted grants from the revenues of the Gold Coast and Nigeria, respectively, with which these mandated areas are fiscally united (see *P.M.C.*, III, 318 ff., and *supra*, chap. xiii, n. 59. *** This came in part from budget surpluses accumulated from previous years.

° Data from League of Nations, *Statistical Information concerning Territories under Mandate*, 1928. Conversion factors from *U.S. Statistical Abstract* (1926), p. 287.

APPENDIX VII

NATIVE WELFARE EXPENDITURES IN MANDATED TERRITORIES*

	Expenditures per Capita (in Dollars)							
	Education		Agriculture		Public Health		Total	
	1921	1926	1921	1926	1921	1926	1921	1926
Iraq	.115	.290	.062	.074	.307	.248	.484	.612
Palestine†	.445	.556	.334	.349	.722	.454	1.501	1.359
Syria	.305	.333	.089	.095	.171	.174	.565	.602
Total Near East	.218	.332	.104	.119	.301	.233	.623	.684
Tanganyika	.003	.032	.009	.051	.077	.164	.089	.247
Ruanda-Urundi	.002	.002	.005	.0004	.001	.002	.008	.004
Togoland (Br.)	.059	.149	.011	.085	.032	.133	.102	.367
Togoland (Fr.)	.023	.031	.010	.036	.038	.071	.071	.138
Cameroons (Br.)	.012	.058	.029	.008	.049	.083	.090	.149
Cameroons (Fr.)	.006	.016	.003	.008	.023	.062	.032	.086
Southwest Africa‡	.588	1.747	1.800	3.011	.281	.314	2.669	5.072
Total Africa	.015	.052	.037	.077	.038	.081	.090	.210
Western Samoa	.330	.898	.549	.343	1.593	2.852	2.472	4.093
Nauru	.939	1.804	.00	.00	2.348	6.766	3.287	8.570
New Guinea	.00	.076	.106	.112	.452	.610	.558	.798
North Pacific Islands	1.379	1.250	2.068	1.893	2.145	1.912	5.592	5.055
Total Pacific	.249	.268	.449	.316	.841	.939	1.539	1.523
Grand total	.078	.144	.063	.096	.129	.150	.270	.390

	Per Cent of Ordinary Revenue Spent For							
	Education		Agriculture		Public Health		Total	
	1921	1926	1921	1926	1921	1926	1921	1926
Iraq	2.215	3.909	1.199	1.007	5.942	3.347	9.356	8.263
Palestine†	4.404	3.993	3.299	2.511	7.144	3.264	14.847	9.768
Syria	8.683	5.894	2.527	1.673	4.886	2.540	16.096	10.107
Total Near East	4.348	4.444	2.066	1.591	5.999	3.111	12.413	9.146
Tanganyika	.380	1.819	1.384	2.939	11.518	9.411	13.282	14.169
Ruanda-Urundi	3.555	3.390	11.110	.847	2.666	5.084	17.331	9.321
Togoland (Br.)	157.190§	14.143	28.580	8.082	85.740	12.627	271.510	34.852
Togoland (Br.)	4.533	4.812	1.983	5.648	7.649	11.088	14.165	21.548
Cameroons (Br.)	2.827	6.478	6.715	.997	11.309	9.302	20.851	16.777
Cameroons (Fr.)	1.818	3.525	.808	1.762	6.666	13.747	9.292	19.034
Southwest Africa‡	2.175	13.085	6.654	22.550	1.039	2.350	9.868	37.985
Total Africa	1.887	5.176	4.682	7.626	4.893	8.023	11.462	20.825
Western Samoa	2.198	6.882	3.664	2.631	10.626	21.859	16.488	52.197
Nauru	4.000	5.000	.00	.00	10.000	18.750	14.000	23.750
New Guinea	.00	2.439	2.679	3.582	11.409	19.588	14.088	25.609
North Pacific Islands	11.578	4.742	17.366	7.183	18.010	7.253	46.954	19.178
Total Pacific	3.863	4.157	6.963	4.910	13.027	14.578	23.853	23.645
Grand total	3.696	4.584	2.989	3.057	6.084	4.785	12.769	12.426

* As the tabulations were obtained from the data in Appendix V and VI, the relevant footnotes apply.

† Excluding Transjordan. ‡ Excluding Caprivi Zipfel. § See Appendix VI, n. ¶¶.

APPENDIX VIII

ECONOMIC DEVELOPMENT OF MANDATED TERRITORIES*

	Miles Railway per 1,000 Sq.Mi.	Foreign Trade per Capita (in Dollars)					
		Total		Exports		Imports	
	1926	1921	1926	1921	1926	1921	1926
Iraq	6.45	31.363	38.066	9.734	15.412	21.629	22.654
Palestine†	54.55‡	37.415	42.998	7.268	7.171	30.146	35.827
Syria	9.46	24.628	28.417	2.517	8.543	22.111	19.894
Total Near East	9.83	28.516	33.987	6.514	11.248	22.001	22.739
Tanganyika	3.06	3.174	6.538	1.708	3.350	1.466	3.189
Ruanda-Urundi	.00	.025	.184	.009	.088	.016	.095
Togoland (Br.)	.00	3.075	5.011	2.314	4.043	.761	.968
Togoland (Fr.)	10.40	1.950	7.791	.748	3.466	1.201	4.325
Cameroons (Br.)	.00	.719	3.613	.239	1.607	.480	2.006
Cameroons (Fr.)	2.25	1.451	5.131	.566	2.681	.885	2.450
Southwest Africa§	4.44	47.300	99.943	26.829	55.090	20.471	44.853
Total Africa	3.31	2.238	5.488	1.169	2.866	1.069	2.622
Western Samoa	.00	95.369	74.239	38.911	42.177	56.458	32.062
Nauru	.00	735.550	1132.261	572.564	904.004	162.986	228.257
New Guinea	.00	20.221	19.311	10.205	12.751	10.016	6.560
North Pacific Islands	.00	25.891	45.785	19.514	26.761	6.377	19.023
Total Pacific	.00	33.428	30.929	18.116	20.226	15.313	10.703
Grand total	4.14	10.453	14.916	3.021	5.899	7.432	9.017

	Revenue per Capita (in Dollars)				Relative Public-Works Expenditures			
	External Sources		Other than External Sources		Per Capita		% (Ordinary) Revenue	
	Loans and Advances Average, 1921–26	Non-recoverable Grants, Average, 1921–26	1921	1926	1921	1926	1921	1926
Iraq	.00	.222	5.179	7.409	.979	.497	18.902	6.689
Palestine†	.00	1.010	10.110	13.917	.779	1.161	7.703	8.342
Syria	1.333	.00	3.509	5.653	.488	1.020	13.918	18.038
Total Near East	.452	2.540	5.024	7.474	.743	.752	14.787	10.057
Tanganyika	.651	.071	.666	1.749	.139	.286	20.996	16.356
Ruanda-Urundi	.016	.00	.045	.047	.007	.010	14.665	21.609
Togoland (Br.)	.00	.00	.037	1.053	.335	.362	9.003	34.347
Togoland (Fr.)	.005	.00	.505	.643	.100	.124	19.831	19.246
Cameroons (Br.)	.00	.262	.439	.902	.130	.157	29.686	17.440
Cameroons (Fr.)	.016	.00	.349	.453	.272	.458	77.770	101.285
Southwest Africa§	.00	.00	27.062	13.355	2.652	2.231	9.803	16.706
Total Africa	.225	.037	.784	1.004	.160	.992	20.440	22.482
Western Samoa	2.430	2.350	14.993	13.047	1.400	2.879	9.343	22.061
Nauru	.00	.00	23.485	36.088	2.818	4.060	12.000	11.250
New Guinea	.064	.045	3.965	3.116	.441	.264	11.112	8.460
North Pacific Islands	.00	16.689	11.911	26.357	2.394	3.474	20.100	13.181
Total Pacific	.231	1.971	6.453	6.441	.852	.811	13.206	12.590
Grand total	.295	.155	2.120	3.135	.342	.403	16.151	12.843

* As the tabulations were obtained from the data in Appendixes V and VI, the relevant footnotes apply. † Excluding Transjordan. ‡ Transjordan, 14.15. § Excluding Caprivi Zipfel.

APPENDIX IX

1. NEAR EASTERN MANDATED TERRITORIES

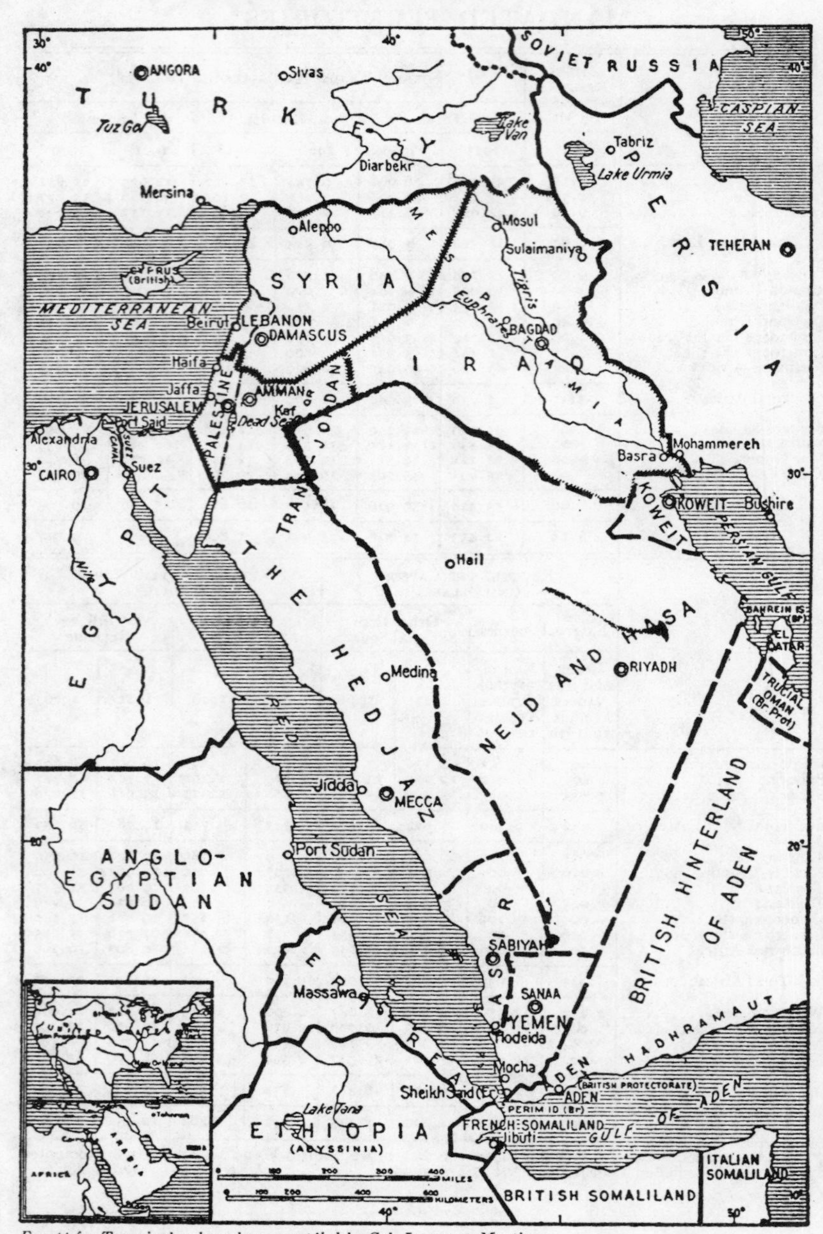

Except for Transjordan boundary, compiled by Col. Lawrence Martin

2. AFRICAN MANDATED TERRITORIES

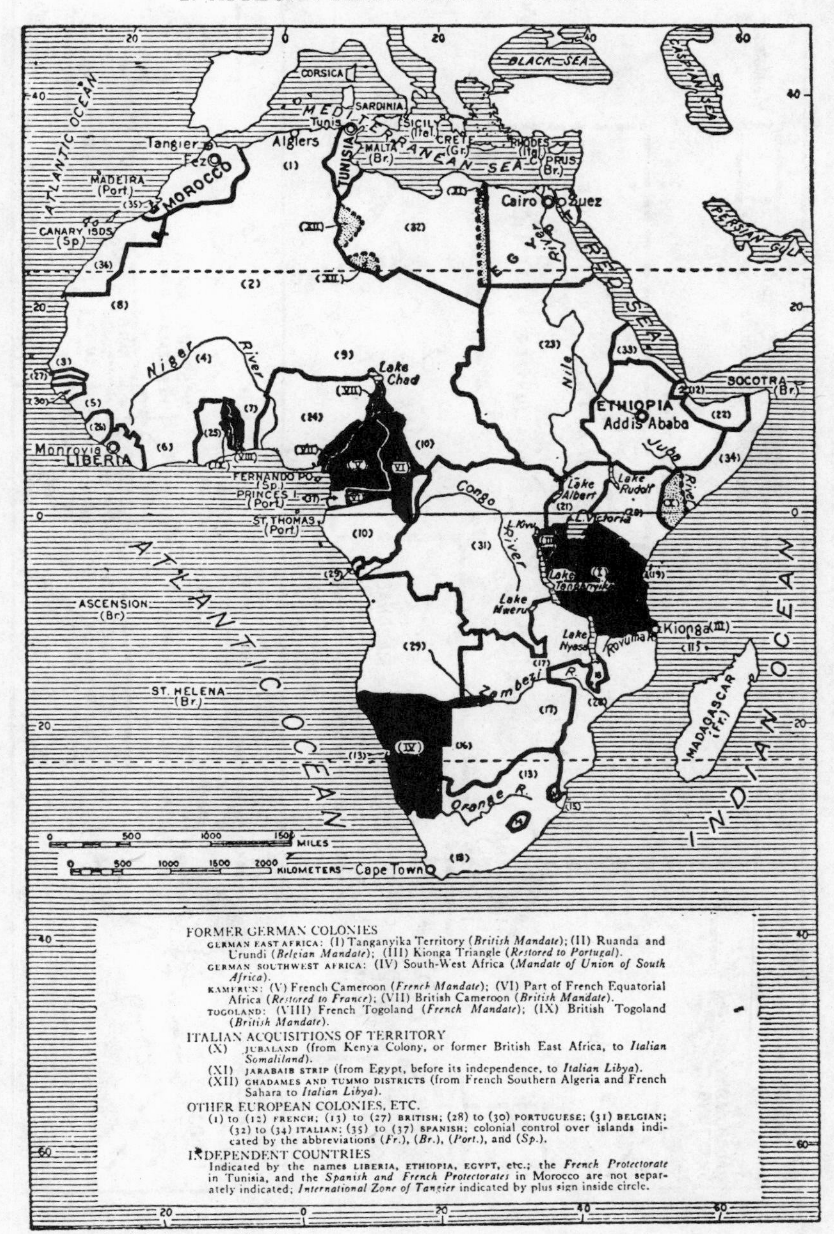

Compiled by Col. Lawrence Martin

3. PACIFIC MANDATED TERRITORIES

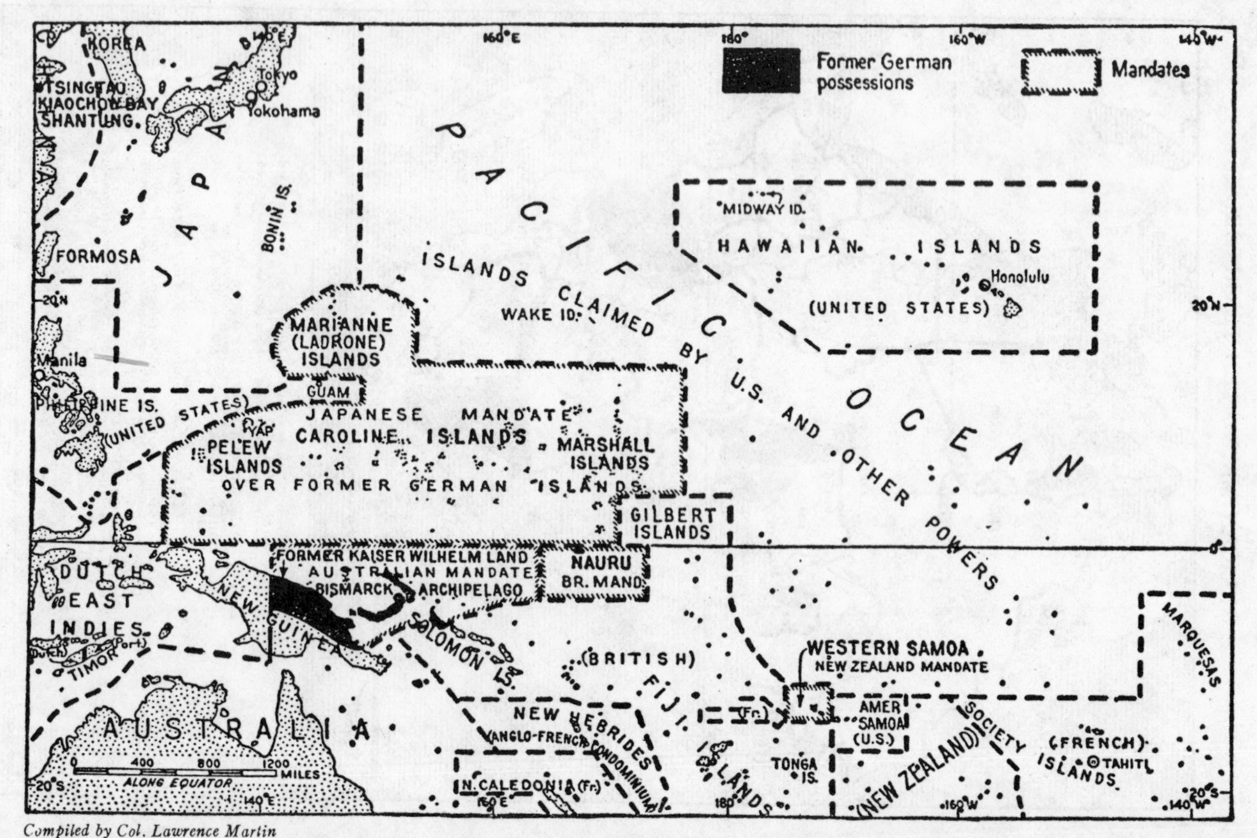

Compiled by Col. Lawrence Martin

BIBLIOGRAPHY

BIBLIOGRAPHY

I. OFFICIAL DOCUMENTS[1]

LEAGUE OF NATIONS

Treaty Series, 1920–28.

Official Journal, 1920–28. (Contains texts of the mandates at time of confirmation, resolutions of the Council, minutes of Council meetings after the fifteenth session, reports of the Permanent Mandates Commission, and observations of the mandatory powers on these reports.)

Minutes of the Council, sess. I–LIV. (Entitled *Procès verbal* for the first eleven sessions. Beginning with the sixteenth session in January, 1922, these have been published as numbers of the *Official Journal*.)

Records of the Assembly, sess. I–IX. (Contains record of debate in plenary sessions and committees. Beginning with the fourth session in 1923 the *Records* have been published as a special supplement to the *Official Journal*.)

Monthly Summary, 1921–29. (Contains a brief account of all League activities for each month and the resolutions of each Assembly.)

Permanent Mandates Commission, Minutes, sess. I–XVI.

Permanent Mandates Commission, Reports to the Council. (Published in the *Official Journal* and also in the *Permanent Mandates Commission, Minutes*, with exception of those for the first, second, and fourth sessions.)

Index to the Records of the Permanent Mandates Commission, sess. I–V and VI–X.

Annual Reports of the Mandatory Powers. (Only those submitted in 1925 have been reprinted as League documents.)

Responsibilities of the League Arising out of Article 22 (Mandates) Report of the Council to the Assembly, 1920. (Published also as an annex to the *Records of the First Assembly*.)

Statistical Information Concerning Territories under Mandate, 1928.

Information Section, The League of Nations, Mandates System (rev., 1927).

GREAT BRITAIN

Statutes at Large.

The Statutory Rules and Orders (rev.).

Parliamentary Debates. (The debates on mandate questions of both the British and Dominion parliaments have usually been reported in the *Journal of the Parliaments of the Empire*.)

Parliamentary Papers.

Correspondence between His Majesty's Government and the United States Ambassador Respecting Economic Rights in Mandated Territories, Cmd. 1226 (1921).

[1] Documents dealing with a particular mandated territory are classified separately.

Report of British Delegation to the Assembly, Cmd. 1807 (1923).
British and Foreign State Papers
Peace Handbooks. (Issued by the Historical Section of the Foreign Office, 1920.)

FRANCE

Journal officiel.
Bulletin des Lois.
Recueil general de jurisprudence, de doctrine et de legislation coloniales et maritime.
La tribune des colonies et des protectorats. (D. Penant, directeur)

UNITED STATES

DEPARTMENT OF STATE. *Treaty Series.* Includes the following treaties relating to mandated territories, No. 664 (Japanese mandated islands); No. 690 (French Cameroons); No. 691 (French Togoland); No. 695 (Syria and the Lebanon); No. 704 (Belgian East Africa); No. 728 (Palestine); No. 743 (British Cameroons); No. 744 (British East Africa); No. 745 (British Togoland).

TARIFF COMMISSION. *Colonial Tariff Policies* (1922).

CONGRESSIONAL DOCUMENTS. *Oil Concessions in Foreign Countries* (68th Cong., 1st sess.), *Senate Doc. 97* (1924). *Conditions of Peace with Germany* (66th Cong., 1st sess.), *Senate Doc. 149.*

GENERAL

BIBLIOTHÈQUE COLONIALE INTERNATIONALE. *Annuaire de documentation coloniale comparée Brussels, 1927.*

———. *La Société des Nations: Revue Mensuelle Documentaire*, Berne, 1918.

II. HISTORY AND ORIGIN OF THE MANDATES SYSTEM

ANONYMOUS. "Windows of Freedom," *Round Table*, IX (December, 1918). 21–35.

———. "Some Principles and Problems of the Settlement," *ibid.*, IX (December, 1918), 88–113.

———. "The Practical Organization of Peace," *ibid.*, IX (March, 1919), 217–48.

———. "America and World Responsibility: First and Second Thoughts," *ibid.*, IX (March, 1919), 249–60.

BAKER, PHILIP. *The Making of the Covenant from the British Point of View*, in Munch, *Les Origines et l'Œuvre de la Société des Nations* (Copenhagen, 1924), II, 55 ff.

BAKER, RAY STANNARD. *Woodrow Wilson and World Settlement.* 3 vols. New York, 1922.

BOWMAN, ISAIAH. *The New World.* New York, 1921.

EVANS, LUTHER H. "Some Legal and Historical Antecedents of the Mandatory System," *Southwestern Political Science Association, Proceedings* (fifth annual convention, March, 1924).

KRAUS, HERBERT, AND RODIGER, G. *Urkunden zum Friedensvertrage von Versailles.* 2 vols. Berlin, 1920–21.

MANABE, TOJI. "Dr. Ariga and the Mandates System," *Gaiko jiho* (*Revue diplomatique*, Japan), XL (1927), 107–21.

MARTIN LAWRENCE. "Maps Showing Territorial Changes since the World War," *International Conciliation* (October, 1925), No. 213.

———. *The Treaties of Peace, 1919–1923.* 2 vols. New York, 1924.

MEYER, LUDWIG. "Zur geschichtlichen Entwickelung des völkerrechtlichen Mandate Systems," *Völkerbundfragen*, 1927.

MILLER, DAVID HUNTER. *The Making of the League of Nations Covenant*, in E. M. House and Charles Seymour, *What Really Happened at Paris* (New York, 1920), pp. 398 ff.

———. "The Origin of the Mandates System," *Foreign Affairs*, January, 1928, pp. 277 ff.

———. *The Drafting of the Covenant.* 2 vols. New York, 1928.

———. *My Diary at the Conference of Paris.* 22 vols. New York, 1928.

POTTER, PITMAN B. "Origin of the System of Mandates under the League of Nations," *American Political Science Review*, XVI (November, 1922), 563 ff.

———. "Further Notes," *ibid.*, XX (November, 1926), 842 ff.

SCHNEE, HEINRICH. "Enstehung und Entwicklung des Mandatsystems," *Zeitschrift für Politik*, XIII (1924), 381–407.

SCHÜCKING, WALTHER. *Der Völkerbundsentwurf der Deutschen Regierung*, in Munch, *Les Origines et l'Œuvre de la Société des Nations* (Copenhagen, 1924), I, 156 ff.

SMUTS, JAN C. *The League of Nations: A Practical Suggestion.* London, 1918. (Reprinted in *New York Nation*, February 8, 1919; and Miller, *The Drafting of the Covenant.*)

TEMPERLEY, H. W. V. *A History of the Peace Conference of Paris.* 6 vols. London, 1920

III. JURISTIC ANALYSES OF THE MANDATES SYSTEM

BAKER, PHILIP J. NOEL. *The Present Juridical Status of the British Dominions in International Law.* London, 1929.

BATY, THOMAS. "Protectorates and Mandates," *B.Y.B.I.L.* (1921–22), pp. 116 ff.

BEMIS, S. F. (ed.). *The American Secretaries of State and Their Diplomacy*, Vol. X. New York, 1929.

BENTWICH, NORMAN. "The Jurisdiction of the International Court of Justice over Concessions in Mandate Territories," *L.Q.R.*, October, 1928, pp. 456–64.

BILESKI, MORITZ. "Kolonialpolitik unter internationaler Kontrolle, Die Arbeit der Mandatkommission des Völkerbundes," *Die Gesellschaft*, I (November, 1924), 169–78.

———. "Bemerkungen zur Mandatspolitik des Völkerbundes," *Zeitschrift für Politik*, XIII (1924), 408–11.

———. "Die Mandat des Völkerbundes," *Zeitschrift für Völkerrecht*, XII (1923), 65–85.

MANABE, TOJI. "Die Entwicklung des Mandatsystems," *ibid.*, XIII (1924), 77 ff.

BOURDARIE, PAUL. "La Question du mandat colonial," *Revue indigène*, 1919.

BRESCHI, B. *La Societe della Nazioni*. Florenz, 1920.

BRIERLY, J. L. *The Law of Nations, an Introduction to the International Law of Peace*. Oxford, 1928.

———. "Trusts and Mandates," *B.Y.B.I.L.*, (1929), pp. 217–19.

BUZA, LADISLAS. "Die rechtliche Natur des Mandates," *Z.O.R.*, 1927.

CANDACE, GRATIEN. "La Question des mandats coloniaux," *Colonies et Marine*, V (June, 1921), 327–37.

CIORCEANU, G. *Les Mandats internationaux*. Paris, 1921.

CORBETT, P. E. "What Is the League of Nations?" *B.Y.B.I.L.* (1924), pp. 127–36.

DICKINSON, E. D. *The Equality of States in International Law*. Cambridge, Mass., 1920.

DIENA, G. "Les Mandats internationaux en droit des gens," *Acad. D.I.*, V (1924), 263 ff.

DUCHÈNE, A. "Les Mandats Français," *Rapport à l'institut colonial International*, 1927, p. 390.

EVANS, LUTHER H. "Are 'C' Mandates Veiled Annexations?" *Southwestern Political and Social Science Quarterly*, VII (March, 1927), 381.

FAUCHILLE, P. *Traité de droit international public*. 4 vols. Paris, 1922–25.

FENWICK, C. G. *Wardship in International Law*. Washington, 1919.

———. *International Law*. New York, 1924.

FERRI, CARLO E. *La Teoria dei mandati internazionali*. Turin, 1927.

FLEICHER, A. A. *L'Analyse juridique du pacte de la Société des Nations*. Paris, 1922.

FLEISCHMANN. "Kolonialmandate," *M.D.G.V.*, 1925.

FRANCESCA, G. M. DE. *La Natura Giuridica dei mandati internazionali*. Pavia, 1926.

FURUKAKI, P. T. *Les Mandates internationaux de la société des Nations*. Lyon, 1923.

GOUDY, H. "Mandatory Government in the League of Nations," *Journ. C.L.* (3d ser.; October, 1919), I, 180 ff.

GSELL-TRUMPI, F. *Zur rechtlichen Natur des Völkerbundmandates*. Glarus, 1928.

HERSHEY, AMOS S. *The Essentials of International Public Law and Organization*. New York, 1927.

HIGGINS, A. P. In Hall's *International Law* (8th ed.). Oxford, 1924.

HOIJER. *Le Pacte de la Société des Nations*. Paris, 1926.

HYDE, C. C. *International Law, Chiefly as Interpreted and Applied by the United States*. 2 vols. Boston, 1922.

KEITH, A. BERRIEDALE. "Mandates," *Journ. C.L.*, IV (February, 1922), 71–83.

———. "The Mandatory System," *ibid.*, VII (November, 1925), 279–81.

LAMPIRE. "De la Nationalité des habitants des pays à mandat de la Société des Nations," *Journal de Droit international*, 1925, p. 54.

LANSING, ROBERT. *The Peace Negotiations, A Personal Narrative.* New York, 1921.
———. "Some Legal Question of the Peace Conference," *A.J.I.L.*, XIII (October, 1919), 640.
LARNAUDE. *La Société des Nations.* Paris, 1920.
LAUTERPACHT, H. *Private Law Sources and Analogies of International Law.* London, 1927.
LEE, D. CAMPBELL. "The Mandatory System," *United Empire*, XIII (February, 1922), 82–91.
———. *Mandates and How They Are Working* (Grotius Society, 1927), Vol. XII.
LEVESQUE, G. *La Situation internationale de Dantzig.* Paris, 1924.
LEWIS, MALCOLM M., "Mandated Territories, Their International Status," *L.Q.R.*, XXXIX (October, 1923), 458–75.
LINDLEY, M. F. *The Acquisition and Government of Backward Territory in International Law.* London, 1926.
MACNAIR, A. D. "Mandates," *Cambridge Law Journal*, III (1928), 149–61.
———. In Oppenheim's *International Law* (4th ed.). London, 1928.
MAKOWSKI, J. "La Situation juridique du territoire de la ville libre de Dantzig," *R.G.D.I.P.*, XXX (1923), 206.
MARGOLITH, AARON M. *The International Mandates* (manuscript thesis). Baltimore: Johns Hopkins University, 1929.
MATHEWS, E. L. "International Status of Mandatory of the League of Nations: High Treason against Mandatory Authority," *Journ. C.L.* (3d ser.; November, 1924), VI, 245–50.
MENDELSSOHN-BARTHOLDI, A. "Kolonialmandate," *M.D.G.V.*, VI (1925), 76.
MILLOT, ALBERT. *Les Mandats internationaux, étude sur l'application de l'article 22 du pacte de la Société des Nations.* Paris, 1924.
MONDAINI, GENNARO. *L'Assetto coloniale del Monda dapa la guerra.* 1921.
PIC, PAUL. "Le Régime du mandat d'après le traité de Versailles, son application dans le Proche Orient," *R.G.D.I.P.*, XXX (1923), 321–71.
POLLOCK, SIR FREDERICK. *The League of Nations.* London, 1920.
REDSLOB, ROBERT. "Le Système des mandats internationaux," *Bull. I.I.I.*, XV (October, 1926), 284 ff.
ROLIN, H. "La Pratique des mandats internationaux," *Acad. D.I.*, V (1927), 495–628.
ROLIN, HENRI. "Le Système des mandats coloniaux," *R.D.I.* (1920), I, 329–63.
ROUGIER, ANTOINE. "La Première Assemblée de la Société des Nations. Les Mandats," *R.G.D.I.P.*, XXVIII, 333–44.
RUTHERFORD, GEDDES W. "Spheres of Influence: An Aspect of Semi-sovereignty," *A.J.I.L.*, XX (April, 1926), 300–325.
SCELLE, GEORGES. "Le Problème juridique de la Société des Nations," *Revue politique et parlementaire*, December, 1919.
SCELLE, GEORGES. "La Société des Nations et l'Assemblée de Genève: La Question des mandats," *L'Action national*, XIV (February, 1921), 211–19.

SCHANZER, C. *Sulla Societa della Nazioni*. 1925.

SCHMITT, C. *Die Kernfrage des Völkerbundes* (Berlin, 1926), pp. 13 ff.

SCHÜCKING, W., AND WEHBERG, H. *Die Satzung des Völkerbundes* (Berlin, 1921; 2d ed., Berlin, 1924), pp. 688–703.

SCHNEIDER, W. *Das völkerrechtliche Mandat*. Stuttgart, 1926.

SEVMOGIEFF, HARALAMBI G. *De la Situation des états Mi-souverain au point de vue du droit international*. Paris, 1889.

SNOW, A.H. *The Question of Aborigines*. New York, 1921.

———. "The Mandatory System under the League of Nations," *Academy of Political Science, Proc.*, VIII, 428 ff.

SOLUS, H. *Traite de la condition les indigìnes en droit prine; colonies et pays de protectorat et pays sous Mandat*, Paris, 1927.

STOWELL, ELLERY C. *Intervention in International Law* (Washington, 1911), pp. 311–16.

STOYANOVSKY, J. *La Theorie générale des mandats internationaux*. Paris, 1925.

STRUPP, K. *Wörterbuch des Völkerrechts*, II (1925), 12 ff.

———. *Grundzüge des positiven Völkerrechts*. Bonn, 1922

VALLINI, A. *Il Mandati internazionale della Societa delle Nazioni*. Milan, 1923.

VAN KOL, H. "Les Mandats coloniaux et la Société des Nations," *Union interparlementaire, Comptes rendus* (1922, 1923), sess. XX, XXI.

VAN REES, D. F. W. *Les Mandats internationaux: I. Le Controle international de l'administration mandataire*. (Paris, 1927); *II. Les Principes généraux du régime des mandats* (Paris, 1928).

VERDROSS, A. *Die Verfassung der Völkerrechtgemeinschaft* (Wien, 1926), pp. 215 ff.

WEHBERG, HANS. "Die Pflichten der Mandatarmächte betreffend die Deutschen Schutzgebietsanleihen," *W.A.*, XXV (January, 1927), 136*–83*.

WILLOUGHBY, W. W., AND FENWICK, C. G. *Types of Restricted Sovereignty and of Colonial Autonomy*. Washington, 1919.

WILSON, G. G. *Handbook of International Law* (2d ed.; St. Paul, 1927), pp. 32 ff., 86 ff.

WINFIELD, PERCY H. In T. J. LAWRENCE, *The Principles of International Law* (7th ed.; New York, 1923), pp. 80 ff.

WOOLF, LEONARD. "Scope of the Mandate under the League of Nations," *I.L.A., Rep.*, Vol. XXIX (1920).

WRIGHT, QUINCY. "Sovereignty of the Mandates," *A.J.I.L.*, XVII (October, 1923), 691–703.

———. "Status of the Inhabitants of Mandated Territory," *ibid.*, XVIII (April, 1924), 306–15.

———. "Treaties Conferring Rights in Mandated Territories," *ibid.*, October, 1924, pp. 786–87.

———. "Some Recent Cases on the Status of Mandated Areas," *ibid.*, XX (October, 1926), 768–72.

IV. POLITICAL AND ADMINISTRATIVE ASPECTS OF THE MANDATES SYSTEM

a) BOOKS

ANDREWS, FANNY FERN. *The Mandatory System* (manuscript thesis, Harvard University). Brief summary printed March, 1923.

AULD, LEONA RUTH. *America and the Mandated Territories* (manuscript thesis, University of Chicago), 1927.

BORCHARD, E. M. "The Problem of Backward Areas and of Colonies," in Duggan, *The League of Nations* (New York, 1919), pp. 201–17.

BOURNE, RANDOLPH S. *Toward an Enduring Peace.* New York, 1916. (Includes articles by John A. Hobson, H. N. Brailsford, and Walter Lippmann on the problem of backward areas.).

BUELL, R. L. *International Relations* (New York, 1925; rev. ed., 1929), chap. xv.

BÜLOW, B. W. VON. *Der Versailler Völkerbund, eine vorläufige Bilanz* (Berlin, 1923), pp. 301–31.

BUXTON, NOEL, AND CONWICK-EVANS, T. P. *Oppressed Peoples and the League of Nations* (London, 1922), chap. iii.

ELLIS, C. HOWARD. *The Origin, Structure and Working of the League of Nations.* New York, 1928.

ERZBERGER, M. *The League of Nations, the Way of the World's Peace* (trans. Bernard Miall; New York, 1919), chap. xi.

FANSHAWE, MAURICE. *Reconstruction, Five Years' Work of the League of Nations.* London, 1925.

GORE, W. ORMSBY-. "Indirect International Supervision," *The League of Nations Starts* (London, 1920), chap. vii.

GOSTAGAR, JOAQUIN RODRIGUEZ DE. *Los Mandatos internacionales en politica colonial.* Valencia, 1928.

HARRIS, JOHN H. *Slavery or "Sacred Trust."* London, 1926.

HURST, SIR CECIL J. B., *et al. Great Britain and the Dominions*, "Harris Foundation Lectures." Chicago, 1928.

JENKINS, E. C. *The United States and the Policy of the Open Door in the Mandated Territories* (manuscript thesis, University of Chicago), 1928.

LEVERMORE, C. H. *League of Nations Year Book.* 1920, 1921, 1922, 1923.

MAANEN-HELMER, ELIZABETH VAN. *The Mandates System in Relation to Africa and the Pacific Islands.* London, 1929.

MARVIN, F. S. *Western Races and the World.* Oxford, 1922.

MOON, PARKER T. *Imperialism and World Politics.* New York, 1926.

OLIVIER, LORD (SIR SYDNEY). "Mandates under the League of Nations," in Marvin, *Western Races and the World* (1922), pp. 249–64.

———. *The League of Nations and Primitive Peoples.* London.

ORTS, PIERRE. *Le System des mandats de la Société des Nations.* Brussel, 1927.

PALACIOS, LEOPOLDO. *Los Mandatos internacionales de la Sociedad de Naciones.* Madrid, 1928.

RAPPARD, WILLIAM E. *International Relations Viewed from Geneva.* New Haven, 1925.

ROBERTS, STEPHEN H. *History of French Colonial Policy, (1870–1925)*, 2 vols., London, 1929. (Cameroons, I, 371–74; Syria, II, 591–602).

SCHNEE, HEINRICH. *Die deutschen Kolonien unter fremder Mandatherrschaft*, Leipzig, 1922. (Translated under the title *German Colonization, Past and Future.* London, 1926.

TOYNBEE, ARNOLD, J. *Survey of International Affairs* (Royal Institute of International Affairs). 3 vols. London, 1920–23, 1924, 1925.

———. *The World after the Peace Conference.* London, 1928.

WARD, MARGARET H. *The Sacred Trust* (manuscript thesis, The Brookings School). Washington, 1929.

WHITE, FREDA. *Mandates.* London, 1926.

WICKERSHAM, GEORGE W. "The Colonial Mandates," in *The Covenanter, an American Exposition of the Covenant of the League of Nations.* New York, 1919.

WORLD PEACE FOUNDATION. *Handbook of the League of Nations*, 1920–24.

———. *League of Nations, Year Book.* 1925, 1926, 1927, 1928, 1929.

b) ARTICLES AND PAMPHLETS

ADDAMS, JANE. "The Potential Advantages of the Mandate System," *Annals*, XCVI (July, 1921), 70–74.

ANDREWS, FANNY FERN. "American Rights and Interests in the Mandatory System," *ibid.*, pp. 95–97.

ANONYMOUS. "The Colonial Mandates," *Anti-Slavery Reporter*, XII (January, 1923), 123–26.

———. "The Mandate System," *Japan Chronicle*, January, 1923, pp. 38 ff., 502 ff.

BATSELL, W. R. "Summary of the Work of the First Session of the Permanent Mandates Commission," *International Conciliation* (October, 1925), No. 213.

———. "The United States and the System of Mandates," *Revue de droit international* (Geneva), II (September, 1924), 264 ff. (Reprinted *International Conciliation* [October, 1925], No. 213.)

BENOIST, JACQUES. "Un Nouveau Régime colonial," *Revue des Sciences politiques*, XL (1920), 721–35.

BRAILSFORD. "Mandates," *New Republic*, XXIII (July 21, 1920), 224 ff.

———, and MADARIAGA, SALVADOR DE. "Can the League Cope with Imperialism?" *F.P.A., Pamphlets*, February 4, 1928.

BUELL, R. L. "'Backward' Peoples under the Mandate System," *Current History*, XX (June, 1924), 386–95.

———. "Forced Labor; Its International Regulation," *F.P.A., Inf. Ser.*, V (January 8, 1930), No. 22.

BÜLOW, B. W. VON. "Völkerbundmandate," *Deutsche Nation*, II (November, 1920), 867–74.

CALDWELL, WILLIAM. *The International Labor Organization and Labor Problems in Mandated Territories* (Institute of Pacific Relations). Honolulu, 1927.

CONDLIFFE, J. B. "Dominions and Mandates," *News Bulletin* (Institute of Pacific Relations; October 16, 1926), pp. 14 ff.

FOREIGN POLICY ASSOCIATION. "Colonial vs. Mandate Administration," *Information Service*, March, 1926.

———. "Functions of the Permanent Mandates Commission," *ibid.*, April, 1927.

FRIIS, FINN T. B. "Mandates and Missions," *International Review of Missions*, October, 1929.

GIBBONS, H. A. "The Defects of the System of Mandates," *Annals*, XCVI (July, 1921), 84–90.

GILCHRIST, H. "The Mandates System," *Advocate of peace*, 1926, pp. 170 ff.

———. *Imperialism and the Mandates System* (League of Nations Non-partizan Association). New York, 1928.

GORE, W. ORMSBY-. "Article 22," *Covenant*, I (July, 1920), 480–90.

GUNZERT, M. "Die Kolonialmandate," *Germania*, June 25, 1925.

HANNIG, E. "Eine Ohrfeige für den Völkerbund; Das Fiasko der Kolonialmandate," *Deutsche Kolonialzeitung*, XXXIX (March, 1922), 11 ff.

HARRIS, J. H. "The League of Nations and the Tropics," *New Europe*, X (April, 1919), 269–75.

———. " 'Native' Races—Trusteeship or Possession," *League of Nations Journal*, I (March, 1920), 86 ff.

———. "The Colonial Office and Native Policy," *New Europe*, 1920.

———. "The Colonial Mandates—Dangers of Delay," *ibid.*, XVI (July, 1920), 33 ff.; *Today and Tomorrow*, III (July, 1920), 106 ff.

———. "A New Colonial Era, for Dependencies, 'Possession' or 'Trusteeship,' " *Contemporary Review*, 1920.

———. "The Challenge of the Mandates," *ibid.*, CXIX (April, 1921), 462–70.

———. "The Colonial Mandates," *ibid.*, CXXII (November, 1922), 604–11.

———. "The Mandates System after Five Years' Working," *ibid.*, February, 1925.

HOCKING, WILLIAM ERNEST. "The Working of the Mandates," *Yale Review*, XIX (Winter, 1930), 244–68.

HUDSON, M. O. "The League of Nations and the Protection of the Inhabitants of Transferred Territories," *Annals*, XCVI (July, 1921), 78–83.

HUGHES, CHARLES EVANS. "Recent Questions and Negotiations," *Foreign Affairs* (U.S.), II (December, 1923), 1–22.

INTERNATIONAL CONCILIATION. "Correspondence. United States and Great Britain on Economic Rights in Mandated Territories," *Pamphlet* (September, 1921), No. 166.

———. "Information Regarding the Mandates System" (Batsell) *Pamphlet* (October, 1925), No. 213.

LEAGUE OF NATIONS UNION. "Mandates in Africa," *Pub. No. 81*. London, 1922.

LEVY, ROGER. "Colonies or Mandates?" *L'Europe nouvelle*, IV (January, 1921), 83 ff.

LUGARD, LORD (SIR FREDERICK). "The Mandates System," *Edinburgh Review*, CCXXXVIII (October, 1923), 398–408.

———. "The Mandates Commission," *Quarterly Review*, Vol. CCXLII (1924).

———. "The Mandate System and the British Mandates," *Journ. R.S.A.*, LXXII (June 27, 1924), 535–50. (Translated, "Das Mandatesystem und die britischen Mandate," *Europäische Gespräche*, XXI [July, 1924], 316–41.)

———. "Mandate," *Encyclopedia Britannica*, 14th ed., XIV, 789.

MCDONALD, JAMES G. "Mandates: America's Opportunity," *Annals*, XCVI (July, 1921), 90–94.

MILLS, M. C. "The Mandatory System," *A.J.I.L.*, XVII (January, 1923), 50–62.

MYERS, DENYS P. "The Mandate System of the League of Nations," *Annals*, XCVI (July, 1921), 74–77.

OLIVIER, LORD (SIR SYDNEY). "The Geneva Assembly and the Question of Mandates," *Contemporary Review*, CXIX (January, 1921), 1–9.

RAPPARD, WILLIAM E. "The Practical Working of the Mandates System," *Journ. B.I.I.A.*, September, 1925, pp. 207 ff.

———. "Zur Sociologie des Mandatsystems," *Zeitschrift für Politik* (1928), No. 1.

RAYNAUD, B. "Les Travailleurs coloniaux et la Legislation internationale," *Revue économique internationale*, III (September, 1924), 285–302.

REGENDANZ. *British Policy in Mandated Colonies*. Berlin, 1929.

REMER, C. F. "The Mandatory System on Trial," *Millards Review*, XVI (March, 1921), 177 ff.

SCHNEE, HEINRICH. "Das Schicksal der deutschen Kolonien und die Weltwirtschaft," *Weltwirtschaft*, XII (January, 1922), 1–4.

SIGER, CARL. "Les Colonies et la Société des Nations," *Mercure de France*, CXLVIII (June, 1921), 776–82.

SNOW, ALPHEUS H. "On Mandatories," *The Nation*. New York, October 18, 1919.

WRIGHT, QUINCY. "The Mandates System and Public Opinion," *Southwestern Political and Social Science Quarterly*, IX (March, 1929), 369–406.

———. "The United States and the Mandates," *Michigan Law Review*, XXIII (May, 1925), 717–47.

V. NEAR EASTERN MANDATED TERRITORIES

1. GENERAL

a) BOOKS

ABI-CHAHLA, H. *L'Extinction des capitulations en Turquie et dans les regions arabes*. Paris, 1924.

AYOUB, CHARLES. *Les Mandats orientaux*. Paris, 1924.

BELL, H. T. MONTAGUE. *The Near East Yearbook*. Chicago, 1927.

CHIROL, SIR VALENTINE. *The Occident and the Orient*, "Harris Foundation Lectures." Chicago, 1924.

HARRIS, N.D. *Europe and the East.* New York, 1926.

JUNG, EUGÈNE. *La Révolte arabe* (2 vols.) Paris, 1925.

KAMPFFMEYER, GEORG. *Damaskus Documents zum Kampfe der Araber um ihre Unabhängigkeit.* Berlin, 1926.

KOHN, HANS. *Geschichte der nationalen Bewegung im Orient.* Berlin, 1928.

LAURENT-VIBERT, R. *Ce Que j'ai vu en Orient; Mesopotamie, Palestine, Syrie, Egypte, Turquie, Notes de Voyage, 1923–24.* Paris, 1924.

LODER, J. DE V. *The Truth about Mesopotamia, Palestine and Syria.* London, 1923.

LOTI, PIERRE. *La Mort de notre chère France en Orient.* Paris, 1920.

LUQUET, J. *La Politique des mandats dans le Levant.* Paris, 1924.

LYAUTEY, P. *Le Drame oriental et le rôle de la France.* Paris, 1923.

MENASSA, GABRIEL. *Les Mandats A et leur application en Orient*, Paris, 1924.

MILLER, W. *The Ottoman Empire and Its Successors, 1800–1922.* Cambridge University Press, 1923.

PERNAT, MAURICE. *La Question d'Orient.* Paris.

PIC, PAUL. *Syrie et Palestine, Mandats française et anglaise dans le Proche-Orient.* Paris, 1924.

POWELL, E. A. *The Struggle for Power in Moslem Asia.* New York, 1924.

TOYNBEE, A. J. "The Islamic World since the Peace Settlement," *Survey of International Affairs* (1925), Part I. London, 1927.

b) ARTICLES AND PAMPHLETS

BENTWICH, NORMAN. "Mandated Territories, Palestine and Mesopotamia," *B.Y.B.I.L.* (1921–22). "Nationality in Mandated Territories Detached from Turkey," *ibid.*, 1926, pp. 97–109.

BERNARD, AUGUSTIN. "Les Populations de la Syrie et de la Palestine d'après les derniers recensements," *Annales de géographie*, XXXIII (January, 1924), 73–79.

BILESKI, MORITZ. "Syrien und Palästina seit Kriegsausgang," *Zeitschrift für Politik*, XVI (1926), 161–70.

EARLE, E. M. "The Turkish Petroleum Company, a Study in Oleaginous Diplomacy," *P.S.Q.*, June, 1924.

———. *Problems of the Near East* (Bibliography). New York, 1924.

FOREIGN POLICY ASSOCIATION. *Survey of Political Trends in the Near East*, 1926 (*Information Service*, March, 1927); 1927 (*ibid.*, March, 1928); 1928 (*ibid.*, May, 1929).

FROIDEVAUX, HENRI. "Les Assyro-Chaldéens et la France," *L'Asie française*, CLXXX (March, 1928), 70–79.

GOADBY, F. M. "Syrians and Palestinians in Egypt," *Journ. C.L.*, VII (February, 1926), 144–45.

KAMPFFMEYER, GEORG. "Urkunden und Berichte zur Gegenwartsgeschichte des arabischen Orients," *Mitteilungen des Seminars für orientalische Sprächen an der Friederich-Wilhelms Universität zu Berlin*, XXVI-XXVII (1924), II, 83–136; XXIX (1926), II, 207–13.

KHAIRALLAH, K. T. "Le Problème du Levant: Les Regions Arabes Liverées, Syrie—Irak—Liban," *Lettre ouverte à la Société des Nations*. Paris, 1919.

KING-CRANE. "Report on the Near East" (American Section, Interallied Commission on Mandates in Turkey), *Editor and Publisher*, LV, No. 27 (December 2, 1922), pp. 1–28.

LYBYER, ALBERT H. "Monthly Review of Current Events in the Near East," *Current History*.

MACCALLUM, ELIZABETH P. "The Near East, a Survey of Political Trends in 1925," *F.P.A., Pamphlets*, 1926.

——— and EARL, E. M. "Trusteeship or Exploitation? An Appraisal of European Stewardship in the New Eastern Mandates," *Asia*, September, 1926.

MASSIGNON, LOUIS. "Le Sort du Proche Orient et le Rôle de la France en Syrie," *L'Europe nouvelle*, XIV (May, 1920), 548–51.

NEWELL, FREDERICK H. *Asiatic Turkey, Its Problems and Resources*, "University of Illinois Bulletins," XVI (March 10, 1919), No. 28.

PHILIPPS, NORMAN. "Iraq, Syria and Palestine," *Near East and India*, XXI (May, 1922), 628–29.

PIC, PAUL. "L'Evolution politique et économique du Proche Orient (Syrie et Palestine) sous le régime des mandats français et anglais," *Revue économique internationale*, IV (October, 1923), 21–50.

TAIRA. "Mandates in the Middle East," *Balkan Review*, IV (January, 1921), 431–38.

TOYNBEE, ARNOLD J. "San Remo and Turkey," *New Europe*, XV (May, 1920), 73–75.

———. "The League in the East," *League of Nations Union, Pamphlets*, London, 1920.

URINOWSKI, WILLIAM. "The Arabs and the Mandates," *Eastern Europe*, V (July, 1921), 298–301.

WORTHAM, H. F. "Europe vs. Asia, a Chapter on Mandates," *Atlantic Monthly*, CXXXI (April, 1923), 556–64.

2. PROPOSED MANDATES

ALBANIA

DURHAM, M. E. "Albania's Fate in the Balance," *New Europe*, XIV (March, 1920), 169–72.

ARMENIA

ADABASHIAN, M. A. "The Armenian Question," *Balkan Review*, III (April, 1920), 216–25.

BLYTH, ESTELLE. "Australia and the Mandate for Armenia," *Near East*, XVII (June, 1920), 903.

BROWN, P. M. "The Mandate over Armenia," *A.J.I.L.*, XIV (1920), 396–99.
HARBORD, MAJOR GENERAL JAMES G. "Report of the American Military Missions to Armenia." *U.S. Senate 66th Cong. 2d Sess. Doc. 266*, Washington, 1920. Reprinted in *International Conciliation* (June, 1920), No. 151.
HECK, LEWIS. "New Avenues of Trade in the Near East," *Asia*, XX, 625–40.
MANDELSTAM, ANDRÉ. "La Société des Nations et les Puissances devant le problème Armenien," *R.G.D.I.P.*, XXIX (1922–23), 301–84, 515–46; XXX, 414–506.
TEHOBARNIAN, ARCHAY. "Armenie," *Revue de Genève*, 1922, pp. 479–94.
TONAPETIAN, P. "Armenia in the Wheel of British Policy," *New Europe*, XIII (January, 1920), 370–73.

ARABIA

HARRISON, P. W. *The Arabs at Home.* 1924.
JACOB, H. F. *The Kings of Arabia: the Rise and Fall of the Turkish Sovereignty in the Arabian Peninsula.* London, 1923.
LAWRENCE, T. E. *Revolt in the Desert.* New York, 1927.
PHILBY, ST. J. B. *The Heart of Arabia.* London, 1922.
———. *Arabia of the Wahabis.* London, 1928.
RIHANY, A. M. *Wise Men from the East and West.* Boston, 1922.
———. *Makers of Modern Arabia.* Boston, 1927.

3. IRAQ

a) OFFICIAL DOCUMENTS

LEAGUE OF NATIONS

Question of the Frontier between Turkey and Iraq (report submitted to the Council by the Commission instituted by the Council resolution of September 30, 1924), Geneva, 1925.

GREAT BRITAIN

Review of the Civil Administration of the Occupied Territories of Al'Iraq, 1914–1918, Bagdad, 1918.
"Review of the Civil Administration of Mesopotamia, 1917–1920" (prepared by Miss Gertrude L. Bell, C.B.E.), *Parl. Pap.*, Cmd. 1061 (1920).
Report on Iraq Administration, 1920–22. *Ibid.*, 1922–23.
Report by His Britannic Majesty on the Administration of Iraq, 1923–24.
Report by His Britannic Majesty's Government to the Council of the League of Nations on the Administration of Iraq for the Year 1925. Ibid., 1926, 1927.
"Iraq. Papers Relating to the Application to Iraq of the Principles of Article 22 of the Covenant of the League of Nations," *Parl. Pap.*, Cmd. 2317 (1925).

IRAQ

Index of the Laws Regulation, Proclamations, etc., Relating to Iraq (issued between October 31, 1914, and December 31, 1926; compiled by C. A. Hooper). Bagdad, 1928.

b) BOOKS

BELL, LADY FLORENCE. *The Letters of Gertrude Bell.* New York, 1927.

BEVAN, E. *The Land of Two Rivers.* London, 1921.

COKE, RICHARD. *The Heart of the Middle East.* London, 1925.

GONTAUT-BIRON, R. DE. *La France et la Question de Moussoul.* Paris, 1923.

HESSE, FRITZ. *Die Mosul Frage.* Berlin, 1925.

HEWETT, SIR JOHN P. *Report for the Army Council on Mesopotamia.* London, 1919.

HOOPER, C. A. *The Constitutional Law of Iraq.* Bagdad, 1928.

———. *L'Iraq et la Société des Nations.* Paris, 1928.

LONGRIGG, STEPHEN. *Four Centuries of Modern Iraq.* Oxford, 1925.

LUKE, H. C. *Mosul and Its Minorities.* 1925.

LYELL, T. *The Ins and Outs of Mesopotamia.* London, 1922.

NEWMAN, MAJOR E. W. POLSON. *The Middle East,* London, 1926.

PHILLIPS, SIR PERCIVAL. *Mesopotamia, Daily Mail Inquiry, at Bagdad.*

STEVENS, E. S. *By Tigris and Euphrates.* London, 1923.

c) ARTICLES

ANONYMOUS. "Great Britain and the Iraq: an Experiment in Anglo-Asiatic Relations," *Round Table,* December, 1923, pp. 64–83.

———. "Current Affairs in Iraq." *Journal of the Central Asian Society,* X (1923), 139–48.

———. "The Iraq Dispute," *Foreign Affairs* (U.S.), III (1925), 687 ff.

———. "The Iraq Recommendations," *ibid.,* IV (1926), 160.

BUCHANAN, GEORGE. "Why Do We Remain in Mesopotamia?" *Nineteenth Century,* XCIII (May, 1923), 764–66.

CHURCHILL, WINSTON. "Great Britain and the Middle East," *Near East,* XIX (June, 1921), 743–47.

———. "Mesopotamia and the New Government," *Empire Review,* XXXVIII (July, 1923), 691–98.

FOREIGN POLICY ASSOCIATION. "The Turco-Iraq Boundary Dispute," *Information Service,* November 5, 1925.

———. "British Interests in Mesopotamia," *ibid.,* November 17, 1925.

———. "American Oil Interests in Mesopotamia," *ibid.,* May 22, 1926.

GORE, W. ORMSBY-. "Great Britain, Mesopotamia and the Arabs," *Nineteenth Century,* August, 1920, pp. 225–38.

LEE, D. CAMPBELL. *The Mandate for Mesopotamia and the Principle of Trusteeship in English Law.* London, 1921.

MACHRAY, ROBERT. "Mesopotamia and Persia," *Fortnightly Review,* CIX (October, 1920), 609–20.

———. "Iraq and Other Arab Problems," *ibid.,* CXII (December, 1922), 881–91.

MILLOT, ALBERT. "Le Mandat anglais pour l'Irak," *R.G.D.I.P.,* XXXII (1925), 79.

PRICE, CLAIR. "Britain's White Elephant in Mesopotamia," *Current History*, XVII (April, 1923), 40–43.

ROBERTS, CHARLES. "Withdrawal from Iraq," *Contemporary Review*, CXXII (April, 1923), 409–15.

WRIGHT, QUINCY. "The Government of Iraq," *A.P.S.R.*, XX (November, 1926), 743–69.

———. "The Mosul Dispute," *A.J.I.L.*, XX (July, 1926), 453–64.

4. PALESTINE AND TRANSJORDAN

a) OFFICIAL DOCUMENTS

GREAT BRITAIN

An Interim Report on the Civil Administration of Palestine during the Period 1st July, 1920—30th June, 1921. London, 1921.

Report on Palestine Administration, July, 1920—December, 1921. *Ibid.*, 1922.

Report by His Britannic Majesty's Government on the Palestine Administration, 1923.

Report by His Britannic Majesty's Government on the Administration under Mandate of Palestine and Transjordan for the Year 1924.

Report by His Britannic Majesty's Government to the Council of the League of Nations on the Administration of Palestine and Transjordan for the Year 1925. *Ibid.*, 1926, 1927.

Report of theHigh Commissioner on the Administration of Palestine, 1920–25.

"Palestine Disturbances, May, 1921" (reports of the Commission of Inquiry with correspondence relating thereto), *Parl. Pap.*, Cmd. 1540 (1921).

"Correspondence with the Palestine Arab Delegation and the Zionist Organization," *ibid.*, Cmd. 1700 (1922).

"Mandate for Palestine" (letter from the Secretary of the Cabinet to the Secretary-General of the League of Nations of July 1, 1922, inclosing a note in reply to Cardinal Gasparri's letter of May 15, 1922, addressed to the Secretary-General of the League of Nations), *ibid.*, Cmd. 1708 (1922).

"Papers Relating to the Election for the Palestine Legislative Council, 1923," *ibid.*, Cmd. 1889 (1923).

"Palestine; Proposed Formation of an Arab Agency; Correspondence with the High Commissioner for Palestine," *ibid.*, Cmd. 1989 (1923).

"Palestine and East Africa Loans, Memorandum Explaining Financial Resolutions," *ibid.*, Cmd. 2696 (1926).

GOVERNMENT OF PALESTINE

Legislation of Palestine, 1918–1925 (compiled by N. Bentwich, attorney-general of Palestine). 2 vols. Alexandria, 1926.

UNITED STATES

Mandate for Palestine. Department of State, 1927.

b) BOOKS

ASHBEE, C. R. *A Palestine Notebook, 1918–1923.* London, 1923.

BATAULT, GEORGES. *Le Problème juif.*

BENTWICH, NORMAN. *Palestine of the Jews, Past, Present and Future.* London, 1919.

CONWAY, W. M. *Palestine and Morocco.* London, 1923.

ERSKINE, MRS. STEWART. *Transjordan.* London.

GOADBY, F. M. *International and Inter-religious Private Law in Palestine.* Jerusalem, 1926.

GRAVES, PHILIP. *Palestine, the Land of Three Faiths.* London, 1923.

HOLDHEIM, GERHARD. *Palästina: Idée, Problème, Tatsachen.* Berlin, 1928.

HOROWITZ, P. *The Jewish Question and Zionism.* London, 1927.

HYAMSON, ALBERT N. *Palestine, the Rebirth of an Ancient People.* New York, 1917.

JOINT PALESTINE SURVEY COMMISSION. *Reports of the Experts.* Boston, 1928.

KAHBAH, H. I. *The Case against Zionism* (Palestine National League). New York.

LAMBELIN, ROGER. *Le Peril juif; l'impérialisme d'Israel.* Paris, 1924.

LOEB, SOPHIE IRENE. *Palestine Awake, the Rebirth of a Nation.* New York, 1926.

MCCRACKEN, W. D. *The New Palestine.* New York, 1922.

MASSEY, W. T. *How Jerusalem Was Won.* London, 1919.

MIGNOT, PIERRE. *Le Problème juif et le principle des nationalités.* Paris, 1923.

PREISS, LUDWIG, AND ROHRBACH, PAUL. *Palestine and Transjordan.* London, 1926.

SIDEBOTHAM, H. *England and Palestine, Essays toward the Restoration of the Jewish State.* London, 1918.

SIMON, L., AND STEIN, L. *Awakening Palestine.* London, 1923.

SOKOLOW, NAHUM. *History of Zionism, 1600–1918.* (Introductions by A. J. Balfour and Stephen Pichon.) 2 vols. London, 1919.

SPIEGEL, MANKA. *Das völkerrechtliche Mandat und seine Anwendung auf Palästina.* Wien, 1928.

STEIN, LEONARD. *Zionism.* London.

STOYANOVSKY, J. *The Mandate for Palestine, a Contribution to the Theory and Practice of International Mandates.* London, 1928.

WEDGEWOOD, J. *The Seventh Dominion.*

WEISL, WOLFGANG. *Der Kampf um das Heilige Land.* Berlin, 1925.

WORSFOLD, W. BASIL. *Palestine of the Mandate.* London, 1925.

c) ARTICLES

AGRONSKY, G. "Lights and Shadows in Palestine Today," *Current History,* XXI (October, 1924), 75–80.

———. "Troubles of the Zionists in Palestine," *ibid.,* XV (October, 1921), 106 ff.

APPEL, DR. ALFRED. "Das Pälestina-Mandat," *M.D.G.V.*, June 7, 1924, pp. 81–88.

BENSUSAN, S. L. "The Position in Palestine," *Review of Reviews* (British), LX (April, 1923), 397–402.

BENTWICH, NORMAN. "Review of Palestine Legislation, 1920–1925," *Journ. C.L.*, Vols. IV–IX.

———. "The Legislation of Palestine, 1918–1925," *ibid.*, VIII, 9–20.

———. "The Application of Jewish Law in Palestine," *ibid.*, IX, 59–67.

———. "The Legal Administration of Palestine under the British Military Occupation," *B.Y.B.I.L.* (1920–21), pp. 139–48.

———. "The Mandate for Palestine," *B.Y.B.I.L.* (1929), pp. 137–43. "The Mandate for Transjordan," *ibid.*, pp. 212–13.

———. "Judicial Interpretation of the Mandate for Palestine," *Zeitschrift für Auslandisches Öffentliches Recht und Völkerrecht*, 1929.

———, AND GOADBY, F. M. "The Antiquities Law of Palestine," *Journ. C.L.*, VI (November, 1924), 251–59.

"DURBIN." "The Transjordan Mandate," *English Review*, July, 1929, pp. 77–81.

GIANNINI, AMEDEDO. "Il Mandati inglese sulla Palestina," *Problemi italiani*, I (1922), 161–82; *Vita internazionale*, XXV (1922), 285–92.

GOADBY, F. M. "The Present Situation with Regard to the Privileges of Foreigners in the Near East," *Journ. C.L.*, VI (November, 1924), 258–71.

GONTAUT-BIRON, P. DE. "France et Palestine," *Correspondent*, CCXCII (July, 25, 1923), 201–23.

HYMAN, COLEMAN, P. "The Mandate and the High Commissioner," *Jewish Chronicle*, October, 1920, pp. 28 ff.

KAPLANSKY, S. "Jews and Arabs in Palestine," *Socialist Review*, XIV (March, 1922), 160–66.

KOHN, HANS. "Die staats und verfassungsrechtliche Entwicklung des Emirate Transjordania," *Archiv für öffentliche Rechte*, April, 1929.

KUHN, A. K. "The Mavromatis Case on Readaptation of the Jerusalem Concession," *A.J.I.L.*, XXII (April, 1928), 383–85.

LUSHY, JACOB. "The New Constitution of the Palestine Jews," *Foreign Affairs* (U.S.), April, 1928, pp. 505 ff.

PRITCHETT, HENRY S. "Observations in Egypt, Palestine, and Greece," *International Conciliation*, December, 1926, No. 225.

SALAMAN, R. N. "The Prospects of Jewish Colonization in Palestine, *Contemporary Review*, May, 1920, pp. 663–72.

SAMUEL, HORACE B. "The Palestinian Problem," *Fortnightly Review*, September, 1920, pp. 402–11.

SHEPSTONE, H. J. "Who Shall Hold the Holy Land? The Question of the Arab and Jew in Palestine," *Review of Reviews* (British), LXVI (July, 1922), 65–73.

Snowden, Ethel. "Palestine under the Mandate," *Empire Review*, XXXI (April, 1924), 392–403.

Stein, Leonard. "The Future of Palestine," *Today and Tomorrow*, III (December, 1920), 351–55.

———. "The Truth about Palestine, a Reply to the Palestine Arab Delegation," *Zionist Organization*, London, 1922.

———. "The Jews in Palestine," *Foreign Affairs*, Vol. IV (March, 1926).

Sydenham of Combs, Lord. "Palestine and the Mandate," *Nineteenth Century*, LXXXIX, 617–29.

Tute, Mr. Justice. "The Law of State Lands in Palestine," *Journ. C.L.*, IX (November, 1927), 165–82.

Wright, Quincy. "The Palestine Problem," *P.S.Q.*, XLI (September, 1926), 381–412.

Xenephon (pseud.). "Transjordan's National Status," *Current History*, XX (July, 1924), 624 ff.

Zangwill, Israel. "Palestine Irridenta," *Jewish Chronicle*, XXIX (November, 18, 1920), 18–21.

Zionist Organization. *The Mandate for Palestine* (memorandum submitted to the Council of the League of Nations, 1922). *Ibid.*, 1923, 1924, 1925, 1926.

5. Syria and the Lebanon

a) official documents

france

Rapport sur la Situation de la Syrie et du Liban, 1922–23.

Rapport provisoire à la Société des Nations sur la situation de la Syrie et du Liban, 1925.

Rapport définitif à la Société des Nations sur la situation de la Syrie et du Liban, 1925.

Rapport à la Société des Nations sur la situation de la Syrie et du Liban, 1926. *Ibid.*, 1927.

Rapport d'Enquête de M. le Conseiller Daclin, magistrat chargé de mission sur les faits d'ordre politique et administratif denoncés à la Société des Nations (manuscript), 1926.

Rapport d'Enquête du Colonel Raynal en retraite chargé de mission sur les faits denoncés à Société des Nations (très parties, manuscript), 1926.

Accusations portées contre le Commandement français, Rapport du General Gamelin, Commandant supérieur des troups du Levant (manuscript), 1926.

Les Crimes commis par les insurgés, redigé par les Bureaux du Haut Commissariat (manuscript), 1926.

haut commissariat de syrie et du liban

Recueil des Actes administrative du Haut Commissariat (5 fascicules, Imprimerie Jean D'Arc). Beyrouth.

La Syrie et le Liban en 1921. Ibid., 1922.

Bulletin économique mensuel (*trimestriel* since 1927) *des pays sous mandat français*. Beyrouth.

UNITED STATES

DEPARTMENT OF COMMERCE. *Syria*, by T. R. Flack. (Supplement to "Commerce Reports," *Trade and Economic Review for 1922*, No. 6.)

b) BOOKS

ABOUSSOUAN, BENOIT. *Le Problème politique syrien*. Paris, 1924.

ALTIAR. *Le Problème Cilicia et l'avenir de la France au Levant*. Paris, 1921.

ANONYMOUS. *La Verité sur la question syrienne*. Stamboul, 1916.

BELL, GERTRUDE. *Syria*. London, 1919.

BOURBON, PRINCE SIXTE DE. *La Syrie et la France*. Paris, 1919.

BURCKHARD, CHARLES. *Le Mandat français en Syrie et au Liban*. Paris, 1925.

CHERIF, IHSSAN EL. *Les Conditions internationals de la Syrie: Analyse juridique du mandat syrien*. Paris, 1922.

———. *Le Mandat en Syrie*. Paris.

DAVID, PHILIP. *Le Congrès Syrien; Un gouvernement arab en Damas*.

FERIET, RENÉ DE. *L'Application d'un mandat, la France, puissance mandataire en Syrie et au Liban*. Paris, 1926.

GONTAUT-BIRON, COMTE R. DE. *Comment la France s'est installée en Syrie, 1918–1919*. Paris, 1923.

———. *Sur les Routes de Syrie après neuf ans de mandat*. Paris, 1928.

JOFFRE, ALPHONSE. *Le Mandat de la France sur la Syrie et le Grand Liban*. Lyon, 1924.

KERILLIS, HENRI DE. *Syrie*. (Articles originally published in *Echo de Paris*, September 28–October 6, 1925.)

LAMMENS, H. *La Syrie, Précis historique*. 2 vols. Beyrouth, 1921.

LUQUET, JEAN. *Le Mandat A et l'organisation du mandat française en Syria*. Paris, 1923.

MACCALLUM, ELIZABETH, P. *The Nationalist Crusade in Syria*. New York, 1928.

MOUTRAN, NADRA. *La Syrie de Demain*. Paris, 1916.

RABBATH E. *L'Evolution politique de la Syrie sous Mandat*. Paris, 1928.

SAMNÉ, GEORGES. *La Question syrienne: exposé—solution—statut politique*. Paris, 1918.

———. *La Syrie*. Paris, 1923.

SFER, PASHA ABDULLAH. *Le Mandat français et les Traditions françaises en Syrie et au Liban*. Paris, 1922.

STEIN, LEONARD. *Syria*. London, 1926.

TABET, J. J. *La Syrie*. Paris, 1920.

WETTERLE, ABBÉ E. *En Syrie avec le Général Gouraud*, Paris, 1924.

c) ARTICLES AND PAMPHLETS

ANONYMOUS. "French Policy in Syria," *European Economic and Political Survey*, August 15, 1927.

———. *Memorandum de protestation presenté par les habitants des territoires annexés illégalement au Sandjak du Mont Liban.* No date.

———. *La France en Syrie et au Liban. Le Mandat devant les Faits.* Paris, 1921.

———. *Ce qui tout Français doit savoir de la Syrie et du Liban.* Paris, 1922.

ARSLAN, EMIR CHEKIB, AND SHABHENDER, A. "Syrian Opposition to French Rule," *Current History*, XX (May, 1924), 239–48.

ASSOCIATION DE LA JEUNESSE SYRIENNE. *Ce qui tout Français doit savoir de la Syrie.* Paris, May, 1922.

BITAS, M. Y. "Gouraud en France," *Correspondance d'Orient*, XV (January, 1922), 16–29.

BOURBON, COMTE SIXTE DE. "La France et la Syrie," *Correspondent*, February 10, 1922, pp. 389–408.

BOWMAN, ISAIAH. "The Syrian Mandate," *Foreign Affairs* (U.S.), I (December, 1922), 161.

CAIX, ROBERT DE. "L'Organisation de la Syrie et du Liban et le mandat français," *L'Europe nouvelle*, September, 1924, pp. 1205 ff.

CATROUX, LIEUT. ÇOL. "Le Mandat français en Syrie, son application à l'état de Damas," *Revue politique et parlementaire*, February 10, 1922, pp. 199–227.

CATTAN, SELIM. "La Costituente siriana," *Rassegna italiana*, October, 1928; January, 1929.

CAYLA, M. "Le Mandat français dans la region d'Alexandrette et dans l'état des Alaouites," *Bulletin de l'Union économique de Syrie*, II (September 30, 1923), 144–54.

CLERGET, P. "La Syrie sous le mandat français," *Revue économique internationale.* Paris, 1923,

DENON, J. "La Question foncière en Syrie et au Liban," *Asie française*, XXIII (February, 1923), 22 ff.

———. "L'Organisation de la fédération des états de Syrie et du Grand Liban sous le mandat français," *Revue des Sciences politiques*, XLVII (July–September, 1924), 345–73.

DUGGAN, STEPHEN. "The Syrian Question," *Journal of International Relations*, April, 1921.

———. "Syria and Its Tangled Problems," *Current History*, February, 1921.

EARLE, E. M. "Syria, Acid Test of the Mandates System," *The Nation* (N.Y.), January 13, 1926.

FLEMING, JACKSON. "Syrian Self-Determination," *Asia*, November, 1919.

FROIDEVAUX, HENRI. "L'Indépendance du Grand Liban," *L'Asie française*, XX (October, 1920), 298 ff.

GHEERBRANDT, J. L. "Syria and the Lebanon," *Asiatic Review*, July, 1927.

GOURAUD, GEN. "La France en Syrie," *Revue de France*, April 1, 1922.

HOGARTH, D. G. "The Burden of Syria," *Nineteenth Century*, February, 1920.

JOHNSON, A. E. "Thumbs Down for Syria," *New Republic*, January 19, 1927, pp. 243 ff.

LICHTENBERGER, ANDRÉ. "La Syrie et Nous," *Opinion*, XV (July, 1922), 773.

McCALLUM, D. "The French in Syria, 1919–1924," *Journ. Central Asian Society*, Part I (1925), pp. 3–25.

———. "The New Land Route to the East," *ibid.*, pp. 44–67.

MURET, MAURICE, "La France en Syrie; la politique du mandat," *Revue de Genève*, July, 1922, pp. 113–25.

POLYZOIDES, A. TH. "Syria's Revolt against France," *Current History*, XVI (July, 1922), 580 ff.

RONDET-SAINT, MAURICE. "L'Etat d'esprit des populations musulmanes de Syrie à l'égard de la France et de sa politique," *Parlement et l'Opinion*, XIII (January, 1923), 171–80.

———. "La France en Syrie," *ibid.*, XII (November, 1922), 2142–63.

RYAN, A. "The Syrian Rebellion," *Contemporary Review*, February, 1926.

SAMNÉ, DR. GEORGES. "La Fédération syrienne et le mandat français," *Correspondance d'Orient*, XV (August, 1922), 449–55.

———. "L'Unité syrienne," *ibid.*, August, 1924, pp. 458 ff.

———. "L'Organisation de la justice en Syrie," *ibid.*, XVI (January, 1923), 16–21.

SFER PASHA ABDULLAH. "Le Mandat français et les traditions françaises en Syrie et en Liban," *Revue hebdomadaire*, August, September, 1922.

SIMON, HENRY. "La Syrie devant le parlement français," *Corresponiance d'Orient*, January, 1925.

TESTIS (pseud). "L'Œuvre de la France en Syrie," *Revue des deux mondes*, LXII (March, 1921) 97–136.

WEILL, GEORGES. "Le Progrès de la Syrie," *Revue économique internationale*, July, 1925.

WEIZL, WOLFGANG VON. "In the Jebel Druze," *Atlantic Monthly*, December, 1925.

WILLSON, BECKLES. "Our Amazing Syrian Adventure," *National Review*, LXXVI (September, 1926), 41–54.

WOODS, H. CHARLES. "The French in Syria," *Fortnightly Review*, October, 1925.

WRIGHT, QUINCY. "Syrian Grievances against French Rule," *Current History*, XIII (February, 1926), 687–93.

———. "The Bombardment of Damascus," *A.J.I.L.*, XX (April, 1926), 263–80.

VI. AFRICAN MANDATED TERRITORIES

1. General

a) books

ANTONELLI, E. *L'Afrique et la Paix de Versailles*. Paris, 1921.

BEER, G. L. *African Questions at the Paris Peace Conference*. New York, 1923.

BUELL, R. L. *The Native Problem in Africa*. 2 vols. New York, 1928.

EVANS, IFOR L. *The British in Tropical Africa*. New York, 1929.

HARRIS, NORMAN D. *Europe and Africa*. Boston, 1927.

JONES, THOMAS JESSE. *Education in Africa, a Study of West, South and Equatorial Africa by the African Education Commission under the Auspices of the Phelps Stokes Fund and Foreign Mission Societies of North America and Europe*. New York, 1922.

———. *Education in East Africa, a Study of East, Central and South Africa by the Second African Education Commission under the Auspices of the Phelps Stokes Fund in Co-operation with the International Education Board*. London.

LUCAS, CHARLES. *The Partition and Colonization of Africa*. Oxford, 1922.

LUGARD, LORD (SIR FREDERICK). *The Dual Mandate in British Tropical Africa*. London, 1923.

MOREL, E. D. *The Black Man's Burden*. London, 1920.

OLIVIER, LORD (SIR SYDNEY). *White Capital and Coloured Labour* (2d ed.). London, 1929.

PELLERAY, E. *L'Afrique occidentale française*. Paris, 1923.

WILLOUGHBY, W. C. *Race Problems in the New Africa*. Oxford, 1923.

WOOLF, LEONARD. *Empire and Commerce in Africa, a Study in Economic Imperialism*, London, 1919.

b) articles

BESSON, MAURICE. "Les Mandats coloniaux," *L'Afrique française*, XXXI (January, 1921), 14 ff.

———. "Le Mouvement colonial, quelques formules nouvelles de colonisation," *ibid.*, XXX (December, 1920), 370 ff.

BISHOP OF ZANZIBAR. "Africa and the Blight of Commercialism," *Nineteenth Century*, CCL (June, 1920), 1074–87.

BRITISH LEAGUE OF NATIONS UNION. "Mandates, Africa," *Publ. No. 81*.

BUELL, R. L. "The Struggle in Africa," *Foreign Affairs* (U.S.), October, 1927, p. 22–40.

———. "The Destiny of East Africa," *ibid.*, April, 1928, pp. 408–26.

———. "Two Lessons in Colonial Rule," *ibid.*, April, 1929, pp. 439–53.

CORRYDON, R. T. "Problem of Eastern Africa," *Journal of the Africa Society*, XXII (1922), 177.

CROZIER, W. P. "France and Her Black Empire," *New Republic*, January 23, 1924, pp. 222 ff.

CUNOW, HEINRICH. "Die Kulturmission der Entente in den früheren deutschen Kolonien," *Neue Zeit*, XL (June, 1922), 313–18.

FULANI BIN FULANI. "Under a Mandate," *New Europe*, XI (July, 1921), 265 ff., 300 ff.

———. "A Suggested Program for Eastern Africa," *ibid.*, X (January, 1919), 12–17.

GRANADOS, GREGARIO. "El Problem colonial africano de la post guerre," *Boletin de la Real Sociedad Geografica*, XXI (March–April, 1924), 102–11.

JOHNSTON, SIR HARRY H. "International Interference in African Affairs," *Journ. C.L.*, XVIII, 26 ff.

———. "Mandates for the Late German Colonies in Africa," *Today and Tomorrow*, III (July, 1920), 97–100.

LEYS, NORMAN. *A Plan for Government by Mandate in Africa.* London, 1921.

LOGAN, RAYFORD W. "The Operation of the Mandate System in Africa," *Journal of Negro History*, XIII (October, 1928), 423–77.

LUGARD, LORD (SIR FREDERICK). "The White Man's Task in Tropical Africa," *Foreign Affairs* (U.S.) October, 1926, pp. 57–68.

MARTIN, CAMILLE. "L'Opinion coloniale allemande et le traité de paix," *L'Afrique française*, XXX (November, 1920), 302–12.

MAURETTE, FERNAND. "La France en Afrique equatoriale," *La Revue de Paris*, XXII (December, 1920), 648–70.

MENDELSSOHN-BARTHOLDI, A. "Die afrikanischen Mandate, Referat für die Deutsche Gesellschaft für Völkerrecht," *Archiv für Politik und Geschichte*, III (August, 1925), 180 ff.

OLIVIER, LORD (SIR SYNDEY). "The British Trust in Africa," *Contemporary Review*, March, 1929.

THIERRY, RENÉ. "L'Afrique de demain," *L'Afrique française*, XXX (December, 1920), 345 ff.

WOOLF, LEONARD. "The League and the Tropics," *Covenant*, I (October, 1919), 28 ff.

2. TANGANYIKA

a) OFFICIAL DOCUMENTS

GREAT BRITAIN

Report on Tanganyika Territory, Covering the Period from the Conclusion of the Armistice to the End of 1920.

Report on Tanganyika Territory for the Year 1921. Ibid., 1922.

Report of His Britannic Majesty's Government on the Mandated Territory of Tanganyika for the Year 1923.

Report by His Britannic Majesty's Government on the Administration under Mandate of Tanganyika Territory for the Year 1924.

Report by His Britannic Majesty's Government to the Council of the League of Nations on the Administration of Tanganyika Territory for the Year 1925. Ibid., 1926, 1927.

"Correspondence Regarding the Modification of the Boundary between British Mandated Territory and Belgian Mandated Territory in East Africa in Continuation of Cmd. 1794," *Parl. Pap.*, Cmd. 1974 (1923).

"Report of the East Africa Commission," *ibid.*, Cmd. 2387 (1925).

"Report of the Commission on Closer Union of the Dependencies in Eastern and Central Africa" (Sir E. Hilton Young), *ibid.*, Cmd. 3234 (1929).

Summary of Proceedings, Conference of Governors of the East African Dependencies, 1926.

Report of Major St. J. Orde Browne, O.B.E. upon Labour in Tanganyika Territory with a Covering Despatch from the Governor. London, 1926.

b) ARTICLES

CAMPBELL, SPENCER. "The Future of Tanganyika," *Fortnightly Review*, January, 1929.

HAYDON, J. R. "Plan for Union of British East African Colonies," *Current History*, March, 1929.

MELLAUD, FRANK. "Eastern Africa—Our Opportunity," *Fortnightly Review*, April, 1929.

TOLLAND, J. PULTNEY. "Tanganyika Territory," *United Empire*, XIV (July, 1923), 436–50.

3. RUANDA-URUNDI

a) OFFICIAL DOCUMENTS

BELGIUM

Rapport sur l'administration belge des territoires occupés de l'est Africa Allemand et specialment du Ruanda et de l'Urundi (pendant les années 1917–1920).

Rapport sur l'administration belge du Ruanda et de l'Urundi pendant l'année 1921.

Rapport sur l'administration belge du Ruanda-Urundi pendant l'année 1922, presenté aux chambres par le ministre des colonies. Ibid., 1923.

Rapport presenté par le gouvernement belge au conseil de la Société des Nations au sujet de l'administration du Ruanda-Urundi pendant l'année 1924. Ibid., 1925, 1926, 1927.

Chambre de représentants (Pecher, Ed.), No. 404. *Projet de loi approvant le mandat conferé à la Belgique sur le territoire du Ruanda-Urundi. Rapport fait au nom de la commission special 1922.* (Includes also *projet de loi* approving the treaty with the United States concerning the mandated territory.)

b) ARTICLES

HORN, M. "Belgium Colonial Administration in the Congo and the New Mandatory Territories," *United Empire*, XIII (March, 1922), 140–57.

JASPER, HENRI. "Le Ruanda-Urundi, pays à disettes périodiques," *Congo*, II (June, 1929), 1–22.

4. British Cameroons and Togo

a) official documents

Reports on the British Sphere of the Cameroons, 1922.

Reports on the British Sphere of the Cameroons for 1922 together with a Covering Dispatch from the Acting Governor of Nigeria.

Reports by His Britannic Majesty's Government to the Council of the League of Nations on the British Mandated Sphere of the Cameroons for the Year 1923.

Report by His Britannic Majesty's Government to the Council of the League of Nations on the Administration of the British Cameroons for the Year 1924. Ibid., 1925, 1926, 1927.

Report on the British Mandated Sphere of Togoland for 1920–1921. Ibid., 1922.

Report by His Brittannic Majesty's Government on the British Sphere of the Mandated Territory of Togoland for the Year 1923. Ibid., 1924.

Report by His Britannic Majesty's Government to the Council of the League of Nations on the Administration of the British Cameroons for the Year 1925. Ibid., 1926, 1927.

Report by the Hon. W. G. A. Ormsby-Gore on His Visit to West Africa during the Year 1926.

b) articles

Cardinall, A. W. "Our Mandate in North Togoland," *Journal of the Africa Society*, XXI (July, 1922), 302–8; XXII (October, 1922), 43–49.

Martin, Camille. "L'Administration des territoires sous le mandat britannique d'après les rapports officiels," *L'Afrique française*, XXXIV (February, 1924), 50–54.

Zache, Hans. "Togo, britisches Mandatsgebiet," *Wirtschaftsdienst*, VIII (November 30, 1923), 1094–95.

5. French Cameroons and Togo

a) official documents

france

Rapport au ministre des colonies sur l'administration des territoires occupées du Cameroun de la conquête au 1er Juillet 1921. Ibid., 1921.

Rapport annuel du gouvernement français sur l'administration sous mandat des territoires du Cameroun pour l'année 1922. Ibid., 1923, 1924, 1925, 1926.

Rapport annuel adressé par le gouvernement français au conseil de la Société des Nations conformément à l'article 22 du acte sur l'administration sous mandat du territoire du Cameroun pour l'année 1927.

Commissariat de la Republique française au Cameroun, Guide de la colonisation de la Republique française au Cameroun. Paris, 1923.

Rapport au ministre des colonies sur l'administration des territoires occupés du Togo de la conquête au 1er Juillet 1921. Ibid., 1921.

Rapport annuel du gouvernement français sur l'administration sous mandat des territoires du Togo pour l'année 1922. Ibid., 1923, 1924.

Rapport annuel adressé pour le gouvernement française au conseil de la Société des Nations sur l'administration sous mandat du territoire du Togo pour l'année 1925. Ibid., 1926, 1927.

Commissariat de la Republique française au Togo, Guide de la colonisation de la Republique française au Togo. Paris, 1924.

b) BOOKS AND ARTICLES

ANGOULVANT, G. "Le Togo, resultes acquis et perspective d'avenir: la question du mandat," *Colonies et Marine*, IV (November, 1920), 663–88.

———. "Togo et Cameroun, les rapports d'ensemble des commissaires de la Republique au ministre des colonies," *ibid.*, V (October, 1921), 699–702.

BESSON, MAURICE. "Nos Deux 'Colonies à mandat,' le Togo et le Cameroun," *Action nationale*, XII (July, 1920), 124–33.

BOUCHERY, E. "Notre Politique Indigène au Togo et au Cameroun," *L'Economiste Européen*, LXVI (August, 1924), 22–24.

CHRISTAL, FRANK. *Quatre Ans au Cameroun* (Société des Missions Evangeliques). Paris, 1923.

GUY, CAMILLE. "Le Cameroun sous le mandat français," *Le Parlement et l'Opinion*, XIII (June, July, 1923), 1221–36, 1345–57.

———. "La France au Cameroun," *L'Afrique française*, XXXII (June, July, 1923), 325–30, 342–45.

MONCHARVILLE, M. "L'Execution du mandat française au Togo et au Cameroun," *R.G.D.I.P.*, XXXII (1925), 58 ff.

PAULIN, HONORÉ, *Le Domaine extérieur de la France, pays à mandat, Cameroun, Togo.* Paris, 1923.

ROUARD DE CARD, F.B.E. *Les Mandats français sur le Togoland et le Cameroun.* Paris, 1924.

VALUDE, P. "Le Mandat français au Cameroun et au Togo," *Parlement et l'Opinion*, XI (August, 1921), 1704–10.

THERY, RENÉ. "La Situation financière de nos mandats africain," *L'Economiste européen*, LXVI (August, 1924), 18 ff.

ZACHE, HANS. "Togo und Kamerun," *Wirtschaftsdienst*, VII (May, 1922), 495 ff.; VIII (December, 1923), 1180 ff.

———. "Togo, französiches Mandatgebiet," *ibid.*, VIII (November, 1923), 1075 ff.

6. SOUTHWEST AFRICA

a) OFFICIAL DOCUMENTS

UNION OF SOUTH AFRICA

Statutes of the Union of South Africa.

Southwest Protectorate. Report of the Administrator for the Year 1919.

Southwest Africa Territory. Report of the Administrator for the Year 1920.

Territory of Southwest Africa. Report of the Administrator for the Year 1921.

Report of the Administrator of Southwest Africa for the Year 1922. Ibid., 1923, 1924.

Report of the Union of South Africa on Southwest Africa for the Year 1926. Ibid., 1927.

Report on the Natives of Southwest Africa and Their Treatment by Germany, 1918.

Commission on Future Form of Government in the Southwest African Protectorate. Capetown, 1921.

b) ARTICLES

ANONYMOUS. "Southwest Africa," *Round Table*, June 1923, pp. 659–65.

———. "The Southwest Africa Mandate," *ibid.*, June 1925, pp. 610–16.

EYMETT. "The Mandate over Southwest Africa," *Journ. C.L.*, 1927, p. 3.

KISKER, H. "Briefe aus Südwest," *Deutsche Kolonialzeitung*, LVIII (September, 1921), 78 ff.

OLIVIER, LORD (SIR SYDNEY). "The League and the Bondelswart Massacre," *New Statesman*, XXI (September, 1923), 631–38.

PERIE, R. "Civilization criminelle," *Paix par le droit*, XXXII (November, 1922), 440 ff.

ZACHE, HANS. "Südwestafrica," *Wirtschafsdienst*, VII (May, 1922), 522–24.

VII. PACIFIC MANDATED TERRITORIES

1. GENERAL

ANONYMOUS. "New Zealand. The Mandates for Samoa and Nauru," *Round Table*, X (1920), 467–77.

BLAKESLEE, G. H. "The Mandates of the Pacific," *Foreign Affairs* (U.S.), September, 1922, pp. 98–115.

HARRIS, JOHN H. "Mr. Winston Churchill and Chinese Indentured Labor in Nauru and Samoa," *Foreign Affairs* (British), IV (November, 1922), 104.

INSTITUTE OF PACIFIC RELATIONS (J. B. Condliffe, ed.). "Problems of the Pacific," *Proceedings of the Second Conference of the Institute of Pacific Relations, Honolulu, 1927* (Chicago, 1928), pp. 192 ff.

League of Nations. Notes on Certain Aspects of the Work of the League of Nations of Interest to the Pacific Countries, Prepared Unofficially by Members of the League of Nations Secretariat, 1927. (Reprinted as an Appendix in Institute of Pacific Relations, *supra*.)

The League of Nations in Relation to the Pacific (prepared by members of the Secretariat for the Conference of the Institute of Pacific Relations, Kyoto, 1929), Geneva, 1929.

SPITZ, LIEUT. COL. "Les Mandats dans le Pacifique, *Revue maritime*, July 1923, pp. 6 ff.

2. NAURU

a) OFFICIAL DOCUMENTS

COMMONWEALTH OF AUSTRALIA

Report on the Administration of Nauru during the Military Occupation and until 17th December, 1920.

Report on the Administration of Nauru, 1921.

Report on the Administration of Nauru during the Year 1922 (prepared by the administration for submission to the League of Nations). *Ibid.*, 1923, 1924.

Report to the Council of the League of Nations on the Administration of Nauru during the Year 1925. Ibid., 1926, 1927.

GREAT BRITAIN

British Phosphate Commission Report and Accounts for the Year Ended 30th June, 1921. (Includes agreement between Great Britain, Australia, and New Zealand in regard to Nauru.)

b) ARTICLES

ANONYMOUS. "The Nauru Mandate," *Round Table*, March, 1923, pp. 401–13.

CHARTERIS, A. "The Mandate over Nauru Island," *B.Y.B.I.L.*, 1923–24, pp. 137–152.

MENDELSSOHN-BARTHOLDY, A. "Nauru," *Deutsche Nation*, III (February, 1921), 114 ff.

WOOLF, L. S. "A Gilbertian Story with a Moral, Sacred and Other Trusts, *Foreign Affairs* (British), III (October, 1921), 58 ff.

3. NEW GUINEA

a) OFFICIAL DOCUMENTS

COMMONWEALTH OF AUSTRALIA

Commonwealth Acts

Reports to the League of Nations on the Administration of New Guinea from September 1914 to 30th June, 1921. Ibid., 1921–22, 1922–23, 1923–24, 1924–25.

Report to the Council of the League of Nations on the Administration of the Territory of New Guinea from July 1st, 1925 to June 30th, 1926. Ibid., 1926–27.

Royal Commission on German New Guinea. Interim and Final Reports of Royal Commission on the Late German New Guinea. Victoria, 1920.

Department of Defence, Report by the Minister of State for Defence on the Military Occupation of the German New Guinea Possessions. Melbourne, 1921.

A Selection of Papers Printed by the League of Nations Relating to the Mandatory System (Especially Those Relating to C Mandates), 1920–1922. (Compiled in Prime Minister's department.) Melbourne, 1923.

New Guinea, Territory of. Laws, Statutes, etc. Expropriation Ordinance, 1920 (and amendments).

b) BOOKS AND ARTICLES

AHERN, F. W. "A Stain on the Southern Cross," *Socialist Review*, XXIV (September, 1924), 71–82.

ANONYMOUS. "Japan and Australia," *Japan Chronicle* (February 17, 1921), pp. 213–14.

BURTON, J. W. "The Australian Mandate in New Guinea," *Studies in Australian Affairs* (issued by New South Wales Branch of the Institute of Pacific Relations, Melbourne, 1928), pp. 218–40.

EGGLESTON, F. W. *The Mandates of New Guinea and Nauru* (data paper, Institute of Pacific Relations, Second Conference). Honolulu, 1927.

———. *The Australian Mandate for New Guinea.* (Issued for the League of Nations by the Institute of Pacific Relations) Melbourne, 1928.

EVANS, LUTHER H. "New Guinea under Australian Mandate Rule," *Southwestern Political and Social Science Quarterly*, X (June, 1929), 1–21.

GRATTAN, C. HARTLEY. "Australia and the Pacific," *Foreign Affairs* (British), October, 1928, pp. 144–49.

LESLIE, ALEXANDER. "An Australian Empire," *ibid.*, VI (July, 1924), 14 ff.

ZACHE, HANS. "Deutsch Neu Guinea," *Wirtschaftsdienst*, IX (January, 1924), 124 ff.

4. WESTERN SAMOA

a) OFFICIAL DOCUMENTS

DOMINION OF NEW ZEALAND

New Zealand Statues

First Report of the Government of the Dominion of New Zealand on the Administration of the Mandated Territory of Western Samoa for the Period from May 1st, 1920, to March 31st, 1921 (prepared by direction of the Minister of External Affairs for the information of the League of Nations pursuant to art. 6 of the mandate). *Ibid.*, 1921–22, 1922–23, 1923–24, 1924–25, 1925–26, 1926–27, 1927–28.

Department of Health, Mandated Territory of Western Samoa (supplementary report for the year ended March 31, 1924).

Report of Visit of Hon. W. Nosworthy, Minister of External Affairs to Mandated Territory of Western Samoa, together with Representations of Citizens' Committee and Replies Thereto, etc., 1927.

Report of the Royal Commission Concerning the Administration of Western Samoa, 1928.

New Zealand, Official Year Book.

b) BOOKS AND ARTICLES

ADAMS, E. C. "The Pearl of the Pacific," *United Empire*, XIII (May, 1922), 296–301.

ALLEN, SIR JAMES. "The Samoan Mandate," *ibid.*, XI (December, 1920), 648–63.

ANONYMOUS. "Geneva and Samoa," *Round Table*, December, 1928.

COCKER, W. H. "The Mandate for Samoa," *New Zealand Affairs* (issued by the New Zealand Branch of the Institute of Pacific Relations, Christ Church, 1929), pp. 179–206.

CONDLIFFE, J. B. *New Zealand in the Making*, London and Chicago, 1930, chap. XIII.

HOLLAND, W. E. *Samoa, a Story That Teems with Tragedy.* Wellington, New Zealand.

———. *Indentured Labour, Is It Slavery?* New Zealand, 1922.

NEW ZEALAND GROUP. *The Mandated Territory of Western Samoa* (data paper, Institute of Pacific Relations, Second Conference). Honolulu, 1927.

TENNENT, HUGH C. "Samoa and Other South Sea Islands as a Problem of the Pacific," *ibid.*

TRIGGS, W. H. "Samoa under New Zealand," *Quarterly Review*, CCXXXVIII (October, 1922), 235–51.

ZACHE, HANS. "Samoa, das Mandatsgebiet," *Wirtschaftsdienst*, IX (January, 1924), 11–12.

5. NORTH PACIFIC ISLANDS

a) OFFICIAL DOCUMENTS

JAPAN

Report of the Administration of Territory under Japanese Mandate, 1920.

Second Annual Report on Japan's Mandated Territory, 1921.

Annual Report to League of Nations on Administration of South Sea Islands under Japanese Mandate for Year 1922. Ibid., 1923, 1924, 1925, 1926, 1927.

b) ARTICLES

BLAKESLEE, GEORGE H. "Japan's New Island Possessions in the Pacific, History and Present Status," *Journal of International Relations*, XII (October, 1921), 173–91.

WOOD, J. B. "Japan's Mandate in the Pacific," *Asia*, XXI (September, 1921), 747–53.

TABLE OF CASES

TABLE OF CASES

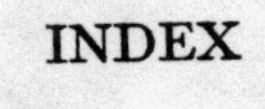
INDEX

INDEX